Women in Mycenaean G

Women in Mycenaean Greece is the first book-length study of women in the Linear B tablets from Mycenaean Greece and the only to collect and compile all the references to women in the documents of the two best attested sites of Late Bronze Age Greece – Pylos on the Greek mainland and Knossos on the island of Crete. The book offers a systematic analysis of women's tasks, holdings, and social and economic status in the Linear B tablets dating from the 14th and 13th centuries BCE, identifying how Mycenaean women functioned in the economic institutions where they were best attested – production, property control, land tenure, and cult. Analyzing all references to women in the Mycenaean documents, the book focuses on the ways in which the economic institutions of these Bronze Age palace states were gendered and effectively extends the framework for the study of women in Greek antiquity back more than 400 years.

Throughout, the book seeks to establish whether gender practices were uniform in the Mycenaean states or differed from site to site and to gauge the relationship of the roles and status of Mycenaean women to their Archaic and Classical counterparts to test if the often-proposed theories of a more egalitarian Bronze Age accurately reflect the textual evidence. The Linear B tablets offer a unique, if under-utilized, point of entry into women's history in Ancient Greece, documenting nearly 2000 women performing over 50 task assignments. From the decipherment of the tablets in 1952 one major gap in the scholarly record remained: a full accounting of the women who inhabited the palace states and their tasks, ranks, and economic contributions. *Women in Mycenaean Greece* fills that gap recovering how class, rank, and other social markers created status hierarchies among women, how women as a group functioned relative to men, and where different localities conformed or diverged in their gender practices.

Barbara A. Olsen is Associate Professor of Greek and Roman Studies at Vassar College, in Poughkeepsie, New York, USA. She received her Ph.D. in Classical Studies from Duke University and her B.A. in Classics from Cornell University. She was appointed the Vanderpool Fellowship from the American School of Classical Studies and was recently a Fellow at the Center for Hellenic Studies.

Women in Mycenaean Greece

The Linear B tablets from Pylos and Knossos

Barbara A. Olsen

LONDON AND NEW YORK

First published 2014
by Routledge
2 Park Square, Milton Park, Abingdon, Oxfordshire OX14 4RN

and by Routledge
711 Third Avenue, New York, NY 10017, USA

First issued in paperback 2017

Routledge is an imprint of the Taylor & Francis Group, an informa business

British Library Cataloguing in Publication Data
A catalogue record for this book is available from the British Library

Library of Congress Cataloging-in-Publication Data
A catalog record has been requested

ISBN 13: 978-1-138-08583-1 (pbk)
ISBN 13: 978-0-415-72515-6 (hbk)

Typeset in Times New Roman
by HWA Text and Data Management, London

Contents

Illustrations

Tables

Figures

Acknowledgements

This project has been a long time in the making, and I am most grateful to those whose support, insights, and time have been so generously given. To start with, I would like to thank the late Judy Ginsburg and the late Lynne Abel who first introduced me to the study of women in antiquity at Cornell, and whose thoughtful, challenging, and patient mentorship has so shaped my scholarship. They are most missed. I would also like to extend my thanks to John Coleman who first introduced me to the Aegean Bronze Age.

I am also most grateful to the American School of Classical Studies at Athens for its support in the form of the Vanderpool Fellowship which was most valuable in this project's early stages. Particular thanks are due to the late Willy Coulson, Bob Bridges, Susan Lupack, Bryan Burns, Brendan Burke, Melissa Moore, Julia Shear, Dave Conlin, and Mireille Lee.

I would also like to extend heartfelt thanks to my graduate department at Duke University for supporting this project in its dissertation form, especially Kent Rigsby, Tolly Boatwright, the late Larry Richardson jr., Gregson Davis, and John Younger who was involved in the early stages of the project. Thanks also are due the Women's Studies Program at Duke for both financial support in terms of the Anne Firor Scott award and to Jean O'Barr and Nancy Rosebaugh for hours of practical mentoring and a lifetime of leading by example. And finally, I would like to offer thanks to Donald Haggis at UNC Chapel Hill for his service on my dissertation committee and for his many useful suggestions.

I have been the grateful recipient of the generosity of numerous scholars who have shared their work and comments with me, notably Sarah Morris, Louise Hitchcock, Anne Chapin, Marie-Louise Nosch, Tom Palaima, Katerina Kopaka, Stephie Nikoloudis, Jim Wright, Judy Hallett, the late Conn Murphy, and the anonymous readers of this volume and my tenure portfolio. This project is much stronger for their insights and suggestions. To Greg Nagy and the Center for Hellenic Studies I owe deep thanks for their generosity in supplying me with a Fellowship for Fall 2011 and Andrea Capra, Cristina Carusi, Sylvian Fachard, Jennifer Gates-Foster, Leopoldo Iribarren, Alex Pappas, and especially Kate Topper for their collegiality, support, and thoughtful commentary.

And to my community at Vassar, I would first like to thank Jon Chenette and the Dean of Faculty office for supplying matching funds with my CHS fellowship and for summer research support. To my students and research assistants, I would like to acknowledge the work and contributions of Tory Wooley, Siddhi Hayes, Jen Gerrish, Zander Malik, and Aaron Hoffman. My appreciation is also due to Steve Taylor who generated the Aegean map appearing in this volume. And to those friends without whose support and encouragement I would be lost, I would like to thank Eva Woods, Miranda Martinez, Eve D'Ambra, Bruce King, Bob Pounder, Robert Brown, Mita Choudury, Susan Quade, Leslie Dunn, Diane Harriford, Susan Zlotnick, Rosemary Moore, Diana Minsky, Barbara Page, and Judy Dollenmayer, with special thanks to Jean Kane, Karen Robertson, Lydia Murdoch, Dorothy Kim, and Gretchen Lieb for their generosity in tirelessly proofing and editing chapter drafts.

My deep thanks are also due to Matthew Gibbons and Amy Davis-Poynter at Routledge for their support and guidance through the publication process; their work has been invaluable in bringing this work to fruition. For aid in securing photograph permissions I would like to thank Carol Hershenson at the University of Cincinnati, Christos Giannopoulos at the Center for Hellenic Studies (Nafplion) and Dr. George Kakavas at the National Museum of Greece for their generous assistance.

Finally I would like to dedicate this volume to Conn Murphy and my parents.

Conventions of Linear B

The following conventions are employed throughout the text in the transliteration of Linear B tablets.

KN	Knossos
PY	Pylos
.1 .2 .3 etc.	Line numbers for a horizontally ruled tablet
.A .B etc.	Line numbers for a partially ruled tablet
.a .b etc.	Line number for an unruled tablet
recto	Front side of a tablet
verso	Reverse side of a tablet
vacat	An empty ruled line
vestigia	Traces of illegible signs remain
inf(ra) mut(ila)	Damaged below
sup(ra) mut(ila)	Damaged above
-	Connecting signs in a word
,	Word divider
[ ]	Missing text
[.]	Text missing a single sign
[a]	Restored text
[[a]]	Erased text (still legible)
< a >	Restorable text omitted by scribal error
ạ	Damaged sign, subscript dot indicates most likely reading

A fuller introduction to the conventions of Linear B transcription can be found in R. Palmer 2008. See also Nakassis 2013.

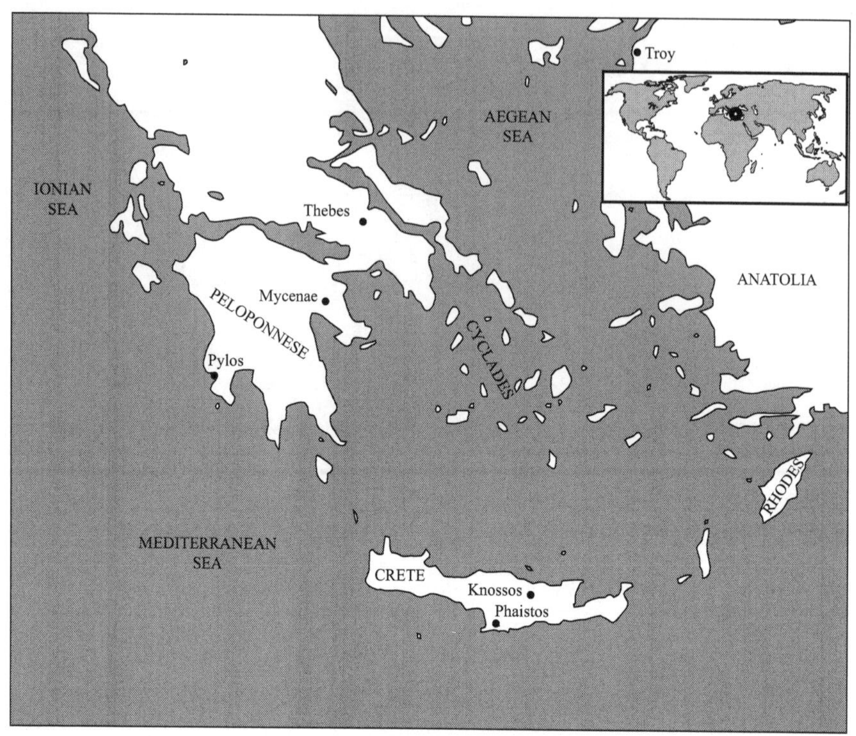

Map of the Aegean Sea

Linear B Tablet PY Tn 316. (Photo credit: Department of Classics, University of Cincinnati)

1 The women of Mycenaean Greece

Introduction

"Cherchez la femme." "Find the woman." This command, to search out an unknown or invisible woman at the heart of a mystery, has particular relevance for the study of women in Greek antiquity – where so often women have been shrouded in myth, notoriety or obscurity. To talk about the actual, rather than mythological, women of Greek antiquity is a complicated task – in order to locate the real women of Ancient Greece one must sift carefully through the historical, epigraphic, and archaeological records, all of which are dominated by the deeds and activities of Greek men. Greek women are consistently – across eras and regions – recorded far less frequently than their male counterparts, both as a consequence of women's near complete exclusion from the political and military arenas and the tendency to locate women in the domestic world, where often their social and economic identities become subsumed under those of their male relatives.

This question of rendering women visible – of recovering them from the documentary and archaeological records – is a task historians of women and gender in the ancient world have been undertaking for four decades now. Women's graves have been excavated, and their names, responsibilities, and rituals have been carefully sifted from inscriptions, orations and the texts of the historiographers. Yet, perhaps nowhere does visibility for women need to be recovered more than in the Greek Bronze Age, whose women have not previously been the focus of a full-length study. Finley unlocked the Homeric world of Odysseus, but what might the Mycenaean world of a real-life Penelope look like? [1]

This book is a study of the women of Mycenaean Greece as they appear in the administrative documents of Late Bronze Age Greece: the Linear B tablets of the 14th and 13th centuries BCE. This is the first study to compile all the references to women in the Linear B tablets from Pylos on the Greek mainland and Knossos on Crete – by far the two best-documented Mycenaean sites – and the first to offer a systematic analysis of the ways in which the economic institutions of these Bronze Age palace states were gendered. This study has three main objectives: 1. to locate the women scattered throughout the records; 2. to identify the mechanisms and rationales that drove the visibility of the women recorded in the documents; and 3. to assess the ways in which Mycenaean women functioned in the economic institutions where they were best attested – production, property holdings, land tenure, and cult practice – in order to determine whether gender practices were uniform in the Mycenaean states or differed from site to site. The study also raises a broader question: what was the relationship of the roles and status of Mycenaean women to their later Archaic and Classical counterparts, and do the often-proposed theories of a more egalitarian Bronze Age hold up to the evidence?

From the tablets of Pylos and Knossos, more than 2000 women emerge – rendering the Linear B tablets one of the largest sets of evidence for women in any period of Greek antiquity. Women surface either as individuals identified by their names and/or titles or as members of aggregate groups.[2] I suggest that these Bronze Age women attested in the tablets do not enter the documentary record randomly, but rather that both sites demonstrate a clear (if idiosyncratic) logic as to which women come to warrant palace attention and hence textual visibility. Overall, I contend that key differences occur between the treatment of women in the Mycenaean and historical periods; while the later evidence primarily places women in the contexts of the *oikos* (family), most of the Linear B evidence registers women who are outside it. And finally, I argue that the two Mycenaean palace states, while not egalitarian in their approach to gender, nonetheless differ not only from the later periods but also from each other. Knossos and Pylos do not share a unified, homogeneous set of gender practices but differ in several important ways in their incorporations of women in their states' economies. I conclude that as early as these earliest of Greek written records, gender already appears a variable institution in Ancient Greece, site-specific and driven by the idiosyncratic needs and histories of each state rather than as a monolithic, unchanging institution for the women of the Mycenaean world.

Gender and Aegean Prehistory

The concept of gender has meaning only as the product of specific historical circumstances. Gender, defined here as the differentiation of society based on perceived sexual difference, conveys different expectations for the roles of men and women in different cultures and functions as *a* primary, if not *the* primary, category of social organization in every known human society.[3] Within a given society, gender establishes a framework for the activities of men and women, governs the mechanisms for the distribution of tasks and goods, sets the political, economic, and institutional roles assigned or denied to men and women, and provides a rationale for the social and economic separation of the sexes.[4] As such, gender functions as a primary, defining trait of cultural identity – one as central as language and religion.

This awareness of the importance of gender as a social variable has been informing Classical scholarship since the early 1970s. Feminist historians, both inside and outside the field of Classics, have insisted on the historical specificity of gender throughout the different periods and *poleis* of Greek antiquity, recognizing that the specific meanings of gender, as with other hierarchical categories, vary across space and time throughout the Greek world.[5] In the historical period, social mores governing gender ideologies and practices differed widely, based on the particular histories of individual city-states. Certainly, no contemporary Classical scholar would declare that a universalized concept of gender was in place throughout the Classical period – even the most cursory of glances at the differences in women's status and lives in fifth-century Sparta and fifth-century Athens would quickly dispel this notion; the differences in the gender practices of Athens and Sparta are substantial and are each rooted in the different historical and institutional circumstances of each *polis*. Both *poleis* evolved the gender systems specific to their own particular societal needs: the high levels of mobility, autonomy, and economic power enjoyed by Spartan women developed to fill needs opened in Spartan society by the vacuum left by the military-centered lives of Spartan men[6] while the nascent democracy at Athens limited all of these to foster a sense of solidarity among citizen men and to protect newly restricted Athenian citizenship requirements – and so barred women from ownership of property and exercise of legal rights including the franchise and the ability to self-represent in court, while social mores strongly discouraged even the circulation of citizen women in public spaces.[7] Consequently, we observe each state developing those specific systems of gender practice which fit its own specific needs and societal ideals.

But how far back do the roots of such widely different gender practices in the Greek world extend? Are these variances in Greek gender practices to be attributed to pressures related to the eighth-century rise of the *polis* which then fractured an otherwise monolithic system of gender throughout Greece or was gender already a fragmented and site-specific phenomenon well before the end of the Early Iron Age (the so-called "Dark Age")?

This study situates these questions in the earliest documented phase of Greek culture – in the palace societies of the Late Bronze Age Aegean (ca. 1400–1200 BCE) – to assess the form or forms which gender assumes several hundred years prior to *polis* development. To answer this question, this text undertakes a study of the two best documented palatial sites of the Late Bronze Age, Knossos on the island of Crete and Pylos on the Mycenaean mainland, focusing on the women of each site to determine whether a *koine* of gender practice was in place or whether, in the earliest written documentation in Greek, gender already displayed regional variances.

History of scholarship on Aegean women: Mythological and iconographic studies

Scholarship has long been interested in the question of women's status and activities in pre-Classical Greece. As much of the literary and archaeological evidence for this period seems to allege that the mythological women of the Homeric epics and the few women known from the real-life Geometric-period (10th–8th century) burials occupied economic and political roles very different from those occupied by 5th-century Athenian women. Several scholars postulated that women enjoyed a higher social rank in the earlier period than they did in historical-era Greece.[8] With the archaeological rediscovery of the Bronze Age (ca. 3000–1100 BCE) civilizations of the Aegean in the late 19th and early 20th centuries, this scholarly "elevation" of the Female was extended backwards to include the newly discovered women of Minoan Crete and Mycenaean Greece. This re-envisioning of women's position in the Aegean led (and still leads) to the commonplace claim that the women of the Late Bronze Age Aegean occupied a substantially higher status than their historical-period descendants. What exactly the nature of this status difference was, however, has been a source of lively debate. Some researchers, influenced by Bachofen's *Mutterrecht* or by Freudian models of societal development, located in the Bronze Age a matriarchal antiquity for Greece, citing such evidence as the mythic traditions recorded in Hesiod's Theogony.[9] These scholars read this myth, with its allusions to an early supremacy of Gaia supplanted ultimately by the patriarch Zeus, as perhaps preserving the memory of a much earlier time when the earthly rule of women was overthrown by men.[10] Other readers were more circumspect: a second line of reasoning, seeking a home for the many memorable women of the mythic tradition, was tempted to locate in Greek prehistory a past where women exercised their voices and political muscles – as Helens, Clytemnestras, and Antigones – at a considerably higher level than did real women of the Athenian *polis*.[11] Under such theoretical influences and faced with the many images of prominent women from the Knossos palace frescoes, this argument joined with Sir Arthur Evans, the excavator of Knossos and the discoverer of the Minoan civilization on Crete, in reading these images as "a sign of a female predominance"[12] in the Bronze Age Aegean.[13]

One hundred years later, an interest in Bronze Age women still remains, but the central questions and methodologies have changed. Early interest in such questions as whether the Minoans were matriarchal or whether their religion centered around a mother goddess[14] have largely given way to discussions of gendered spaces, women's participation in cult and ritual, and public images of power.[15] Currently, research on Aegean women is being conducted through three main avenues of research: through art historical approaches which privilege iconographic evidence, through archaeological investigations of material culture and burial sites,[16] and through analysis of the Linear B tablets.

Research on the women of Minoan Crete,[17] particularly in light of the absence of translatable texts in the Minoan language, has relied heavily on iconographic studies. These studies have tended to privilege images from fresco, and to a lesser extent, glyptic and small sculptures (figurines) over other forms of evidence.[18] These investigations have ranged in subject matter from women's activities in religious ritual,[19] to representations of women in public and domestic spaces,[20] to studies on women's clothing,[21] and their possible participation in athletic scenes.[22] A few recent studies have also addressed the difficulties of recognizing girls in Minoan art.[23] As a result of this research, several patterns in the way Minoan art portrays women may be identified:[24] First and foremost, Minoan iconography consistently places women in public, never domestic, contexts where they often occupy prominent spatial positions.[25] Second, Minoan iconography depicts women of different social ranks, with status hierarchies emphasized on both the Grandstand and Sacred Grove frescoes, each of which depict two categories of women: some large and well-differentiated and others who, like the men depicted on both frescoes, appear on a much smaller scale as an undifferentiated mass of painted heads. Finally, when taken as a whole, Minoan women do not appear to occupy a fully equal standing with Minoan men even in Minoan art; women go missing from several important pictorial media – for example, stone vase reliefs,[26] ivory figurines, and portrait seals[27] – and are absent from the scenes most generally associated with Minoan hierarchy or administration such as the single standing (male) figures of the portrait seals[28] or the "ambassadors" in the Avaris (Tell el-Dab'a) frescoes from Egypt – frescoes widely considered to be of Aegean origin or inspiration.[29] Instead, Minoan art more commonly locates its women in prominent roles in cult practice, perhaps even eclipsing the roles of Minoan men in particular rituals.[30]

Images of women from the Mycenaean (Greek) mainland are somewhat different. Mycenaean images place some women in positions of power (for example as priestesses), but overall prominence in artistic images shifts to Mycenaean men, who as Kokkinidou and Nikolaidou note often appear in heavily militarized contexts.[31] As yet, no Mycenaean women are seen occupying prominent positions at the expense of accompanying men. Mycenaean art also introduces a new locus for displaying women unattested in Minoan Crete as it adds a new trope for women, displaying them also in the domestic realm; over 70 figurine representations of women caring for children are attested in a significant change from the exclusively public Minoan images of women.[32]

From these studies, we can gain some access to the ways in which these two societies address issues of gender. It is clear that these two societies approach gendered scenes differently and idiosyncratically, if not in practice, at least in representation. Not only are these neighboring societies not identical in their presentations of a gendered world, but each demonstrates its own specific approach to representing women in the public and domestic spheres: Mycenaeans conceptualized and structured gender in one manner; Minoans in another. Or more simply, gender appears to convey different meaning in each society: Minoans seem more invested in locating women in an official, civic context while Mycenaeans place greater emphasis on framing women within the family. Yet these two societies did not exist in isolation from each other, and the central theoretical question of this study is what is the historical result when one society comes to dominate another whose gender roles and ideologies differ from that of the governing society.

Iconographic studies are not, of course, without their own methodological difficulties, particularly if one's goal is to recover the lived realities of actual Bronze Age women. Sara Immerwahr has identified succinctly the central problems in relying on the frescoes as evidence for "real life": the ambiguous portrayal of prominent figures who cannot be distinguished as definitively human or divine, that is, as women or goddesses;[33] the impossibility of distinguishing between ritual, generic, or daily-life scenes as it is not yet clear how many of these options are exercised in Aegean iconography; the degree to which palatial frescoes depicting elite members of society do or do not accurately reflect life outside the palace; and difficulties in sorting out gender hierarchies as in some scenes women appear central and in others men do.[34] Obviously, iconography alone is insufficient to recover the everyday, lived realities of actual Bronze Age women. In his discussion on the lack of warfare scenes in Minoan art, Charles Gates makes the larger point regarding the relationship between iconography and lived reality: "Pictorial art is not – or better, need not be – a direct representation of society, but instead function[s] as a set of ideological statements whose messages vary according to context and audience."[35]

So, art can enrich but not of itself answer our questions. To investigate our topic, we need textual evidence which might provide a glimpse of Bronze Age women and their actual, day-to-day activities. Use of textual evidence, however, necessitates a much smaller chronological and geographical window of study. Because of the untranslated state of Linear A – and because of the abbreviated nature of most Linear A records – the historical realities of Minoan women before the period of Mycenaean administration on Crete are currently unrecoverable. Only the Linear B tablets are readable, and they limit the chronological scope for investigation of Aegean women to the final phase of the Bronze Age (1400–1200 BCE) – the period of the Mycenaean palaces of the mainland and the period of the Mycenaean administrative presence on (formerly Minoan-controlled) Crete. Furthermore, currently only two sites have produced a sufficiently large corpus of Linear B tablets to permit the large-scale investigation of women: Pylos on the Mycenaean mainland with 1107 tablets and Knossos on Crete with 3369.[36] It must be noted that the tablets from Knossos date from the period of Mycenaean governance of (at least parts of) Crete. As a consequence, they cannot be used as direct evidence for women's lives in indigenous Minoan society; rather they reflect the social organization and economic activities of the hybridized Minoan-Mycenaean society that was Mycenaean Knossos (which may even provide some evidence of Minoan holdovers into the Mycenaean era). Nonetheless, even with these chronological limitations, for both these sites, the tablets are rich sources of demographic evidence for the women of Mycenaean-era Greece, with nearly 2000 women securely attested in their combined corpora.

The content of the Linear B tablets: The Mycenaean economy

The content of the Linear B tablets is entirely administrative and economic.[37] The tablets record economic transactions (transfers, allocations, collections, etc.) considered to be of direct interest to the palatial governments which commissioned them; no non-palatial records are known from Pylos and Knossos nor any documents with anything other than an administrative context – such as, for example, letters, chronicles, or hymns.[38] Nearly all the tablets conform to one of three categories: inventories of goods and property holdings;[39] production goals and records; and records of outflow, such as rations and offerings.[40] As such, the

Linear B tablets act not as simply random windows into the Mycenaean world, nor as spontaneous or free-floating threads of evidence, but rather as mediated texts, filtered through the interests and responsibilities of both the scribes themselves and by the palace elites which commissioned them.

Since we are working, then, with evidence specifically pertaining to elite, palatial economic interests, a short survey of current perspectives into the workings of the Mycenaean economy seems useful. The nature and workings of the Mycenaean economy have been a key area of research across the 60 years of decipherment. Scholarship has long noted that the closest models for this pre-monetary economy are not the city-states of Archaic and Classical Greece so much as much as those of the palace states of the Bronze Age Near East, in that both share an emphasis on redistribution of goods, commodities, and labor by a central administration, palace- or temple-centered in the Ancient Near East, palace-centered for the Mycenaeans.[41]

And so, as the centers of redistributive economies,[42] the palaces were the main economic nuclei of both Knossos and Pylos. The scope of the palatial economy embodied in the tablets is consequently broad as the palaces controlled the lion's share of the Bronze Age states' economies, particularly the import and export of goods.[43] The tablets from both centers indicate that the palaces were closely monitoring a variety of industries and commodities, including the textile industry in all stages of production (from counts of herds to wool production to the finished textiles themselves), the manufacture of luxury products such as perfumed oil, the organization of land management, the distribution of metals, the rations given to dependent personnel, the management of multiple species of livestock, the production of foodstuffs, and the distribution of olive oil, gold, and other materials to the (Greek and Minoan[44]) gods. Early studies[45] once attributed near-complete domination of all aspects of the Mycenaean economy to the palaces;[46] more contemporary analysis would modulate this reading, noting that many areas of the economy and the vast majority of the population of the Mycenaean states do not come to enter the tablets,[47] and that we are more likely working under a system whereby the palaces act as the largest economic driver, but "para-palatial" or extra-palatial regions of the economy also play a significant role.[48] Under this model, then, we should read the tablets as reflecting the palatial area of the Mycenaean economy; much of the non-palatial economy remains outside the scope of our evidence. Nakassis sums up the situation usefully: "The Mycenaean palaces, then, rather than monopolizing virtually all economic activity, were engaged in mobilizing goods and services that benefitted the ruling elite."[49]

In addition to moving away from extreme models of palace control of state economies, models for the degree of hierarchical, political, and social organization have also shifted. Again, the earlier reading had attributed greater agency to the elite, here elite political officials, than current models, which stress a less stratified and more complex series of interactions among palace and regional officials and the rest of the Mycenaean population.[50] Again, missing sectors of the economic hierarchy are stressed, as is the multi-dimensional or overlapping nature of various officials' purviews,[51] with the result that more current emphasis focuses on the relationship between the palaces and the groups, officials, and individuals with whom they interact.[52]

Women in the Mycenaean economy: The Linear B tablets

The Greek Bronze Age predates the invention of the alphabet but not the rise of recorded data. Writing and written documents emerge in the Aegean basin in the first half of the 2nd millennium BCE, first in the form of Cretan Hieroglyphic (also known as Pictographic) on the island of Crete in the 18th century BCE and then shifts to the – still-untranslated – syllabic script known as Linear A (well-documented by the 15th century BCE as the major writing system of the Minoan civilization at its peak in the New Palace period). In this writing system, specialized scribes kept records by inscribing clay tablets with a combination of syllabic signs, drawn images (ideograms), and numerical tallies to keep records of economic transactions of interest to their palace and local administrations.[53]

Following the collapse of Neopalatial Crete in the 15th century BCE and the consequent loss of the Linear A script, a new syllabic script emerged in the Aegean, Linear B, deciphered in 1952 by Michael Ventris, who proved it to be a syllabic script representing the Mycenaean dialect of Ancient Greek. Found both at mainland citadel and palace sites and replacing the earlier Linear A at the now Mycenaean-administered site of Knossos on Crete, Linear B adopted many of the conventions of Linear A, continuing to spell words out via their component syllables alongside the ongoing use of ideograms and tallies. Clay continued to be the main media in use, at least for records intended to be kept for relatively short times,[54] and tablets were frequently stored in administrative centers, most typically palaces. When these palaces were destroyed, fires broke out and, fortunately for the modern researcher, baked the once semi-hardened clay tablets to kiln-like temperatures, inadvertently preserving these once short-term records for more than 32 centuries.

Once more, the primary impetus for creating these records was administrative and economic, allowing the palace administrations to track its varied interactions with an increasingly hierarchical and stratified Mycenaean population. On these records, the scribes would frequently list the names and titles of people either supplying or receiving goods and/or commodities for the palaces, the types of commodity involved in the exchange, and a tally of the number of units exchanged. From these records, we can reconstruct at least parts of those areas of the economy most regulated and recorded by palace scribes. Two palace sites emerge with vastly more documentation than the others: Pylos in the South-Western Peloponnese with more than 1100 tablets surviving and Knossos on Crete with more than 3000.

While the tablets have too often been dismissed as impenetrable or been subject to accusations of being the ancient equivalent of shopping lists,[55] the two corpora are actually rich sources for the social structures of Aegean proto-history. In fact, they provide a degree of demographic detail not replicated in later Greek history until well into the Hellenistic period. Of the nearly 5000 total tablets from

Knossos and Pylos, more than half provide evidence of the names, occupational responsibilities, and property holdings of real, rather than mythological, Bronze Age women and men.[56] Furthermore, as property and commodity holdings are typically quantified, we can estimate a relative sense of the listed individual's proportionate economic import vis-à-vis other members of his or her society. Overall, we see a high degree of centralization in the palace economies of the Aegean, with the palaces maintaining direct or indirect control over much of the economic activity within their states. Furthermore, these economies are maintained via a regimented hierarchy of personnel displaying a level of specialization unsustainable after the destruction of the palaces ca. 1200 BCE.

This economic evidence is particularly useful for the study of Bronze Age women. For a time period previously dependent on the vagaries of iconographic representations or on dubiously sexed burials for our understanding of social organization,[57] the tablets provide numerous and invaluable prosopographical details, documenting women's names, titles, professions, and, through the materials variously allotted to or collected from them, a sense of women's relative importance within the societies to which they contribute, a resource whose importance to the social historian cannot be overestimated.[58] This situation, where women are rendered visible to the historian by means of their economic roles, stands in marked contrast to Classical Athens, for instance, where what visibility women accrue stems from their roles within the domestic or religious spheres.

Returning to the Late Bronze Age, it remains ironic that, while women's importance has tended to be overread in the iconography, it has for the most part been marginalized in previous studies of Linear B administration. In many syntheses, the focus has been primarily on male officials with women mentioned only briefly in discussions of specific groupings of tablets such as the personnel series[59] or as religious officials.[60] This is particularly unfortunate as the tablets are a valuable primary source from which to access women's role in the palatial economy. To date, in the 60 years following the decipherment of Linear B,[61] only seven studies have been specifically dedicated to women's activities in the Mycenaean economy.

The first study to address the functions performed by women in the tablets was published in 1958, within six years of Ventris's announcement of decipherment. In this study, Tritsch primarily addressed the workgroup women of the personnel series from Pylos.[62] Tritsch noted that a wide variety of occupational tasks were assigned to these women and opened the debate as to whether these low-status workers were to be understood as slaves or free. Tritsch argued that these women were free female contract labor who traveled to Pylos as refugees from the disturbances throughout the Aegean in the Late Bronze Age in order to seek paid employment; this theory is no longer widely accepted.

The women of the tablets received only one direct study throughout the 1960s and 1970s in the form of Deger-Jalkotzy's article on the parentage of the thirteen slave women listed on the tablet PY An 607.[63] Otherwise throughout these two decades, women were addressed not in studies exclusively devoted to women per se but via treatments of areas of the economy in which women made prominent appearances, for example, in work outlining the stationing and rationing of workers and in monographs devoted to specific institutions such as religion and industries such as textile production, where we are indebted to Killen's decades of careful and insightful study.[64]

This period also saw the publication of two of the most influential reference texts in Linear B research: the revised 2nd edition of Ventris and Chadwick's 1956 landmark study *Documents in Mycenaean Greek*[65] and Lindgren's invaluable prosopographical study *The People of Pylos*,[66] both published in 1973. Although neither of these texts has chapters or discussions devoted solely to women, both works are indispensable for researchers addressing Bronze Age prosopography and social and administrative structure.

The 1970s also saw a burgeoning interest in women's history within the discipline of Classics, an interest which grew rapidly and in multiple directions upon the publication of Pomeroy's 1975 landmark *Goddesses, Whores, Wives, and Slaves*.[67] These new directions of inquiry into women's historical realities in Ancient Greece took a variety of forms, ranging from monographs on women's legal, domestic, and economic status, to sourcebooks of primary materials relating to women's lives in antiquity, to thematically driven essay collections.[68] In the 1970s this growing interest in women's history was concentrated on women of the historical period but expanded in the 1980s to include the women of Greek pre- and proto-history alongside their Archaic and Classical counterparts.

Billigmeier and Turner's 1981 article,[69] published in the essay collection *Reflections of Women in Antiquity*, was the first study to reflect this renewed interest and was designed for a largely non-specialist audience and remains perhaps the most widely read treatment of women in the Linear B tablets.[70] In this survey of the evidence pertaining to women's socio-economic roles in the tablets, Billigmeier and Turner concentrated on bringing to light the variety of occupations held by women throughout the major palatial sites, noting divisions between sacerdotal women and artisans. In particular, they emphasized aspects of the tablets where men and women appeared to enjoy a somewhat egalitarian status and made the now-contested claim that "women in Mycenaean Greece may have enjoyed a more equal socio-economic status than they did in Classical Hellas."[71] However, this reading fails to note the dependent rather than free status of most of the female laborers and neglects to quantify the holdings associated with the different groups of women referenced in the tablets, thereby excluding from its treatment the evidence most pertinent to determining the status of the women of this study.

In 1983, Carlier published a short but first-rate article, "La femme dans la société mycénienne," among the papers of the conference *La Femme dans les Sociétés Antiques*;[72] it offered a well-grounded and judiciously presented survey of the types of information the tablets can and cannot provide about women in Mycenaean society.[73] This study first addressed the evidence for women in the state hierarchy – the role played by priestesses in palace society and the continuing difficulties in clearly identifying a Mycenaean queen – and then sampled the evidence for craftswomen at Knossos and Pylos on a site-by-site basis. Perhaps most importantly, Carlier first raised the possibility of differences in gender practices between the two sites, noting that in the Knossian texts recording women and children, greater attention was given to subdividing the age groups of the children accompanying the workgroup women than at Pylos, and that Knossos employed a wider variety of descriptive terms for women than did Pylos.

Uchitel further expanded the context in which the women of the Linear B tablets were studied in 1984. [74] He compared the records of Mycenaean women at Pylos and Knossos with those of the Near Eastern archives from Lagash and Ur.[75] This article focused primarily on the status of the women of these records using the Near Eastern records as comparanda for the Aegean and argued based on (somewhat slim) internal evidence and through analogy with the Near Eastern material, that the women of Pylos and Knossos should not be considered to have been slaves but rather corvée workers.[76] Of additional value is Uchitel's lucid and concise methodological discussion of the Aegean personnel tablets and his treatment and elucidation of parallel sources.

The final major inquiry into women's roles in the Aegean Bronze Age documents in this period of renewed interest was John Chadwick's 1988 article "The Women of Pylos," published as part of the essay collection *Texts, Tablets, and Scribes*.[77] Like Carlier, Chadwick offered a circumspect treatment of the women of the tablets, specifically the palatial craftswomen. In this study, Chadwick compiled and presented all the extant texts pertaining to the craftswomen of the Pylos A series (Aa, Ab, and Ad), identifying them by their workgroup titles (frequently proposing and commenting on suggested etymologies for these terms) and by location. He also identified the calculations involved in the supply of rations to these workers, noting the standardized nature of the rations. On the larger question of the status of these workers, Chadwick quite effectively refuted Tritsch's refugee theory, instead arguing in favor of regarding these women as "menial dependents, virtually if not legally slaves, many of them probably acquired through Greek trading posts in the Aegean."[78] It should be noted that this investigation was nearly exclusively devoted to the women of Pylos; Chadwick only briefly referenced the Knossos evidence, but noted one important difference between the women mentioned at the two sites: the location-derived adjectives (the so-called "ethnics") which occasionally accompany women's workgroups were exclusively derived from Crete in the Knossos archives while at Pylos women's ethnics appeared to derive exclusively from the Eastern Aegean and the Greek mainland.

Kokkinidou and Nikolaidou's sweeping 1993 synthesis Η αρχαιολογία και η κοινωνική ταυτό ητα του φύλου Προσεγγίσει στην αιγαιακή[79] was the first systematic investigation to reformulate the social evolution of Aegean Prehistory with gender as its primary axis of investigation. This study postulated that an increase/intensification of warfare led to an increasingly stratified social hierarchy as the Bronze Age progressed, a social hierarchy particularly delineated along gender lines, and that the more "egalitarian" societies of the Early and Middle Bronze Age were replaced by a more militaristic, hierarchical, and consequently patriarchal one in the Late Bronze Age. Kokkinidou and Nikolaidou draw the majority of their evidence from archaeological material, but they also briefly discuss the Linear B data, which they characterize as reflecting primarily an androcentric and hierarchical political system under the control of the male *wanax* ("king") and an evident task differentiation between the sexes which they attribute to an indoor/outdoor division of labor. Additionally, they discuss palatial religion, which they contend also became dominated by (male) hierarchical structures such as the priesthood. While I am reluctant to accept all aspects of their polarized pre-militaristic – egalitarian and militaristic – patriarchal theory of gendered social development, their discussion of religion is especially relevant to this project. Furthermore, their contention that women only acquire status through priesthood is addressed in Chapters 5 and 7, a contention I argue may be more accurate for the women of Pylos than for the women of Knossos.

From the late 1990s to the present, scholarship on women has evolved to include studies focused on recovering the lived realities of Bronze Age women and on recovering how Bronze Age social and political institutions were differently gendered for men and women. This scholarship has assumed three forms: 1. discussions of gender practices within specific Bronze Age social institutions, 2. textual studies not expressly devoted to women per se but where women figured prominently, 3. investigations employing ethnographic analogies to shed light on Aegean women and/or theoretical discussions about framing a methodology for studying Bronze Age women.[80] This first category – investigations of gender practice within Bronze Age institutions – has largely concerned the family unit[81] while the second category – studies of specific institutions where women are predominant – has been spearheaded by Killen's great corpus of work illuminating the textile industry at Knossos. Killen's work on the textile industry is currently being expanded by Burke and Nosch, addressing the mechanics of the industry and the work performed by female laborers.[82] Finally, Lupack's ongoing work on cult sanctuaries and their personnel continues to tease out the complex economic interactions between cult personnel and their polities – especially pertinent to the study of Mycenaean women is her attention to the roles and economic activities of sanctuary priestesses.[83]

While these various studies each help to illuminate some aspect of gender organization in the Mycenaean world, we nonetheless remain left with a disjointed and patchwork view of women and gender in this time period. While it is, of course, helpful to have an understanding of the evidence for women's activities in specific subsets of the tablets, or to tease out the complexities of how gendered iconography – both of women and of goddesses – is employed, we are still in urgent need of a broader narrative, one which helps illuminate the wider contexts occupied by women in the tablets and which helps to decipher at least some of the rules and patterns of Mycenaean gendered practices. In short, we have located and analysed many pieces of this puzzle, but we need a frame. At present, several key questions remain unanswered – and largely unposed: Who are the women visible in the tablets, how do they become visible, and are they broadly representative of the women of their states? What is the relationship between the various women recorded in the tablets at each site? Do they share a similar status as women or do the categories of gender, class, and/or other variables intersect to create hierarchies among women? Do the rules and practices governing women's activities in their states' economies vary across sites or is the status and economic role of women relatively homogeneous in the Mycenaean world? Iconography hints at differences;[84] do the texts confirm these? These questions all require answering, we need to take the tablets from each site as a whole, and this disparate evidence needs to be fitted into a more coherent narrative if we are to reach any overall understanding of how the category of woman functions in each of these palace states.

In addition to addressing these currently unasked questions, we also need to correct perhaps the largest methodological flaw in the previous scholarship; nearly all of the previous works share the tacit assumption that the different Mycenaean polities were essentially similar in their structures and institutions, and that the Linear B tablets reflected a Mycenaean *koine* not only of language but also of society. This methodological trait is particularly characteristic of previous studies of women's roles in the tablets and creates, I argue, a misleading impression of a single, monolithic conception of gender in place at all the different states of the Late Bronze Age Aegean. No previous study has juxtaposed the experience of the women recorded on the tablets across sites. Some studies have been confined to one site (generally Pylos) but the question of how similar gender practices are between Linear B-administered Pylos and Knossos has not yet been raised.

In fact, only recently have scholars begun to question the homogeneity of the so-called Mycenaean experience. Kopcke's paper ("The Argolid in 1400 – What Happened?")[85] prompted a discussion at the 1994 *Politeia* conference which led to Palaima's challenge for the future direction of Linear B studies:

> One of the challenges facing Linear B scholars in the next twenty or thirty years – and one we are coming to terms with now – is really to try to see, with the variations in information that are available from site to site, what the regional differences are even in the documentation for administration and economic and social structure from site to site. So it is very tempting to take the documentation that we have from Pylos – say texts Un 718 and Er 312 – and extrapolate from them universally….We should indeed not expect that Mycenae will conform to the pattern we see in the Linear B texts from Pylos….*We should also not expect that Mycenaean Knossos is going to conform to the pattern that we see at Pylos* [emphasis added]. So it is a real challenge to figure out region to region what is going on in the period of full palatial culture. [86]

This emphasis on site differentiation has not previously been applied to scholarship on women in the Late Bronze Age. What has been lacking in these studies of women in the tablets has been an attention to the potential site-specificity of gender practice in the Late Bronze Age. Surely, we cannot assume that gender practices are uniform across all Bronze Age sites, particularly given the unique historical circumstances of Pylos and Knossos. Instead we must allow for the possibility that Knossos and Pylos both functioned as unique and idiosyncratic political entities, which may well have made significantly different choices in their orderings of their gendered practices and structures.

This tendency to homogenize the social and administrative practices of Knossos and Pylos is understandable, if unfortunate. As Olivier has succinctly noted, there are many similarities in the scribal and administrative practices of these two states: documents are written and presented in a nearly identical fashion, the same ideograms are in use, and the same subject matter is addressed.[87] The similarities between the sites extend further than the mechanics of the texts; as Olivier noted, the economic system, which permitted the palace to assess and redistribute agricultural products or semi-finished ones, seems to have been absolutely identical on Crete and in Messenia. Nearly all the traces of economic activity (religious, military or civil) in one palace find their equivalent at least partially in the other.[88]

Olivier, however, went on to note that while the two sites appear very similar on a macroscopic level, when examined on a more microscopic level, distinct differences in the recording practices and themes emerge between Knossos and Pylos. In particular, he noted significant archival differences between the two sites (including wide ranges in numbers of scribes, findspots, and signs per tablets).[89] Differences have also been noted in the organization of various industries and personnel including the varied treatment of smiths, and the obligations related to sanctuary lands, the management of the perfume industry, and the attention paid to children's age grades at Knossos.[90] These studies strongly suggest that the specific mechanisms of the palace economy are not uniform throughout all Mycenaean polities but instead are adapted to suit best the local needs of each state. Perhaps the notion of local variation should not come as a surprise to us, particularly given the different historical circumstances of Pylos and Knossos[91] – those of Pylos, where a Mycenaean administration governed a Mycenaean population, and those of Knossos which, by the time of the Linear B tablets, witnessed a Mycenaean administration which superseded an earlier Minoan one and governed a co-mingled population of Greeks and ethnic Minoans.

The question of Mycenaean Crete

Knossos, before the end of the Late Minoan IB period (traditionally dated to ca. 1450 BCE),[92] had been the administrative center of one of at least five *Minoan* states – where Minoan populations had been governed by Minoan administrations.[93] Observable during the Minoan palatial period are distinctly and uniquely Minoan practices in architecture, ceramics, religion, social organization, and its system of scribal organization, which kept records in the Linear A script.

Widespread destructions of administrative buildings at the end of the LMIB period irrevocably changed the nature of Minoan Crete and the site of Knossos. These destructions have largely been attributed to the coming of Mycenaeans from the mainland who remained and grafted a Mycenaean administration onto what had previously been Minoan-governed Crete.[94] While there continues to be much debate over the exact mechanisms which governed this assumption of power on Crete by Mycenaean Greeks and whether they occurred concurrent with the LMIB destructions or in the following LMII period, certainly by the time the Knossos Linear B tablets were inscribed, Knossos and the parts of Crete under its control were unquestionably under Mycenaean administration.[95]

Yet the Mycenaean-administered palatial state of Knossos is an entity unparalleled on the Mycenaean mainland. At Mycenaean Knossos, we encounter not a state like Pylos, where an ethnic Mycenaean population is governed by a Mycenaean administration, but rather a hybrid society of both ethnic Minoans and ethnic Mycenaeans under the authority of a Mycenaean administration.[96]

One of the major issues current in Aegean research is the question of how Mycenaean was Mycenaean-administered Crete.[97] Under this investigative rubric, archaeologists are focusing attention on questions of assimilation and of cultural survivals, asking what happened to Minoan culture in the period of Mycenaean administration. These investigations have devised a number of paradigms for interrogating material culture in order to identify the degree to which Minoan cultural traits are retained or displaced under Mycenaean administration. Scholarship is divided on the question of Minoan assimilation into Mycenaean "culture." Davis and Bennet see Mycenaeanization as "a relatively homogenous cultural *koine* that covered most of the southern Aegean at the end of the Late Bronze Age,"[98] one which had the capacity for absorbing and acculturating non-Greek-speaking populations, especially non-Mycenaean elites. As evidence for a *koine* of Mycenaean culture, they cite the relative homogeneity of material culture during LH/LM III and read "the language of the Linear B tablets – almost indistinguishable from Knossos to Thebes – [as] used as a marker of elite Mycenaean identity."[99] (The central problem with this reading, of course, is that it notes the linguistic unity of the script used by the various palace scribes; yet unity of scribal language does not necessarily demand a similar level of *cultural* homogeneity in the social, political, and economic behaviors of the different Mycenaean states and their inhabitants.)

On the other hand, the persistence of Minoan ceramic and architectural styles on Crete would seem to indicate the continued survival of at least some indigenous Minoan artisanship and technologies into the period of Mycenaean administration. Additional Minoan cultural survivals seem to be indicated in the sphere of religion; various tablets from Knossos record local Minoan divinities receiving offerings along with Olympians, votive traditions persist, and Minoan burial patterns continue deep into the Mycenaean period. Two textual studies have also tracked the degree of assimilation for Minoan men by examining the geographical contexts where Minoan men's names are given to boys and where Mycenaean ones seem to have been preferred.[100] (Driessen has also argued on the basis of later literary evidence that the process of Hellenization on Crete should be regarded as a slow, centuries-long process.)[101] It seems clear that at least some elements of an earlier Minoan culture persist and are co-existent with Mycenaean cultural traits, at least as far as religion, technology, and the social organization of men are concerned.

But is this also true for the social organization of Cretan women? More to the point, how do the social and cultural choices of Minoan society fare under a Mycenaean Greek administration? Would our model be one of broad cultural assimilation to the gender mores and practices of the Mycenaean administration or do elements of Minoan cultural practices persist? To answer this question, we might look to see how closely the gender patterns of Knossos conform to those of mainland Pylos. Closely patterned similarities might argue for a high degree of assimilation of Minoan gender roles and practices into Mycenaean ones while significant differences might argue for the holdovers of at least some aspects of a more Minoan approach to gender organization, persisting even a century or so after the initial Mycenaean dominance of Knossos. This is particularly significant if the theorized higher status for women in Minoan Crete than in mainland Greek society is valid;[102] should this be true, we would have a scenario in which a society with a relatively low status for women assumes dominance over another which accords women a higher social status. So what did political dominance by Mycenaeans mean for the women of previously Minoan Crete? The answer to this question may offer another entry point into the assimilation/persistence debate.

The structure and scope of this study

Uchitel writes concerning the Sumerian texts of the Ur III period, "we have to keep in mind that Sumerian economic texts were not written for the purpose of sociological research, but for the very practical reason of registration of actual work-teams"[103] under the control of the administration of Ur. This caveat also applies to the range of evidence present in the Linear B records. Keeping this in mind, we must acknowledge the futility of using the Linear B tablets to answer all our questions about Mycenaean palatial society. A more viable and valuable approach to the tablets, then, lies in the careful framing of questions which the tablets can answer, rather than those they cannot. Therefore, for this study, the central research question posed is "is the treatment of women in the economic records from Pylos and Knossos the same?" – a question that the tablets can address. This central question is posed across the two sites in terms of how women's status compares to that of men at each site, the ways in which women's status tiers are arranged and structured and the ways in which well-documented institutions shared by both sites (e.g. land tenure and religion) are gendered.

Consequently, this study focuses mainly on the economic activities of women at these two sites and uses their Linear B tablets as its primary source for women's participation in economic matters. In assessing this evidence, I contend that the different historical circumstances of Mycenaean Pylos and Mycenaean-Minoan Knossos have produced very different gendered economic structures at the two sites. In particular I ask the question, how closely do the economic activities of women at a purely Mycenaean site like Pylos conform to those of women at a hybridized Mycenaean-Minoan site like Knossos? Do we see women's production and property holdings taking roughly the same form at both sites – indicating a high level of correspondence – or do they differ significantly? I argue that a high level of correspondence would indicate that an indigenous Minoan gender system had been largely assimilated into that of the Mycenaean administration while a high level of difference would indicate that even under Mycenaean political domination, Crete continues to be governed by its own idiosyncratic system of gender.

Toward this end, I focus on the ways they manage their subordinate populations: women. Women are the focus of this project because it is here with women where gender-based status differences are visible – far more visible than among men within patriarchal societies. Due to the patriarchal organization of both Knossos and Pylos, the men of the two states appear largely the same; at both sites, men comprise the highest civic and ruling elite, own or control the majority of commodities and resources, and are fully integrated throughout all the arenas of palatial social, political, and economic life. To see difference, we must look to the marked, rather than unmarked, social category; to the ways in which the socially subordinated sex is incorporated into palace society, for it is here where we may observe variances in the degrees of access to resources, and in patterns of ownership, social and economic mobility, task-assignments, etc. In a mathematical analogy, if men are considered to have full (100 percent) access to all areas of ancient economic life (commodities, property, social and political institutions, etc.), differences in gender practice will not be particularly visible between one site or another. If, however, women at one site have 75 percent access to men's activities, and women at another have 20 percent, we might speculate that different ideologies about women and their social roles are at work in these two societies.

Throughout this study, I focus on areas of visible difference – seeking to identify the types of access and relative economic status of the women at Pylos and the women at Knossos – both vis-à-vis men in their societies, and then vis-à-vis each other. Practically, and due to the methodological issues inherent to the fragmented Knossos corpus, this translates to first identifying the ways in which various economic institutions at Pylos are organized by gender and then contrasting the more limited evidence from Knossos with the patterns recoverable at Pylos. As the evidence of both archives indicates the overall subordinate position of women,[104] I ask not whether women were dominant or even equal participants in the political arena of Late Bronze Age palatial society— since it seems certain that they were not – but rather whether there was a common system of gender organization in place in the Late Bronze Age Aegean or rather discrete, site-specific systems such as those present in the historical period. In what ways is gender constructed in these two centers, what gender roles do women occupy, how do the palaces incorporate women into their economies, and does gender construction – in the forms of gender roles and gender ideologies as recoverable from both the textual and iconographic evidence – look the same on Mycenaean Crete as it does on the Mycenaean mainland? I argue that not only does gender play a major role in governing the range and scope of women's roles in both palatial economies, but also that each site makes different and locally specific choices in the ways it structures women's production and control over goods and commodities.

This book addresses these questions by examining both the quantitative and qualitative evidence pertaining to women's economics in the tablets, with emphasis on the specifics of each palatial site. Toward this end, I limit my discussion to only those women who can be established *qua* women with a high degree of security,[105] and I concentrate on the ways in which task assignments and property holdings create and reinforce status hierarchies both between men and women and among women. Throughout, I identify what gender patterns are in place at each site with respect to such social and economic institutions as property holdings (including land holding), production and task assignment, and religion, and compare each site's pattern for engendering each institution within the other's in order to identify similarities and differences. As mentioned above, the evidence allows a greater chance at reconstructing and modeling gendered patterns at Pylos; the Knossos evidence does not allow such modeling, but can be used as a counterpoint to the patterns observed at Pylos.

Above all, I argue that even as early as Late Bronze Age Greece, gender is already a site-specific and locally distinct institution, governed by the needs and ideologies of a particular community at a particular historical moment. Toward this end, this book comprises several thematic chapters which explore different facets of women's economic activities at both sites. Chapter 2 establishes the criteria by which I identify women in the tablets and discusses the ways in which both Knossos and Pylos are revealed as gender-segregated and patriarchal societies. The remaining chapters address the ways in which gender affects specific palatial institutions critical to the economies of both sites. Chapters 3–5 investigate the roles that production and property holding play in creating and reinforcing status hierarchies among elite and non-elite women at each site. Chapter 3 discusses the evidence for low-status women at Pylos, women who are defined exclusively through their production activities, while Chapter 4 discusses the property holdings of elite Pylian women as well as the criteria which appear to justify their more elite status. Chapter 5 discusses production and property at Knossos and identifies the ways in which women's hierarchies at Knossos differ from those of Pylos. Chapters 6 and 7 each focus on the two specific institutions where men and women at both sites are recorded in sufficient numbers to assess how gender affects the involvement of the sexes vis-à-vis each other: Chapter 6 addresses men's and women's investiture into the land tenure systems of Pylos and Knossos while Chapter 7 surveys the evidence for the gendering of cult offices and the ways in which religion relates to the creation and sustaining of social hierarchies.

I conclude with a discussion of the ramifications of this gender-centric investigation[106] as they pertain to the study of women's economic history within Greek antiquity, especially with respect to low-status women, and within Bronze Age studies to address the ways in which newly visible gender practice impacts questions such as the structure of the larger palatial economy and the Hellenization of Late Bronze Age Crete.

Notes

1 Moses I. Finley's seminal 1954 study *The World of Odysseus* explored the palace-centered societies of the Homeric epics, set in the 10th–8th centuries BCE and established much of the social, economic, and cultural backdrops of the worlds of the epics. My project pushes back from the mythological world of Homer to the real-life palace societies the epics purport to describe, the palace societies of the Mycenaean Greek Bronze Age from the 14th to the late 13th centuries BCE to investigate and establish the social contexts experienced by actual rather than mythological women, drawing from documentary rather than epic sources.

2 These circumstances presage that of, for example, later Classical Athens where certain women – either those most revered, such as Athenian priestesses like Lysimache, or those most notorious, such as the former slave Neaira – appear as named and differentiated individuals while the vast majority enter the historical record in the collective, as girls or matrons in the practice of cult, as mourners lamenting family losses, or as widows grieving the loss of husbands in war.

3 Feminist historical scholarship has long emphasized the central role occupied by gender in human social organization from its emergence as a field in the 1970s via such work as Ortner 1974, and continuing to the present with recent studies such as Judith Bennett 2006. Early scholarship like Ortner's tended to emphasize human universality of ideology and experience while newer scholarship such as Bennett's instead insists on the necessity for focused and sustained attention to cultural specificity in the study of gender.

4 Research on gender and gendered societies which began within the discipline of history in the 1970s within ten years spread to other disciplines occupied with past societies, coming to Classical History in the mid-1970s, Aegean Bronze Age studies in the early 1980s and to Anthropology-based Archaeology in the mid-1980s with the work of Conkey and Spector 1984 and Gero and Conkey 1991. Useful review articles on the origins of feminist scholarship within anthropological archaeology include Wylie 1996; Gilchrist 1991; and R. Wright 1996a. For the state of scholarship on women in Ancient Greece, see Katz 2000.

5 The attention to local gender practices was the impetus behind the 2004 Feminism and Classics IV Conference, "Gender and Diversity in Place" hosted at the University of Arizona, Tucson. (Papers are published online at *Diotima* (www.stoa.org/diotima).)

6 On gender roles and ideologies in Spartan society: Bradford 1986; Cartledge 1981; Fantham, Foley, Kampen, Pomeroy and Shapiro 1994; Kunstler 1987; and Zweig 1993.

7 On the rationale behind gender relations at Athens: Cohen 1989; Foxhall 1995; Foxhall 1989; and Walters 1993. The major exception to these restrictions comes in the form of Athenian religion: Connelly 2007.

8 Scholarship alleging a higher status for Greek women in the Homeric era: Arthur 1981; and Leduc 1992. On women of the Geometric period: Coldstream 1995; Smithson 1968; and Whitley 1996.

9 Gimbutas 1999, 1997, 1974 has been the most vocal proponent of this position; she posits a matriarchal Minoan culture that came to be conquered by patriarchal Indo-European Mycenaeans. She reads this supposedly matriarchal Minoan culture as part of the larger culture of "Old Europe" which she regards as uniformly peaceful and matriarchal. Gimbutas argues that the preponderance (in her view) of female figurines from prehistoric Europe indicate the ascendancy of a Mother Goddess at the center of the "Old European" pantheon and that in turn the rule of a female figure in heaven is paralleled by the rule of mortal women in matriarchal societies throughout late Neolithic Europe. See also: Dexter and Polomé 1997; and Christ 1998. In recent years, several feminist prehistorians, notably Talalay 1994, 1993 and Meskell 1995 have called Gimbutas's interpretations into question, noting that the culture of "Old

Europe" is significantly less than uniform or monolithic or that Gimbutas's evidence – primarily consisting of figurines once thought to be predominantly female – is instead more frequently androgynous or of indeterminate gender. For histories and critiques of prehistoric matriarchal theories: Georgoudi 1992; Meskell 1995; and Tringham 1994.

10 This myth has strong ethnographic parallels in Amazon societies: Bamberger 1974.

11 This theory emerged with the *Palace of Minos* (Evans 1930, vol. 3: 227) and reemerged in feminist studies of the 1980s: Billigmeier and Turner 1981: n. 81; and Ehrenberg 1989.

12 "Women among the Minoans, as is well illustrated by their occupation of all the front seats of the Grand Stands, took the higher rank in Society, just as their great Goddess took the place later assigned to Zeus." Evans 1930: 227. Immerwahr 1983 echoes this statement, noting that "the frescoes from Knossos certainly suggest a female bias," but Nixon 1983 rightly criticizes dependence solely on iconography to read a high status for Minoan women.

13 The evidence most commonly cited by proponents of this position is the Women in Blue, the Sacred Grove, Temple, and Grandstand Frescoes.

14 Scholarship has also investigated Mycenaean women, but to a lesser degree; the gender dynamics of Mycenaean society have largely been treated as a foil for the allegedly "female-centered" Minoan culture and dismissed as entirely patriarchal in nature: Kokkinidou and Nikolaidou 1993: n. xx.

15 Kopaka 2009; Dyczek 1992; Hägg and Marinatos 1981; Marinatos 1995, 1993, 1987a, 1987b.

16 For example, Acheson 1999 on longevity in the Bronze Age which revealed sex-based differences in life expectancy: 32 years for Late Bronze Age women and 40 for men. Cavanagh and Mee 1998 also note that male burials outnumber female in Mycenaean society, offering as possible explanations a higher level of female than male infanticide or a declination to bury unmarried or widowed women. Lisa Little's anthropological investigation into family relations in the graves at Mochlos is eagerly anticipated.

17 For clarification purposes, I am treating as "Minoan" all material up to the LMIB destructions on the island. I use the term "Mycenaean Crete" to identify the hybridized society of the LM II and LM III periods in which the island is being administrated in the Greek Linear B script. See Driessen 1990 for definitively fixing LM II as administered in Linear B (Room of the Chariot Tablets). As no women are mentioned in the Room of the Chariot Tablets texts, all Knossian references will date to the LM III period.

18 Alexandri 1994; Lee 1995.

19 *Supra*, note 13.

20 Hitchcock's work on gendered spaces in the Minoan world is typical of the increased sophistication of recent iconographic studies through careful attention to detail and strict methodology; she observes that rather than operating as part of a fluid gender system, gender roles in Minoan art tend toward clear definition and delineation: Hitchcock 2000, 1997.

21 Jones 1998.

22 Damiani Indelicato 1988; Younger 1995, 1976.

23 Rehak 2007; Rutter 2003.

24 While iconography cannot permit the full recovery of day-to-day lived realities, it can provide useful insight into societal norms and expectations: Weingarten 1999.

25 Marinatos 1995: 584–85; Olsen 1998.

26 Warren 1969: 174–81; Hood 1978: 142–50; Younger and Rehak 2008: 152.

27 E. Davis 1995: 11–20.

28 E. Davis, citing the evidence of portrait seals notes, "it must be significant that only men and not women appear on the portrait seals. And it is primarily men who

are shown as single standing figures with attributes, the way men in the 'priest-robes' are shown. This suggests that men functioned in the Minoan hierarchy or administration in a capacity that was not shared by females." E. Davis 1995: 16. Likewise, Thomas 1999 notes that several major narrative vessels are entirely male-populated, including the Master Impression, the Deer Hunt, the Harvester Vase and the Boxer Rhyton.

29 Wachsman 1987; Rehak 1996.

30 Immerwahr 1983 notes that this apparent emphasis on women over men might reflect the dominance of a female divinity and her priestess at a religious ritual.

31 Kokkinidou and Nikolaidou 1993.

32 Olsen 1998, followed by Rutter 2003.

33 Exceptions to this trend are relatively few: human (as opposed to divine) women can be identified if they are wearing a sealstone – the mark of an administrator – on their wrists; a female figure is likely to be a representation of a goddess, on the other hand, if she is seated on a throne and surrounded by non-anthropomorphic characters such as griffins, monkeys, genii, etc. Otherwise, the distinction is very difficult to defend. Rehak 1995.

34 Immerwahr 1983.

35 Gates 1999.

36 A major archive at Thebes is currently being excavated and published; Chania is also producing a small, but extremely interesting, tablet cache.

37 The workings of the palatial economy and palatial industries continue to be a central topic of investigation in Bronze Age research. Discussions (non-gender-themed) of the Mycenaean palatial economy include: Earle 2002; Chaniotis 1999; Cline 1994; Halstead 1992; Morris 1986; Killen 2008, 1985; Olivier and Palaima 1988; R. Palmer 1994; Shelmerdine 2008a, 2008b, 2006, 1985; Shelmerdine and Bennet 2008; Sherratt and Sheratt 1991; Sjöberg 1995; Uchitel 1988.

38 "Les textes inscrits sur les tablettes sont toujours des comptes. On n'a aucun contrat, aucune lettre, aucune chronique, aucun hymne religieux, aucun texte littéraire. Ce point fondamental étant rappelé, il faut ajouter que les comptes mycéniens sont de types assez variés: on a des cadastres [land registers], des recensements [inventories], des rôles fiscaux, des rentrées d'impôt, des distributions de rations, des listes d'offrandes, etc." Carlier 1983: 9.

39 These goods and holdings include both imported goods and those produced for export. Shelmerdine 1998: 292.

40 Uchitel 1988: 20, 23.

41 Ventris and Chadwick 1956: 106; Killen 2008: 159.

42 The palaces' role as redistributive centers has long been recognized: Finley 1957a.

43 Killen 1985: 252.

44 For studies on Minoan-Mycenaean divinities: Gérard-Rousseau 1968; L. Palmer 1981; Yamagata 1995.

45 Nakassis 2013: 1–20, provides an excellent survey of the evolving scholarship on the nature and structures of the Mycenaean economy.

46 Sjöberg 1960: 109–144.

47 Nakassis 2013: 2–16.

48 Nakassis 2013: 2. See also Bennet 2007: 190; Galaty and Parkinson 2007: 26.

49 Nakassis 2013: 2.

50 Bennet 2001: 25–26.

51 Bennet, 2007: 195. Nakassis 2013: 2–20.

52 De Fidio 2001; Nikoloudis 2006, 2008b; Nakassis 2013: 3.

53 A few non-transactional usages of Linear A are also known, such as short inscriptions on so-called offering tables found at shrines throughout the island.

54 Longer-term records are thought to have been transferred to more costly surfaces, such as papyrus.

55 For example, Facaros and Pauls 2003: 109. Rather than as shopping lists I suggest they should probably be thought of as akin to contemporary corporate phone logs in that they typically provide, in abbreviated form, details of a transaction including the name, title, and location of the relevant official, the form of commodity and its specific size. The obvious advantage of this model is in its focus on the real people involved in real transactions at a specific moment in time.

56 The majority of the tablets where men and women are not mentioned are typically either illegible or very fragmentary; the Pylian and Knossian texts most commonly reference not only the commodities involved in a given transaction but the humans involved in these transactions as well.

57 In the late nineteenth and early twentieth centuries – arguably the most prolific period for the excavation of Bronze Age cemeteries – burials were typically sexed not by anthropological examination of skeletal remains, but rather by Victorian/Edwardian notions regarding the sexual distribution of grave goods. Graves containing weapons were commonly sexed as male, while graves with jewelry were sexed as female without further physical investigation. This causes great distortion in the evidence particularly on Crete where, "no clear index of distinction between male and female [grave gifts] may be established." D'Agata 1999: 52. Consequently, it has largely been impossible to link burial property conclusively with one sex or the other. Fortunately, recent research has begun to sex Bronze Age graves based on skeletal remains: Cavanagh and Mee 1998: 165–171.

58 Numerous recent textual studies of women of the Mesopotamian Bronze Age provide useful comparanda for research on Bronze Age Aegean women. In particular: Lerner 1986; Uchitel 1984.

59 These tablets roster and record rations for personnel dependent on the palace. They are generally identified as belonging to the A series and are discussed more extensively in Chapters 2, 3, and 5.

60 Cline 2011; Shelmerdine 2008a; Dickinson 1994.

61 For the story of Linear B's decipherment, see Pope 2008.

62 Tritsch 1958.

63 Deger-Jalkotzy 1972.

64 For a discussion of Killen's work on the palatial textile industry, see Chapters 3 and 5, *passim*.

65 Ventris and Chadwick 1956, 1973.

66 Killen 1985: 252.

67 Pomeroy 1975. Among the early 1970s, "pre-Pomeroy" studies: Ortner 1974; Richter 1971; Slater 1974; Thomas 1973; de Ste. Croix 1970.

68 Notable works on women's legal, domestic, and economic status in Greek antiquity include Cohen 1989; Cole 1981; Gould 1980; Just 1989; Lefkowitz 1983; Schaps 1979; Sealey 1990. Sourcebooks include: Kraemer 1988; Lefkowitz and Fant 1992. Essay collections include: Cameron and Kuhrt 1983; Foley 1981; Hawley and Levick 1995; Schmitt Panel 1992; Peradotto and Sullivan 1984; Pomeroy 1991.

69 Billigmeier and Turner 1981.

70 Interestingly, this interest in women in Aegean prehistory predates the beginnings of feminist archaeological inquiry within anthropology, where gender was also primarily investigated through economic evidence. Feminist archaeological inquiry within anthropology began with a co-authored four-page article in 1984 where Conkey and Spector offered suggestions for investigating gender in prehistoric societies through an economic framework focused on task-differentiation: Conkey and Spector 1984.

71 Billigmeier and Turner 1981: 10.

72 Carlier 1983.

73 Among the lacunae he places the education of free young women, matrimonial customs, and the role of wives. Carlier 1983: 31.

74 Uchitel 1984.

75 For a more general comparison between the Mycenaean and Near Eastern archives: Uchitel 1988.
76 This contention is addressed in depth in Chapters 3 and 5.
77 Chadwick 1988.
78 Chadwick 1988: 92.
79 Kokkinidou and Nikolaidou 1993.
80 Most prominent among this research is the work of Barber and Nosch on women and textiles in Aegean prehistory: Barber 1997, 1994, 1991; Nosch 2012, 2011, 2008, 2003; and Nosch and Gillis 2007. For non-textile related investigations, see also Ehrenberg 1989: 50–54; Kopaka 1997; Nordquist 1995; R. Wright 1991.
81 For women in the family, see Hiller 1989; Olsen 1998; Rutter 2003; and Budin 2011, the latter of which examines kourotrophic imagery in Bronze Age Mediterranean iconography, including Mycenaean and Minoan art.
82 Burke 2011, 1999, 1997; Nosch 2000, 1997b, 1997a. Nosch's work with experimental archaeology reproducing ancient textile techniques and technologies continues to offer particularly promising insights into this critically important industry.
83 Lupack 2008a, 2007a, 2007b, 1999.
84 For example, the Mycenaean mainland maintains a significant interest in gendered scenes of mother and children, while Mycenaean Crete does not: Olsen 1998.
85 Kopcke 1995.
86 Palaima 1995a: 93.
87 Olivier 1984: 12.
88 Olivier 1984: 12.
89 On differences in scribal habits across the two sites: Olivier 1984. See also Bartonek 1983: 19–22; Tegyey 1987.
90 For the treatment of smiths and sanctuary lands: Olivier 1984. For the perfume industry: E. D. Foster 1980; Shelmerdine 1985, 1984. For age grade variances: Tegyey 1987. Also: J. Bennet 1990, 1988b; Hooker 1987a; Ilievski 1983; Shelmerdine 1988.
91 Another critical difference between the two is the different dates of their archives in the LH/M III phases of the Mycenaean era. The Pylos tablets are, save five tablets, a chronologically unified archive dating to the end of the LH IIIB period (generally dated ca. 1200 BCE); the Knossos tablets, on the other hand, are more complicated. The unity of the main body of the Knossos tablets remains heavily debated and no consensus has yet been reached as to whether they derive from one destruction or many; likewise their date. While they are at least a century earlier than the tablets at Pylos, the Knossos tablets have been variously dated ranging from LH II to LH IIIA1 (for the Room of the Chariot Tablets texts) to LH IIIA2-LH IIIB for the larger set. For recent discussions on the state of the debate over the date and unity of the Knossos tablets, see Driessen 2008; and Shelmerdine and Bennet 2008: 292, 310–11, 320.
92 On traditional and revised datings for the Late Bronze Age, see Dickinson 1994; Manning 1995; Warren and Hankey 1989.
93 Palaces have been discovered at Knossos, Phaistos, Malia, Kato Zakro, and recently at Galatas.
94 There continues to be debate over the exact time that Mycenaean administration was imposed on Crete, but as recent research by Driessen indicates, as early as LM II, the Greek language as evidenced by the Linear B script was already well established on Crete: Driessen 1990: 115–125. Whether the coming of the Mycenaeans to Crete should be dated to the LM IB destructions or to the LM II phase continues to receive lively debate. Among those arguing against an LM IB are Driessen and McDonald, who argue for internal rather than external causes for the disintegration of Minoan society during LM IB and cite as support for their contention that other than at Knossos, LM II occupation remained scarce for most sites on Crete. Driessen and McDonald 1997: 389.

95 For the evidence of Mycenaeans at LM II Knossos: Driessen and McDonald 1984; Driessen 1990: 115–125. For a dissenting view, see Niemeier 1983, who contests reading LM II Knossos as Mycenaean. To my mind, Driessen's establishment of a LM II date for the Linear B tablets in the Room of the Chariot Tablets severely problematizes Niemeier's argument.

96 Studies on ethnicity in the Aegean Bronze Age have taken two major forms: theoretical and methodological discussions and archaeological studies of Mycenaean and Minoan interactions via the physical evidence. Major recent theoretical and methodological discussions: S. Jones 1997; Hall 1997; Sherratt and Sherratt 1998, and Bennet 2008. Notable among studies focusing on the interactions of ethnic Minoans and ethnic Mycenaeans on Crete is D'Agata 1999: 47–55. D'Agata notes (*pace* Popham, Catling and Catling 1974: 253) that the two ethnic groups remain sufficiently distinct during LMII – LM IIIA1 to be using different cemeteries at Knossos, associating in particular the cemeteries at Mavrospelia and Gypsadhes with Minoan burials.

97 Important recent overviews of this question include de Fidio 2008; Preston 2008; D'Agata and Moody 2005; and Driessen and Farnoux 1997; and Driessen and Langohr 2007.

98 J. Davis and J. Bennet 1999: 113.

99 J. Davis and J. Bennet 1999: 115. In this position, Davis and Bennet echo Tsountas and Manatt 1966, who argue for the "ultimate homogeneity" of mixed-population Mycenaean cultures under a dominant Greek rubric.

100 The prosopographical studies of Firth 1993 and Baumbach 1979 each indicate that assimilation differed for men across the parameters of space and social status. Firth, examining the naming patterns for men at Crete, noted a strong correlation between Mycenaean male names and identification and social rank, observing that 80 percent of the high-ranking male officials at Knossos had Greek rather than Minoan names. Baumbach, in her investigation of the naming patterns of shepherds, noted that these low-ranking men had names which were 80 percent non-Greek (Minoan). Taken in conjunction, these two studies seem to demonstrate the disproportionate rankings of Minoan- and Mycenaean-identified men, with greater social status associated with Greek names on Mycenaean-administered Crete. A similar study is not possible with women's names at Knossos as too few are extant to be statistically significant.

101 Driessen 1998–99: 83.

102 Ehrenberg 1989.

103 Uchitel 1984: 273.

104 None of the upper-ranking officials who can be definitely identified are female, nor do women hold any of the larger estates of the land recorded in the palatial systems.

105 A detailed delineation of these criteria appears in Chapter 2.

106 This project intersects in particular with many of the theoretical issues raised by feminist archaeological research within the fields of anthropology and history, notably the ongoing work on the incorporation of women into status hierarchies and the role of gender in social stratification as well as the structures and rationales governing male/female task differentiation; see especially: Ehrenberg 1989; Lerner 1986; Spector 1993; Tringham 1994; R. Wright 1996a, 1996b.

2 Identifying and contextualizing women in the tablets[1]

Introduction

The Linear B tablets from Knossos and Pylos offer a rare opportunity for the study of women's economic history in the ancient Aegean.[2] These documents, which were commissioned and collected by the administrations of these Mycenaean palace states in the Late Bronze Age, were serendipitously preserved by the very fires that destroyed their palaces – fires that preserved the clay fabric of the tablets as if in a kiln. Therefore, these accidentally preserved documents, deciphered again some 32 centuries after their initial loss, are to historians of gender an invaluable cache of historical documents recording the lived economic and public roles of actual, rather than idealized, women. With the exception of the papyrological records of Hellenistic Egypt, these texts, in both the quantity and quality of information they preserve, provide the most extensive documentation of women in the historical record of any period in Greek antiquity. Consequently, study of these tablets serves to enlarge the scope of scholarship on women in Ancient Greece by allowing the inclusion of Mycenaean women in our discussions of women in Greek antiquity and offers a valuable early counterpoint to the more frequently discussed (and less well-documented) women of the Archaic and Classical periods.

Locating women in the Linear B tablets

Before any discussion of women's roles and activities in the Linear B tablets can be initiated, it is first necessary to establish which persons can be recognized with certainty as women – and to limit the field of discussion only to those individuals who can be definitively identified as women.[3] This task requires careful attention, as the usual means of identifying women in (alphabetic) Greek texts are further complicated by the conventions of the syllabic Linear B script.[4] Isolating the presence of women in alphabetic Greek texts can be a thorny matter in itself; the choice of Greek to use the masculine plural to refer to groups including both men and women and the fact that Greek does not always allow the sexing of names based on their endings alone (as many Greek names of either sex end in –ω or –ις) highlight only two of the methodological obstacles to the secure identification of women in Greek texts. The complexity of the situation is only heightened by the requirements for writing Linear B; in particular, the requirement of Linear B that all words be rendered in syllabic form (either naturally occurring syllables or those artificially rendered to fit the script) and that all syllables end with a vowel can make the normalization of a Mycenaean Greek word back into its phonetic counterpart difficult. This is especially the case in Linear B's omission of final sigmas, which can serve to blur critical distinctions between such nominal endings as -ης and -η or -ας and -α and hence to obscure the gender of the named individual. And lastly, due to the particular history of Knossos with its co-mingled Greek and non-Greek populations bearing names either Greek in form or with apparent Minoan language origins further complicates the sexing of persons; it is surely not reasonable to assume that non-Greek words would follow Greek conventions for signaling gender. All of these are legitimate concerns that illustrate the inherent challenges of the evidence, and most careful attention is required to distinguish between male and female persons in the Mycenaean archives. Fortunately for the modern researcher, the ancient scribes seemed to have shared many of these concerns, employing in their texts several practical solutions through which they could (and we can) identify the sex of individuals or groups in the tablets, with a high degree of security. Of these, three primary conventions allow an individual to be securely sexed as female: the addition of the Linear B ideogram for woman (MUL); the use of a gender-specific familial, occupational and/or official title; and the use of the feminine variant of an identifiably Greek name.

Method 1: The MUL ideogram

The simplest and most secure means for distinguishing the sex of an individual is to locate a personal name or a title accompanied by the ideogram for either MAN or for WOMAN (Figures 2.1 and 2.2). These ideograms – schematic line drawings of either a man or a woman – are transliterated using the standard scholarly convention for rendering Linear B ideograms with their equivalent Latin terms. Hence, the convention is to render these ideograms in textual transliterations as VIR ("man") and MUL (for *mulier* "woman"). When the scribes provide these ideograms, the task of detecting women in the tablets is much simplified.

Figure 2.1 MUL Ideogram

Figure 2.2 VIR Ideogram

In addition to being the simplest convention to convey gender, the MUL ideogram is also the most common means for signaling the presence of women on a tablet. Of the 199 tablets at Knossos that preserve mentions of women, 71 employ the MUL ideogram and it can reasonably be restored in lacuna on another 52 tablets. Similarly, MUL appears on 84 tablets and can reasonably be restored on another 11 of the 208 Pylian texts mentioning women.[5] Overall, more than half of the women who can be identified in the tablets are identifiable through the usage of MUL either alone or in conjunction with women's names or titles. This seems to be the solution that both Knossian and Pylian scribes most frequently employed to sidestep any difficulties involved in sexing potentially ambiguous names or titles.

The MUL ideogram in the Pylos tablets

As noted above, 84[6] of the extant tablets from the mainland site of Pylos use the MUL ideogram to signal that their tablets record women.[7] These 84 tablets employing the MUL ideogram record a total of approximately 1100 women mentioned either as individuals or as members of collective groups. [8] The Pylian texts use MUL to signal "woman" in two different ways: either on its own or accompanying the women belonging to aggregate workgroups. In all instances at Pylos in which is it used, MUL refers to women of low social rank.

The MUL ideogram is almost exclusively the domain of the A series (or personnel series) tablets from Pylos, a series devoted to the tallying and rationing of low-ranking palace workers. Outside the personnel series, only three additional texts use this ideogram: the clay tablet-transport basket label PY Wa 114, which recorded rations allocated to workgroup women in Pylos's outer province,[9] PY Wa 1008, a sealing so fragmentary it preserves only the MUL and a three-sign word fragment, and the much-discussed offering tablet PY Tn 316.[10]

As a modifier for women's workgroups at Pylos, MUL appears in the two subseries of the personnel tablets Aa and Ab, which respectively record the group strength and rations provided for workgroups of female laborers and their children.[11] In these personnel series tablets the MUL ideogram is used in conjunction with workgroup designations in four ways: with women's occupational titles, with adjectives identifying the geographic ("ethnic") origins of workgroup women, with place names identifying the current location of the workgroups, or to identify (unnamed) women in the service of elite male officials. These titles always appear in the nominative feminine plural. In these series, the ideogram serves to reinforce the entirely female composition of these workgroups.[12] The following section offers a brief introduction to each of these workgroup designations. (Table 2.1 lists all occupational usages of MUL at Pylos.)

Of these four types of workgroups, those identified with task designations are most common; MUL commonly appears alongside the occupational titles. Many of these titles normalize clearly into Greek and can be easily read and translated; other titles are less clear etymologically but can still be recognized as task designations due to their usages of agent suffixes, most notably the feminine variant of –ευς,

Table 2.1 Women's titles identified by MUL at Pylos

Workgroup designation	*Normalized (ethnics and tasks)*	*Tablet*
a-*64-ja	*Aswiai* ("women of Asia/Lydia")	PY Aa 701, PY Ab 515
a-ke-ti-ra2 / a-ke-ti-ri-ja	*asketriai* "finishers/decorators"	PY Aa 717, PY Aa 815, PY Ab 564, PY Aa 85, PY Ab 1099, PY Un 219.04
a-pi-qo-ro	*amphiqoloi* "attendant-women"	PY Aa 804
a-pu-ko-wo-ko	a*mpukworgoi* "headband makers"	PY Ab 210
a-ra-ka-te-ja	*alakateiai* "spinning women"	PY Aa 89, PY Aa 240
e-ke-ro-qo-no	*enkheroquoinoi* "women wage-earners"	PY Aa 854, PY Ab 1100
e-ke-ro-qo-no o-pi-ro-qo	*enkheroquoinoi* "unassigned/remaining women wage-earners," *opiloquoi* "supernumerary"	PY Aa 777, PY Ab 563
e-wi-ri-pi-ja	*Ewipiai* ("women from Εὔριπος," ethnic adj.	PY Aa 60
ka-pa-ra2	description of women cloth-worker(s), ethnic or descriptive term	PY An 292.02, PY Aa 788
ki-ma-ra	description of women, possibly ethnic adj.	PY Aa 63
ki-ni-di-ja	*Knidiai* ("women from Κνίδος)," ethnic adj.	PY Aa 792, PY Ab 189, PY An 292.04
ki-ri-te-wi-ja	a class of women with a religious function	PY An 607
ki-si-wi-ja	"Chian women;" ki-si-wi-ja ethnic adj., describing women	PY Aa 770
ki-si-wi-ja o-nu-ke-ja	"Chian women o-nu-ka makers"	PY Ab 194
ko-ro-ki-ja	ethnic adj. describing women	PY Aa 354, PY An 292.03, PY Ab 372
ku-te-ra3	"*Kytherai* (cf. PN: Κύθερᾳ)," ethnic adj.	PY Aa 506, PY Ab 562
ku-te-ra3 ka-pa-ra2	"Kytheran textile workers;" ka-pa-ra2 (above)	PY Aa 788
me-re-ti-ra2/ me-re-ti-ri-ja	*meletriai* "flour-grinders"	PY Aa 62, PY Aa 764, PY Ab 789
mi-ra-ti-ja	*Milatia*i ("women of Miletus)," ethnic adj.	PY Aa 798, PY Ab 382, PY Ab 573, PY Ae 634
mi-ra-ti-ja a-ra-[ka-]te-ja	*Milatiai* ("women of Miletus) spinning women"; a-ra-ka-te-ja (above)	PY Ad 380
ne-we-wi-ja	adj., describing women textile-workers	PY Aa 695, PY Ab 560
no-ri-wo-ko	"nori-workers" (*–worgoi*)	PY Aa 98
o-pi-ro-qo	*opiloquoi* "remaining, supernumerary"	PY Ab 899

Workgroup designation	*Normalized (ethnics and tasks)*	*Tablet*
o-ti-ra2/o-ti-ri-ja	"*-triai* workers" (name of a trade: *-triai*)	PY Aa 313, PY Ab 417+1050
pa-wo-ke	*pan-worges* "maids with a variety of tasks"	PY Aa 795, PY Ab 558
pe-ki-ti-ra2	*pektriai* "wool-carders"	PY Ab 578
ra-mi-ni-ja	*Lamniai* ("women of PN: Λῆμνος," ethnic adj.	PY Ab 186
ra-pi-ti-ra	*raptriai* "sewing women" [ῥάπτριαι]	PY Ab 555
ra-qi-ti-ra2	*laqutriai* description of women; women's trade not identical with ra-pi-ti-ra2	PY Ab 356 + 1049
ra-wi-ja-ja	*lawiaiai*, description of women	PY Aa 807, PY Ab 586
re-wo-to-ro-ko-wo	*lewotrokhowoi* "bath-attendants"	PY Aa 783, PY Ab 553
ri-ne-ja	*lineiai* "linen-workers	PY Aa 94, PY Aa 96, PY Aa 772, PY Ab 379, PY Aa 93, PY Aa 76
(ri-ne-ja?) pa-ke-te-ja	*lineiai* "linen-workers;" pa-ke-te-ja (a women's trade – obscure, perhaps "measurers")	PY Aa 662, PY Ab 745, PY Ab 746
?si-to-ko-wo	*sitokhowoi* "grainmeasurer(s)?"	PY An 292.01
[ ]-ti MUL	too fragmentary for identification	PY Ae 629
ti-nwa-si-ja	"Tinwasian women," ethnic adj.	PY Aa 699, PY Ab 190
ti-nwa-ti-ja i-te-ja	"Tinwasian weaver women," ethnic adj.; *histeiai* "weavers"	PY Ad 684
to-sa-me-ja	"to-sa-me-ja women," description of woman, probably a trade	PY Aa 775+0956, PY Ab 277
ze-pu2-ra3 ri-ne-ja	"Zephyrian women linen-workers/flax-weavers"; *lineiai*; ze-pu2-ra3, ethnic adj. from PN: Ζεφυρία	PY Aa 61
Women's workgroups identified by their location		
e-pi-jo-ta-na (PN) MUL	"women at PN: e-pi-jo-ta-na"	PY Aa 95
me-ta-pa (PN) MUL	"women at PN: me-ta-pa	PY Aa 752, PY Aa 779, PY Ab 355
ne-wo-pe-o (PN) MUL	"women at PN: ne-wo-pe-o"	PY Aa 786, PY Ab 554
pi-we-re (PN) MUL	"women at PN: pi-we-re"	PY Aa 1182

-εια written in Linear B as e-ja. As discussed further in Chapter 3, the vast majority of task-derived titles at Pylos relate either to the Pylian textile industry or to food-preparation and maintenance of the palace environs. The entry on PY Aa 62 is typical of a task-identified workgroup recorded with the MUL ideogram.

PY Aa 62
me-re-ti-ri-ja MUL 7̣ ko-wa 10 ko-wo 6
"7̣ women flour-grinders, 10 girls, 6 boys"

This tablet records a workgroup of seven adult women who are identified by the task-designation me-re-ti-ri-ja, a feminine nominative plural term. As on all tablets of the Aa series, the name of the workgroup is the first piece of information recorded; in this instance the workgroup bears the occupational title me-re-ti-ri-ja, which is derived from the Linear B term for flour (me-re-u-ro) and transliterates as *meletriai* "flour-grinders."[13] Inclusion of the ideogram MUL reinforces that the women described by this term are adult women. The tablet also lists the sub-adult children who accompany the adult women of the workgroup, listing ten girls with the term ko-wa (κόραι *korwai)* "girls,"[14] and six boys as ko-wo (κοῦροι *kouroi*).[15] It is not known at what age the children come to be considered adults; the Pylos archives offer no further clarification on the child/adult divide. (This is perhaps unsurprising as, even in historical Greece, standards for the transition from childhood to adulthood – or even a common definition of childhood – were often opaque, and, when articulated, were generally particular to specific eras and locales.[16]) This tablet is typical of the abbreviated nature of most of the data encoded in the personnel series tablets. The Aa series provides consistently the following information: the name of the workgroup and its working strength in terms of the numbers of adult women, and sub-adult girls and boys,[17] whereas the Ab tablets repeat the tally of the workgroup and add a record of the subsistence-level[18] rations allocated to the group as well.

The second type of women's workgroup at Pylos modified by MUL is identified by an origin-derived ("ethnic") adjective in the feminine nominative plural;[19] on tablets of this type the descriptor adjective replaces the task-titles of the workgroups discussed above. In these workgroups the group name derives not from the type of work performed but rather by the ethnic heritage and/or geographical origin of the workgroup.[20] PY Aa 792 is a typical example of an ethnic-titled workgroup:

PY Aa 792
ki-ni-di-ja MUL 21 ko-ẉạ 12 ko-wo 10 *DA* 1 *TA* 1
"21 Cnidian women, 12 girls, 10 boys, 1 DA, 1 TA"[21]

This tablet uses much the same formula as PY Aa 62, with the ethnic adjective ki-ni-di-ja substituting for the task-derived title. As with PY Aa 62, the name of the workgroup is the first piece of evidence recorded; here the term ki-ni-di-ja as the functional name of the workgroup. (Ki-ni-di-ja is morphologically a nominative plural and is thought to be derived from the place name Κνίδος ("Cnidos") and the use of MUL once more serves to reinforce the female composition of the workgroup.)

The third way that the MUL ideogram is used at Pylos to designate women's workgroups is by modifying a workgroup identified not by an occupational or ethnic title but rather by the location of the group within the Pylian state. Such workgroup locations involve one of three areas: Pylos proper (that is, the palace center) or either of its two provinces, conventionally referred to as the Hither and Further Provinces. This is a less common means of identifying workgroups, but for these tablets the MUL ideogram signals that the workers located in a particular village are female. PY Aa 752 illustrates this form of subgroup well:

PY Aa 752
me-ta-pạ MUL 7 ko-wa 3 ko-wo 3 *TA* 1
"At Metapa, 7 women, 3 girls, 3 boys and 1 TA"

This tablet refers to a workgroup of seven women at the site of Metapa,[22] accompanied by three girls, three boys and one TA supervisor. On tablets of this type, it is not possible to reconstruct the type of production this workgroup engages in, unless the corresponding Ab or Ad tablets should provide this information. It would appear that the location alone suffices to identify this group of women – and we might presume that the task this group engaged in was considered readily apparent to the recording scribe. Location-identified tablets are useful in allowing us to ascertain how the palace monitored and maintained workgroups in both near and distant locations.

In three additional instances at Pylos, MUL is used to modify a workgroup whose title derives not from occupation, origin, or current location, but from an adjectival variant of the name of prominent male officials. Otherwise the formulaic construction remains much the same:

PY Aa 785
a-da-ra-te-ja MUL 1 TA 1
"1 Adrasteian woman, 1 TA"

On this tablet the man's name Adrastos has been transformed into a feminine adjective *Adrasteia*. As he is recognizable from several other tablets as a prominent official,[23] we should best understand the woman assigned to this "workgroup" as one of his members of staff.

Finally, three last Pylian texts employ the MUL ideogram to account for unnamed and untitled women; these tablets are unique within the Pylian corpus.[24] PY Wa 1008, a sealing impression rather than a tablet, is very fragmentary and preserves only the MUL ideogram on the upper line of the sealing and an otherwise unattested string of symbols (o-si-to[ ) on the lower. PY Wa 114, a basket label discussed at length in Chapter 3,[25] preserves the MUL ideogram in conjunction with the words me-ni-jo ("monthly ration") and pe-ra2-ko-ra-i-ja ("of the further province") – presumably listing the entire monthly rations allocated to the workgroup women (hence the use of MUL) in the Further Province; the expected enumeration is not preserved. The remaining text on which the MUL ideogram stands alone is the familiar tablet PY Tn 316, which lists unnamed women as part of the allotments sent to various divinities at Pylos, echoing the other, unnamed women of the workgroups also recorded simply as "woman/women".

To reiterate, then, an inclusion of the MUL ideogram on a tablet serves to secure unquestionably the sex of the recorded persons as female. Used solely at Pylos as a marker for low-status, unnamed women, it secures our identification of the personnel of the Aa and Ab series workers as women alongside the women of Tn 316, Wa 1008, and Wa 114.

The MUL ideogram in the Knossos tablets

As previously noted 71 of the 199 tablets at Knossos which mention women preserve the inclusion of the MUL ideogram.[26] These tablets record a total of at least 1200 women. The Knossian conventions for using MUL are closely similar to the Pylian; both sites use MUL to modify occupational and ethnic titles, as well as workgroups identified by place names and workgroups belonging to men whose names appear in the genitive. Table 2.2 lists all occupational usages of MUL at Knossos. For example, KN Ai 739 provides the MUL ideogram in contexts of both occupational title and workgroup location:

KN Ai 739
.1: ra-su-to , 'a-ke-ti-ri-ja' MUL 2
.2: ko-wa 1 ko-wo 1
"At Lasunthos, 2 decorator women, 1 girl, 1 boy"

Knossos, however, records at least one additional context for the MUL ideogram not in use at Pylos; it appears as an affix to low-ranking women's names and may possibly also indicate the presence of women within family units.

Of the 82 known women's names at Knossos, 66 are identifiable as women from the MUL ideogram accompanying their names. This usage of MUL along with women's names is unique to Knossos; Pylos reserves naming for more elite women than those signaled by the MUL ideogram, women attributed status titles and/or property. These 66 named women at Knossos are recorded on a total of eight tablets, all of which belong to the Knossian personnel series (the Ag, Ai, Ak, and Ap tablets).[27] Most of these tablets provide simply a list of women's names, each of which is accompanied by the MUL ideogram.[28] Only one of these tablets (KN Ap 5748 + 5901 + 5923 + 8558) provides more than a list of women's names; this tablet lists women, their daughters and a specific type of cloth – TELA-1+TE.[29] None of the remaining seven[30] tablets provides any information on property holdings or occupational responsibilities – on these MUL simply accompanies names, helping to fix them as women. For a full listing of these names, see Table 2.3.

Despite the lack of additional economic details on the tablets which link MUL and women's names, these tablets remain useful to scholarship on Knossian women in that they allow us to sex non-Greek names as female. MUL is particularly useful for establishing women's names at Knossos as most of these names do not readily normalize into Greek feminine names. In fact, most of the names known for women at Knossos do not appear to be Greek names at all – a circumstance that in all likelihood renders a great deal of further Knossian women invisible to contemporary scholarship. In fact, of the 82 names we can now sex as belonging to women, only six of them would otherwise be visible to us as indisputably Greek feminine forms. These are ke-ra-me-ja "*Kerameia*" (Κεραμεῖα),[31] pa-i-ti-ja "*Phaistia*" (Φαιστία),[32] pi-ra-ka-ra "*Philagra*" (Φίαγρα),[33] pu-wa "*Purwa*" (Πύρρα),[34] te-qa-ja "*Theqaia*" (Θηβαῖα),[35] and wo-di-je-ja "*Wordieia.*"[36] Most of the named women with the MUL accompanier appear only once in the tablets.

The question of whether MUL appears as an identifier of women in family units at Knossos remains in question. Eight tablets appear to use the MUL ideogram to refer to unnamed women within families.[37] These tablets begin their entries with a man's name, along with children and a woman referred to not by name but by an unaccompanied MUL. KN Ag 1654 is a typical example of this usage of MUL:

KN Ag 1654
qe-ri-jo VIR 1 MUL 1 ko-wa[
"*Qe-ri-jo* (MN: *Qerion?* [Θηρίων]woman (wife?), 1 girl ..."

Recently, however, Hiller has called into question the authenticity of these tablets as genuine historical documents; it now appears likely that these tablets are scribal exercises rather than real documents.[38] (Consequently, due to the insecurity of this evidence, these tablets and the women listed upon them are excluded from my tabulations and are not incorporated in my discussions of the Knossos evidence.)

MUL Used alone

Only one text from Knossos uses an unmodified MUL outside family units. In this instance, KN Wn 8752, MUL is found below an imprinted sealing. No other information is recorded and it seems unlikely that we will ascertain the purpose of this record.

In sum, at both Knossos and Pylos the MUL ideogram appears to have been used exclusively to modify low-status women – either to record unnamed women within workgroups or, at Knossos, to record rosters of named women who otherwise have no visible economic presence in the tablets. And so arises a skewed visibility for lower-ranking women in the tablets; at both sites in which MUL offers us a rock-solid means of identifying persons at Knossos and Pylos as women, their frequent lack of differentiation (for the workgroup women) or missing contexts (for the named women at Knossos) will limit our ability to

Table 2.2 Women's occupational titles identified by MUL at Knossos

Workgroup designation	*Normalized*	*Tablet*
a-ke-ti-ri-ja or	*asketriai* "decorators/finishers"	KN Ak 7001, KN Ai 739
a-ze-ti-ri-ja (variant)	*asketriai* "decorators/finishers"	KN Ap 694.03, KN E 777, KN Ln 1568 lat a, KN M 683, KN Xe 544, KN Xe 657, KN X 7737
a-mi-ni-si-ja	*Amnisiai* "women from Amnisos," ethnic adj. from PN: Amnisos	KN Ai 825
a-no-qo-ta [MUL]	"women belonging to MN: a-no-qo-ta"	KN Ak 615
a-no-zo-jo	"women belonging to MN: a-no-zo-jo"	KN Ak 627+7025+fr.
a-ra-ka-te-ja	*alakateiai* "spinning women" [ἠλακάτη "distaff" Od. iv. 135+]	KN Ak 5009+6037+8588, KN Lc 531+542
da-te-we-ja	ethnic or occupational term describing women, exact sense uncertain KN Ak 612, KN Lc 540+8075, KN L 594, KN Xe 5891	
da-wi-ja, ne-ki-ri-de	"*da-wian* women ne-ki-ri-de workers;" da-wi-ja ethnic women of PN: da-wo; ne-ki-ri-de obscure occupational term	KN Ak 780+7004+7045+7767
do-e-ra	*doela* "slave-woman, maid-servant, bondwoman" [δούλη Il. etc]	KN Ap 628+5935.01, KN Ap 628+5935.03
do-e-ra (belonging to a-pi-qo-i-ta)	*doelai* "slave-women / servants belonging to MN: a-pi-qo-i-ta"	KN Ai 824
e-ne-re-ja	description of women: "makers of e-ne-ra"?	KN Ak 638, KN Ai 762+fr.
[ ]ja	too fragmentary for identification	KN Ai 338, KN Ak 7006, KN Ak 7030+9664+frr., KN Ak 7830+fr., KN Ak 8444
[ ]jo-jo MUL]	too fragmentary for identification; women identified by a MN in the genitive	KN Ak 7827 + frr.
ka-pa-ra2	description of women cloth-worker(s), ethnic or descriptive term - exact sense uncertain	KN Ak 5009+6037+8588
[ ]ke-ja	too fragmentary for identification	KN Ak 620+6028+fr.
ko-so-jo [MUL]	"woman of MN: ko-so-jo (gen.)"	KN Ap 637.02

Workgroup designation	*Normalized*	*Tablet*
ko-u-re-ja	"makers of ko-u-ra (textile type)"	KN Ak 643, KN Ap 694, KN Lc 548, KN Lc 550+7381, KN Lc 0581
ne-ki-ri-de	"women ne-ki-ri-de workers;" ne-ki-ri-obscure occupational term de	KN Ln 1568. lat a, KN Ws 8152
ne-we-wi-ja	adj., describing women textile-workers	KN Lc 560+7587+7815
o-du-ru-wi-ja	"Women of o-du-ru-we/Zakro" ethnic adj. from PN: o-du-ru-we (Zakro?)	KN Ai 982
pa-i-ti-ja	"*Phaistian* women"; ethnic adj. from PN: Phaistos	KN Ak 828
pe-ki-ti-ra2 (tab: pe-ke-ti[ )	*pektriai* "wool-carders" [Cf. δμωαι; ... εἴρια πείκετε Od. xviii, 316]	KN Ld 656
qa-mi-ja	"Women of qa-mo," ethnic adj. (PN: qa-mo)	KN Ak 613
[ ]-ra [MUL]	too fragmentary for identification	KN Ai 825
[ ]re-ja [MUL]	too fragmentary for identification	KN Ai 752+753
ri-jo-ni-ja	"women of ri-u-no," ethnic adj.	KN Ak 624
se-to-i-ja (PN) [MUL]	"women at PN: se-to-i-ja"	KN Ak 634+5767
[ ]te-ja-ne [MUL]	obscure term	KN Ai 7962+7969
ti-wa-ti-ja	"*Tinwasian* women," ethnic adj.	KN Ap 618+623+633+ 5533+5922
to-te-ja	"women to-te-ja workers" (a woman's trade)	KN Ak 611, KN X 7846
we-ra-te-ja or we-ra-ti-ja (variant)	ethnic or occupational term describing women	KN Ap 618+623+633+ 5533+5922, KN Ak 784+8019
we-we-si-jo [MUL]	workgroup identified by MN: we-we-si-jo	KN Ak 622, KN Ak 9173+9459+9001

Table 2.3 Women's names at Knossos identified by the MUL ideogram

Name	Tablet
*18-to-no	KN Ap 639.04
a-*79	KN Ap 618+623 +633+ 5533 + 5922.02
a-de-ra2	KN Ap 639.11
a-ma-no	KN Ap 5748+5901 +5923+8558.01
a-nu-wa-to	KN Ap 639.14
a-qi-ti-ta	KN Ap 639.12
a-to-me-ja	KN Ap 639.02
a-wa-ti-ka-ra	KN Am 827+7032 +7618
a3-du-wo-na	KN Ap 769.01
da-te-ne-ja	KN Ap 639.02
du-sa-ni	KN Ap 639.03
du-tu-wa	KN Ap 639.13
e-ti-wa-ja	KN Od 681, KN Ap 639.08
i-du	KN Ap 639.07
i-ta-ja	KN Ap 769.02, KN Xe 537
i-ta-mo	KN Ap 618+ 623 +633+5533+ 5922.01
[ ][i-ta-no	KN Ap 769.01
[ ][ja	KN Ap 694.01
[ ][ja-mi-nu	KN Ap 5547+ 8162.01
[ ][ja-mu-ta	KN Ap 5864.05
[ ][ja-si-ja	KN Ap 639.14
ka-*56-so-ta	KN Ap 769.01
[ ][ka-na	KN Ap 5864.03
ka-na-to-po	KN Ap 639.09
ke-pu	KN Ap 639.13
ke-ra-me-ja "*Kerameia*" Κεραμεῖα	KN Ap 639.07
ki-nu-qa	KN Ap 618+623 + 633+5533+ 5922.01
ki-zo	KN Ap 5748+5901 + 5923+8558.01
ko-pi	KN Ap 639.01
ku-tu-qa-no	KN Ap 639.09, KN Da 1161+7187
[ ][-ma	KN Ap 5864.04
ma-ku[ ]	KN Ap 639.03
[ ][-me-no	KN Ap 639.01
[ ][-na	KN Ap 5864.03
[ ][ni-ta	KN Ap 5748+ 5901 + 5923+8558.03
o-ri-mo	KN Ap 5748+5901 +592+8558.02
o-sa-po-to	KN Ap 5748+5901 + 5923+8558.03
pa-i-ti-ja "*Phaistia*" Φαιστία	KN Ap 639.04
pa-ja-ni	KN Ap 639.02
pi-ja-mu-nu	KN Ap 5748+5901 +5923+8558.02
pi-ra-ka-ra "*Philagra*" Φΐλαγρα	KN Ap 639.04
pu-wa "*Purwa*" Πύρρα	KN Ap 639.11
pu-zo	KN Ap 5748+5901 +5923+8558.02
[ ][-ra	KN Ap 5864.02
ru-ta2-no	KN Ap 639.12
sa-*65	KN Ap 639.10
sa-ma-ti-ja	KN Ap 639.08
sa-mi	KN Ap 639.10
sa-ti-qi-to	KN Ap 639.09
[ ][si	KN Ap 5748+5901 + 5923+8558.01
si-ne-e-ja	KN Ap 639.12
si-nu-ke	KN Ap 639.11
[ ][ta2-no [ ][	KN Ap 5864.06

Name	*Tablet*
te-qa-ja "*Theqaia*" Θηβαῖα	KN Ap 5864
ti-no	KN Ap 5748+5901 +5923+8558.02
tu-*49-mi	KN Ap 639.07
tu-ka-na	KN Ap 639.10, KN Ap 639.11
tu-ka-to	KN Ap 639.08
tu-zo	KN Ap 639.01, KN C 7698+7892+ 8223+frr.

Name	*Tablet*
u-jo-na	KN Ap 639.10
u-pa-ra	KN Ap 639.12
wa-ra-ti	KN Ap 639.13
wi-da-ma-ta2	KN Ap 639.09, KN Ln 1568
wi-ja-na-tu	KN Ap 769.02
wi-so	KN Ap 639.04
wo-di-je-ja "*Wordieia*"	KN Ap 639.03

recover more of their lived realities beyond their labor and rations. In contrast, no MUL ideograms ever appear with women of higher social standings; they become visible via their names and titles instead.

Method 2: Use of gender-specific family title

Apart from use of the MUL ideogram, there are several other methods by which women become visible in the tablets. One such method is to locate and identify familial titles that indicate a woman's relationship to her kin. Women can be identified by family title: "mother" (ma-te *mater*);[39] "daughter" (tu-ka-te *thugater*/θυγάτηρ or its abbreviation TU);[40] "girl" (ko-wa *kore* which seems to double as "daughter" within workgroup contexts);[41] or by "old women" (ka-ra-we *grawes*).[42] These titles are typically found in the personnel series at both Knossos and Pylos and are often used to identify members of otherwise undifferentiated collective workgroups.[43] Nowhere do any of the family titles appear accompanied by a specific woman's name. Instead, in all instances family titles are used to add specific information about individuals within their workgroup units.

At Pylos, 63 texts – all of the personnel series' Aa and Ab subseries – record counts of girls (ko-wa *kore* "girl"). All of these texts locate these girls within workgroup contexts where they are being counted as part of the total strength of the workgroup (the Aa series) and are being provided rations (the Ab series) along with the rest of the group. For a complete list of references to girls at Pylos, see the ko-wa entries in Appendix A: All references to Pylian women.

The second family title for women used at Pylos, ma-te (*mater* "mother"), is found on the much-discussed tablet PY An 607.[44] This tablet seems to record the parentage of a number of female do-qe-ja do-e-ra workers (exact function unknown).[45] The tablet lists the occupation title of both the mother (ma-te) and father (pa-te) of these workers; in all cases these workers' mothers are slaves (do-e-ra) while their fathers hold titles as varied as smith (ka-ke-u) and slave (do-e-ro). (The title ma-te has one additional attestation at Pylos on PY Fr 1202, where it refers not to a human mother but rather a divinity known as ma-te-re te-i-ja or "divine mother.")

At Knossos, "girl" (ko-wa) continues to be the most-used family-related term, cited on 75 extant tablets. All of these texts (with the usual exception of the X series texts which, by definition, are too fragmentary to reassign to specific subseries) are located within the personnel series subsets Ag, Ai, Ak, and Ap. As at Pylos, none of the young women bearing this title are ever named; all are recorded in workgroup contexts and all accompany adult women (presumably their mothers). As mentioned above, girls in workgroups at Knossos are further differentiated within the workgroup along the lines of age-grade and training level. Girls appear to move through four different stages ("younger girl," "older girl," "under instruction," and "instructed") before they reach adulthood, at Knossos. At no point do girls at either site appear on (fully legible) tablets unaccompanied by adult women.

Four Knossos texts also use the term tu-ka-te "daughter" *thugater* (θυγάτηρ) or its abbreviation "TU." This term has two usages in the tablets. It can be used within "family" contexts as per KN Ap 637 where an unnamed adult woman (signaled by the MUL ideogram) and two daughters follow a man's name in the genitive case (ko-so-jo). It can also be used in a workgroup context, where it is used to describe (and count) daughters of adult women in the personnel series workgroups. Three tablets fit this pattern: KN Ap 639 which provides a list of over 50 named women with their daughters and sons, KN Ap 5748 + 5901 + 5923 + 8558 which lists women, their unnamed daughters and cloth allotments, and KN Ap 629 which provides a count of workers' daughters who have either just reached or are about to reach adulthood:

KN Ap 629
.1: tu-ni-ja 'TU' MUL 4 NE 'DI' 3 'KO 1' ri-jo-no 'TU' MUL 3 ko-wo 3[
.2: do-ti-ja 'TU' MUL 4 NE 'DI' 6 [ ] *vacat* [
.3: *vacat* [
"At Tu-ni-ja, Daughters: 4 women, 3 young women under instruction, 1 boy; at Ri-jo-no, Daughters: 3 women, 3 boys; at Do-ti-ja, Daughters: 4 women, 6 young women under instruction ...."

The tablet provides an accounting of only the daughters of workgroup women at the sites of tu-ni-ja, do-ti-ja, and ri-jo-no. On this tablet, the TU abbreviations serve to indicate the full number of daughters who are then divided into two subgroups of adult women (identified by the MUL ideogram and their number) and of younger women still in the process of completing their training (identified by the two abbreviations NE "young" and DI "under instruction" also with their number). No further information on these daughters is provided, but presumably the palace had an interest in tracking the whereabouts of women on the cusp of adulthood.

Knossos uses one additional age-grade-derived title: ka-ra-we (*grawes* "old women"). While ka-ra-we is not exactly a family title, it reveals similar attention to rank by age as do ko-wa and "daughter." Ka-ra-we is attested on two incomplete/fragmentary tablets (KN Ap 694 and KN Ap 5868 + 8220) where it refers to women workers within workgroup contexts.

Method 3: Use of gender-specific occupational title

A third method for recovering women in the tablets is to locate occupational or professional titles that take gender-specific forms. This technique is particularly useful for identifying, by isolating their occupational title, those women who are not listed in conjunction with the MUL ideogram. Most of these occupational titles employ either the feminine agent ending *–e-ja* (-eia) or the ethnic ending *-i-ja* (-ia).

Occupational titles can be found either accompanying personal names or standing alone as substantives. These titles may occur either in the singular or in the plural; when they are found in their plural forms, they generally designate single-sex workgroups described by their assigned tasks, such as decorators, bath-attendants, food-preparers and the like. In these instances it is not possible to differentiate any of these women as individuals.

At Knossos, six additional occupational designations can be securely assigned to women by dint of their grammatical structure. Like the designations which were assignable by an accompanying MUL, these additional titles can be either ethnic- or task-based. Some of these titles can be readily normalized into Greek such as do-e-ra "slave/servant woman" (*doela* δούλη)[46] or i-je-re-ja "priestess" (*hiereia* ἱέρεια).[47] One additional title can be identified as an ethnic adjective for women – e-ra-ja,[48] with three more titles describing specific types of textile workers – e-ro-pa-ke-ja,[49] ko-ru-we-ja,[50] and te-pe-ja.[51] One further occupational title remains too fragmentary for identification: (ko-ro-ko[ ).[52]

At Pylos, eight additional titles for women can be identified on the basis of textual context as a result of their appearance as genitive plurals in the Ad series. As at Knossos, several of these titles are workgroup designations: e-ke-ro-qo-no ("wage-earners" *enkheroquoinon* from * ἐγχειρόποινος),[53] ri-ne-ja (*lineiai* "flax-workers," "linen-weavers"),[54] and the textile-related titles ka-ru-ti-je-ja[55] and te-pe-ja.[56] As these titles refer to the mothers of the sons who are being counted in the Ad series, we can securely identify these titles as belonging to women. Otherwise, the *–eia* endings of ri-ne-ja, ka-ru-ti-je-ja, te-pe-ja would also provide a sufficient basis for sexing these titles.

Four other women's titles grammatically recoverable from Pylos occur in very different contexts from the above workgroups. These titles are all known from tablets outside the Aa, Ab and Ad contexts, where the workgroups are mainly attested and tend to be listed in terms of the commodities the titled women control. These additional four titles also share another feature: all four are religious titles.[57] These titles are i-je-re-ja ("priestess" *hiereia* [ἱέρεια]),[58] ka-ra-wi-po-ro ("keybearer [*klawiphoros*]),[59] and two specialized forms of sacred slaves – do-e-ra i-je-re-ja ("slave of the priestess")[60] and te-o-jo do-e-ra ("slave of the god").[61] Frequently, these women are also identified by both their names and their titles. In fact, nearly all of the named women at Pylos are religious functionaries holding one of these four titles.

Method 4: Use of feminine name form[62] *– Table 2.4*

The final method through which women become visible to us is isolating gender-specific variants of personal names. Obviously, this method can only be employed when names take an identifiably Greek form; we surely cannot expect Minoan names to follow Greek conventions for signaling sex through the ending of a name.[63] (We cannot yet identify whether Minoan naming conventions employ masculine and feminine variants.) Under these circumstances, I have opted for very conservative criteria for sexing names in the archives as female. Consequently, the only names that can be recovered through their forms alone must be either identifiably Greek or follow Greek structural patterns. As a result, I allow only two circumstances whereby a name can be identified as belonging to a woman: 1. where the name ends with a feminine form that varies from the masculine by more than a final sigma (I allow only the variant *–eia* which can never be confused with its masculine counterpart *–eus)* and 2. where the feminine ending can be readily differentiated from an attested masculine name, such as ke-sa-da-ra "Kessandra" vs. ke-sa-da-ro "Kessandros." We can also resupply in limited contexts women's names from tablets whose contexts clearly establish all the figures on that text as uniformly female.

Using these criteria, we can identify an additional thirteen women at Pylos; another seven names seem very likely to be female as well. This method also adds thirteen women's names to the roster of identified women at Knossos. (Table 2.4 lists these women across the two sites.) Of the Knossian women, five are named with words using Greek *–eia* endings; eight others are recoverable from KN Ln 1568, a tablet which lists exclusively female names and their cloth holdings.[64] Contextually, we can also identify four additional names as belonging to women.

From this survey, we can see the rough borders of a class/status system coming into focus. At least two tiers of status levels for women seem to be present: low-ranking women identified with the MUL ideogram (likely as they were so anonymous to the scribes recording them that no differentiation into individuals was necessary or desired) and named women of higher status who appear without a MUL adjunct. This will stand in contrast to men, for whom three social ranks emerge: low-ranking palace dependents, independent contractors, producers, and merchants, and the men who comprise the administrative elite of the state.

Women's contexts in the Linear B tablets

With secure means for identifying women in the tablets established now, we can turn to the types of evidence the tablets preserve about their activities in the Pylian and Knossian states. First and foremost, the Linear B tablets record primarily the administrative activities of the palaces, particularly where they intersect with the economic sphere. What is best attested about women in Linear B is their

Table 2.4 Women's names at Pylos and Knossos identified by name form (and not by MUL)

Name	*Tablet*	*Name*	*Tablet*
Pylos		*Knossos*	
*34-ke-ja	PY Fn 187.19	*56-po-so	KN Ln 1568
*35-ke-ja	PY Eb 871	di-qa-ra	KN Ap 628 +5935.02
a-*65-ja	PY Vn 34 + 1191 + 1006 + fr.02	di-wi-je-ja	KN Xd 97 + 284
a-pi-e-ra *Amphiera*	PY An 1281.08; PY Fn 50.13	e-ti-wa-ja	KN Od 681
		ki-si-wi-je-ja	KN Xd 98 + 196
a-pi-te-ja	PY Fn 187.01	ku-tu-qa-no	KN Da 1161 + 7187
a-ro-ja	PY Fn 187.20		
a3-pu-ke-ne-ja	PY Fn 079.01	na-e-ra-ja	KN Ln 1568
e-ti-je-ja	PY Vn 851.10	pe-ri-je-ja *Perieia*	KN Uf 1031 + 5738
e-ti-ri-ja	PY Vn 851.09		
ka-pa-si-ja *Karpathia*	PY Vn 851.12	po-i-ra	KN Od 690
ka-pa-ti-ja *Karpathia*	PY Ep 539.09	po-ni-ke-ja *Phonikeia*	KN Ln 1568
ke-i-ja	PY Qa 1303	po-po	KN L 513, KN L 567, KN L 648, KN Ln 1568, KN Od 689, KN Xe 524
ke-sa-da-ra *Kessandra*	PY Fg 368; PY Fg 828; PY Mn 1368; PY Xa 1380		
ku-ri-na-ze-ja	PY Fn 187.07	qe-pa-ta-no	KN Ln 1568
ma-ra-me-na[	PY Vn 34 + 1191 + 1006 + fr 06	qi-na	KN Ld 584
		ru-ki-ti-ja *Luktia*	KN Ln 1568, Xd 314
me-ta-ka-wa *Metakalwai*	PY An 1281.12	ru-nu	KN Ln 1568
mi-jo-qa	PY Fn 867; PY Fn 50.12; PY An 1281.11	ru-sa-ma	KN Ln 1568
		ta-su	KN Ln 1568
		tu-zo	KN C 7698+7892+ 8223+frr.
pi-ro-pa-ta-ra *Philopatra*	PY Vn 34 + 1191 + 1006+ fr 05	wa-wa-ka	KN Ln 1568
re-u-ka-ta-ra-ja *Leuktraia*	PY Vn 851.12		
]-ru-ke-ja	PY Vn 851.05		
te-do-ne-ja	PY Vn 851.10		
wi-ri-ke-ja	PY Vn 851.08		
wo-di-je-ja *Wordieia*	PY Ub 1318; PY Vn 34 + 1191 + 1006 + fr.01		

occupation: 48 different occupations/task titles for women are attested between Knossos and Pylos. Interestingly, unlike the (later) literary sources, the tablets betray a distinct bias toward women of the lower classes, recording approximately 2000 low-status workers, 200 female religious functionaries, seven women who appear to be wives or daughters of high-ranking male officials at Pylos and a few dozen women of middle and elite rank at Knossos.

The information the Linear B tablets provide about women differs significantly from historical period accounts of women. In particular, the Bronze Age evidence offers very different information about women's public activities than Classical Athenian sources, where most of our historical evidence for women derives from mentions in lawsuits, orations, or infrequent inscriptions or dedications; compounding the problem, the historiographers likewise tend to elide most of the specifics of women's daily lives. Overall, the Athenian evidence regarding women tends to be more ideological and prescriptive rather than idiosyncratic and specific, focusing more on women in general rather than on individual women. Typically, the Athenian evidence locates them primarily either within the oikos ("household") structure – ironically, the area the Bronze Age tablets mention the least[65] – or as collective participants in those cult rituals specific to girls and women.[66]

Finally, the tablets remain silent on many of the primary areas related to women's economic roles in the later evidence. In particular, the tablets are blind on the material best attested later: the role of women within the oikos, whether or not a required kyrios ("legal guardian") institution is in force, inheritance requirements, the usage of dowry or brideprice in conducting marriages, or any other insights for the legal standing of women within family contexts.[67] Of the seven economic matters pertaining to Classical Athenian women discussed by Schaps in his venerable monograph on women in the Classical economy – property holding, acquisition of property through gifts or inheritance, rights of the epikleros (an heiress lacking brothers), the kyrios institution, wills and dedications, dowry, and women's economic rights under the law[68] — only the most public of these institutions, the types and structures of property control, is referenced in the Linear B tablets.

In contrast to the Classical-era texts, the Linear B texts record the economic activities of women in public and civic – rather than domestic – contexts. Pylian and Knossian women participated in the economic spheres of palatial life by means of their labor, their property holdings, and their roles in cult practice. The major point of convergence between the Classical-period and Bronze Age texts relates to women's involvement in this last circuit, the area of religion. But while many of the Classical texts focus on women's roles in religious rituals,[69] the Linear B tablets record instead the tasks and responsibilities sacerdotal women perform as they relate to economic matters; thus, the tablets' record of women's religious involvement concentrates on the economic (rather than the ceremonial) aspects of their jobs by tracking the personnel, cult material, and sanctuary assets entrusted to their care.

Now that we have established ways to identify women mentioned in the tablets, we must turn to the larger question of how these women are incorporated into the palatial economies of both Knossos and Pylos. To begin to answer this question, we first need to ask the central question of how significant gender is as a categorical divider in these polities; that is, do men and women as a whole receive similar treatment throughout the archives or does gender act to separate the sexes into two different economic spheres?

Pylos and Knossos as gender-segregated societies

Throughout the tablets from both palatial centers, careful attention is paid to differentiating men and women. The archives render gender visible via the textual conventions previously mentioned – through the use of ideograms and gender-specific titles which eliminate much of the potential confusion in recording male and female workers in the Linear B script. Yet the differentiation between the sexes is not limited to the sexing of particular individuals; the differentiation between the sexes extends to the contexts men and women occupy – consistently at both Pylos and Knossos, men and women occupy different archival and economic contexts.

The first area where men and women occupy different contexts is perhaps the most simple – the individual Linear B tablet itself. Even at this most basic level of archive organization, men and women are generally isolated into male- and female-only tablets and the tablets that list both sexes together remain relatively rare.

At Knossos, of the 1,329 tablets that mention humans, only 32 tablets mention both men and women on the same tablet. (Otherwise, the remaining 1297 tablets record humans in a single-sex environment, either exclusively male or exclusively female. Similarly, at Pylos, only 34 of the 631 tablets where humans can be identified record members of both sexes. (Table 2.6 enumerates the different tablet series at Pylos recording men and women.) It seems evident that even at this most elemental level of organization, men and women are not presented as occupying the same conceptual spaces. (Tables 2.5 and 2.6 provide the breakdown of tablet counts by sex within each series.)

This isolation of the sexes continues into the next level of archival organization – the tablet series. Even prior to the decipherment of Linear B, scholars recognized that various tablets were employing common ideograms (the drawn rather than spelled objects which are frequently tallied on the tablets). On the basis of these ideograms, tablets were assigned to series groupings identified by a capital letter, such as A for tablets using the VIR (man) or MUL (woman) ideograms or D for tablets with ideograms of livestock. Following decipherment, these capital letter series were subdivided into smaller series distinguished by use of the originally assigned capital letter plus a new lower case letter. Tablets were then assigned to these series based on the nature of their specific content.[70] And so at Pylos, the Aa series came to denote those tablets which list tabulations of women identified by the MUL ideogram and a task-based descriptor (along with their children); likewise the Ab series lists the rations assigned to the workgroups known from the Aa series, and the Ad series lists the total number of adult and adolescent sons of the workgroup women from the Aa and Ab series.

Table 2.5 Knossos series tablets recording men and women.

Total tablets[1]	*Series*[2]	*Men only*[3]	*Women only*[4]	*Men and women*[5]
7	Ag	2	—	5
35	Ai	5	27	3
86	Ak	3	86	7
11	Am	10	—	1
13	Ap	—	13	—
33	As	33	—	—
1	Bg	1	—	—
57	B	58	—	—
15	Ce	6	—	—
19	C	19	—	—
121	Da	118	1(?)[6]	—
81	Db	78	—	—
34	Dc	34	—	—
44	Dd	43	—	—
42	De	36	—	—
28	Df	28	—	—
13	Dg	13	—	—
6	Dh	6	—	—
72	Dk	67	—	—
62	Dl	53	3	—
15	Dm	2	—	—
18	Do	12	—	—
10	Dp	2	1	—
29	Dq	25	—	—
33	D	29	0	1(?)[7]
32	E	9	1	—
123	Fh	35	1	—
15	Fp	3	2	1
29	F	8	—	—
69	Ga	15	1	—
30	Gg	—	2	—
2	Gm	1	—	—
3	Gv	1	—	—
8	G	—	2	—
21	K	4	—	—
54	Lc	3	8	—
32	Ld	7	2	1

Total tablets[1]	*Series*[2]	*Men only*[3]	*Women only*[4]	*Men and women*[5]
6	Le	2	—	1
1	Ln	—	—	1
117	L	15	5	4
23	Mc	9	—	—
11	M	1	1	1
51	Nc	6	1	—
50	Np	5	—	—
9	Oa	1	2	—
49	Od	10	1	3
20	Og	1	—	—
8	Pp	4	—	—
23	Ra	9	—	—
157	Sc	28	—	—
18	Sd	1	—	—
16	Sf	1	—	—
24	So	4	—	—
29	Uf	21	2	—
25	U	5	—	—
63	Vc	54	—	—
4	Vd	3	—	—
66	V	43	—	—
11	Wm	3	—	—
1	Wn	1	—	—
21	Ws	2	—	—
217	Xd	62	4	—
42	Xe	11	2	3
515	X	56	5	—
2	Z	1	—	—

Notes

1 Total number of tablets in series (includes tablets too fragmentary to identify sex of mentioned individuals).
2 Includes only series which record people in some capacity.
3 Includes only those tablets where men can be securely identified.
4 Includes only those tablets where women can be securely identified.
5 Includes only those tablets where both men and women can be securely identified.
6 The name *ku-tu-qa-no* is a woman's name (WN) in KN Ap 639; there is no way to know if the *ku-tu-qa-no* is the same or a different individual. Otherwise no women are attested anywhere in the Knossos sheep tablets (the Da series).
7 Possible mention of a women's occupational title.

Table 2.6 Pylos series tablets recording men and women.

Total tablets[1]	*Series*[2]	*Men only*[3]	*Women only*[4]	*Men and women*[5]
49	Aa (Personnel)	—	49	—
50	Ab	—	41	—
9	Ac	9	—	—
40	Ad	40	—[6]	—
19	Ae	14	4	1
45	An	43	2	—
2	Aq	1	—	1(?)[7]
4	Cc	3	—	—
41	Cn	30	—	—
67	Ea	56	1	—
98	Eb	41	21	—
6	Ed	4	—	2
4	En	7	—	6
15	Eo	7	—	6
6	Ep	1	—	5
5	Eq	4	—	—
2	Er	2	—	—
16	Es	16	—	—
4	Fg	1	2	—
20	Fn	5	—	4
52	Fr	6	1	—
2	Gn	2	—	—
2	Ja	1	—	—
28	Jn	23	—	—
1	Jo	1	—	—
13	La	2	1	—
17	Ma	11	—	—
25	Mb	2	—	—
14	Mn	4	1	1
100	Na	26	—	—
2	Nn	1	—	—
3	On	2	—	—
4	Pa	4	—	—
1	Pn	1	—	—
26	Qa	14	3	—

Total tablets[1]	*Series*[2]	*Men only*[3]	*Women only*[4]	*Men and women*[5]
32	Sa	20	—	—
12	Sh	1	—	—
13	Ta	2	—	—
2	Tn	1	—	—
4	Ub	2	—	1
24	Un	12	1	3
5	Va	2	—	—
12	Vn	4	—	3
19	Wa	3	2	1
23	Wr	3	—	—
54	Xa	6	2	—
93	Xn	3	—	—

Notes

1 Total number of tablets in series. Includes tablets too fragmentary to identify sex of mentioned individuals.
2 Includes only series which record people in some capacity.
3 Includes only those tablets where men can be securely identified.
4 Includes only those tablets where women can be securely identified.
5 Includes only those tablets where both men and women can be securely identified.
6 Women are mentioned as the mothers of the men being counted on this tablet but they themselves are not counted.
7 Several women secure on this tablet, perhaps one man.

When we examine those tablet series that mention humans, it becomes immediately apparent that men and women are disproportionately represented throughout them.

Human beings are recorded in 47 different tablet series at Pylos. When the sex of people mentioned in these tablets is assessed, it becomes evident that approximately three-quarters of these series – 35 out of 47 – are predominately, if not entirely, the domain of men.[71] These series include the livestock holdings of the Cc and Cn series; the recordings of temenos ("precinct") holdings of the Er series; metal allocations in the Ja, Jn, and Jo series;[72] various foodstuff allotments in the Ma and Mb series; armor and chariots in the Sa and Sh series; utensils in the Ta and Tn series; indeterminate holdings on the V series (which lacks ideograms) and the fragmentary Xn series; as well as various miscellaneous (and as yet unidentifiable) allotments in the Na, Nn, On, Pa, and Pn series. Only two of the tablet series at Pylos deal exclusively with women (excluding the male children who frequently accompany them), the aforementioned Aa and Ab series. A third series, the four-tablet PY Fg series, which deals with large rations of grain and figs, has two tablets mentioning women and a third mentioning men[73] The Pylian texts provide only two major groupings where we see substantial numbers of both men and women present throughout the series: the A series, or personnel tablets, which (as discussed above) record tallies of, and rations given to, low-status dependent palace workers[74] and the E series, which enumerates the land register at Pylos where the size of allocated land is measured in units of GRA (wheat).[75] Otherwise, the image that arises from a series-by-series survey of the Pylian tablets is of a society where men and women occupy different economic spheres.

A similar situation is observable at Knossos. The archives at Knossos partition into 65 discrete series involving men and women. As at Pylos, nearly three-quarters of these series record men's activities predominately.[76] At Knossos, tablet series which record exclusively men include the personnel tablets of the Bg and B series; the livestock holdings of the Ce and C series recording horses, sheep, oxen, pigs, and goats; the sheep tablets of the D series – the largest series in the Knossian corpus, tracking more than 100,000 sheep on a total of 895 tablets (this is presumably the basis of Knossos's large textile industry); the rations (including olives, barley, and olive oil) of the F series; the vase tablets of the K series; the Ra weapons series tablets; chariots and armor in the Sc, Sd, Sf, and So series; wine and amphorae of the U series; and the miscellaneous allotments of the Mc, Np, Od, Og, Pp, V, W, and X series. A dozen series contain both men and women; three of these are personnel tablets (A series) listing workers and three belong to the X series – a catchall category for tablets too fragmentary to be assigned to any of the thematic series. The remaining series where we observe men and women receiving or possessing similar commodities are the Fp offerings of olive oil; the G series rations tablets; the cloth tablets of the L series; the Uf orchard series; and again among the miscellaneous allotment series M, Nc, Oa, and Od. Only three series are exclusively devoted to women. One of these (Ap) is a personnel series designation; the remaining two are subsets of the G ration series; however, as so few of the tablets in these series are legible (four out of thirty-eight), it seems premature to make assumptions regarding the overall gender composition of the series. Overall, the Knossos tablets also seem to reflect a largely gender-segregated society, although possibly with a slightly higher degree of fluidity than at Pylos.

The observation that palatial society was segregated by gender is not unique to this study; iconographic studies have long noted differences in representation and placement for men and women in Aegean art. Studies on fresco painting, in particular, have observed the attention given to distinguishing between women and men through the use of color conventions, i.e., by using the familiar Egyptian red vs. white skin coloring for men and women respectively, or by emphasizing differences in male and female dress.[77] Many frescoes depict members of one sex exclusively, such as the Ladies in Blue fresco from Knossos or the various male-only battle scenes excavated at the Palace of Nestor at Pylos. (This trait continues into other media as well; the sarcophagi from Tanagra depict only women as does the group of dancers from Palaikastro, while carved stone vases carry exclusively male-figured scenes.[78]) Otherwise, in the few frescoes where we see both groups of men and groups of women, we observe very little interaction between the sexes as they tend to occupy distinctly gendered spaces. A particularly illustrative example of this tendency is the Knossos Grandstand fresco where the two sexes are drawn as distinct clusters of men and women. In fact, painted depictions of women and men together are limited to three stock scenes: bull leaping frescoes,[79] procession frescoes,[80] and scenes of cultic ritual such as the Haghia Triada sarcophagus.[81]

Returning to the textual evidence, I would contend that simply noting that these societies demonstrate segregation between the sexes is not enough. It is necessary to examine what, if any, are the ramifications of this segregation. Simply put, is gender inherently hierarchical in Mycenaean palace society? Are the different spheres occupied by men and women separate but largely analogous to each other or does difference in the Late Bronze Age lead to a "separate and unequal" scenario?[82] To answer this question, we must examine the economic contexts men and women occupy.

Gender as a hierarchical category

As noted above, significantly more series are devoted to the activities of men than to those of women. This disparity continues into the overall representation of the sexes throughout the archives. The combined archives of Knossos and Pylos record approximately 2000 women throughout their corpora while the total number of recorded men is around 5000. Consequently, we may surmise that the tablets reflect societies where men's production and holdings were more significant than those of women (assuming consistent rates of tablet survival).

Thus far, we have established that women are less frequently mentioned than men and that they, as a sex, are not equally represented throughout the tablet series. Neither of these conditions in and of itself, however, reveals whether this translates to an inferior social status for Knossian or Pylian women vis-à-vis their countrymen. To understand whether "fewer mentions" leads to "less access," we need to examine more closely the civic and economic organization of Knossos and Pylos. Toward this end, I offer here a brief overview of the property holdings of, and civic titles associated with, men and women at both centers.

Examination of the property holdings of men and women reveals that Separate does indeed translate as Unequal for women at both Knossos and Pylos. Property holding patterns at both Knossos and Pylos show substantial differences across gender lines. If we were to regard the relative numbers of men and women recorded in the archives as translating directly into economic clout, we might expect women to hold the same types of commodities as men but at approximately 30 percent the amount, reflecting the proportion of women vis-à-vis men in the tablets. This is not at all the case. At both sites, women's property holdings differ from men's not just in scale but also in substance;[83] the records from both sites indicate that women's property and commodity holdings are significantly more limited than men's in both size[84] and scope.

At Pylos, men of all social rankings control a wide range of properties and commodities. Among the various property holdings attributed to Pylian men are personnel (including slaves),[85] livestock (sheep, goat, cattle, pigs),[86] land,[87] foodstuffs (wheat,[88] barley,[89] olives,[90] olive oil,[91] figs,[92] wine,[93] cheese[94]), bronze,[95] skins[96] and leather goods,[97] textiles,[98] wool,[99] linen,[100] furniture and cult implements,[101] gold and terracotta vessels,[102] spices,[103] ivory,[104] armor,[105] chariots and chariot parts,[106] and a number of as-yet-unidentified commodities.[107]

Women's property holdings at Pylos are significantly more limited. Table 2.7 lists women's holdings at Pylos. At Pylos, women's holdings break down into two different configurations: property held by sacerdotal women and property held by laywomen. Sacerdotal women are documented in control of male and female slaves, land leases, and in one particular instance shrine bronze.[108] Laywomen are attested with foodstuffs (barley, wheat, figs, and olives), a small allocation of leather goods including shoes, and the unidentified commodities *146 and KA. (Women's property at Pylos is addressed extensively in Chapter 4.)

A similar situation is in effect at Knossos, where Knossian men are attested in possession of a similarly wide range of holdings. Knossian men appear as the holders of female[109] and male[110] slaves, other personnel,[111] orchards and other land holdings,[112] a variety of types of finished and unfinished textiles,[113] leather skins,[114] livestock (sheep, goats, cattle, and pigs),[115] foodstuffs (wheat,[116] barley,[117] olives,[118] oil,[119] and figs[120]), spices and unguents,[121] terracotta, bronze or gold vessels,[122] wool,[123] linen tunics,[124] horn,[125] swords, armor, chariots both functioning and under repair,[126] metal ingots,[127] other types of assorted weaponry,[128] horses,[129] and a number of as-yet-unidentified commodities.[130]

In contrast, the property holdings of Knossian women are more limited (although not as limited as the holdings of Pylian women). At Knossos, women are attested as exerting control over various textiles, foodstuffs such as wheat and oil (sometimes in extremely large quantities), wool, raw and worked linen, and land, in the form of orchards. (Women's holdings at Knossos are listed on Table 2.8 and the topic is featured in Chapter 5.)

This brief summary highlights the importance of identifying differences in gender organization by focusing on the women of these sites. At both sites men, as the unmarked gender category, appear to be fully invested through all aspects of the property system. In fact, at neither site do women hold a single commodity to which men do not also share access; rather we observe a property system whereby women's property holdings are systemically inferior to those of men. Furthermore, we see the near complete exclusion of women from access to and control over luxury goods, weaponry and chariots, as well as metals,[131] all of which can be considered status markers of a ruling Late Bronze Age elite.

This subordination of women in economic circles is also mirrored in the civic realm. A brief survey of civic and occupational titles[132] again reveals substantial differences between the sexes. At both sites, men and women perform widely distinct tasks and hold different occupational titles, and they enact different and discrete roles within the family unit[133] and religious structures. Again, these variances are fundamentally different; again, they are not merely a matter of scale. Women are completely excluded from many tasks and titles; significantly, all of the highest governmental offices at both Knossos and Pylos fall into this category. None of the members of the ruling elite, identifiable by name and/or by title, are women. We observe no women at either Pylos or Knossos recorded as wa-na-ka,

Table 2.7 Women's holdings at Pylos

Commodity/holding	*Holder*	*Tablet/tablet series*
Slaves – sex unknown	ka-ra-wi-po-ro-jo @ Pylos (Woman's Religious Title "Keybearer")	PY Ae 110
Slaves – women[1]	i-je-re-ja @ Pylos ("Priestess")	PY Ae 303
Slaves – women[1]	i-je-re-ja @ pa-ki-ja-na	PY En 609, PY Eo 224
Slaves – men	Named women mi-jo-qa and a-pi-e-ra	PY Fn 50
Slaves – men	Named woman ka-pa-ti-ja (the ka-ra-wi-po-ro)	PY Ep 539
Slaves – men	i-je-re-ja	PY Ep 539
Barley – HORD	Named women mi-jo-qa and a-pi-e-ra	PY Fn 50
Barley – HORD	Named woman a3-pu-ke-ne-ja	PY Fn 79
Barley – HORD	Named women a-pi-te-ja and *34-ke-ja	PY Fn 187
Barley – HORD	a-ke-ti-ra2 (Women's Occupational Title)	PY Fn 187
Figs	Named women a-pi-te-ja and *34-ke-ja	PY Fn 187
Figs	a-ke-ti-ra2 (Women's Occupational Title)	PY Fn 187
Olives	Named woman a3-pu-ke-ne-ja	PY Fn 79
Wheat and figs rations	Numerous Women's Workgroups	*passim* Ab series
Commodity *146[2]	Named woman ke-sa-da-ra	PY Mn 1368
Commodity KA[3]	a-ke-ti-ri-ja (Women's Occupation Title)	PY Un 219
Leather shoes – pe-di-ra	Named woman wo-di-je-ja	PY Ub 1318
Bronze (temple bronze)	ka-ra-wi-po-ro (Woman's Religious Title "Keybearer")	PY Jn 829
Land leases (or "land under obligation")	te-o-jo do-e-ra	*passim* Ea, Eb, En, Eo Ep series[4]
Land leases (or "land under obligation")	do-e-ra i-je-re-ja pa-ki-ja-na ("Female slave of the priestess at Pa-ki-ja-na")	PY En 609.16
Land leases (or "land under obligation")	i-je-re-ja ("priestess")	PY EB 297, PY Eb 339 + PY Eb 409, PY Eb 1176, PY En 609.16, PY En 609.18, PY Eo 224.6, PY Eo 224.8, PY Ep 539.7, PY Ep 539.8, PY Ep 704.3, PY Ep 704.5

continued ...

Table 2.7 continued

Commodity/holding	*Holder*	*Tablet/tablet series*
Land leases (or "land under obligation")	ka-pa-ti-ja (WN) the ka-ra-wi-po-ro	PY Ed 317
Land leases (or "land under obligation")	ki-ri-te-wi-ja (Collective Group)	PY Eb 321 + PY 327+PY Eb 1153, PY Ep 704.4
γέρας lease – ke-ra o-na-to	i-je-re-ja[5]	PY Eb 416
Communal land (ke-ke-ma-na ko-to-na)	ka-pa-ti-ja (WN) the ka-ra-wi-po-ro	PY EB 338, PY Ep 704.7
"Freehold" land(?)[6] (e-to-ni-ja ko-to-na)	i-je-re-ja	PY Eb 297, PY Ep 704.5

Notes

1 PY Ae 303 reads .a i-je-re-jo .b pu-ro i-je-re-ja do-e-ra e-ne-ka ku-ru-so-jo MUL 14[ ] ("At Pylos, 14 slave-women of the priestess on account of the sacred gold.")
2 As yet unidentified.
3 As yet unidentified.
4 See the chapter on land for detailed breakdown on land leases and their holders.
5 The priestess seems to be in possession of this type of land grant as she is credited with giving this lease to the woman named u-wa-mi-ja.
6 Unclear if this type of land is actually held by the priestess. Whether the land she holds is freehold land which she holds on behalf of her divinity as she claims or is leased communal land as the village claims is at the heart of the one legal dispute recorded in the tablets. Otherwise, the tablets list only men as e-to-ni-jo holders.

ra-wa-ke-ta, e-qe-ta, or te-re-ta, or among the "collectors"[134] – the highest civic offices at both sites.[135]

Consequently, even such a brief survey as this one must ring the death knell for any stray notions of either a matriarchal or egalitarian social structure in the Late Bronze Age Aegean, as nowhere do we see women achieve dominance or even parity in the political, economic, or symbolic realms; rather, the evidence leaves us with no other option than to regard both Knossos and Pylos as societies which were patriarchal in their social, economic, and political organizations.

Patriarchal organization at Pylos and Knossos

Recently, the medieval historian Judith Bennett has argued for the dusting off and revival of the term patriarchy, a term most commonly associated with 1970s feminist theory, as the most useful term to designate societies which demonstrate persistent gender inequities which systemically disadvantage women.[136] Under her reading, then, patriarchy is a system in which "women's persistent economic disadvantages [are] integral"[137] rather than coincidental, or in Allan Johnson's phrasing, "a society is patriarchal to the degree that it promotes male privilege, by being male dominated, male identified, and male centered."[138] Additionally,

Table 2.8 Women's holdings at Knossos

Commodity/holding	*Holder*	*Tablet/tablet series*
Finished cloth		
Cloth – TELA + te-pa	Various Named Women (WNs)	KN Ap 5748, KN Ln 1568
Cloth – TELA-1	da-te-we-ja (Women's Occupational Title)	KN L 594
Cloth – TELA-1	Named Woman ru-nu	KN Ln 1568
Cloth – TELA-1 pa-we-a	a-ra-ka-te-ja (Women's Occupation Title "spinning women")	KN L 531
Cloth – TELA-2	Named Woman po-po	KN L 513
Cloth – TELA-2	Named Woman qi-na	KN Ld 584
Cloth – TELA-2+PU	ko-ru-we-ja (Women's Occupational Title)	KN L 472
Tunics – TUN+KI	da-te-we-ja (Women's Occupational Title)	KN L 594
Linen		
Linen – ri-ta	Named Woman po-po	KN L 567
Linen pieces – ri-ta- pa-we-a	da-te-we-ja (Women's Occupational Title)	KN L 594
Wool		
Wool	Named Woman do-ti-ja	KN L 520
Wool	Named Woman po-ni-ke-ja	KN Ln 1568 lat. B
Wool	Named Woman e-ti-wa-ja	KN Od 681
Wool	Named Woman po-po	KN Od 681
Wool Type *164	Named Person ka-ma?[1]	KN L 520
Livestock[2]		
Sheep (?)[3]	ku-tu-qa-no	KN Da 1161
Oxen (?) – BOS-ZE	tu-zo[4]	KN C 7698
Wheat		
Wheat – GRA 100 units[5]	ki-ri-te-wi-ja (Collective Group)	KN E 777
Wheat – GRA 110 units	ki-ri-te-wi-ja (Collective Group)	KN E 777
Oil		
Oil V4 (6.4 liters)	i-je-re-ja a-ne-mo (Priestess of the Winds)	KN Fp 1+31
Oil 1 unit (28.8 l.)	i-je-re-ja a-ne-mo (Priestess of the Winds)	KN Fp 13

continued ...

Table 2.8 continued

Commodity/holding	*Holder*	*Tablet/tablet series*
Oil S1 V3 (14.4 l.)	i-je-re-ja a-ne-mo @ PN u-ta-no (Priestess of the Winds @ u-ta-no)	KN Fp 13
Oil	ki-ri-te-wi-ja (Collective Groups)	KN Fp 363
Coriander Spice – 10 units	ma-ri-ne-we[6]	KN Ga 713+94
Slave Woman	ma-ri-ne-we	KN Ga 713+94
Vessel – *209-VAS A	ma-ri-ne-we	KN Ga 713+94
Land		
Land 5 DA	Named Woman]ka-wi-ja	KN Uf 79
Land – Orchard Plot	Named Woman pe-ri-je-ja	KN Uf 70

Notes

1 The identification of the term ka-ma remains controversial, with suggestions of a man's name, a woman's name or a toponym all proposed. *Diccionario* 1: 309. I find the term inconclusive.
2 Livestock holdings for women are not securely attested on any Knossian tablet.
3 The name ku-tu-qa-no is a woman's name (WM) in KN Ap 639; there is no way to know if the ku-tu-qa-no is the same or a different individual on KN Da 1161. Otherwise, no women are attested anywhere in the 120+ Knossos sheep tablets (the Da) series.
4 Tu-zo may be a man's name; if tu-zo is a woman, she would be the sole woman in a series that otherwise records exclusively men.
5 This is a particularly large amount – 9,600 l. wheat – and is identified on the tablet as a monthly allotment.
6 Variously identified either as a collective of women of a local divinity. As we cannot be certain if these references are to real women, the holdings of ma-ri-ne-we are not included in Chapter 5's discussion of women's property holdings as Knossos.

Bamberger has established a checklist of observable criteria to allow researchers to classify any given society as egalitarian or patriarchal.[139] Among her list of societal features indicating a patriarchal organization of societies is the limited access for women to goods and commodities, positions of rank, and participation in high symbolic rituals. For our purposes, the combined weight of women's diminished economic viability and women's exclusion from the highest political offices at both Knossos and Pylos firmly identifies both palace societies as patriarchal and places women at both centers as socially and economically subordinate to men. Thus from even this brief analysis of women's holdings and their consequent relationship to the ruling elite, I argue that there is clear conceptual movement from women as first unequally represented, to women having lesser access to commodities and positions, and finally for women to occupy a position of social subordination in terms of civic autonomy and economic maneuverability.

Thus, even from this brief survey, we can claim that at both Bronze Age palaces, gender acts as a major category of social organization, circumscribing and influencing the daily lives and economic standings of both men and women. The archives from both palaces reveal strictly gendered societies where an individual's sex opens or limits access to various occupations and to specific commodities or resources and ultimately governs his or her access to civic office, control over property, and public functions. In short, gender is constructed at both Bronze Age palaces in a way so that men and women largely experience their societies in very distinct ways.[140]

The question that must next be addressed is whether the two functional patriarchies of the island of Knossos and mainland Pylos remained similar in their patriarchal organizations or, due to their different historical circumstances, experienced and structured their systems of women's subordination in different ways. Would real and significant differences exist between the gender organizations of Pylos with its Mycenaean Greek administration and population and that of Knossos where a Mycenaean administration governed a hybridized Mycenaean and Minoan citizenry?

The remainder of this study addresses this question.

Notes

1 All text transliterations are current with *PTT* for Pylos and Killen and Olivier 1989 for Knossos.
2 For a discussion of the major scholarly inquiries on women in the tablets, see the Introduction to this study.
3 Mycenaean Greece seems to have observed a strict gender binary with naming conventions reinforcing the differentiation of male and female.
4 R. Palmer 2008 offers a thoughtful overview to the conventions of the Linear B script and the challenges inherent to using the tablets; see also Duhoux 2011 for methodological concerns.
5 The ideogram VIR ("man") is used at Knossos on 110 tablets and at Pylos on 112.
6 An additional 12 tablets remain too fragmentary to allow a tabulation.
7 Presumably additional tablets used the ideogram, but their state of preservation leaves the part of the table where MUL would appear lacunose. For the purposes of this study, only tablets where the ideogram is clearly legible are assessed and tallied.
8 Some women, particularly those belonging to collective workgroups and those listed in the E series land register may be listed twice.
9 Palaima 2011a, 2003.
10 PY Tn 316 is addressed in Chapter 7: Women and religion at Knossos and Pylos.
11 An additional subseries of the personnel tablets at Pylos – the Ad series – also references the workgroups of the Pylos Aa and Ab women by tallying the numbers of their adolescent and adult sons.
12 Women's workgroups at Pylos are discussed in greater detail in Chapter 3.
13 Etymologies and translations for workgroup titles used at Pylos are discussed extensively in Chapter 3.
14 Ventris and Chadwick also note that ko-wa is used for the nominative singular, plural, and dual (to prevent confusion with ko-wo "boy") and cites as comparanda κούρη [Il. vi, 420+], κόρη [Attic] and κόρα [Arcadian]. Ventris and Chadwick 1973: 557.
15 Ko-wo functions as the nominative singular, dual, and plural as well as the dative singular for *korwos, -oi, -oi* meaning "boy/son" or in the plural "children;" cf. κοῦρος [Od. xix, 523], κόρος [Attic], and κῶρος [Doric]: Ventris and Chadwick 1973: 557.
16 Cohen and Rutter 2007.
17 Some occupational titles may also be found (accompanied by the MUL ideogram) in the two summary tablets of the An series which deal with female workers.

18 R. Palmer 1989.

19 The ethnic adjectives of the Pylian A series have received a fair amount of scholarly attention. Most scholars have noted that the ethnics largely refer to places in Western Asia Minor (Lydia, Miletus, Halicarnassos, Cnidos, etc.) or islands in the Eastern Aegean such as Lemnos. See Shelmerdine 1998 for a discussion of the ethnics in context of the Eastern Aegean. Other major texts dealing with ethnics include Chadwick 1988: 78–84, 91–92; Lindgren 1973; *Diccionario,* passim; Ventris and Chadwick 1973, passim.

20 It was once thought that these titles referred either to the ethnic ancestry of women or to the immediate provenance of these workers. For reasons discussed in Chapter 3, the ancestry-based hypothesis is the more tenable one as ethnics are never linked at Pylos to the current locations of the workers.

21 This translation from Ventris and Chadwick 1973: 158. The annotations TA and DA appear to refer to supervisors within the group and are discussed in detail in Chapter 3.

22 Metapa is the name of one of the Nine Towns of Pylos' Hither Province but has not been conclusively identified with any known site. For the towns of the Hither and Further Provinces: John Bennet 2011; Lang 1988: 185–212.

23 Cf. Adrastos in Chapter 3.

24 Two additional tablets of the Ae series (PY Ae 629 and PY Ae 634) also use the MUL ideogram; both are in very fragmentary condition but may have the remnants of titles preceding their better preserved ideograms.

25 Cf. 68–69.

26 We may presume additional tablets used the ideogram but their state of preservation is not sufficient to be able to read the ideogram now; for our purposes here, I am counting only those tablets which are currently legible.

27 The remaining 16 names are recoverable through other means, discussed below.

28 For example:
KN Ap 769:
.1:]i̩-ta-no MUL 1 ka-*56-so-ta MUL 1 a3-du-wo-na MUL 1
.2:]wi-ja-na-tu MUL 1 i-ta-ja MUL 1

29 Discussed further in Chapter 5: Women at Knossos.

30 KN Am 827 + 7032 + 7618; KN Ap 618 + 623 + 633 + 5533 + 5922; KN Ap 628 + 5935; KN Ap 639; KN Ap 769; KN Ap 5547 + 8162; KN Ap 5864.

31 KN Ap 639.07.

32 KN Ap 639.04. Pa-i-ti-ja seems to function in different contexts both as a woman's name and as a women's ethnic title (KN Ak 828).

33 KN Ap 639.04.

34 KN Ap 639.11.

35 KN Ap 5864.04.

36 KN Ap 639.03.

37 KN Ag 87, KN Ag 88 + 7033, KN Ag 91, KN Ag 1654, KN Ag 7000, KN Ai 63, KN Ai 321, KN Am 827 + 7032 + 7618, and KN Ap 637.

38 Hiller 1989.

39 The term ma-te is mostly seen in the human context on Py Un 207. For usage of this term in divine context (notably the dative phrase ma-te-re te-i-ja "Mother of the gods"): Gérard-Rousseau 1968: 1381; *Diccionario* Vol. I: 429–430.

40 Killen 1966; Hiller 1989.

41 The tablets from Mycenae add another family title to the repertoire: infant girl (*ki-ra or *gila*). *Docs2*: 554.

42 Cf. γρηύς Od. 1. 191+. *Docs2*: 551.

43 TU and ka-ra-we are specific to Knossos; ko-wa features in both corpora.

44 Uchitel 1984: 257–282; Gérard-Rousseau 1968: 79–81; Hiller 1989. This text receives further treatment in Chapter 7: Women and religion at Knossos and Pylos.

45 Do-qe-ja has been proposed as a feminine theonym. See Chapter 7 for additional discussion.
46 KN Ai 1036, KN Ai 1037, KN Ap 628 + 5935, KN Gg 713 + 994.
47 KN Fp 1 + 31, KN Fp 13.
48 KN Ap 639.05.
49 KN Lc 534 + 7647 + 7818, KN Ld 595.
50 Kn L 472.
51 KN Lc 549, KN Le 641 + frr.
52 KN Ak 5553.
53 PY Ad 691.
54 PY Ad 687.
55 PY Ad 671.
56 PY Ad 921.
57 The role of women in religion at both sites is discussed in detail in Chapter 7.
58 PY Ae 303, PY Eb 416 [PY Ep 704.02], PY Ed 317, PY Ep 704.02, PY Ep 704.03, PY Ep 704.05, PY Qa 1289, PY Qa 1300, PY Un 6 v1, PY Eb 297 [PY Ep 704.05], PY Eb 339 + 409, [PY Ep 704.03], PY Eb 1176, PY En 609.16, PY En 609.18, PY Eo 224.06 [PY En 609.16], PY Eo 224.08 [PY En 609.18]. [Brackets indicate recapitulation tablets repeating the data of the previous text.]
59 PY Ae 110, PY Eb 338 [PY Ep 704.07], PY Ed 317, PY Ep 704.07, PY Jn 829, PY Un 6 v2, PY Vn 48.07.
60 PY Ae 303, PY En 609.16, PY Eo 224.06 [PY En 609.16].
61 Attested to on 31 tablets. For complete listing, see Appendix A: Women in the Pylos Tablets.
62 A fair amount of scholarship has been devoted to the study of Mycenaean personal names. Among these onomastic studies are studies of the structure of Mycenaean names: Garcia Ramon 2011: 253–298; Palaima 1999: 370, n.14; Neumann 1994; Landau 1958. For discussion of Mycenaean vs. Classical Greek names: Ilievski 1979b: 134–146. For prosopographical studies useful to analyses of Bronze Age social structures: Ilievski 1992; Baumbach 1979, 1983; Lindgren 1973; Landenius Enegren 2008.
63 For a discussion of the methodological difficulties posed by the ambiguity inherent in many Mycenaean name forms: Palaima 1999: 367–375.
64 Of the women's names recovered from KN Ln 1568, three are grammatically feminine: ru-ki-ti-ja, na-e-ra-ja, and po-ni-ke-ja, but the analogous treatment of the other figures of this tablet allows the recovery of 9 additional non-Greek women's names: *56-po-so; wa-wa-ka; wi-da-ma-ta2, po-po, ta-su, ko-re-wo, ru-sa-ma, qe-pa-ta-no, and ru-nu.
65 Scholarship has largely approached women's roles in the Classical period from an Athenocentric and oikos-based perspective and has focused on the complexities of women's legal and social status as daughters, wives, mothers, and heiresses. Studies tend to investigate either the ideological or economic components of women's investiture within the oikos structure, emphasizing women's exclusion from the political realm [Patterson 1987; Walters 1993; Katz 1995] or exploring the social and economic organization of the family structure [Schaps 1979; Patterson 1998, 1991; Pomeroy 1995; Gould 1980; Katz 2000].
66 Connelly 2007: 31–33.
67 Consequently, we cannot currently verify if these even exist as institutions in the Bronze Age or if they are inventions of the Dark Age or Archaic period.
68 Schaps 1979.
69 Connelly 2007: 57–84.
70 For the classification of the different Linear B series: Hooker 1980: 36–37 or Ventris and Chadwick 1973: 50–51.
71 Of the total 47 series, the tablets of 36 of these series record only men. Nine additional series have two or fewer tablets that mention women.

72 A single Jn tablet (Jn 829) includes a mention of a lone woman among a group of male officials. This tablet is discussed in both Chapter 4 and Chapter 7.

73 On none of these tablets, however, do both men and women appear.

74 While the Pylos A tablets include both men and women, the sexes are mostly segregated into discrete subseries: the Aa and Ab subseries for women and the Ac, Ad, Ae, and Aq for men. Only the An series records both men and women.

75 Both of these series will be explored in greater detail. The A series' personnel tablets are discussed in Chapter 2, and the land-holding tablets are examined in Chapter 6.

76 Thirty-seven of the series at Knossos record men exclusively while in another ten series women appear on two or fewer tablets.

77 For color conventions in Aegean art: S. Immerwahr 1990; Hood 1985: 21–26; Marinatos 1995: 577–85; for gender and costume: Lyberopoulou 1978; for gender distinctions in glyptic art: Alexandri 1994.

78 Rehak and Younger 1998: 115.

79 The sex of the jumpers is still disputed. For bibliography on gender and bull-leaping: Damiani Indelicato 1988; Younger 1995, 1976.

80 Peterson 1981.

81 The frescoes from Akrotiri are a notable exception to the rule and we frequently see scenes with both men and women. Some scenes, though, are single-sex: the saffron-gatherers, the House of the Ladies, etc. (Akrotiri is, of course, not a Mycenaean era town and will be excluded from this study.)

82 Costin notes, "… there are no known cases of complex society – modern or historic – in which a gendered division of labor is not a critical factor in the domestic and political economies and because gendered relations of production are tied into other complex social and political relations." Costin 1991: 111.

83 Nosch notes that titled men and women receive different types of compensation from their polities, with women generally receiving commodity *120 and figs, while titled men tend to be compensated with land or other goods. Nosch 1997b: 397.

84 In many areas the preservation state of the tablets or scribal habit makes impossible an exact tally of the size of women's holdings vis-à-vis men's. The few areas where we are able to quantify the size of property holdings (such as land holdings discussed in depth in Chapter 6) seem to indicate women's holdings are rarely larger than 5 percent of men's.

85 *Passim* PY A series.

86 *Passim* PY Ae, PY An, PY Cc, and PY Cn.

87 *Passim* PY Ea, Eb, Eo, Ep, and Er series.

88 *Passim* PY Es series.

89 PY Fn 50, PY Fn 29.

90 PY Fn 29.

91 PY Fr 1184.

92 PY Un 2.

93 PY Un 2, PY Un 1321.

94 PY Un 718.

95 *Passim* PY Jn series.

96 PY Ub 1316.

97 PY Ub 1318.

98 PY La 1393.

99 PY Un 249.

100 *Passim* PY Na series.

101 PY Ta 709.

102 PY Tn 316, PY Vn 130.

103 PY Un 2.

104 PY Va 482.

105 PY Sh 736, PY Vn 10, PY Wa 1148.

106 *Passim* PY Sa series, PY Va 15.
107 *Passim* PY Ma, PY On 300, *passim* PY Pa, PY Qa series. For a useful discussion of the economics of the PY Ma series: Lejeune 1979: 147–150.
108 The distribution, or possibly loan, of temple bronze by the ka-ra-wi-po-ro on PY Jn 829 in conjunction with the otherwise male local officials has received much scholarly attention. Two notable studies on this tablet are Leukart 1979: 183–187 and Hiller 1979: 189–195. This and other holdings of the ka-ra-wi-po-ro are addressed in detail in Chapter 7: Women and religion at Knossos and Pylos.
109 KN Ak 615, KN Ak 9173 + 9459 + 9001, KN Ai 1036.
110 KN Ai 5976 + 8268 + frr., KN B 822, KN B 988.
111 KN Am 821, KN Am 827 + 7032 + 7618, KN As 602, KN As 605, KN As 1518 + 1529, KN As 602 + 650 + 1639 + fr., KN As 605 + 5869 + 5911 + 5931 + frr., KN As 1518 + 1529, KN B 809, KN B 812, KN B 818.
112 *Passim* KN Uf series.
113 *Passim* KN Lc, Ld, Le, Mc and M series.
114 KN As 1518 + KN As 1529.
115 *Passim* KN C and D series.
116 *Passim* KN E series, KN F 854.
117 KN F 51, KN F 153.
118 KN F 854.
119 *Passim* KN Fh series.
120 KN F 841.
121 KN Oa 878.
122 KN K 773 + 1809, KN K 775, KN K 875.
123 *Passim* KN Od series; KN Og 4467.
124 *Passim* KN L series.
125 *Passim* KN Sd series.
126 KN Sd 4403 + 5114, KN Sf 4420, *passim* KN So series.
127 KN Oa 878.
128 KN Ra 1543, *passim* KN Sc series.
129 *Passim* KN Sc series.
130 KN U 109 + 7499, KN U 172.
131 The one exception to this is the keybearer on PY Jn 829.
132 Women's Occupations are addressed in Chapters 3 and 4.
133 Olsen 1998.
134 Kyriakidis 2010; Bennet 1992; Rougemont 2008, 2004, 2001; Killen 1995.
135 These positions are further discussed in Chapter 3.
136 Judith Bennett 2006: 21.
137 Judith Bennett 2006: 15.
138 Johnson 2005: 5.
139 Bamberger 1974: 263–80.
140 One particular social institution serves as the major exception to this rule. See Chapter 7: Women and religion at Knossos and Pylos.

3 Women and production at Pylos

Introduction

In the two Bronze Age polities of Pylos and Knossos women contributed to their palatial economies by means of the production of goods or through the control of property. At both sites, the majority of women who are recorded in the tablets appear in these two fields; thus, participation in either production or commodity exchanges emerges as the primary means by which women become visible in the Linear B records.

As women are recorded in a variety of textual contexts throughout the tablets, how might the tablets be best used to recover the activities and commodities controlled by Mycenaean women? I contend that the most fruitful means to understand how gender patterns operate for women in the Bronze Age states is first to start on a local level, recovering all of the references to women in the economy of each state and then to identify patterns in such well-documented economic institutions as production, commodity holdings, land tenure, and religion. Moreover, since the transactions involving women are so frequently enumerated, by focusing on the sizes and types of transactions women are involved in, we can gain insight into the gendered patterns at play inside each state and recover some of the means through which social rank and status was defined for Pylian and Knossian women.

Chapters 3, 4, and 5 investigate the ways in which Pylian and Knossian women are integrated into their respective economies: first by juxtaposing the roles women enact as members of the workforce and as property holders with those of men, and then by comparing the treatment of women between the two sites. I begin here with a brief discussion of the ways both sites structure men into their labor forces. While men are integrated into a three-tiered social hierarchy comprised of the ruling elite, middle-status independent workers who exercise control over property, and low-ranked laborers whose standing is that of palace dependents, women at both sites are recorded in only two distinct economic categories: low-ranked laborers and mid-status administrative officials. At Pylos, this creates two groupings of women: women defined by their production activities and women defined by their property holdings. Women located in these two categories occupy different hierarchical positions; property holders occupy a distinctly higher status than laborers.

This chapter explores the evidence for women's activities as laborers at the site of Pylos. It compiles the references to women's tasks and workgroups throughout the tablets of this mainland palace site and offers a rationale for understanding women in this category – by far the largest subset of the women documented at Pylos – as a slave labor force, whose labor and status are entirely defined by their relationship to the palace and its administration.

Gender and the palatial workforce

The tablets from Knossos and Pylos record approximately 7000 people who contribute to the palatial economies – approximately 5000 men and 2000 women between the two sites.[1] These individuals, who constitute the palaces' labor forces, enter the archives in two related capacities: we see them recorded in terms of a.) their role in production and b.) the property and commodities under their control. As a product of the economic focus of this evidence, tracking individuals in terms of tasks and holdings provides an opportunity to examine the gendered workings of the two palaces' worker populations.

At both Knossos and Pylos gender plays a central role in organizing the labor force; all aspects of production appear to have been segregated along gender lines. Nowhere in the tablets from either center do we observe men and women working in conjunction with each other to produce any product or commodity; instead their production activities are separated by sex to create either all-male or all-female groups of workers. Furthermore, labor is gender-segregated not only by clustering women and men into single-sex workgroups, but also by tasks and titles. Labor is highly specialized in the Mycenaean economy;[2] throughout the archives at both sites, the assignment of tasks and titles to men and women demonstrates a high degree of gender specificity, and occupational designations are nearly always assigned to one sex or the other. For example, we see only female bath-attendants and flour-grinders and only male shepherds and bronze-smiths. Furthermore, the gender specificity of tasks seems to extend across sites; no tasks are specific to one sex at one site and assigned to the other sex at the other. In fact out of the 200 or so known occupational titles assigned to men and women, only five "work" designations are used to describe members of both sexes: priests/priestesses, "slaves of the god," (ordinary) slaves, stitchers, and weavers.[3] With the exception of these five terms, all other recorded titles can be assigned to men or women exclusively. This division of labor along gender lines functions to create two distinct social and economic spheres – one for women and another for men.

Gender does appear to have provided the primary organizational rationale for the distribution of tasks, but it is not the only factor. A number of hierarchical concerns also come into play with respect to these two different economic spheres. Two primary areas of economic hierarchies are observable: the first between the sexes – where men's economic activities take higher priority than women's – and the second between members of the same sex. Overall, we see two levels of task differentiation; first, by gender which separates men and women into different economic categories, and then, within each sex, by economic status which differentiates between the ruling elite, property holders, and dependent laborers. Interestingly, intra-sex status hierarchies are not structured in the same way but rather take different forms for men and women. For men, we see three different levels of title and task differentiation: men's titles establish them as members of the ruling elite, religious functionaries alongside independent craftsmen who are compensated by the palace for their labor or products, and palace dependents. This is true of the hierarchical organization of men at both Knossos and Pylos.

For women, the economic and task hierarchy is somewhat different. At both sites we observe instead a two-tiered system of economic status: female property holders or other types of autonomous women – differentiated by use of their names or individual titles – and the mass of dependent women, working directly for the palace as collectives. As Chapters 3–5 demonstrate, these intra-gender hierarchies are differently constructed across Pylos and Knossos. I begin with a brief summary of men's tasks and holdings in the tablets.

Men's production and property holdings

From the first flurry of publication that followed Michael Ventris' decipherment of Linear B up to the present, a tremendous amount of Linear B scholarship has been devoted to identifying the economic activities of men in the tablets.[4] As much work has been devoted to this topic – and since this section is not original to my research – I will not replicate here previous studies on men's exact property holdings and tasks performed; instead, this section explores how men's economic activities functioned on a more macroscopic level and the hierarchical organization of men in the Knossos and Pylos archives.

The documents from Knossos and Pylos reveal attention to hierarchies among the male workers within their polities.[5] Both sites employ a three-tier schema for the structure of men in the workforce. Men at these sites fall into three status categories: the ruling elite, low-status palace dependents, and middle-status independent workers and functionaries who contribute to the palatial economy but do not appear as dependent on it.

Elite men

For the purposes of investigating the status hierarchies among men at both centers, I am defining as elite those men who occupy the governmental structures of the Mycenaean state, from the local to the state level. In addition to their administrative functions, these men also tend to have large property holdings (particularly with respect to luxury or precious commodities), large supervisory responsibilities, and personal staff in their sole employ.[6]

Much research has been directed at identifying the members of the ruling elite and at ranking them hierarchically.[7] Reconstructing the exact roles and functions of officials in the Linear B tablets remains a knotty and somewhat unproductive task; as Morpurgo Davies writes, "the basic administration and organization of the Mycenaean state had a certain degree of complexity which called for specialized terminology … [which] seems to have disappeared together with the end of the Mycenaean palaces."[8] Consequently, the more specialized terms are often only accessible in their most broad readings. Nonetheless, we can reconstruct at least part of the palaces' administrative and economic structures through both internal scrutiny of the tablets and from linguistic analysis of economic terms and titles.[9]

At both sites, men categorically dominate the administrative structure, holding all the positions of the ruling elite from the local to the state level. At both Knossos and Pylos, the most important official is the *wanax* (wa-na-ka) who maintains a pre-eminent role in the palatial records, exerting control over the civic, economic, and religious spheres. At Pylos, where his name appears to be e-ke-ra2-wo (*Enkhelyawos*),[10] he also possesses the most extensive property holdings of any human figure in the tablets – property which includes major land holdings as well as specialist craftsmen in his employ. While there is full consensus on the etymology of the term as Φἄναξ,[11] its exact interpretation continues to be a focus for debate. Interpretations range from "king" to "religious authority" to the less common reading of the *wanax* as a divinity.[12] Nonetheless, Palaima's designation of the *wanax* as "the central figure of authority in Mycenaean society" seems the best means to express the various civic and religious components presided over by the *wanax*.[13] Currently, no female counterpart for the wa-na-ka has been securely identified at either site.[14]

The second-highest ranking figure at both sites bears the title *lawagetas* (ra-wa-ke-ta). The ra-wa-ke-ta, like the wa-na-ka, has also received a good deal of scholarly attention.[15] The term, most commonly understood to normalize as *λαFαγέτας, appears to be a derivation from λαός which is generally understood to mean at this stage of the Bronze Age either "collective folk of armed warriors"[16] or "people;" ra-wa-ke-ta by extension is understood to mean "leader of the people," most commonly in the form of the highest-ranking military leader of a Bronze Age State.[17] Nikoloudis has recently proposed *lawagetas* as a figure who can mobilize and command human labor for specialized tasks.[18] Like the *wanax*, the *lawagetas* appears to have been recorded by name as well; at Pylos the *lawagetas* seems to be named we-da-ne-wo (*Wedanewos*),[19] and can, like the *wanax*, be recorded either by name or title. Additionally, the *lawagetas* has personnel assigned to him (designated by the adjective ra-wa-ke-si-jo) as well as a temenos (also described by ra-wa-ke-si-jo). His *temenos* is significantly smaller than that of the *wanax*, but he is the only other human to possess a *temenos* in his own right. He also contributes to cult offerings to Poseidon, but once again on a smaller scale than the *wanax*.[20] In terms of the relationship of the *wanax* and the *lawagetas*, the *lawagetas* seems to occupy the second position of rank in palatial society and would appear to derive his status from his military associations.[21] Again, no female counterpart for this title is attested.

In addition to the *wanax* and the *lawagetas*, other important officials include the *heqetai* (e-qe-ta-i), regarded as companions, also possibly of a military nature, to the *wanax*; the *telestai* (te-re-ta) who hold large amounts of land and who may hold a religious function as well, officials bearing the title *basileus* (qa-si-re-u) who appear in the Mycenaean period more as a local chief-type, and who often appear in an industrial context;[22] ko-re-te (pl.) and po-ro-ko-re-te (pl.) who seem to be local officials,[23] and local "councilmen"[24] identified by the term ke-ro-si-ja. Neither site reveals women occupying any of these positions.

Middle-status men

The vast majority of men attested in both archives occupy the middle-ranked category. As with elite men, middle-status men seem to be organized in much the same way at both palaces. This category – the largest hierarchical grouping for men – includes all men in the tablets who are neither palace dependents, slaves, or members of the administrative elite.[25] Men who occupy this somewhat composite category include craftsmen, religious functionaries, small landholders, and the economic administrators commonly referred to as "collectors".[26] These men appear to be defined in the tablets by both their production and by their holdings. Craftsmen of this rank include smiths, heralds, rowers, weavers, and cooks; religious functionaries include priests (i-je-re-u) and "slaves of the god" (te-o-jo do-e-ro).[27] Overall, nearly 90 titles between the two sites belong to this category.

Workers in this category tend to be identified by both their titles and their holdings. Middle-ranked men can be listed in one of two ways: firmly within their occupational contexts or in ways which appear more peripheral to their production and tasks.[28] That is, we observe tablets where men are identified by their titles and receive or contribute allotments directly related to their occupational assignments, for example, shepherds whose sheep are tallied and bronze-smiths who receive measured allotments of bronze,[29] or else we see tablets where the linkage between the commodity allotted and the task performance is less direct. Land allotments granted to cooks and to priests or wheat allotments best exemplified this situation. In the latter arrangement, the rationale governing the task and the allotment is not always clear; plausible explanations include the idea of products or holdings given as payment in kind,[30] where grain and land are exchanged for labor or commodities; or, we might be witnessing the use of the title not to refer to work related to that title in specific, but rather to distinguish between individuals bearing the same name.

It is difficult to discern what, if any, hierarchical relationships the men of this rank have vis-à-vis each other,[31] but overall they remain fundamentally different from the other two ranks in their lack of political responsibilities (which separates them from elite-status men) and in that they often have access to land holdings and receive substantially larger and more varied commodity allotments than do dependent workers (who only receive subsistence rations). Overall, we should understand these workers as fitting into the palace economy in four distinct ways: 1.) As specialized craftsmen who work for the palace (or palatial officials) and whose labor is deemed important enough to compensate with more substantial holdings than their daily subsistence would require.[32] 2.) As independent contractors with workshops and holdings outside of direct palatial control.[33] This is certainly the way we should interpret the weaver who on PY Un 1322 receives more than 60 times the amount of wheat allocated to each female weaver who serves as a palace dependent. He surely is being allotted payment for materials produced by a workshop under his control as this amount is too exorbitantly large to represent any rations given as compensation for individual labor. 3.) As religious officials for whom the performance of their duties (rather than material production) warrants compensation by the state, often in the form of land grants. 4.) And as "collectors" who serve as the economic backbone of the state, overseeing many mid-level transactions and supervising lower-ranking personnel.[34]

Lower-status men

The final status category for men at both sites is comprised of two types of workers, palace dependents and privately held slaves (δοῦλοι/do-e-ro).[35] In both instances, these men do not appear to possess any independent legal standing or any property or commodity holdings beyond their immediate sustenance.[36] Additionally, men of this standing are rarely seen differentiated by name, by parentage, or by any other marker;[37] they tend to be clustered together into collective groups identified only by VIR and a place name and/or occupational title. Furthermore, both groups appear to have little to no autonomy as either the palace or their "owners" seem to assign and direct their labor either in the form of workgroups, or to assign them as a group to a particular task, such as the rowers from Pylos.[38] It is not entirely clear how men come to attain this status, although at least two mechanisms seem to be alluded to in the tablets. Slaves can either be purchased,[39] or they can inherit their servile status from their (slave) mothers; throughout the personnel series tablets from both Knossos and Pylos, it would also appear that men who are sons of women who are palace dependents inherit their mothers' status, and, as palace dependents, the palace carefully monitors their numbers and rations, and also directs their production activities in their adult lives.[40] Far fewer men than women are recorded in this rank.

Overall, then, we observe a three-tier status hierarchy for the men who contribute to the palatial economy at Knossos and at Pylos; female workers are integrated into both palace systems in a substantially different manner.

Women's production and property holdings

While men at Knossos and Pylos dominated their states' economies in both the size and variety of their property holdings and in the breadth of their occupational titles, women's contributions to the economies of both palatial sites were also considerable. Between the two sites, women assumed nearly 50 different occupational designations, and women's production activities, particularly textile production, were of vital importance to the Aegean economy.[41] Furthermore, in addition to production activities, women at both sites exercised significant control over property and commodities.

In the 60 years following the decipherment of Linear B in 1952, only a handful of studies have investigated women's integration into the Late Bronze Age workforce. These studies have assumed two forms: investigations into women's labor as evidenced in a specific tablet series (usually either the personnel series or textile management tablets at either site) or as survey articles designed to render women's occupations and activities accessible to a non-Linear B specialist audience.[42] While all these studies have been instrumental in shedding light on the topic of palatial women, they have produced the unintended consequences of creating impressions of cultural unity between the two sites with women occupying a common social and economic status at Knossos and Pylos and of fostering a rosier image of egalitarianism between the sexes. [43] A more quantitative approach to the evidence would suggest otherwise.

The documentary evidence clearly indicates that women's incorporation into the palatial economies differs significantly from that of men. We continue to observe status hierarchies among members of the same sex, but the ways in which women documented in the tablets are ranked hierarchically is different from the organizational structure governing men. While men are configured into a three-tiered hierarchy, the status structure for Knossian and Pylian women is instead two-tiered. Rather than conforming to men's system of elite, middle- and low-ranked personnel, the women documented in the tablets inhabit one of only two categories: low-status laborers or middle-status persons with some degree of property control, economic autonomy, and/or supervisory responsibilities. The third category available to men – that of the ruling elite – is not one where women appear; the nearest we have to "elite" status women are seven, high-ranking wives who have no titles or major property holdings of their own.[44] None of the officials who compose the administrative elite at either Knossos or Pylos can be identified securely as women.

As previously mentioned, the most visible category of women in the tablets from Pylos is the over 750 low-status female laborers who are organized into collective workgroups.[45] This stands in direct contrast with palatial men who are most visible in the guise of independent, mid-status craftsmen. It also provides a counterpoint to most later documentary evidence in that instead of the upper-class bias of most historiographical and archival sources, we have far more references in the Linear B tablets to women of the lower social strata than we do for middle- or upper-ranked women. Women occupying the lower-status category are typically recorded as unnamed members of collective workgroups identified by task, location, or ethnic descriptors in conjunction with the MUL ideogram previously discussed in Chapter 2. With few exceptions, women occupying this social rung are associated with no property holdings beyond their subsistence rations and are entirely defined by their production activities.

Women in the Pylos workforce

Introduction to the personnel tablets[46]

At Pylos, the main sources of evidence on low-status women are the personnel tablets of the A series which record the stationing, tallying, and rationing of low-ranking laborers in the service of the palace and its officials. The personnel series at Pylos consists of seven subsets, the Aa, Ab, Ac, Ad, Ae, An, and Aq series; the subsets Ac, Ae, and Aq deal exclusively with male personnel, as do 43 of the 45 An series tablets. Female personnel are recorded in the Aa, Ab, and Ad series, and on the two remaining An tablets PY An 292 and PY An 607. One additional document outside the personnel series has bearing on low-status women workers at Pylos, the basket label PY Wa 114 which records the monthly rations for women of the Further Province at Pylos. (A second Wa tablet, PY Wa 1008, records a lone MUL ideogram on a tablet too fragmentary to provide any other information.) The A series seems to have been particularly well preserved at Pylos; Chadwick suggests that we may have recovered about 80 percent of the overall series.[47] The Pylos personnel series is by far and away the largest evidentiary set in the Linear B tablets addressing Late Bronze Age women, and the remainder of this chapter addresses its nearly 150 tablets documenting women in the palace workforce.

The Aa series records adult women who comprise each workgroup along with underage girls and boys (likely their daughters and sons).[48] As mentioned in Chapter 2, these tablets typically open with the name of the workgroup expressed as a feminine adjective which is either task- or location-derived ("ethnic"); a small number of the Aa tablets omit their task titles and instead offer a place name as the designation for the workgroup. The Aa series is comprised of two different sets: the so-called Major Aa set and the Minor Aa set,[49] each written in a different hand. Scribe 1 wrote the Major Aa set which consists of tablets Aa 240–1182; this set records only workgroups of women in residence at Pylos and the Hither Province (Pylos itself and the west coast of Messenia). The Minor Aa set in turn was written by Scribe 4. This set consists of Aa 60–98 and records women exclusively of the Further Province (Leuktron and the Parmissos plain).[50]

The closely related Ab series once more records counts of workgroup women and their accompanying children but also lists the amount of wheat (GRA) and fig (NI) rations provided to each workgroup; this series lists the rations for the workgroups of the Major Aa set (the workgroups of Pylos and the Hither Province). The amount of rations assigned is constant throughout the Ab series: adult women receive 2 T units of both wheat and figs, and all children (regardless of sex or age) receive 1 T unit of both commodities.[51] Following the generally accepted equivalences proposed by Ventris and Chadwick, the rations received by adult women translate to 19.2 l. of each commodity and that received of each by children at 9.6 l.[52] All Ab tablets were written by a single scribe (Hand 21). Of the workgroups known from the Major Aa set, 22 have a corresponding Ab tablet, three or four Aa tablets have no known Ab tablet, and a few Aa tablets may have more than one corresponding Ab rations text.[53]

No Ab rations tablets are in existence for the Minor Aa set (workgroups of the Further Province). Instead, the palace seems to have monitored the rationing of the Further Province women as a whole rather than workgroup by workgroup as the fragmentary clay tablet-transport basket label PY Wa 114 would attest:[54]

PY Wa 114
.1 me-ni-jo , MUL
.2 pe-ra3-ko-ra-i-ja , ḳọ[
"Monthly rations for the women of the Further Province …"

As this label implies, the palace is keeping a record of the entire provisioning of the Further Province's women, rather than maintaining records specific to each Further Province workgroup. It is unclear how closely the palace may have scrutinized the rations provided to women of the Further Province. Are we to suppose that a second Ab set of tablets was to have been kept for this group at the palace that did not survive? Or does this sealing label represent the full extent of palatial involvement in the rationing of these women? Palmer had theorized that the female workgroups of the Further Province drew their subsistence rations from the Further Province capital of Leuktron and that the palace had no direct or indirect role in supplying these workers.[55] Killen, criticizing Palmer's interpretation, has argued that the presence in the archives at Pylos of the above sealing which pertains to monthly rations in the Further Province reveals at least some level of interest on the part of the palace site in the rationing of its more distant workers as would its monitoring of these workers in the Aa series.[56] Was it that the palace was responsible for the furnishing of the rations, but that they were doled out and recorded on the local level – perhaps at Leuktron, the capital site of the Further Province? This hypothesis seems to be a reasonable one given the careful attention to preserving the ration records of the Hither Province and the presence of only a brief notation dealing with the monthly allocation of rations for the full worker population of the Further Province. Either way, the absence of a Further Province Ab set will indeed limit our evidence pertaining to the Further Province and may circumscribe our ability to recover evidence as detailed as that of the Hither Province.

The third series pertaining to the workgroup women at Pylos – the Ad series – tallies the adult sons of the women of both the Major and Minor Aa sets.[57] These men are drawn out of their mothers' occupations (although they continue to be referred to as the sons of the titled women) and are instead reassigned by the palace to other tasks, possibly including conscription into Pylos's army or navy.[58] These tablets correspond closely to the workgroups mentioned in the Aa and Ab series; only two Ad tablets (PY Ad 326 and PY Ad 921) have no counterparts in the Aa or Ab series.[59]

The exact temporal relationship between the three series remains not entirely understood. It has long been recognized that the tallies of workers on the Aa and Ab series do not always correspond exactly; in fact, as Chadwick notes, "… there are fourteen cases where the pair of Aa/Ab tablets survives with the figures complete, and in all but two cases there is a discrepancy."[60] Since the two series are obviously discussing the same women, these discrepancies warrant explanation. Chadwick also notes a pattern between the two series: "If the 14 sets with both an Aa and an Ab are compared, there is a net change of 1.2% of the women and 9.3% of the children (both losses)."[61] The most likely explanation for the slight difference in the tallies is that the two series were each written at different times of the year, and that the differences reflect births, deaths, and/or the transfer of underage girls to adult status. It is not currently possible to decide whether Aa was the earlier series and that the population was diminishing or if Ab was the earlier and therefore the population was increasing.

Geography seems to have been the main organizational factor for the scribal tracking of these workers. Women whose workgroups are based at Pylos or in the Hither Province are recorded in series Aa, Ab, and Ad which note the number of personnel in each workgroup, the rations each workgroup receives in wheat and figs corresponding to the size of each group, and the number of sons of the women of each workgroup who have reached adulthood. The Further Province women are recorded in only the Aa and Ad series; no separate rations series is in existence for these women, although the lacunose portion of the sealing label Wa 114 seems to record the full provisioning for these women.

Women's tasks in the personnel series

Specific identifications of the tasks performed by each workgroup is dependent on two principal variables: the textual contexts in which the workgroup titles occur and the readiness with which a specific term can be reasonably normalized into a familiar Greek word.[62] As the Pylian A series maintains the identical textual contexts for each workgroup (total count of laborers, rations provided, and tallies of adult and adolescent sons), we are largely dependent on etymological interpretations to shed light on the task assignments of women in Pylian palatial society; these etymologies may be based on Homeric mentions of related terms, derived from other Linear B terms, or reconstructed from later Greek words. Consequently, we are left with an assortment of terms which range from the etymologically transparent, to those with etymologies from known roots where we can be reasonably certain, to terms whose etymologies remain obscure and meanings elusive. As much as possible, I will confine my argument to those terms of which we can be at least reasonably secure, if not in their exact meanings, at least in their general labor category.

Overall, at Pylos we observe 51 different workgroups,[63] performing at least 27 tasks.[64] These tasks consist of textile production, food-processing, domestic service or palace maintenance, and terms too poorly understood to assign to any of the above categories. Table 3.1 records all the workgroups listed for women in the Pylos texts by site assignment; Appendix A lists each mention of women at Pylos by name, title, and commodity exchanged.

Textile production[65]

The majority of workgroups whose task assignments can be identified fall under the category of textile production. At Pylos, female textile workers were widely dispersed throughout the Hither and Further Provinces (including Pylos itself) and numbered more than half of the total female worker population. These textile

Table 3.1 Women's workgroups by location*

Pylos and Hither Province

Pylos

Textile workers

pe-ki-ti-ra2 (T) (7)
a-ra-ka-te-ja (T) (21)
a-ra-te-ja **[mi-ra-ti-ja]** (T) (-)
i-te-ja **[ti-nwa-ti-ja]** (T) (9)
ri-ne-ja pa-ke-te-ja (T) (9/2+2)
a-pu-wo-ko (T) (8)
o-nu-ke-ja **[ki-si-wi-ja]** (T) (6/7)
ra-pi-ti-ra2 (T) (38)
a-ke-ti-ri-ja/a-ke-ti-ra2 (T) (38)
ka-pa-ra2-de **[ku-te-ra]** (T?) (24)
ne-we-wi-ja (T) (21)

Food production/domestic upkeep

me-re-ti-ri-ja/me-re-ti-ra2 (FP) (6)
re-wo-to-ro-ko-wo (DU) (38/37)
a-pi-qo-ro (DU) (32)

Etymologically obscure

pa-wo-ke (DU) (4)
o-ti-ri-ja/o-ti-ra2 (EO) (21)
ra-qi-ti-ra2 (EO) (6)
e-ke-ro-qo-no (EO) (-)
o-pi-ro-qo (EO) (8)
e-ke-ro-qo o-pi-ro-qo (7)

Ethnic (no task title)

a-*64-ja (UN – unknown task) (35)
ki-ni-di-ja (UN) (21)
ko-ro-ki-ja (UN) (8/9)
ku-te-ra3 (but see above) (UN) (28)
mi-ra-ti-ja (plus 1 above) (UN) (16)
ra-mi-ni-ja (UN) (7)

Collector's workgroups

a-da-re-te-ja (1)
me-ki-to-ki-ri-ta (1)
ka-ru-ti-je-ja (-)

Other Hither Province sites

Pylos ke-re-za

Collector's staff

we-we-si-je-ja (T) (22/16)

Etymologically obscure

ra-wi-ja-ja (EO) (28)

e-u-de-we-ro

Textile workers

ri-ne-ja (T) (6/8)

Lousos (ro-u-so)

Textile workers

a-ke-ti-ri-ja/a-ke-ti-ra2 (T) (32)

Ethnic (no task title)

mi-ra-ti-ja (54)

me-ta-pa

Task unknown

MUL (7)
MUL (5/3)

ne-wo-pe-o

Ethnic (no task title)

MUL (8/7)

o-wi-to-no

Etymologically obscure

to-sa-me-ja (EO) (8)

pi-we-re

Ethnic (no task title)

MUL (7)

Leuktron and Further Province	**e-pi-ko-e**
Leuktron	*Textile workers*
Textile workers	ri-ne-ja (T) 14
ri-ne-ja [a-*64-ja] (T) (-)	
a-ke-ti-ri-ja/a-ke-ti-ra2 (T) (12)	**ke-e**
	Textile workers
Food production	ri-ne-ja (T) (6)
/domestic upkeep	
me-re-ti-ri-ja/me-re-ti-ra2 (FP) (7)	**po-to-ro-wa-pi**
	Textile workers
Etymologically obscure	ri-ne-ja (T) (4)
no-ri-wo-ko (EO) (8)	
ki-ma-ra (EO) (3)	**Pylos Lauranthias (ra-u-ra-ti-jo)**
	Textile workers
(Not Listed = Leuktron)	ri-ne-ja **[ze-pu2-ra]** (T) (- Ad)
Textile workers	
a-ra-ka-te-ja (T) 37	**Corinth (ko-ri-to)**
Ethnic (no task title)	*Textile workers*
e-wi-ri-pi-ja (UN) (16)	te-pe-ja (T) (- Ad)
Other Further Province sites	**Damnia (da-mi-ni-ja)**
e-pi-jo-ta-na	*Textile workers*
Textile workers	ri-ne-ja (T) (-1)
ri-ne-ja (T) (8)	

* Location and ethnic terms are shown in bold

workers were organized into highly specialized groups; if we count terms whose meanings appear to be relatively secure, it appears at least 12 different titles were in use for textile-producing workgroups. Textile-involved workgroup titles could be very specific and identify workers who produced specialized garment-types or more general referring simply to "weavers" or "carders." Of the 12 occupational titles which appear relevant to textile production, seven can be read with relative certainty, and the remaining five titles offer compelling reasons to consider them among the textile-related tasks. Among the secure designations are: a-ra-ka-te-ja ("spinners"), *i-te-ja ("weavers"), o-nu-ke-ja, ("makers of o-nu-ka cloth") pe-ki-ti-ra2 ("carders"), ri-ne-ja ("linen-workers"), ri-ne-ja pa-ke-te-ja ("specialized linen-workers"), and te-pe-ja ("makers of te-pa cloth"); the five moderately secure textile-related titles are a-ke-ti-ri-ja ("finishers/decorators"), a-pu-ko-wo-ko ("headband-makers"), ra-pi-ti-ra2 ("stitchers"), ka-pa-ra2-de (unknown), and ne-we-wi-ja (also unknown).[66] These titles refer to functions including spinning, weaving, and flax-working, as well as the production of specialty cloths. It is not uncommon for there to have been more than one workgroup for each title; for example, linen-workers (ri-ne-ja) are subdivided into nine separate groups based on the ethnic background or current location of the workers. This section presents and discusses the personnel series evidence for the different textile-related workgroups at Pylos. First discussed are the secure terms followed by the terms whose identification as textile producers may be reasonably certain.

Two securely identified workgroup titles pertain to the earliest stage of textile production: thread preparation, with women's workgroups assigned to carding wool (pe-ki-ti-ra2) and thread spinning (a-ra-ka-te-ja). These are the earliest stages where Pylian women enter textile production; the raising and shearing of sheep and the growing and harvesting of flax appear to be tasks performed exclusively by men.

CARDERS/PE-KI-TI-RA2

Wool-carding is assigned to women bearing the title pe-ki-ti-ra2. Pe-ki-ti-ra2 should normalize as *pektriai* with a derivation from the verb πέκω; this term has Homeric parallels[67] and seems to clearly indicate a task assignment as "carders."[68] One workgroup is attested.[69] This workgroup belongs to the Major Aa set and has a complete set of Aa, Ab, and Ad tablets. The Aa series table, although fragmentary, opens in the manner typical of the Aa series with a feminine plural adjective:

PY Aa 891
pe-ki-ṭị[-ra2 MUL]
"wool-carders x women"

The ideogram MUL, the number of adult women, and tallies of associated boys and girls are lacunose. This tablet belongs to the Major Aa set all of which are written by Scribe 1 and refer to workgroups based within Pylos and the Hither Province; consequently, we can reasonably place even a workgroup with so fragmentary a title within the immediate region of Pylos. Furthermore, since this is a tablet of the Major Aa set, we can expect that an Ab monthly rations tablet would also have been prepared for this workgroup, an Ab tablet which in this instance has been preserved:

PY Ab 578
.a GRA 2 T 4 TA
.b pu-ro , pe-ki-ti-ra2 MUL 7 ko-wa 4 ko-wo 4 NI 2 T 4
"At Pylos, 7 women wool-carders, 4 girls, 4 boys: wheat 230.4 l., figs 230.4 l., 1 TA"

From this intact text we can assess the overall size of the wool-carders workgroup. This tablet confirms what had already been surmised from its Aa tablet – the workgroup is indeed located in the Hither Province, moreover at the site of Pylos itself. Seven adult women comprise this workgroup, one of the smallest groups at Pylos. Accompanying the adult women are eight children (four girls and four boys). [70]

PY Ab 578 also provides a tally of the total wheat (GRA)[71] and fig (NI) subsistence rations allotted to this workgroup; all workgroups receive equal amounts of GRA and NI. A few words need to be said about Linear B conventions for tallying numbers: As Linear B numbers are typically written after the commodity they modify, the tablet's notations of GRA 2 *T* 4 and NI 2 *T* 4 translate as wheat and fig allotments of 2 full units plus 4 T units of each commodity. (A T unit is a fractional unit one-tenth the size of a "full" unit.) Therefore, this workgroup has a sum total of 24 T units (2 full units = 20 T plus the 4 T units). These full and T units have conventionally been assigned equivalences in contemporary metric values of 96 l. per full unit and 9.6 l. per fractional T unit.[72] This particular pe-ki-ti-ra2 workgroup would thus be receiving a total ration of 230.4 l. of each staple (24 T x 9.6 l.). These rations break down as following: 2 T of each commodity are provided for each adult woman and 1 T per child.[73] Therefore, we see 14 T units for the combined adult women and 8 T for the children for a total of 22 T units (or 2 full units and 2 T units); converting to modern measurements, this tablet assigns a total of 211.2 l. of each commodity to the seven women and eight children composing this workgroup, accounting for all but 2 T (19.2 l.) of the total 230.4 l. allotted to this group.

The tablet also has an annotation of TA on line 2, and 2 T units (19.2 l.) need to be accounted for. Palmer noted that the presence of a TA notation on a rations tablet consistently results in an "extra" 2 T rations allotted to a workgroup, and speculated that a TA mention referred to an additional adult whose presence warranted the addition of 2 T (the standard ration for an adult woman) to the workgroup's rations. More specifically, he speculated that the TA functioned as an abbreviation for a woman bearing the title ταμία. While Palmer initially read TA as a woman functioning as an escort for the group,[74] more recent scholarship prefers a reading of TA as denoting a female supervisor for the workgroup. The question remains, however, whether the TA is a title given to one of the women already designated by the MUL ideogram or if it refers to an additional woman who joins the group as a supervisor and is not included among the tallied women. If we follow Killen's suggestion that the TA is already counted with the other seven women of the workgroup, then we should understand her as receiving a double ration of 4 T rather than the standard 2 T amount.[75] If she is not included among the seven counted MUL women, then she would receive the same 2 T ration as the women she is thought to be supervising.[76] This reading leaves open the question, however, of why a woman elevated to the position of group supervisor would receive only the same subsistence rations as the others within the workgroup instead of a larger amount? Killen addresses this question by proposing that TA women may have received a double ration to T 4, if they were already included in the total number of MUL on the tablet. This seems a reasonable solution to the problem, allowing for slightly higher monthly rations for an intra-group supervisor.

PY Ad 694
pe-ki-ti-ra2-o ko-wo VIR 4 ko-wo 3
"Four (adult) sons of the carders (women), 3 boys"

This Ad tablet records not the women who comprise the pe-ki-ti-ra2 workgroup, but rather their sons, both adult and adolescent. Adult sons are signaled by addition of the VIR ideogram in conjunction with ko-wo (κοῦροι); younger sons are identified with an unadorned ko-wo. We should understand these men as having been siphoned out of the women's workgroups, presumably because they reached an age too great to continue to be placed with their mothers.[77] It would appear that they are being tallied in preparation for assignment to a new task (no sons perform their mothers' tasks as adults); their task is unspecified here, but it is thought that these men were to be reassigned to military or naval service for the Pylian state.[78]

SPINNERS/A-RA-KA-TE-JA

Returning to the textile industry, the next workgroup title referring to thread-preparation workers is a-ra-ka-te-ja. Chadwick's etymology for a-ra-ka-te-ja as deriving from ἠλακάτη "distaff" is widely accepted and the term is understood to mean "women who spin."[79] At least three different workgroups of a-ra-ka-te-ja are attested in the Pylos archives.[80] Two of these workgroups seem to have been located at the center of Pylos itself; the third workgroup was located in the Further Province.[81] One of these Pylos-based workgroups is further differentiated by the ethnic term mi-ra-ti-ja "Milatian" (apparently a variant of "Milesian"). These workgroups are fairly large in size, with workforces of 21 and 37 adult women assigned to the two workgroups where the workgroup size is legible.

Two tablets document the first a-ra-ka-te-ja workgroup: PY Aa 240 and PY Ad 677.[82] The Aa tablet belongs to the Major Aa set, written by Scribe 1, which pertains exclusively to workgroups of Pylos and the Hither Province. As a Major Aa tablet workgroup, we might expect to find a corresponding Ab rations tablet, but in this particular instance, the Ab tablet does not survive.[83]

PY Aa 240
a-ra-ka-te-ja MUL 21 ko-wa 25 ko-wo 4 TA 1[
"21 spinning women, 25 girls, 4 boys, 1 TA"[84]

PY Ad 677
pu-ro a-ra-ka-te-ja-o ko-wo VIR 30 ko-wo 9
"At Pylos, sons of the spinning women: 30 adult men, 9 boys"

This workgroup is slightly larger than average, with 21 adult women and 29 children. Interestingly, the proportion of boys and girls in this workgroup seems rather uneven, with 25 girls of the 29 children on the Aa tablet. The Ad tablet confirms that this group is located at the Pylian center itself. (While Pylos is typically the location of workgroups whose location is not specified on the Major set Aa and Ab tablets, it is useful to have confirmation from the Ad series whose entries generally offer the most complete description of the workgroups.) This tablet also records a high number of sons who have transitioned into adulthood: 39 adult and adolescent sons. The large number of adult sons may indicate that this is a fairly long-established workgroup as sufficient time has elapsed to allow the majority of the a-ra-ka-te-ja-o ko-wo to mature into adults.

The second workgroup of a-ra-ka-te-ja workers is attested by a single Ad tablet.[85] As this workgroup is located at Pylos, we should surmise that we are missing both an Aa and an Ab tablet for this workgroup.[86]

PY Ad 380
pu-ro mi-ra-ti-ja-o a-ra-te-ja-o ko-wo 3
"At Pylos, sons of the Milatian spinning women: 3 boys"

In this group, the workgroup is described by two terms in the feminine genitive plural: the task title a-ra-ka-te-ja-o (here misspelled by the scribe as a-ra-te-ja-o) and the ethnic adjective mi-ra-ti-ja-o. In the nominative feminine, mi-ra-ti-ja seems to offer a normalization of *Milatiai*, presumably "women of Miletus."[87] This collective is one of three groups of Milatian women attested at Pylos; in the two remaining groups no task title appears in conjunction with the ethnic/location-derived adjective.

The function of the ethnic adjectives in specifying these low-status personnel series workers continues to elicit discussion. It had been previously suggested that the ethnic designations play a dual role in the texts, referring both to the ancestral origin of the women as well as to whatever specialty task the women from that provenance were most commonly considered expert.[88] In this reading, then, use of the ethnic title functions as a scribal shorthand to signify, in addition to a place of origin, a specialty occupation for the women of the workgroup so obvious as not to require listing, that is, a one-to-one correspondence between site of origin and specialized craft. Under this theory, women from Miletus would be understood as spinning specialists – but this theory of origin-based specializations does not adequately account for the evidence. While one can readily imagine local specialties in tasks such as weaving or embroidering, it is difficult to imagine a task as common and mundane as spinning having so distinct a regional flavor as to warrant the singling out of the women of a particular region as specialists. Furthermore, if we were to understand *Milatiai* as always indicating specialized spinners, the presence of a second distinct group of mi-ra-ti-ja workers also located at Pylos is difficult to explain. Why, if the two groups were assigned to the same task, were the two workgroups of *Milatiai* not combined into a single group? Almost certainly, we should understand the presence of two separate groups of *Milatiai* at Pylos as indicating two separate task assignments. It is also interesting to note that while the center of Pylos maintains at least two a-ra-ka-te-ja groups in close proximity, they do not appear to integrate the "ethnic" women throughout the two groups but rather continue to maintain them as separate units.

The third workgroup of a-ra-ka-te-ja women is attested by only one tablet (PY Aa 89); it belongs to the Minor Aa set. As a Minor Aa tablet, it was written by Scribe 4 and records workers in the Further Province. Also, as a Minor set tablet, no Ab tablet would have been present. An Ad tablet could conceivably have been written, but if so, it is no longer extant.

PY Aa 89
a-ra-ka-te-ja MUL 37 ko-wa 26 ko-wo 16 TA 1
"37 spinning women, 26 girls, 16 boys 1 TA"

This workgroup is fairly large, with 37 adult women, 42 children and a TA. Chadwick has noted a pattern in the recording done by Scribe 4, noting that "the absence of a place name in the tablet of the Minor Aa set indicates an assignment to Leuktron,"[89] and we should then assign this workgroup to Leuktron, the capital of the Further Province. If so, it seems likely that we should understand this workgroup to be the main thread-supplier for Leuktron's administrative population.

WEAVERS/I-TE-JA

In addition to workgroups occupied with thread-preparation, we can also recover the titles of additional workers whose task assignments within the textile industry are known. Weavers are employed under the title of i-te-ja normalizing as *histeia* ("weaver") from ἵστος ("loom").[90] One workgroup of female weavers is documented at Pylos. As the Aa tablet belongs to the Major set, this group could be attested in all three (Aa, Ab, and Ad) series; all relevant tablets are extant[91] although only the Ad tablet specifies their task assignment.

PY Aa 699
ti-nwa-si-ja MUL 9 ko-wa 4 ko-wo 3 DA 1 TA [1
"9 Tinwasian women, 4 girls, 3 boys 1 DA 1 TA"

PY Ab 190
.a GRA 3 [[T 9]] DA TA
.b pu-ro ti-nwa-si-ja MUL 9 ko[-wa]2 ko-wo 1 NI 3 [[T 9]]
"At Pylos, 9 Tinwasian women, 2 girls, 1 boy: 288 l. wheat, 288 l. figs, 1 DA 1 TA"

PY Ad 684
lat. sup.
a-pu-ne-we e-re-ta-o ko-wo
r.
pu-ro ti-nwa-ti-ja-o i-te-ja-o ḳọ-wo VIR 5 ko-wo 2
"At Pylos, sons of the *Ti-nwa*-sian weavers (sons of rowers at A-pu-ne-we) 5 men, 2 boys"[92]

Women weavers constitute a smaller number of workers than do their spinning counterparts, with nine adult women attested in both the Aa and Ab tablets. They continue to receive standard rations and their adult and underage children are tracked in the same way as other female A series workers. This workgroup is again composed of women who are described with an ethnic adjective; in this instance the ethnic term is ti-nwa-si-ja, a term with a clear derivation from the place name *ti-nwa-to. *Ti-nwa-to is referenced in other texts[93] as a location which contributed a large assessment of gold to the palace and which appears to have been closely associated in the tablets with the seven districts that composed the Further Province.[94] Notably, ti-nwa-si-ja is one of only two ethnic adjectives for women throughout the Pylos corpus which is derived from the name of a location under Pylian control.[95] It is also interesting to note that these ethnically-identified women do not remain at their origin-site within the Pylian state, but have instead been transferred to the palace environs. This should settle the question of whether the ethnics refer to the initial origins of the workgroup women or to their current location. Clearly, the ethnics must refer only to origins as here we observe women bearing a Further Province ethnic who have been relocated to the Hither Province palace center of Pylos.

This workgroup differs slightly from the a-ra-ka-te-ja (spinning) and pe-ki-ti-ra2 (carding) workgroups in that on both the Aa and Ab tablets not only a TA but a DA is attested ("ti-nwa-si-ja MUL 9 ko-wa 4 ko-wo 3 *DA* 1 *TA* [1]"). If we calculate the rations amount using the standard 2 T for adult women, 1 T for children, and the added 2 T received by a TA, an additional 5 T rations of both wheat and figs remain. As DA is recorded in a similar manner as TA, occupying the same line and generally preceding TA in the listing, it seems reasonable to read DA as another abbreviation for a type of workgroup supervisor. Furthermore, since the addition of a TA results in an additional ration of 2 T for a group and the presence of a DA results in an additional ration of 5 T, it would appear that a DA is a higher ranked supervisor than a TA.

Near Eastern records provide support for this reading, as frequently supervisors of different ranks can be seen assigned to specific workgroups.[96] It has been suggested that the disparity in allotments reflect a difference in sex between the two "supervisory" personnel: Palmer suggested that the DA should be understood as a male supervisor accompanying a lower-ranked female TA supervisor.[97] On the other hand, Chadwick reads both DA and TA as referring to female supervisors of these workgroups,[98] but Carlier notes that while DA and TA would both seem to indicate supervisory personnel, nothing on the tablets provides direct information as to the sex of either figure;[99] however as no additional personnel is added to the workgroup tally – and certainly no VIR appears – I think most plausible is to understand the DA as referring to one of the women of the workgroup, who like the TA draws a secondary ration as part of her supervisory responsibilities.

There are three additional points of interest pertinent to this weavers' workgroup. The first relates directly to tablet PY Ad 684 that mentions not only the mothers – as is the usual convention – of the tallied sons but also their fathers. ("At Pylos, sons of the *Ti-nwa*-sian weavers (sons of rowers at A-pu-ne-we): 5

men, 2 boys").[100] It is extremely rare in the tablets for the fathers of low-status workers to be recorded (or even present); it should perhaps be noted here that these children seem to be the products of long-term familial relationships, if not actual marriages, and that the children here seem to inherit the low social status of both their mothers and their fathers. This tablet also provides strong evidence that the palace arranged the "marriages" of at least some of its lower-status workers; it is difficult to envision any other arrangement in which women form partnerships en masse with a group of men who are also collectively assigned to a single task. Also, the listing of only the women as *Tinwasiai* also argues against these "marriages" either predating palace influence or as existing in complete independence of it; otherwise why would the "husbands" not share the same ethnic heritage as their "wives"?

The second point relates to the small number of women assigned as weavers. Why if, as is generally held to be true, textile production was of such importance to the Bronze Age economy does the best-attested palatial site record only nine women weavers? Certainly that 25 of the total 51 workgroups at Pylos (and 25 of the 31 groups with reasonably secure task identifications) are devoted to textile production should support the claim for the importance of textile production; where then are the rest of the weavers? While it is possible that some of the 20 undetermined groups may have held assignments as specialized types of weavers, there is also substantial evidence indicating a large-scale weaving industry external to the palace, and these nine female weavers are not the only weavers recorded in the Pylian corpus.

The third point of interest is related to this issue and pertains to the gender assignment of the task of weaving. Weaving is one of the five occupational designations Pylian women share with Pylian men and is one of only two which directly relate to production activities.[101] However, as PY Un 1322 demonstrates, male and female weavers do not seem to occupy analogous social positions.

PY Un 1322 + fr.
.1] GRA [
.2:]ṇọ[ ]ọ-no[ ] GRA 6̣ ṆỊ [
.3: de-ku-tu-wo-ḳọ[ ]o-no GRA 2̣ NI 2
.4: ị-ṭẹ-ẉẹ , o-ṇọ [ ] GRA 12
.5: we-a2-no[ ]-no re-po-to *1̣4̣6̣ GRA 5
.6: we-[ ]no[ ]*1̣4̣6̣ G̣ṚẠ 1̣5̣
.7: (*vestigia*)
1: Wheat [
2. payment: 576 l. Wheat x l. Figs
3: "to the net maker(s)" payment: 192 l. Wheat, 192 l. Figs
4: to the weaver, payment: 1152 l. Wheat
5: for fine robes: 480 l. Wheat
6. ....1440 l. Wheat

This tablet provides a fragmentary list of payments (o-no) from the palace to a series of specialized (male) craftsmen, among whom is a weaver (i-te-we, *histewei*, the dative singular of *histeus*).[102] It is unclear what, if any, the relationship of the male weavers is to the female weavers (who do not appear on this tablet), but it seems clear that the women who belong to the weaving workgroup referenced in the A series enter the Pylian economy in a very different manner than does the male weaver of PY Un 1322. On this tablet payment (o-no) of wheat and figs are made to "net-makers" (de-ku-tu-wo-ko) presumably for nets rendered, and to i-te-we who is compensated on lines 3 and 4. On line 4 he is compensated with 480 l. of wheat for we-a2-no re-po-to, *weanon lepton* or "fine robes."[103]

This tablet differs from that of the women in that the relation between his finished product and payment are made explicit; production and delivery of the "fine robes" provide the rationale for his 480 l. in compensation. No commodity for exchange is listed with his allotted 12 GRA units on line 3; quite possibly the additional 15 GRA of line 5 is directed to him as well. What is most interesting about this record is that there is no indication that this unnamed weaver is kept on the palace staff or supported (even partially) by its ration system in the same way as the personnel series workgroup. Attention to the size of the allotted GRA moreover reveals that very different models of production were assumed by men and women holding the same occupational title. While the female weavers of the A-series are low-status palace dependents, the male weaver of PY Un 1322 is surely not, as the amount of wheat he receives in return for his products is well beyond the usual ration system where women (and men) each receive T 2 units (19.2 l.) of wheat per month; his line 3 allotment of 1152 l. of wheat – 60 times the monthly rations of a workgroup woman – should indicate that his grain allotment is not intended for his personal monthly subsistence. Rather, the allotment size would indicate the presence of at least one large, independent weaving workgroup which exchanged finished goods with the palace in exchange for large-scale allotments of wheat. This may explain why only one small group of female weavers is attested in palace employ as this tablet would seem to indicate that there was almost certainly a larger, extra-palatial industry which fulfilled much of the palaces' weaving needs.

As the tablets of the Aa, Ab, and Ad series tend to conform closely to the recording formulas preferred by each series, I am opting to relegate to the footnotes all texts which follow the standard formulas. Only texts which diverge from the usual formats will be quoted directly in the text from here on. Unless otherwise noted, all translations are mine.

LINEN-WORKERS/RI-NE-JA

The largest subset of securely-identifiable textile workers are linen- or flax-workers bearing the title ri-ne-ja;[104] this title is etymologically transparent, normalizing as the adjective *lineiai* (*λίνειαι) from λίνον "flax/linen."[105] Scholarship has not previously reached a consensus as to whether these workgroups work with raw flax or with processed linen.[106] (I prefer the identification of these women as "linen-workers" for reasons discussed in the following section.[107]) At least nine different workgroups at eight different locations are recorded. These workgroups are recorded in several different ways: two groups are described with ethnics and workgroup locations, six are described only by their location, and a final group entitled pa-ke-te-ja ri-ne-ja refers to a more specialized form of linen-worker.

The two linen-working workgroups which are described with both an ethnic adjective and a place name are the a-*64-ja ri-ne-ja group at Leuktron[108] and the ze-pu2-ra-o- ri-ne-ja group at Pylos Lauranthias, both of which are Further Province locations. Both groups are attested by a single tablet in the Aa series.

PY Ad 326[109] provides the sole documentation for the one ri-ne-ja workgroup at the Further Province capital of Leuktron – recording the 12 sons of the a-*64-ja (*Aswiai)* linen-working workgroup. [110] If the reading of the ethnic is correct, Asia Minor may have served as the provenance for these workers; ethnics with associations with the Eastern Aegean and Asia Minor will appear frequently as descriptors of the female laborers of the Pylos personnel series. Interestingly, this is also the first tablet that places a group with an ethnic designation outside the Pylian center; in this case the group is located at Leuktron, the capital of Pylos's Further Province. As its Aa tablet has not survived, we can glean no specific information about the size of the workgroup;[111] however, from the relatively low number of sons on the Ad tablet, we might expect no more than 15 adult women in the original workgroup.

The second of the ri-ne-ja workgroups listed with both an ethnic designation and a place name is recorded on PY Ad 664, which tallies the seven sons of the ze-pu2-ra-o ri-ne-ja at the location of Pylos Lauranthias.[112] Again, the group bears an ethnic identifier in addition to the trade name – in this instance, ze-pu2-ra-o, the genitive plural of *Dzephurai*. Once more, an Asian provenance seems to be indicated in Ζεφυρία; Ζεφυρία is attested by Strabo as an archaic name for Halikarnassos.[113] Finally, like its counterpart previously discussed, this workgroup is also located outside the main center of Pylos in the Further Province site of Pylos Lauranthias; despite the similarities in name, this site is not the palace site (pu-ro) nor even within the same province. While this is the only tablet to supply the full place name Pylos Lauranthias, a second tablet of the Minor Aa series also appears to record the same workgroup:

PY Aa 61

pu-ro ze-pu2-ra3 MUL 26 ko-wa 15 ko-wo 10 DA 1 TA 1

"At Pylos, 26 Dzephuraian women, 15 girls, 10 boys, 1 DA, 1 TA"

As a Minor Aa tablet this group of ze-pur2-ra3 women must then be in Pylos's Further Province, which precludes us from identifying this pu-ro as the (Hither Province) locale of Pylos proper; the opening word pu-ro requires explanation. I think the best solution to this problem is to read the pu-ro as a shorthand for pu-ro ra-u-ta-ri-jo (as this would be the only Pylos that Scribe 4 – assigned to the Further Province – could possibly be recording) and to associate this Aa tablet with PY Ad 664, as both reference a Dzephuraian workgroup located at Pylos Lauranthias.

Six additional groups of linen-workers are attested by their locations alone. For all these groups, the location name serves as the workgroup title in all series but the Ad which alone provides the added datum of task-designation; without the Ad tablets to accompany these workgroups we would be unable to identify their task assignments. All but one of these groups are stationed in the Further Province; only the workgroup at e-u-de-we-ro is located in the Hither Province. The remaining ri-ne-ja workgroups are stationed at the Further Province sites of da-mi-ni-ja,[114] e-pi-jo-ta-na, e-pi-ko-o, ke-e, and po-to-ro-wa-pi. At all of these five locations, these ri-ne-ja workgroups are the sole workgroups present. Most of these groups are recorded in minimalist fashion with few additional details. Atypically, all the associated tablets are extant. (As these tablets provide no new data to the ri-ne-ja records save for the group locations, their tablet citations have been relegated to the footnotes.)

The lone Hither Province workgroup at e-u-de-we-ro[115] is attested with great brevity on all three of its associated tablets.[116] Of these tablets, only the Ad identifies the task performed by the female workgroup as linen-working. The workgroup size is quite small, ranging from six to eight adult women across the Aa and Ab tablets. It is not clear why this workgroup has acquired an additional DA supervisor on its Ab tablet.

The Further Province ri-ne-ja workgroups are recorded very uniformly. The linen-working group at e-pi-jo-ta-na[117] is typical of the place name identified groups. Both tablets are extant.[118] Perhaps the only detail of note is the small size of the workgroup. Similar is the e-pi-ko-o group,[119] which is only notable in the usage of two locative forms for the place name.[120] The single workgroups based at ke-e[121] and po-to-ro-wa-pi[122] closely follow suit; each workgroup has both tablets preserved.[123] The last group which is identified by location only – the group at da-mi-ni-ja – diverges somewhat from the other location-based linen workgroups and is attested on two tablets.[124] While the Aa tablet assumes the canonical form,[125] the corresponding Ad tablet provides an additional detail in that it identifies the task assigned to the linen-workers' sons.

PY Ad 697
a e-re-[ ]qe-ro-me-no
b da-mi-ni-ja ṛị-ne-ja-o ko-wo VIR
"At Damnia, sons of the linen-workers... Men ('willing to row' or 'becoming rowers')"[126]

These men are being assigned as rowers – one of the lesser-status tasks performed by men in the Pylian corpus. This tablet is important in that it confirms the interest of the palace in reassigning the sons of the workgroup women to new task assignments; it also strongly implies that the bodies and labor of these sons are the palace's to command.

The ninth and final type of linen-worker is somewhat more difficult to apprehend. This designation involves the conjunction of two trade titles – pa-ke-te-ja and ri-ne-ja – to describe what appears to be a more specialized type of linen-worker. This type of worker is attested on at least three A-series tablets, which presumably deal with the same workgroup. The record of this workgroup breaks with more typical personnel records in that its Aa roster tablet has two corresponding Ab tablets; despite this peculiarity, all use the conventional format.[127] Lindgren raises the central question here: what additional meaning does pa-ke-te-ja confer upon the term ri-ne-ja?[128] Regarding pa-ke-te-ja as an ethnicon seems unfeasible in light of its -e-ja, rather than –i-ja, ending. Two suggestions seem viable both in terms of etymology and context – Ventris and Chadwick's proposed "measurers" and Ruijgh's "washers" (φάκτειαι);[129] when combined with ri-ne-ja, their respective senses would be either "linen-measurers" or "flax-washers." In a divergent reading, Olivier and Nosch read the term as indicating a workgroup in the service of the Collector pa-ke-ta,[130] a figure otherwise unknown in the Pylos tablets although the term is used for a man's name at Knossos.[131]

MAKERS OF SPECIFIC FORMS OF CLOTH/O-NU-KE-JA AND TE-PE-JA

Two other occupational designations for female textile workers seem to derive from the names of the specialized cloth they produce: o-nu-ke-ja and te-pe-ja women after the textiles o-nu-ka and te-pa. The derivation of o-nu-ke-ja from the cloth type called o-nu-ka seems transparent; o-nu-ka is attested as a technical name for a specific type of cloth which appears on eight Knossos tablets. O-nu-ke-ja should then probably be understood as "women who make o-nu-ka."[132] A single o-nu-ke-ja workgroup is known.[133] As this workgroup is located in the Hither Province, we should expect three associated tablets; all are extant.[134] Again, we see a specialized workgroup modified with a second title: here, the ethnic ki-si-wi-ja. As with many of the ethnics, consensus has been achieved in identifying this term as a feminine ethnic adjective, but again, the exact provenance giving rise to this term remains under debate. The most frequent normalizations of this term are *Ksiwiai* as the adjective deriving from an unknown toponym **Ksiwos* and the more common *Kswiai* as an ethnic adjective deriving from the island Χῖος. [135] Like the previously discussed mi-ra-ti-ja, a-ra-ka-te-ja, and ti-nwa-ti-ja i-te-ja, this ethnic-titled workgroup is small in size and is based at the center of Pylos itself. This workgroup also appears to have acquired a DA as of the recording of the Ab tablet.

Te-pe-ja workers are recorded in much the same way. Like the o-nu-ke-ja, the work-title for the te-pe-ja is derived from the specific textile they produce (te-pa). Te-pa cloth (or the worker title te-pe-ja) is attested at all four major tablet-producing palace sites in the Mycenaean Bronze Age (Knossos, Pylos, Mycenae, and Thebes), and seems to refer to a particularly heavy type of cloth locally produced at all of these sites.[136] Te-pa is so frequently mentioned a commodity that it can also be rendered in the tablets by a standardized abbreviated form: TELA+TE (where the abbreviation TE is adjoined to TELA, the ideogram for cloth). At Pylos, only one surviving tablet documents a single workgroup[137] of te-pa workers.[138] Interestingly, this workgroup does not seem to be based at Pylos but rather at the somewhat more distant Further Province site of *Korinthos*.[139] The lack of an ethnic title in the Ad tablet (which often provides this information) may indicate that this workgroup is not organized on ethnic lines.

In addition to the more secure textile occupational titles discussed, three additional titles likely refer to textile workers: a-ke-ti-ri-ja, a-pu-ko-wo-ko, and ra-pi-ti-ra2.

HEADBAND-MAKERS/A-PU-KO-WO-KO

The least-contested of these occupational terms is a-pu-ko-wo-ko. This title should normalize as *ampukworgoi* which would seem to refer to "headband makers."[140] It has been suggested that these "headbands" may have been intended for horses, and that leather rather than cloth was the preferred medium. A single workgroup is attested on two tablets;[141] the Aa tablet is missing, but the presence of the Ab tablet indicates that this group would belong to the Major Aa set of the Hither Province.[142] There is not much to distinguish this workgroup; it is relatively small with only eight adult women assigned to Pylos. However, the Ad tablet provides an additional datum; the *O* which precedes the VIR 5 on line a is an abbreviation for the term o-pe-ro ("missing") and indicates that not all the men presumed to belong to these workgroups were present for the tally. Again, the fact that the palace is tracking the whereabouts of absent men underscores the palace's proprietary interest in these men as workers.

STITCHERS/RA-PI-TI-RA2

The second group likely to be textile workers is designated ra-pi-ti-ra2. One workgroup is attested[143] on a single Ab tablet.[144] This group again is located at the Pylian center and is one of the largest workgroups attested at Pylos. (The largest workgroup in the Pylos archives is the Lousos-based mi-ra-ti-ja with 54 women; this group of 38 ra-pi-ti-ra2 joins two other workgroups – the re-wo-to-ro-ko-wo and the a-ke-ti-ri-ja – in a three-way tie for second place.) Like the previously discussed term i-te-ja, this occupational title is one of the five occupational titles that have masculine and feminine variants in the Pylos archives. Ra-pi-ti-ra2 is structurally parallel with the man's trade ra-pte (*ῥαπτήρ), and the feminine form ra-pi-ti-ra2 should normalize as *raptriai* (ῥάπτριαι); both terms convey the sense of "people who stitch."[145] While the masculine variant ra-pte is attested on 11 tablets at Pylos – among them seven land tenure tablets – its feminine counterpart is attested on only one, PY Ab 555. Yet, like the non-analogous relationship exhibited by i-te-ja/i-te-u (female and male weavers), the structurally parallel ra-pte and ra-pi-ti-ra2 demonstrate no functional parallels. They appear on no tablets together nor even within the same tablet series. Even their remuneration takes entirely different forms; while men described as ra-pte-re receive land allotments from the central polity, ra-pi-ti-ra2 receive no more than the standard subsistence rations of wheat and figs. Like i-te-ja/i-te-u, there again appears to be no correspondence between men's and women's similarly named production activities. Lindgren offers a plausible reconciliation between the masculine and feminine variants of this term, reading the two terms as indicating "tailors" where the women *raptriai* are sewing cloth and the male *raptere* are stitching leather, perhaps as saddlers.[146]

DECORATORS/FINISHERS A-KE-TI-RI-JA

The final category of workers whose role in textile production is generally accepted is designated by the term a-ke-ti-ri-ja, variant a-ke-ti-ra2. This term was originally translated by Chadwick as *asketriai* ("seamstresses") which he associated with the term ἀκέστρια,[147] but more recently Killen's reading of *asketriai* (ἀσκήτριαι) as textile "decorators" has gained greater acceptance; as decorators, it would seem they are women who apply ornaments to woven cloth and thus function as finishing workers in the field of textile processing.[148] At least three workgroups are known, ranging in size from 12 to 38 adult women, stationed in at least three different sites including two Hither Province sites (Pylos and Lousos) and the Further Province capital of Leuktron.

The first a-ke-ti-ri-ja workgroup, the group located at Pylos, is attested on three tablets;[149] this group is recorded with the alternate spelling a-ke-ti-ra2.[150] This workgroup is one of the largest workgroups attested in the tablets, composed of 38 adult women and 49 children accompanying the workgroup; an additional 27 older sons are listed in the Ad tablet; the lack of an ethnic title suggests these women originated within the Pylian state. The second a-ke-ti-ri-ja workgroup is similarly large and is one of only two workgroups recorded at the site of ro-u-so (Lousos), one of the nine towns of Pylos's Hither Province.[151] This group is attested on two tablets; the Ad tablet is missing.[152] It is interesting to note the large sizes of the groups stationed at Lousos; this a-ke-ti-ri-ja workgroup contains 32 adult women while Lousos's other group, the 54 women of the mi-ra-ti-ja workgroup mentioned below, is even larger. I suggest that Lousos may have functioned as a second large textile-producing site as more than 170 women and children were stationed there.[153] The final workgroup entry for a-ke-ti-ri-ja in the personnel series tablets at Pylos locates the third group at the Further Province's capital of Leuktron.[154] As a Minor Aa set tablet, only Aa and Ad tablets could record this group. Both are extant.[155] The a-ke-ti-ri-ja group at Leuktron is significantly smaller than its Hither Province counterparts. Judging from the low number of adult sons associated with this workgroup on PY Ad 290, it may have only been recently formed at the time of the destructions.

A-ke-ti-ri-ja workers, unlike all the lower-status female workers discussed thus far, also make two appearances on tablets outside the personnel series.[156] They appear on PY Fn 187 and on PY Un 219 where they receive allotments of barley (HORD) and KA, respectively. The property allotments of this workgroup are addressed in Chapter 4.[157]

TEXTILE WORKERS RECOVERABLE FROM CONTEXT ONLY

Finally, two additional workgroups have been proposed as textile workers: ka-pa-ra2-de and ne-we-wi-ja. Each title is represented by a single workgroup.

The ka-pa-ra2-de group[158] differs from the occupational titles discussed above in that it is not described by an occupational – *eiai* ending but rather a generic feminine plural – *ades*.[159] No satisfactory etymology identifying it as a task-derived title has yet been proposed; Killen offers the suggestion that it may be based on the man's name ka-pa-ra2,[160] but as the term appears among known textile occupations at Knossos[161] a textile association seems more likely. The term is attested on a Major set Aa tablet and an Ad tablet; [162] it also appears on one of the two An series tablets which mention female workgroups:

PY An 292
.1: si-to-ko-wo
.2: ka-pa-ra2-de MUL 24 ko-wo 10
.3: ḳọ-ro-ki-ja[ ] MUL 8 ko-wo[
.4: ki-ni-di[-ja MUL] 21 ko[-wo
.5: (INFRA MUTILA)

While the An series typically records groups of male workers, PY An 292 preserves a roster of the working strength of several female workgroups; three of these groups (the ka-pa-ra2-de, ko-ro-ko-ja, and ki-ni-di-ja) are well attested in the Aa, Ab, and Ad texts. The workers mentioned on line 1, the si-to-ko-wo, are more obscure. Si-to-ko-wo is often taken to mean "grain-measurers" or "grain-pourers" from the Mycenaean term si-to which appears in conjunction with the barley ideogram at Knossos and the wheat ideogram at Mycenae.[163] The gender of the "grain-measurers" is not known, although the otherwise clearly feminine terms on the rest of the extant tablet would seem to render their identification as a women's workgroup fairly plausible.[164]

Returning to the ka-pa-ra2-de workers, we have evidence of a single mid-sized group based at Pylos; its Ad tablet also signals that this workgroup is ethnically homogeneous as it is composed of workers described with the genitive ku-te-ra-o. This ethnic seems to normalize as *Kutherai*, perhaps indicating an origin on the island of Kythera. A second group of workers of *Kutherai*, also stationed at Knossos, is discussed below.[165]

The final group thought to be textile workers are the ne-we-wi-ja. The title's normalization and etymology remain disputed. The -wi-ja ending has led some to regard it as an ethnicon;[166] Chadwick largely dispels this reading, noting that its usage at Knossos lessens the odds of this term being an ethnic, as no ethnic adjectives have yet been demonstrated to have been in use at both sites. (Chadwick, however, does not offer another reading of this word.)[167] Morpurgo Davies favors reading ne-we-wi-ja as an occupational term, citing its mention in clear textile-related contexts at Knossos.[168] Killen expands upon this reading, cautiously proposing viewing them as "spinners."[169] Lindgren notes that both interpretations fit the occupational contexts of the Aa, Ab, and Ad series.[170] I have placed it among the textile workers based on the strength of the mentions at Knossos. One workgroup is known,[171] attested on three tablets.[172]

DISCUSSION OF TEXTILE WORKGROUPS AT PYLOS

In summary, a number of points regarding the A series evidence for textile production warrant comment:

1 Textile production is the largest task category in which the workgroup women of the personnel series were occupied as evidenced by both the numbers of occupational titles and distinct workgroup units. Of the 24 occupational titles in use at Pylos, half are related to textile production. Textile production likewise occupies 60 percent of the total tallied women in the A series; of the 705 women whose tallies are legible in the personnel series, at least 325 were assigned to textile-related activities.[173] These 325+ women issue from 24 different workgroups, nearly half of the 51 known workgroups at Pylos.

2 The geographical distribution of the textile-related groups appears significant. Table 3.1 provides a roster of women's workgroups at Pylos by location and by occupational category. Textile production is the only production category located in all four possible geographic locales referenced in the Pylos tablets (a. Hither Province capital site of Pylos Proper, b. Hither Province non-capital sites, c. Further Province Capital site of Leuktron, and d. Further Province non-capital sites).

   Moreover, textile workgroups are not evenly distributed throughout these four locations; the evidence reveals a concentration of textile workers around the two capital centers. Of the 14 textile-producing workgroups of the Hither Province, 11 are based at the Pylian center accounting for 182 of the total 262 Hither Province textile workers. In the Further Province, Leuktron also houses the majority of its province's textile workers, employing at least 49 of the 74 women assigned to this occupational category.[174]

3 In addition to the overall concentration of textile workers at the provincial centers, the subset of textile workers who also receive an ethnic designation are also disproportionately clustered. Six textile workgroups carry ethnic titles; four are assigned to the Hither Province and two to the Further Province. All four ethnically-identified Hither Province workgroups (a-ra-ka-te-ja mi-ra-ti-ja, i-te-ja ti-nwa-ti-ja, ka-pa-ra2-de ku-te-ra, and o-nu-ke-ja ki-si-wi-ja) are assigned to Pylos itself. In the Further Province, the ri-ne-ja a-*64-ja workgroup is stationed at Leuktron while a second group of ri-ne-ja, the ri-ne-ja ze-pu2-ra at Pylos Lauranthias, are the sole "ethnic" textile workers to be stationed outside their province capital.

4 The final note of interest relates to the stages of textile production attested in the personnel series tablets. Pylos proper, hosting 11 of the 24 textile workgroups, likewise boasts the widest distribution of textile tasks and stages. Pylos houses both "specialty" cloth-workers and well as workers

> dedicated to specific stages of production. Pylos's local labor force of single-task textile workers include carders (pe-ki-ti-ra2), two groups of thread spinners (a-ra-ka-te-ja),[175] weavers (i-te-ja), women who sew (ra-pi-ti-ra2), and decorators (a-ke-ti-ri-ja), representing the five essential stages for the transformation of raw wool and linen into finished cloth. Furthermore, the stationing of standing workgroups dedicated to single-item production tasks may imply the presence of a small-scale assembly line for textile production at the palace center. As discussed above, a significantly larger extra-palatial textile industry is strongly implied on PY Un 1322 (which records the large allotment of wheat to an unnamed male weaver); I suggest these six stage-specific workgroups function as the palace's own permanent textile workers, maintaining and replacing the textiles used by the palace itself.

In addition to these more generic textile workers, five additional groups of more specialized workers were stationed at Pylos; some of these specialized workgroups seemed to have been named after the specific types of cloth they produced. These include the o-nu-ke-ja ("women who make o-nu-ka"), and apparently the ka-pa-ra-de2 and the ne-we-wi-ja, all of which currently elude any interpretation more specific than "cloth-workers." The remaining two textile groups are the a-pu-wo-ko, thought to specialize in headband production, and the ri-ne-ja pa-ke-te-ja, a specialized type of linen-workers, possibly dedicated to measuring. Of these five "specialized" workgroups, only two (ka-pa-ra-de2 and ne-we-wi-ja) employ more than ten workers. These specialty workers may also have been devoted specifically to the needs of the palace for luxury garments; their numbers appear too small to constitute a workforce intended for the production of goods for widespread distribution or export.

In the Further Province, Leuktron employed at least three textile workgroups, an a-ra-ka-te-ja, an a-ke-ti-ri-ja, and a ri-ne-ja a-*64-ja. In these three workgroups the beginning and end stages of production (spinning and decorating) are accounted for; the third group is simply named after the commodity they work with – ri-no "flax/linen." This workgroup also has an additional ethnic – a-*64-ja – signaling an origin perhaps from Anatolia. If we assume that the presence of these three workgroups at Leuktron was not random but governed by a specific rationale, we might then understand these ri-ne-ja as performing the intermediate production tasks that would bridge the labor gap between the spinners and the decorators at this site. If we accept this reading, we should then fix ri-ne-ja as "linen-workers" rather than "flax-workers" and understand them as functioning as (linen-)weavers and (linen-)seamstresses; assuming levels of multi-functionality within this fabric-identified workgroup eliminates a need for workgroups of weavers and seamstresses at Leuktron and adequately explains their absence. In this case, we might also understand Leuktron as being fairly self-sufficient in terms of its textile production. The sole discordant note might be the large number of spinners (37), rivaling the numbers of the much larger textile industry at Pylos; a possible explanation for their number is suggested below.

Outside of the provincial capitals, the face of textile production changes significantly. Instead of a standing workforce of stage-specific and specialty-cloth workers, the norm becomes a single workgroup of unspecialized textile workers typically identified only by the fabric they work with. This is best exemplified in the Further Province where a single group of textile workers is stationed in each of seven towns. These workers are not identified with a single stage of production; instead six of these seven groups are named solely by their assigned fabric – linen. (The seventh town-based workgroup is identified by the fabric term te-pe-ja.) Again, I think we should understand the absence of any further specificity in describing these workers as indicating that these ri-ne-ja were engaged in all stages of linen cloth manufacturing, from spinning and weaving to sewing and finishing. As none of these workgroups are particularly large – the largest is the 14 ri-ne-ja at e-pi-ko-e – I surmise that their production might have been designed to suit local needs, perhaps providing for their village administrators. This may also have been the case for the te-pe-ja workers although we should not rule out the possibility that their finished cloth may have been forwarded on to either Leuktron or Pylos.

Textile production in the Hither Province villages takes a somewhat different form from that of the Further Province towns. Textile workgroups are stationed at the three villages of Pylos ke-re-za, e-u-de-we-ro, and Lousos, and it is likely that the unidentified workgroups based at me-ta-pa, ne-wo-pe-o, o-wi-to-no, and pi-we-re were also devoted to textile production. Two different models of production seem to be in place. The smaller villages such as e-u-de-we-ro, and possibly the untitled workgroups as well, function similarly to the Further Province in that smaller groups of workers are identified with the generic ri-ne-ja and are probably also serving local needs. The remaining two sites with textile workgroups seem to house a more complex local textile industry. Lousos, with its 32 decorators (and 54 mi-ra-ti-ja) seems to be functioning not as a site engaged solely in local production, but rather as a large second-tier textile-producing site in that it employs more than one workgroup consisting of specialized workers. Pylos ke-re-za is the one outlier with neither of its two workgroups clearly assigned to textile production.

Overall, we should understand a comprehensible rationale governing the choices made in stationing these textile groups throughout the provincial capital and villages whereby the smaller sites are provided with a small textile force to supply their needs locally, while Pylos itself maintains both a standing assembly line textile force and specialized workers devoted exclusively to the production of specialty and luxury products. In no instances are work targets provided for any of the workgroups.

Food production and palace maintenance

In addition to textile production, the other major category for women's labor at Pylos involves tasks related to food-processing or domestic service either as personal attendants or in tasks related to maintaining the palace and its water supply. Once more we see women assigned to aggregate workgroups that are again recorded in the personnel Aa, Ab, and Ad tablets. The women in the food and domestic service workgroups are tracked and rationed in an identical manner to the textile workers, and once more their children are tracked and reassigned in the Ad tablets. No discernable difference in the textual treatment of these two groups of women is visible, and despite their different task assignments, we should understand all of these workgroup women as sharing a common, indivisible status.

Three occupational titles can be read relating to food-processing and domestic upkeep with a reasonable amount of certainty. These terms are identified either from mentions in the Homeric poems or through etymological reconstruction. The me-re-ti-ri-ja were assigned food-production tasks, with household management activities performed by the re-wo-to-ro-ko-wo and a-pi-qo-ro *amphiqoloi* (the Homeric ἀμφιπόλοι). One might hear echoes of these titles in Homeric verbs describing the tasks of the female palace attendants of Odysseus, Alcinoos, and Nestor, whose staff provide food, personal attendance on more elite folk, and maintain the facilities of the shining palaces.

Food-processing

The primary food-production workers at Pylos seem to be the me-re-ti-ri-ja (*meletriai*), reconstructed as *μελέτριαι ("flour-grinders").[176] The tablets reference two such workgroups, one at Pylos and the other at Leuktron; it is significant that the food-processing workgroups are only based at the capital of each Province. The Pylos-based workgroup[177] is attested on two tablets, both of which follow the standard Aa and Ab series format.[178] This workgroup is relatively small – only six adult women – considering that it is the only group of food workers among all the Pylos-based workgroups. The second group[179] of flour-grinders is based at Leuktron and is known from two tablets.[180] Again, this workgroup is relatively small with seven tallied women. Neither group of me-re-ti-ri-ja carries an ethnic identification.

Domestic and household maintenance

Two workgroups are charged with domestic or household maintenance responsibilities. As both are located at the main site of Pylos, it seems reasonable to understand these workers as comprising the maintenance/attendant staff for the palace complex.[181]

Of the workers charged with palatial management responsibilities, the larger group is the re-wo-to-ro-ko-wo with 37/38 women assigned here. This term is thought to normalize as *lewotrokhowoi* from the Homeric λοετροχόος[182] and bears the same translation as "bath-attendants," or perhaps more specifically, "bath-pourers."[183] One workgroup is known[184] and is attested by the full complement of A series tablets.[185] It is interesting to note how closely the name of this workgroup conforms to its Homeric counterpart. It seems logical that these workers are based at Pylos itself as one might expect only the main palatial center to have the facilities and the need for a relatively large standing force of women assigned to water-gathering and bath-related activities. Certain scholars have thought the number of re-wo-to-ro-ko-wo to have been excessively high for a palace with a single excavated bathtub. Tritsch has suggested that in order to keep such a large force occupied, the re-wo-to-ro-ko-wo may have served as nurses charged with washing the palace's wounded.[186] Carlier disagrees, finding sufficient work in the transport and heating of water and in the washing of the palace's linen, to keep such a workforce sufficiently occupied.[187] Finally, Chadwick regards these women as holding the "task of providing all domestic water-supplies,"[188] which seems a likely reading considering the large size of this workgroup. I find both a combined reading of Carlier's and Chadwick's interpretations to be a reasonable resolution of this term.

The second category of household worker also has Homeric parallels; the workers referred to as a-pi-qo-ro *amphiqoloi* seem to be the Mycenaean equivalents of the Homeric ἀμφιπόλοι.[189] Lindgren notes that this term is "generally accepted as a *general* [original emphasis] female occupation designation: 'waiting-women', 'serving-women', and 'attendants';"[190] Carlier considers these attendants to be "personal servants."[191] Two personnel series tablets[192] record this large workgroup of 32 adult women and 41 accompanying children.[193] Like the re-wo-to-ro-ko-wo workers, this group is also based at the main center of Pylos, and its large size makes it likely that this group comprised the main body of workers attending on the more elite members of the palace and their needs. These workers are also named on a non-personnel series tablet, one of only three workgroup designations at Pylos to receive mention outside the A series tablets. A-pi-qo-ro women receive this outside mention on the olive oil tablet PY Fr 1205, and this reference receives additional discussion in Chapter 4.

Discussion of food and palace staff at Pylos

Several points relating to kitchen and domestic workgroups warrant comment:

1.) Workers assigned to food-processing and janitorial or maintenance chores are the most centralized of the various occupational categories in the Pylian A tablets, located entirely at the two provincial capital sites. Pylos alone houses both workgroups of these occupational types; at Leuktron only a food-processing workgroup is attested. This concentration of domestic labor around the major centers is unlikely to be accidental.

2.) The types of labor attested in this occupational subset all share a logistic commonality: the types of labor represented under these titles are menial, repetitive, and potentially unending – tasks which are necessary full time and year-round. These three categories of domestic workgroups manage between them to fulfill many of the permanent labor and water needs of a large complex with both administrative and quartering functions. Based on their presence solely at the capital site of Pylos and taking into account their specific occupational responsibilities, I would suggest that we think of these workgroups (a-pi-qo-ro, me-re-ti-ri-ja, and re-wo-to-ro-ko-wo) as constituting the full-time, regular domestic staff of the palace itself as their task assignments would exactly fulfill the ongoing feeding, watering, and cleaning of a palace which incorporates a throne room complex, "royal" quarters, a large staff of specialized craftsmen, and a system of contained storage areas. Such a palace would require continual replenishment of a flour supply, a staff to attend to the personal requirements of its elite, and a force to clean and maintain the palace's water supply (for drinking water, for bathing, or for laundering).[194] As all these needs would have been perpetual, a full-time staff would have been needed to accomplish these tasks, a staff likely composed of the domestic workgroups attested to in the A series. Between them, these workgroups could well fulfill such needs as providing a regular supply of milled wheat to feed the palace's administrators (the me-re-ti-ri-ja), and furnishing the daily domestic requirements of a large administrative complex by tending the palace's water-related tasks as either bath-workers or launderers (the re-wo-to-ro-ko-wo), and supplying a staff of personal attendants (the a-pi-ro-qo) for the palace's ruling elite.

Leuktron houses only a me-re-ti-ri-ja workgroup; absence of a janitorial/attendant staff may indicate that there is no major administrative building at this site which would require such staff. No other sites of either province are assigned a milling or maintenance workgroup.

Etymologically obscure workgroups

In addition to tasks related to textile production and domestic management, the Pylos archives record another ten workgroup titles. The nature of these task assignments cannot be ascertained, however, as their etymologies remain too obscure to permit their particular specialization to be determined. Titles placed in this category include those whose etymologies can be only partially reconstructed, those whose etymologies cannot be recovered at all, and those whose reconstructed etymologies remain too vague to provide any real indication of their labor category.

Among the occupational titles where only a partial etymology can be reconstructed is no-ri-wo-ko.[195] Etymologically, this title indicates a feminine trade with its ending in *–worgoi (-ergoi)*; no-ri remains obscure, but the overall sense of the word seems to be "no-ri-workers." Based on a parallel mention at Thebes, no-ri-wo-ko may well be another textile-production-related term. One workgroup is known,[196] which is located in the Further Province and attested by an Aa[197] and an Ad tablet.[198] This workgroup is based at the site of Leuktron, one of five total workgroups known at that site. Although its total of eight adult women seems relatively small when compared with some of the groups stationed at Pylos proper, this is the second largest workgroup attested to at Leuktron, after the 12 women of the a-ke-ti-ri-ja ("decorators") workgroup. If this should be a textile-related term, it would be the fourth known textile-related group at Leuktron.

Two more etymologically obscure terms are constructed with the feminine task ending *–triai*: o-ti-ri-ja (variant: o-ti-ra2) and ra-qi-ti-ra2. One Hither Province o-ti-ri-ja/o-ti-ra2 workgroup is known,[199] attested with the full three tablet complement.[200] The sense of this term remains elusive, although Ruijgh's proposed etymology from ὄρτριαι, ὄρνυμι with its sense of "women who move (something)" has merit.[201] With 21 adult women attested on both the Aa and Ab tablets, this group is the eighth largest of the 27 Pylos-based groups. If Ruijgh's proposal of "movers" is correct, this workgroup may have been related to the three domestic/maintenance workgroups also based at Pylos.

The second workgroup using the *–triai* ending is ra-qi-ti-ra2. This group is not etymologically the same as the similarly spelled ra-pi-ti-ra2.[202] Ruijgh's early proposal of "store-keepers"[203] is largely considered implausible; a more plausible reading is "thresher-women,"[204] although not universally accepted. One small workgroup (six adult women) is known,[205] located at the Pylian center.[206] Should this reading be correct, this would be the second group of food-preparation workers at Pylos.[207]

Another workgroup of uncertain assignment – the to-sa-me-ja – uses the agent ending *–eia*, the feminine equivalent of the masculine *–eus*. This small workgroup is attested as being at the village of o-wi-to-no.[208] This workgroup is attested to on three tablets, although only one combines both the title to-sa-me-ja and the place name o-wi-to-no.[209] The sense of to-sa-me-ja remains unknown.[210] For this set, the title to-sa-me-ja is restored to the Aa and Ab tablet based on the evidence of the corresponding Ad tablet which links both the place name o-wi-to-no and the trade title to-sa-me-ja. This is the only workgroup attested to at o-wi-to-no, a town of the Hither Province. It is possible that this workgroup pertains to textile production if we view the workgroup situation at o-wi-to-no as analogous to that of the other (non-capital) villages in the Pylos archives; the workgroups (whose tasks can be recovered) at all 13 of the other village sites are textile workgroups. If textile production functions as the default assignment for the provincial workgroups, this to-sa-me-ja group may share a similar duty, but as yet we cannot be certain.

A further workgroup is described with the term ki-ma-ra.[211] No workable etymology for this term has been proposed, although this term could potentially be an ethnicon or an occupational designation.[212] (Only a place name can be ruled out as Ad 668 indicates that the group is based at Leuktron.) Two tablets document a single ki-ma-ra workgroup.[213]

The two remaining trade titles known from Pylos are the most difficult to understand. These two titles – o-pi-ro-qo-no and e-ke-ro-qo-no – appear to be connected either in sense or function although their precise relation to each other is not exactly clear. The nature of this confusion stems from the tendency of various personnel series tablets to use these titles either independently or jointly, apparently to modify each other in these instances. When appearing independently they are most commonly interpreted to mean "remaining/unassigned workers"[214] for o-pi-ro-qo-no and "wage-earners"[215] for e-ke-ro-qo-no; when combined the prevailing sense is that of "unassigned wage-earners."

At least four tablets seem to treat o-pi-ro-qo-no and e-ke-re-qo-no as separate titles, whereby the two terms are either used independently of each other or are linked by the enclitic *–que* ("and"). From these four tablets, we can identify two separate workgroups: one o-pi-ro-qo-no group[216] and one e-ke-re-qo-no group.[217] While the Aa and Ab tablets which record these two workgroups follow the standard format, the Ad tablet which mentions both workgroups diverges from the usual treatment of this series. Instead of the expected tally of the adult sons of a single women's workgroup, this tablet records the adult sons of women identified with three different titles (e-ke-ro-qo-no, pa-wo-ko, and o-pi-ro-qo). The titles of these women are linked by *–que* which should imply that these titles are conceptualized by the scribe as being three distinct types of workers.[218] It remains possible that these workgroups are linked here because these groups may be in some way related, perhaps as three kinds of generic or floating laborers.

In addition to the "unassigned" o-pi-ro-qo-no workers and the (assigned) e-ke-ro-qo-no "wage-earners," we also see the third category of "unassigned wage-earners" or e-ke-ro-qo-no o-pi-ro-qo. While both of their etymologies are less than certain, the apparent flexibility of these two groups in being assigned either separately or together might imply that these two groups may function as floating workers rather than as single-task specialists. One workgroup of "unassigned wage-earners" is known at Pylos.[219] This group is evidenced by one complete tablet (PY Aa 777[220]) and another that seems to refer to the same workgroup but remains too fragmentary for certainty (PY Ab 1100[221]). If these two texts do in fact refer to the same workers, one wonders how workers come to be "unassigned" within so tightly regulated an economy as that of Pylos. Several explanations seem possible: 1.) These workers were only recently acquired by the palace and have not yet been trained in a specialty. 2.) These workers were trained in tasks that had been completed and were waiting to be reassigned. 3.) These were seasonal workers in the off-season. 4.) These workers had been reassigned for disciplinary or other reasons. 5.) The palace opted to have a small standing labor force ready for whatever odd tasks might arise – to my mind the most likely explanation. 6.) These workers are farmed out to third-parties who pay their wages to the palace but who are currently between assignments.

An obvious question concerns the exact relationship of these three groups to each other. They seem to be closely associated in that their sons are tallied together – the only such instance in the Pylos personnel tablets; they are also, however, sufficiently distinct as to warrant the use of three different titles although two of these titles (e-ke-ro-qo-no and o-pi-ro-qo-no) can be combined. Should we understand this tablet indicating a hyper-specialization of these three tasks? Or, conversely, is the slippage between the categories evidence that these terms are so general that they can be combined and reassigned without changing their basic task assignments? I see no way as yet to untangle this confusion.

The title pa-wo-ke differs from the other obscure titles discussed above in that while its etymology appears rather clear, its task assignment nevertheless remains vague. This occupational category is attested to on three personnel series tablets;[222] a single workgroup is known.[223] Etymologically, it seems highly probable that this term normalizes as Chadwick's proposed *pan-worges* (πάνϝοργες). Chadwick understood *panworges* to mean "maids of all work"[224] or some type of generic, all-purpose laborer. Other readings of this term translate it as "ancillary workers," "general workers," "extra hands," or "household-workers."[225] Affiliated with the equally elusive e-ke-ro-qo-no and o-pi-ro-qo women on PY Ad 691, it may be that these workers may also function as floaters, performing whatever random tasks might arise. As none of the A series texts provide any insight into the genre of task these workers perform, we should not rule out the possibility that these women may have been among the large numbers of textile workers at Pylos. Context within other tablet series may further support this reading, for example the wool-tablet PY La 0632:

PY La 0632
[ ] pa-wo-ko LANA[
"… of the all-purpose workers, WOOL["

It is possible that this mention of the term pa-wo-ko on a wool tablet might suggest a possible task assignment within wool-working if the word-string pa-wo-ko does indeed refer to the same group of workers mentioned in the personnel series.[226]

The final titled workgroup at Pylos, the ra-wi-ja-ja,[227] attested on three Hither Province tablets,[228] has inspired the largest amount of debate, both with regard to its proposed etymology and to the implications that its possible etymologies raise for the overall status of the women of the personnel series. Early proposed readings[229] have largely given way to Chadwick's etymology off the Homeric ληιάδες[230] as *lawiaiai* "captive women"[231] acquired either during raids or bought on the slave markets – a reading also echoed by Ruijgh and accepted by Chantraine.[232] (No major challenges to this reading have been offered in recent years.) If we accept this reading, then it would seem we are dealing here with *recent* captive women, as they have not yet been assigned to an occupational task; it is also interesting to note that they are not identified by a singular ethnic (assuming they all originated in the same place). Also of interest is that this workgroup is not based at the Pylian center proper but in the outer locale of Pylos Kereza. This is the largest workgroup assigned to Pylos Kereza and the third largest of all the non-Pylos-based workgroups.

By definition, titles designated as obscure resist a large amount of summary analysis. Three points warrant mention: 1.) Of the ten obscure titles, three may perhaps be tentatively assigned to other labor categories – the no-ri-wo-ko and perhaps the to-sa-me-ja to textile production and the o-ti-ri-ja to domestic upkeep, possibly lowering the total of completely unrecoverable titles to seven. 2.) Workers bearing "obscure" titles are disproportionately concentrated at the two provincial capitals; six groups consisting of at least 36 workers[233] located at Pylos, and Leuktron houses 11 women within two more workgroups. Only two groups of etymologically unrecoverable workers are situated outside these two locales: the eight to-sa-me-ja at o-wi-to-no and the 28 ra-wi-ja-ja at Pylos ke-re-za; both sites fall within the Hither Province. This clustering at the capital sites may be significant, particularly in that neither the workers currently understood as extraneous nor those thought to have maintenance duties are assigned outside the palace site itself. It would seem that Pylos is not stationing "unnecessary" or "floating" workers in the villages or in the Further Province, but is instead concentrating them at the largest center of administration. Indeed, no outlying site is attested to as maintaining a contingent of unassigned workers. Might this indicate that only the palatial site is sufficiently complex as to require a floating staff of workers who can be assigned to miscellaneous, quotidian tasks? And that all secondary and tertiary sites are only equipped with workers whose tasks are clearly assigned and, one presumes, deemed particularly necessary in that locale?

Workgroups identified by ethnic titles (tasks unknown)

In addition to the variety of task-titled workgroups discussed in the previous section, a significant number of workgroups are identified not by the name of the tasks they perform, but rather by the ethnic ancestry of their workers.[234] Ethnics use adjectives derived from place names with endings in i-ja rather than the e-ja more frequently seen with occupational titles. All but three of the workgroups bearing ethnic titles are assigned to the site of Pylos. Ten different ethnic adjectives either substitute for or modify the occupational titles used to name workgroups within the Pylian state; these ethnics follow here in alphabetical order.

The ethnic adjective a-*64-ja is used to modify women belonging to two separate workgroups: the first, the Further Province workgroup of a-*64-ja linen-workers based at Leuktron which was discussed above, and a second Hither Province workgroup based at Pylos and identified solely with the ethnic. As already mentioned, the term a-*64-ja appears to normalize as *Aswiai* and should mean "women of Asia," thought to indicate Lydia.[235] Of the two different Aswian workgroups, the Pylos-based group,[236] preserved on three tablets, PY Aa 701, Ab 515, and Ad 315,[237] is one of the largest groups at the palace site. As is typical of the ethnically-titled workgroups, the ethnic term occupies the same textual positions as the occupational title. Since the Ad tablet, from the series which tends to list the most complete designation for workgroups, does not supply their task designation, there is no way to tell if this workgroup, like its counterpart at Leuktron, is devoted to flax-working or even to textile production. While some have suggested a direct correlation between ethnic affiliation and task assignments, whereby all women of a specific ethnicity perform the same task,[238] no textual evidence exists to support this claim. In fact, as discussed below, there are strong textual grounds to dissociate common ethnicity and shared task assignments among the Pylos workgroups.

The next ethnic title is e-wi-ri-pi-ja, attested on a single Aa tablet. There is full scholarly consensus in reading e-wi-ri-pi-ja as an ethnicon.[239] The term is thought to normalize as *Ewiripiai*, deriving from the place name Εὔριπος,[240] a town of the Hither Province at Pylos. One workgroup[241] of women bearing this ethnicon is attested to on a single Minor set Aa tablet.[242] While this tablet does not name the location of this workgroup, we can ascertain that, on account of its Scribe 4 authorship, it must be a village of the Further Province at Pylos.[243] Furthermore, while the ethnic e-wi-ri-pi-ja is one of only two in the Pylian corpus which refers to an origin within either of Pylos's provinces,[244] it is interesting to note that these women are at work not in their eponymous village but have been transferred to another Pylos-controlled location which, in this instance, is in a different province. This situation exactly parallels that of the ti-nwa-si-ja weavers discussed on p. 77 who also originated within one location under Pylian control but who likewise were transferred to another location for their labor activities. This transfer of women originating within the Pylian state to secondary locales within the state should surely argue against Uchitel's corvée labor model in which he proposed that the women of Mycenaean states have their labor co-opted by the state and perform their labor in their home villages.[245]

The third ethnic workgroup title is ki-ni-di-ja, used to denote a single, medium-sized workgroup[246] attested to on four tablets; this workgroup is located at Pylos itself. Three of these tablets are the expected Aa, Ab, and Ad texts; [247] the fourth is the summary tablet PY An 0292 which mentions 3 other workgroups.[248] Ki-ni-di-ja seems transparent as *Knidiai*, most likely referencing an origin at Κνίδος.[249]

The ethnic term ki-si-wi-ja has already been discussed (p. 86). It likely indicates *Kswijiai* "Chian," with an intervocalic sigma still present. This ethnic appears in conjunction with a single workgroup at Pylos also described with the textile-producing title o-nu-ke-ja.

The ethnic ko-ro-ki-ja is attested on four tablets, including on PY An 292.[250] The place name the ethnic title derived from has not yet been identified with certainty.[251] One workgroup is known.[252]

The sixth ethnic adjective in use at Pylos is ku-te-ra3; as mentioned above in the discussion of the ka-pa-ra-de workers this term seems to normalize as *Kytherai,* from the island of Kythera/Κύθερα. Two workgroups are known, the previously mentioned ka-pa-ra-de ku-te-ra3 group and a second group identified by ku-te-ra3 alone;[253] the latter group is attested to on three tablets.[254] This workgroup is relatively large for an ethnically organized group. It is possible, due to the large number of sons who have reached adulthood, that this may have been one of the longer-established workgroups at Pylos. If this workgroup and the ku-te-ra3 ka-pa-ra-de do indeed originate from Kythera, they would be the only known ethnic workgroups without antecedents either in the Eastern Aegean/Anatolian coast or the immediate Pylian environs. Furthermore, when the total number of Kytheran women from the two workgroups are combined, they total 52 adult women, rendering Kytheran women the second largest group of ethnically-identified women at Pylos.

There is another feature of interest relating to the Kytheran women at Pylos. Two separate workgroups of women of the same ethnic background are recorded; only one of these workgroups has a separate occupational listing. These two Pylos-based workgroups of Kytheran women bear directly on Lindgren's theory that all women of a common ethnicity are associated with a craft specialty specific to their originating locale, whereby ethnic women from one location might all be considered to be famed for their weaving while women from another provenance would be renowned for their sewing.[255] As this theory requires a unity of tasks among women bearing the same ethnic title, the presence of two distinct Kytheran workgroups based at the same site (Pylos) creates a problem. If we were to accept a commonality of task assignment between all Kytheran women, and since we have already encountered a workgroup of Kytheran women described with the occupational title ka-pa-ra-de, we would need to understand this second group of Kytheran workers as ka-pa-ra-de as well. This would then place two separate groups of Kytheran ka-pa-ra-de in the Pylos texts, a circumstance that would be unremarkable were these two groups to be assigned to different sites within the Pylian state, for instance, with one of these workgroups based in the Hither Province and the other in the Further Province in order that they might fulfill the specific production needs of each province. These two groups of Kytheran women, however, are both located at the same site – the capital site of Pylos proper. If all these Kytheran women are assigned to the same task, it is difficult to explain why two separate workgroups would be necessary (or why one group carries an occupational title and the other does not). A more likely explanation for these two distinct groups at the same location would be that two separate tasks were assigned to these women. Additionally, throughout the Pylian personnel series, we see no redundancy of occupational assignments within any of the sites where the workgroup women are stationed; at each site all workers performing the same task are assigned to a single, unified workgroup. The one exception to this rule is the presence at Pylos proper of both an a-ra-ka-te-ja and an a-ra-ka-te-ja mi-ra-ti-ja workgroup, but even this exception proves the rule – we have two groups because a second is needed to separate a (newly-arrived?) group of ethnically-designated women from the major group. Consequently, the rationale behind creating two distinct groups of women of the same ethnicity and performing the same task would require a justification no one has yet proposed. I view the best solution to be the simplest; there are two workgroups of Kytheran women at Pylos because they are performing two different tasks.

The seventh ethnic title – mi-ra-ti-ja – is used to describe three workgroups: one accompanied by an occupational title and the other two unmodified. The first workgroup, the Pylos-based a-ra-ka-te-ja mi-ra-ti-ja ("Milatian spinning-women"), was documented on the tablet PY Ad 380 and has been discussed above (p. 75). The second mi-ra-ti-ja workgroup is attested on three tablets where the ethnic acts as the sole descriptor for these women;[256] like its occupationally-titled counterpart, this workgroup is also based at Pylos. This is the second instance in the personnel series where women bearing the same ethnic title are separated into two distinct workgroups at the same location, one with an additional task annotation and one without. Again, I understand the presence of two separate workgroups at a single site bearing the same ethnic adjective as additional confirmation that these women were assigned to separate tasks; had they performed the same tasks, they could easily have been all assigned to a single workgroup.

The final workgroup of mi-ra-ti-ja women is located at ro-u-so (Lousos) also in the Hither Province.[257] This workgroup is attested on two tablets; no Ad tablet has survived.[258] There are several interesting features of this workgroup. First, this workgroup is one of the three ethnically-designated workgroups of the personnel series which is not based at the Pylian center, the more common location for the ethnic workgroups. It is also the only one to have a non-Pylos Hither Province location; it is located in the town of Lousos, one of only two workgroups assigned there. Second is the size of this workgroup – it is the largest workgroup recorded in the entire A series with 54 adult women and 57 underage children accompanying them. The large size of this workgroup is perhaps not coincidental; the *Milatiai* are the largest contingent of workgroup women at Pylos with at least 70 women indicated; as the tally for the third workgroup has not been preserved, the actual number of mi-ra-ti-ja at Pylos would have been even larger.

The eighth ethnic title also appears to have an Eastern Aegean origin: ra-mi-ni-ja (*Lamniai*) apparently from the island of Λῆμνος.[259] One single tablet[260] preserves this small Pylos-based workgroup.[261]

The ninth ethnic title in use – ti-nwa-si-ja – has previously been discussed (p. 77). It is used in conjunction with the occupational title i-te-ja ("weaver") at Pylos and is attested on three tablets. Its provenance is unknown, but from internal evidence in the tablets it appears to be a possession of Pylos as it contributes a large amount of gold to the Pylian state (PY Jo 0438). Along with e-wi-ri-pi-ja, this ethnic appears to be one of only two ethnics with an internal Pylian origin.

The tenth and final ethnic title in use in the Pylos A-series is ze-pu2-ra3; this title is used for a single workgroup, the ri-ne-ja ("flax-workers") at the Further Province site of Pylos Lauranthias (pp. 80–81). Ze-pu2-ra3 seems to normalize as *Dzephurai,* possibly indicating an origin of Ζεφυρία, an alternate name for Halicarnassos attested to in Strabo.

Attention to the locations, task assignments, and origins of the ethnically-designated workgroups reveals several important patterns:

1. The ethnics in use in the Pylian personnel series derive from provenances both within and without the Pylian state. Of the ten ethnics in use either singly or in combination, the majority appear to derive from outside Pylos's geographical territory. Only two ethnics derive from locations within the region of Pylian control: e-wi-ri-pi-ja from the place name *Euripos,* known from An 610 to be a town of the Hither Province, and ti-nwa-si-ja, which derives from ti-nwa-to, a location which appears to contribute large commodities of gold to the palace. The remaining eight ethnic titles appear to be associated with different regions/islands far from the sphere of Pylos's influence; at least seven of these have plausible etymological links to Eastern Aegean locations, either East Aegean islands or regions of western Asia Minor. (These "foreign" ethnics are discussed in point 4.)

2. As noted above, no workgroup bearing an ethnic title remains at the provenance which gives rise to its ethnic. This is obvious in the case of those "foreign" ethnics which derive from outside the Pylian state, but the two workgroups whose personnel originate within regions under Pylian control also conform to this pattern. Both these workgroups, the ti-nwa-si-ja and e-wi-ri-pi-ja, are transferred to secondary locations where their labor activities are performed: the Hither Province-originating e-wi-ri-pi-ja perform their tasks at the Further Province capital of Leuktron, and the ti-nwa-si-ja, thought to originate from an

island under the aegis of Pylos, do their weaving at the palace site of Pylos itself. As it would be easy for the palace to simply leave these two groups in their place of origin, it would appear that an administrative choice has been made to place these workers in a location other than that of their origin. While relocating the ti-nwa-si-ja workers may have had a practical reason – we are not certain how far away ti-nwa-to is – the transfer of a Hither Province workgroup to a Further Province location seems more suggestive of a policy decision to locate ethnic workers at a location other than their home village.

3. The task assignments of these ethnically-designated workers do not necessarily correspond to their ethnicity for reasons discussed above. There is also no overwhelming reason to assume all workers of a certain ethnicity continue to perform the same specialized tasks across their various workgroups as evidenced by the two distinct Pylos-based *Kytherai*. Nonetheless, these ethnic workers seem to have some correspondences in their tasks: none of the ethnic workers can be identified as working in a workgroup devoted either to food production or domestic upkeep, and, in all instances where the task of the ethnic workgroup is identified, ethnically identified workgroups are assigned to textile production. Six workgroups of ethnic workers are expressly identified as textile workers (spinners, weavers, linen-workers, ka-pa-ra-de, and o-nu-ka makers), while the tasks of the remaining eight groups remain uncertain. I think it likely that these eight groups are likewise occupied with textile work, but the absence of explicit documentation must be duly acknowledged.

4. The 14 ethnically identified workgroups, which correspond to ten separate ethnic titles, are not evenly distributed throughout the two provinces but rather are disproportionately concentrated at the regional centers, particularly at the site of Pylos itself. Pylos itself houses ten of the ethnic workgroups, which accounts for 156[262] of the 226[263] known ethnic workers. Furthermore, these ethnically identified workers make up nearly 40 percent of the total workgroup women at Pylos, underscoring their importance as a key component of the palace's dependent female labor force. Outside of the capital site, the Hither Province houses one additional workgroup of ethnic women at Lousos, which employs a large number of a-ke-ti-ri-ja ("decorators") and appears to be the second largest (after Pylos) node of textile production in the Hither Province, as it stations the largest workgroup in the personnel series, a workgroup of mi-ra-ti-ja women 54 strong. The assignment of these women to a major textile site strengthens the possibility that these mi-ra-ti-ja can be understood as textile workers themselves. Otherwise, none of the smaller Hither Province villages which have been assigned personnel series women house an ethnically identified workgroup.

This concentration of ethnically identified workers at the provincial capital site is repeated, albeit on a smaller scale, at the Further Province center of Leuktron which houses two such workgroups: the ri-ne-ja a-*64-ja and the e-wi-pi-ri-ja; these two workgroups comprise two of the total seven workgroups at Leuktron. As the tally of the ri-ne-ja a-*64-ja is lacunose, we cannot offer an estimate of the relative proportion of ethnic workers among Leuktron's workforce, although we might note that the e-wi-ri-pi-ja workgroup is the second largest (legible) workgroup at the site. Likewise in the Hither Province, one outlying site in the Further Province also accommodates an ethnic workgroup: the ri-ne-ja ze-pu-ra2 at Pylos Lauranthias. As this is the sole mention of Pylos Lauranthias, and since the workgroup is only known from its Ad tablet, it is not possible to ascertain whether this group is exceptional in size or is located at a textile center. The rationale that would account for the stationing of a *Dzephurian* (Halicarnassian?) workgroup at this particular locale also remains unclear.

Proposed etymologies for the "foreign" ethnics appear to cluster their provenances in locations in the Eastern Aegean or Ionian coast; among the locales proposed as origins for these ethnics are Miletus, Lydia, Halicarnassos, Cnidos, and Lemnos. While the originating locale for these ten ethnics remains contentious, and it is likely that not all of these proposed etymologies are correct, it is striking that so many of the "foreign" ethnics have associations with the Eastern Aegean, either the islands or the western coast of Asia Minor.[264] This clustering has struck many as significant and has frequently factored into the debate on women's overall status in the personnel series workgroups; discussion of the status of these women concludes this chapter.

Workgroups known from location alone

The final group of low-status laborers from Pylos are the women of workgroups that are identified only by place name at which they are stationed; no further ethnic or task-derived titles are listed for these workgroups. Four workgroups at three different locales are recorded in this way; these groups are all very small, and none has more than eight adult women. All of these workgroups are located in the Hither Province; it is unclear if we should draw any additional significance from this datum.

Two location-identified groups are located at the village of Metapa, one of the nine towns of the Hither Province.[265] The first[266] of these two workgroups is attested on a single Aa tablet[267] and consists of seven women. The second workgroup is also attested by an Aa tablet as well as an Ab tablet; this second workgroup is slightly smaller than the first.[268] It may be possible that the two Aa tablets refer to one, rather than two distinct workgroups, but it seems more reasonable to regard them as separate workgroups at the same site based on the scribe's decision to separate them into two Aa series tablets.

The next location at which an otherwise unidentified workgroup is based is ne-wo-pe-o. Like me-ta-pa, ne-wo-pe-o is another of the seven towns that make up the Hither Province.[269] Again, no task assignment can be recovered, even though its Ad tablet is sufficiently well-preserved as to include its full heading. Like the two groups at me-ta-pa, this workgroup is also relatively small.[270] It is attested on three tablets.[271]

The final site name used in lieu of an ethnic or occupational term is pi-we-re. This term would seem to normalize as * Πιερεῖ [272] A single tablet[273] mentions another small workgroup stationed here;[274] as this tablet is of the Major Aa set, pi-we-re must be located within the Hither Province at Pylos.

These four workgroups have a number of features in common. First and foremost, they are the only workgroups attested at their sites. Second, their production activities and their ethnic origins are unknown. If, however, we might extrapolate from the example of the outlying villages of the Further Province who, when they house a single workgroup at their sites, house single workgroups of textile workers, then we should understand these location-identified workgroups belonging to far-flung Hither Province villages to also be of textile workers. Third, in all four cases, these workgroups based in minor outlying villages each contain only a small number of women. These three facts leave open – and unanswered – several important questions: 1. Are the women of these workgroups indigenous to these villages or have they been transferred here by a central authority? 2. If they have indeed been transferred here, might the small size of the groups be designed to make it easier for a small community to maintain control of these women? 3. Is it only coincidental that all of these workgroups are lacking an Ad tablet, or are these groups so newly formed that there has not been sufficient time for the sons of these women to have matured into adulthood? 4. Do these women share the same relationship to their polity that the women in the occupational and ethnic workgroups do? To this final question, I would answer yes; they do seem to be accounted and rationed in much the same way. The other questions must all remain open at this time.

Workers assigned to "collectors"

Finally, four A series workgroups remain. These entries are identified with the terms a-da-ra-te-ja,[275] me-ki-to-ki-ri-ta,[276] ka-ru-ti-je-ja, and we-we-si-je-ja and are presented in the same way as the workgroups discussed above. Each of the first two workgroups consists of a single woman.

PY Aa 955
me-ki-to-ki[-ri-ta MUL

PY Ab 575
pu-ro me-ki-to-ki-ri-ta MUL 1 ko-wo [
"At Pylos, women belonging to Megistokrites: 1 woman, x boy(s)"

This Pylos-based "workgroup" consists of a single woman and at least one underage boy; no Ad record of adult sons is in existence.

Initially, it was not clear how the term me-ki-to-ki-ri-ta should be understood. As it lacks an occupation e-ja or an ethnic i-ja ending, it was most frequently understood to be either the name of the workgroup's sole woman (Megistokrita)[277] or a feminine adjective derived from a man's name (Megistokrites).[278] As the women of these workgroups appear to be of the lowest social status within Pylos, and naming seems to be reserved in the tablets for persons of rank, this second reading seems the more plausible, whereby a female dependent of the palace (for it is the palace who is monitoring her subsistence) might have had her labor allocated to a particular man, possibly a low-level palace official. It should be noted, however, that no such man is attested to by this name in the Pylos archives.

The second lone-woman "workgroup" is presented much in the same way:

PY Aa 785
a-da-ra-te-ja MUL 1 TA 1
"1 Adrasteian woman, 1 TA"

PY Ab 388
.a GRA T 4
.b pu-ro a-da-ra-te-ja MUL [ ] 1 NI T 4 TA
"At Pylos, Adrasteian women: 1, 38.4 l. wheat, 38.4 l. figs"

Etymologically, this entry has one additional interpretative possibility than its counterpart: the e-ja ending couple possibly indicate an otherwise unknown trade term. More likely is that a-da-ra-te-ja is, or derives from, a personal name, either the woman's name Adrasteia[279] or as a feminine adjective from the man's name Adrastos,[280] whereby this tablet would be referencing an "Adrasteian woman." The Pylos tablets do make mention of the man's name Adrastos who appears on two tablets in the genitive case. An Adrastos is mentioned on PY Aq 218 as the father of a man named a3-ko-ta who is under obligation to bring a number of men upon summons, and on PY An 656, as the father of an e-qe-ta named di-ko-na-ro. Olivier has argued that Adrastos should be regarded as among the Collectors at Pylos.[281] As children frequently inherit their parents' status in the tablets, this Adrastos should be a person of high status. It is not clear if these two mentions refer to the same person, but the possibility must be entertained that one or both these men may be the eponym for this "group" entry. Again, I suggest that the model in place here may be that of a worker dependent upon the central administration for her subsistence rations who has been assigned to a ranking man for labor related to either his personal or state civic duties, i.e., a servant of an official who requires only a single staff member. This would solve the issue of why the workgroup is so small, and also provide a mechanism whereby Collectors and other ranking men come to acquire the personnel we often see attested for them.

The remaining two workgroups in the Pylian corpus also appear to be composed of workgroup women assigned to a particular collector, the ka-ru-ti-je-ja and we-we-si-je-ja groups. The ka-ru-ti-je-ja workgroup's title derives from the name of its owner *Karustios*[282] and is known only from an Ad tablet, PY Ad 671, which tracks the older sons of this workgroup.[283] (As no Aa or Ab has survived for this group, we do not know the size of this workgroup.)

The we-we-si-je-ja group, belonging to the Major Aa set at Pylos, likewise derives its name from the name of the man we-we-si-jo[284] who also appears on three Jn tablets in the role of collector.[285] (Chadwick's once accepted proposal of a derivation from ειρεσιώνη "wool-workers" from εἶρος "wool"[286] has been shown to be linguistically untenable.)[287] A single workgroup is known,[288] and all three tablets are extant.[289] It is important to note that the Ab tablet places the workgroup at a site referred to as pu-ro ke-re-za; this is not indicating the site of Pylos proper, but rather the secondary site of Pylos Kereza, apparently an important second-tier, textile-producing locale. The exact location of Pylos Ke-re-za is unknown, but, based on its scribal hand, it must fall within the Hither Province. Of note is the wider degree of variance in the number of the workers; we witness a change of six in the counts of adult women between the Aa and Ab tablets in this set; while the tallies of women on the Ab tablets are on average slightly smaller than the tallies on the Aa series, the 30 percent decrease between the two series is higher than average.

If Olivier and Nosch's proposal is correct, we might add the workgroup of pa-ke-te-ja ri-ne-ja to this classification as well.[290]

Additional labor categories

Finally, there are two last categories of labor that occupy low-ranking women at Pylos. Neither of these labor categories is organized into the personnel series workgroups per se. The first of these two labor categories pertains to the role of the workgroup women in their status as primary child-care providers, responsible for all underage offspring regardless of sex.[291] Nowhere in the tablets are adult men listed with children in their care as they carry out their assigned duties. As the proportion of women to children in the personnel series is roughly 1:1,[292] this duty would have been substantial.

The second category of low-ranking female workers is that of slave to various religious functionaries. Three tablets of the Ae subseries, a series which otherwise tallies low-status male personnel at Pylos, refer to low-ranking women outside of the workgroups referenced in the Aa, Ab, and Ad tablets. Unfortunately, two of these tablets are in poor condition, and the third tablet (PY Ae 303) breaks in mid-tally. On these tablets, women outside of the workgroup sets are tallied. The two most fragmentary of these tablets have preserved little more than the MUL ideogram and a number:

PY Ae 629
]-ti MUL 20[

PY Ae 634
]ọ o MUL 7 [

It is striking to note, that even on tablets this abbreviated, and belonging to a different series, that the women appear to be tallied in much the same way as the workgroup women: the women are attributed to someone or someplace else, they are unnamed, undifferentiated and counted in the same way, grouped together under the ideogram MUL with the tabulation following. On PY Ae 303, a tablet which is also discussed in Chapter 4, 14 women explicitly called slaves in the employ of a priestess are tallied:

PY Ae 303

.a i-je-ro-jo

.b pu-ro , i-je-re-ja , do-e-ra , e-ne-ka , ku-ru-so-jo MUL 14[

"At Pylos, 14+ female slaves of the priestess on account of the sacred gold"[293]

While this tablet presents a number of unusual features, particularly in reference to the e-ne-ka i-je-ro-jo ku-ru-so-jo ("on account of the sacred gold") and in the attribution of these women to a specific single individual – the priestess at Pylos in this case – again the similarities to the workgroup women are notable. In particular, this tablet resembles one of the Aa series: in both cases the women are treated as a collective unit, with no attention paid to distinguishing them in any way, they are presented by their occupational title (in this instance, do-e-ra), their location is noted, and they are tallied with the MUL ideogram and a number. Even the attribution of these slaves to a particular owner may not isolate these slave women from the workgroup women; if we accept the proposal that the women referred to as me-ki-to-ki-ri-ta, a-da-ra-te-ja, and we-we-si-je-ja are in fact women belonging to specific male officials whose labor is regulated by the palace, attribution of these slave women to another public official – the priestess – seems in many ways a parallel treatment of these two sets of women. In fact, the epigraphical similarities between these slave women and the workgroup women would appear to place them at a similar status level – as workers whose strength is monitored by the palace administration and who contribute to it either directly – as in the case of the workgroup women – or indirectly, by serving a public official whose activities in turn benefit the Pylian state.

Discussion of low-status female workers at Pylos:

The personnel series tablets from Pylos document the integration of low-status women's workgroups into a highly specialized economy. The economy into which these women are incorporated spans two provinces, 16 sites, and reveals a pattern of centralization around the two province capitals, the Palace site of Pylos itself for the Hither Province and Leuktron for the Further Province. Across the two provinces, the personnel series attests 42 different workgroup titles from which derive fifty distinct workgroups, which regulate the labor of 705 tallied women.[294] Adding in the cult staffers identified by MUL increases the total to 746 women. Of these 42 titles, 13 directly relate to textile production[295] for a total of 24 workgroups,[296] which account for at least 325 women.[297] (If we add in the collectors' workgroups, generally understood to also relate to textile production although this relationship is clearer at Knossos than Pylos, we should add at least 25 women to this category.) Food-production and attending or maintenance tasks occupy the women of three[298] task titles, translating to five workgroups of 83 adult women; another ten titles remain etymologically obscure (ten workgroups, 93 women). The final two categories of workgroup women (ethnic and untitled) seem likely to be textile workers, but due to the lack of more explicit evidence have not been factored in among the more securely identified textile producers. Eight distinct ethnic titles are in use in the Pylos A series. Seven are used singly (seven workgroups, 161 women), and six are used in combination with occupational titles (six workgroups, at least 40[299] women). Four groups of untitled workers are known (27 women).

Discussion of workgroups by location[300]

Production activities, however, are not the sole axis along which the workgroup women are organized. What would be the result if we analyze these workgroups not only by their production categories but also by site assignment? Is there a rationale behind the assignment of specific types of workers to individual sites? This section discusses the physical distribution of women's workgroups across the four zones of Pylos's economic geography: 1.) the Hither Province capital of Pylos, 2.) the remaining Hither Province villages, 3.) the Further Province capital of Leuktron, and 4.) the remaining Further Province villages.

Pylos

The main site of Pylos, containing the palace and its environs, houses the greatest number and variety of workgroups.[301] It is the only site to house textile workers, food preparation workers, maintenance workers, and ethnically homogeneous workgroups. In all, Pylos employs 27 distinct women's workgroups (excluding the two single-woman workgroups, both of which are also Pylos-based), under 25 titles totaling 421 adult women. Of these workgroups, at least 11[302] are devoted to textile production, which employs 182 women *in toto*. Five workgroups engage in single-task specialties: a-ra-ka-te-ja ("spinners"),[303] pe-ki-ti-ri-ja ("carders"), i-te-ja ("weavers"), ra-pi-ti-ra2 ("stitchers"), and a-ke-ti-ri-ja ("decorators"); three work in single fabrics only: ri-ne-ja ("linen-workers"), ri-ne-ja pa-ke-te-ja ("linen-measurers"), and o-nu-ke-ja ("workers who make specialty o-nu-ka cloth"). The two remaining titles have more obscure assignments within the field of textile production: the a-pu-wo-ko, thought to perhaps be "headband makers" and the ka-pa-ra-de whose tasks remain unknown. The overall image of textile production at Pylos is two-fold. On the one hand, the palace seems to employ a staff of standing assembly-line style piece-workers assigned to continuous labor on a specific stage of textile production; the finished products of such single-stage workers appear to be forwarded on to the workers specializing in the next stage of production (i.e., spinners to carders to weavers to stitchers to decorators). On the other hand, we see specialized workers who work in a single fabric medium. It is quite possible that the assembly-line workers are engaged in the production of the bulk of the palace's textile needs while the specialized workers may be engaged in producing textile for elite or luxury consumption. As the total rations for the textile workers at Pylos amount to approximately one-half that of the total grain compensation of Pylos's lone known male weaver (they receive 364 l. collectively, to his 760 l.), I find it unlikely that their lower level of production would constitute a large-scale, export-driven production mode rather than that their production is oriented toward filling the daily textile needs of the Pylian administration and its dependents.

In addition to its textile workgroups, Pylos also maintains a standing staff of domestic workers. Pylos houses a workgroup of women engaged in food-processing, the me-re-ti-ri-ja ("flour-grinders); as only a small number (six) of these women seem to have been employed, we might surmise that the palace required only a small number of women to fulfill its milling needs. Two additional workgroups of food-processors may also be active, should we accept Lindgren's etymology of ra-qi-ti-ra2 as "thresher-women"[304] and the identification of the si-to-ko-wo as women as correct. Pylos also employs workgroups assigned to attending and maintenance tasks and is the only location within the personnel series to do so. Two workgroups are known: the re-wo-to-ro-ko-wo occupied with the palace's water-supply (possible either as bath-workers or launderers), and the a-pi-qo-ro who function as the palace's attendant women. A third type of domestic worker may also have been present at the palace, if the proposed reading of o-ti-ri-ja as "movers" were to be accepted.

Pylos' janitorial staff well out-numbers its food workers – at least 70 workers are attested to in the two domestic worker groups whose tallies are preserved. I understand the large number of these workers present at the Pylos site to indicate that these workers constitute the daily maintenance staff required by an administrative building as complex as the Ano Englianos palace; conversely, the absence of attendant/janitorial workers at any of the remaining 15 sites underscores my theory that these are types of workers specific to the palace site and elite. As no other site maintains a large administrative complex, there would be no need for any of these workgroups elsewhere.

Pylos also stations the vast majority of the ethnically-identified workgroups, housing ten of the thirteen such workgroups in the personnel series, accounting for 70 percent of its total ethnic workers. Six of these workgroups are known from their ethnic alone, four others – the a-ra-[ka]-te-ja mi-ra-ti-ja, i-te-ja ti-nwa-ti-ja, ka-pa-ra2-de ku-te-ra, and o-nu-ke-ja ki-si-wi-ja – appear in conjunction with an occupational title. Combined, these workers constitute 157 of the total 421 women at Pylos, nearly 40 percent of its total workgroup population. The origins of these ethnic workers at Pylos seem distinctly Eastern Aegean in origin (Lydia, Miletos, Chios, Cnidos, and Lemnos), with two exceptions: ti-nwa-to, a territory paying tribute to Pylos, and Kythera, which perhaps we should associate as well with the Eastern Aegean as it would be a likely stop for any east-sailing military or mercantile expedition. As only two other "foreign" ethnics are attested in the personnel series, and as these two are assigned to separate sites (mi-ra-ti-ja to Lousos and ri-ne-ja a-*64-ja to Leuktron), it would seem that the level of concentration demonstrated at the palace site is disproportionate and likely to be significant. Why might this be? Two explanations seem possible: 1.) these workgroups are too new to have achieved a task assignment – a situation which seems hardly likely as many of these groups have sons who have reached adulthood, or 2.) the palace has made a deliberate choice not to disperse these workgroups randomly throughout the smaller village sites – possibly either for specific production or security purposes.

Returning to the larger production categories in place at Pylos, we should address the six additional workgroups reluctantly designated as "obscure." Without drawing too heavily on difficult and highly contested etymologies, the issue of the three interrelated workgroups e-ke-ro-qo-no, o-pi-ro-qo-no, and pa-wo-ke perhaps suggests another organizational factor unique to the Pylos site. The apparent interchangeability and generic task assignments for these workgroups would seem to imply that Pylos kept on hand not only workers with clear and stable task assignments, but also workers with more flexible occupational assignments. That these unassigned or floating workers receive the same subsistence rations as the other workgroup women should imply that these are permanent workers of the same status level as the rest of the workgroup women and that the palace compels not only specialized laborers but "floating" workers as well.

Finally, Pylos also provides rations for the two "workgroups" composed of one woman each. As these are rationed in identical proportions with the other workgroup women, their status should also be the same. As discussed previously, I prefer the theory that these women constitute the small staff of specific male officials ("collectors") who utilize their labor although in some way they still remain under the aegis of the palace administration from which they draw their rations. Staff under the aegis of a "collector" also seems to be the situation for the workgroup of women designated ka-ru-ti-je-ja.

The Hither Province

The seven remaining Hither Province villages demonstrate a fair amount of uniformity in their workgroup assignments. Two of the Hither Province villages each house two workgroups, 50 or more women at each site; the other five sites house a single group[305] consisting of fewer than ten workers.[306] The two dual-workgroup villages are Pylos ke-re-za and Lousos, both apparently secondary textile centers of the Hither Province. Pylos ke-re-za houses one collector's group (we-we-si-je-ja) of 22 and a second group (ra-wi-ja-ja) with 32 women. If we accept Chadwick's reading of this second group as "captives," then it is possible that Pylos ke-re-za functioned as a containment location for the women most recently acquired by the Pylian state.

Lousos also has two workgroups, 32 women belonging to the a-ke-ti-ri-ja ("decorators") workgroup which, after ri-ne-ja ("linen-workers"), is the second most widely dispersed occupational title in the Pylos tablets, appearing at three sites (Pylos, Lousos, and Leuktron). Lousos's second workgroup is the largest of the archives, the 54 women who compose the third known mi-ra-ti-ja workgroup; the other two mi-ra-ti-ja workgroups are Pylos based. If this ethnic workgroup is also engaged in textile production, Lousos would be second only to Pylos in the total number of textile workers, surpassing even the Further Province's capital site Leuktron.[307] The remaining five villages each host a single workgroup, workgroups named by a textile production title at e-u-de-we-ro, the etymologically obscure to-sa-me-ja workgroup at o-wi-to-no and the untitled workgroups of me-ta-pa, ne-wo-pe-o, and pi-we-re. Based on analogy with the single-workgroup sites of the Further Province, it seems reasonable to understand these village workgroups also as textile workers; no lone workgroup is attested to at any site engaged in any task other than textile production, that is, no single workgroup of food-processors, janitorial staffers, or ethnic workers is attested to at any location in either province. At any rate, it would appear that the palace had a significant vested interest in the labor of the Hither Province workgroups as these detailed tally and rations records were stored in the palace itself.

Leuktron and the Further Province

The Further Province demonstrates the same capital-centered modality as the Hither Province, with fully half of its 14 workgroups clustered at Leuktron. These 14 workgroups occupy 83 of the Province's 116 workers (72 percent of the province's attested workgroup women).[308] As at the larger capital site of Pylos, Leuktron has the widest distribution of workers of its province, with textile workers, millers, and ethnic workers represented. Three types of textile workers are present: spinners, linen-workers of the ethnic title a-*64-ja, and decorators. Through these three groups of textile workers, Leuktron may well have been self-sufficient in its textile needs, as these groups are devoted to the initial, intermediate, and ending stages of textile manufacturing. In terms of domestic laborers, Leuktron houses a workgroup of seven grain millers (me-re-ti-ri-ja), a group which is actually larger than its Pylian counterpart. Unlike Pylos, Leuktron houses no janitorial or maintenance workers, nor does the remainder of the Further Province. Leuktron also stations a single ethnically homogeneous workgroup of ethnic workers, in this instance a workgroup of women (e-wi-ri-pi-ja) bearing an ethnic title derived from a Hither Province town who have been transferred to the Further Province capital, the only known such transfer. (Two obscure workgroups – ki-ma-ra and no-ri-wo-mo – are also attested at Leuktron with a combined eleven women belonging to these two groups.)

Outside of Leuktron, seven Further Province sites house a single workgroup each which range in size from four to fourteen workers among the four workgroups whose full tallies are preserved. All of these workgroups work in the manufacture of textiles. Five sites record workgroups of ri-ne-ja workers; at the site of Pylos Lauranthias the ri-ne-ja workgroups also bear the otherwise unattested ethnic ze-pu-ra2. The seventh village workgroup holds a more specific textile title, the cloth-derived term te-pe-ja. No other workgroup type is attested to in the Further Province villages; it would appear that textile workgroups are the *sine qua non* of the smaller villages.[309] Are these textile workgroups sustaining their villages or are their products being transferred to the larger sites? It would appear that the palace itself had a distinct interest in the activities of these workers as it maintained tallies of these workgroups' workers and adult sons on a sealing stored at the palace. This interest, however, appears somewhat diminished in comparison to the Hither Province, as nothing indicates the palace kept the same detailed rationing records for these groups. The actual distribution of rations for these workers seems to have taken place locally within the Further Province as Pylos only maintained a record of the total rations provided to all of the workgroups rather than records detailing the rationing of each group.

Therefore, if we conceptualize the economic geography of the workgroup women as encompassing four zones (the Hither Province capital of Pylos, the remaining Hither Province villages, the Further Province Capital of Leuktron, and the remaining Further Province villages), several clear patterns emerge: 1.) the women of the workgroups are concentrated at the provincial capitals, especially at Pylos, 2.) the capital sites are the only locations where all three categories of workers (textile, domestic, and ethnic) are located, 3.) the secondary sites of both provinces house much smaller numbers of workgroups and workers than might proportionately be expected – typically only a single workgroup; 4.) the overall rationale for the distribution of workgroups in the Pylian state seems to follow set rules: a.) all sites require a standing textile-producing labor force, despite the size or location of the site, most frequently devoted to linen production; b.) capital sites alone may acquire a small group of millers, presumably to provide the ground grain required to support the local administration and their subordinates; c.) janitorial and maintenance workers are limited to the main palace site itself and most likely function as the domestic labor force for the palace complex; d.) homogeneously ethnic workgroups may follow one of two patterns: optimally, they are to be concentrated at the major sites or, if circumstances necessitate they be placed outside the palace region; no more than one ethnic workgroup can be assigned to any site. Additionally, no homogeneously ethnic workgroup originating within the sway of the Pylian state may remain at its initial site of origin. Possible explanations for these rationales are addressed below.

Status of the workgroup women

The observations and theories above all bear upon the central issue of the relationship between the women of the workgroups and the administration that monitors them. What precisely is the relationship of these women to the central administration? That these nameless women are assigned to labor intensive, repetitive, and time-consuming tasks reinforces their low rank in Pylian society. That the palace provides them with subsistence rations indicates that they are reliant upon the palace in some way but the nature of that reliance remains a subject of considerable controversy. Three competing explanations have been offered:[310] 1.) The workgroup women are independent contractors who have set up shop at Pylos and the foodstuffs allotted to them constitute payment for their labor. 2.) These women labor under a corvée system and are compensated with food rations for the weeks/months in which they work for the palace. 3.) These women are slaves of the palace, possibly acquired either by purchase or captured in military raids in the Eastern Aegean. This section addresses the strengths and weaknesses of these three theories.

The independent contractor model[311]

Tritsch[312] proposed that all the workgroup women be understood as skilled craftswomen who have settled in the region of Pylos for economic benefit. Under this model, rations constitute payment in kind for these workers. This model could explain why we see both local and foreign ethnics used to describe workgroup women in that it allows for skilled workers from any region to travel to and settle at a palace. This reading, however, does not adequately explain other problematic evidence.

First, this explanation does not explain why workers sufficiently skilled to hire themselves out to the highest bidders would then work for only subsistence rations of figs and wheat, while other skilled workers in the archives are compensated with more valuable commodities and goods. Second, it does not account for why the palace keeps account of missing workers or why it allocates to itself the right to assign the adult sons of these women to particular tasks; one would expect that free contractors – and their children – would choose their own professions. Third, it does not offer any explanation for the large population of Eastern Aegean workers working alongside presumably local Pylian village women; contrast this situation to Knossos, all of whose "ethnic" workers are local to Crete. Fourth, this reading does not provide adequate explanation for the workgroups only identified by village names; if the palaces are so interested in hiring specialized workers, why is so little attention paid to identifying the presumably skilled-labor category of the women of the smaller Hither and Further Province village workgroups? And, finally, and perhaps most damningly, this interpretation provides no explanation for the absence of adult countrymen accompanying the many groups of women and children from both Pylos and the Eastern Aegean, an absence underscored by the necessity for the group "marriages" of the Ti-nwa-sian women and local Pylian men on PY Ad 684. This lack of adult male companions is especially glaring, if we remember how crisis-laden the Aegean was at the end of the LH IIIB period – a moment when so many coastal cities and islands are sufficiently worried about safety and security as to, for example, enlarge their walls and secure their water supplies. It is hard to picture how so many women would be willingly traveling with their children and without male relatives at so precarious a moment. We should abandon this model on two grounds: these women were almost certainly not willing travelers, and highly sought after and specialized contractors should receive more than subsistence rations for their wages.

The corvée labor model

Uchitel, in comparing Aegean workgroup women with Near Eastern workgroup women, proposed that the well-attested corvée system of the Near Eastern palaces might be the same system in place at the Aegean palaces.[313] Under this system, men and women provide infrastructure labor to the palaces for several weeks/months each year, and in turn, are provided with subsistence rations for that time period. This interpretation accounts well for the rations provided to the workgroup women and also to the palace's prerogative in assigning tasks for their adult sons – presumably it would have corvée requirements for both the women and men of its state. It also explains the incorporation of women from the Hither and Further Provinces as members of the Pylian workforce.

This interpretation, however, has three major weaknesses. It does not explain why the palace assigns tasks to the adult sons of the workgroup women and not their husbands or other male relations as well. This exemption is difficult to reconcile with the thoroughness of the palace in co-opting the labor of the workgroup women and their sons. The second objection pertains to the preponderance of foreign ethnics in the personnel series. Why are there more foreign women among the workforce than there are women from local outlying villages? One would presume that Pylian-born women would greatly outnumber any population of recent immigrants. Similarly, how would the palace acquire the right or ability to demand labor from foreign women? Finally, if the labor system was corvée, why does the palace not allow women to engage in their work at their village of origin? Why are the workgroups bearing the two ethnic terms from within the purview of Pylos each put to work in a different locale rather than performing their assignments within their place of origin as is the more common practice for textile corvée practices in the Near East?

The slavery model

The third interpretation posits that all the women of the workgroups are direct palace dependents, "servants" if not actual slaves.[314] This argument has evolved over time; initially this proposal was based on the title of one of the workgroups – the women belonging to the aggregate workgroup entitled ra-wi-ja-ja – in an attempt to derive *lawiaiai* from the Homeric term ληιάδες "captive women." Chadwick in particular promoted this argument, citing also the several Eastern Aegean ethnic adjectives to identify them as slave women who were prizes of war, and consequently the presence of this term was regarded as dispositive, thus securing the servile status of the women. I would contend, however, that we have better reasons – grounded in the tablets – to accept the slave theory:

1. The low social standing of the women of the workgroups is apparent from their low-paid, repetitive, labor-intensive work and their treatment as an undifferentiated mass; understanding their low social standing to be that of slaves provides an explanation why the palace provides only subsistence rations for these women, transfers them to secondary – that is non-native – locations for their work, and monitors and assigns the labor of their children. Regarding them as slaves also helps explain the analogous treatments in the recording of the slave women of the Ae series and the workgroup women – as workers tallied only according to their labor, as nameless and colorless representations of the MUL ideogram.

2. The presence of the ethnic-titled workgroups has often been cited by those in favor of the slave interpretation, with the argument that enslavement would be the most likely mechanism by which Pylos would have large numbers of Eastern Aegean women and children among its dependent labor force, in particular

women unaccompanied by any adult male kinsmen.[315] Two mechanisms for how these women and children would have come to be acquired as slaves at Pylos have been offered: the first following a Homeric model that these women and children would have been acquired through war or raiding with their male kin put to the sword upon the capture of their home villages, and the second, somewhat less dramatic, reading which proposes that these women and children were slaves purchased in an Eastern Aegean slave trading center. I am not sure we need to exclude or adhere to either possibility beyond that the palace at Pylos was able to acquire – through trade or direct action – a large contingent of slave women from the islands and Western Asia Minor. This explanation squares with the preponderance of ethnic adjectives derived from the names of Eastern Aegean islands and coastal cities (or islands passed en route to the east like Kythera). This reading also provides an explanation for women who remain "unassigned" yet rationed, as only fully dependent people would still be rationed while assigned to no set task.[316] It also explains why these women continue to be described as foreigners rather than as assimilated residents even though sufficient time seems to have elapsed for several of their sons to reach their maturity.[317]

Those are the standard arguments in favor of the slavery hypothesis. I would add two more to them:

3. The geographical locations of the workgroups also seem to support the enslavement hypothesis.[318] Of all the workgroups at Pylos, 28 are concentrated at the center of Pylos itself (including nine of the groups with Eastern Aegean titles). In contrast, the remaining nine sites where workgroups are stationed share between them only 15 groups; furthermore, only two ethnic-titled workgroups are based outside of Pylos proper – one at the site of Lousos and the other at the corollary site of Pylos Lauranthias. Leuktron, the capital site of the Further Province, has four workgroups, Lousos and Metapa,[319] both in the Hither Province, each have two workgroups, as does the site of Pylos Kereza. The final four sites where workgroups are located (Ko-ri-to, Ne-wo-pe-o, O-wi-to-no, and Pi-we-re) have only a single workgroup each. We do not know the rationale by which these groups were assigned to a specific area. While it is possible that groups were assigned to specific regions only on basis of labor necessities, these choices could also be viewed as strategic, especially since the workers assigned to these smaller sites seem to be performing the same tasks. If controlling the population of workgroup women and children was one of the goals of their site assignments, these choices make considerable sense. Nearly two-thirds of the workgroups are based in the largest population center – the site most able to absorb and control a large number of dependents, that is, the palace site at Pylos. The palace site also accounts for all but two of the foreign (ethnic) workgroups. Furthermore, the site which absorbs the second largest number of workgroups – the Further Province's capital Leuktron – is the second most populated and regulated site, and it is only required to maintain four workgroups. It is interesting that Leuktron also houses one of the two remaining ethnic workgroups. Furthermore, if we read these women as not just dependents but slaves,[320] these choices make even greater

sense as they would seem to allow the palace and outlying villages to maximize their control over these workers.

4. Finally, to my mind the most compelling reason to regard these women as slaves arises from the identical treatment received by all the workgroup women. From the palace perspective, we should understand all the workgroup women to be considered indivisible in status; all personnel series women are assigned, monitored and rationed in the same way – and all women see their children co-opted into palace-directed labor as well. Thus, I would argue if we can ascertain the servile, servant or free status of some of the workgroup women we can extrapolate from them to ascertain the status of all. I contend that it is the task assignments themselves that should establish the servile status of the women. While textile workers might presumably be co-opted for short-term work assignments (with set production goals and/or time limits – none of which appear in the Pylos tablets), it is extremely difficult to view the palace's millers and attendant staff under the same rubric. As personnel attendance, water tending, and palace maintenance are for all purposes perpetual and "uncompletable" labor, surely we should understand these workers as operating under perpetual servitude. As the remaining workgroup laborers appear indivisible from the palace laborers, I argue we should extrapolate the same status for them. Location, rations, control of children and task assignments to my mind constitute a preponderance of evidence – and thus we should regard the largest subset of visible women in the Pylos tablets as slave labor.

And so, returning to the "captives" interpretation of ra-wi-ja-ja, this reading would serve to *further* strengthen the slave identification. "Captive/booty" women would then not be the only slave women in the Pylian workforce, but would be the ones most recently acquired and not yet assigned. Maintaining this group at Pylos ke-re-za rather than at the palace site might be a result of a desire on the part of state elites to isolate this group from the majority of servile women as part of the acculturation/enslavement process. One remains to wonder if this may not have been the same mechanism used to acquire the other workgroups, particularly those bearing Eastern Aegean ethnics.

Postscript on women's labor at Pylos

So having established that the largest documented group of women in the Pylian Linear B corpus should most reasonably be considered to be slaves, we must also note the virtual absence of non-servile women in the documented labor force at the site. We have no references to the labor of low-ranking women who are not direct palace dependents. Where are the wives and daughters of the farmers, shepherds, and craftsmen of the tablets? Why are they – who presumably also spend their lives in production and labor activities – not visible in the records? Perhaps the best answer is that they are not visible under their own names and via their individual activities. While arguments from silence are always problematic, the model of the historical Greek poleis like Athens is appealing – whereby women within the *oikos*/family structure often did not have an independent economic identity of their own and were subsumed under the auspices of their male guardians and/or relatives. Perhaps then the silence on the labor of non-workgroup women is because such women do not occupy an independent economic status and therefore could not conduct transactions with the palace as individual, autonomous actors, and as such would not attract the attentions of the palace scribes as their labor and sustenance did not fall under the direct control of the palaces. Only the labor of women outside the *oikos* structure at Pylos comes to be documented in the tablets, causing the most socially marginal of the working women to become the most visible of all women to the textual record.

Notes

1 Important recent overviews on the workings of Mycenaean palace economies include Shelmerdine and Bennet 2008; J. Bennet 2007; and Shelmerdine 2006.
2 On the specialization of Linear B labor terms, see Morpurgo Davies 1979: 87–109.
3 Only two social status institutions/markers seem to be able to outweigh gender: cult officialdom and enslavement. The two occupational titles "stitcher" and "weaver," as shown on pp. 76–69 (weavers) and pp. 83–84 (stitchers) function very differently when applied to men and women.
4 Important works on men's economic activities in the tablets include: Bennet 1988b: 19–42; Carlier 1995, 1987; Gillis 1997; Hiller 1988; Hooker 1987b; Killen 1985; Kopaka 1997; Laffineur 1995: Vol. I, 189–200; Lindgren 1979; Morpurgo Davies 1979; Nordquist 1995; Rehak 1995b; Thomas 1995; Wright 1995.
5 Nakassis warns that this palace representation might not adequately account for activities taking place outside of full palace control or may imply a more rigid and static hierarchy among officials with more-overlapping concerns: Nakassis 2013: 15–19. While this remains an important caveat in using the Linear B evidence, I would contend that we can still extract from the tablets, a sense of how the palatial elite defined their understanding of power and status relationships within the Mycenaean states, and that is what we may recover here.
6 Nakassis 2013: 5–14 for a useful survey of elite male officials in the Linear B documents.
7 For an overview of the relationship of elite male officials, see Shelmerdine and Bennet 2008: 290–303; Bennet 1985: 231–48; Hooker 1987b: 258–267; Morpurgo-Davies 1979: 98–99; Palaima 1995b; for a discussion of Mycenaean social hierarchies visible via burial and mortuary customs: Voutsaki 1995: 55–63. But also note Nakassis 2013: 14–19, on the dangers of attributing strictly defined, rather than overlapping, relationships among officials recorded in the tablets.
8 Morpurgo-Davies 1979: 104. cf. Lindgren 1979: 81–86.
9 Iconography is of little assistance in this task as Aegean art lacks visual representations of a recognizable ruler. E. Davis 1995: 11–19.
10 Lindgren 1973: Part II, 150–155.
11 Hooker 1987b: 258; Lindgren 1973: Part II, 150; Palaima 1997: 406–412, 1995b: 119–139; Webster 1960: 11; Morpurgo Davies 1979: 96.
12 Much discussion has been focused on the subject of Aegean kingship and the particular function the wanax played; in particular, see Rehak 1995; Palaima 1995b. Interpretations of the term wa-na-ka ((ἄναξ "lord") range from interpretations that identify the wanax as a human king [Baumbach 1979: 143–160; Ventris and Chadwick 1973: 120; Ruijgh 1967: 381; Gérard-Rousseau 1968: 232–23; Hiller and Panagl 1976: 280; Lejeune 1958: 313; Lindgren 1973: Part II, 150–155; Olivier 1959: 179; Shelmerdine 1985: 77; Sutton 1970: 214. Interpretations reading wanax as

"king with priestly functions": Palaima 1995b: 119–139, 1997: 407–12; G. Thomas 1976: 93–116. Others read wanax as an important figure in the palatial administration but shy from identifications with kingship: Hooker 1987b: 259, and Morris's well-reasoned discussion which argues for the strong association of the wanax as a figure with primarily cultic functions: Morris 2004: 1–24. Less accepted readings have tried to locate the wanax in the divine sphere as a divine "lord" (either consistently throughout the texts or to refer to human lords in some contexts and divine ones in others): Chadwick 1985: 197; van Leuven 1979: 113; Webster 1960: 11. *Diccionario* also favors this reading and further suggests that the divinity so designated may refer to Poseidon; *Diccionario*: Vol. II, 400–401.

13 As he writes, "the wanax is the central figure of authority in Mycenaean society. This much is clear from: a. studies of the references to wanax in the Linear B tablets; b. interpretation of the history of the use of the term wanax in Homer and later Greek; c. reconstruction of the development of the institution of kingship from the end of the Bronze Age through the Archaic to Hellenistic period. The wanax has substantial holdings among which are the largest and most exclusive land holdings – the enormous *temene* which are held by only two other elite officials; wa-na-ka also is attested as the possessor of a number of highly specialized craftsmen who deal in luxury goods. In addition to his civic responsibilities and holdings, the position of wa-na-ka also appears to entail a religious component, as he appears in several texts which have strongly religious character; he appears as both the donor and recipient of offerings." Palaima 1995b: 122–23. This article is the most succinct discussion of the linguistic and textual evidence pertaining to the wanax to date. On the wanax and his staff, see also: Palaima 1997.

14 Two words have periodically been propounded as possibly indicating a queen in the Linear B texts: wa-na-sa and po-ti-ni-ja. Wa-na-sa, per se, is not attested in the tablets, but some had suggested that the adjective wa-na-se-wi-ja should be understood to mean "of or for the Queen." Ventris and Chadwick 1973: 335; cf. Lindgren 1973: Part II, 155. More recently, wa-na-sa and wa-na-se-wi-ja have been rightly dissociated from associations with any sort of queen figure; the interpretation of po-ti-ni-ja as indicating a queen remains disputed, despite the Aegaeum conference dedicated to this very question: Laffineur and Hägg 2001.

15 For additional bibliography and discussion of the ra-wa-ke-ta, see *Diccionario*: Vol. II, 230–231, and Lindgren 1973: Part II, 133–35.

16 Palaima 1995b: 129. Cf. Driessen 1985: 169–93; and Lindgren 1973: Part II, 134–36.

17 Adrados 1968: 559–573; *Docs2*: 579; Heubeck 1969: 535–544. For the relationship between military association and rank in palatial society, see Palaima 1999: 367–375 and Driessen and Schoep 1999: 389–401.

18 Nikoloudis 2008a, 2008b, 2012.

19 Lindgren 1973: Part II, 135.

20 Lindgren 1973: Part II, 135.

21 "...the wanax and the lawagetas seem to have clearly distinguished spheres of influence, responsibility and prestige," with the wanax deriving his status from religious associations and the lawagetas from military ones. Palaima 1995b: 129.

22 Palaima 1995b: 124. Cf. *Diccionario*: 189–191; Lindgren 1973: Part II, 126–130. Morpurgo Davies has offered a convincing argument for the evolution of the Mycenaean sense of qa-si-re-u (basileus) from "local chieftain" to the Classical "king," arguing that the term originally recalled a local official under the command of the wanax and palace, which, following the collapse of the palaces and all central authorities, became the local term for the most powerful official and gradually intensified its meaning over time. Morpurgo Davies 1979: 98–99.

23 Palaima translates the ko-re-te and po-ro-ko-re-te as "… 'mayors' and 'vice-mayors' whose local duties, especially in connection with the major second-order centers within the palatial regional administration of Bronze Age Messenia, are clearly and

systematically registered in the texts (e.g., PY Jn 829). It is attractive to posit that these officials are directly responsible to the central palace – and appointed, controlled, rewarded and sustained by it." Palaima 1995b: 124.

24 Additional terms which have been identified as referring to the administrative elite include: da-mo-ko-ro, a-to-mo, du-ma, and mo-ro-qa; terms with less certain identifications include: ke-re-mo, e-re-u-te-re, i-je-ro-wo-ko, o-pi-ka-pe-e-we, o-pi-ko-wo, o-pi-su-ko, pa-da-je-u, pa-de-we-u; u-wo-qe-ne, u-wo-qe-we. Morpurgo Davies 1979: 98–99.

25 Nakassis 2013 suggests an alternate division of the Mycenaean social hierarchy: the palatial elite, the regional elite, and the lower classes, Nakassis 2013: 15. Our groupings overlap on the elite category, whereas I would assign the middle category to non-dependent craftspeople, moving much of his middle category to the elite ranks; he would include non-dependent craftpersons among the lower classes, while I reserve the lowest rank only for palace dependents and their children.

26 For additional studies on "middle-status men" see: Bloedow 1997: 438–447; Costin 1991: 1–56; Gillis 1997: 505, n. 3; Palaima 1999: 367–375. See also Nosch 1997 for a careful and well-reasoned discussion of the differences between the remuneration of male and female artisans.

27 On the mid-ranked status of "divine slaves," see Hiller 1989: 40–65.

28 Lindgren 1979: 82.

29 For a source discussion and bibliography on bronze-smiths: see Gillis 1995.

30 Nosch 1997: 397–405.

31 The hierarchies among religious functionaries are the major exception to this rule.

32 Palaima 1997, 1995b.

33 Gillis 1995: 505–513.

34 For bibliography on the men known as "collectors": John Bennet 1992: 65–101; Driessen 1992: 197–214; Killen 1995; Olivier 2001.

35 I distinguish between the terms "slave of the god" (te-o-jo do-e-ro/ra) and "ordinary" slaves (do-e-ro/do-e-ra) as the former title refers to individuals of higher status who have a clear religious affiliation and who are allotted land leases. "Ordinary" slaves appear as the dependents of specific individuals or the state, and appear to have no property holdings or legal standings of their own.

36 Cf. Hiller 1988: 53–68.

37 The men assigned to the ke-ro-si-ja on PY An 261 and PY An 616 are the exception as they are listed only as a group on 616 but are differentiated by name on 261.

38 Hocker and Palaima 1993: 297–317; Palaima 1999, 1991. For other men conscripted into military service, see Ventris and Chadwick 1973: 188–193; Dickinson 1999: 21–25; Driessen and MacDonald 1984: 49–74.

39 KN Ai 1037.

40 For example, the adult sons of the workgroup women recorded in the PY Ad series.

41 Barber 1994, 1991. Burke (1997: 412) also argues that the Bronze Age textile industry was particularly suited to palace control. Much work has been done on textile organization in the tablets, most notably by Killen: Killen 1995, 1988, 1984, 1979, 1974, 1966.

42 See Chapter 1 for discussion.

43 Billigmeier and Turner 1981.

44 Women's property holdings at Pylos are the subject of Chapter 4.

45 Billigmeier and Turner estimate the number of these women at over 1400, following Tritsch, but their number in actuality includes both women and their children, not women alone: Billigmeier and Turner 1981:3; Tritsch 1958: 402–445. Nosch 2003 and Chadwick 1988 are more in line with the 750 tally.

46 Major works on the women of the personnel series include Carlier 1983; Chadwick 1988; Lindgren 1973. These three works lay much of the foundation for studies of women in the personnel series; all three provide careful, thoroughly documented

analyses of the textual evidence pertaining to these workers. Other valuable treatments of this series include: E.L. Bennett 1956b; Billigmeier and Turner 1981; Chadwick 1976: 79–83; Hooker 1980: 101–106; L. Palmer 1963: 113–124; Palaima 1984; Tritsch 1958; Uchitel 1984.

47 Chadwick 1988: 62.

48 Carlier 1983: 18. See also Uchitel 1984: 257–258.

49 For discussion of composition and features of the Major and Minor Aa sets, see Chadwick 1988: 62–63.

50 Carlier 1983: 14–15.

51 Comparison of the ration tablets from both Pylos and Knossos would indicate that male and female palatial dependents receive roughly the same caloric rations in both systems. Chadwick 1979: 21–33.

52 For the Mycenaean measuring system pertaining to dry measures, the following equivalences are accepted: 1 (full) unit GRA = 10 T = 60 V = 240 Z. Following their translations into modern measures, we arrive at 1 GRA = 96 l., 1 T = 9.6 l., 1 V = 1.6l., and 1 Z = .4 l. R. Palmer 1989.

53 Chadwick 1988: 62–63. The reasons for the recording of more than one Ab tablet for an Aa series text are not clear.

54 Palaima 2011a; 2003: 153–194 figs. 8.1–8.9, 161 fig. 8.5, and 178–180.

55 L. Palmer 1963: 113.

56 Killen 1988: 170.

57 These are not the same sons referred to in the Aa and Ab series; the Aa and Ab boys are underage while the Ad tablets record post-pubescent adolescent and adult sons.

58 Carlier 1983: 19.

59 Chadwick 1988: 63.

60 Chadwick 1988: 64.

61 Chadwick 1988: 67.

62 A third variable also exists: state of preservation. I have also omitted from this discussion those A-series texts which are too fragmentary to recover any mention of a specific workgroup: Aa 759; Aa 860; Aa 863; Aa 987; Aa 1178; Ab 468; Ab 559; Ab 581; Ab 582; Ab 584; Ab 585; Ab 946; Ab 978; Ab 1102; Ab 1103; Ab 1109; Ab 1112; Ab 1113; Ab 1115; Ad 681; Ad 700; and Ad 1450.

63 Chadwick identifies 49 separate workgroups; I count 51, dissociating Chadwick's long me-ta-pa and e-ke-ro-qo-no workgroups each into two smaller ones for the reasons addressed on pp. 92–93. Chadwick 1988: 49–60. Each of the workgroups I mention is footnoted with its corresponding number in Chadwick's identification scheme.

64 This number excludes ethnic titles and workgroups identified by location alone as well as the title si-to-ko-wo which seems likely to refer to women but which cannot yet be verified.

65 Important works on textile organization within the Linear B tablets include: Burke 1998, 1997; Nosch 2003, 1997; Hooker 1980: 83–100; Killen 1984; Lindgren 1973; Melena 1975; Morpurgo Davies 1979: 98–99.

66 To the list of textile-related workers, Morpurgo Davies (1979: 100) tentatively added de-ku-tu-wo-ko, following Chadwick's proposed "net-makers." I have omitted this term as I find neither its context nor proposed etymologies sufficiently convincing to identify it as an occupational title assigned specifically to women.

67 πέκω has Homeric attestations: (Cf. *Od.* xviii, 316). Ventris and Chadwick 1973: 570.

68 Chadwick 1988: 82, following Killen 1974. This reading for pe-ki-ti-ra2 as "carders" is widely accepted, cf. Ventris and Chadwick 1973: 570; Killen 1984: 58; Lindgren 1973: Part II, 114–15; *Diccionario:* Vol. II, 97. (As Billigmeier and Turner 1981 closely follow the Ventris and Chadwick 1973: glossary, their interpretations of the various terms are not separately cited here.)

69 Chadwick labels this workgroup Group 21 of the "Major Aa" set: Chadwick 1988: 53–54.

70 Further bibliographic studies on Children in Ancient Aegean: General Studies: Gates 1992: 161–171; Rutter 2003. For age grades: E. Davis 1986: 399–406; Koehl 1986; Withee 1992. For children in the palatial workforce: Chadwick 1988: 43–95; Killen 1981: 37–45; Olsen 1998.

71 But see R. Palmer who argues for an identification of wheat with the HORD ideogram and barley for the GRANUM ideogram: R. Palmer 1992: 475–497. For convention, I use the GRA = wheat identification.

72 Supra, fn. 52.

73 Chadwick 1988: 67.

74 L. Palmer 1963: 116.

75 Killen 1983b: 121–126.

76 Carlier 1983: 28–29; Chadwick 1988: 67–70.

77 It would seem that the ko-wo of the Ad tablets and the ko-wo of the Aa/Ab tablets are not the same boys, rather that the boys of the Aa/Ab series are of a younger age-grade than the Ad boys who are deemed old enough to be reassigned by the palace to tasks other than those performed by their mothers.

78 For the conscription of men into the Pylian army and navy, see Palaima 1999, 1991.

79 Chadwick justifies the identification of a-ra-ka-te-ja as a textile-related occupation on two grounds. First he notes that this title also appears in the context of textiles and textile production at both Knossos (Ak 5009, Lc 531) and at Thebes (Of 34.2), and second on etymological grounds as the term is "certainly to be reconstructed as *alakateiai* cf. ἠλακάτη 'distaff', which would imply spinning…" Chadwick 1988: 79. This interpretation of "spinning-women" is shared by Ventris and Chadwick 1973: 533; Chadwick and Baumbach 1973: 200; Killen 1984: 58; Lindgren 1973: Part II, 23–24; *Diccionario*: Vol. 1, 93–94. See *Diccionario* for additional texts following this reading. L. Palmer's (1963: 114) early suggestion of a-ra-ka-te-ja as an ethnicon has largely been dismissed on etymological grounds as the e-ja endings do not appear to have been used as ethnics, cf. Lindgren 1973: Part II, 24.

80 Chadwick 1988: 79.

81 The workgroups belonging to specific locations are enumerated in Table 3.1.

82 This workgroup corresponds to Chadwick's Group 5: Chadwick 1988: 49.

83 It is possible that the fragmentary tablet Ab 581 which lists a ration amount of 6 full units and 1 T of wheat and figs might correspond to this a-ra-ka-te-ja workgroup as it is the only Ab tablet which implies a ration amount sufficiently large enough to supply this group. Chadwick notes that if this were to be the case, the workgroup would have had to have been reduced in size as compared to the Aa tablet: Chadwick 1988: 49.

84 This translation is from Ventris and Chadwick 1973: 158.

85 Chadwick includes Ad 380 with his Group 15: Chadwick 1988: 52. I find the attribution of this tablet to this workgroup cluster as less secure than his other a-ra-ka-te-ja tablet assignments. The other tablets he places in his Group 15 list only the ethnic adjective mi-ra-ti-ja; neither a-ra-ka-te-ja nor any other task-derived title is present.

86 Two additional workgroups of mi-ra-ti-ja women are known (see Table 3.1); in both these groups no task-title appears in conjunction with the ethnic. However, as both of these workgroups have an extant Ad series tablet, it does not appear possible to link either of those workgroups with this mi-ra-ti-ja a-ra-ka-te-ja.

87 Later, Μιλήσιοι: Ventris and Chadwick 1973: 561.

88 Billigmeier and Turner 1981: 5; Lindgren 1973: Part II, 92.

89 Chadwick 1988: 58.

90 The identification of i-te-ja as **isteia* (with its genitive plural i-te-ja-o * ἱστειάων) as deriving from *istos* ἵστος "loom" has been unanimously accepted by Mycenaean scholarship; see *Diccionario:* Vol. I, 288–289 for a full list of citations. Lindgren expands on the traditional reading of "weaver", adding "loom-women" and "loom-workers" as possible clarifications of this term. Lindgren 1973: Part II, 58.

91 Chadwick labels this workgroup Group 27. Chadwick 1988: 55.

92 Ventris and Chadwick 1973: 161.
93 See PY Fn 324, PY Jo 438 and PY Xa 633 for additional mentions of ti-nwa-to.
94 Chadwick 1988: 83–84. Chadwick also allows for the possibility that ti-nwa-to may have been an overseas possession of the Pylian state, proposing Zakynthos and Kythera as the only nearby islands which could conceivably have been capable of contributing a sufficiently high measure of gold. Heubeck offers another possibility: that if ti-nwa-si-ja normalized instead as *Thinwasiai* using the suffix **wat* from a name **Thinwon(t)s* 'sandy" (which may survive in the term Στενύκλαρος, the name of the upper Messenian plain bordering on Arcadia) and if the name refers to a mountain pass, "perhaps it was in Mycenaean times applied to the hill country immediately to the north of the Messenian valley." Heubeck 1976: 130.
95 The other local ethnic is e-wi-ri-pi-ja.
96 Chadwick 1988: 67–68.
97 L. Palmer 1963: 116.
98 Chadwick 1988: 67.
99 Carlier 1983: 15.
100 Ventris and Chadwick 1973: 161.
101 The four remaining joint titles are "slave/servant," "slave/servant of the god," "priest/priestess," and the other production-related term ra-pte/ra-pi-ti-ri-ja "stitcher."
102 Ventris and Chadwick 1973: 506. Again we see unanimous agreement on the interpretation of this term. *Diccionario*: Vol. I, 289.
103 The term we-a2-no appears in the dative plural we-a2-no-i on PY Fr 1225 and is the apparent precursor of the Homeric ἔανος (*Il. xxi*, 507): Ventris and Chadwick 1973: 590. re-po-to is transparent as *lepton* λεπτόν "fine, thin": *Diccionario:* Vol. II, 240–41; Ventris and Chadwick 1973: 579.
104 While the textile industry of Knossos seems to be primarily wool based, the textile industry of Pylos seems to prefer flax as the material basis for textiles. Killen 1984, 1979, 1964.
105 There is full consensus on the identification of this term as *λίνειαι "linen-workers" and/or "flax-workers." Ventris and Chadwick 1973: 580; Lindgren 1973: Part II, 138; *Diccionario*: Vol. II, 255.
106 Ruijgh 1967: 214, n. 83.
107 Killen also prefers "linen-workers" to "flax-workers". Killen 1984: 58.
108 Chadwick's Group 38 of the Minor (Further Province) Aa set. Chadwick 1988: 8.
109 PY Ad 326
re-u-ko-to-ro ri-ne-ja-o a-*64-ja-o ko-wo VIR 3 ko-wo 9
"At Leuktron, sons of the Aswian linen-workers: 3 men, 9 boys.)
110 The sign*64 is frequently interpreted as **swi*, but as full consensus has not been reached, I follow the convention of identifying the sign by its originally assigned number.
111 As a further province tablet, no Ab rations tablet would have been recorded.
112 PY Ad 664
pu-ro ra-u-ra-ti-jo ze-pu2-ra-o ko-wo ri-ne-ja-o VIR 4 ko-wo 3
"At Lauranthias, Pylos, sons of the Zephyrian (Halicarnassian?) linen-workers: 4 men, 3 boys"
113 Chadwick 1988: 84: "Place names such as Ζεφύριον and Ζεφύριον are recorded in many parts of the Aegean. But in view of the other links in this series with the eastern Aegean, their connexion with Halikarnassos (Strabo 14.16 (656); Steph. Byz. s.v.) may be significant, since a Mycenaean settlement is known to have existed in the area." See also Heubeck 1985: 123–138, 135. Uchitel (1984: 258) proposes an alternative reading of ze-pu2-ra-o as the genitive of a man's name ze-pu2-ro (attested to on PY Ea 56) and translates this tablet as "Pylos, 'Rawaratian' sons of female flax-workers of Zephyros, 4 men, 3 boys." But from the evidence of the Ea tablet, ze-pu2-ro would appear as a figure of only modest status and there is no compelling reason

either to view him as a man who commands a staff or even to connect him with these women. Moreover no other tablet offers both a man's name and an occupational title to identify a workgroup.

114 Olivier 2001: 148 has alternately suggested an identification as a Collector's workgroup for this set, but from mentions in the B series, I consider location to be a more likely source of this workgroup's designation.

115 Chadwick's Group 29 of the Major (Further Province) Aa set: Chadwick 1988: 56.

116 PY Aa 772
e-u-de-we-ro MUL 6 ko-wo 4 TA 1
"At Eudeiwelos, 6 women, 4 boys, 1 TA"

PY Ab 379
.a GRA 2 T 8 TA DA
.b e-u-de-we-ro MUL 8 ko-wa 2 ko-wo 3 NI 2 T 8
"At Eudeiwelos, 8 women, 2 girls, 3 boys, 268.8 l. of wheat , 268.8 l. figs, TA DA"

PY Ad 670
e-u-de-we-ro , ri-ne-ja-o ko-wo VIR 4 [
"At Eudeiwelos: sons of the linen-workers, 4 men …"

117 Chadwick's Group 43 of the Minor (Further Province) Aa Set. Chadwick 1988: 58.

118 PY Aa 95 +fr.
e-pi-jo-ta-na MUL 8 ko-wa 8 ko-wo 7 DA 1 TA 1
"At Epijotana 8 women, 8 girls, 7 boys 1 DA 1 TA"

PY Ad 687
]e-pi-ja-ta-ni-ja ri-ne-ja-ọ ḳọ[-wo VIR
"Sons of the Epijatanian linen-workers (women) .... Men"

119 Chadwick's Group 44 of the Minor (Further Province) Aa set. Chadwick 1988: 59.

120 PY Aa 94
e-pi-ko-o MUL 14 ko-wa 5̣ ko-wo 8 DA 1 TA 1
"At Epikoe, 14 women, 5 girls, 8 boys, 1 DA 1 TA"

PY Ad 672
e-pi-ko-e ri-ne-ja-o ko-wo VIR 4 ko-wo 3
"At Epikoe, sons of the linen-workers, 4 Men 3 boys"

121 Chadwick's Group 46 of the Minor (Further Province) Aa set. Chadwick 1988: 59.

122 Chadwick's Group 48 of the Minor (Further Province) Aa set. Chadwick 1988: 59.

123 PY Aa 93
ke-e MUL 6 ko-wa 9 ko-wo 6 DA 1 TA 1
"At ke-e, 6 women, 9 girls, 6 boys, 1 DA, 1 TA"

PY Ad 295
ke-e , ri-ne-ja-o , ko-wo VIR 8 ko-wo 5
"At ke-e, sons of the linen-working women: 8 men, 5 boys"

PY Aa 76
po-to-ro-wa-pi MUL 4 ko-wa 4 ko-wo 3 DA 1 TA 1
"At po-to-ro-wa-pi, 4 women, 4 girls, 3 boys, 1 DA 1 TA"

PY Ad 678
po-to-ro-wa-pi ri-ne-ja-o ko-wo VIR ko-wo 1 [
"At Po-to-ro-wa-pi, sons of the linen-workers: 1 man, 1 boy"

124 Chadwick's Group 42 of the Minor (Further Province) Aa set. Chadwick 1988: 59.

125 PY Aa 96

da-ṃị[-ni-ja MUL] .1 ko-wa 13 DA 1 TA 1
"At Damnia, 1 woman, 13 girls, 1 DA 1 TA"

126 This translation is from Ventris and Chadwick 1973: 161.

127 PY Aa 662
pa-ke-te-ja MUL 9 ko-wa 5 ko-wo 11
"9 women measurers/washers, 5 girls, 11 boys"

PY Ab 745
.a GRA T 5
.b pa-ke-te-ja , ri-ne-ja MUL 2 ko-wo 1 NI T 5
"2 women linen-measurers, 1 boy, 48 l. figs"

PY Ab 746
.a GRA T 5
.b pa-ke-te-ja , ri-ne-ja MUL 2 ko-wa 1 NI T 5
"2 women linen-measurers, 1 girl, 48 l. figs"

128 L. Palmer 1963: 444.

129 Ventris and Chadwick 1973: 499, 567; Ruijgh 1967: 78. See also Lindgren 1973: Part II, 112; *Diccionario*: Vol. II, 70–71. Killen 1983a: 80 – a reading Chadwick prefers: Chadwick 1988: 82.

130 Olivier 2001: 148; Nosch 2003:15.

131 KN U 4478.

132 *Diccionario*: Vol. II, 30; Lindgren 1973: Part II, 103; *Docs2:* 564. Chadwick goes further to speculate that o-nu-ka cloth refers specifically to ornamented or decorated cloth and that the women involved would be specialized decorators: Chadwick 1988: 81. Killen concurs: Killen 1984: 58. Palmer once again serves as the minority opinion on this term, reading o-nu-ka as a cloth made of wool-thread: L. Palmer 1963: 293.

133 Chadwick's Group 10 in the Major Aa set from Pylos: Chadwick 1988: 50.

134 PY Aa 770
ki-si-wi-ja MUL 6 ko-wa 4 ko-wo 6 TA 1
"6 Chian/Kswian women, 4 girls, 6 boys, 1 TA"

PY Ab 194
.a GRA 3 TA DA
.b pu-ro] ki-si-wi[-ja] o-nu-ke-ja MUL 7 ko-wa 3 ko-wo 6 NI 3
"At Pylos, 7 Chian/Kswian women who make o-nu-ka, 3 girls, 6 boys, 288 l. wheat, 288 l. figs, 1 DA 1 TA"

PY Ad 675
pụ-ro ki-si-wi-ja-o o-nu-ḳẹ-jạ-o ko-wo VIR 3 ko-wo 5
"At Pylos, sons of the Chian/K̇swian o-nu-ka makers: 3 men, 5 boys"

135 The identification of ki-si-wi-ja as the ethnic adjective pertaining to Χῖος is dependent on the assumption that **ksw* developed into **kh(w)* as proposed by Chadwick in Ventris and Chadwick 1973: 156. This reading had been initially criticized, but more recent philological studies by Heubeck and Killen on the formation of ethnics in Mycenaean would render this more plausible: Heubeck 1985: 135; Killen 1983a: 88. On strength of their research and citing analogical parallels such as the classical Greek adjective Ἄσιος as deriving from the Mycenaean form Ἀσία Chadwick has more recently defended, and to my mind successfully, his earlier identification of ki-si-wi-ja as Chian. For his complete argument, see Chadwick 1988: 80; cf. *Diccionario*: Vol. I, 364.

136 Near-consensus places them as textile workers: *Diccionario*, Vol. II, 332; Chadwick, "Women of Pylos," 81; Killen, 1966: 105–109; Lindgren 1973: 142–43; Ventris and Chadwick 1973: 585. The most skeptical voice is Morpurgo Davies who lists them in

the category of "probably textile workers:" Morpurgo Davies 1979: 100. In light of the abundant evidence which identifies te-pa as a major cloth type, even this note of caution seems unnecessary.

137 Chadwick's Group 47 of the Minor set (Further Province locations). Chadwick 1988: 59.

138 PY Ad 921
ko-ri-to te-pe-ja-o ko-wo VIR [[3ọ]] ko-wo 1
"At Corinth, sons of the te-pa making women: [[30]] men, 1 boy"

139 This is not the Isthmian Corinth.

140 The etymology of a-pu-ko-wo-ko as *ἀμπύκοργος generally accepted. The exact sense of this term, however, is less certain with both "headband-makers for women" and "headband-makers for horses" suggested. *Diccionario:* Vol. I, 90; Killen 1984: 58; Lindgren 1973: Part II, 22–23; Ruijgh, 1967: 65; Ventris and Chadwick 1973: 533.

141 Chadwick's Group 19 of the Major Aa set. Chadwick 1988: 53.

142 PY Ab 210
a. GRA 3 T 6 ṬẠ [
.b a-pu-ko-wo-ko MUL 8 ko-wa 7 ko-wo 8 NI 3 T 6 [
"8 women head-band makers, 7 girls, 8 boys: 345.6 l. wheat, 345.6 l. figs, TA"

PY Ad 671
.a ka-ru-ti-je-ja-o-qe O VIR ̣5
.b pu-ro , a-pu-ko-wo-ko pa-ke-te-ja-o-qe VIR ̣3 ko-wo ̣4
"At Pylos, 3 adult sons and 4 boys of the head-band makers, and the 'measurers' and the sweepers, missing (o-pe-ro) 5 men"

143 Chadwick's Group 23 of the Major Aa set. Chadwick 1988: 54.

144 PY Ab 555
.a GRA 16[
.b pu-ro , ra-pi-ti-ra2 MUL 38 ko-wa 20 ko-wo 19 NI 16 [
"At Pylos, 38 sewing women; 20 girls, 19 boys: 1536+ l. wheat, 1536+ l. figs"
There appears to be a typographic error on this tablet as the amounts of wheat and figs are not identical. Chadwick 1988: 54.

145 Ventris and Chadwick 1973: 407, 578; Killen 1984: 58. See *Diccionario*: Vol. II, 221 for additional bibliography.

146 Lindgren 1973: 133–35; Ruijgh 1967: 113; Ventris and Chadwick 1973: 409. "Stitcher" has largely superseded earlier readings such as "torchbearer" and "scribe;" see *Diccionario:* Vol. II, 221–23 for additional bibliography.

147 Ventris and Chadwick 1956: 387; Ventris and Chadwick 1973: 529.

148 *Diccionario*: Vol. I, 42–43; Chadwick 1988: 78; Killen 1984: 58; Morpurgo Davies 1979: 99.

149 PY Aa 815
a-ke-ti-ra2 MUL 38 ko-wa 33 ko-wo 16 DA 1 TA 1
"38 decorators, 33 girls, 16 boys 1 DA, 1 TA"

PY Ab 564 + 1105
pụ-ro a-ke-ti-ṛạ2 MUL [ko-]ẉạ 34 [
"At Pylos, decorators: x women, 34 girls"

PY Ad 666
pu-ro a-ke-ti-ra2-o ko-wo VIR 20 ko-wo 7 [
"At Pylos, sons of the decorators: 20 men, 7 boys"

150 Chadwick, Group 2 of the Major set at Pylos: Chadwick 1988: 48. It is possible that PY Ab 1105 which reads]ko-wa 34[might belong to this group, as it appears the only workgroup large enough to fit an entry of 34 girls.

151 Chadwick's Group 34 of the Major Aa set. Chadwick 1988: 57.

152 PY Aa 717
ro-u-so , a-ke-ti-ri-ja MUL 32 ko-wa 18 ko-wo 8 DA 1 TA 1
"At Lousos, 32 decorators, 18 girls, 8 boys, 1 DA, 1 TA"

PY Ab 1099
ro-u-so a-ḳẹ[-ti-ra2 MUL
"At Lousos, decorators..."

153 This echoes Killen's theory of Lousos's function as a sub-capital of the Hither Province. Killen 1984: 59.
154 Chadwick's Group 35 of the Minor Aa set: Chadwick 1988: 57.
155 PY Aa 85
a-ke-ti-ri-ja MUL 12 ko-wa 16 ko-wo 8 DA 1 TA 1
"12 decorators 16 girls, 8 boys, 1 DA 1 TA"

PY Ad 290
re-u-ko-to-ro a-ke-ti-ra2-o ko-wo VIR 2 ko-wo
"At Leuktron, sons of the decorators: 2 adult men, 1(?) boy"

156 They are one of only three such occupational designations.
157 This is the workgroup title whose property holdings are most securely attested.
158 Chadwick's Group 8 of the Major set at Pylos: Chadwick 1988: 50.
159 *Diccionario*: Vol. I, 315 raises the possibility that ka-pa-ra2-de is an ethnic term; if this is indeed an ethnic, it would be the lone ethnic employing an –a2-de rather than the usual -i-ja ending, and would therefore be unparalleled at either Knossos or Pylos.
160 Killen 1983b: 121–126.
161 KN Ak 5009 + 6037 + 8588.
162 PY Aa 788
ka-pa-ra2-de MUL 24 ko-wa 8 ko-wo 2 DA 1 TA 1
"24 women cloth-workers 8 girls, 2 boys, 1 DA 1 TA"

PY Ad 679
.a ka-pa-ra2-do [
.b pu-ro ku-te-ra-o ko-wo VIR 6 [[o-pe-ro VIR 8]]
"At Pylos, sons of the Kytheran cloth-makers: 6 men [[missing 8 men]]"

163 For discussion of wheat, grain, and barley, see R. Palmer 1992: 475–497.
164 The lack of definitive evidence fixing the si-to-ko-wo as women, however, has led me to omit them from Table 3.1 and from tabulations and concluding discussions of women's production at Pylos.
165 Kytheran workgroups are discussed further on pp. 96–97.
166 L. Palmer 1963: 436; Ruijgh 1967: 183. For full bibliography, see *Diccionario:* Vol. I, 471–72.
167 Chadwick 1988: 81.
168 Morpurgo Davies 1979: 100.
169 Killen 1984: 58; Killen and Olivier 1966: 54.
170 Lindgren 1973: Part II, 100–101.
171 Chadwick's Group 16 of the Major Aa set: Chadwick 1988: 52.
172 PY Aa 695
ne-we-wi-ja MUL 21 ko-wa 10 ko-wo 6 DA 1 TA 1
"21 textile working women, 10 girls, 6 boys 1 DA 1 TA"

PY Ab 560
pu-ro , ne-we-wi-ja ṂỤḶ [
"At Pylos, women textile workers...."

PY Ad 357
ne-we-wi-ja-o ko-wo VIR 6 o-pe-ro VIR 3
"Sons of the textile workers: 6 men, missing 3 men"

173 As seven of the workgroup tallies are lacunose, the total number of adult female workers may have been considerably higher; three of these lacunose workgroups were assigned to textile production.

174 These numbers do not attempt to correct for the numbers of women in lacunose tallies.

175 One of these a-ra-ke-te-ja groups is also modified with the ethnic mi-ra-ti-ja.

176 Chadwick reads me-re-ti-ri-ja as an "occupational term, [which is] clearly an agent noun in /*-tria*/ or its Mycenaean variants, cf. a-ke-ti-ra2, o-ti-ra2, pe-ki-ti-ra2, ra-pi-ti-ra2, ra-qi-ti-ra2. It would seem certain that this is derived from the base * μελ/μολ 'to grind' found in Latin *molo* and many other languages, since it is supported by *me-re-u-ro* / μέλευρον 'flour'. Since the corresponding forms of later Greek are ἀλετρίς and ἄλευρον, it is tempting to derive these from a zero grade of the same root (cf. μέχρι, ἄχρι), but it is possible that two roots of similar meaning have become contaminated. In any case ἆλευρον (Alcaeus) seems to form a link between the Mycenaean and the later forms." Chadwick 1988: 81. This identification is dependent, of course, on the interpretation of me-re-u-ro as μέλευρον "flour." Chadwick has made strong arguments for this interpretation, beginning with Chadwick 1954: 14, and subsequent authors have largely accepted this reading for me-re-ti-ri-ja: *Diccionario* 1993: Vol. II, 437–38, 560; Killen 1984: 58; Morpurgo Davies 1979: 103; Ventris and Chadwick 1973, and Lindgren, *People of Pylos* 1973: Part II, 95–96, with minor reservations.

177 Chadwick's Group 14 of the Major Aa set. Chadwick 1988: 51.

178 PY Aa 764
me-re-ti-ri-ja MUL 6 ko-wa 8 ko-wo 1
"6 flour-grinding women, 8 girls, 1 boy"

PY Ab 789
a GRA 2 T 1[
b "pu-ro" me-re-ti-ra2 MUL 6 ko-wo 6 ko-wo 3 NI 2 T 1[
"At Pylos, 6 flour-grinding women, 6 boys , 3 girls: 201.6 l. wheat, 201.6. l. figs

179 Chadwick's Group 41 of the Minor Aa set of the Further Province. Chadwick 1988: 58.

180 PY Aa 62
me-re-ti-ri-ja MUL 7 ko-wa 10 ko-wo 6
"7 flour-grinding women, 10 girls, 6 boys"

PY Ad 308
re-u-ko-to-ro me-re-ti-ra2[-o VIR
"Sons of the flour-grinding women at Leuktron: [x men"

181 This reading expands upon Killen's. Killen 1984: 58.

182 Cf. λοετροχόοι [*Od.* xx, 297+]. *Docs2:* 580.

183 *Diccionario* 1993: Vol. II, 250–51; Lindgren 1973: Part II, 137; Ruijgh 1967: 241; Ventris and Chadwick 1973: 580. Chadwick and Killen prefer "bath-pourers:" Chadwick 1988: 83 and Killen 1984: 58.

184 Chadwick's Group 26 of the Major Set. Chadwick 1988: 55.

185 PY Aa 783
re-wo-to-ro-ko-wo MUL 38 ko-wa 13 ko-wo 15 DA 1 TA 1
"38 women bath-attendants, 13 girls, 15 boys, 1 DA 1 TA"

PY Ab 553
.a GRA 11 T ̣1 DA TA
.b pu-ro , re-wo-to-ro-ko-wo 37 ko-wa 13 ko-wo 15 NI 11 T 1

"At Pylos, 37 (women) bath-attendants, 13 daughters, 15 sons, 1056 l. wheat, 1056 l. figs, DA, TA"

PY Ad 676
pu-ro re-wo-to-ro-ko-wo ko-wo VIR 22 ko-wo 11
"At Pylos, sons of the bath-attendants 22 men, 11 boys"

186 Tritsch 1958: 440.
187 Carlier 1983: 16.
188 Chadwick 1988: 83.
189 Ἀμφιπόλοι [*Od.* i. 331]. Ventris and Chadwick 1973: 532.
190 Lindgren 1973: Part II, 21. Cf. *Diccionario* Vol. 1, 84; Ventris and Chadwick 1973: 480.
191 Carlier 1983: 78. Killen concurs with a reading of "domestic servants." Killen 1984: 58.
192 PY Aa 804
a-pi-qo-ro MUL 32 ko-wa 26 ko-wo 15 TA 1
"32 attendant women, 26 girls, 15 boys, 1 TA"

PY Ad 690
pu-ro a-pi-qo-ro ko-wo VIR 10 ko-wo 4 [[o VIR 3]]
"At Pylos, sons of the attendant women, 10 men, 4 boys [[missing 3 men]]"

193 Chadwick's Group 3 of the Major Aa set at Pylos. Chadwick would also assign the fragmentary rations tablet PY Ab 580 to this group. See also, Carlier 1983: 48–49.
194 Presumably cooks would have been required full time at the palace complex as well; the limited evidence for cooks in the tablets seems to indicate that this task was assigned to men. (cf. PY Eb 177 + 1010; PY Ep 613 + 1131; and KN As 608 + 625 + 5870 + 5942.)
195 Morpurgo Davies reads this title, on evidence of TH Of 36, as a textile-related term. Morpurgo Davies 1979: 388.
196 Chadwick's Group 40 of the Minor Aa set of the Further Province: Chadwick 1988: 58.
197 PY Aa 98
no-ri-wo-ko MUL 8 ko-wa 10 ko-wo 5
"no-ri-workers: 8 women, 10 girls, 5 boys"
198 PY Ad 669
re-u-ko-to-ro , no-ri-wo-ko-jo ko-wo VIR 5
"At Leuktron, sons of the no-ri-workers: 5 men"
199 Chadwick's Group 18 of the Major Aa set at Pylos: Chadwick 1988: 53.
200 PY Aa 313
o-ti-ri-ja MUL 21 ko-wa 12 ko-wo 8 DA 1 TA 1
"21 women o-triai workers, 12 girls, 8 boys, 1 DA 1 TA"

PY Ab 417 + PY Ab 1050
.a GRA 6[
.b pu-ro , o-ti-ra2 MUL 21 ko[-wa ko-wo] 8 NI 6 [
"At Pylos, o-triai workers: 21 women, x girls, 8 boys, 576+ l. wheat, 576+ l. figs"

PY Ad 663 +674
o-ti-ra2-o ko-wo VIR [ ] ̣5 ko-wo 7
"Sons of the o-triai workers: 5 men, 7 boys"

201 Ruijgh 1967: 341. Lindgren also prefers this reading: Lindgren 1973: Part II, 109. Other commentators take no position on o-ti-ri-ja beyond identifying it as a feminine occupation: *Diccionario* Vol. II, 53–54; Chadwick, 1988: 82; Ventris and Chadwick 1973: 566.

202 The correspondence of ra-pi-ti-ri-ja and ra-qi-ti-ra was originally proposed by Bennett 1956: 131. This reading has been discarded on both textual and linguistic grounds by Chadwick: "In view of the difference in the size of the groups this cannot be an alternative spelling of *ra-pi-ti-ra2* as was at first thought. … Moreover, the alternation of *p* and *q* could not be explained, since the labio-velar is preserved intact, even before consonants. No plausible interpretation has been proposed." Chadwick 1988: 82–83.

203 Ruijgh 1967: 346.

204 Lindgren 1973: Part II, 134. For additional discussion, see *Diccionario* Vol. II, 224.

205 Chadwick's Group 24 of the Major Aa set at Pylos: Chadwick 1988: 54.

206 PY Ab 356 + 1049

.a GRA 2 T 2 DA

.b pu-ro, ra-qi-ti-ra2 MUL 6 ko-wa 3 ko[-wo]1 NI 2 T 2

"At Pylos, 6 ra-qi-ti-ra2 women, 3 girls, 1 boy: 211.2 l. wheat, 211.2 l. figs, DA"

PY Ad 667

pu-ro , ra-qi-ti-ra2-o ko-wo VIR 2

"At Pylos, sons of the ra-qi-ti-ra2 women, 2 men"

207 If the si-to-ko-wo were to be identified definitively as women, we could have a third workgroup of food workers at the Pylian center.

208 Chadwick's Group 32 of the Major Aa set of the Hither Province: Chadwick 1988: 56. It is possible, however, that PY Aa 775 and PY Ab 277 in fact may refer to two separate workgroups at o-wi-to-no. If so, this could explain the disparity in numbers of adult women and boys on these two tablets.

209 PY Aa 775 + fr. + 956

o-wi-to-no[MUL]4 ko-wa 2 ko-wo 10 DA 1 TA 1

"At o-winthos, 4 (to-sa-me-ja) women, 2 girls, 10 boys, 1 DA, 1 TA"

PY Ab 277

.a GRA 3 DA TA

.b o-wi-to-no MUL 8 ko-wa 5 ko-wo 2 NI 3

"At o-winthos, 8 (to-sa-me-ja) women, 5 girls, 2 boys, 288 l. wheat, 288 l. figs, DA, TA"

PY Ad 685

o-wi-to-no to-sa-me-jạ-ọ ko-wo VIR 3 ko-wo

"At o-winthos, sons of the to-sa-me-ja women: 3 men, 1(?) boy"

210 The identification of to-sa-me-ja has been speculated about only in the most general of terms; Lindgren, Ventris and Chadwick 1973, and *Diccionario* all identify it simply as a feminine occupational title. *Diccionario* Vol. II, 368; Lindgren 1973: Part II, 148; Ventris and Chadwick 1973: 587. Palmer's reading of to-sa-me-ja as an ethnicon has been largely ruled out: L. Palmer 1963: 114, 459. Chadwick has also raised the possibility of its being a possible derivative of a man's name, citing the case of the term a-da-ra-te-ja as a potential parallel. Chadwick 1988: 79.

211 Chadwick's Group 39 of the Minor Aa set of the Further Province at Leuktron. Chadwick 1988: 58.

212 *Diccionario*: Vol. I, 359.

213 PY Aa 63

ki-ma-ra MUL 3 ko-wa 5 ko-wo 4 DA 1 TA 1

"3 ki-ma-ra women workers, 5 girls, 4 boys, 1 DA 1 TA"

PY Ad 668

re-u-ko-to-ro ki-ma-ra-o ko-wo VIR 4

"At Leuktron, sons of the ki-ma-ra women: 4 men"

214 This interpretation normalizes o-pi-ro-qo as *opiloquoi, -on*, offering a translation as "remaining" or "supernumerary" workers; cf. ἐπίλοιπο [Pind.+]. Ventris and Chadwick 1973: 565. Chadwick fine tunes this reading to indicate women not yet allocated to particular duties. Chadwick 1988: 81. Killen concurs: Killen 1984: 58.

215 Palmer proposes a normalization of *enkheroquoinon* deriving from * ἐγχειρόποινος. Palmer 1973: 416. Killen modifies the term to "salaried workers": Killen 1984: 58. See also Lindgren 1973: Part II, 43–44 for additional bibliography and discussion. No other plausible explanations for this title have been offered, but we should remember that the exact nature of the palatial compensation system for workers remains unclear, that is, whether a palatial wage-based remuneration system was in place or if the palace simply relied on the redistribution of goods to compensate its labor force. Consequently, the term "wage-earner" must be used with caution.

216 PY Ab 899
.a GRA 2 T 2
.b pu-ro o-pi-ro-qo MUL 8 ko-wa 3 ko-wo 3 NI 2 T 2
"At Pylos, 8 unassigned women, 3 girls, 3 boys, 211.2 l. wheat, 211.2 l. figs"

PY Ad 691
.a e-ke-ro-qo-no-qe , pa-wo-ko-qe
.b pu-ro o-pi-ro-qo ko-wo [[ ]] VIR 9
"At Pylos, sons of the wage-earners, the all-purpose workers, and the unassigned workers: 9 men"

217 PY Aa 854
e-ke[-ro-qo-no MUL
"Women wage-earners, x women"

PY Ab 563 + 581 + 1112 + 1113 + 1506 + frr.
.a]G̣ṚẠ 6 T 1 [
.b pu-ro , e-ke-ro-qo-no MUL [ ] 1̣ [ko-]ẉạ 5 [ ] ḳọ-ẉọ 5 Ṇ Ị 6 T 1̣[
"At Pylos, [25] women wage-earners, 5 girls, 5 boys, 585.6 l. wheat, 585.6 l. figs"

218 There continues to be some division in scholarship as to whether the three titles on PY Ad 691 (e-ke-ro-qo-no, pa-wo-ko, and o-pi-ro-qo) refer to three distinct workgroups or whether one of the terms is used to modify the others. Ruijgh favors reading them as indicating three separate workgroups, while Lindgren, in contrast, argues that the –qe's should be ignored and takes o-pi-ro-qo-no as a modifying term. Ruijgh 1967: 261, 295; Lindgren 1973: Part II, 105. I concur with Ruijgh and view them as separate units in PY Ad 691, as the addition of -qe would appear to be significant, while I see them as linked terms on PY Aa 777 where no -qe separates the two.

219 Chadwick's Group 17 of the Major Aa set. Chadwick 1988: 52.

220 PY Aa 777
a e-ke-ro-qo-no
b o-pi-ro-qo MUL 7 ko-wa 3 ko-wo 4 DA 1 TA 1
"Wage-earners: 7 unassigned women 3 girls, 4 boys, 1 DA 1 TA"

221 PY Ab 1100
a pu-ro
b e-ke-ro-qo-no[MUL
"At Pylos, wage-earners…"

222 PY Aa 795
pa-wo-ke MUL 4 ko-wa 2 ko-wo 1 TA 1
"4 women all-purpose workers, 2 girls, 1 boy, 1 TA"

PY Ab 558 *recto*
.a GRA 1 T 8 TA DA
.b pu-ro , pa-wo-ke MUL 4 ko-wa 2 ko-wo 1 NI 1 T 8

Recto: "At Pylos, all-purpose workers 4 women, 2 girls, 1 boy: 172.8 l. wheat, 172.8 l. figs, DA, TA"

PY Ad 691
a e-ke-ro-qo-no-qe pa-wo-ko-qe
b pu-ro o-pi-ro-qo ko-wo [[ ]] VIR 9
"At Pylos, sons of the unassigned women and the wage-earners (?) and the all-purpose workers: 9 men"

223 Chadwick's Group 20 of the Major Aa set at Pylos. Chadwick 1988: 53.
224 Chadwick 1967: 115–117; Killen 1984: 58.
225 See *Diccionario*, Part II, 92–93 for complete bibliography. See also Lindgren 1973: Part II, 113–114 for a discussion regarding the strengths and weaknesses of the various interpretations.
226 This is the third and final workgroup title to warrant mention outside the personnel series at Pylos. This reference is further discussed in Chapter 4.
227 Chadwick's Group 25 of the Major Aa set at Pylos. Chadwick 1988: 54–55.
228 PY Aa 807
ke-re-za, ra-wi-ja-ja MUL 26 ko-wa 7 ko-wo 7 DA 1 TA 1
"At (Pylos) Kereza, 26 ra-wi-ja-ja women 7 girls, 7 boys, 1 DA 1 TA"

PY Ab 586
.a GRA 7 T 7 DA TA [
.b pu-ro ke-re-za , ra-wi-ja-ja MUL 28 ko-wa 9 ko-wo 5 NI 7 T 7 [
"At Pylos Ke-re-za, 28 ra-wi-ja-ja women, 9 girls, 5 boys: 739.2 l. wheat, 739.2 l. figs, 1 DA, 1 TA"

PY Ad 686
.a o-u-pa-ro-ke-ne-ṭọ , ka-wo-ta-ra-[ ]pọ-ṛọ
.b pu-ro ke-re-za , ra-wi-ja-ja-o ko-wo VIR 15
"At Pylos Kereza, sons of the ra-wi-ja-ja women: 15 men; [A]lkawon the... did not present himself."

229 Earlier readings included the identification of ra-wi-ja-ja as an ethnicon (Lindgren 1973: Part II, 136; Palmer 1963: 452), a place-derived name (i.e. from *Lawos-land*: Heubeck 1969: 543), and as deriving from the term λήιον (Dor.) "cornfield" whereby ra-wi-ja-ja would refer to a type of grain-worker (Tritsch 1958: 428, followed by Uchitel 1984: 275).
230 *Il*. xx. 193. Cf. Ion. ληίη; Dor. λάα; Att. λεία. Ventris and Chadwick 1973: 163, 407.
231 Chadwick 1988: 54–55.
232 Ruijgh 1967, 626; Chantraine, 1968, Vol. 3, 626.
233 The tally of the independent e-ke-ro-qo-no workers is lacunose.
234 It is clear that the ethnics refer to the origin of the workgroup women rather than the location in which they perform their tasks as several tablets place women described by an ethnic title at sites other than those from which the ethnics arise.
235 This is, of course, dependent on the assumption that *64 = *swi*.
236 Chadwick's Group 6 of the Major Aa set at Pylos. Chadwick 1988: 49.
237 PY Aa 701
a-*64-ja MUL 35 ko-wa 11 ko-wo 1ḍ4 DA 1 TA 1
"35 Aswian women, 11 girls, 14 boys 1 DA 1 TA"

PY Ab 515
.a GRA 10 DA TA
.b pu-ro , a-*64-ja MUL 35 ko-wa 12 ko-wo 11 NI 10
"At Pylos, 35 Aswian women; 12 girls, 11 boys: 960 l. wheat, 960 l. figs, DA TA"

PY Ad 315 + 1450 + fr.
pu-ro a-*64-ja-o ko-wo VIR [ ] 12 ḳọ-wo 6
"At Pylos, sons of the Aswian women: 12 men, 6 boys"

238 *Pace* Lindgren 1973: Part II, 92, following Ruijgh 1967: 139. See also Heubeck 1985: 123–138, 135.

239 *Diccionario:* Vol. I, 267.

240 Ventris and Chadwick 1973:547; Ruijgh 1967: 172. Euripos is listed as the location for a work unit of nine men on PY An 610.6.

241 Chadwick's Group 45 of the Minor Aa set of the Further Province (non-Leuktron locations). Chadwick 1988: 59.

242 PY Aa 60
e-wi-ri-pi-ja MUL 16 ko-wa 11 ko-wo 7 DA 1 TA 1
"Ewiripiai/Euripian women: 16 women, 11 girls, 7 boys, 1 DA, 1 TA"

243 Chadwick 1988: 58.

244 The other is the ti-nwa-si-ja i-te-ja workgroup discussed on pp. 76–77.

245 Uchitel 1984.

246 Chadwick's Group 9 of the Major Aa set at Pylos. Chadwick 1988: 50.

247 PY Aa 792
ki-ni-di-ja MUL 21 ko-ẉạ 12 ko-wo 10 DA 1 TA 1
"21 Cnidian women, 12 girls, 10 boys, 1 DA, 1 TA"

PY Ab 189
.a GRA 6 T 7 TA DA
.b pu-ro ki-ni-di-ja MUL 20 ko-wa 10 ko-wo 10 NI 6 T 7
"At Pylos, 20 Knidian women, 10 girls, 10 boys: 643.2 l. wheat, 643.2 l. figs, 1 TA, 1 DA"

PY Ad 683
pu-ro ki-ni-di-ja-o ko-wo VIR 5 ko-wo 4
"At Pylos, sons of the Cnidian women: 5 men, 4 boys"

248 PY An 292
.1 si-to-ko-wo
.2 ka-pa-ra2-de MUL 24 ko-wo 10
.3 ko-ro-ki-ja[ ] MUL 8 ko-wo[
.4 ki-ni-di[-ja MUL] 21 ḳọ[-wo
.5 (INFRA MUTILA)

249 There is near full consensus on this identification. Ventris and Chadwick 1956: 148; Ruijgh 1967: 168; Ventris and Chadwick 1973: 554; Chadwick 1988: 80; *Diccionario*: Vol. 1, 360.

250 PY Aa 354
ko-ro-ki-ja MUL 8 ko-wa 4 ko-wo 1 DA 1
8 Korokian women, 4 girls, 1 boy 1 DA

PY Ab 372
.a GRA 2 T 7 TA DA
.b pu-ro ko-ro-ki-ja MUL 9 ko-wa 2 [[ ]] NI 2 T 7
"At Pylos, 9 Korokian women, 2 girls, 259.2 l. wheat, 259.2 l. figs, TA, DA"

PY Ad 680
.a pu-ro
.b ko-ro-ki-ja-o ko-wo VIR 5
"At Pylos, sons of the Korokian women: 5 men"
For the full text of PY An 292, n. 248.

251 *Diccionario:* Vol. I, 384–85; Chadwick 1988: 80; Ventris and Chadwick 1973: 556.

252 Chadwick's Group 11 of the Major Aa set at Pylos. Chadwick 1988: 51.
253 Chadwick's Group 12 of the Major Aa set at Pylos. Chadwick 1988: 51.
254 PY Aa 506
ku-te-ra3 MUL 28 ko-wa[
"28 Kytheran women x girls"

PY Ab 562
pu-ṛọ ḳụ-te-ra3[MUL
"At Pylos, Kytheran women ["

PY Ad 390
pu-ro ku-te-ra-o ko-wo [ ] VIR 22
"At Pylos, sons of the Kytheran women: 22 men"
255 Lindgren 1973: Part II, 92. Followed by Billigmeier and Turner 1981: 5.
256 PY Aa 1180
.a pu-ro ,
.b mi-ra-ti-ja MUL [
"At Pylos, Milatian women …."

PY Ab 573
.a GRA 5 T 1 DA TA
.b pu-ro , mi-ra-ti-ja MUL 16 ko-wa 3 ko-wo 7 NI 5 T 1
"At Pylos, 16 Milatian women, 3 girls, 7 boys, 489.6 l. wheat, 489.6 l. figs, 1 DA, 1 TA"

PY Ad 689
.a a-so-qi-ịẹ-ịạ
.b pu-ro mi-ra-ti-ja-o ko-wo VIR 2 ko-wo
"At Pylos, sons of the Milatian women: 2 men, (1) boy"
257 Chadwick's Group 35 of the Major Aa set at Pylos. Chadwick 1988: 57.
258 Aa 798
ro-u-so mi-ra-ti-ja MUL 54 ko-wa 35 ko-wo 22 DA 1 TA 1

Ab 382
GRA 16 T 8 DA TA
ro-u-so mi-ra-ti-ra MUL 54 ko-wa 31 [ ] ko-wo 20 NI 16 T 8
"At Lousos, 54 Milatian women, 31 girls, 20 boys, 1612.8 l. wheat, 1612.8 l. figs, 1 TA, 1 DA"
259 The identification of ra-mi-ni-ja with *Lamniai* is widely accepted. Ventris and Chadwick 1956: 149; Tritsch 1958: 406; Ventris and Chadwick 1973: 578; Chadwick 1988: 82; *Diccionario*: Vol. II, 218–19.
260 PY Ab 186
.a GRA 2 T 4 TA DA
.b pu-ro , ra-mi-ni-ja MUL 7 ko-wa 1 ko-wo 2 NI 2 T 4
"At Pylos, 7 Lamnian women, 1 girl, 2 boys, 230.4 l. wheat, 230.4 l. figs, 1 TA, 1 DA"
261 Chadwick's Group 22 of the Major Aa set at Pylos. Chadwick 1988: 54.
262 Excluding the a-ra-te-ja mi-ra-ti-ja workers whose tally is lacunose.
263 The Further Province's ri-ne-ja ze-pu2-ra workgroup at Pylos Lauranthias workgroup is also lacunose.
264 *Pace* Carlier who dismisses the origins idea arguing that only four ethnic adjectives directly pertain to the Aegean islands: Carlier 1983: 16. If one expands the category from "Aegean islands" to "the Eastern Aegean", the numbers increase to seven, raising the total proportion of foreign ethnics to 70 percent of the total ethnics in use at Pylos.

265 While all sources agree that me-ta-pa is a toponym located in the Hither Province, and a normalization as *Μετάπα is largely accepted [*Diccionario*: Vol. I, 423–24], its precise location is not known. Chadwick, on evidence of PY Jn 829 and PY Vn 20 postulates that Me-ta-pa's "position in the north of the Province suggests a location in the area of modern Kyparissia." Chadwick 1988: 85.

266 Chadwick's Group 30 of the Major Aa set of the Hither Province. Chadwick 1988: 56.

267 PY Aa 752 + fr.
me-ta-pa MUL 7 ko-wa 3 ko-wo 3 TA 1
"At Metapa (Hither Province) 7 women, 3 girls 3 boys 1 TA"

268 PY Aa 779
me-ta-pa MUL 3 ko-wo 1 TA 1
(lat.inf.)
a-te-re-wi-ja
"At Metapa, 3 women, 1 boy, 1 TA
At Aterewija..."

PY Ab 355
me-ta-pa MUL 5 [
"At Metapa, 5 women…"

269 The specific location of ne-wo-pe-o remains unclear. Ventris and Chadwick 1973: 563; *Diccionario:* Vol. I, 473.

270 Chadwick's Group 31 of the Major Aa set of the Hither Province. Chadwick 1988: 56.

271 PY Aa 786
ne-wo-pe-o MUL 8 ko-wa 3 ko-wo 2 *TA* 1
"At Newopeo, 8 women 3 girls, 2 boys, 1 TA"

PY Ab 554
.a GRA 2 Ṭ[
.b ne-wo-pe-o MUL 7 ko-wa 5 ḳọ-wo 5 NI ?[T
"At Newopeo, 7 women, 5 girls, 5 boys, 192+ l. wheat, 192 + l. figs"

PY Ad 688
ne-wo-pe-o ko-wo VIR 4 ko-wo 2 [
"At Newopeo: 4 adult sons, 2 [boys]"

272 *Diccionario*: Vol. II, 430; Chadwick 1988: 85. An alternate reading has raised the possibility of pi-we-re as an occupational designation, but a toponym seems more likely. Lindgren 1973: Part II, 117–18.

273 PY Aa 1182
pi-we-re MUL 7 ko-wo 2

274 Chadwick's Group 33 of the Major Aa set of the Hither Province at Pylos. Chadwick 1988: 57.

275 Chadwick's Group 1 of the Major Aa set at Pylos. Chadwick 1988: 49.

276 Chadwick's Group 13 of the Major Aa set at Pylos. Chadwick 1988: 51.

277 Cf. Μεγιστοκλῆς, Ἀγαθόκριτοι. Ventris and Chadwick 1973: 560, also Lindgren 1973: Part II, 94, 177.

278 Killen 1983a: 66–99.

279 Chadwick 1988: 78; cf. Ἀδρήστεια (*Il.* ii, 828): Ventris and Chadwick 1973: 528.

280 Killen 1983a: 66–99; Uchitel 1984: 259, n. 4.

281 Olivier 2001: 148.

282 This identification of ka-ru-ti-je-ja as a collector's workgroup was first proposed by Killen 1983b and followed by Chadwick 1988: 49 and Olivier 2001: 148 and is widely accepted, superseding earlier proposals such as Chadwick 1964: 323 based on καλλύνω ("to clean, make beautiful") and κάλλυνθρον ("broom"), with a functional translation as "sweepers/cleaners."

283 PY Ad 671
.a ka-ru-ti-je-ja-o-qe O VIR 5̣
.b pu-ro , a-pu-ko-wo-ko pa-ke-te-ja-o-qe VIR 3̣ ko-wo 4̣
"At Pylos, 3 adult sons and 4 boys of the head-band makers, and the measurers and the sweepers, missing: 5 men."

284 Killen 1979: 176.

285 PY Jn 431.13, PY Jn 658.2, and PY Jn 725.3. Olivier 2001: 147.

286 Ventris and Chadwick 1973: 412; Tritsch 1958: 248; L.R. Palmer 1973: 115

287 Rougemont 2001: 134.

288 Chadwick's Group 28 of the Major Aa set. Chadwick 1988: 55.

289 PY Aa 762
ke-re-za , we-we-si-je-ja MUL 22 ko-wa 6 ko-wo 11 DA 1 TA 1
"At Kereza, 22 women belonging to we-we-si-jo, 6 girls, 11 boys , 1 DA 1 TA"

PY Ab 217
.a GRA 5 T 1 TA ḌẠ [
.b pu-ro ke-re-za we-we-si-je-ja MUL 16 ko-wa 5 ko-wo 7 NI 5 T 1 [
"At Pylos Ke-re-za, 16 women belonging to we-we-si-jo, 5 girls, 7 boys, 489.6 l. wheat, 489.6 l. figs, 1 DA 1 TA"

PY Ad 318 + 420 + frr.
pu-ro , ke[-re-]ẓạ ẉẹ-we-si-je-ja-o ko-wo VIR 8̣ ko-wo 7
"At Pylos Kereza, sons of women belonging to we-we-si-jo: 8 men, 7 boys"

290 Olivier 2001: 148; Nosch 2003: 15.

291 Olsen 1988: 90.

292 Nosch 2003: 17; 2001: 39, no.10.

293 This translation from Ventris and Chadwick 1973: 166.

294 These counts exclude the two single-women "workgroups" and those workgroups whose tallies have not been preserved.

295 Another nine titles are also suspected to be textile-related, but their etymological justifications are weaker than these 24. The suspected titles are: to-sa-me-ja , no-ri-wo-ko, and the seven unmodified ethnics – a-*64-ja, ki-ni-di-ja, ko-ro-ki-ja, ku-te-ra3, mi-ra-ti-ja, ra-mi-ni-ja, and e-wi-ri-pi-ja.

296 If the discussed ethnics and the untitled workgroups of the Hither Province villages are understood to be textile workgroups, the total number of textile workgroups expands to 38 of the total 50 groups.

297 This number excludes the women of the workgroups only suspected as textile workers as well as the women who belong to the three secure workgroups whose tallies are lacunose.

298 Two additional titles may belong to the domestic laborer category: o-ti-ri-ja and ra-qi-ti-ra2.

299 Two of the ethnic/occupational workgroups have lacunose tallies. The tallies of these six workgroups have already been factored in above, among the textile workers.

300 For a parallel discussion of the importance of location on workgroup organization and assignments, see also Killen 1984: 57–61.

301 Killen also notes the high level of specificity demonstrated by the workgroup women at Pylos: Killen 1984: 58.

302 Excluding women in the collectors' groups who are not explicitly designated as such.

303 Pylos has two different groups of a-ra-ka-te-ja workers: one with the additional ethnic mi-ra-ti-ja and the other without.

304 Lindgren 1973: Part II, 134. For further discussion, see *Diccionario*: Vol. II, 224.

305 Metapa may have two groups of seven and five women or the Metapa tablets may be referring to the same group. Given the current state of the evidence, it is not possible to conclusively distinguish between these two possibilities.

306 See also Killen 1984: 58 on the small sizes of workgroups located outside of Pylos and Leuktron.

307 Killen also notes the anomalous treatment of Lousos on the texts; as a solution Killen proposes that Lousos perhaps be understood as a "sub-capital" of some kind in the Hither Province which functioned as a center for finishing work. Killen 1984: 59–60.

308 See also Killen for the concentration of Further Province workgroups at Leuktron: Killen 1984: 58.

309 Killen concurs that the less specialized nature of the subordinate location workers implies that these workers be understood as performing all tasks related to textile production rather than acting as single-task specialists. Killen 1984: 58–59.

310 See Carlier's well-reasoned summary presentation of previous theories, Carlier 1983: 16–20.

311 Billigmeier and Turner's interpretation that these independent contractors are refugees is a subset of this model. Billigmeier and Turner 1981: 4–5.

312 Tritsch 1958: 405–445.

313 Uchitel 1984: 260. Uchitel does not differentiate between the Pylos and Knossos systems, but treats them as fairly analogous in their social structures.

314 This is the prevailing view in scholarship: Carlier 1983: 16–20; Chadwick 1976: 79; Killen 1984: 52; Shelmerdine 1998: 295.

315 Chadwick 1976: 80.

316 Some have also wanted to tie the "captives" reading of ra-wi-ja-ja as evidence for the slave status of these women viewing them particularly as prizes of war. The etymology is plausible but not definitive. A stronger argument for slavery, to my mind, is the common status of all the workgroup women, at least some of whose titles imply perpetual, menial labor. That only one group may be termed "captives" to my mind does not remove slave status of the workgroup women but implies that this group would consist of recent captive women.

317 Shelmerdine 1998: 295. Shelmerdine leaves open the question of how these foreign women came to be at Pylos, as either attracted or conscripted to Pylos.

318 Palmer (1963: 117–118) suggested that these women were moved to the Hither and Further provinces to protect them in a state of emergency, but see Hooker who notes, upon closer examination, that while these workers were indeed spread out in a variety of locales, none of them were located in the Further Province: Hooker 1982: 210–217.

319 Carlier reads Metapa as "le chef-lieu de l'un des districts de la province proche." Carlier 1983: 26, n. 34.

320 A position shared by Hooker 1982: 211.

4 Women and property holdings at Pylos

Introduction

In Archaic and Classical Greece, few social practices involving women varied as broadly from state to state as the ability to command and control property holdings. By law, wives in Classical Athens could own no more than their personal clothing and jewelry[1] – exceptions were granted only to priestesses and other female cult officials[2] – while the Gortyn law code offered extensive protections to the interests and property of heiresses.[3] Few ancient voices, however, were as contentious as Aristotle's on the subject with his outraged insistence that Spartan women's ownership of more than a third of all Spartan land would rapidly lead to female lawlessness and the collapse of the Spartan state.[4] (It didn't.) Did patterns similar to these apply to women in the Mycenaean states? What forms of property did Mycenaean women command – and who were the women who controlled them?

Laboring in the low-status collective workgroups was not the only way women entered the economic records of Pylos; Pylian women also contributed to the economy through their control over various resources and commodities. In the economy of Pylos, access to and control over property and commodities served to establish, define, and reinforce status distinctions among all members of the Pylian community. Property holdings functioned as the differentiating line between lower-status men and women within the Pylian state and their middle- and upper-status counterparts insomuch as one of the markers of low social rank was the lack of tangible, non-subsistence-related goods. While Pylian men can be further subdivided between the middle- and upper-status ranks based on elite administrative assignments, it is specifically the control over property and commodities which distinguishes the elite class of women from their workgroup counterparts. This chapter investigates the (non-landed) properties and commodities in the control of women at Pylos by examining the size and nature of their holdings as well as the mechanisms by which the elite among women would seem to acquire their property.[5]

Women's property holdings at Pylos

Women who exercise control over property holdings constitute the elite among women at Pylos; no other women are recorded in the Pylian texts other than laborers or property holders. These more elite women are consistently referenced in the tablets in very different ways than the women of the workgroups and a great gulf exists in status between these two categories of Pylian women. Unlike the workgroup women of the personnel series, female property holders are recorded not in terms of their fecundity, subsistence, or production responsibilities – all topics which indicate a state of dependence on the palace – but rather in terms of the amounts and varieties of materials they control. These women are carefully differentiated in the tablets; unlike the unnamed women of the workgroups, a woman in control of property is typically recorded as a distinct party,[6] identified by her particular title, name, or both. Furthermore, their holdings are generally attributed to them as individuals, unlike the workgroup women whose rations are assigned to them as a collective.

Such differences in the recording of the two categories of women listed in the Pylos tablets underscore their status differences as well. For women at Pylos, only two status options are documented: low-ranking palace dependents or "elite" women. It must be noted, however, that the so-called elite women do not have the same status or attributes as the elite among men; "elite" women conform more closely to the status of mid-ranked men in terms of the property holdings, official titles, obligations to the state, and in their distribution throughout the corpus. Consequently we should understand the female property holders of Pylos as middle-ranked members of the Pylian state, as the elite only among women rather than the elite of the entire population of Pylos.

How the concept of "property ownership" was understood or governed in the Mycenaean world remains largely an open question. Our current state of evidence offers little help in defining what ownership might mean at this time, that is, if properties were, for example, immutably and inviolably in the hands of the individual (or individual family), or if the state retained ultimate command over all materials in its jurisdiction. Such theoretical considerations remain outside the scope of the Linear B documents which focus instead on more empirical and quotidian concerns. What the documents do reveal in great clarity, however, are the details of transactions transferring or conferring properties and commodities to and from the hands of individuals, groups, and the palace elites. For this reason, I am opting away from the term "ownership" (which implies a long-term and inviolable relationship between the possessor and the property) to use instead the term "holdings" (which emphasizes more the functional relationship between the holder and the commodity, that is who has it now for purpose of transfer or receipt) and to regard as a property holder any individual or group exerting sufficient control over commodities and materials as to be deemed responsible for its receipt, delivery, assignment or transfer.

If we then define property holding as the independent allocation to women of resources or properties not directly related to their subsistence, we can identify approximately 100 female Pylian property holders; these women may be identified by name or title.

Property holdings of titled women

The largest subset of women who have property holdings in the Pylos texts are titled women, that is, women who are primarily identified by their occupational designations. These women may also be identified by their names, but the use of their names tends to be in addition to, rather than in lieu of, their titles. Titled women typically have larger holdings than their named-only counterparts, in terms of both the quantities and the varieties of their holdings. They are also the only women at Pylos to be listed in possession of land – a topic explored more extensively in Chapter 6. Nine feminine titles appear to designate women recorded with property and/or commodity holdings at Pylos; six of these titles have clear cult associations.

Female cult officials

The majority of mentions of titled women with property holdings refer to the holdings of female cult officials. These officials are identified with the titles of i-je-re-ja ("priestess"), ka-ra-wi-po-ro ("keybearer"), ki-ri-te-wi-ja (translation disputed), te-o-jo do-e-ra ("slave of the god"), do-e-ra i-je-re-ja ("slave of the priestess"), and do-e-ra ka-ra-wi-po-ro ("slave of the keybearer").

Priestesses

The women who control the greatest amount of material goods at Pylos bear the title i-je-re-ja "priestess" (ἱέρεια).[7] Priestesses appear to be the most important women mentioned in the Linear B tablets from either site. They may be identified either by name or title, and always appear in the singular. The holdings and property of priestesses are mentioned 17 times over a span of 13 tablets which belong to the personnel (A) series, the land tenure (E) series, the sanctuary holdings of the Un series, and the miscellaneous commodities of the Qa series. [8]

At Pylos, priestesses are attested with control over land,[9] textiles,[10] the as yet unknown commodity *189,[11] and both male[12] and female personnel.[13] While it is unclear how many priestesses are present in the Pylos tablets, two priestesses are specified by name (ka-wa-ra and e-ri-ta), and the title appears without an associated name 12 additional times throughout the corpus.[14]

ERITHA/E-RI-TA

Of the named priestesses, e-ri-ta, whose name should normalize as *Eritha,* seems to have been the more significant. *Eritha* is recorded in the land tenure series on PY Ep 704[15] in possession of two parcels of land:

PY Ep 704 lines 3, 5–6

.3 e-ri-ta , i-je-re-ja , o-na-to , e-ke , ke-ke-me-na, ko-to-na , pa-ro , da-mo , to-so , pe-mo GRA T 4

.5 e-ri-ta , i-je-re-ja , e-ke , e-u-ke-to-qe , e-to-ni-jo , e-ke-e , te-o , da-mo-de-mi , pa-si , ko-to-na-o ,

.6 ke-ke-me-na-o , o-na-to , e-ke-e , to-so , pe-mo GRA 3 T 9

3. "Eritha the priestess has a leased plot (o-na-to) of communal land (ke-ke-me-na ko-to-na-o) from the damos, so much seed: 38.4 l. wheat

5–6. Eritha the priestess has and claims a freehold holding (e-to-ni-jo) for her god, but the damos says that she holds a leased plot (o-na-to) of communal land (ke-ke-me-na ko-to-na-o), so much seed: 374.4 l. wheat"

One of these holdings is a leased plot of communal land (o-na-to ke-ke-me-na ko-to-na)[16] of modest size (line 3). It measures T 4 GRA, or of sufficient size that 38.4 liters of grain were required to seed it. It is the second smallest of the five plots recorded on this tablet. The second plot attributed to e-ri-ta is much larger (374.4 l.), but the type of this holding was in active dispute in the records themselves. While her local administration (da-mo) contended that it was a plot of leased communal land (o-na-to ke-ke-me-na ko-to-na) – and presumably taxable – e-ri-ta in turn argued that it was "freehold" (e-to-ni-jo) land belonging to her god (te-o) rather than her personal property.[17] (Like so many other ancient legal disputes, we do not know how this one was resolved.) In either case, the size of this holding is substantial, underscoring the priestess's importance to the damos which allocated her land and the palace who monitored this transaction.

As PY Ep 704 recapitulates the information on two Eb series tablets, we can also identify the figure known as the priestess at Sphagianes (i-je-re-ja pa-ki-ja-na) as *Eritha*. (The T 4 holding on this tablet is the same as that of the i-je-re-ja pa-ki-ja-na on PY Eb 339 + PY Eb 409.)[18] Under this designation, she receives another three mentions on two land tenure tablets; she appears in possession of two types of holdings: personnel and land allotments.[19] The final land holding in the direct control of the priestess at pa-ki-ja-ne is recorded on En 609, where she is attested as the holder of a leased plot (o-na-to) requiring 28.8 liters of seed to sow it – the largest plot of any of the 13 officials mentioned on the tablet.[20]

Her personnel "holdings" take the form of two sanctuary functionaries. These functionaries incorporate her title into theirs as do-e-ra/ro i-je-re-ja pa-ki-ja-ne "slaves of the priestess at pa-ki-ja-na." Both of these slaves are named: a man te-te-re-u (*Tetreus*) and a woman e-ra-ta-ra. Both are attested in possession of small land allotments. Tetreus the δοῦλος of the priestess possesses a leased plot of communal land (o-na-to ke-ke-me-na ko-to-na) which measures 4.8 liters on PY Eb 1176[21] while e-ra-ta-ra, a δούλη, holds a leased plot measuring 9.6 liters on PY En 609.[22] What is interesting is that while both listings indicate that these personnel belong to the priestess, their land holdings appear to have been administered in their own right rather than as additional possessions of the priestess. There is strong evidence to think of the "slave" designation of this series as a ceremonial title; "slaves of the priestess" – and later, "slaves of the keybearer" and "slaves of the god" – share none of the attributes of the slave women of the personnel series; these cult slaves are instead recorded as distinct individuals by their names and allotted land holdings, rather than the aggregate designations of the workgroup women who receive only subsistence rations. As such, this further reinforces the economic prominence of this priestess, in that even her underlings are sufficiently important to draw public land holdings.

KA-WA-RA

The second named priestess, ka-wa-ra, is recorded on the miscellaneous commodity tablet PY Qa 1289 with a lacunose amount of the commodity *189.[23] A second tablet (PY Qa 1300) records an additional 2 units of *189 being allotted to a priestess.[24] Unfortunately the name of this priestess is in lacuna, but it would seem that the woman in question is likely also ka-wa-ra as the structure of this tablet appears identical to the one on which she is named.

UNNAMED PRIESTESSES

We see five additional mentions of priestesses who remain unmodified by either name or location. As these are mostly land series tablets, it is likely that the priestess in question is indeed e-ri-ta but no concrete link is yet present. The largest holdings attributed to an unnamed priestess are attested on PY Ed 317 which records enormous leased plots of land in the joint possession of the priestess, the female official entitled ka-ra-wi-po-ro, an e-qe-ta (an elite male official), and the priest we-te-re-u – combined holdings which measure an enormous 2073.6 liters of grain.

PY Ed 317
.1 o-da-a2 , i-je-re-ja , ka-ra-wi-po-ro-qe , e-qe-ta-qe [[ ]]
.2 we-te-re-u-qe , o-na-ta , to-so-de , pe-mo GRA 21 T 6
"And so, the priestess and the keybearer and the e-qe-ta ("follower") and Westreus (a priest) [hold] leased-plots, so much seed: 2073.6 l. wheat"

Unfortunately, as these plots are not differentiated by individual holders, we cannot ascertain how much of this leased land can be attributed specifically to the priestess; this is particularly unfortunate, as this wheat measure on this tablet is the second largest of all the land holdings at Pylos, surpassing those of the *lawagetas* and second only to that of the *wanax*. A second land tenure tablet attests another aspect of the management of land resources by priestesses: PY Eb 416[25] records an allotment of land to a female slave of the god (te-o-jo do-e-ra) named u-wa-mi-ja (*Huamia*)[26] not from communal lands but as a 24 l. lease described as ke-ra i-je-re-ja, a γέρας or "gift of honor" from the priestess.[27] As the only such mention of this term in the land tenure tablets, it is difficult to know exactly what a ke-ra entails, but this tablet would seem to indicate that the priestess was in a position from which she had sufficient control over at least some of her holdings that she could reassign them at her discretion.

Further personnel attributed to an unnamed priestess are documented on two tablets: the land tenure tablet PY EP 539 and the personnel tablet PY Ae 303. PY

Ep 539.7 records a personnel holding of the priestess in the form of a do-e-ro named me-re-u who has a small (3.2 liter) land lease;[28] this tablet, like the others mentioning slaves in the control of priestesses, confirms that the land in question is in the possession of this do-e-ro rather than the priestess who controls him. The title "slave of the priestess" used in the E series clearly differentiates these slaves from "ordinary" slaves of the personnel series, who remain nameless and control no property, by setting them on a parallel footing with the te-o-jo do-e-ro-i ("slaves of the god') – a cult title indicating a significantly higher social status than that of genuine slaves.

The second tablet which documents personnel in the control of a priestess is unique within the Pylian corpus. As mentioned in the previous chapter, PY Ae 303 records 14 women designated by the ideogram MUL and the title i-je-re-ja do-e-ra ("slaves of the priestess").[29] The tablet also notes that these women are present at Pylos, rather than at pa-ki-ja-na, and adds the datum e-ne-ka i-je-ro-jo ku-ru-su-jo ("on account of the sacred gold"). The significance of this additional prepositional phrase is not entirely clear. It would appear to offer an explanation for their transfer to the control of the priestess or perhaps to signal that their task was related to the treasury; it is also possible that this tablet is signaling that this was the means by which they were acquired. I am doubtful that these 14 women referred to on this tablet should be considered to share the same status as the similarly titled "slaves of the priestess" mentioned in the land tablets. The slave women in Ae 303 are recorded in much the same way as the other low-status women of the personnel tablets: their names are not mentioned, they are tallied with an accompanying MUL ideogram (an ideogram which never appears in conjunction with women of more elite status at Pylos), and they are not attested with any property of their own. From this evidence, then, it would appear that the priestess(es?) possessed two different groups of subordinate personnel: people for whom the title "slave of the priestess" denoted an actual servile status related to tending the priestess and her sanctuary and those for whom it functioned as a kind of low-level honorific on a par with the ceremonial title "slave of the god." In either case, the assignment of multiple personnel to the jurisdiction of the priestess is securely attested.

In addition to land and personnel holdings, priestess(es) are also attested in possession of commodity holdings. In addition to the commodity *189 holdings of the priestess ka-wa-ra already mentioned, priestesses are also recorded with textile holdings. PY Un 6, a tablet whose recto records allotments of animals provided to divine figures including Poseidon, lists on its verso allotments to a priestess and ka-ra-wi-po-ro of TELA+te cloth.[30] (The te affix indicates that the cloth in question is te-pa cloth, the specialty cloth produced by the te-pe-ja women of the personnel series.[31]) These two women are the only officials listed on the verso, and the sizes of their allotments are unfortunately lost.

Ka-ra-wi-po-ro/"Keybearer"

In addition to the priestesses, the official known as the ka-ra-wi-po-ro also commands significant property at Pylos. A title with unmistakable religious connotations, this term normalizes as *klawiphoros* ("keybearer")[32] and seems to be either a specialized type of priestess or a separate religious official of approximately the same standing as priestesses. Unlike the title i-je-re-ja "priestess" which has a masculine variant in i-je-re-u "priest," ka-ra-wi-po-ro are always female. Otherwise the treatment of the keybearer in the tablets is quite similar to that of priestesses. The ka-ra-wi-po-ro occupy many of the same tablet series as do priestesses – occasionally in parallel contexts[33] – and like priestesses may be recorded by name, by title, or with both terms in conjunction. So closely are these two types of female cult officials linked, they appear together on nearly half the tablets which record the ka-ra-wi-po-ro. As with priestesses, it is uncertain how many keybearers are referenced, although the name of one keybearer, ka-pa-ti-ja, which normalizes as *Karpathia,* is clearly identifiable on several tablets both in conjunction with and apart from her title. It is not currently possible to discern whether this Karpathia is the sole ka-ra-wi-po-ro at Pylos or if she is one of many. (For convenience, and in the absence of any other named keybearers, I will regard Karpathia as the sole ka-ra-wi-po-ro in this chapter.) Property, personnel, and commodity holdings are attributed to the keybearer on nine tablets belonging to the personnel (A), land tenure (E), cult offerings (Un), unknown commodity (V), and bronze (Jn) series. The first four of these series also record property in the control of priestesses, and the holdings of the keybearer(s) are largely similar in both size and scope. The ka-ra-wi-po-ro controls personnel (do-e-ro/ra ka-ra-wi-po-ro-jo),[34] land holdings,[35] textiles,[36] and foodstuffs (barley).[37] Slaves of the ka-ra-wi-po-ro seem to be exactly analogous to those of the priestess, with her named slaves of higher rank (do-e-ro ka-pa-ti-ja) in the Ep series functioning as land-lease holders while her lower-ranked slaves (also recorded as do-e-ro/ra ka-pa-ti-ja) remain unnamed and tallied as a group in the Ae series.The land holdings of the keybearer are similar to that of the priestess as well. In her own right, Karpathia holds leases (o-na-ta) of two communal plots (ke-ke-me-na kot-to-na) of lacunose size on PY Eb 388, an entry recapitulated on Py Ep 704. On PY Ed 317, she appears in conjunction with the priestess and other cult officials in control of plots measuring a combined 2073.6 l.; as already mentioned this aggregate holding is not further differentiated by holder. This is particularly regrettable as none of the sizes of the ka-ra-wi-po-ro's land holdings are extant, rendering any direct comparison with the size of the priestess's lands unachievable. The ka-ra-wi-po-ro also closely parallels the priestess in terms of her textile holdings. As mentioned above, women are the sole recipients of TELA+te cloth on the verso of PY Un 6; they are the tablet's only recipients. Both amounts are in lacuna. In contrast, PY Un 443 + PY Un 998 offers the first instance where a holding of the keybearer's is not echoed by a similar holding of the priestess. On this tablet Karpathia – without title – appears with three male officials who are allotted measures of wool, barley, and wheat; Karpathia receives 2 units of HORD,[38] the only HORD allotment of this tablet. A second unparalleled mention comes from the Vn series – a series which lists tallies exclusive of ideograms. On PY Vn 48 the ka-ra-wi-po-ro is recorded solely by title among a list of at least nine low- to mid-level officials; five unspecified items are attributed to her, the second largest amount of this tablet. These last two tablets seem to reinforce the status of the ka-ra-wi-po-ro as a mid-level rather than an elite official as these mentions seem to associate her with only middle-status men and to record her holdings in a similar fashion.

The final tablet on which the ka-ra-wi-po-ro appears is the most significant: PY Jn 829 from the J series which is distinguished by the use of the AES bronze ideogram.[39] This tablet consists of a three-line introductory heading followed by a sixteen-line body section.

PY Jn 829
.1 jo-do-so-si , ko-re-te-re , du-ma-te-qe ,
.2 po-ro-ko-re-te-re-qe , ka-ra-wi-po-ro-qe , o-pi-su-ko-qe , o-pi-ka-pe-'e-we-qe'
.3 ka-ko , na-wi-jo , pa-ta-jo-i-qe , e-ke-si-qe , a3-ka-sa-ma
.4 pi-*82 , ko-re-te , AES M 2 po-ro-ko-re-te AES N 3
.5 me-ta-pa , ko-re-te AES M 2 po-ro-ko-re-te AES N 3 [ ] *vacat*
(etc.)
1–3 "Thus the ko-re-te-re (official along the lines of 'mayors'), the officials known as du-ma-te-qe, theko-re-te-re ('under-mayors'), the keybearer(s?), the overseers of figs, and the overseers of hoes contribute temple /sacred bronze for points for spears and javelins.
4. From pi-*82 (place name), the 'mayors': 2 M units Bronze; the 'vice-mayors' 3 N units Bronze
5. From me-ta-pa (place name), the 'mayors': 2 M units Bronze; the 'vice-mayors' 3 N units Bronze"

The heading indicates that bronze is to be contributed for the forging of points for arrows and spears from six different types of officials; the remainder of the tablet enumerates the specific contributions of officials designated by two of these six titles.[40] The contributions of the remaining four types of officials are not recorded here. These officials occupy different status levels: the ko-re-te and po-ro-ko-re-te are the local administrative elite,[41] the o-pi-su-ko-qe and o-pi-ka-pe-we-qe would seem to be local agrarian supervisors, assuming their tentative identifications as overseers of figs and hoes, respectively, are correct,[42] the fifth official classification du-ma-te remains obscure,[43] and the remaining official mentioned is the ka-ra-wi-po-ro. It would seem that these six classifications of officials are not linked so much by a shared social or administrative status but by their proximate access to bronze via their respective official responsibilities. Thus the farm overseers might have a ready supply of metal in their tools available for contribution while a keybearer could access the bronze locked away for her safekeeping, bronze which presumably was shrine property. This is the only instance in the Pylos corpus where we see in female hands a commodity so vital as bronze, and it is interesting that the hands in question belong to a female religious functionary.

Ki-ri-te-wi-ja

The third group of female officials recorded with property holdings are the ki-ri-te-wi-ja.[44] This title is different from either i-je-re-ja or ka-ra-wi-po-ro in that the term ki-ri-te-wi-ja always appears in the plural and the women who compose this group are never named or differentiated as individuals. Like the term ka-ra-wi-po-ro, ki-ri-te-wi-ja has no masculine equivalent. This title is attested four times at Pylos, and these women are recorded as holding land leases in the E series[45] in much the same way as the priestess and keybearer. They also appear on the fragmentary PY Un 1426 + 1428 – a tablet which records massive amounts of foodstuffs allotted to officials at Pylos, including the *wanax,* the highest ranking figure in the state; their amount, however, is in lacuna. Finally, while their association with Pylian cult is not as transparent as with the priestesses and keybearer, they also seem to have some sort of religious affiliation – an affiliation which would appear to be secured by PY Ep 704 which lists them in conjunction with known religious officials such as the priestess, keybearer, a female "slave of the god", and a male functionary at the cult center of pa-ki-ja-na.[46] As no lay officials are otherwise present on this tablet, it seems logical from context to also regard the ki-ri-te-wi-ja as belonging to the sphere of cult. Lending further support to their identification as religious functionaries is PY An 607 which presents the ki-ri-te-wi-ja in contexts with otherwise unknown slaves of various gods, but this tablet is particularly ambiguous and poorly understood.[47]

"Sacred slaves"

The three last categories of female cult officials with property holdings have already been mentioned; these are the named women who bear the word do-e-ra "slave" as part of their titles. These women, carrying the specialized titles of te-o-jo do-e-ra "slave of the god"[48] or slaves of the priestess or keybearer (in the texts mentioned on p. 136–140), occupy a different social status than ordinary slaves or the workgroup women and are always named and recorded with property holdings. Both te-o-jo do-e-ra (pl.) and slaves of religious functionaries possess the same type of holdings – land leases in the E series.[49] Te-o-jo do-e-ra are much more numerous, with over 50 of these women attested. As with the slaves of the priestess or keybearer, a masculine variant (te-o-jo do-e-ro) is also known.

Discussion of cult officials and property

Several patterns emerge regarding the ways in which female cult officials controlled their property holdings. All these titled women are in possession of leased land; for the ki-ri-te-wi-ja, te-o-jo do-e-ra, and do-e-ra of the priestess and the keybearer these leases constitute their only property recorded in the Pylos tablets. In contrast, the holdings of both the priestesses and keybearer are more varied, with personnel, cloth, foodstuffs, and land among their goods. In terms of property alone, it would appear that a status hierarchy was in effect even among these "elite" women. Priestesses and keybearers occupy the highest rung of the social ladder for Pylian women, while "slaves of the god" and slaves of priestesses come substantially lower in terms of their economic power. The location of the ki-ri-te-wi-ja in the status hierarchy remains uncertain, but it seems reasonable to place them between the three types of "sacred slaves" and the priestess and keybearer.[50]

All of these cult functionaries seem to display autonomy in their property holdings. All property and commodities seem to be allocated to each of these officials in their own right, by name or joint title in the case of the ki-ri-te-wi-ja, despite whatever standing in the functionary hierarchy each of these women occupy. Importantly, the property holdings even of women who are designated slaves of the priestess or keybearer belong to them rather than their superiors. While these women appear to occupy the lowest rung of the property-holding hierarchy, it is important to note that they too rank among the economically autonomous women at Pylos.

A greater level of economic and administrative autonomy seems to have been accorded to the two highest ranking female cult officials, the priestess and the keybearer. In addition to their various land holdings and their standing personnel of servile (such as the slaves assigned to the priestess "on account of the sacred gold" on PY Ae 303) and those of higher, ceremonial status (the land-receiving do-e-ra-i of the PY E series), both officials are attested in circumstances which underscore their undisputed control of property: the priestess who is in a position to issue a ke-ra (γέρας) lease to one of her underlings and the keybearer being called upon to contribute the bronze in her charge to the state; in neither case does the functionary need to act through a brokering middleman – or male guardian – nor is the commodity presented as belonging to anyone other than her. And perhaps the best argument for regarding priestesses as figures with legal and economic autonomy lies in the dispute between e-ri-ta and the damos over the status of the larger plot of land on PY Ep 704; that she directly represents herself, without a kyrios (guardian), in what appears to be a local legal dispute would seem to establish her as a legally independent personage in direct command of the commodities and property allocated to her or else why would the scribe choose to record the dispute and directly record her claim? It is unclear how much we should make of this direct personal representation here as even in Classical Athens, priestesses were exempt from the kyrios requirement in order to fulfill, unhampered, the requirements of the cult practices entrusted to their care.[51] Consequently, it is not possible to judge whether priestesses alone in the Pylian state functioned kyrios-free, but certainly the high correlation between property holdings and functionary status would seem to argue for a privileged relationship between religious affiliation among women and access to important goods and resources – with one important caveat: we must remember that all the land involved here is leased land; no women are attested with any long-term ownership of land at Pylos.

The second major issue pertaining to the institutionalized property holdings of functionary women relates to the forms which these holdings take. Should we understand these holdings as being owned or merely administered by these officials, that is, are their holdings conceived as their own property or as connected with their official tasks and responsibilities? Again, this is a difficult question to untangle; the line between personal and official holdings is not always clearly defined in the tablets, although two cases involving Pylian priestesses seem to illustrate both extremes. First of all, the issue of official versus personal use seems to be at the heart of the e-ri-ta freehold/leased land dispute.[52] Once again, the priestess e-ri-ta makes the claim that her land is e-to-ni-jo, or freehold, land belonging to her god – a clearly official form of land holding – while the local damos in turn contends that is an o-na-to, or leased plot, in her possession – a circumstance that would seem to convey obligations directly upon her person. I read the very possibility of such a dispute as indicating that the priestess could have property in both an official and a personal capacity – otherwise there would be nothing for these two entities to dispute. On the other hand, the addition on PY Ae 303, the tablet which records the 14 slave women designated by the ideogram MUL and the title i-je-re-ja do-e-ra, of the phrase e-ne-ka i-je-ro-jo ku-ru-su-jo "on account of the sacred gold" underscores that this group of women belong to the priestess entirely in her official capacity; the term "sacred gold" can surely be interpreted in no other way. Also clearly official are the bronze holdings of the keybearer. I would expect that we should also understand the textile allotments to both the priestess and the keybearer in an official light, as the textiles necessary for either their shrines themselves or the shrine personnel in their employ, and that we should perhaps regard at least most of the property attributed in the tablets to functionary women to have been allocated in their official capacities.

Titled laywomen

In addition to the cult functionaries discussed above, a small number of other women identified by titles appear with property holdings in the Pylos tablets. These titles are consistently occupationally-derived, and all are mentioned in conjunction with the MUL ideogram as the titles of dependent workgroup women known from the personnel series. One of these mentions securely associates property to the a-ke-ti-ri-ja; the remaining two mentions, the a-pi-qo-ro and the pa-wo-ko, are possible but not definitive.

The sole secure association of titled workgroup women with commodity holdings are those of the a-ke-ti-ri-ja ("decorators");[53] they are mentioned with commodity holdings on PY Fn 187 and PY Un 219. The Fn tablet belongs to a series which Killen has convincingly demonstrated is devoted to recording the allocation of barley and other foodstuffs for religious festivals sponsored by the Pylian palace.[54] The a-ke-ti-ri-ja appear in the dative plural on the 15th line of this 23-line tablet where they receive allotments of barley along with a number of titled individuals who appear to be low-level religious functionaries[55] – underscoring the overall cultic character of this tablet series. Of the 20 allottees, the a-ke-ti-ri-ja receive the second lowest portion recorded on the tablet – 16 l. of barley. (The highest amount allocated is 48 l.)

On PY Un 219, the a-ke-ti-ri-ja appear midway through line 4 of a 17-line tablet and receive the unknown commodity KA.[56] This tablet otherwise records allotments given to mid- and high-level palace functionaries as well as to a few divinities. It is not possible, however, to gauge the relative importance of the a-ke-ti-ri-ja mentioned on this tablet as only one other personage receives a KA allotment – a herald on line 3. Most problematic about this tablet is the impossibility of ascertaining whether this mention of a-ke-ti-ri-ja pertains to one of the four such workgroups from the personnel series or to an entirely female group of decorators. (If the second option is correct, it is possible that these decorators may not even be employed in textile production but that they may devote their decorating activities to a different medium.) What is unmistakable is that in both mentions the a-ke-ti-ri-ja appear in conjunction with cult-related personnel and activities. This can hardly be accidental; the Pylos tablets seem to document a strong linkage between religious affiliation for women and access to properties or commodities. One might surmise that these decorators may have been in attendance on a shrine complex;[57] if so, they may have been granted access to commodities and products not ordinarily accessible to other low-ranking workgroup women as a result of their presence in activities related to the tending of cult.

The second non-functionary title to appear in conjunction with a commodity is a-pi-qo-ro on the Olive Oil tablet PY Fr 1205:[58]

PY Fr 1205
a-pi-qo-ro-i , we-ja-re-pe OLE +PA S 2 V 4 [
"To the attendants, sage scented oil for anointing: 22.4 l."[59]

This tablet, one of the 51 tablets of the Fr series – a series which exclusively deals with cult-related disbursements of olive oil to various divinities and human religious personnel, records the allotment of sage scented olive oil (OLE in conjunction with the ligature PA, the abbreviation for pa-ko-we *sphakowen* "scented with sage"[60]) which is suitable for anointing,[61] to a group of *amphipoloi*, a title also known from the personnel series at Pylos where, in conjunction with the MUL ideogram, it refers to a group of low-status workgroup women.[62] The issue arises in the precise identification of the *amphipoloi* in the Fr tablets in that it is not clear that this mention of a-pi-qo-ro refers to the same group of women as the personnel series, or, for that matter, refers to women at all. In the absence of a gender-specific ideogram here it should be remembered that the term ἀμφιπόλος grammatically can be either masculine or feminine. It is clearly a feminine term in the personnel series where it is accompanied by the MUL ideogram. Is this also the case here? *LSJ* notes that the primary attestations in Greek literature of this term place it exclusively as a feminine substantive meaning "handmaid" or "waiting woman." These are the readings attested in both Homer and Hesiod;[63] only later do we get attestations placing these female figures in specialized religious contexts as "handmaids of the gods" or "priestesses."[64] However, *LSJ* also notes masculine attributions for ἀμφιπόλοι; as early as Pindar, it can also indicate (male) "attendant" or "follower."[65] Later usages also show the same elevation of the term to functionary status ("priest, sacrist") in Euripides and Philodemus.[66] Lindgren has offered two possible interpretations for these oil recipients: as (human) "servants of a god/shrine" or as members of the divine sphere as "the Two Servants/Handmaidens."[67] To my mind, given the clear religious context of the Fr series as well as the lack of specifying ideogram, both these readings are plausible as would be the readings that place them as male functionaries or divinities as well. If we were to read these as attendant women of some stripe, bearing in mind that this interpretation is not entirely secure, we should perhaps consider it significant that the *amphipoloi*, like the a-ke-ti-ri-ja, only receive commodity holdings when they appear in an overtly religious context.

Even more problematic is the mention of pa-wo-ko on the wool tablet PY La 632:

PY La 632
pa-wo-ko LANA[

Assuming the rather tenuous proposition that the word-string pa-wo-ko is indeed referring to *pan-worges*,[68] this workgroup (?) would have some connection to wool working; nonetheless it is important to note that this term could also be a masculine form as well. As no secure linkage between this mention and the personnel series workgroup can be made, nor even the identification of this term as referring to women, it is perhaps best to dissociate this reference from our examination of women's property holdings at Pylos.

Overall, the property holdings of titled "lay" women are vastly more limited than their functionary counterparts. While cult officials are attested with control over a variety of resources, including that most precious commodity of land, the holdings of the occupationally-titled women are severely more limited, consisting of a single secure mention and referring to a relatively small amount of a given commodity. Nonetheless, the institutionalized property holdings of these two otherwise distinct groups converge in one major aspect: all titled women attested with property of any kind at Pylos receive property in contexts which are directly linked to cult-related practice. Religious affiliation either via official functionary status or by the inclusion of lay women into cult contexts appears to be the justification for extending access to and control over commodities for titled women of otherwise very distinct social standings, rendering it the lone institutional setting where Pylian women control goods and resources in parallel ways to Pylian men.

Property Holdings Of Named Women

Property is also controlled by several women identified by their names rather than a religious or occupational title. These named women are recorded on eight tablets scattered throughout the Pylian texts; unlike the Ab rations tablets or the land holdings of the E series, tablets which document the holdings of these named women do not constitute a single, unified subseries but are instead distributed more randomly throughout the Pylos corpus.[69] Like the titled women discussed above, the women identified by name are allocated their holdings directly. However, when the specific holdings of the named women are examined more closely, significant differences emerge in both quality and quantity as compared to their titled counterparts. While the property attributed to the titled women largely assumed two distinct forms (land and movable goods belonging to female religious officials and non-subsistence related foodstuffs provided for non-sacerdotal women when they enter cult contexts), the holdings of the named women tend to be less unified. There seem to be at least four distinct ways in which these titled women hold property, and at least one of these arrangements involves the property holdings of women who are of high social rank.

Named women of low to middle status

Women receiving food allocations

Two of the named women with property associations are recorded on PY Fn 187,[70] a tablet which lists allotments of barley and/or figs to 21 recipients, many of whom have clear associations with cult locales or personnel.[71] As mentioned above, the Fn series records the allotments of barley and other foodstuffs on the occasion of religious festivals. The recipients of these commodities are varied although the relationship to cult is evident throughout; the commodities of barley and figs on this tablet are allotted to both persons involved in cult practice and to cult localities such as pa-ki-ja-ne and the shrine of Poseidon. Among the human recipients are male officials such as four heralds (ka-ru-ke) and an unspecified number of priests of Poseidon (po-si-da-i-je-u-si),[72] two undisputedly masculine names (a-ma-tu-na, and te-qi-ri-jo-ne), several masculine words which are likely either men's names or men's titles (au-to-*34-ta-ra, de-do-wa-re-we, i-so-e-ko, o-pi-ti-ra-jo), several individuals of uncertain gender (a-ro-ja and ku-ri-na-ze-ja), a possible divinity,[73] a feminine occupational title in the plural (a-ke-ti-ri-ja, in one of their two property-related mentions), and what appear to be the names of two otherwise unknown women (a-pi-te-ja on line 1 and *34-ke-ja on line 19). The tablet's allotments range in size from 2 full units (192 l.) on line 1 down to V 3 (4.8 l.) received by both te-qi-ri-jo-ne and a-ro-ja on lines 12 and 20, respectively. What is perhaps most significant, is that the largest amount on this tablet, 192 l. of figs and presumably the same amount of barley,[74] is assigned to a woman, a-pi-te-ja on line 1, markedly more than any other figure here. The second allotment to a woman, *34-ke-ja receiving 14 l. of barley and figs, is more proportionate to the remaining figures on this tablet. It is not clear how much weight we should give to this tablet as a record of personal property, as it entails what appears to be a one-time distribution of small amounts of foodstuffs on the occasion of a religious festival,[75] but what seems significant is the reinforced relationship between cultic settings and women's allocations.

A third named woman who is allotted commodities appears on a second PY Fn tablet: PY Fn 79.[76] Killen, building on the work of Perpillou and Chadwick, has made a strong argument for understanding this tablet as recording distributions of barley and olives to cult workers involved in a five-day festival.[77] This tablet has a less varied recipient list than did PY Fn 187, listing men's names on 14 of its 15 lines and a single woman's name (a3-pu-ke-ne-ja) on the remaining line. This tablet is somewhat unusual in its tabulation formula in that the tallies of all commodities follow rather than precede their ideograms, and the amounts of each foodstuff do not correspond in size. The HORD allotments range in size from 64 l. down to 8 l., with five individuals, including a3-pu-ke-ne-ja, tied for the top amount and three for the lower. Seven individuals, including all four who received the 64 l. barley allotment, additionally receive one full unit of olives. What is interesting about this tablet pertains to what is known about the recipients named here. As Perpillou observed, five of the male names on this tablet are repeated on PY Fn 50 – a tablet which records allocations to sanctuary workers.[78] It seems logical to regard the remaining workers on this tablet in the same light, particularly as they appear to all be rationed in the same way at the same festival, and to regard the lone woman of this tablet, a3-pu-ke-ne-ja, as another instance of a female cult attendant receiving commodities in her own right as a result of her relationship to Pylian religious practice. As her holdings are somewhat more substantial than either the workgroup women or the named women of PY Fn 187 (a-pi-te-ja and *34-ke-ja), it may be correct to think of a3-pu-ke-ne-ja as holding a cult position of middle rank, perhaps on a par with figures such as te-o-jo do-e-ra ("slaves of the god").

Thus, of the eight non-titled women who are attributed property holdings at Pylos, two have as their "holdings" only relatively small quantities of foodstuffs; the holdings of two of these women are comparable to the rations provided to the workgroup workers while the third operates on an only slightly larger scale (approximately three times as much) than the women of the workgroups. Cult affiliation certainly seems to be the mechanism by which these women come to have any personal allocations at all, but even within this context we see no indication of major amounts of property being allocated to these women. Only four non-titled women at Pylos may have holdings of any significance: a-pi-te-ja, a-pi-e-ra, and mi-jo-qa, and ke-sa-da-ra.

Mi-jo-qa and A-pi-e-ra

I turn next to the property holdings of two additional women: a-pi-e-ra and mi-jo-qa who both appear on tablets PY An 1281 and PY Fn 50. PY Fn 50[79] is composed of three different paragraphs of information. The first paragraph (lines 1–3) is concerned with the allocation of foodstuffs to the qa-si-re-wi-ja, officials who typically appear in connection with metals, the second paragraph (lines 4–9) with the allocation of barley to known cult workers, and the third paragraph (lines 11–14) records the distribution of food to the dependent personnel of ranking cult officials.[80] A-pi-e-ra and mi-jo-qa each appear in the third paragraph in the genitive case[81] as the "owners" of slaves (do-e-ro) (lines 12–13). A second, more fragmentary, tablet (PY Fn 867[82]) makes a similar reference to a slave of mi-jo-qa who also receives barley. On both these tablets, a-pi-e-ra and mi-jo-qa appear in an analogous fashion to their male counterparts in both recording practices and holdings.

PY An 1281[83] opens with a two-line header "i-qe-ja Potnia …at her seat,"[84] which is then followed by its 11-line body. Each of these body lines consists of a personal name typically in the dative case[85] followed by a second name which is masculine and nominative; after the names the VIR ideogram follows and either the numerals for one or two. It seems apparent that the nominative men are being attributed to the people[86] who appear in the dative. The two names mi-jo-qa and a-pi-e-ra are mentioned twice on this tablet in the opening position and seem to be recorded in the same way as the other opening names. A-pi-e-ra is assigned to a man on both lines 8 and 13, and mi-jo-qa appears with men on lines 7 and 11.

From context, it would appear that mi-jo-qa and a-pi-e-ra are conceptualized as being on a similar tier with the mid-ranking male officials who also appear on these tablets. Significantly, all three of these tablets are directly connected to cult practice; known sanctuary workers appear on both Fn tablets while the An tablet connects these women with the cult of Potnia.[87] Since in all three instances, the type of holdings these two women are in possession of is personnel, and due to the close correlation of all these tablets with cult-related personnel and activities, Killen's identification of mi-jo-qa and a-pi-e-ra as priestesses must certainly be correct; priestesses are the only women at Pylos attested to as owning slaves.[88]

Kessandra

Thus far, all the women in control of property in the Pylos tablets have been explicitly and closely connected to cult practice. A single exception to this rule exists: the woman named ke-sa-da-ra (*Kessandra*).[89] Ke-sa-da-ra appears on five tablets at Pylos: An 435, Fg 368, Fg 828, Mb 1380, and MN 1368 (twice). She is one of the few women at Pylos who can be sexed solely on the basis of her name. (As a masculine variant would take the form ke-sa-da-ro, the -ra ending in this case can be more than reasonably taken to indicate a feminine ending.) While the Mn tablet attributes to her the as yet unknown commodity represented by sign *146[90] and the Xa tablet preserves only a mention of her name, the strength of her economic status is revealed by the two Fg tablets which allocate to her large quantities of wheat and figs:

PY Fg 368
ke-sa-da-ra GRA 5̣ NI 5
"Kessandra: 480 l. wheat, 480 l. figs"

PY Fg 828
ke-sa-da-ra GRA 5
"Kessandra: 480 l. wheat"

These two tablets are excellent examples about the hazards of taking an impressionistic rather than numerical approach to the material. At first glance, if one were only to address the name and the ideogram, it might appear that this tablet is a ration tablet on a par with the Ab series. The amount of wheat and figs she receives, however, is more than 25 times the amount of wheat and figs a workgroup woman would receive. Clearly, ke-sa-da-ra occupies a very different position in the Pylian economy than other women who receive the same commodities as rations. These are the largest, and perhaps only, real property holdings attributed to a Pylian woman not expressly of religious standing. So what are we to make of her? Might she be a supervisor in charge of the distribution of food to the workgroup women or perhaps she controls a workshop of her own to receive such a massive quantity of food?

The two remaining tablets in the Pylos Fg series may shed some light on this question. The one complete tablet (PY Fg 374) records the allocation of one full unit (96 l.) each of wheat and figs to ko-ka-ro the unguent-boiler. The other PY Fg 253 records the allotment of a massive quantity of both figs and grain (192 full units + 7 T units or 18,499.2 l.) to an only partially preserved figure [ ]-ra-so-ro. The enormous size of this last allocation might well support the idea that at least some members of this series are receiving food rations (as wheat and figs are the usual subsistence foods at Pylos) for large regions or workgroups. As so little information is available from the tablets related to *Kessandra*, it is very difficult to understand why she seems to differ so widely from the other 1200 women in the Pylos tablets. At this juncture, I lean toward viewing her as a local rations supervisor (perhaps as one of the DA or TA figures of the personnel series), a reading also shared by Nakassis in light of PY An 435 which records allocations of men by a-ko-so-ta, likely to her.[91] Under any circumstances, she is operating at a significantly different societal level than the low-status laborers or the functionary women. The question remains, why is she the only such woman in the Pylos archive?

Elite wives: high social status but little economic autonomy

Circumstances regarding the final set of named women in the Pylos tablets diverge widely from the named women discussed above. Seven women compose this remaining category of women within the Pylos archives – wo-di-je-ja, a*64-ja, pi-ri-ta, pi-ro-pa-ta-ra, o-[.]-o-wa, and ma-ra-me-na. Six of these appear on PY Vn 34 + 1191 + 1006 + fr. (discussed below) while one of their number – wo-di-je-ja – is referenced a second time on PY Ub 1318 which also adds the name of the remaining woman in this category (a-pe-i-ja). (I have put them in bold for convenience.)

PY Ub 1318 + frr.

.1 au-ke-i-ja-te-we , ka-tu-re-wi-ja-i di-pte-ra 4 [ ]ḍị-pte-ra 2 au-ke-i-ja-te-we , o-ka , di-pte-ṛạ[

.2 au-ke-i-ja-te-we o-pi-de-so-mo ka-tu-ro2 , di-pte-ra 4 ka-ne-ja wo-ro-ma-ta 4
.3 me-ti-ja-no , to-pa , ru-de-a2 , ḍị-pte-ra 1 a-re-se-si , e-ru-ta-ra , di-pte-ṛạ 3 wo-di-je-ja , pe-di-ra 2
.4 we-e-wi-ja , di-pte-ra ,10 wi-ri-no , we-ru-ma-ta , ti-ri-si , ze-u-ke-si 1
.5 wi-ri-no , pe-di-ro , e-ma-ta 4 e-ra-pe-ja , e-pi-u-ru-te-we , E 2
.6 a-pe-i-ja , u-po , ka-ro , we-[ ]-ja 1 u-po , we-e-wi-ja , e-ra-pe-ja E 1
.7 mu-te-we , we-re-ne-ja , ku[ ]pe-re 1 mu-te-we, di-pte-ra , a3-za pe-di-ro-i , 1
.8–.10 *vacat*

1 "To Au-ke-i-ja-te-we (MN, dat.), for saddlebags (?), prepared hides: 4; .... prepared hides: 2; to au-ke-i-ja- te-we, for straps (?), prepared hides: ....
2 To au-ke-i-ja-te-we, bindings for straps, prepared hides: 4; containers made of basketry: 4
3 To me-ti-ja-no (*Metianor*), *ru-de-a2* of a container, prepared hides: 1; red leather *a-re-se-si*, prepared hides: 3; to **wo-di-je-ja** (***Wordieia***, WN, dat.), sandals: 2
4 Pigskins (?), prepared hides: 10; ox-hide wrappers, pairs: 1
5 Oxhides, sandal laces: 4; deerskin *e-pi-i-ri-te-we*: e 2
6 To **A-pe-i-ja** (WN, dat.), under fringes (?) ... 1; under pigskins (?), deerskins: e 1
7 To mu-te-we (*Murtewei?*, MN, dat.), lambskins ... : 1; To mu-te-we, prepared hides, goatskin, for sandals: 1"
8 blank

This tablet is interesting for several reasons. On its most basic level, it records the allocation of leather goods to several individuals, many of whom are also referenced on other tablets. The tablet's formula is typically comprised of a personal name in the dative, followed by a description of the leather good to be prepared, frequently followed by di-pte-ra ("prepared hides"), and a tally of these hides, or, with the dative personal name followed by the type of animal the skin derives from, the intended use of that skin, and the tally. At least five people are mentioned as the intended recipients of the finished goods – three men and two women. The apparent commissioner of the greatest amount of leather goods on this tablet, the man au-ke-i-ja-te-we (dat.) to whose commodities the first two lines of the tablet refer, is known from three other tablets at Pylos. He appears on PY An 1281,[92] the same tablet that mentions both mi-jo-qa and a-pi-e-ra, as the contributor of a man identified by the VIR ideogram; the man's name is in lacuna, but this entry is exactly parallel to all others on the tablet. He also appears as the owner of slaves who receive HORD allotments on PY Fn 50[93] – a tablet which again features mi-jo-qa and a-pi-e-ra also as owners of slaves. From these three tablets, this individual would appear to be a significantly placed official who is deemed sufficiently important that the palace tracks the location and rations for his slaves and keeps records of relatively small amounts of leather goods he commissions for, presumably, his personal use.

While neither the man mu-te-we nor the woman a-pe-i-ja appear on any other extant tablet, the remaining two people mentioned on PY Ub 1318, me-ti-ja-no (*Metianor*)[94] and wo-di-je-ja (*Wordieia*), would seem to occupy a rather interesting position in Pylian society. But who are they and what is their significance on this tablet? Why are both named, why do their names appear closely linked even though their holdings are different – moreover, why are their commissions of relatively minor amounts of leather goods recorded in the tablets at all? To approach these questions, it is necessary to also investigate the second tablet on which they both appear, PY Vn 34 + 1191 + 1006 + fr. – the tablet which also provides the remainder of the named women at Pylos. As with the above tablet PY Ub 1318 which closely links me-ti-ja-no and wo-di-je-ja by listing them and their holdings on the same line, Vn 34 + 1191 + 1006 + fr. also offers a similar treatment, with both me-ti-ja-no and wo-di-je-ja mentioned again in the same order as on the Ub tablet.

PY Vn 34 + 1191 + 1006 + fr.
.1: me-ti-ja-no-ro wo-di-je-ja 1
.2: ka-e-sa-me-no-jo , a-*64-ja 1
.3: e-to-mo-jo o-[.]-o-wa 1
.4: de-ki-si-wo-jo pi-ri-ta 1
.5: a-ta-o-jo pi-ro-pa-ta-ra 1
.6: qa-ko-jo ma-ra-me-na[1] *vacat*
.7: pe-ra2[1] *vacat*
.8: a-[1
.9 ḍụ-[ ] jo-jo [1
.10 [ ]wa-o , o-[1
inf. mut.

This tablet appears to present a list of personnel but in a distinctly different manner than did the A series personnel tablets. On this tablet, all people are named. Each line begins with a man's name in the genitive case, followed by a woman's in the nominative; all women's names are followed by the numerical marker for one. While none of these women's names are replicated on other tablets (except for wo-di-je-ja), at least three of the six men's names are attested elsewhere in the Pylian texts. These other attestations serve to establish the standing of these men as ranking officials, with some prominence in Pylian society.[95] If, then, the men who begin each line of PY Vn 34 + 1191 + 1006 + fr. function as elite members of Pylian society, how are we to understand the nominative women whose names follow these men's on each line of PY Vn 34 + 1191 + 1006 + fr.? The fact that each woman is named seems significant; at Pylos the practice of naming women usually signals an affiliation within the ranks of "elite" women at the site. Furthermore, the one-to-one linking of a genitive man's name and a nominative woman's on each line seems to imply a close linkage in the relationship between these men and women. At least one of these pairs from PY Vn 34 + 1191 + 1006 + fr. is repeated on another Pylian tablet – PY UB 1318 discussed above – where the pair of me-ti-ja-no-ro and wo-di-je-ja (line 1 of PY Vn 34 + 1191 + 1006 + fr.) appear on line 3 of PY Ub 1318 where both are the intended recipients of leather goods. Hiller has proposed that we understand the nominative women of Vn 34 + 1191 + 1006 + fr. as the wives of the genitive men;[96] this seems to me to be the most reasonable reading insofar as it accounts for the choice to identify all figures by name, as well as the elite standing of the men in question, the repetition of the relationship between me-ti-ja-no-ro and wo-di-je-ja who appear on the same line on two different tablets, and the similarities in the scale and nature of the goods both commission on Ub 1318.

How do these wives then compare to the priestly women vis-à-vis their investiture into Pylos's property structures? Priestesses certainly seem to demonstrate a high level of economic autonomy – is this also true for the more socially elite wives? While the seven women recorded in this category do not provide much of a sample size, nonetheless they seem to be treated quite differently from the clerics. These wives would appear to occupy a high level of prestige – presumably they were aristocrats – but their high social status does not seem to translate to a similarly high level of economic status. Put simply, these women have no major property holdings allocated to them as distinct individuals – the most we hear of their holdings is a pair of sandals being prepared for one of them – and consequently no real economic authority or autonomy. In this regard, these women seem very analogous to Odysseus's Penelope, who also maintains a high social standing as the wife of Ithaca's king, but has no direct claim herself on the family property.

Conclusions

While production activities were disproportionately the milieu of low-status women, more elite Pylian women entered the institution of property holdings only under very specific circumstances – notably, and with one sole exception, via official standing within the sphere of religion.

Unlike the women of the workgroups, women listed as religious functionaries enjoyed a much higher level of visibility and economic autonomy at Pylos, an autonomy perhaps best underscored by the priestess e-ri-ta who represented herself in a legal dispute with her local *damos*. In many ways, religion functioned as the great gender equalizer in terms of the control over property at Pylos; this was the sole venue in the Pylos tablets where women demonstrated any economic power in their own right.

Female religious functionaries entered the sphere of property holdings in several ways; approximately 95 percent of the 120 women attested to with property holdings at Pylos belong to this category. Lower-ranked cult figures such as the te-o-jo do-e-ra ("slaves of the god") along with the slaves of priestesses and keybearers are recorded in control of various land leases. More elite cult figures such as priestesses and the keybearer had significantly broader holdings, ranging from slaves, both male and female, to foodstuffs, textiles, and commodities as important as bronze. This included property which they administered on behalf of their divinities – including shrines and their contents – as well as property allocated to them in their own names. Furthermore, they also functioned as supervisors to free personnel. The most significant of their holdings, of course, were their land-leases. Priestesses and other female cult officials were the only women at Pylos with attested access to land holdings. Typically referred to both by their names and titles, these women seem to have been envisioned by the palace primarily within their official capacities; these are the only women who were not recorded in terms of either their marital arrangements or fecundity.

The access that religious affiliation provided to property was not limited solely to female cult officials. In more limited circumstances, women whose titles indicate task assignments within more secular arenas were also provided with small holdings – largely in the form of food allotments – when they took on supporting functions at cult centers.

Only eight women were attested to outside the spheres of menial production or religious affiliation. These included the anomalous and elusive *Kessandra* who appeared with property holdings – including large quantities of grain – on four tablets, and the wives of high-status Pylian officials. While these women seem to have elite family connections, nonetheless they have no property of significance in their command – only small amounts of personal items – circumstances which sharply divided these socially elite women from their economically elite sacerdotal counterparts.

This distinction between high social status and economic independence and autonomy is an important one, especially for our understanding of women's economic power at Pylos as it appears to explain why certain women function as the economic elite while others do not. At Pylos, it seems very clear that there existed a strong institutional rationale for elevating a woman to the status of property holder. To be granted access to property holdings at Pylos, a woman had to have made a significant public contribution to the welfare of her state. As some 95 percent of the women who acceded to this status were cult officials, it would seem that religion functioned as the primary avenue whereby women could meet this requirement and hence enter the most important economic sphere of their state – the institutionalized control over personnel, commodities, and property. It is also important to note that women's economic autonomy and social ranking do not appear to travel together; instead we see women attached to elite men with high social standing but limited economic autonomy while priestesses – who never appear linked to male political officials – maintain control of land, commodities and personnel. At Pylos, it would appear that only the institution of religion could trump gender, allowing certain women greater economic viability and access than their otherwise invisible peers.

Notes

1 Just 1989; Patterson 1998, 1991.
2 Connelly 2007.
3 Kristensen 1994.

4 *Pol.* 1270a20.
5 Land holdings of Pylian women are extensively addressed in Chapter 6.
6 The single exception is the religiously-associated women designated by the title ki-ri-te-wi-ja who always appear in the plural.
7 Consensus has been achieved on the identification of *i-je-re-ja* as the Greek ἱέρεια "priestess." Carlier 1983: 12; *Diccionario*: Vol. 1, 273–74; Ventris and Chadwick 1973: 547; Lindgren 1973: Part II, 561; Morpurgo Davies 1979: 93; etc. For detailed discussion of the texts referring to priestesses and other female religious functionaries see Chapter 7: Women and religion at Pylos and Knossos.
8 PY Ae 303; PY Eb 297; PY Eb 339 + 409; PY Eb 416; PY Eb 1176; PY Ed 317; PY En 609; PY Eo 224; PY Ep 539; PY Ep 704; PY Qa 1289; PY Qa 1330; PY Un 6.
9 See Chapter 6 for tablets pertinent to the land holdings of priestesses.
10 PY Un 6.
11 PY Qa 1289, PY Qa 1300.
12 PY Ep 539.07, PY Ep 539.08
13 PY En 609.16, PY Eo 224.06.
14 Some of the unnamed priestess references surely refer to either ka-wa-ra or e-ri-ta for reasons discussed on pp. 136–139.
15 PY Ep 704
1: o-pe-to-re-u , qe-ja-me-no , e-ke , ke-ke-me-na , ko-to-na , to-so , pe-mo[ ] GRA 2 T 5
2: u-wa-mi-ja , te-o-jo , do-e-ra , o-na-to , e-ke-qe , i-je-re-ja , ke-ra , to-so , pe-mo GRA T 1 V 3
3: e-ri-ta , i-je-re-ja , o-na-to , e-ke , ke-ke-me-na , ko-to-na , pa-ro , da-mo , to-so , pe-mo GRA T 4
4: ki-ri-te-wi-ja , o-na-to , e-ko-si , ke-ke-me-na , ko-to-na , pa-ro , da-mo , to-so , pe-mo GRA 1 T 9
5: e-ri-ta , i-je-re-ja , e-ke , e-u-ke-to-qe , e-to-ni-jo , e-ke-e , te-o , da-mo-de-mi , pa-si , ko-to-na-o ,
6: ke-ke-me-na-o , o-na-to , e-ke-e , to-so , pe-mo GRA 3 T 9
7: ka-pa-ti-ja , ka-ra-wi-po-ro , e-ke , ke-ke-me-no , o-pe-ro-sa , du-wo-u-pi , wo-ze-e , o-u-wo-ze ,
8: to-so , [pe-mo GRA]4
16 For detailed discussion of specific land holdings, see Chapter 6.
17 This holding is also repeated on PY Eb 297 with this line quoted exactly save for the now omitted name of the priestess. At Pylos, the PY Ep series recapitulates the shorter documents of the Eb series for reasons that are not entirely clear. See Chapter 6 for discussion.
18 PY Eb 339 + 409
.a i-je-re-ja , pa-ki-ja-na , e-ke-qẹ [o-na-to , ke-ke-me-na] X
.b ko-to-na , pa-ro da-mo [to-so-de]pe-mo GRA T 4
"The priestess at pa-ki-ja-na has a leased plot (o-na-to) of communal land (ke-ke-me-na ko-to-na-o) from the damos, so much seed: 38.4 l. wheat."
19 The types of land holdings at Pylos are presented in detail in Chapter 6; for etymologies, measurement translations, and discussions of terms please refer to Chapter 6.
20 PY En 609.18: [i-je-re-ja pa-ki-ja-na o-na-]to , e-ke , to-so-de , pe-mo GRA *T* 3
21 PY Eb 1176
.a te-te-re-u , i-je-re-ja , pa-ki-ja-na , do-e-ro
.b e-ke-qe , o-na-to , ke-ke-me-na , ko-to-na , pa-ro , da-mo , to-so-de[pe-mo GRA V 3
"Tetreus the male slave of the priestess at pa-ki-ja-na has a leased plot (o-na-to) of communal land (ke-ke-me-na ko-to-na-o) from the damos, so much seed: 4.8 l. wheat."

This tablet is recapitulated on PY Ep 539.8 where the location of pa-ki-ja-na is omitted from the priestess's title.

22 PY En 609.16:
[e-ra-ta-ra i-je-re-ja do-e-ra]pa-ki-ja-na , o-na-to , e-ke , to-so-de , pe-mo GRA T 1.
"Eratara the female slave of the priestess at pa-ki-ja-na has a leased plot (o-na-to) of communal land (ke-ke-me-na ko-to-na-o) from the damos, so much seed: 9.6 l. wheat.

23 PY Qa 1289:
ka-wa-ra i-je-re-ja *189 [

24 PY Qa 1300
i-]je-re-ja *189 2.

25 PY Eb 416
.1 u-wa-mi-ja , te-o-jo , do-e-ṛạ , ẹ[-ke-]qe , i-je-ṛẹ[-ja] ḳẹ-ṛạ ọ[-na-to
.2 to-so-ḍẹ pe-mo GRA T ?2 V ?3 [ ] (*vacat*) [

26 *Diccionario*: Vol. II, 393; Ventris and Chadwick 1973: 589; Lindgren, *People of Pylos*, Part I, 123.

27 Ventris and Chadwick 1973: 553 cites a parallel usage in Homeric Greek: γέρας ὅ τι δῆμος ἔδωκεν [*Od.* vii, 150].

28 PY Ep 539.7:
me-re-u , i-je-re-ja , do-e-ro , o-na-to , e-ke , pa-ro , [ ]ṛẹ-ma-ta , ka-ma-e-ẉẹ o-u-qe wo-ze to-so pe-mo GRA[ ] V 2

29 PY Ae 303:
.a i-je-ro-jo
.b pu-ro , i-je-re-ja , do-e-ra , e-ne-ka , ku-ru-so-jo MUL 14[
"At Pylos, 14+ female slaves of the priestess on account of the sacred gold."
This translation is from Ventris and Chadwick 1973: 166.

30 PY Un 6 *verso*:
v1:]i-ịẹ-ṛẹ-ịạ TELA+ ṬẸ [
v2: ka-]ra-ẉị-pọ-ṛọ TELA + ṬẸ [

31 Cf. Chapter 3 for discussion of te-pe-ja workers at Pylos.

32 The term ka-ra-wi-po-ro has been identified with the Doric κλᾳδοφόρος (Attic κλειδοῦχος "priestess"), translated literally as "keybearer," by Ventris and Chadwick. Billigmeier and Turner 1981: 7; Carlier 1983: 12; *Diccionario*: Vol. I, 324–25; Ventris and Chadwick 1956: 396; Ventris and Chadwick 1973: 551; Hooker 1987a: 313–315; Morpurgo Davies 1979: 93. Lindgren notes the general acceptance of this term as indicating a cult official with duties pertaining to the administrative and economic aspects of cult management. Lindgren 1973: Part II, 72–73. See also Chapter 7.

33 For example, the tablets PY Ed 317 and PY Un 6 which associate them and their holdings more closely than any other figures on these tablets.

34 PY Ae 110, PY Ep 539.9.

35 PY Eb 338, PY Ed 317, PY Ep 704.7–8.

36 PY Un 6.

37 PY Un 443 + 998.

38 The ideogram rendered as HORD has long been identified as barley, but research by R. Palmer makes a strong case for understanding this ideogram as wheat instead. R. Palmer 1992: 475–97. As with the case for GRA/"Wheat", I continue with the traditional reading for HORD as "barley" throughout this text.

39 PY Jn 829
1: jo-do-so-si , ko-re-te-re , du-ma-te-qe ,
2: po-ro-ko-re-te-re-qe , ka-ra-wi-po-ro-qe , o-pi-su-ko-qe , o-pi-ka-pe-'e-we-qe'
3: ka-ko , na-wi-jo , pa-ta-jo-i-qe , e-ke-si-qe , a3-ka-sa-ma
4: pi-*82 , ko-re-te , AES M 2 po-ro-ko-re-te AES N 3
5: me-ta-pa , ko-re-te AES M 2 po-ro-ko-re-te AES N 3[ ]*vacat*
6: pe-to-no , ko-re-te AES M 2 po-ro-ko-re-te AES N 3

7: pa-ki-ja-pi , ko-re-te AES M 2 po-ro-ko-re-te AES N 3
8: a-pu2-we , ko-re-te AES M 2 po-ro-ko-re-te AES N 3
9: ạ-ke-re-wa , ko-re-te AES M 2 po-ro-ko-re-te AES N 3
10: ṛọ-ụ-so , ko-re-te AES M 2 po-ro-ko-re-te AES N 3
11: ḳạ-ra-do-ro , ko-re-te AES M 2 po-ro-ko-re-te AES N 3
12: ri-]jọ, ko-re-te AES M 2 po-ro-ko-re-te AES N 3
13: ṭị-mi-to-a-ke-e , ko-re-te AES M 2 po-ro-ko-re-te AES N 3
14: ra-]wa-ra-ta2 , ko-re-te AES M 2 n 3 po-ro-ko-re-te AES N 3
15: sa-]ma-ra , ko-re-te AES M 3 n 3 po-ro-ko-re-te N 3
16: a-si-ja-ti-ja ḳọ-re-te AES M 2 po-ro-ko-re-te N 3
17: e-ra-te-re-wa-pi , ko-re-te AES M 2 po-ro-ko-re-te N 3
18: za-ma-e-wi-ja ; ḳọ-re-te AES M 3 N ̣3 po-ro-ko-re-te N 3
19: e-re-i , ko-re-te AES M 3 N ̣3 po-ro-ko-re-te N 3
20–23: (*vacat*)

40 Discussed in Ventris and Chadwick 1973: 357–358, 511–514. Palaima 2009: 528.

41 The po-ro-ko-re-te and the ko-re-te are the two groups of officials enumerated on lines 4–19.

42 For this reading of o-pi-su-ko-qe, see Ventris and Chadwick 1973: 357, 565; for o-pi-ka-pe-we-qe, Ventris and Chadwick 1973: 357, 512, 565. These readings are generally, but not entirely, accepted with greater credence given to the interpretation of o-pi-si-ko-qe. For discussion, see *Diccionario:* Vol. II, 39, 42.

43 Du-ma-te is the plural form of du-ma, an official title whose precise identification remains one of the more contested occupational terms in Linear B scholarship. Theories include interpretations as a cult official (Lejeune 1958: 190), an official with similar responsibilities to the ko-re-te-re (L. Palmer, 1963: 89, 415), as related to the da-ma-te (Ruijgh 1967: 384), as an administrator (Gérard-Rousseau 1968: 83), and as a cult figure (Olivier 1960: 38). For further discussion, see *Diccionario*: Vol. 1, 195–196.

44 Both the exact etymology and sense of the term ki-ri-te-wi-ja remain murky although most scholarship agrees in placing it among cult officials on strength of its textual context. Bennett 1956b: 132; Ventris and Chadwick 1956: 397; Ventris and Chadwick 1973: 554; Lejeune 1958: 86; L. Palmer 1963: 223; Ruijgh 1967: 129; Lindgren 1973: Part II, 81; Morpurgo Davies 1963:148–149; R. Palmer 1992: 475–497. The only major dissenting voice is Gérard-Rousseau who reads them solely as a privileged class of women. Gérard-Rousseau 1968: 133–134. This term is also discussed in greater detail in Chapter 7: Women and religion at Pylos and Knossos.

45 PY Eb 321 + 327 + 1153, repeated on PY Ep 704.04.

46 Billigmeier and Turner 1981: 7; Ventris and Chadwick 1973: 167. Further discussion of their identification as religious officials can be found in Chapter 7: Women in religion at Pylos and Knossos.

47 To my mind the most lucid reading of this difficult tablet is Hiller's. Hiller 1989: 45–46.

48 There is near scholarly consensus in reading the terms te-o-jo do-e-ra and te-o-jo do-e-ro as "servant (male or female) of the god." For etymologies, definitions, and further commentary, see Lindgren 1973: Part II, *35*. A total of 45 servants of the god are known at Pylos: 22 men and 23 women. Still under debate is their social rank. Some scholars have regarded this as an honorific title describing cult-associated persons of high rank as they are named, and have land holdings: Billigmeier and Turner 1981: 7. Others, including Carlier, view them as actual slaves "in the strictest sense" in that their status was hereditary and they "accomplished production tasks in the service of a sanctuary." Carlier 1983: 12–14. Lindgren takes no position on this issue, but I concur with Billigmeier and Turner, that based on the elite nature of their holdings that the inclusion of the term "slave" in their titles be understood as a ceremonial rather than functional addition.

49 Discussed in greater detail in Chapter 6: Women and land tenure at Pylos and Knossos.

50 Lindgren 1973: Part II, 38–39.

51 Connelly 2007; Sourvinou-Inwood 1995.

52 PY Eb 297, repeated on PY Ep 704.05–6.

53 Etymological and interpretational considerations for the a-ke-ti-ri-ja are discussed in Chapter 3, p. 84.

54 Killen 2001: 435–43.

55 For text of PY Fn 187, *infra,* n. 70.

56 PY Un 219 + frr.
.1 e-ke-ra-ne , tu-wo 2 O 1[
.2 pa-de-we , O 1 pa-de-we , O 1
.3 ka-ru-ke , PE 2 KA 1 O 6
.4 te-qi-jo-ne , O 1 a-ke-ti-ri-ja-i , KA 1
.5 a-ti-mi-te , O 1 da-ko-ro-i , E 1
.6 di-pte-ra-po-ro , RA 1 O 3 ko-ṛọ[ ] 1̣
.7 ạ-na-ka-te , TE 1 po-ti-ni-ja[
.8 e-[ ] U 1 e-ma-a2 , U 1 pe-[
.9 a-ka-wo-ne , MA 1 pa-ra-[ ]2
.10 ra-wa-ke-ta , MA 1 KO 1 [ ]ME 1 O 1 WI 1
.11 KE 1 [ ] (*vacat*)
.12–.17 (*vacat*)

57 Similarly, Killen suggests that they may have "carried out some special form of decorating in connection with religious ritual." Killen 2001: 436.

58 See Chapter 3 for discussion of the a-pi-qo-ro in the personnel series.

59 These calculations follow the standard convention for translating Mycenaean liquid measures whereby 1 full unit equates to 28.8 l.; S = 1/3 a full measure for 9.6 l., V = 1/6 a S measure for 1/6 l.; and Z for ¼ a V measure for 0.4 l.

60 Ventris and Chadwick 1973: 568.

61 We-ja-re-pi, a nominative singular neuter adjective describing oil, is thought to normalize as *u-aleiphes* "for anointing". Ventris and Chadwick 1973: 590.

62 PY Aa 804, PY Ad 690.

63 *LSJ*, 93: *Od.* 1.331, 6.199.

64 *LSJ*, 93: E.*IT* 1114 (Euripides, *Iphigenia at Tauris*); *IG* 14.2111.

65 *LSJ*, 93: Pindar, *Olympian* 6.32

66 *LSJ*, 93: Euripides, Fragment 982; Phld, *D* 1.13.

67 Lindgren 1973: Part II, 21. Bennett in turn reads them as human cult attendants – specifically as servants attached to a goddess or sanctuary: Bennett 1958: 4. In contrast, Gérard-Rousseau and Stella opt to move them out of cult contexts to view them either more along the lines of the Homeric *amphipolos* "servante, suivante," (Gérard-Rousseau 1968: 37) or more specifically as the servants of the queen and the royal family (Stella 1965: 127). I see no reason why so technical a reading as "royal staffers" is necessary, as the term *amphipolos* seems to be a fairly generic term for attendant women of all stripes. Furthermore, neither Gérard-Rousseau's nor Stella's reading to my mind take sufficient account of this tablet's placement in the Fr series; as this series is so consumed with the activities of cult, dissociating these individuals from cult related activities seems problematic and in direct conflict with the function of this series.

68 I share Lindgren's skepticism regarding this connection: Lindgren 1973: Part II, 113.

69 The range of tablet series represented here is broad, consisting of three tablets from the Fn series, two from the Fg series, and a single tablet each from the An, Mn, and Xa series.

70 PY Fn 187
.1 a-pi-te-ja ḤỌṚḌ [ ] NI 2
.2 po-si-da-i-jo-de HORD[ ] NI T 1

.3 ka-ru-ke HORD [ ] F̣ẠṚ
.4 pạ-ki-ja-na-de HORD T 1[ ] NI T 1
.5 ka-ru-ke HORD T 1 V 3 ṆỊ T 1 V 3
.6 de-do-wa-re-we HORD T 1
.7 ḳụ-ṛị-na-ze-ja HORD T 2 NI T 2
.8 u-po-jo-po-ti-ni-ja HORD T 5̣ NI T 4
.9 o-pi-tu-ra-jo HORD T 3
.10 au-to-*34-ta-ra HORD T 1
.11 a-ma-tu-na HORD T 1
.12 te-qi-ri-jo-ne HORD V 3
.13 u-do-no-o-i HORD Ṭ 3
.14 po-te-re-we HORD Ṭ 4 NI T 4
.15 a-ke-ti-ri-ja-i HORD T 1 V 3
.16 ka-ru-ke HORD T 1 V 3
.17 i-so-e-ko HORD T 2 [[Ṿ 3]]
.18 po-si-da-i-je-u-si HORD T 1 V 3
.19 *34-ke-ja HORD T 1 V 3 NI T 1 V [
.20 a-ro-ja [HORD] V 3
.21 ka-ru-ke ḤỌṚḌ Ṭ 1̣ Ṿ 3̣
.22 (*vacat*)
.23 (*vacat*)

71 The most extensive treatment of this tablet to date is Killen 2001: 435–436.
72 Ventris and Chadwick 1973: 574.
73 This is dependent on the acceptance of Killen's suggestion of u-po-jo po-ti-ni-ja as a divine figure. Killen 2001: 436. The status of the figure(s) entitled po-ti-ni-ja continues to be debated, cf. the publication of the recent conference on the same theme: Laffineur and Hägg: 2001.
74 The number of units of barley a-pi-te-ja receives is in lacuna, but as all figures who receive barley and figs on this tablet receive the same amount of each commodity, we can surely reconstruct her barley allotment based on the extant amount of her fig allotment.
75 Killen 2001: 436.
76 PY Fn 79
1: a3-pu-ke-ne-ja HORD T 6 V 4 OLIV 1[
2: a-ki-re-we HORD T 5
3: du-ni-jo , ti-ni-ja-ta HORD V 5
4: to-sa-no HORD T 6 V 4 OLIV 1
5: ne-e-ra-wo HORD T 6 V 4 OLIV 1
6: a-e-se-wa HORD T 6 V 4 OLIV 1
7: ka-ra-so-mo HORD V 5 [[OLIV]]
8: wa-di-re-we HORD T 2 V 3 OLIV T 7
9: pe-qe-we HORD T 1 V 4
10: ze-u-ke-u-si , i-po-po-qo-i-qe HORD 1 T 7 V 3
11: te-ra-wo-ne HORD V 5
12: to-wa-no-re HORD T 6 V 4 OLIV 1[
13: e-to-wo-ko-i HORD T 5 V 1
14: a-ki-to HORD T 2 V 3 OLIV 1
15: a3-ki-a2-ri-jo HORD T 1 V 4
77 Killen 2001: 438–41; Perpillou 1976: 65–78; Chadwick 1976: 118–19.
78 Perpillou 1976: 65–78.
79 PY Fn 50 + fr.
.1 a-ki-to-jo , qa-si-re-wi-ja HORD[
.2 ke-ko-jo , qa-si-re-wi-ja HORD [
.3 a-ta-no-ro , qa-si-re-wi-ja HORD T [

.4 me-za-ne HORD V 2 a3-ki-a2-ri-jo V 2[
.5 me-ri-du-te HORD V 3 mi-ka-ta HORD V 3
.6 di-pte-ra-po-ro HORD V 2 e-to-wo-ko V 2
.7 a-to-po-qo HORD V 2 po-ro-du-ma-te HORD V 2
.8 o-pi-te-u-ke-e-we HORD V 2 i-za-a-to-mo-i HORD V 3
.9 ze-u-ke-u-si HORD V 4
.10] (*vacat*)
.11 au[-ke-i-]ja-te-wo , do-e-ro-i HORD T 1
.12 mi-jo[-qa] do-e-ro-i HORD V 3
.13 a-pi-ẹ-ṛạ do-e-ro-i HORD V 3
.14]-ẉọ[ ]ṇẹ[do-e-ro-]i HORD T 3
.15–.19 *vacat*

80 Killen 2001: 436–438. In his identification of the individuals of the second section as cult workers, Killen draws upon the work of Olivier 1960: 114–19.

81 It is their a-endings in the genitive here which fixes their gender as feminine. Killen 2001: 438; Olivier 1960: 134–135. This runs in direct contradiction of Lejeune and Lindgren who both read mi-jo-qa as a masculine name, while Lindgren goes further to read *Amphieras* for a-pi-e-ra as well. Lejeune 1958: II, 72, no. 39; Lindgren 1973: Part I, 29, I 79, II 37. Lejeune's reading of mi-jo-qa and Lindgren's reading of both names as masculine works well for the second tablet which mentions both in the dative case (PY An 1281), but surely Olivier and Killen are correct from the genitive forms on PY Fn 0050. Ventris and Chadwick 1973 and *Diccionario* concur with Olivier and Killen: Ventris and Chadwick 1973: 532, 561; *Diccionario:* Vol. 1 81, 451–52.

82 PY Fn 867
.0 sup. mut.
.1 i-qe[HORD
.2 pa-na-re-jo [HORD
.3 a-ki-to-jo , qa[-si-re-wi-ja HORD
.4 mi-jo-qa , do-e-ro [HORD
.5 do-ri-je-we [HORD
.6 me-ri-du-ma-si [HORD

83 PY AN 1281 + frr. + fr.
.1 po-]ti-ni-ja , i-qe-ja
.2]-mo , o-pi-e-de-i
.3 a-ka , re-u-si-wo-qe VIR 2
.4 au-ke-i-ja-te-we [[i-qẹ-jạ ṾỊṚ]]
.5 o-na-se-u , ta-ni-ko-qe VIR 2
.6 me-ta-ka-wa , po-so-ro VIR 1
.7 mi-jo-qa[ ]e-we-za-no VIR 1
.8 a-pị-e-ṛạ to-ze-u VIR 1
.9]-a-ke-ṣị , po-ti-ni-ja , re-si-wo VIR 1
.10 au-ke-i-jạ-ṭẹ-ẉẹ[ ]ro VIR 1
.11 mi-jo-qa , ma-ra-si-jọ[ ] VIR 1
.12 me-ta-ka-wa , ti-ta-ra[ ] VIR 1
.13 a-pi-e-ra , ṛụ-ḳọ-ro VIR 1
.14–.15 *vacat*

84 Ventris and Chadwick 1973 proposes that o-pi-e-de-i be read as two words *opi hedei* "at her seat" (i.e. shrine or temple) [ἕδος *Il.* v, 360+]. Ventris and Chadwick 1973: 565.

85 A single man's name appears not in the dative, but in the nominative: o-na-se-u on line 5.

86 Or to divinities, as po-ti-ni-ja is named twice.

87 Killen 2001: 438.

88 Killen 2001: 438.

89 Also discussed in Garcia Ramon 1992 and Nakassis 2013: 287.f

90 PY Mn 1368
sup. mut.
.1 ḳị-[ ]-ṭọ ., [
.2 ke-sa-da-ra , e-[*146
.3 ke-sa-da-ra i-no[*146
inf. mut.

91 Nakassis 2013: 287.

92 *Supra,* n. 83.

93 *Supra*, n. 79.

94 *Mestianor* is also grammatically possible. Ventris and Chadwick 1973: 561.

95 A-ta-o (*Antaos)* is featured as the major figure on the personnel tablet PY An 340 where he appears as contributor of 16 named men. The tablet's heading establishes that all the men are pa-ro a-ta-o-jo, and each individual line is introduced by his name in the genitive followed by the man he is providing for this tally. That all these men are named should indicate that they belong to the category of mid-ranked men at Pylos. As they are all in a-ta-o's employ, this should place him as a fairly elite official. He also appears on PY Fn 324 as a recipient of HORD, as does ka-e-sa-me-no who appears on line 2 of PY Vn 34 + 1191 + 1006 + fr. above. It is not entirely clear that the de-ki-so-wo of line 4 is the same individual identified as a-no de-ki-si-wo on PY Cn 254, listed in possession of 80 sheep. E-to-mo-jo and qa-ko-jo appear only on PY Vn 34 + 1191 + 1006 + fr.. For the normalization of a-ta-o as *Antaos*, see Ventris and Chadwick 1973: 535.

96 Hiller 1989: 48.

5 Women at Knossos

Production and property

Introduction

While in the Pylian economy, as discussed in Chapters 3 and 4, a wide gulf existed between the women identified as either laborers or property holders, the Linear B tablets from Knossos display a more multi-tiered approach to women's labor and ownership. We see a more complicated labor system, with slave women, personal servants, and ostensibly free corvée workers distributed throughout the tablets, and women's property holdings do not reveal the same close correlation with cult as at Pylos. Overall, women appear to have been more broadly integrated into the economy of Mycenaean Knossos than at Pylos, with production and property as less distinct and more overlapping categories. This chapter investigates the forms both of these institutions take at Knossos and contrasts the Knossian evidence on these subjects with the better-preserved (and understood) evidence from Pylos.

The Knossos Linear B tablets

Excavations at Knossos have to date produced more than 3300 Linear B tablets, more than three times the number of tablets from Pylos, but the Knossos tablets have proved far more reticent in disclosing their contents to scholarly scrutiny. Many of the conditions that render the smaller Pylian corpus accessible are missing at Knossos. For example, instead of the unified archives of Pylos – stored in a carefully sorted two-room, ground-level complex at the Ano Englianos palace at Pylos, carefully compiled and chronologically unified,[1] the Knossos tablets date from at least two – and potentially as many as five – different destructions, have often fallen from upper storeys, are only rarely intact, and seem to have never been sorted by scribes or officials into a coherent whole. The dating of these tablets has also remained a subject of lively controversy. At least two different time-frames are represented. Driessen has demonstrated – convincingly to all but a few staunch holdouts – that the tablet collection found in the Room of the Chariot Tablets dates to an earlier phase of Mycenaean administration at Knossos, to the L(ate) M(inoan) II period, at least 50 years earlier than the rest of the tablets – whose unity remains in heated dispute; for our purposes, however, it should be noted that none of these tablets reference women either by name, title, or ideogram, and hence remain outside the scope of this study. The remainder of the tablets derive from later destruction(s); while their date has long been disputed, all should place from the middle of the 14th century BCE to perhaps the first few decades of the 13th. As such they provide insight into the middle time range of Mycenaean Crete, and offer a glimpse into how the Mycenaean presence is interacting on Crete at this time.

Landenius Enegren summarizes well the major challenges of working with the Knossos tablets:

> Primarily the nature of the preservation of the tablets differs from that of Pylos. Of the c. 3400 Knossos documents, 75% are incomplete and 56% average less than 5 signs, the average number of signs being 7.7. At Pylos we have c. 1100 documents of which 50% are incomplete, 33% have less than five signs, and the average number of signs per tablet is 25. Because of the minimalistic nature of many Knossos tablets, interpretation of the Knossian data as evidence for prosopograhy is more complicated. Possible cross-references most certainly, in some cases, have been lost. Moreover, because the tablets are so fragmentary, headings and/or ideograms are frequently missing. This renders it more challenging to ascertain individual interrelationships and/or assign a person or a group of persons to a specific profession or industrial activity or sector, even when the Scribal Hand serves as a pointer to the activity of specific area concerned.[2]

These difficulties are formidable and prevent the forms of modeling and narrative synthesis permitted by the prosopographical data from Pylos. The Knossos material is by no means unusable, but a tighter methodological framework needs to be applied.

We are indebted to the work of several intrepid scholars in the disentangling of the social and economic institutions documented in the Knossos tablets. Herculean labor into the extremely complicated workings of the textile industry has been performed by J.T. Killen in more than four decades of study, Nosch and Burke are continuing this process through the combined forces of textual study, artifact analysis, and experimental archaeology, and Landenius Enegren's now-published, long-awaited masterstroke on Knossian prosopography is an invaluable addition to the study of social structure of Mycenaean Knossos. From their work, we are able to see aspects of a Mycenaean economy on Crete that is heavily invested in the production of textiles, that is also mobilizing large labor resources, and that is administering outer villages in relationship to the palace center. (Knossos does seem to be more decentralized than Pylos, however.) An investigation into the women of Knossos would be all but unthinkable without their labors; I am deeply indebted to all of these scholars and draw on them heavily in this chapter.

Women and production in the Knossos tablets

As at Pylos, much of the evidence relevant to women's economics at Knossos derives from their production activities, and, particularly, their participation as members of low-status workgroups. This economic category accounts for the majority of women mentioned in the Linear B texts at Knossos. These texts share a number of features with their Pylian counterparts but demonstrate significant variations as well.

Knossian workgroup women feature prominently in the palace's personnel series tablets. These low-ranking women appear in nearly 140 tablets of the Ai, Ak, and Ap series, which record workgroup women along with their children. In contrast to Pylos, however, Knossian workgroup women also have a large presence outside the personnel series, particularly in the textile-focused L series texts. The types of information the Knossos tablets provide about the workgroup women is rather different from that of the Pylos Aa, Ab, and Ad series texts; only the Aa texts seem to have a Knossian counterpart.

Most of the evidence pertaining to Knossian female laborers derives from three subsets of the Knossos personnel tablets (Ai, Ak, and Ap) and from the textile subseries L(1), Lc, Ld, and Le. Of the 63 total mentions of female laborers,[3] 34 are from the personnel series texts, 15 from the L series, and the remainder are from brief mentions in the E, G, Od, Og, Ws, Xe, and X series. The usual difficulties in working with the highly fragmentary Knossos texts apply: for example, although nearly 140 tablets belong to the seven major series above (Ai, Ak, Ap, L(1), Lc, Ld, and Le), only approximately 30 are sufficiently preserved to allow the recovery of the occupational titles of the women they record.

As at Pylos, women recorded as belonging to the collective workgroups are identified in a variety of ways – by the use of the MUL ideogram, by title, or by ethnic – but in contrast to Pylos, low-ranking female laborers at Knossos are also occasionally identified by name. While at Pylos, the recoverable occupations of the workgroup women fit into four categories of labor (textile production, maintenance and attendant duties at the palace site, food-processing and preparation, and staffers assigned to mid- to high-ranking male officials), at Knossos every woman whose duties can be identified works in the sphere of textile production.

Textile production at Knossos[4]

Estimates place more than 1,000 women at work in the textile industry of Knossos.[5] The textile industry at Knossos occupies by far and away the largest proportion of tablets of any industry attested there. This industry is far more decentralized than its counterpart at Pylos,[6] and is recorded in detail in all stages. As Bennet writes, "there are extensive records for every stage of production, involving all aspects of the industry from [the husbandry of] animals (D series) through shearing (Dk/Dl), wool allocations (Od), cloth production targets (Lc), cloth deliveries (Le) and cloth storage (Ld [1]), to the workgroups themselves."[7] The scope of this industry can be ascertained from the sheer numbers of animals involved – over 100,000 sheep documented on approximately 900 tablets.[8] While men seem to have been involved in the initial and final stages of textile production – men served as the shepherds, shearers, and fullers[9] – all the intermediate work of producing cloth was assigned to women. In tracking the work of women at Knossos, we are heavily indebted to Killen's lifetime of invaluable study; I draw heavily from his work in this chapter.

Major evidence for women's activities in textile production derives from both the personnel (A) and textile (L) series. These provide somewhat different information than did the major Pylian series that recorded textile workers. While the three Pylian series provided tallies of women and their children (Aa), the rations provided to said women and children (Ab), and a separate tally of the older sons of the workgroup women (Ad), only the Aa has a close parallel at Knossos with similar treatment in the Ak series. As each of the Knossos series brings with it specific inherent methodological strengths and difficulties, I provide here a brief introduction to each of the major sets which record Knossos's low-status female labor force.

Women are rostered at Knossos in two main series – the Ai and Ak.[10] The Ak series is most closely equivalent to the Pylos Aa; both are devoted to recording the working strength of each workgroup. As with the Pylos Aa texts, the Knossos Ak typically record the name of the workgroup, the supervisors known as DAs and TAs if present,[11] the location of the workgroup, and a tally of the adult female workers and the underage children who accompany them. Unlike the Pylos tablets, however, the Knossos Ak series further divides the children, both boys and girls, on account of their ages – sorting them into the four categories of "older girl," "older boy," "younger girl," and "younger boy." (Periodically, older girls are further divided into ones "undergoing training" and "training completed" categories.) A little over 90 Ak tablets are preserved to some extent; of these, approximately one-fifth are sufficiently preserved to be of use.

The second class of tablets that records women's workgroups at Knossos is the Ai series; this series is on the whole in poorer condition than the Ak. Of the 35 total Ai tablets, only three are complete, and in only two instances (e-ne-re-ja and a-ke-ti-ri-ja) do we have corresponding Ai and Ak tablets for the same workgroup. It may have been that the Ai tablets were intended as rations tablets for the Ak workgroups, but the evidence is not conclusive. In contrast to Pylos, where the Ab series was explicitly devoted to recording rations provided by the palace to workgroups and their children, similar evidence from Knossos is largely lacking throughout the corpus. Only five tablets of the Knossos Ai series record any form of food distribution; unlike the Pylos Ab tablets which record distributions of GRA (wheat) and NI (figs), these five tablets mention only the distribution of GRA. All five of the Ai tablets are extremely fragmentary; none of them provide a full description for the workgroups they would appear to track. Unfortunately, the poor state of the evidence makes it impossible to determine whether these tablets refer to a customary practice whereby the palace regularly supplied its female workers with rations throughout all the different village and central workgroup locations or if these five tablets refer to an exceptional relationship between the palace and these unrecoverable workgroups. Killen argues for the likelihood that the Ak tablets "served as a basis for calculating the amount of the monthly rations to be allocated to each group"[12] – which would make sense for a series that tracks two levels of children's age grades in addition to adult women – but whether these rations are regularized or sporadic remains open. Killen notes that at least one tablet – KN E 845 – may well list monthly rations for one of the workgroups assigned to a-no-qo-ta on Ak (2) 614,[13] and if so, we may have at least some of the Knossos workgroups receiving regular monthly rations.

The final personnel series at Knossos relevant to its workgroup women consists of the 13 tablets of the Ap series. This series differs from the Ai and the Ak in that it typically records low-ranking women by name and ideogram in addition to a few occupational designations. [14] None of these tablets are intact.

The L series tablets also mention female laborers but in a more oblique way. This class, distinguished by its use of the textile ideograms *159 and *164, inventories textiles.[15]

The first of these series is the Lc. Lc tablets are records of targets for cloth production for workgroups which set specific textile product goals for the workgroups to fulfill (in an unknown amount of time).[16] These tablets belong to two sets, Lc (1) written in hand 103 and Lc (2) with rectos written by hand 113 and versos by 115.[17] Killen notes a geographic distinction between the two sets, with the Lc(1) groups referring to weaving workgroups in central Crete – at Knossos, Phaistos, Tylissos, etc., and the Lc(2) tablets dealing with groups at Kydonia and points west.[18] These records set their projections for cloth production based upon the size of the workgroup in question; as such they have some overlap with the Ak tablets which list the size and strength of textile-assigned workgroups. To cite Killen's example regarding the relationship between these two series:

> The Ak tablets … are likely to have provided the information about the *working strength* of each group that the palace would have needed to have before it when it was calculating what production targets it should set for the women. It is difficult to doubt, for instance, that it was on the basis of the information provided on Ak(1) 612 (or a similar Ak record relating to a different year), i.e. that the group of da-te-we-ja contained nine adult women, that the palace decided that the 'stint' for this workgroup, for whatever period it is that the Lc(1) records cover, should be nine units of cloth.[19]

Killen notes that the only secure overlap between these two series concerns the Lc(1) and Ak(1) records – both of which pertain to women's workgroups based in the central region of Crete.[20] If the Lc records set target goals for women's production, the completed materials are accounted for on the Ld (1) and Le series. The Le tablets in hand 103 – the same hand as the Lc(1) tablets – record the receipt of cloth from the Lc (1) central Cretan workgroups;[21] these tablets refer specifically to the delivery of the finished cloth. The Ld (1) tablets are more complicated. The Ld(1) series, which as a whole is concerned with the storage of the cloth projected in the Lc tablets and delivered in the Le, has been divided by Killen into two sets, a major of "store records" and a minor of "delivery records;"[22] the only set relevant to this study is the minor which accounts for three tablets which mention women workers.[23]

Ultimately, then, the Knossos tablets could provide a full production lemma for cloth, ranging from the women who make the cloth (rostered in the Ak tablets), to the projected amount of cloth they were expected to produce (recorded in the Lc (1) tablets), to the delivery of said cloth (Le series), and its storage (Ld (1) series.) Due, however, to the poor state of preservation of these series – symptomatic of the Knossos corpus as a whole – no more than two of these stages are preserved for any of the recorded workgroups – a frustrating preservation record at best.

A final caveat: as Carlier rightly notes, the evidence from Knossos pertaining to women's production is extremely difficult largely due to the vagaries of preservation;[24] consequently I do not attempt the same sort of modeling of the evidence that the Pylos texts provided. And so, the aim of the remainder of this chapter is more comparative in focus, that is, to investigate how closely women's economic activities at Knossos conform to the better-understood ones at Pylos.

Titled women in textile production

Textile production seems to occupy possibly an even larger role in the Knossian economy than it does in the Pylian – with more than 1200 tablets dedicated to its stages – and this primacy is reflected in the tasks assigned to the workgroup women of Knossos. Textile production seems to be the only occupation of all the workgroup women at Knossos, consuming the labor of all women identified both by occupational titles and ethnics across a variety of sites in central Crete. At least 16 occupational titles can be recovered from the Knossos tablets; all appear to pertain to textile production – an activity that encompasses ten ethnic titles as well. This section presents all the legible evidence for women's textile production at Knossos.

The first group of textile workers securely attested at Knossos is the a-ra-ka-te-ja women – a workgroup title also attested at Pylos. As discussed in Chapter 3, the term is thought to derive from ἠλακάτη "distaff" and to refer to "spinning-women."[25] A-ra-ka-te-ja workers are recorded on two tablets, one from the Ak personnel and the other from the Lc series which sets the production stint for the workgroup.

KN Ak 5009 + 6037 + 8588
.a]ka-pa-ra2 [
.b] ko-wa , ṃẹ[
.c ạ-ra-ka-te-ja , / ko[
a]ka-pa-ra2 (cloth-working) women[
b] girls [
c]spinning women [

This tablet, pieced together from three joins, seems to be listing the women and children comprising at least three different occupational groups. The titles of only two of these groups have been preserved: ka-pa-ra2 (probably the same title as the ka-pa-ra2-de known at Pylos) and the a-ra-ka-te-ja. As this tablet suffers from the same poor state of preservation as most of the Knossos tablets, not much can be recovered about the size, location, or composition of this workgroup. It is, however, interesting that both legible entries refer to textile workers. The second tablet sets the work assignment for this workgroup.

KN Lc 531 + 542
.a] 'pa-we-a ko-u-ra' *161 TELA-1 15[
.b]ạ-ra-ka-te-ja tu-na-no TELA-̣1 1 [
a:] cloaks of ko-u-ra CLOTH: 15 [
b:] spinning women: tu-na-no CLOTH: 1["

This tablet lists the amount of finished textiles that the a-ra-ka-te-ja are projected to produce: 15 cloaks (pa-we-a)[26] of ko-u-ra[27] cloth and one unit of tu-na-no[28] cloth. (Pa-we-a ko-u-ra is the typical cloth type mentioned in the Lc series.[29]) It would appear that these two tablets are referencing the same workers. I, however, find this second tablet particularly odd in that while the women in question are spinners by occupation, they are being assigned to a different stage of textile production, namely the weaving of specialized cloth types. I am not aware of any study which addresses this particular question, and I offer a theory of my own below. The next type of textile worker recorded at Knossos – pe-ki-ti-ra2 or "wool-carders" – is also attested to at Pylos.[30] Unfortunately, the usual preservation problem applies. Only one tablet appears to mention this type of worker, and part of the word string is lacunose.

KN Ld 656
1: pe-ki-ti[ra2
2: re-u-ḳọ[
"carders …. white"

On this delivery tablet, we might presume that the white items mentioned on line 2 (re-u-ko) would be carded white wool, if these workers are operating solely within their own occupational milieu. However, if these workers are appearing, like the a-ra-ka-te-ja, outside the strictest boundaries of their occupational title, the item in question may be re-u-ko-nu-ka cloth, a term that recurs in nine other Ld tablets. If this is the case, I continue to find it very interesting that women identified by a title that implies a single-task stage within the contexts of textile production appear to be performing tasks outside that specific designation.

Several titles for textile workers appear to be derived from the types of cloth they produce. None of these textile types have been plausibly etymologized; it may be that these names descend from Minoan technical terms. These occupation titles include te-pe-ja, e-ne-re-ja, ko-u-re-ja.

The term te-pe-ja, also attested at Pylos and Thebes, has a clear derivation from the cloth named te-pa, thought to be a particularly heavy, locally-produced type cloth. The occupational term should therefore be translated as "women who make te-pa."[31]

KN Le 641 + frr.
.1 o-a-po-ṭẹ , de-ka-sa-to , a-re-i-jo , o-u-qe-po[
.2 pa-i-ti-ja , 'PE' TELA+TE ?2 MI TELA-1+TE 1?4 da-wi-ja 'PE' TELA-x+TE 1[
.3 do-ti-ja ṂỊ TELA+TE 6 qa-mi-ja TELA-1+TE 1[
.4 ko-no-so te-pe-ja 'MI' TELA+TE 3 tu-ni-ja TELA-1+TE 1 [
.5 vac. [ ] vac. [
.6 vac. [ ] vac. [

On this tablet,[32] which has as its opening heading "And thus a-po-te (man's name) received from *Areios* and not from ….," deliveries of finished cloth from various women's workgroups are recorded; the te-pe-ja appear on the fourth line delivering 3 units of te-pa cloth (further described with the prefix MI). The tablet specifies that these te-pe-ja workers are Knossos-based; the inclusion of the ko-no-so only with this group seems to imply the remaining groups are located elsewhere. It is again interesting to note that these are not the only women on this tablet producing te-pa cloth; five other groupings of women – none of whom are explicitly called te-pe-ja – also deliver this same material.[33]

Three very fragmentary tablets attest to another type of textile worker identified by the title ko-u-re-ja. This title, unique to Knossos, appears transparent as "producers of ko-u-ra," a type of cloth recorded on some 20 tablets from the archives at Knossos, Pylos, and Mycenae.[34] Two of the tablets locate these workers in the personnel series; it is not clear how many workgroups of ko-u-re-ja these tablets refer to.

KN Ak 643
.a] ko-no-so [
.b]ko-u-re-ja / [
"At Knossos, ... ko-u-ra makers..."

KN Ap 694
.1]ịạ , ko-u-re-ja MUL ̣1[
.2] ka-ra-we MUL 1[
.3] a-ze-ti-ri-ja MUL 1[
.4] *vacat* [
1: 1[ ] ko-u-ra making woman
2: 1 old woman
3: 1 decorator

The final ko-u-re-ja tablet (KN Lc 581) lists 30 units of wool in conjunction with these workers.

KN Lc 581
recto
.a] 'pa-we-a' TELA -4 40[
.b]no , / ko-u-re-ja LANA ?30[
verso] to-u-ka ḶẠṆẠ [

As a projection tablet, this tablet may refer to raw material allotted to the ko-u-re-ja for their production activities; presumably a target amount was listed in the lacunose sections. The title e-ne-re-ja appears similar to ko-u-re-ja. This title, unused at Pylos, is thought to mean "makers of e-ne-ra,"[35] and appears on two personnel series tablets. KN Ak 638, while fragmentary, appears to follow the standard format for a workgroup tablet, listing the location of the workgroup – in this case Amnisos – as well as the children who accompany its adult women workers. (This is the typical format for an Ak tablet, listing a feminine occupational title in conjunction with the underage children accompanying their mothers. This tablet is also sufficiently preserved to identify the workgroup's location.)

KN Ak 638
1 'e-ne-re-ja['
2 ko-wa[
3 a-mi-ni-so / ko-wo[

The second tablet, KN Ai 0762 + fr., is too fragmentary to provide much information but appears from the conjunction of the term e-ne-ra and MUL to be another reference to this or an additional e-ne-re-ja workgroup.

KN Ai 762 + fr
]ra-ma-na , / e-ne-ra MUL[

No project, delivery, or storage tablets are known for this workgroup.

The textile workgroup title e-ro-pa-ke-ja, attested to at Mycenae as well as at Knossos, has no extant attestations in the personnel series, but, like ko-u-re-ja, appears with textile production goals set for it in the KN Lc series.

KN Lc 534 + 7647 + 7818
.1 pa-we-a , ko-u-ra '*161' TELA -1 10[
.2 e-ro-pa-ke-ja , tu-na-no TELA -1 ̣1[

Again we see target amounts set for the standard types of cloth for this series – pa-we-a ko-u-ra and tu-na-no – ten units for the ko-u-ra type and one for the tu-na-no. The second tablet that mentions this group (KN Ld 595) records the storage and receipt of chitons (TUN+KI) produced by this workgroup.

KN Ld 595
1:]e-ro-pa-ke-ja o TUN+ KI[
2: pe TUN+ KI 8 [

This record notes both the eight chitons produced and delivered as well as those chitons that remain outstanding (literally, "missing" o-pe-ro). The exact sense of the abbreviation PE remains unclear.

The title ko-ru-we-ja follows this pattern as well whereby the workgroup can be reconstructed from its textile delivery tablet.[36] This subset of workers is attested only on a single L series tablet that records the exchange of 84 pieces of a specialized cloth type.[37]

KN L 472
]ko-ru-we-ja TELA-2+PU 84

The special PU affix on the TELA ideogram signals a different type of cloth here; the PU is an abbreviation for pu-ka-ta-ri-ja "of double thickness."[38] This is a frequently mentioned type of cloth in this series, appearing on 37 tablets. It is interesting to note the large size of the cloth delivery here; large delivery amounts are a typical feature of this series.

The title ke-ri-mi-ja is another title used in context with textiles; this workgroup is only attested in the Lc series at Knossos, although it does appear in workgroup contexts at Pylos.[39]

KN Lc 535 + 538
.1 ta-ra-si-ja pa-we-a [
.2 ke-ri-mi-ja tu-na-no [
.3 to-sa pe-ko-to [
"So much *piece-work* of the *ke-ri-mi-ja*: x cloaks of *ko-u-ra* type,x tu-na-no cloths, x pe-ko-to cloths"[40]

The above translation, from Ventris and Chadwick (1973), restores ko-u-ra in the lacuna in line 1 as pa-we-a is generally linked with ko-u-ra on other documents. If this restoration is correct, and I am inclined to think it is, then once more we see a further distancing, or at least not a one-to-one correspondence, between worker title and cloth type with more than one group of workers (here the ke-ri-mi-ja) associated with ko-u-ra cloth, the same cloth type after which the ko-u-re-ja workers received their title.

The women known as ne-ki-ri-de also appear from context and analogy to be textile workers; their workgroup is attested on four tablets, one of which identifies them as a workgroup unit of the Ak series.

KN Ak 780 + KN Ak 7004 + KN Ak 7045 + KN Ak 7767
.1 da-wi-ja , ne-ki-ri-de MUL 2 PE VIR 2
.2 ko-wa me-wi-jo[ ]1
.3 ko-wo me-ẉị[-jo-]e 3
"2 Dawian ne-ki-ri-de women, two 'last year's' men, 1 younger girl, 3 younger boys"

This (mostly preserved) tablet is an excellent example of the ways in which the Ak series at Knossos functions as an analog to the Aa at Pylos. Here, the da-wi-ja ne-ki-ri-de workgroup is recorded along with their underage children and two sons who have come of age. There are a few textual differences between the two series, however. The most significant of these differences is that the Knossos tablets differentiate the workgroups' children by age, grouping them into the categories me-zo (plural me-zo-e) from μείζων to signal the presence of "older" children and me-u-jo (plural me-u-jo-e) from μείων for "younger" children.[41] We have insufficient data to surmise the age at which children pass from "younger" to "older" but this attention to children's ages seems to be reflected as well on the Minoan-inspired frescoes from Akrotiri[42] and in the depiction of boys on the Warrior Vase. Nor are there good parallels at Knossos to the remainder of the A series tablets at Pylos – in the Knossos tablets, specific rations given to each group are not typically recorded, nor do we know the fate of the collectives' adult sons.

This tablet is slightly unusual for an Ak tablet in that it provides not just the workgroup title (ne-ki-ri-de) but also an ethnic (da-wi-ja);[43] the Knossos tablets generally use only one marker to signify a workgroup. This tablet includes, in addition to women and children, a count of *PE* VIR, literally "last year's men." This odd phrase probably refers to the sons of these women who reached adulthood the previous year and who, for reasons unknown, continue to be counted with their mothers. While the meaning of the title remains obscure, two of the four tablets on which these workers appear have clear connections to textiles and their production. The first is the rather long tablet KN Ln 1568 which records on its recto the names of at least sixteen women and their cloth holdings, and on its verso, two women's occupational titles (a-ze-ti-ri-ja and ne-ki-ri-de) in conjunction with allotments of wool under the jurisdiction of two individuals bearing women's names. The exact purpose of the tablet is somewhat unclear but the first series of allotments of finished cloth and the second set of entries dealing with wool seem to fix the term ne-ki-ri-de (as well as a-ze-ti-ri-ja) as being textile-related professions. As an O series tablet records a transfer of a full unit of wool from a man named a-mi-ke-te-to to ne-ki-ri-de workers (here in the dative plural form ne-ki-ri-si), it is tempting to read this tablet as referring to a transfer of raw material to these craftswomen for their working.

KN Od 687
.1 ṭị-ra
.2 a-mi-ke-te-to ne-ki-ri-si LANA 1

A final reference to these workers (and to their connections to wool) can be found on the sealing KN Ws 8152:

1: LANA supra sigillum
2: ne-ki-
3: -ri-de

Overall, this evidence might allow us to view these workers not simply as generic textile producers but possibly as specialists in wool-working.

The last title known only from the L series tablets is ne-we-wi-ja. This term, however, is also attested as a workgroup title at Pylos, so its attribution as a workgroup title is certain. Like many of the other workgroups described above, this workgroup is also mentioned while setting its production stint of ko-u-ra cloth pieces.

KN Lc 560 + KN Lc 7587 + KN Lc 7815
.1 pa-we-a ko-ụ[-ra
.2 ne-we-wi-ja / [

So while an appearance in the L series tablets is perhaps the surest guarantee that a workgroup is engaged in textile production, six titles from outside the L series would also seem to identify women assigned to these tasks. Three derive from the personnel series (a series that often cross-references the L series workers); the remaining three come from the E series tracking grain distributions and the X series, which encompasses all tablets too fragmentary to assign to any of the other headings.

The first such group of task-titled workers are the a-ke-ti-ri-ja (variant spelling a-ze-ti-ri-ja). These workers are the best attested of all the collective workgroup members at Knossos. This title, also appearing at Pylos, as mentioned above has been understood to mean "decorators."[44] Not only are these workers the most frequently mentioned of all the workgroup women with appearances on ten tablets, they also have the widest distribution across the tablet series at Knossos, attested to in six different letter subsets. Three mentions belong to the personnel series.

KN Ai 739
.1 ra-su-to , 'a-ke-ti-ri-ja' MUL 2
.2 ko-wa 1 ko-wo 1
"At Lasunthos, decorators: 2 women, 1 girl, 1 boy"

KN Ak 7001
1: a-]ḳẹ-ti-ri-ja , MUL 1[
2: me-]ẉị-jo-e 4 [[ko-wa]] [
3:] *vacat* [
"... Decorators: 1 woman, 4 younger ...."

KN Ap 694
.1]jạ , ko-u-re-ja MUL ̣1[
.2] ka-ra-we MUL 1[
.3] a-ze-ti-ri-ja MUL 1[
.4] *vacat* [
1: 1[ ] ko-u-ra making woman
2: 1 old woman
3: 1 decorator

These three tablets provide some insight into the workings of the a-ke-ti-ri-ja/a-ze-ti-ri-ja workers at Knossos. It seems that this occupation may be represented by several workgroups, some based at Knossos and others at outer sites like Lasunthos. It is interesting to note that all of these workgroups seem to be very small. It may be that the a-ke-ti-ri-ja workgroups run smaller than other women's collectives; KN E 777 may give some support to this hypothesis.

KN E 777
recto
.1 ko-no-si-ja / ki-ri-te-wi-ja-i LUNA 1 GRA 100[
.2 a-mi-ni-si-ja LUNA 1 GRA 100 [
.3 pa-i-ti-ja LUNA 1 GRA 100[
verso
.1 a-ze-ti-ri-ja GRA 1̣0̣[

This tablet records on its recto the monthly rations (LUNA) of wheat being allotted to ki-ri-te-wi-ja women at the sites of Knossos, Amnisos, and Phaistos with each site receiving 9,600 l. wheat. Two different models have been suggested to account for this allocation: payment in kind for services rendered, or as rations provided for the sustenance of these women – the LUNA might support the second reading. If the former explanation is correct, this is a massive amount of wheat being allocated to women of high religious and social status.[45] If, on the other hand, we view these allocations as representing rations, we have enough to supply 500 persons at each site for a month. Assuming the function of the verso of this tablet is the same as its recto, the a-ze-ti-ri-ja women (whose site is unspecified) are receiving either a payment in kind or subsistence rations which, at 960 l. wheat, is one tenth of the amount given to the groups on the recto, and an amount sufficient to ration only 50 workers for a month. Assuming all things being equal, this may indicate that the size of the a-ze-ti-ri-ja workgroup is only one-tenth the size of the other groups. In terms of task assignments, while Chadwick had preferred translating the term as "nurses,"[46] this term is attested in much the same way as other, more readily identifiable textile workers in the L and M series. The verso of KN Ln 1568, discussed above in conjunction with ne-ki-ri-de workers, records the a-ze-ti-ri-ja, in contexts with wool under the supervision of a named woman, and KN M 683[47] lists a-ze-ti-ri-ja women in conjunction with 9 full measures of wool. These two tablets make a compelling case for assigning this workgroup to the genre of textile production. The final three tablets are too fragmentary to provide further insight into this occupational designation. Tablets KN Fh 8504 and KN X 7737 both list no more than a full or partial mention of the title itself, but surely its inclusion into the Fh series which records the distribution of oil to a variety of people and divinities should indicate that the a-ke-ti-ri-ja were also in possession of an oil allocation (and possibly the GRA allocation listed above). The final two tablets KN Xe 544 and KN Xe 657 remain too brief to attribute to any specific series. It is perhaps noteworthy that this designation is also the most frequent designation for women workers at Pylos. Furthermore, at both sites, this is one of the few groups where women make appearances outside of their primary production activities.

Another workgroup that can reasonably be assigned to textile production is composed of women identified by the term ka-pa-ra2-de.[48] No assistance in identifying this term can be gained from etymology beyond the nominative feminine plural *–ades* ending. It is possible that we may have a Minoan occupational term here. This workgroup has been thought to be a textile producer largely due to the presence of another known textile workgroup (a-ra-ka-te-ja) on its only extant tablet:

KN Ak 5009 + KN Ak 6037 + KN Ak 8588
.a]ka-pa-ra2 [
.b] ko-wa , ṃẹ[
.c ạ-ra-ka-te-ja , / ko[
a]ka-pa-ra2 (cloth-working) women[
b] girls [
c]spinning women [

The tablet appears to be following the usual conventions for a workgroup tablet, recording the title of the workgroup and their children, broken down by age-grade (as the me[ ] attests).

The next workgroup to fit this category is composed of to-te-ja women, attested to on two tablets. This title is also used at Pylos where it identifies a workgroup of textile producers. This title is clearly preserved on a tablet in the Knossos Ak subset class; another fragment has been assigned to the X. The Ak tablet is one of the better preserved of its series:

KN Ak 611
.1 to-te-ja , TA 2 'DA 1' MUL 10[ ]ḍẹ-di-ku-ja MUL 1[
.2 ko-wa , / me-zo-e 4 [ ] ko-wo , / me-wi-jo ̣1[
.3 *vacat*
1. to-te-ja workers 2 TA, 1 DA; 10+ women; 1 trained woman [
2. 4 older girls, 1 younger boy

This tablet underscores the greater emphasis the Knossos scribes place on the differentiation of workers by the three markers of sex, age, and training status than do their counterparts at Pylos. It is interesting to note that the number of women undergoing "training" (de-di-ku-ja) on this tablet is significantly smaller than the numbers of adult (and presumably trained) women and older girls (who presumably have not begun this formal training). The other tablet thought to refer to to-te-ja workers is KN X 7846. This reading is dependent on restoring the syllabogram ja to the lacuna on the tablet's second line. Even if this restoration should be correct, this tablet is still too broken to provide any real information.

Kn X 7846
.a]ẉọ-a [
.b]*161 , to-te-[

One last title is used to refer to women in the workgroups at Pylos, but this term is not actually an occupational term but rather a status term. Ka-ra-we, also attested in the Pylos archives, refers to "old women" normalizing as *grawes* from γρηῦς.[49] These women can be integrated as members of a larger workgroup, as indicated by KN Ap 5868 + 8220 where 6 ka-ra-we women are counted alongside women in training and boys.

KN Ap 5868 + 8220
.1 ?ko-]ṇọ-ṣị-ja / to-sa MUL 26 di[
.2]7 ko-wo 9 ka-ra-we MUL '6 [
lat. inf.
] e-u-[
"... total women 26 (under instruction?) ... 7 boys, 6 old women"

In some instances, however, the title ka-ra-we seems to be treated as an independent title functioning to identify certain women in the same manner as do occupational-based titles:

KN Ap 694
.1]jạ , ko-u-re-ja MUL 1̣[
.2] ka-ra-we MUL 1[
.3] a-ze-ti-ri-ja MUL 1[
.4] *vacat* [
1: 1[ ] ko-u-ra making woman
2: 1 old woman
3: 1 decorator

These two tablets appear somewhat contradictory with regard to task assignment; the former seems to indicate they are absorbed into workgroups and presumably carry out whatever task that group is assigned while the latter seems to treat older women as a category unto themselves. It is not yet clear how this difference can be resolved.

The assignment of children of a variety of ages to the workgroup women also seems to indicate that Knossian women also functioned as the primary child-care providers of their society.[50]

Ethnically-identified women in the Knossian workforce

At Knossos, at least ten ethnic titles are also used to designate low-status workgroup women. Unlike the Pylos archives where most of the ethnic adjectives were derived from far-off place names, all the identifiable ethnics in use at Knossos appear to be local to Crete. The ethnics seem to be used in much the same ways as the occupational titles and appear in both the personnel and textile series. The ethnics do require one methodological caveat, however; these terms are used very frequently throughout the archives to describe both persons and things deriving from specific places. In order to avoid inadvertently including ethnics which refer to objects rather than female workers, I am treating as legitimate references to women only those ethnics which a.) are accompanied by the MUL ideogram, b.) appear in the personnel series, or c.) appear in the textile series in analogous fashion to the occupational groups discussed above.

Ten ethnics appear in both the personnel and textile series. These ethnics are da-wi-ja, pa-i-ti-ja, qa-mi-ja, ri-no-ni-ja, ti-wa-ti-ja, and five titles which appear together on the same G series tablet: da-*22-ti-ja, ja-pu2-wi-ja, *56-ko-we-i-ja, ku-do-ni-ja,[51] and ku-ta-ti-ja.

The ethnic adjective da-wi-ja derives from the place name da-wo (thought to be Haghia Triadha) and is used to identify women on five tablets. The first, KN Ak 780 + 7004 + 7045 + 7767, appears in conjunction with the occupational term ne-ki-ri-de and has been introduced above. On this tablet the ethnic *Dawian* is used to identify the origin, and likely current location, of these ne-ki-ri-de workers accompanied by their sons and daughters. The term also appears on three L series tablets.

KN Lc 526
.1] 'pe-ko-to' TELA -1+TE ̣1̣0 TELA -2+TE 14[
.2]ḍạ-wi-ja / tu-na-no TELA -1 3 LANA [

This tablet once again lists the production target for this workgroup,[52] with at least three different types of finished product expected: the familiar tu-na-no TELA-1 type, the TELA-2 type, and a new type of te-pa cloth modified by the term pe-ko-to.[53] This term da-wi-ja also appears on KN Lc 7549,[54] but as it is the only complete word on this tablet, it is not possible to say much more about this mention. The final textile series tablet records women identified by several different occupational and ethnic terms involved in the (eventual) transfer of various types of finished cloth:

KN Le 641 + frr.
.1 o-a-po-te , de-ka-sa-ṭọ , a-re-i-jo , o-u-qe-po[
.2 pa-i-ti-ja , 'PE' TELA +TE ̣2 MI TELA -1+TE 1̣4 da-wi-ja , PE TELA -x+TE 1[
.3 do-ti-ja , MI TELA +TE 6 qa-mi-ja TELA -1+TE 1[
.4 ko-no-so te-pe-ja MI TELA +TE 3 tu-ni-ja TELA -1+TE 1 [
.5–.6: *vacat*

The first line of this tablet "a-po-te (MN) did not received from Areios (MN)" indicates that this is an inventory tablet. The remaining lines on this cloth delivery tablet list the amount of finished cloth that remains undelivered by each workgroup. These workgroups are all based in different locations and are identified by the ethnics of the female producers in five out of six instances.[55] The remaining mention of da-wi-ja also seems to indicate the workgroup women themselves as this is a tablet belonging to the series that allocates raw wool to workers for processing into finished products:

KN Og 180
recto
.1 pa-i-ti-ja M 130[
.2 da-wi-ja M 60[
verso
.1]-to M 4̣0[
.2 M 4̣[

The ethnic adjective pa-i-ti-ja, derived from pa-i-to "Phaistos," is one of the most common ethnic adjectives in the Knossos archives. In most cases, it is used to modify things, but in three instances it is used as a descriptor for women: on the personnel tablet KN Ak 828 and on the same two tablets that listed the da-wi-ja women presented immediately above: KN Le 641 and KN Og 180. In this two last instances the amounts of product associated with the Phaistian women was equal or greater than that of the da-wi-ja. The remaining personnel series tablet rosters a workgroup of Phaistian women and their children:

KN Ak 828
.1 pa-i-ti-ja , DA 1 TA [
.2 ko-wa me-zo-e di-da-ka[
.3 ko-wo me-zo-e di-da[
"Phaistian woman 1 DA 1 TA ..., older girls, under instruction .... older boys, under instruction"

For reasons discussed further on p.188, we should perhaps view these as women indigenous to and still located at Phaistos. Finally, pa-i-ti-ja also makes a brief appearance on the roster tablet KN Ap 639 to describe the origin of a small group of named women.

The ethnic qa-mi-ja, which also appears in conjunction with textiles on KN Le 641, derives from the place name qa-mo. While this title and its variants appear on eighteen tablets, only four (including KN Le 641) refer to qa-mian women. (The location of qa-mo is not known.) Two personnel tablets and an additional textile series tablet record these workers.

KN Ak 613
.1 qa-mi-ja / TA 1 DA 1 ṂỤḶ [
.2 ko-wa , / me-u-jo-e 9 ko-wo[
lat. sup.
] 7̣ T 1[
"qa-mi-ja women: 1 TA, 1 DA, x women, 9 younger girls, x boys"

KN Ap 5876 + 5928 + 5971 + 6068 +fr.
.1] ko-wo , DỊ qa-mi-ja ko-wa 'DI' 3 ko-wo DI 3̣[
.2] 'DI' 1 ri-jo-no ko-wo DI 2 [
.3] *vacat* [
"… 4 boys under instruction, 3 qa-mi-ja girls under instruction, 3 boys under instruction,
… 1 [boy/girl] under instruction, 2 ri-jo-no boys under instruction"

KN Ak 613 is clearly following the standard format for workgroups, listing the working strength of female workers and their children, while the Ap tablet provides a tally of "trained" children emanating from several workgroups. The final tablet mentioning qa-mi-ja workers records the amount of tu-na-no cloth they are expected to produce.

KN Lc 543
.1 TELA -1+TE 11[
.2 qa-mi-ja / tu[-na-no

The ethnic ri-jo-ni-ja is attested on a single tablet tallying a workgroup of women in the personnel series.[56] The location of ri-jo-no remains unknown.

KN Ak 624
.1 ri-jo-ni-ja , TA [ ] 'DA [ ]' [
.2 ne di 3 ko-wa , / me-zo-e [
.3 ko-wo , di 3 ko-wo , me-zo-e 1̣[
Ri-jo-nian women: x DA, x TA ...; 3 young women under instruction, x older girls..., 3 boys under instruction, x older boys."[57]

The final ethnic title for women attested in the personnel series is ti-wa-ti-ja.

KN Ap 618 + 623 + 633 + 5533 + 5922
1: a-pe-a-sa / i-ta-mo , 'do-ti-ja' MUL 1 ki-nu-qa '*56-ko-we' MUL 1 [
2: ṭị-wa-ti-ja / a-*79 'a-no-qo-ta' MUL 3 ko-ma-we-to MUL 2 we-ra-te-ja MUL 2 [
"Absent women: Itamo (WN) at Do-ti-ja; Ki-nu-qa (WN) at Ko-ko-we
3 Tiwatian (?) women: a-*79 (WN) (belonging to) A-no-qo-ta (man's name); 2 women (belonging to) Komawen (man's name); 2 We-ra-teian women"

This tablet differs from those of the Ak series on several grounds: it tracks absent rather than present women, it identifies them by name, and it records the ethnic heritage of at least some of the women. This tablet would indicate that the palace at Knossos monitors its female workers as closely as it does its male.

Ethnic titles for women occur in one additional place in the Knossos tablets; a ration tablet of the G series records the monthly rations provided for four different groups of ethnically-identified female workers:

KN G 820 + fr vi-70
.1] [.]-ṇạ , e-ko-si , a-pi , ku-do-ni-ja / pạ-sa 'ki-ri-ta' LUNA 1
.2 ja-]pu2-wi-ja-qe , *56-ko-we-i-ja-qe ḶUNA 4
.3 da-]*22-ti-ja , ku-ta-ti-ja-qe , po-ti-ni-ja-we-ja , a-pu , ke-u-po-de-ja
.4] LUNA 4
"... have in the region of Kudonia all the barley; one month's *rations*
Women of Ja-pu-wi-ja and *56-*ko-we*: four months *rations*
Women of da-*22-to, and *Ku-ta-to,* women belonging to the mistress, women of ke-u-po-da (MN)*:* four month's rations"[58]

This tablet identifies four feminine ethnics: *56-ko-we-i-ja, da-*22-ti-ja, ku-ta-ti-ja, and ja-pu2-wi-ja (as well as a place name, Kudonia/Chania, where the women receiving these rations are located). The first three ethnics are otherwise unattested. The title ja-pu2-wi-ja appears on a separate textile tablet where it records both cloth production targets for this workgroup as well as the unprocessed wool they would use in this task.

KN Lc 541 + 5055 + 7104 + 8045
.a TELA -1+TE 22 LANA 15̣4
.b ja-pu2-wi-ja

In addition to their more common usage as a reference to women's current locations, ethnics can also serve as designations themselves in order to identify specific female workers.[59] (See also ku-do-ni-ja immediately above.) The lengthy tablet KN Ap 639 records a long list of women by name; lines 4 and 5 track women from Phaistos and E-ra.

KN Ap 639
.0 *sup. mut.*
.1 [.]-me-no X MUL 1 tu-zo X MUL 1 ko-pi X MUL 1̣ [
.2 a-to-me-ja MUL 1 da-te-ne-ja MUL 1 X pa-ja-ni MUL 1 [ ] p̣ị[
.3 wo-di-je-ja MUL 1 ko-wo 1 du-sa-ni X MUL 1 ma-ku[
.4 pa-i-ti-ja X MUL 1 pi-ra-ka-ra X MUL 1 *18-to-no , / TU MUL 2 wi-so ṂỤḶ 1 X
.5 e-ra-ja MUL 7 ko-wa 1 ko-wo 1
.6 to-sa MUL 45 ko-wa 5 ko-ẉọ 4
.7 ke-ra-me-ja X MUL 1 ko-wo 1 tu-*49-mi X MUL 1 i-du X ṂỤḶ[
.8 tu-ka-to X MUL 1 e-ti-wa-ja MUL 1 sa-ma-ti-ja X MUL 1 ṣị-[
.9 ku-tu-qa-no X MUL 1 wi-da-ma-ta2 X MUL 1 ka-na-to-po X MUL 1 sa-ti-qị-ṭọ MUL 1
.10 tu-ka-na X MUL 1 sa-*65 X MUL 1 u-jo-na X MUL 1 sa-mi MUL 1
.11 ạ-de-ra2 X MUL tu-ka-na X MUL 1 pu-wa MUL 1 X si-nu-ke X MUL 1
.12 [a-]qi-ti-ta X MUL 1 si-ne-e-ja MUL 1 X u-pa-ra MUL 1 X ru-ta2-no MUL[1
.13 ḍụ-tu-wa MUL 1 ko-wa 2 ke-pu MUL 1 ko-wa 2 wa-ra-ti MUL[1
.14]j̣ạ-si-ja MUL 4 a-nu-wa-to MUL 1[

Women workers attributed to male collectors

Occasionally, female workers will not be identified by their titles or ethnics, but by the name of an individual man. Six men fit this category. All the men in question can be identified as collectors at Knossos, men who play an important role in the hierarchy of the Knossian economy.[60] Collectors serve as the middlemen of Mycenaean economies, supervising both regions and transactional categories at both states. Most commonly they appear under their own names, and we often see them mediating the transition from local production to state holdings throughout the archives. At both Knossos and Pylos these collectors are assigned workgroup women; the workgroups are designated with a feminine plural form of the male collectors' names.[61] It is important to note at Knossos – a site which does explicitly identify some of its low-ranking women as slaves (see p.185–186) – that these women here belonging to named collectors are not indeed termed slaves. I think it most reasonable to read these women as the staff/servants of these men for whom they perform menial labor. Despite their unusual monikers, these workgroups otherwise are presented in the tablets much like the other personnel series workgroups.

The first women's workgroup bearing a man's name in lieu of a title is the group attributed to a-no-qo-ta. A-no-qo-ta appears as a prominent collector in the Knossos tablets, appearing on at least eight tablets.[62] He is associated with several different types of holdings: several hundred sheep, large grain rations, and male as well as female personnel.[63] He is recorded in command of a workgroup of women; the task assignment of his workers is unspecified.

KN Ak 615
.1]a-no-qo-ta MUL 30 [
.2] ko-wa me-zo-e 6 ko-wa me-ụ[
.3] ko-wo me-ẓọ-e ̣3 ko-wo me-u-jọ[
L LAT. INF.
]ạ-pe-a-ṣạ 24[

This group seems to be a particularly large workgroup[64] with 30 adult women present and another 24 missing (a-pe-a-sa). He is also mentioned on the previously discussed KN Ap 618 + 623 + 633 + 5533 + 5922[65] as the possessor of two missing women on this roster tablet. Unfortunately, none of the tablets that mention a-no-qo-ta give an indication of his own title or specific standing in the overall hierarchy at Knossos. He does, however, on the strength of his other holdings appear to be far more than merely an overseer for this workgroup.

A second man is recorded on this same tablet[66] as the possessor of two missing women. This is the man ko-ma-we (*Komawens*) on line 2.[67] (He is recorded on this tablet in the genitive form ko-ma-we-to.) Like a-no-qo-ta, ko-ma-we appears on a variety of tablets with similar holdings ranging from livestock (goats, sheep, pigs), wool, and male personnel. His title is also unknown.

Returning to the Ak workgroup series, we see an otherwise unattested man as the purported "owner" of another workgroup. A-no-zo-jo, a man's name in the genitive case has a workgroup of women at the site of da-*22-to:

KN Ak 627 + 7025 + fr
.1 da-*22-to , / a-no-zo-jo TA 1 'DA 1' MỤḶ[ ]9 PE di 2
.2 ko-wa / me-zo-e 7 ko-wa / me-wi-jo-e 10
.3 ko-wo / me-zo-e 2 ko-wo / me-wi-jọ-e 10
"At da-*22-to, a-no-zo's women: 1 TA, 1 DA, 9+ women, 2 older women under instruction; 7 older girls, 10 younger girls, 2 older boys, 10 younger girls."

Five tablets document the textile workgroup of the man da-te-wa. His workgroup is designated da-te-we-ja and is documented on both the Ak personnel and L textile series tablets.

KN Ak 612
.a TA 1 'DA 1' MUL 9
.b ko-wa., / me-zo 1 ko-wa / me-u-jo 1
.c da-te-we-ja / ko-wo me-zo 1 [[ḳọ-ẉọ ṃẹ-]]
"da-te-we-ja (women): 1 TA, 1 DA, 9 women, 1 older girl, 1 younger girl, older boy["

On this tablet we see a small – 9-member – workgroup of women in the charge of da-te-we-ja along with their underage children; this tablet also includes the TA and DA syllabograms; their numbers are roughly the same as seen at Pylos – usually no more than one of each. Children are once more differentiated into the "older" and "younger" categories. Nosch has noted that while we see a nearly 1:1 woman : child ratio at Pylos, Knossos tends to run closer to 3:1.[68]

Simply being able to identify da-te-we-ja as a Collector's workgroup does not necessarily provide much information about the types of tasks performed by these workers. Fortunately, this term is also attested in the L cloth series where two texts associate these workers with cloth production.

KN Lc 540 + 8075
.a 'pa-we-a' ko-u-ra TELA -1 3[
.b da-te-we-ja / [

KN L 594
.1] ri-ta , pa-we-a
.2]da-te-we-ja TELA -1 1 TUN+KI 1

Both these tablets record cloth produced by the da-te-we-ja women. On Kn Lc 540 + 8075 the workgroup's assignment of producing three units of the usual product associated with the Lc series, pa-we-a ko-u-ra cloth, is recorded. On KN L 594 the commodities are pieces of linen cloth (ri-ta pa-we-a) and one chiton. The second tablet belongs to a series – L (1) – we have not yet encountered. The L

(1) series, written by the familiar hand 103, deals with records of linen cloth, more specifically the receipt of linen cloth items from outlying villages.[69] On this tablet, one unit of linen cloth (ri-ta pa-we-a) and one chiton are recorded as received. One additional tablet, KN Xe 5891 has been assigned to the catchall X series as it is too fragmentary to identify its series placement:

KN Xe 5891
da-te-we-ja[

(A final tablet which mentions the term da-te-we-ja, but it is unlikely that the term refers to women.)

KN D 8174
.1 [ ]-si-jo-jo / ko //OVIS-Ṃ[
.2 ḍạ-te-we-ja [

This tablet is from the largest tablet series at Knossos – the sheep tablets which number approximately 900 tablets and record some 100,000 sheep between them. On this tablet, the first line records a man's name in the genitive case in the position of the collector; he is collecting rams on this tablet. More confusing is the clearly legible da-te-we-ja on the second line in the position where shepherds' names normally occur. If this is referring to the same da-te-we-ja workers as the A and L series tablets, this would be the only instance among 900 tablets where a.) women function as shepherds, and b.) where a plural group functions as the recorded shepherd. Granted, while ambiguous and confusing tablets often seem the hallmarks of the Knossos archive, the term here is more likely either a feminine or neuter plural adjective, modifying sheep or another lacunose noun.

Two tablets attest to the workgroup holdings of the collector named we-ra-to.[70] We-ra-to also appears as the overseeing collector on the livestock tablet KN De 1136 that records missing sheep.[71] His women's workgroup – we-ra-ti-ja (variant spelling: we-ra-te-ja) – is attested on two tablets in the Knossos personnel series. As this title receives no mentions outside the Knossos Ak and Ap series, its production responsibilities cannot be independently corroborated as textile workers; however, if we assume a commonality of function for all the Ak workgroups, by analogy we might reasonably associate these women as assigned to textile production also.[72]

KN Ak 784 [+] 8019
.1]we-ra-ti-ja [ ]2
.2]me-zo-e , di-da-ka-re[ ]11
.3]me-zo-e , di-da-ka-re[ ]1̣5̣

On this tablet, we-ra-ti-ja functions as the occupational title for a women's workgroup that counts among its members both boys and girls undergoing their occupational training. The other tablet which mentions them is the now-familiar KN Ap 618 + 623 + 633 + 5533 + 5922 which notes the absence of two we-ra-te-ja women among others.[73]

KN Ap 618 + 623 + 633 + 5533 + 5922
1: a-pe-a-sa / i-ta-mo , ‘do-ti-ja’ MUL 1 ki-nu-qa ‘*56-ko-we’ MUL 1 [
2: ṭị-wa-ti-ja / a-*79 ‘a-no-qo-ta’ MUL 3 ko-ma-we-to MUL 2 we-ra-te-ja MUL 2 [
“Absent women: Itamo (WN) at Do-ti-ja; Ki-nu-qa (WN) at Ko-ko-we
3 Tiwatian (?) women: a-79 (WN) … (A-no-qo-ta MN); 2 of Komawens’ women; 2 We-ra-teian women”

The final male collector attested to in possession of an Ak series women’s workgroup is we-we-si-jo (Werwesios). Werwesios is the best attested of the men who hold women’s workgroups, appearing on nearly 40 tablets in the Knossian archives. Olivier goes so far as to classify him as an “international collector.”[74] He has access to huge commodity holdings, overseeing the collection of several thousand sheep from various shepherds in the KN D series; he also has holdings of cloth,[75] wool,[76] and miscellaneous unidentified commodities. He seems to have two workgroups of women attributed to him in the archives as well.

KN Ak 622
.1 we-we-si-jo-jo [
.2 ko-wa , me-zo-e [
.3 ko-wo[
“Belonging to We-we-si-jo: [x women], older girls, [ ] boys[”

KN AK 9173 + 9459 [+?] 9001
.1 ?we-]we-si-jọ[
.2] ko-wa [
.3] ko-wo [
“Belonging to We-we-si-jo: [x women], girls, [ ] boys[”

It is interesting to note that of these collectors’ workgroups, only one is explicitly assigned to textile production (da-te-we-ja).

Women identified with the term do-e-ra

The last major category of low-status women workers at Knossos are women who are explicitly titled slaves (do-e-ra for singular and plural).[77] Women bearing the title do-e-ra are attested on four tablets, all in the personnel series. All of these tablets mention both the term do-e-ra and the name of her owner. Unfortunately, three of these tablets are very lacunose and do not provide as much evidence for this institution as one might hope.

KN Ai 1036
.1]*56-so-jo , / a-mi-ni-so , // do-e-ra
.2] *vacat*
"Belonging to ...sos (?) at Amnisos, a (sing?) female slave"

Here, we get the location of the two individuals, the port village of Amnisos. Otherwise this tablet does little more than provide an attestation for this title. KN Ap 628 + KN Ap 5935 appears to be of equal merit:

KN Ap 628 + 5935
.1a vac. [
.1b]-ja , / a-ke-wo 'do-e-ra' MUL 4 [[ko]][
.2]-ro , / do-e-ra ṂỤḶ 1 di-qa-ra[
.3]ne-o , / do-e-ra MUL[
"... female slaves of Alkeus, 4 women [
... female slaves of [man], 1 (named?) di-qa-ra
... female slaves of [... neos – man] x women"

KN Ai 1037 identifies the mechanism by which at least one woman becomes a slave:

KN Ai 1037 + fr.
1: do-]e-ra we-ka-sa[
2:] , qi-ri-ja-to , [

If we accept the restoration of [do-]e-ra on line one, and the normalization of qi-ri-ja-to as *quriato* following πρίατο,[78] we have a record of a slave purchase here.[79] This is the only tablet indicating a purchase of a slave woman; in most cases they seem to inherit the status from their mothers. The final tablet which mentions female slaves at Knossos appears very similar to the workgroup tablets of the Ak series.

KN Ai 824
.1 a-pi-qo-i-ta / do-e-ra MUL 32 ko-wa , me-zo-e 5 ko-wa me-wi-jo-e 15
.2 ko-wo me-wi-jo-e 4
"*Amphiquhoitas*: 32 female slaves, 5 older girls, 15 younger girls, 4 younger boys"[80]

On this tablet the phrase a-pi-qo-i-ta do-e-ra seems to operate as the functional title of what is presumably a workgroup (from its roster of women and children) identified by a man's name.[81] Like many of the men in the Ak series, a-pi-qo-i-ta (variant spelling a-pi-qo-ta) is also attested in other areas of the archives than just the personnel series. While not attested on as many tablets as his Ak series counterparts, a-pi-qo-ta nonetheless has varied holdings including male slaves, [82] goats,[83] and sheep.[84] Rougemont and Killen both consider a-pi-qo-i-ta a collector;[85] if so, his is the only collector's workgroup in which the women are explicitly identified as slaves.

From these four tablets we might obtain a somewhat impressionistic image of the status of slaves/servants at Knossos. All four of these tablets seem to refer to privately held slaves; we have no tablets explicitly recording any women who appear to be direct palace slaves. Slaves of particular individuals, however, seem to enter the Knossian economy in a variety of ways. Some appear to be privately held and to remain outside the workgroup system in place at Knossos[86] while others seem to be fully integrated into the workforce such as the do-e-ra belonging to a-pi-qo-i-ta on KN Ai 824. It is interesting to note that of all the women belonging to specific men at Knossos – both the slaves and those apparently free – only one group, that of da-te-we-ja can be identified as working in cloth production.

Summary discussion of low-status women's production

The evidence pertaining to low-status female workers at Knossos is far more heterogeneous with that of Pylos. Part of this is a preservation problem; we can only read the titles of workers on fewer than half of the total extant personnel series tablets from Knossos, due to their extremely poor state of preservation. These 26 workgroups at Knossos may reflect only the tip of the proverbial iceberg of women's actual role in production at Knossos,[87] but unfortunately they are all the current state of the evidence permits us to recover. Even from this disjointed evidence, however, some initial differences in the ways in which the workgroup women of Knossos and Pylos are recorded emerge.

1 The first difference that emerges is in naming practices. Whereas at Pylos, low-ranking women were never named, at Knossos we have roster tablets listing the names of several dozen low-ranking laborers. It is the titled women – workgroup laborers and priestesses[88] – who remain unnamed at this site.[89]
2 The organization of workgroups and tracking of workgroups also differs. In general, workgroups at Knossos tend to be somewhat smaller than those of Pylos, and the Knossian scribes are more attentive to ages of the workgroups' underage children. There is also no solid evidence that Knossos supplied food rations to its low-ranking workers – a difference that might have important ramifications for determining the status of Knossos's female workers.
3 Knossos also differs from Pylos in the types of documentation it keeps on the workgroup women. While we see similar formulae in the Knossos Ak and PY Aa personnel tablets – women's occupational and/or ethnic titles and tallies of adult women and their children – the rest of the data diverges. While Pylos seems to have used these tallies to determine the amount of rations each workgroup required, Knossos seems to have recorded the working strength of each group not to feed them but to set production targets for their labor.
4 Whereas at Pylos, all the women of the workgroups shared the same social status, at Knossos, the tablets distinguish between three sets of workgroup women: one set of workers identified explicitly as do-e-ra (slaves) of specific male collectors, non-slave workers assigned to male collectors, and the remainder consisting entirely of textile workers. Textile workers were not identified as slaves, presumably because they were not.[90]

5 Knossos does not seem to demonstrate as high a degree of craft specialization as Pylos. Whereas at Pylos, workgroup women were assigned to at least three categories of labor (textile production, maintenance and attendant duties at the palace site, and food-processing), at Knossos all women whose tasks can be ascertained worked in textile production.[91] Furthermore, Knossos seems to take this idea of uniformity of assignment for these textile workers to such an extreme that we see even women whom one would expect to be assigned to a single, early stage of production (such as the a-ra-ka-te-ja "spinners" or pe-ki-ti-ra2 "carders") assigned to producing the same types of finished cloth as are women whose titles imply a specialization in either late-stage tasks or specialized cloth types. I find the convergence of these two facts – that workgroups are composed solely of textile workers and that all of these workgroups are required to produce the same, finished products – as significant.

6 Among the textile workers, we see hints of hierarchies too, with some of the women appearing to hold positions of responsibility: the "overseers" qi-na and po-po[92] fit this category well – again, implying that not all women involved in textile production are chattel labor.

7 Another key difference lies in the origins of workgroup women at both sites. While both sites document large numbers of ethnically-identified women, all of the Knossian female textile workers hail from Cretan locations and conduct their work while based at their home villages.[93] We see no women with foreign origins as we did at Pylos, nor an effort to move locally-originating women to new worksites.

8 Explicit production targets are set for only the workers at Knossos, a major divergence that establishes that the textile industry at Knossos was not operating in the same way that it did at Pylos. First and foremost, Knossos sets clear production targets for the women who belong to its textile workgroups, most of whom appear to work in their home villages. These production targets – along with the receipt and storage tablets – are unprecedented for the workgroup women at Pylos who seem to have no end to their labor, be they textile workers or palace maintenance and attendant workers. Killen and Nosch also read the setting of these targets as an indication that the work of Knossian textile producers may have had a distinct and finite end when their targets were met, rather than being full-time, year-round work. This idea is further supported by Nosch's work in experimental archaeology recreating Aegean textile-making; she suggests that the workload set for the village textile workgroups might take up to six months to fulfill[94] – a substantial burden, to be sure, but not a perpetual one.

Status of workers at Knossos: Corvée laborers

As we turn to the question of the social status of Knossian textile workers, it would seem that the category of "low-status woman" is not nearly as monolithic in the Knossian economy as in the Pylian, and instead, we see evidence for several different status tiers present within this larger category.

At the lowest end of the economic hierarchy at Knossos are the workgroup women identified as belonging to specific men. It would appear significant that only some of these women are expressly labeled as do-e-ra, or “slaves,” and I think we should understand two categories of dependent women to be encompassed here: actual slave women and “semi-free” menials whose social standing is somewhat higher than that of the slave women. Their identities as autonomous economic entities seem deeply suppressed; they are not even named on roster tablets. These women have no property holdings; they themselves are the holdings of their owners, and either their owner’s name or do-e-ra stands as their sole identification. It is interesting to note that collectors’ women are the only women at Knossos who are – with one exception, the workgroup designated da-te-we-ja – situated outside the textile series. In fact, I see no reason to read the remaining collectors’ women as textile workers: likely they are the menial attendants of high-ranking officials.

When we examine the standing of the workgroup women, a number of interesting points emerge. There appears to be no significant difference between the women identified with occupational titles and those with ethnic adjectives; in fact, the correlation between these two groups of women is so close that the two titles occasionally overlap to describe the origin and task assignment of a specific workgroup. From analysis of the ethnics, all the women organized into Knossos’s workgroups are local women. Moreover, rather than Pylos’s clustering of the workgroup women at its provincial capitals, Knossos’s textile workers most commonly remain in their originating villages instead of being moved to a secondary location.[95] In short, the Knossian model is one where groups of local women are set textile production targets in their villages for prearranged amounts of work;[96] presumably these women fulfilled the production targets set by the palace within their own communities without the disruptions evidenced in the Pylian tablets.

Under this system at Knossos, we see a greater degree of flexibility of products produced by each workgroup – many of whom produced two or even three different types of products regardless of their official task designation. I read this as indicating that Knossos co-opted specialist and local workers throughout its dependent villages to produce standardized textile goods on a standardized level throughout the state.[97] Presumably then, when each production stint was finished, the specialist women returned to their tasks for which their workgroups were named – why else retain both their original title and these production goals?

This hypothesis would seem to gain support from the absence of workgroups at Knossos devoted to the kinds of task categories known from Pylos which are, by definition, perpetual in nature – tasks such as maintaining the palace water supply, personal attendant activities, or food-processing. Assignments to any of these categories would necessitate understanding these workgroup women as composing a full-time, year-round palace staff; this is precisely what we do not see at Knossos. I suggest that a different structure and rationale governing the organization of women's workgroups at Knossos may have been at work, as the diffuse and locally-based workgroups of Knossos do not seem to imply, to my mind, the same state of complete and perpetual service to and dependence upon the Knossian palatial administration that the personnel records of the Pylos A series document. What then might this different structure have been? In addressing this question, it is useful to compare the workgroup situation of Knossos with those of the Bronze Age Near East.[98]

In 1984, Uchitel[99] documented the ways in which the institution of corvée[100] labor functioned in the states of Lagash and Ur, focusing specifically on the treatment of women in the Sumerian records. He noted that corvée labor for Near Eastern women generally involved several elements: 1. The short-term conscription of low-status free women as members of single-sex work-teams. 2. The presence of children alongside their conscripted mothers – often with assigned supervisors accompanying them. 3. Subsistence rations provided by the state (only) during their period of service. He suggested that the Aegean states of Knossos and Pylos were also governed by this mechanism. While I find this suggestion untenable for the Pylos evidence, as I think the texts strongly indicate a state of on-going slavery for the women of the Pylos workgroups rather than any short-term co-option,[101] all three of his conditions fit the idiosyncrasies of the Knossian evidence quite well,[102] with the corvée system at Knossos opting against the widespread shifting of the population to different locales. This suggestion particularly helps explain the apparent uniformity of the task assignments and provides and explanation for the target tablets – unlike at Pylos where women's labor on behalf of the state appeared unending, the Knossos tablets strongly imply that local women's labor was commandeered by the state for part of the year in order to produce textiles, and the work continued until set production goals were met. If Nosch's estimate of three to six months of labor per production target is correct,[103] corvée textile production would consume one-quarter to one year's worth of village women's time, suiting the needs of Knossos's textile industry while allowing them to commit the rest of the year's labor to sustain themselves and their families.

Women and property at Knossos

At Knossos, women are attested in possession of the following types of property: cloth, wheat, oil, wool, linen both raw and finished, land, and possibly livestock holdings. While these categories encompass many of the materials recorded in the Knossos tablets, as a whole the holdings of Knossian women are very limited when compared to those of Knossian men. Knossian men control the following types of property: female and male slaves, various cloth types (finished and unfinished), leather skins, non-slave personnel (men and women), livestock (sheep, goats, cattle, pigs – with numbers of animals reaching the hundred thousands), a variety of foodstuffs (wheat, barley, olives, olive oil, figs), spices and unguents, vessels (gold, bronze, and terracotta), wool, linen, tunics and a variety of cloth pieces, horn (for working), swords, metal ingots, chariots and chariot parts, assorted weaponry, horses, armor and a few as yet unidentified commodities.

But, while the holdings of Knossos's women in no way compete with those of Knossian men, how do they compare to that of Pylos's women? Does the institution of property at Knossos demonstrate the same close correlation to religious office as it does at Pylos? Who are the female property holders at Knossos, and do they occupy similar status tiers to their counterparts at Pylos?

Property holdings of sacerdotal women

As at Pylos, female religious functionaries at Knossos continue to occupy the category of "elite" women. There is a major difference, however, between the economic clout of functionary women at Pylos and at Knossos. While the vast majority of economically autonomous women at Pylos were cult officials, at Knossos female functionaries make up a significantly smaller percentage of the local "elite" women. Unlike the six different categories of female religious officials at Pylos, only two types of female cult functionaries (priestesses and the ki-ri-te-wi-ja) are attested to at Knossos.

The highest-ranking class of female religious functionaries – the priestesses – receive only three mentions at Knossos in two tablets: KN Fp 1 + 31 and KN Fp 13; the latter provides two mentions of priestesses. The KN Fp series deals exclusively with the distribution of oil in cult contexts – recipients are either divinities or human cult officials. Both tablets record the monthly distribution of olive oil to shrines of various divinities and to religious officials. In all three instances, the priestesses in question are described with the title a-ne-mo i-je-re-ja (*anemon hiereia* "priestess of the winds"). There are at least two different priestesses of the winds; KN Fp 13 mentions on line 3 one priestess (presumably at Knossos) who receives 28.8 l. of olive oil and a second at the village of u-ta-no who receives 14.4 l.

KN Fp 13
.1 ra-pa-to 'me-no' , *47-ku-to-de OLE V 1 pi-pi-tu-na V 1
.2 au-ri-mo-de OLE V 4 pa-si-te-o-i S 1 qe-ra-si-ja S 1
.3 a-ne-mo-i-je-re-ja OLE 1 u-ta-no , a-ne-mo-i-je-re-ja S 1 Ṿ 3
1: "In the month of Lapatos: to *47-ko-to: 1.6 l. oil, to Pi-pi-tu-na: 1.6 liters
2: To Aurimo: 6.4 l. oil; to all the gods: 9.6 liters; to qe-ra-si-ja: 9.6 liters
3: To the priestess of the winds: 28.8 l. oil; At Utanos (PN), to the priestess of the winds: 14.4 liters"

KN Fp 1 + KN Fp 31
.1 de-u-ki-jo-jo 'me-no'
.2 di-ka-ta-jo / di-we OLE S 1
.3 da-da-re-jo-de OLE S 2
.4 pa-de OLE S 1
.5 pa-si-te-o-i OLE 1
.6 qe-ra-si-ja OLE S 1[
.7 a-mi-ni-so , / pa-si-te-o-i S 1[

.8 e-ri-nu , OLE V 3
.9 *47-da-de OLE V 1
.10 a-ne-mo , / i-je-re-ja V 4
.11 *vacat*
.12 to-so OLE 3 S 2 V 2
1. "In the month of Deukios:
2. To Diktaion Zeus: 9.6 l. oil
3. To the Daidaleion: 19.2 l. oil
4. To Pa-de: 9.6 l. oil
5. To all the gods: 28.8 l. oil
6. To qe-ra-si-ja: 9.6 l. oil
7. Amnisos, to all the gods: 9.6 l. oil
8. To Erinys: 4.8 l. oil
9. To *47-da-: 1.6 l. oil
10. To the priestess of the winds: 6.4 l. oil
11. (blank)
12. (total) 112 l. oil"

The priestess on KN Fp 1 + 31 receives 6.4 l. of oil on behalf of her cult. It is uncertain whether this priestesses is one of the two mentioned on KN Fp 13, receiving on this tablet a different offering amount in a different month or if this tablet references an entirely different individual altogether; it is possible that the mention of Amnisos in line 7 carries over to all references following it. As the priestesses receive these disbursements in conjunction with other shrine complexes or with specific gods, we should perhaps understand this allotment as falling under her official responsibilities rather than being allotted to her for personal use. No other holdings are attested in the control of priestesses in the Knossos archives.

Two tablets reference the second religious title assigned to Knossian women, ki-ri-te-wi-ja. KN E 777 records the monthly allotment of wheat provided to groups of ki-ri-te-wi-ja women at three different sites – Knossos, Amnisos, and Phaistos. These three sites are the three most important sites in the Knossian archives. These allotments are likely to have been intended as monthly rations based on their size and the inclusion of the LUNA. The ration amounts are very large – 9,600 l. of wheat per group, per month. If we apply the Pylian ration ratio (for workgroup women), these are ration amounts for 500 women.

KN E 777
recto
.1 ko-no-si-ja / ki-ri-te-wi-ja-i LUNA 1 GRA 100[
.2 a-mi-ni-si-ja LUNA 1 GRA 100 [
.3 pa-i-ti-ja LUNA 1 GRA 100[
1: "Women of Knossos (for the *ki-ri-te-wi-ja* women): ration for one month 9,600 l. of wheat
2: Women of Amnisos: ration for one month 9,600 l. of wheat
3: Women of Phaistos: ration for one month 9,600 l. of wheat"

The second tablet (KN Fp 363) mentioning the ki-ri-te-wi-ja provides the strongest support for the identification of ki-ri-te-wi-ja as a religion-affiliated term. KN Fp 363 belongs to the Olive Oil series at Knossos – a series devoted to recording offerings of olive oil to religious sites and officials. On this tablet, the lacunose offering to the ki-ri-te-wi-ja shares a line with an offering of oil (OLE) to be paid/delivered (qe-te-a) to various locations and persons, including, on Line 2 to the ki-ri-te-wi-ja and to the shrine (i-je-ro) of da-*83-ja-de.[104] As the amount is lacunose, it is of course impossible to assess the relative importance of the ki-ri-te-wi-ja vis-à-vis the other recipients on this tablet. (Di-wo-pu-ka-ta is thought to be a man's name or title; te-re-no in the first line remains obscure.)

KN Fp 363
.1 qe-te-a , te-re-no OLE [
.2 da-*83-ja-de / i-je-ro S 2 ki-ri-te-wi-ja , [
.3 di-wo-pu-ka-ta S 2 [
.4] *vacat* [
"Oil to be paid [ ] to the Daidaleon shrine: 19.2 l.; to the ki-ri-te-wi-ja [ ] to the man named di-wo-pu-ka-ta 19.2 l. units [ ];"

Overall it is interesting to note the differences in the holdings of the sacerdotal women attested to at Pylos and those of Knossos. Two major differences are immediately striking: 1.) The female religious structure of Knossos does not appear to be as varied or fleshed out as that of Pylos.[105] No mention is made of the other eminent female official known from Pylos – the ka-ra-wi-po-ro "keybearer" – or the large number of lower level officials – the "slaves" either of "the god" or of the priestess and keybearer. 2.) No mention is made of land being attributed to either of the cult functionaries at Knossos. In fact, there is little indication of the priestesses having a broader economic role in the Knossian state; and no personnel, land, or shrine property are associated with female cult officials.

Property holdings of lay women at Knossos

In contrast to Pylos, where we see nearly all of the property attributed to women in the hands of cult officials, the majority of the property associated with women at Knossos is linked with low- to middle-status women. While the titled women of the workgroups seem to have had some access to property and commodity holdings,[106] the middle-status, property-holding women at Knossos are most frequently identified not by their titles but by their names. Unfortunately, like so many other of the people who appear in the Knossos tablets,[107] many of these names appear as *hapax legomena*.

The commodity most commonly attributed to women at Knossos (either via allocation or collection) is cloth. At least 18 women on tablets KN Ap 5748 + 5901 + 5923 + 8558 and KN Ln 1568 are listed in conjunction with cloth holdings.

KN Ap 5748 + 5901 + 5923 + 8558
.1]si 1 TU 1 ki-zo 1 MUL 3̣ ṬẸḶẠ[-1+TE] ạ-ma-no[
.2]1 o-ri-mo MUL 3 TELA-1+*TE* 1 pu-zo ti-no pi-ja-mu-nu ṂỤḶ[
.3]ni-ta , o-sa-po-to MUL 3 TELA[1]+*TE* 1 [
.4] *vacat* [

This tablet rosters at least seven women by their names with holdings of te-pa cloth (TELA+TE). No information beyond names and cloth amounts can be recovered, although one of the women is apparently accompanied by a daughter. KN Ln 1568 is similarly themed except on this tablet both named men and named women are associated with te-pa cloth.

KN Ln 1568
.1a mi-ja-ro , E , PA , 4 E , PA 6 E , PA 12
.1b *56-po-so 1 wa-wa-ka 1 TELA -1+TE 1 ru-ki-ti-ja PE TELA +TE 1 wi-da-ma-ta2 , MI
TELA -1+TE 1
.2a E, PA 12 E PA 4 E , PA 4
E, PA 8
.2b po-po PE TELA -1+TE 1 ta-su MI TELA +TE 1 ko-re-wo MI TELA +TE 1 di-*65-pa-ta
MI TELA +TE 1
.3a PA 12 PA 11 PA 12
.3b ru-sa-ma PE TELA -1+TE na-e-ṛạ-ja PE ṬẸḶẠ +TE 1 qe-pa-ta-no PE TELA +TE 1
.4a PA 8
.4b]tu-na-no ru-nu TELA -1 1̣ [ ] TELA -x 1
.5 pạ-ṛọ no-si-ro TELA -x+TE 3
.6 da-wo to-sa te-[ ] [[ṃị ṬẸḶẠ-+ṬẸ]] pa-ra-ja ṂỊ TELA –x +TE 7 [
lat. inf.
a: a-ze-ti-ṛị-ja ne-ki-ri-de [
b o-pi ma-tu-ẉẹ o-nu-ke LANA 1 o-pi , po-ni-ke-ja[

Seven women can be securely identified on this tablet – po-ni-ke-ja (“*Phoinikeia*”); po-po; ru-ki-ti-ja (“*Luktia*”); ru-nu, ru-sa-ma, wi-da-ma-ta2; and na-e-ra-ja, and another three (qe-pa-ta-no, *56-po-so, wa-wa-ka) also seem likely to be women. Otherwise, three men’s names can be securely read (di-*65-pa-ta, ko-re-wo, no-si-ro); the gender of the names ta-su and ma-tu-we remains unclear. Perhaps the most significant aspect of this tablet is the rather unremarkable way it presents the similarities of men’s and women’s textile holdings; it seems to treat this circumstance as relatively ordinary.

KN Od 681 also seems to link men’s and women’s property at Knossos:

.a ‘e-na-po-na , o-nu , pa-i-ti-jo’ e-ti-wa-ja-qe ḶẠṆẠ [
.b ‘qo-ja-ṭẹ a-pu-do-ke , ti-ra [

This tablet deals with the allocation of raw wool, presumably at Phaistos. While the first two words of line 1 are somewhat unclear, they seem to refer to obligated transactions involving wool. The second line of this tablet records a MN (qo-ja-te) who "paid" or "rendered" (a-pu-do-ke) ti-ra (a word describing wool). The remaining word on the tablet – e-ti-wa-ja-qe near the end of line 1 – is more puzzling. In this term the woman's name e-ti-wa-ia is suffixed with the enclitic *que* "and" which seems to link e-ti-wa-ja with some other concept on the tablet; it may be that both she and qo-ja-te are involved in making this payment. In either case, we see members of both sexes incorporated into this wool transaction indicating that both people are considered to have enough of a stake in the possession of this commodity that both are considered liable for its transfer.

In contrast to the solid evidence for women's textile holdings, the evidence pertaining to women's holdings in livestock is shaky at best. Two (KN C 7698 + 7892 + 8223 + frr., KN Da 1161 + 7187) tablets may record women owning oxen and sheep. The C series tablet records on its only surviving line the phrase tu-zo BOS ZE 1 ("tu-zo: 1 yoke oxen"). It is the sex of the individual tu-zo that is at issue here. The personnel series tablet KN Ap 639 includes the name tu-zo among a roster of women; furthermore, tu-zo is also accompanied by the MUL ideogram, all convincing evidence that the tu-zo of KN Ap 639 is a woman. But is this the same tu-zo? All the other names listed throughout the 90+ tablets of the KN C series are unquestionably men. Might there coincidentally be two individuals whose names translated into Linear B in the same way?[108] That may be the likelier explanation; otherwise we have the anomalous situation of a sole female cattle owner.

A similar situation arises on the sheep tablet KN Da 1161 + 7187 + fr.:

.a]we-we-si-jo OVIS-M 300 [
.b]ku-tu-qa-no / pa-i-to[

This tablet records the transfer of 300 rams from the shepherd ku-tu-qa-no at Phaistos to the collector we-we-si-jo (MN). Here we have the same problem; KN Ap 639 also records a ku-tu-qa-no, again with a MUL ideogram. If this were to be the same individual, ku-tu-qa-no would be the sole woman attested on a series of over 900 tablets. It is not entirely beyond the realm of possibility that a woman is in the immediate possession of any of these animals – she could be perhaps an exception to the pattern or she could be standing in for a missing or deceased male relative – but the atypicality of women to appear as livestock holders in a large and well-documented series (nearly 900 tablets) should not be dismissed.

Thus far, the evidence for women's property holdings at Knossos has been rather sparse. Religious functionaries are attested to only with holdings pertaining to their cult activities or rations for their personnel while the holdings of laywomen seem limited mainly to small quantities of textiles and do not appear to be significantly different from those of the women who comprise the collective workgroups. Livestock holdings are inconclusive at best, and overall, women do not seem to wield any major economic clout through their control of property.

The four remaining property holders change this picture dramatically in terms of both the substance of their holdings and their role in production; two women are attested to as land owners and two others show more than a passive role in commodity holdings. KN Ld 584 discusses the holdings of the woman qi-na, identifiable as a woman from the dative ending of her name.

KN Ld 584
.1 po-]ki-ro-nu-ka 'o-pi-qi-na' TELA-2 4
.2 pa-]ro , e-ta-wo-ne-we 'o-nu-ka' TELA -2 5
lat.inf.
]to-sa TELA 15
1: "In the charge of Qi-na, *po-ki-ro* -type o-nu-ka cloth: 4 units CLOTH type 2
2. Responsible for o-nu-ka cloth, the man E-ta-wo-neus: 5 units CLOTH type 2
below: total CLOTH: 15 units"

This tablet refers to textile holdings of o-nu-ka and po-ki-ro-nu-ka types in the control of two individuals – the man e-ta-wo-ne-we and the woman qi-na. Both these individuals follow prepositions that strengthen their claim to the materials. E-ta-wo-ne-we follows pa-ro[109] and qi-na o-pi;[110] both are used in the tablets to convey "responsible for" or "in the charge of." Taken together these two phrases indicate a closer connection with the materials than simple allotment; they seem more likely as the producers of these products, or possibly even the supervisors of the workshops themselves.

The next woman attested to with property holdings at Pylos is the best-attested woman at the site: the woman named po-po. Her name appears among a listing of female textile holders on the previously discussed KN Ln 1568 which solidifies her identification as a woman. Po-po also appears on two secure L series textile tablets, one O series tablet, and a miscellaneous X series tablet. She appears in a supervisory capacity with control over (o-pi) the raw materials of textile production in three tablets (KN L 567,[111] KN L 648,[112] and KN Od 689[113]) where she has control over linen on the two L series tablets and wool on KN Od 689.[114] The wool tablet preserves the amount of wool in her charge – four full units, a fairly large quantity. The fourth tablet (KN Xe 524[115]) is too fragmentary to preserve the commodity she controls here. All these tablets along with the roster tablet KN Ln 1568 are written by the same scribe, Hand 103. As scribes frequently document the same regions and persons, it seems that all these texts refer to the same person, the woman identifiable as such on Ln 1568.[116]

The final tablet (KN L 513[117]) on which she appears is a fairly standard tablet recording textiles owed; on this tablet po-po is expected to transfer 4 units of cloth. Overall, the evidence concerning po-po seems to confirm her status as a workshop supervisor; she receives the preposition most suited to those in charge, and she is shown with both the raw and finished materials for textiles – all of which seems to identify her as one of the highest-status women in textile production.

One other major category of property holdings is also attested as being in women's hands – that most important of all resources in an agrarian economy –

land. Land holdings are attributed to two Knossian women: ka-wi-ja on KN Uf 79 and pe-ri-je-ja on KN Uf 1031 + KN Uf 5738. These two women comprise approximately 10 percent of all known landowners at Knossos and are discussed in greater detail in the following chapter on women's land-holding patterns in the Linear B tablets.

Conclusions

Unlike at Pylos, the line between lower-status women and economically autonomous mid-status women at Knossos is not so clearly defined. While a large gap can be identified between the workgroup "slaves" at Pylos and the religious functionaries, the gap seems smaller at Knossos, largely because the women who belong to Knossos's workgroups do not appear to all be at as low a social rung as their counterparts at Pylos; the difference between being co-opted into short-term corvée labor and permanent slavery is a substantial one.

This difference between the gender organization of Pylian and Knossian institutions persists into the area of property holdings as well. While the gulf between property holders and producers was wide at Pylos, and, with one exception, the only women attested with property holdings belonged to the sphere of religious officialdom, we see much greater variability in the category of "middle status women" at Knossos. Some of these property holders seem barely higher than workgroup women while others have extensive property holdings and/or supervisory responsibilities. In any case, the rigid hierarchical concerns that differentiated sharply between female laborers and property holding sacerdotal women at Pylos, do not seem to be in place at Knossos. Also, unlike at Pylos where the linkage between religious status and property control was at least circumstantially strong, the rationale governing the elevation of certain women to property holdings and supervisory positions at Knossos must remain opaque; it may be related to inheritance, service, or talent – but certainly religion should be eliminated as the central institution granting economic license to Knossian women. Finally, two last considerations should be noted with respect to women's property holdings at Knossos. It is quite likely that the women currently identified as property holders are but a small subset of the full numbers of property-controlling women at Knossos. Two factors may contribute to this: 1.) The dismal state of tablet preservation at Knossos which allows us to read with any degree of clarity approximately one-quarter of its tablets. 2.) Our inability to distinguish both Mycenaean- and Minoan-derived names for women. While we can identify Greek-derived names for women under certain circumstances, outside of the personnel series, we have very little chance of recovering Minoan-language ones. It seems extremely likely that many women would have had such names. Studies of the naming practices of Knossian men certainly indicate the persistence of Minoan language names,[118] and we should expect the same for Minoan women. Unfortunately, however, as we do not yet understand if the Minoans had gender-based naming conventions, or what these might have been, we should expect that a large percentage of Minoan-named women will continue to be invisible to us. What is significant to note, however, is that even with suspected gaps in our knowledge about Knossian women in the Mycenaean era, the little evidence we do have strongly suggests that women's investiture in production and property is conceptualized and institutionalized in a very different way on Mycenaean Crete than it was on the mainland.

Notes

1 Save for four tablets. Nakassis 2013: 32.
2 Landenius Enegren 2008: 13.
3 This number reflects only the number of tablets sufficiently preserved to allow the recovery of the occupational title; a total of 349 tablets actually belong to these six series.
4 Major bibliography on the Knossos textile industry: Killen 1995, 1988, 1984, 1979, 1974, 1966.
5 Killen 1984: 52, followed by Shelmerdine and Bennet 2008: 306.
6 Shelmerdine and Bennet 2008: 306.
7 Bennet 1988b: 26.
8 Bennet notes that this enormous number of sheep may well have involved "the majority of the available sheep livestock in central and west-central Crete." Bennet 1988b: 31–32.
9 Killen 1988: 173. The term ka-na-pe-u (κναφεύς) is the attested term for "fuller." *Docs2*: 550.
10 A third class Ag is often included among the roster series; however, as recent research suggests that these texts are not genuine documentary records but rather scribal exercises, I have omitted them from my study. Hiller 1989: 40–65.
11 The workgroups supervisors referred to with the abbreviations DA and TA are discussed in Chapter 3.
12 Killen 1988: 168–69.
13 Killen 1988: 169.
14 Killen 1988: 167–183.
15 Hooker 1980: 95.
16 Killen 1988: 167.
17 Olivier 1967.
18 Killen 1988: 167.
19 Killen 1988: 168–69.
20 Killen cites as an analog the Ab rations which only exist for the major Aa set at Pylos, although he does suggest that the palace at Knossos may have kept (non-surviving) records of the western workgroups whose projections are recorded on the Lc (2) tablets as well. Killen 1988: 170.
21 Killen 1979: 154.
22 The major set consists of what Killen classifies as "store records," that is, tablets on which the source of the cloth is not indicated. As this level of detail is beyond the scope of this study, I refer the reader to Killen 1979: 151–154.
23 Ld 584, Ld 595, Ld 656.
24 Carlier 1983: 20.
25 For the etymology and interpretation of the term a-ra-ka-te-ja, see Chapter 3, n. 79.
26 Pa-we-a has been identified as *pharwea* from the Homeric φᾶρος ("piece of cloth"). Its identification as "cloaks" is somewhat arbitrary. Ventris and Chadwick 1973: 313–14. Killen simply identified pa-we-a as a specific variety of woolen textile. Killen 1988: 177.

27 Ko-u-ra is a technical term for a specific type of cloth (of unknown type). This term gives rise to the occupational term ko-u-re-ja "women who make ko-u-ra" discussed below.
28 The exact sense of tu-na-no, like many of the technical terms used in the archives to refer to textiles, is unknown.
29 Killen 1979: 153.
30 Derivation from πέκω is widely accepted. Chadwick 1988; Ventris and Chadwick 1973: 570; Killen 1984, 1974: 58; Lindgren 1973: Part II, 114–15; *Diccionario:* Vol. II, 97.
31 Te-pe-ja are discussed further in Chapter 3, pp. 82–3.
32 As the exact sense of many of these tablets is less than secure, and as in many cases it would be overreading to assign a specific translation to an ambiguous text, I have elected in many cases to paraphrase the general sense of these tablets from Knossos rather than mistranslate nominatives as datives or genitives in an attempt to convey movement of these commodities. I am also opting to paraphrase several of the longer tablets from Knossos, particularly those which provide only lists of names.
33 If all are to be understood as te-pe-ja workers, I find the burying of the occupational term in the fourth line an odd choice.
34 Morpurgo Davies 1979: 100.
35 Ventris and Chadwick 1973: 543 followed by Morpurgo Davies 1979: 100.
36 This title has long been recognized as a textile-workgroup term. Killen 1983a: 81; followed by Landenius Enegren 2008: 73.
37 This term is tentatively assigned also by Morpurgo Davies to the realm of textile work. Morpurgo Davies 1979: 100.
38 Cf. πτυκτός, πυκνός. *Docs2:* 575.
39 PY An 42.
40 Ventris and Chadwick 1973: 316. For further discussion of the term ta-ra-si-ja and its implications for the organization of the overall textile industry at Pylos, see Killen 1988: 181.
41 This scribal difference has long been recognized: Uchitel 1984: 257–282.
42 Ellen Davis has noted that the children at Akrotiri are differentiated into age groups distinguishable by their hair styles. E. Davis 1986: 399–406.
43 Derived from the place name da-wo, surmised to be the site of Haghia Triadha.
44 For etymology and interpretation of the term a-ke-ti-ri-ja, see Chapter 3, p. 84.
45 The ki-ri-te-wi-ja women and their role within the religious hierarchy of Pylos are discussed in Chapters 4 and 7.
46 Ventris and Chadwick 1973: 214.
47 KN M 683
.1a] a-ze-ti-ri-ja
.1b]te-o o-nu-ke LANA 9 M 2
.2]ti-mu-nu-we *146 30
48 This title is also attested to at Pylos.
49 *Od.* 1. 191. Ventris and Chadwick 1973: 551.
50 Olsen 1998: 90.
51 Ku-do-ni-ja is not a true ethnic but rather a place name ending in –ia substituting for a title ending in –ia.
52 Ventris and Chadwick 1973 provide a minority reading on this text, treating the ethnic simply as a place marker, translating this tablet as "From Da-wo: Ten edged cloths (Type A) of pe-ko-to, 14 edged cloths (types B)...; Three cloths of tu-na-no type, x measures of wool." *Docs2*: 315. I find this reading inadequate to explain the adjectival form of da-wi-ja and its similar presentation to the occupational titles in placement and function.
53 This term is not well understood. Ventris and Chadwick 1973: 315, 570.
54 KN Lc 7549

.a] vest. [
.b]da-wi-ja tu[

55 The sixth, the workgroup identified by the occupational term te-pe-ja, is accompanied not by the ethnic "Knossian" but rather by the place name "Knossos" itself.
56 The masculine equivalent ri-jo-no appears on KN Ap 5876 + 5928 + 5971 + 6068 +fr. to describe boys "under instruction."
57 Ventris and Chadwick 1973: 164.
58 Based on the translation of Ventris and Chadwick 1973: 215 which offers "Women of da-*22-to, and *Ku-ta-to,* belonging to the mistress, from *Ke-u-po-do:* four month's rations" for line 3.
59 Except for line 7 where the women are not named while their number is recorded.
60 For studies on "collectors": John Bennet 1992: 65–101; Driessen 1992: 197–214; Landenius Enegren 2008; Killen 1995; Olivier 2001; Rougemont 2008, 2001.
61 Killen 1983a.
62 Landenius Enegren 2008: 60.
63 KN Da 1289, KN Dq 45, KN Dq 440, KN E 847 + 5739 + 7341 + fr iii, KN Vr 173, and KN X 1051.
64 Although at Knossos, workgroup size is very difficult to ascertain as so many of the tablets are lacunose where numbers might appear.
65 KN Ap 618 + 623 + 633 + 5533 + 5922
1: a-pe-a-sa / i-ta-mo , 'do-ti-ja' MUL 1 ki-nu-qa '*56-ko-we' MUL 1 [
2: ṭị-wa-ti-ja / a-*79 'a-no-qo-ta' MUL
3 ko-ma-we-to MUL 2 we-ra-te-ja MUL 2 [
"Absent women: Itamo (WN) at Do-ti-ja; Ki-nu-qa (WN) at Ko-ko-we3 Tiwatian (?) women: a-79 (WN), ... (A-no-qo-ta MN); 2 of Komawens' women; 2 We-ra-teian women"
66 KN Ap 0618 + 0623 + 0633 + 5533 + 5922.
67 Landenius Enegren 2008: 60.
68 Nosch 2008: 17.
69 Ventris and Chadwick: base this interpretation (rightly, I think) on the occasional inclusions of place names and the terms o-pe-ro 'debt' and a-pu-do-si 'delivery.' Ventris and Chadwick 1973: 314.
70 Landenius Enegren and Killen concur on identifying this workgroup as belonging to a collector. Killen 1983: 82; Landenius Enegren 2008: 56.
71 Killen 1983: 82; Landenius Enegren 2008: 56.
72 "The whole AK series seems to be connected with textiles." Morpurgo Davies 1979: 100.
73 This tablet is further discussed on p.179 in conjunction with worker women belonging to two of the men listed on this tablet (a-n-qo-ta and ko-ma-we).
74 Olivier 2001: 155, after Killen 1975: 176–9.
75 KN Lc 7392 + 7398.
76 KN Od 502.
77 Some commentators prefer the translation of "servant" for do-e-ra. See *Diccionario:* Vol. 1, 186–87.
78 *Od.* 1, 430 of buying a slave: Ventris and Chadwick 1973*:* 577; see also Ilievski for further discussion on slave-purchasing in the tablets. Ilievski 1979: 161–169.
79 KN B 0822 and KN B 0988 also record purchases of slaves; in both these texts the purchased slaves are male. Olivier 1987: 479–498.
80 Ventris and Chadwick 1973: 164.
81 Uchitel notes a slight irregularity on this tablet in that a-pi-qo-i-ta does not appear in the expected genitive form a-pi-qo-i-ta-o "(slaves) belonging to Amphiphoitas" but rather the dative "to (for) Amphiphoitas." Uchitel 1984: 260.
82 KN C 915.
83 KN C 0915.

84 KN C 0941 + 1016 + FR.
85 Killen 1994: 76–77; Rougemont 2009.
86 KN Ai 1036.
87 The total of 26 is the combined total of the occupationally and ethnically titled workgroups; it does not include the women attributed to specific ranking men (either with or without the term do-e-ra.)
88 Discussed in chapter 7.
89 This is not the case for Knossian men who appear with both names and titles on 111 tablets. For further textual differences between the two corpora, see Carlier 1983: 20–22.
90 Killen also suggests differences in status between the women of the KN Ak series. Killen 2001: 172.
91 Nosch 2003: 21.
92 Discussed below, p. 195.
93 Nosch 2003: 21.
94 Nosch 2003. Killen 2001 suggests three months instead. Either way, both concur on a workload with a definite ending.
95 Nosch 2003: 21.
96 For discussions of the ta-ra-si-ja work allocation system for textile production at Knossos, see Nosch 2011, 2000, 1998.
97 Nosch also notes that the workgroup women of Knossos remain in their home villages. Nosch 2003: 21.
98 Especially since Knossos does not appear to conform to mainland Greek practices here.
99 Under this system, men and women are obligated to provide infrastructure labor to the palaces for several weeks/months each year and in turn are provided with subsistence rations for that time period. Uchitel 1984: 282.
100 For additional references to corvée labor, see Wright 1996b: 79–110.
101 See chapter 3 for discussion of Uchitel's theory as it applies to Pylos.
102 I find Uchitel's reading of the do-e-ra as the corvée workers to be mistaken, as they are few in number and their task assignment is never stated. I think his contention, however, best suits the workgroup women instead.
103 Killen 2001 suggests three months instead.
104 Daedalus is a tempting resolution of da-*83-ja-de, but of course, cannot be verified.
105 Acknowledging, as always, the limits and difficulties of the Knossos corpus.
106 Of the titled women discussed above, only three are listed in conjunction with commodity holdings of any type – the da-te-we-ja, the ne-k-ri-de and the a-ke-ti-ri-ja. At least two of these alleged holdings (the da-te-we-ja association with sheep on KN D 8174 and the a-ke-ti-ri-ja's mention with large amounts of wheat on KN E 777) are insecure at best; only the wool allocations to both the ne-ki-ri-de and an a-ke-ti-ri-ja on KN Ln 1568 and the apparent oil allotment of the a-ke-ti-ri-ja on KN Fh 8504 appear to reflect genuine holdings.
107 Lindgren 2008.
108 This certainly is the view of Ventris and Chadwick 1973: 588.
109 Pa-ro *paro* "from or at the hands of (a person)" [παρά Homer +; πάρο Alcaeus, fr. 130]. Ventris and Chadwick 1973: 568–69.
110 O-pi *opi*, at KN with personal names "n the charge or house of (a supervisor)"; at PY with animals "responsible for, in charge of"[* ὀπι- in οπιθεν, ὀπώρα, etc]. *Docs2*: 565. Godart 1969: 39–65 leans toward a translation of "chez" for opi.
111 KN L 567
.1 o-pi / po-po [
.2 o-pi / a3-ka-ra 'ri-ṭạ'[
112 KN L 648
.1 ri[-ta pa-we-a
.2 o-pi / po-po[

113 KN Od 689
.1 ne-wo
.2 o-pi , po-po LANA 4

114 The final tablet, KN L 513 on which a person named po-po is mentioned appears to refer to an entirely different person; Killen notes that 1.) this tablet is written in a different hand (H. 209) and 2.) belongs to a series that records only men among its participants. As this figure is likely a man – and certainly not the woman of the preceding paragraphs – this po-po is excluded from this study. Killen 1968: 637–638.

115 KN Xe 524
sup. mut.
.1]ọ-pi po-po[
.2]o-pi ta-qa-ra-te[

116 Landenius Enegren concurs with identifying po-po as a woman on these tablets. Landenius Enegren 2008: 66.

117 KN L 513
recto
.a qe-te-o TELA -2 [
.b po-po TELA -2 4 [
verso [[a-mi-si-ja TELA -1 12]][

118 Geographical proximity to the center of power seems to play a major role in influencing whether a man at Knossos would be assigned a Minoan or Mycenaean name; approximately 70 percent of men in the vicinity of the palace are named with Greek names, in the provinces only 30 percent. Baumbach 1983: 3–10.

6 Women and land tenure at Pylos and Knossos

Introduction

In the ancient Mycenaean economy, no higher markers of status existed than command and control of such elite properties as metals, subordinate personnel, and arable land. Through control of these assets, ancient elites effectively could drive a controlling share of the internal and external power mechanisms of a state's economy through their domination and direction of agriculture, import and export trade, military[1] personnel and materiel, and command and co-opt the support of their subordinates and allies via allotments of personnel and resources. The previous chapter has detailed the very limited control women at Pylos and Knossos exercised over the first two of these elite holdings – metals and personnel – but the issue of land tenure requires special attention.

Land tenure as an institution receives considerable attention at both Pylos and Knossos, with both palaces producing tablets providing detailed records of land-holding practices. (As usual, however, the Pylian texts are more numerous and accessible than the Knossian.) These land tenure records are particularly useful for a study of social organization in palatial society in that they allow us to track and quantify the holdings of specific named and titled individuals. Above all, the land tenure records underscore the deeply hierarchical nature of Mycenaean society,[2] with access to land carefully structured to engender and reinforce the power of social and ruling elites.

The importance of controlling land in an agrarian economy[3] cannot be overstated. As Palmer observed, "agriculture was the basis of ancient society and the structure of power should be reflected in the arrangements governing the ownership and use of land."[4] Certainly, access to, and control of, arable land would have been highly important in these Late Bronze Age economies,[5] allowing individuals the opportunities to provide sustenance for themselves and their families and, in the cases of ownership or long-term tenure, to allow individuals the possibility to secure their own and their descendants' ranks and economic futures. Land also carries connotations of status and regional power, separating "owners" from "lessees," and thus it creates among individuals systems of autonomy or dependence. However, to date, no studies have yet addressed the relationship between land tenure and gender nor questioned whether land tenure might be differentially structured for Mycenaean men and women. Determining whether men and women have the same access to this critical resource, especially in light of the security and status it can convey, is central to our understanding of Knossian and Pylian women's economic clout within their societies.[6]

The operative question, then, is whether gender asymmetry also governs the investiture of men and women in the land-tenure systems of both polities, a question which must be addressed through three component parts. 1.) Do men and women both have access to all forms of land holdings? 2.) Are men and women, when they control the same type of holding, incorporated into this system for the same structural reasons? This is to say, do land holders of both sexes exhibit the same range of titles and occupational designations or is there an occupational bias governing *which* men and women have access to land? 3.) Within each type of land holding, do men and women control parcels of comparable size, or does one sex receive larger allotments than the other?

The answers to these questions are consequential. If a.) gender asymmetry is detectable in the land-tenure system, and b.) this asymmetry is sufficiently significant to create gender-based hierarchies (where one sex has less access to this resource than the other), then c.) we should expect this to have serious implications for men's and women's economic power and status in each polity. If we are to regard land as an important economic indicator, which seems likely given both the high proportion of tablets devoted to this theme and the amount of detail many of these tablets provide, and if gender distinctions create a marked difference in women's and men's access to so central an asset as land, we must expect severe limitations on the economic opportunities of the less-enfranchised sex. Thus, determining whether land tenure functions as a gendered institution at Knossos and Pylos, with either egalitarian or differential investiture of men and women, is vital to our understanding of women's economic opportunities at these two administrative centers.

Land tenure patterns at Pylos

Land tenure records form a major thematic component of the Pylian archive; the 252 tablets dealing with land and property constitute more than one-fifth of the extant Pylos corpus.[7] These records are found exclusively in the Pylian E-series, a series distinguishable by the use of the GRANUM (wheat)[8] ideogram on its tablets, and trace seven different types of land-holding arrangements in operation at Pylos, including those under public and private control. Throughout the E series at Pylos seven different types of land tenure arrangements are attested, ranging from the large estates in the possession of the wanax and the ruling elite to extremely small plots of leased land in the (short-term) control of lower-level functionaries. The full range of land tenure categories are temene, ka-ma, ko-to-na (unmodified), ki-ti-me-na ko-to-na, and ke-ke-me-na ko-to-na, e-to-ni-jo and o-na-ta.[9] Additionally, as this series uses recorded measures of GRA as a way of referring to the sizes of the holdings in question, this series also provides a rare opportunity to offer a case study involving *quantifiable* male and female property holdings.

Introduction to the E series land registry[10]

The E series[11] tablets from Pylos function as a form of land registry,[12] and its 205 tablets provide a detailed inventory of the Pylian land-tenure system. This large and complex set, valuable for both quantitative and qualitative purposes, records individual land holders by both their names and occupational titles; it is one of the few series to consistently use both identifiers in tandem. These tablets also identify which of the seven types of known land holdings these individuals control, and, when land is leased, the individual or institution from whom the lease derives.[13] In addition to names, titles, and holding arrangements, the entries also list an amount of wheat (ideogram GRA with subunits T and V). This amount of wheat functions in some way as a measure of the size of the parcel of land.[14] (Calcuations follow the equivalences established by Ventris and Chadwick in *Docs2* for GRA and its two submeasures T and V; GRA translates to 96 l. wheat, T to 9.6 l. wheat, and V to 1.6 l. wheat.)[15]

Sutton in particular stresses the unique value of these documents as "our best guide to the structure of Mycenaean society"[16] from the demographic details they preserve. It is in this abundance of demographic evidence that the land series is most useful for a study of the relationship between gender and social hierarchy. Because these tablets regularly identify an individual both by name and title, they allow us to identify the sex of the land holder,[17] either from the masculine or feminine forms of their occupational titles or from the oblique forms of their names. And a sample size of over a hundred land holders, seven different types of land tenure arrangements, and numerically quantifiable holdings provide a unique opportunity to assess holding patterns using gender as the major category of analysis.[18]

The set of land tenure records at Pylos consist of tablets from the Ea, Eb, Ed, En, Eo, Ep, and Er subseries. [19] The vast majority of these texts derive from the closely related Ea, Eb, En, Eo and Ep subsets. These tablets are the work of three scribes: one for the Ea series, a second for the Eb and Eo series, and a third for the En and Ep series.[20] These series all record transactions of land and present similar formats for each entry. The entry format is typically:

Personal name (PN) title "holds" land holding from "damos" (or PN) WHEAT amount.
PN title e-ke or e-ke-qe land holding pa-ro da-mo[21] (or PN) GRA amount

The Ea subset is the simplest of these series, typically recording only one or two land holders per tablet.[22] The Ea series records land leased out by the damos or private individuals as well as the tenure of private, unleased land. The four remaining subheadings Eb, En, Eo and Ep typically have much longer entries than the Ea series. But while the Ea series covers a variety of land-holding options, the four remaining series are all thematically defined: Eb and Ep list holdings of ke-ke-me-na land, whereas En and Eo list holdings of ki-ti-me-na land. But these are not their only differences from the Ea series. These four series are our only instances throughout the various Linear B corpora where we have duplicate versions of information. The Eb and Ep series duplicate each other, with the shorter tablets of the Eb series recapitulated in the longer Ep tablets. Similarly the Eo and En series echo each other, with the longer En tablets each reiterating several shorter Eo tablets. The rationale behind this duplication is not immediately apparent. Various theories have been proposed to explain why this redundancy occurred, but scholarly consensus has not yet been reached; some of the thornier methodological issues related to the doublet series are discussed here.

The two sets of duplicate entries record different types of land holdings. The Eo/En series record holdings of one particular type of land: ki-ti-me-na land. The ki-ti-me-na series (Eo/En) record the names of individuals who hold ki-ti-me-na land apparently in their own right and the individuals who lease plots of it from them. Ki-ti-me-na holdings are generally large estates, second only to the *temene* of the wanax and other high officials. The En series are the longer tablets, encapsulating the shorter Eo series tablets. The texts make a clear distinction between those who actually control ("own") the ki-ti-me-na estates and those who only lease it; the "owners" lead off each tablet in the Eo tablets and each section in the En tablets with their names in the genitive case. These "owners" are then followed by lists of those who lease land from them. From the amounts of GRA attested, it is clear that the ki-ti-me-na are large holdings and that the individual plots of land leased out are substantially smaller. In short, this series identifies ki-ti-me-na holders by name as well as those who hold leases from them.[23] The gendered nature of these holdings is addressed further below.

The Eb/Ep tablets are similar to the above En/Eo but instead of recording ki-ti-me-na holdings, they list leases (o-na-to) of the land type identified as ke-ke-me-na. These holdings tend to be much smaller than the ki-ti-me-na holdings discussed above and also have a long (Ep) and a short (Eb) series.

Three additional E series subheadings record land tenure-related information: the Ed, the Eq, and the Er records.[24] These are all very short series and when combined number only 13 tablets. The five tablets of the Ed series are in many ways similar to the Ea holdings mentioned above; they tend to be brief, composed of one or two lines recording leases (o-na-ta) of ke-ke-me-na land. The primary difference in these holdings from the Ea series is that the Ed holdings are held not by individuals but by groups. These groups tend to be comprised of high-ranking persons such as ka-ma holders (discussed below), the te-re-ta (elite male officials), and the elite of the religious establishment: priests, priestesses and keybearers. These holdings tend to be very large (running into the tens of thousands of liters of wheat), but it is not possible to differentiate the holdings of individual lessees because the totals are combined amounts. The Eq series is more difficult. Out of a total of five tablets, three are too fragmentary to identify gender or holding types, and the remaining two tablets are on different themes. One of these (PY Eq 213) records the amounts of wheat coming from specific locales (with no people recorded); only the remaining one (PY Eq 146) records the land holdings of human members of the Pylian state. This tablet, broken in several places, records a small number of o-na-to holders who are factored into my overall calculations.

The final E series tablet relevant to land holding is the Er subseries which records two types of land holdings (which appear non-transactional) held by the wanax and other high-ranking palace officials. This is a small subseries, limited to two tablets: PY Er 312 and PY Er 880. In this series, the records have no sentence structure, consisting simply of the officials' titles, the type of holding they have, and an amount of wheat.

In addition to the E series material, there may be another source of evidence for land ownership at Pylos encoded in one of the constructions that comes to be used occasionally as a formula to indicate place names. These are addressed briefly on pp. 214–15.

While the land tenure tablets from Pylos may perhaps seem at first glance a corpus too disparate or unruly to allow us to recover any aspects of the social structure underlying it, when one approaches the tablets with a focus on gender, clear and consistent patterns emerge: women's investiture into the land-holding systems of Pylos is substantially and systematically more limited than men's.

Methodological considerations and the Pylian E-series

Before resuming discussion of the roles gender plays in the structure and organization of the land-tenure system, we must address the limits and controversies inherent to this evidence. The E series continues to pose several methodological difficulties to the researcher, even after now 60 years of continued investigations. Many of these topics are still under discussion and, in general, scholarly consensus has not often been attained. I offer here a brief discussion of some of the controversies associated with these tablets and a summary of the scholarship that has addressed these issues. Some of these issues are related to internal matters within the E series tablets; others are related to the tablets and their broader administrative contexts. I address the internal questions and then some of the broader-context questions.

1. Perhaps ironically, although the E series tablets constitute a land registry, these tablets differ from their Near Eastern counterparts in that the Pylos E series does not identify where the plots of land they record were located. All scholars seem to be in agreement that the Pylian cult center of pa-ki-ja-na (Sphagianes) is one of the locations documented in the E tablets; the numbers and locations of other sites are somewhat less certain. Sutton offers a lower limit of at least two different communities (including pa-ki-ja-na)[25] while Killen offers an upper limit of no more than five different localities (again including pa-ki-ja-na).[26] Hooker identifies a second major difference from the cuneiform archives, noting that not only do the tablets not record the location of plots of land, they also do not identify exactly who was in possession of each plot of land.[27]

2. A second question that has long perplexed scholars is the existence of what appear to be duplicate versions of two subseries. It has long been recognized that the Eb and Ep series duplicate each other. (The shorter tablets of the Eb series are repeated in the longer Ep tablets.) Similarly the Eo and En series echo each

other, with the longer En tablets reiterating several shorter Eo tablets. Scholarship is still divided as to which versions take priority. Ventris and Chadwick take the position on the two separate recensions that the longer tablets (Ep and En) may well represent later, more polished versions of the shorter Eb and Eo tablets.[28] Aligned with this view is that of E. L. Bennett, who approached the controversy in 1956 by examining those instances where the two sets differed in an irregular way. He argued that formulae on the longer tablets tended more toward regularity than did those on the shorter tablets and attributed this to active normalization by the scribe copying the tablets.[29]

Other scholars argue instead that the longer tablets predate the shorter. Carpenter suggests that the En series was already in existence when the Eo series was written by tracking where blank lines occur in the Eo series vis-à-vis the En. He suggests that the longer versions may have been a master copy and that at some time it was necessary to re-order the records, perhaps as a form of index.[30]

Still other scholars have questioned whether these series should be read as equivalents at all. Much of this school of thought has focused on the verbs employed in the longer and shorter "versions": e-ke on the longer tablets and e-ke-qe on the shorter. Previously the difference between the two forms had been overlooked and they were largely regarded as identical; e-ke-qe was identified as e-ke with an attached enclitic. As such they may not be full equivalents but rather two different verbs.

Bennett's later research may provide a solution to this last problem. In 1983, he supported his earlier reading by autopsy of the tablets themselves and noted that the page tablets of the Ep and En series had noticeably narrower widths than those of the Eb and Eo. From this he argued that the scribes writing the longer tablets were economizing on space to fit longer Eb and Eo lines on shorter Ep and En ones. This reading explains neatly the apparent omissions of some signs on the longer versions. It also provides a solution to the e-ke vs. e-ke-qe problem by proposing e-ke not as an equivalent for e-ke-qe but as an abbreviation for it.[31]

For our purposes, the issue of priority is not of central concern although Bennett's solution would seem the most plausible of the explanations to date. Regardless, for statistical purposes in this study, the values on duplicate tablets factor only once into the calculations below.

The remaining controversies related to the E series tablets have to do with their broader social and administrative contexts:

3. It is also uncertain exactly when the tablets were written vis-à-vis the destruction of the Palace of Nestor. Hooker and Bennett both suggest that these tablets may have antedated the destruction by only a few weeks.[32] This raises the question of how typical the evidence encapsulated in the tablets may be; if they are indeed a product of a state-of-emergency at Pylos and, therefore, the product of particularly cramped space, our measurements may be much smaller than they might be otherwise, under a "peaceful" setting. For this study, again, this is not of paramount importance. After all, we do not know the exact measurements of our

units; for our purposes, it is the relative proportions that are of greatest significance. Even under an alleged state-of-emergency,[33] allotment decisions would be based on social hierarchy and so should still be indicative of the recipient's overall standing in the community.

4. The ultimate ownership of the land has not yet been firmly established. Several scholars have proposed that the land-tenure system be understood as governed under a feudal model.[34] One theory holds that the connection of the wanax and lawagetas with apparently restricted land holdings implies some type of feudal system where kingly authority rested in part on possession of landed wealth.[35]

Others have been more reticent to identify Pylian land tenure practices under the feudal rubric. Both Killen and Nosch stress that we simply do not have sufficient evidence to state definitively whether the palace indeed controlled all land holdings, but both do note that the evidence strongly suggests the palace as a major land holder with, in all likelihood, the ability to impose its will on its subjects. This seems the most prudent reading; the evidence as it is currently understood is insufficient to support or reject the feudal model.[36]

5. The remaining questions have generated perhaps the most commentary: why did the palace compile these records in the first place? And, referring to the relationship between the palace and the land-tenure system, how much control did the palace exercise?

Three different models are favored. The first model argues for a high degree of palatial control over internal economic matters, including land tenure.[37] Others view the palace as possessing effective, if not total, control, capable of imposing its will when it so chooses.[38] Palaima has suggested that palatial administrations should best be understood as monitoring rather than strictly controlling all internal affairs (although this model was developed with Mycenaean Crete in mind).[39] Overall, however, while the debate on palatial control of land tenure remains open, it remains clear that at the very least these tenure systems fall under the rubric of palatial interests if not actual, direct control.

On the question of why the palace compiled these records, several theories have been espoused (or pre-emptively rejected):

1 As a cadastral survey (rejected): Killen rules out the possibility of reading these tablets as part of a wider cadastral survey since the tablets provide no information about the precise location of the plots vis-à-vis others in the same area.[40]
2 As a legal registry made to enable the palace to arbitrate any disputes over ownership of land. Killen makes the same objection as above: no precise locations of plots are mentioned.[41]
3 As a basis of a remuneration system where either goods or services were expected to be rendered by the holder in return for use of the land and where the size of the contribution was in some way linked to the size of the plot.[42] Killen elaborates further:

Two obvious possibilities suggest themselves: either a.) that this is palace-owned land, perhaps land allocated to its holders in return for services to the center and held on condition that the holders would continue to provide some form of services, together with some of the produce of the land; or, alternatively, b.) that it is land not owned by the palace, but from whose holders the center was still capable of extracting taxes in the form of produce and services in respect of their holdings. It is not possible on present evidence to decide definitively between these alternatives; but such evidence as we have on the matter strongly favors the first possibility.[43]

Land holding categories at Pylos

Seven categories of state-allotted land holdings are attested in the Pylian land tablets, differentiated by the terms te-me-no, ka-ma, ko-to-na (unspecified), ki-ti-me-na ko-to-na, ke-ke-me-na ko-to-na, o-na-ta, and e-to-ni-jo. The first way to assess the question of gendered representation in the Pylian land-tenure system is to ascertain whether men and women are attested with equal access to all of the seven types. The tablets answer this question resoundingly in the negative. Men at Pylos are attested in possession of all seven known land tenure types, but only one of the seven holdings (o-na-ta) can be definitively placed also in the hands of Pylian women. (A second category – e-to-ni-jo – remains contested; the ancient evidence's sole instance where it is linked to a woman was the subject of an active dispute between the priestess *Eritha* and the damos discussed below.) As no previous study has addressed the relationship between gender and land tenure, the following section offers an overview first of the apparently masculine-specific land tenure categories and then moves to the two categories of land tenure where evidence of both men's and women's control appears either secure (o-na-ta) or likely (e-to-ni-jo).

Categories of land held exclusively by men

Men, whose gender can be securely determined by the form of their names and from a wide variety of titles, possess land at Pylos in all seven known land tenure arrangements. Furthermore, five types of land holdings – *temene*, ka-ma, ko-to-na (unmodified), ki-ti-me-na ko-to-na, and ke-ke-me-na ko-to-na – appear to have been limited exclusively to male holders at Pylos. (No women's names or titles appear among the lists of holders currently extant.) This section surveys these five formal categories of land tenure as well as an additional designation which appears also to refer to land and its ownership. (The sixth type of land allocation (e-to-ni-jo) remains unclear as to its gender attribution, while the seventh and final type of land holding at Pylos – leased land described by the term o-na-to – is the lone category where both men and women are attested.)

TEMENE

Temenos land (te-me-no) appears as the largest and most prestigious of the Pylian land holdings. As a category of land, *temene* are the only classification of land in the Bronze Age whose terminology survives into the historical period where the term shifts somewhat to signify land belonging to the precinct of a god.[44] In the Linear B tablets however, *temene* are exclusively the property of the most elite of Pylos's officials and are distinguishable from other types of land holdings by their remarkably large size. Despite their size, however, *temene* are barely referenced in the tablets. A single tablet (PY Er 312) mentions a total of three land holdings along with their measurements and possessors, two of which are explicitly called te-me-no; these possessors include two individuals and one small collective. All these temenos holders are male.[45]

PY Er 312.1–6
.1 wa-na-ka-te-ro , te-me-no [
.2 to-so-jo pe-ma GRA 30
.3 ra-wa-ke-si-jo te-me-no GRA 10
.4 (*vacat*)
.5 te-re-ta-o[ ]ṭọ-ṣọ p̣ẹ-ma GRA 30
.6 to-so-de,te-re-ta VIR 3
1. Belonging to the wanax, a temenos [
2. so much seed 2,880 l. wheat
3 "Belonging to the lawagetas, a temenos 960 l. wheat
4. *(blank)*
5. Belonging to the telestai, so much seed 2,880 l. wheat
6. so many telestai, 3 men"

This type of land holding appears to be the most exclusive of all the Pylian lands as access to *temene* seems to have been limited to the highest members of Pylos's administrative elite. Only the two highest-ranking officials at Pylos hold *temene* in their own right: the *wanax* (Homeric and Classical ἄναξ)[46] and the ra-wa-ke-ta *lawagetas* (λαγέτας)[47] whose two *temene* by far exceed all others' land holdings in terms of their GRA measurements: 2,880 l. and 960 l., respectively. (In contrast, the average leased o-na-to holding allocated to women in the tablets is 25.6 l.) The collectively-held *temenos* is of similar size (2,880 l. total) and is held by three unnamed te-re-ta (*telestai* from τελεστής) whose status as male is underscored by the accompanying VIR ideogram.[48] It is interesting to note that their combined total is the same as that of the *wanax* and their individual averages equal that of the *lawagetas* at 960 l. each, further underscoring the elite status of these men.[49]

No mention is made of any sort of elite female figure such as either a "queen," priestess, or ranking administrator in this context.

KA-MA

The second land category exclusive to men are the ka-ma holdings. This category continues to remain poorly understood and its etymology in dispute. It would appear to refer to worked land; context seems to indicate that it carries with it some form of obligation to the damos, perhaps in the form of percentage of its yield.[50] It is not clear how this form of holding differs from *temene*,[51] but as the attested ka-ma tend to be much smaller in size, it seems to be a less elite land category. Evidence for ka-ma holdings stems from two sources in the tablets: mentions of ka-ma as a functioning form of land tenure, complete with a wheat measure, or more indirectly, from mentions of ka-ma-e-u ("man who has a ka-ma") or its plural ka-ma-e-we; ka-ma or ka-ma-e-u references appear on twelve Pylian texts bearing one of the following formulae:[52]

PY Ea 28 + fr.
ti-ri-da-ro / ra-pte , e-ke , ka-ma GRA[ ] *vacat*
"Ti-ri-da-ro the stitcher has a ka-ma land holding: x l. Wheat"

PY Eb 842
.a sa-sa-wo , e-ke-qe , o-na-to , ka-ma-e-u
.b e-pi-qe , to-e , te-ra-pi-ke to-so-de , pe-mo GRA 1 *T* [5
"Sa-sa-wo holds a lease as a kama-holder, and in return for this he works / *serves;* so much seed: 144 l. wheat"[53]

At Pylos ten men hold ka-ma whose sizes cluster around values of 120 l. wheat although one man ne-qe-u (PY Eb 493 / PY Ep 613.1) has a much larger holding (969.6 l. wheat) on which he is liable for certain duties termed o-pe-ro.[54] The occupational titles of the ka-ma holders in the E series are quite disparate; holders include a te-o-jo do-e-ro ("slave of the god"), an e-da-wo (builder),[55] a ko-to-no-o-ko (ko-to-na holder), an i-je-ro-wo-ko (a type of priest),[56] an a-si-to-o-po-qo (cook) and a ra-pte (stitcher). This holding does not appear to be circumscribed by occupation;[57] the sex of the holders, however, shows a much more consistent pattern – all of the holders are male. Women are not recorded as holding or working any ka-ma in the Pylian corpus. Outside the E tablets, two[58] tablets mention the titles ka-me-u and ka-ma-e-we.[59] On both these tablets the sex of the ka-ma-e-we is unequivocal; the ideogram VIR accompanies both titles.

KO-TO-NA (UNSPECIFIED)

Ko-to-na holdings are mentioned more frequently than either te-me-no or ka-ma at Pylos and represent one of the few aspects of the land-tenure system at Pylos where some consensus has been reached. Ko-to-na are generally understood to refer to κτοίνα "plots."[60] Ko-to-na can be listed either without any additional modifier, or, more frequently, by the two qualifiers ki-ti-me-na and ke-ke-me-na.[61]

The four tablets which list "unspecified" ko-to-na (that is, ko-to-na not designated as either ki-ti-me-na or ke-ke-me-na) record only male names as both the recipients and granters of ko-to-na. PY Ea 109 and PY Ea 823 are representative of this type of holding.

PY Ea 109
a-pi-a2-ro , e-ke , su-qo-ta-o , ko-to-na GRA 2 *T* 5
"A-pi-a2-ro (MN) has a plot of land from/ belonging to the swineherd(s): 240 l. Wheat"

PY Ea 823
ru-ko-ro-jo , ko-to-na , ra-wa-ke-si-jo-jo , GRA *T* 6 [
"Lugros's (MN) plot of Lawagersian (adj.) land, 57.6 l. Wheat"

Both of these tablets record a transaction in which an individual man (a-pi-a2-ro and ru-ku-ro) comes to hold a ko-to-na from another holder (the swineherd(s) or the *lawagetas*). Similarly the treatment on PY Ea 270 where the man a-pi-a2-ro has a second plot, this time from a man named pe-re-qo-no identified as one of the oxherds (qo-qo-ta-o); on this tablet his holding is 57.6 l. wheat, significantly smaller than his 240 l. ko-to-na on PY Ea 109. (The remaining tablet in this set PY Ea 812 records a ko-to-na in the possession of a man named Eumedes (e-u-me-de), a perfume maker (a-re-po-zo-o), of moderate size: 172.8 l. wheat.

KI-TI-ME-NA KO-TO-NA

The two remaining ko-to-na categories are recorded as being held in two different forms: as ki-ti-me-na ko-to-na and ke-ke-me-na ko-to-na. Despite the large amount of scholarship these two terms have generated over the last sixty years, their exact meanings and etymologies continue to resist secure definition.[62] The most widely accepted readings associate them respectively as "privately held" and "centrally held plots." Both types are apportioned by their holders/owners to individuals or to small groups. The tablets clearly and consistently distinguish between holders of ki-ti-me-na estates ("owners") and those to whom smaller parcels of ki-ti-me-na plots are allotted; those to whom the subdivided parcels are allotted are most commonly identified as lessors.[63] The formula for ki-ti-me-na holdings is PN (personal name) "holds" (e-ke) "ki-ti-me-na land." This is a different formula than for lessees: PN "holds" (e-ke) a "lease of ki-ti-me-na land" (o-na-to ki-ti-me-na-o ko-to-na-o).

Ki-ti-me-na holdings are recording in the Pylos Ea, En and Eo subsets. A representative tablet detailing ki-ti-me-na holdings is PY Eo 247 (recapitulated in a somewhat different order on PY En 74):

PY Eo 247
.1 a3-ti-jo-qo , ki-ti-me-na , ko-to-na , to-so-de , pe-mo GRA 1[*T* 5 *V* 4
.2 e-ko-to , te-o-jo , do-e-ro , e-ke-qe , o-na-to , pa-ro , a3-ti-jo-qe , ko-to-no-o-ko GRA T[1
.3 ko-ri-si-ja , te-o-jo , do-e-ra , e-ke-qe , o-na-to , ki-ti-me-na , ko-to-na , a3-ti-jo-qe GRA *T* 5
.4 i-pa-sa-na-ti , te-o-jo , do-e-ra , e-ke-qe , o-na-to , pa-ro , a3-ti-jo-qe GRA *T* 2

.5 ku-*63-so , te-o-jo , do-e-ro , e-ke-qe , o-na-to , pa-ro , a3-ti-jo-qe GRA *T* 1
.6 ta-ra-to , te-o-jo , do-e-ro , e-ke-qe , o-na-to , pa-ro , a3-ti-jo-qe GRA *T* 1
.7 we-te-re-u , i-je-re-u , e-ke-qe , o-na-to , pa-ro , a3-ti-jo-qe GRA *T* 5
.8 *vacat*
1. "The *private plot* of a3-ti-jo-qo, so much seed: 150.4 l. wheat
2. Hektor, male slave of the god, holds a lease from a3-ti-jo-qo, holder of a ktoina: 9.6 l. Wheat
3. Korisia, female slave of the god, holds a lease from a3-ti-jo-qo: 48 l. Wheat
4. i-pa-sa-na-ti (e-pa-sa-na-ti on PY EN0074) , female slave of the god, holds a lease, from a3-ti-jo-qo: 19.2 l. Wheat
5. ku-*63-so male slave of the god, holds a lease, from a3-ti-jo-qo: 9.6 l. Wheat
6. ta-ra2-to , male slave of the god, holds a lease from a3-ti-jo-qo, 9.6. Wheat
7. we-te-re-u (Westreus) , priest , holds a lease, from a3-ti-jo-qo: 48 l. Wheat"

As with the rest of this series (and the En series which recapitulate several of the shorter Eo tablets) the opening line provides the heading, here the name of the individual (or, on occasion, group) who holds the ki-ti-me-na ko-to-na in their own right and then, on the following lines the names and titles of the individuals to whom they lease it to in plots (o-na-ta). In all cases, the quantities of land as measured in seed grain continue to be tracked.

At Pylos, ki-ti-me-na holdings are second in size only to the *temene* and range from 105.6 to 796.8 liters of wheat. (When the wanax's ki-ti-me-na holdings – he has private lands planted with trees on PY Er 880[64] – are included, the upper measure leaps to 4800 liters of wheat.)

Despite the continuing discussion over the exact definition of the term ki-ti-me-na, a gender-centered analysis clearly indicates that it is a gender specific form of land holding.[65] Twenty individuals are documented with ki-ti-me-na ko-to-na holdings.[66] and it is probable that at least one other group possesses ki-te-me-na estates. All the ki-ti-me-na estate holders are male;[67] nineteen are identified by masculine names, some of which are further modified by male occupational titles such as qo-u-ko-ro-jo (oxherd), me-ri-te-wo (beekeeper), and su-qa-ta-o (swineherd).[68]

This apparent gender specificity whereby no women hold ki-ti-me-na ko-to-na is important for our understanding of women's economic opportunities at Pylos; these are, after all, the largest parcels of land in private control. These holdings also provide our most plausible instance of ownership (or at minimum, a case for the autonomous, long-term control) of land. The exclusion of women from this form of holding suggests important economic and social consequences as this system effectively precludes women from large private holdings. Additionally, since no women function as lessors, it decreases the likelihood that any Pylian women could have wielded economic power over men as landlords.

KE-KE-ME-NA KO-TO-NA

The remaining form of ko-to-na holdings are the ke-ke-me-na ko-to-na. These holdings are attested in the Ea, Eb, and Ep subseries. Very little is well understood about ke-ke-me-na holdings; most of our evidence refers not to ke-ke-me-na holdings in their own right, but rather to leases of ke-ke-me-na holdings. PY Ea 809 offers an example of a record of a lease of ke-ke-me-na land from its "owner" the wheelwright of the *lawagetas*:

PY Ea 809 + 1483
.a ra-wa-ke-si-jo-jo , a-mo-te-wo
.b ke-]ṛẹ-te-ụ e-ke , o-na-to , ke-ke-me-na , ko-to-na[ ]G̣ṚẠ T 2
"*Kresteus* holds a lease of communal land from the Lawagetas' wheelwright, 19.2 l. wheat"

If we model ke-ke-me-na ko-to-na under the same rubric as ki-ti-me-na ko-to-na, we may identify as the possessors of ke-ke-me-na ko-to-na the individuals or institutions that act as lessors. If this is indeed the case, the distributors of these leases may be considered the "owners" of ke-ke-me-na holdings. In addition to the damos which doles out the majority of these leases, 12 men, sexed by name and title, are attested in this capacity.[69] (The mention of ka-pa-ti-ja on PY Ep 704.7 in possession of two plots of land designated ke-ke-me-no (dual) seems to be a mistake for o-na-ta ke-ke-me-na-o as her land carries with it an obligation to the damos, an obligation associated not with ke-ke-me-na land held outright but with leases of such land; the fact that she is nowhere attested as doling out leases of this land further argues for understanding her holding as a lease rather than as an estate.)

COMPOUND PLACE-NAMES

Another possible source of information on Pylian land holdings may come from a less obvious source – compound place-names. Regions and villages are attested throughout the Pylian archives; among these names are a small number of compound place-names which combine a name in the genitive with one of two words: wo-wo or wo-wi-ja. Wo-wo should normalize as *worwos* and its identification as the Linear B equivalent of ὅρος "boundary" seems secure.[70] Wo-wi-ja has been proposed as the plural form worwia from ὅρια "borders."[71] An example of this type of tablet would be PY An 424, which provides a listing of male workers and officials being tallied in Pylos's Hither Province:

PY An 424 + fr. + fr.
.1 p̣i-*8̣2̣ , ra-pte-re , VIR 12 pu-ka-ẉọ , VIR 6 te-u-ta-ra-ko-ro[VIR
.2 ka-ra-ḍọ-ṛọ , ra-pte-re VIR [ ]1 sa-ri-nu-wo-te , ra-pte-re VIR 10[
.3 ke-ra-ti-jo-jo , wo-wo , me-ri-du-ma-te VIR 2 da-ko-ro VIR 2 [

This tablet, belonging to the personnel series at Pylos, tracks male workers known as ra-pte-re (likely to be "stitchers" from ῥάπτηρ),[72] me-ri-di-ma-te (possibly related to work with honey "me-ri"), pu-ka-wo, da-ko-ro, and te-u-ta-ra-ko-ro at various locales including ka-ra-do-ro (*Kharadros*, one of the nine towns of Pylos's Hither Province), sa-ri-nu-wo-te, and a third location, introduced on the final line as ke-ra-ti-jo-jo wo-wo. This last term offers a rare periphrastic means of signaling location, a man's name in the genitive case coupled with the term wo-wo "border," roughly "Keratios's territory," a formula used with other men's names on 14 other tablets using compound place-names. These tablets derive from five series: the An which records male workers by location and title,[73] the Cn series which records sheep, pigs, and goats, their owners and their locations,[74] the La series which tracks transfers of wool and lists no human names,[75] the Mn series which lists only place names,[76] and the Na series which records amounts of linen coming from various locations.[77] In these formulaic constructions, it is men's names without exception which appear in the genitive (ke-ra-ti-jo-jo on PY An 424, wa-no-jo (four times) on PY Cn 40 and (twice) on PY Cn 599, ne-wo-ki-to on PY An 656, ka-pe-se-wa-o on PY Cn 453+836, o-re-e-wo (5 times) on PY Cn 600, mo-ro-ko on PY La 635 and lacunose names on PY An 615 and PY Cn 437). Interestingly, none of these men's names appears elsewhere in the Pylian corpus; their sole appearance in the tablets remains in the encoding of their names into place names. I suggest that this phenomenon may indicate the conceptualization of these men as the human (since none of these names are theophorics) owners, or perhaps better, founders of these regions (as nothing in the tablets necessitates identifying these men as still living at the time of compilation, these compound names may well represent ancestral eponyms). It is important to note that none of these regions are identified by a woman's name; this may provide additional support for the contention that land ownership at Pylos is the prerogative of Pylian men only. This concludes this survey of land types held exclusively by men.

Categories of land held exclusively by women

No land-holding category is recorded as being held exclusively by women.[78]

Categories of land with undeterminable holders

One category of land holding is difficult to fully classify under a gendered schema – e-to-ni-jo land – as the evidence available remains inconclusive. This holding is mentioned three times in the Pylian corpus and it seems to be a holding type free from incurred obligations; it is often translated into English as "freehold" land. It is attested as the holding type of a god in PY An 724 where it belongs to e-nwa-ri-jo who is generally identified as Ares on the basis of his epithet Ἐνυάλιος.[79] Another holding of this type is that of the man a-pi-me-de (Ἀμφιμηδής) attested on the duplicate tablets PY Ep 539.14 and PY Eb 473.

PY Eb 473
1: a-pi-me-de , e-ke-qe , e-to-ni-jo , ke-ke-me-na-o , ko-to-na-o
2: to-so-de , pe-mo GRA 4 *T* 6
"Amphimedes holds an e-to-ni-jo of communal (ke-ke-me-na) plots, so much seed, 441.6 l. wheat"

This tablet (and its duplicate reiteration on PY Ep 539) records the man a-pi-me-de in possession of an e-to-ni-jo of ke-ke-me-na plots and also provides the size of the holding in wheat – a fairly large measure of 441.6 l. wheat. A-pi-me-de appears to be a figure of some prominence at Pylos, attested on two additional Pylos land tenure tablets as the owner of three male do-e-ro ("slaves") named to-wa-te-u (PY Eb 1188), e-ni-to-wo (PY Eb 1187), and wi-dwo-i-jo (PY Eb 1186), who each receive land leases (o-na-ta) from the da-mo.[80] As no evidence exists that "ordinary" slaves warrant land leases in this series the only do-e-ro we see in possession of land leases are te-o-jo do-e-ro ("slaves of the gods"), slaves of priests or priestesses or staff belonging to elite individuals (such as the potter and fuller of the wanax) it stands to reason that a-pi-me-de should also be regarded as a highly elite Pylian man in that even his servants warrant access to the Pylian land-tenure system. From this evidence, it would appear that e-to-ni-jo should be regarded as an unusual and elite form of land holding, associated with divinities and elite men.

It is with the third mention of the term e-to-ni-jo that the matter becomes more complicated. On the duplicate tablets PY Ep 704.5 and PY Eb 297, the priestess e-ri-ta (*Eritha*) contends that she holds an e-to-ni-jo (freehold) on behalf of her god; the damos disagrees, instead characterizing the land in question as plots of communal land (o-na-ta ke-ke-me-na-o ko-to-na-o). The two tablets that provide this information are near echoes of each other, agreeing on most of the text ("the priestess holds and claims that (her) god holds the e-to-ni-jo") with a counterclaim offered by the damos/ko-to-no-o-ko-de ("plot holder") that the land indeed is held as o-na-ta ("plots") of ke-ke-me-na land, and as such would be bound by the obligations inherent in the o-na-to system (which seem to be exempt in the e-to-ni-jo arrangement).

PY Eb 297
.1 i-je-re-ja , e-ke-qe , e-u-ke-to-qe , e-to-ni-jo , e-ke-e , te-o
.2 ko-to-no-o-ko-de , ko-to-na-o , ke-ke-me-na-o , o-na-ta , e-ke-e
.3 GRA 3 *T* 9 *V* 3
"The priestess, and she holds (this), and she claims that (her) god holds the *freehold (?)*; but the actual plot owner (the village in PY Ep 704) says that he/she (merely?) holds the *lease of communal plots*: so much seed: 377.6 l. wheat"[81]

PY Ep 704.5–6
.5 e-ri-ta , i-je-re-ja , e-ke , e-u-ke-to-qe , e-to-ni-jo , e-ke-e , te-o , da-mo-de-mi , pa-si , ko-to-na-o
.6 ke-ke-me-na-o , o-na-to , e-ke-e , to-so , pe-mo GRA 3 *T* 9

"Eritha the priestess holds and she claims that (her) god holds an e-to-ni-jo, but the damos says that she has a plot of ke-ke-me-na ko-to-na (a communal plot): so much seed: 374.4 l. wheat"

This dispute is most typically understood as *Eritha* declaring that the land is a sacred possession and is therefore "tax-free" (e-to-ni-jo) while the damos declares that it is subject to certain obligations (either in the form of "taxes" or services).[82] This conflict, the only dispute recorded in the tablets, seems to have been unresolved at the time this tablet was recorded; it likely exists because the recording scribe – faced with two powerful, competing entities, a priestess and the damos – either lacked the will or the authority to decide whose claim took priority and simply recorded both claims as items to be dealt with at some later time. In addition to offering no hint of how this dispute was resolved, these two tablets also provide no reason as to why the damos is contesting *Eritha's* claim.[83] While two explanations spring readily to mind: 1.) that the property does indeed belong to the god but that it is not among the freehold holdings, 2.) that the land under dispute is *Eritha's* personal property and she is attempting to evade liability by re-glossing the land as a divine freehold, there is simply not enough evidence here to resolve this issue. This is unfortunate, as this is the lone instance in which a woman may be in possession of e-to-ni-jo land, but the dispute renders void any attempt to associate it with this priestess definitively. Yet, surely the claim itself by the priestess would indicate that at least one member of Mycenaean Pylos believed that at least one woman could plausibly be linked with e-to-ni-jo holdings and so perhaps e-to-ni-jo land might be glossed as a land type likely, if not certainly, controlled by women.

Categories of land held by men and women

O-NA-TA

The final category of holding, o-na-ta or "leased land," differs from the land tenure categories discussed above in that multiple tablets document significant numbers of men and women as lease holders. The tablets record 95 Pylian individuals holding o-na-ta (leases of either ki-ti-me-na or ke-ke-me-na ko-to-na): 33 women and 62 men; these numbers dwarf that of holders of all other land categories, rendering o-na-ta the most common and accessible land tenure arrangement at Pylos. There appears to be no difference between o-na-ta originating from ki-ti-me-na or ke-ke-me-na ko-to-na in terms of parcel size, gender of holder, or in scribal recording practices. Two aspects of o-na-ta have attracted a fair amount of scholarly attention to date: the extremely small sizes of some of these plots and the sense they are held with certain obligations to the damos.[84]

O-na-to has long been identified as a neuter noun whose plural form is o-na-ta. It is conventionally translated as "lease," as it appears to constitute a kind of subordinate title to the use of particular fields.[85] Its etymology, however, remains less than obvious. It is conventionally etymologized as ὄνατον, a noun which does not survive into classical Greek.[86] Attempts have been made to connect ὄνατον with the verb ὀνίνημι "to confer a benefit upon" either in the active ὀνίνημι or the middle ὀνίναμαι.[87] In most readings, attempts have been made to reconcile the functional meaning of o-na-to, as a subordinate land holding, with the idea of a conveyed benefit. Ventris and Chadwick attempted to resolve this by suggesting that onaton may have originally meant "a plot of land given to a retainer as a reward, cf. *Od.* xiv 62–7."[88] Dunkel takes this even further, reading o-na-to as implying a "certain ownership" or "rental from individuals."[89] Lane has recently challenged the reading of "lease", offering instead an etymology from ὠνή with an interpretation of the term as "beneficial" or "profitable."[90] While this etymology is certainly tenable, it is very difficult to resolve its meaning within the context of the tablets where it consistently refers to smaller plots of land subdivided and allocated from either the da-mo or an important "private" individual, land which appears reserved for the use of the allocatee rather than passing into his or her permanent possession. Krigas's reading is the most widely accepted and resolves both the sense of "benefit" from ὠνή with the functional use of the term in the tablets, by combining the two, with a reading whereby lease holders receive their leases in return for certain services offered to the central government.[91] This seems the most reasonable interpretation of the term and will be used throughout this chapter as "lease which carries certain obligations." In terms of status, lease holders (o-na-te-re) are unquestionably of lower social rank than te-re-ta (pl.) (*telestai*). This is certainly borne out based on the relative size of the land holdings in their control. Te-re-ta (pl.) hold the large ki-ti-me-na "estates" (ke-ke-me-na originate largely from the damos) which are subdivided into the much smaller o-na-ta of the o-na-te-re ("lease-holders").[92] O-na-te-re also seem to be of lower status than ka-ma-e-we. PY An 724 associates a ka-ma holding with e-qe-ta (pl.) (officials of high rank, closely associated with the wanax and lawagetas on this and other texts), PY An 616 lists ka-ma-e-we in association with male personnel, and formulaic constructions on PY Eb 156+157, PY Eb 842, PY Eb 862, and PY Ep 613 + 1131.7 routinely identify ka-ma-e-we (ka-ma holders) in secondary possession of o-na-ta. For example, PY Eb 156 + 157.1:

PY Eb 156.1
1a: wo-ze-qe
1: e-u-ru-wo-ṭạ , te-o-jo , do-e-ro , ka-ma-e-u[e-ke-qe o-na-to]to-so-de , pe-mo GRA 1[*T* 3
"Eurwotas / e-u-wo-ta the slave of the god, (being a) ka-ma-holder has and works an o-na-to, so much seed: 124.8 l. wheat"

In no cases is the formula reversed where persons primarily described as o-na-te-re hold ka-ma. Further, PY Ed 0236 offers a summary table of the (presumably full) o-na-ta holdings of ka-ma-e-we, measuring in at a huge 30 units T2 V3 or the equivalent of 2904 l. wheat.

While the aggregate size of o-na-ta holdings on PY Ed 236 is quite large, individual o-na-to tend to run quite small in size with some holdings measuring as little as 1.6 l. wheat (the smallest possible holding at Pylos: V 1). The extremely small sizes of these fields have disconcerted several scholars. Hooker has considered these leases impossibly small and has suggested that the "cultivation of such small plots (could) hardly have been economic," and that "such a practice (would be) hard to reconcile with the general picture of a well-organized system." From this data, Hooker then concludes that the situation at Pylos must have been abnormal and argues that these small land holdings are indicative of a "state-of-emergency" at Pylos. Under this postulated state of emergency, the holdings are abnormally small because all the holders are being squeezed into a small, but safe, area, rather than being out in the presumably exposed open.[93] However, as the weight of scholarly opinion at present runs against the State of Emergency hypothesis[94] (and no clear locations are provided, cramped or otherwise), perhaps another explanation is necessary. Among possible explanations for the small sizes of o-na-ta are: 1.) that extra-palatial/extra-demotic structures for obtaining additional sustenance are in place at Pylos, but since they are outside the scope of palatial jurisdiction, they are also outside the scope of palatial monitoring; 2.) that we have simply grossly underestimated the values of wheat expressed by T, V, and full units, which would render this entire debate moot; or 3.) that the yield of these holdings is intended to supplement, not sustain, nutritional and/or income needs of their holders. For purposes of this study, it is the proportions of the holdings that are most useful in that they supply a *relative* sense of individuals' rankings in the social hierarchy of the state, but these remain open questions requiring further investigation.

Perhaps the most significant difference between o-na-ta holdings and all other land tenure arrangements is that o-na-ta are the primary, if not sole, component of the Pylian land allotment system which grants women as well as men access to this critically important resource. Additionally, o-na-to seem to be held by both men and women in very similar ways; the most common formula employed on Eb, Ep, En, and Eo tablets reads "Name and title holds an o-na-to of either ke-ke-me-na land from the damos or ki-ti-me-na land from a specific individual or group"; no difference in scribal treatment for male and female o-na-te-re is discernable and men and women generally appear side by side on these tablets throughout these series. (These four series represent fully two-thirds of the series at Pylos in which both men and women appear documented on the same tablet.)[95] In these tablets, nearly 100 lease holders are documented; approximately one-third of these lessees are women.

Fifteen tablets document the workings of the o-na-ta system at Pylos. The composite tablet PY En 74 records the leasing of o-na-ta plots from larger plots of ki-ti-me-na land belonging to three individuals, listed in the genitive case as ru-*83-o, a3-ti-jo-qo, and pi-ke-re-wo.[96]

PY En 74 + frr.
.1 ru-*83-o , ko-to-na , ki-ti-me<-na> , to-so-de , pe-mo GRA 1 *Ṭ* [5
.2 o-da-a2 , o-na-te-re , ru-*83-o , ko-to-na , e-ko-si
.3 pe-ki-ta , ka-na-pe-u , wa-na-ka-te-ro , [o-]na-to , e-ke , to-so-de , pe-mo GRA *T* 1

.4 mi-ra , te-o-jo , do-e-ra , e-ke , to-so-de , pe-mo GRA *T* 1
.5 te-se-u , te-o-jo , do-e-ro , o-na-to , e-ke , to-so-de , pe-mo GRA *T* 4
.6 ma-re-ku-na , te-o-jo , do-e-ro , o-ṇạ[-to e-ke to- so-de]pẹ-mo GRA *T* 1
.7 e-ko-to , te-ọ-jo , do-e-ro , o-na-to , e-ke , to-so-de , pe-mo GRA *Ṿ* 3̣
.8 ma-*79 , te-ọ-jọ , ḍọ-e-ra , o-na-to , e-ke , to-so-de , pe-mo GRA *V* 3̣
.9 e-*65-to , te-o-jo , do-e[-ro] , o-na-to , e-ke , to-so-de , pe-mo GRA *V* 1
.10 *angustum*
.11 a3-ti-jo-qo , ko-to-ṇạ , ki-ti-me-na , to-so-de , pẹ-ṃọ GRA 1 *T* 5 *V* 4
.12 o-da-a2 , o-na-te-re , e-ko-si , a3-ti-jo-qọ , ko-to-na
.13 e-pa-sa-na-ti , te-o-jo , do-e-ra , o-na-to , e-ke , to-so-de , pe-mo GRA *T* 2
.14 ku-*63-so ṭẹ-o-jo , do-e-ro , o-na-to , e-ke , to-so-de , pe-mo GRA *T* 1
.15 ta-ra2-to , te-o-jo , do-e-ro , o-na-to , e-ke , ṭọ-so-de , pe-mo GRA *T* 1
.16 we-te-re-u , i-e-re-u , o-na-to , e-ke , to-so-de , pe-mo GRA *T* 5
.17 e-ko-to , te-o-jo , do-e-ro , o-na-to , e-ke , to-so-de , pe-mo GRA *T* 1
.18 ko-ri-si-ja , te-o-jo , do-e-ra , o-na-to , e-ke , to-so-de , pe-ṃọ GRA *T* 5
.19 *angustum*
.20 pi-ke-re-wo , ko-to-na , ki-ti-me-na , to-so-de , pe-mo GRA 2 *T* 6
.21 o-da-a2 , o-na-te-re , e-ke-si , pi-ke-re-wo , ko-to-na
.22 a3-wa-ja , te-o-jo , do-e-ra , o-na-to , e-ke , to-so-de , pe-mo GRA *T* 1
.23 pe-ki-ta , ka-na-pe-u , wa-na-ka-te-ro , o-na-to , e-ke , to-so-de , pe-mo GRA *T* 2
.24 ko-ri-si-ja , te-o-jo , do-e-ra , o-na-to , e-ke , to-so-de, pe-mo GRA *T* 5

1. "The ki-ti-me-na ("private") plots belonging to ru-*83-o (MN), so much seed, 144 l. wheat
2. Thus, the lease-holders (o-na-te-re) hold plots belonging to ru-*83-0:
3. pe-ki-ta (MN), the wanax's fuller holds a lease, so much seed: 12 l. wheat
4. mi-ra (Smila?), female slave of the god holds (a lease), so much seed: 9.6 l. wheat
5. Theseus, male slave of the god, holds a lease, so much seed: 38.4 l. wheat
6. ma-re-ku-na, male slave of the god, holds a lease, so much seed: 9.6 l. wheat
7. Hektor, male slave of the god, holds a lease, so much seed: 4.8 l. wheat
8. ma-*79, female slave of the god, holds a lease, so much seed: 4.6 l. wheat
9. e-*65-to, male slave of the god, holds a lease, so much seed: 1.6 l. wheat
10. *(blank)*
11. The ki-ti-me-na ("private") plot belonging to a3-ti-jo-qo, so much seed: 150.4 l. wheat
12. Thus, the lease-holders hold plots belonging to a3-ti-jo-qo:
13. e-pa-sa-na-ti, female slave of the god, holds a lease, so much seed: 19.2 l. wheat
14. ku-*63-so male slave of the god, holds a lease, so much seed: 9.6 l. wheat
15. ta-ra-to2, male slave of the god, holds a lease, so much seed: 9.6 l. wheat
16. we-te-re-u (Westreus), priest, holds a lease, so much seed: 48 l. wheat
17. Hektor, male slave of the god, holds a lease, so much seed: 9.6 l. wheat
18. ko-ri-si-ja (*Korinsia*?), female slave of the god, holds a lease, so much seed: 48 l. wheat

19. *(blank)*
20. The ki-ti-me-na ("private") plot belonging to pi-ke-re-wo (*Pikreus*?), so much seed: 249.6 l. wheat
21. Thus, the lease-holders hold plots belonging to pi-ke-re-wo:
22. a3-wa-ja, female slave of the god, holds a lease, so much seed: 9.6 l. wheat
23. pe-ki-ta, the wanax's fuller, holds a lease, so much seed: 19.2 l. wheat
24. ko-ri-si-ja (*Korinsia*?), female slave of the god, holds a lease, so much seed: 48 l. wheat[97]"

PY En 74 lists 16 o-na-ta along with their holders and their sizes; 13 individuals are in possession of these plots. (Three individuals – e-ko-to Hektor), a male slave of the god, ko-ri-si-ja (*Korinsia*), a female slave of the god and pe-ki-ta, the ka-na-pe-u ("fuller") of the wanax each have two plots.) The o-na-to holders include eight men and five women, all identified both by name and title. The male o-na-te-re are identified with three heterogeneous titles, six of these are designated as te-o-jo do-e-ro ("slave of the god"), and the remaining two are comprised of a priest and the wanax's fuller (ka-na-pe-u *knapheus* wa-na-ka-te-ro). All five women carry the same title: te-o-jo do-e-ra ("slave of the god"). The o-na-ta plots range in size from the smallest possible land measurements – the V 1 (1.6 l.) of wheat held by the male slave of the god e-*65-to – to the combined 96 l. held by the female slave of the god ko-ri-si-ja in the form of two separate o-na-ta, one of ki-ti-me-na land belonging to a3-ti-jo-qo and the other from pi-ke-re-wo. These two holdings each equal the 48 l. plot of the priest *Westreus* (we-te-re-u) who is attested on seven additional land tablets in individual possession of another four o-na-ta measuring a total of 656.8 l. wheat and sharing joint possession with three other o-na-te-re whose combined land holdings clock in at 2073.6 l. wheat.[98]

The apparent egalitarianism of the o-na-ta holdings on this tablet, however, offers no positive grounds from which to position a discussion on the financial basis of women's potential economic power; it is critical to remember that these plots of land are short-term leases of property which continue to belong to someone other than the woman holding the lease. Women's land holdings remain under lease rather than under women's ownership. Contrary to Billigmeier and Turner's reading of women of the E series as *land-owners*, closer examination of the land-tenure system at Pylos offers no evidence for women at Pylos possessing any land on a long-term basis or owning any land in their own right; the evidence situates women only as lessees.[99]

Furthermore, lacking documentation suggesting ownership or long-term possession of land, it seems we must eliminate the possibility that women had opportunities to acquire land, either through purchase or inheritance. Consequently, the possibility for a Pylian woman to disburse land to her children also seems most unlikely. All of these factors strongly imply that land holding was structured in a manner designed to limit female control over land; perhaps this might betray anxiety regarding women's long-term control over land as a facet of Pylian gender ideology.

So while at first glance, the scattering of men's and women's names and titles throughout the E series tablets might create the impression that holding patterns appear gender neutral,[100] a closer analysis of land-holding categories – and their sizes – reveals that access to land at Pylos was not remotely a gender-neutral institution. Pylian men had access to a wide variety of land-holding arrangements while women's access to land was limited to just one category, that of leased land. For Pylian women, land leases, the lowest rung on the land tenure ladder, seem to have functioned as the land-holding glass ceiling.

But did gender also impact the internal workings of the land-leasing system at Pylos? Were men and women incorporated differently within the o-na-to system? The following discussion argues that this is indeed the case, that close analysis of both the occupations of the o-na-te-re and the proportionate sizes of their holdings reveal disproportionate investment of men and women even within the lease-holding system with women's tenure substantially more limited than their male counterparts.

Occupational titles of o-na-ta holders

Occupational titles, as one of the only three variables attested in the land lease tablets – personal name and land size being the other two – can provide us with some insight into which members of the Pylian state were granted access to the o-na-ta system; this is particularly useful to a study of Mycenaean gender relations as these female lessees of o-na-ta are the only women at Pylos with attested control over land resources. But what exactly is the relationship between women's occupational titles and their access to leasable land? Webster once postulated a connection between women's workgroups and land tenure at Pylos, whereby service in a workgroup was in some way recompensed with land, but he was uncertain exactly what that connection might have been.[101] In actuality and upon closer examination, however, there is no correlation between the women who hold land leases and the dependent women who function as members of the collective workgroups and who are compensated with subsistence rations at most. The women of the workgroups and the women who hold land are mutually exclusive; there is no overlap between the two sets by name, title or location. But when female lease holders are analyzed in light of their occupational titles, a pattern readily emerges; every single woman listed on land tenure tablets falls under the rubric of religious officialdom. This once more refutes the claim of Billigmeier and Turner that "secular women of high social status" appear at Pylos; they cite the example of "the land holder Kessandra at Pylos (Fg 368 and Fg 82)" whom they identify as a landholder devoid of religious connections.[102] But nowhere does Kessandra appear among the land holdings of the E series. This seems to have been the result of a misreading of the two tablets in question; these Fg series tablets, while they do record GRA holdings, also record Figs, and should be understood not as records of land but rather as food rations.

Returning to the E series, while seven of the entries are too fragmentary to allow the recovery of names or titles, the remaining 66 list at least 33 women (some are mentioned several times) who bear one of six titles: i-je-re-ja ("priestess"), ka-ra-wi-po-ro ("keybearer"), ki-ri-te-wi-ja, te-o-jo do-e-ra ("female slave of the god"), do-e-ra i-je-re-ja ("slave of the priestess"), or do-e-ra ka-ra-wi-po-ro ("slave of the keybearer").[103] The majority of these land holders are "slaves of the gods," recorded 54 times in the E series tablets. Some of these sacerdotal women are attested with more than one o-na-to.

As a caveat, we should remember that it remains possible that some of these women may have controlled additional land that is not mentioned in the tablets. It seems plausible that the priestess and the keybearer(s?) may have had charge of some sort of sanctuary, but it is interesting that it is not recorded here among the E series tablets.

The case for the priestess *Eritha* (e-ri-ta) controlling additional territory is suggestive. She is referred to on PY Eb 297 [PY Ep 704.5] as a ko-to-no-o-ko(-de), a term also used to describe men with ko-to-na holdings, and she may provide our sole example of a woman in a position to disburse land. On PY Eb 416 [duplicated on PY Ep 704], she doles out an otherwise unattested form of land holding, a ke-ra or *geras*-lease (a different form of holding from the o-na-ta leases granted by the (male) ki-ti-me-na estate holders), to the woman u-wa-mi-ja (Huamia), a te-o-jo do-e-ra. The ke-ra o-na-to is generally understood as a lease given as a gift. But is this a gift of "owned land" or is it a secondary disbursal of land already leased to her? It is important to note that for this one exception, the context for this atypical holding is to be located in the religious realm; it is surely not coincidental that the sole (alleged) female "landlady" is a high-ranking religious functionary whose position may well be exceptional because of her religious function.

In contrast to the pattern where women lessees are always religious officials, male lease-holdings are identified with a broader range of titles, including stitchers, shepherds, and fullers, to servants of the gods and priests. (Additional titles of male o-na-to holders include: a-ke-ro (herald), a-re-po-zo-o (perfumer), di-ra-po-ro (unknown), do-e-ro a-pi-me-de-o (slave of Amphimedes), do-e-ro i-je-re-ja (slave of the priestess), do-e-ro ka-pa-ti-ja (slave of Karpathia the keybearer), e-te-do-mo (unknown),[104] i-ja-te (physician), i-je-ro-wo-ko (some form of sacred official), mi-ka-ta (unknown), qe-ja-me-no (unknown), ra-pte (stitcher), and the elite officials known as te-re-ta.) Several other men are recorded without a titular modifier. Interestingly, and in direct contrast to the female o-na-to holders, no direct relationship whatsoever can be discerned between men's titles and their types of land holding (including both leased and non-leased land) at Pylos.[105] Some men are clearly part of the religious hierarchy at Pylos (priests, slaves of gods and human cult officials, etc.), some others are functionaries attached to men of elite rank (for example the wanax's fuller and e-te-do-mo or the servant of a-pi-me-de-o), while others such as the ra-pte-re ("stitchers") of PY Ea 29, Ea 813, and PY Ea 754 are well attested in the o-na-to tablets yet have no obvious connection to either the civic or religious hierarchy. It would appear that no single type of occupational title functioned as a defining signifier in land tenure for men in the way that it did for women for whom a clear relationship between titles and land holdings is discernible – only women with religious functions hold land, and more specifically, only leased land. From this evidence we may infer at least one element of Pylian gender ideology: women were not envisioned as the normative land holders. I suggest that the land-holding system is based on the assumption that men are to be the normative land holders; the land-tenure system is far more inclusive where men are concerned, allowing a wide variety of permutations in both holding types and occupational designations. Women's holdings are far more anomalous; only those women with official positions in the religious sphere were incorporated into the land-holding system. It may be for this reason that the scribes so carefully document each woman by naming her religious title as an explanation for why she has access to a resource otherwise not available to women.

The idea of religion as the locus where the "normal" roles of this otherwise strictly gender-segregated society break down, has strong parallels in later Greek practice as well. Even Classical Athens, with its ideological rhetoric advocating the virtues of female seclusion,[106] was reluctant to interfere within the boundaries of religious practice, allowing priestesses command over their divinities' temene and cult properties.[107] Furthermore, the argument that religion is the overriding factor in superseding "normative" gender roles is further supported by the tablets' total silence on land holding by any of the other female officials or workers; no woman bearing any of the other 32 professional titles at Pylos[108] holds an o-na-to, only those holding one of the six religious titles.

Anna Morpurgo Davies once asked "whether there was a clear distinction between religious and civil powers" in the Mycenaean state;[109] with respect to land holding, this question must be answered along gender lines. We observe no distinction within land tenure between men with civil and religious titles, but in the case of female officials, however, a clear distinction is made between religious and lay persons. At Pylos, the only women who hold land are religious officials.

Size of o-na-ta holdings.

In addition to the differences in the occupational makeup of the men and women lease holders, gender-based difference can be observed in the lease-holding system: the average size of women's holdings as attested are smaller than those belonging to men.

When the holdings are approached as quantitative evidence, an interesting result occurs with gender difference once more playing a key organizational role. By analyzing the GRA seed values and proportions themselves, it becomes clear that women only controlled a very small amount of the total land recorded in the land tenure tablets from Pylos. The aggregate holdings of the 149 individuals whose sex can be determined – 116 men[110] and 33 women – throughout the E series land tenure tablets[111] amount to 33,558.4 l. of seed grain used to measure the seven known forms of land allotments and holdings (temene, ki-ti-me-na, ke-ke-me-na, and unmodified ktoina, ka-ma, e-to-ni-jo and o-na-ta); the 33 women attested in this system constitute 22 percent of land holders but, when their combined seed measurement of 1734.4 l. out of the total 33,558.4 attested is assessed, only 5.2

percent of all recorded lands at Pylos can be found under women's control. (In arriving at these calculations, I have counted amounts on all tablets in which the sex of the holder and amount of allotment are extant; additionally, I have counted amounts listed on the duplicate entries only once and have excluded all summary tablets where a single total is given for multiple land holders.)

Disparity in allotment size also applies within the "more egalitarian" o-na-ta (lease-holding) system – the one type of land holding controlled by both men and women. Excluding *Eritha* the priestess, the keybearer, and the ki-ri-te-wi-ja, no woman exceeds 1 full unit GRA, that is, no woman receives a lease for a parcel of land larger than 96 l. wheat. More than half of the female lease holders hold land in the 14–28 l. range. For men, if we again exclude the holdings of groups and priests, several dozen men cluster in the 96–192 l. range. Women's o-na-to plots average 25.6 l. of wheat in size; while male lessees run slightly higher with 38 liters, leaving the women with approximately two-thirds of men's holdings on average.[112] To arrive at these values for the o-na-to averages: 28 women lessees hold a total of 716.8 l. for an average of 25.6 l each while 62 men hold a total of 2358.4 l. for an average of 38 l. each.[113] Hooker has proposed that size of tenure was directly linked to social status;[114] if this is indeed accurate, we have here quantitative evidence for the inferior status of women in the social and economic spheres at Pylos.

Land tenure at Pylos – conclusions

Pylos's pattern, where "ownership" holdings are exclusively the domain of men, and with exceptions granted for women only in the instance of high religious rank, is congruent with later Greek practices. In classical Athens, for example, women's economic holdings were extremely limited, consisting (with very few exceptions) of her dowry, which infrequently included land holdings. In those instances where land was ostensibly possessed by a woman, control over that land would not have been her prerogative but rather that of her (male) kyrios.[115] Only priestesses were exempt from this rule, presumably due to their responsibilities in tending to the economic affairs of their goddesses, responsibilities which included the disbursal and management of sanctuary land.[116]

It is impossible to say whether identical rationales are in place for these exceptions in both the Late Bronze and historical periods, but, at very least, both seem to reveal an operative restriction on women's control of property (explicit in the historic period texts, and implicit through the otherwise complete absence of any women among the 40 odd lease-givers at Pylos). From these accounts, we see clearly that the large "private estates" of *temene* and ki-ti-me-na ko-to-na never fall into women's hands but remain an exclusively male form of property holding, a finding that may suggest that if the institution of inheritance exists at this time (or at very least the inheritance of land), property passes solely through the male line; large, leasable estates belong to men only, and the tablets record no women with the ability to disburse private land holdings. This situation strongly implies two things: Pylian women did not inherit land or pass it to their children, and no mechanism existed at Pylos whereby women could achieve economic dominance or even autonomy through state-allotted land.

Land tenure at Knossos

Gendered land-holding patterns at Knossos cannot be quantified as readily as those from Pylos. To begin with, Knossos has no series which function similarly to the Pylos E series land cadastre where scribes who used GRA as a standard of measurement carefully recorded the specifics of the land-tenure system, detailing individual holders, their titles, and the sizes of the plots. At Knossos, the local version of the E series uses GRA not as a standard of land measurement but rather as a commodity in its own right and as such is more similar to the non-land E series at Pylos. Therefore, while the (rest of the) E series at Pylos has as its raison d'etre the quantification of land size as measured in wheat, the E series of Knossos uses the ideogram in a more literal fashion; the Knossos E series exists to monitor the disbursement of wheat *qua* wheat and in no way appears connected to land tenure.[117]

The absence of a land-focused E series at Knossos, however, does not entirely prevent an investigation of the role played by gender in the Knossian land-tenure system, but it does circumscribe it considerably. References to land tenure, like much of the Knossos evidence, tend to appear more obliquely and more randomly, and the modeling or quantifying of the evidence that the Pylos evidence permits is largely a pipedream at Knossos. While much of the evidence is disappointing – for example the several Knossian tablets which mention familiar holding categories like ka-ma, ke-ke-me-na, or ki-ti-me-na but which, due to their poor state of preservation record little else[118] — one series at Knossos does deal exclusively with land holdings: the nearly 20[119] tablets of the Uf series which record the ownership/stewardship of groves of fruit-trees. These tablets, like much of the Knossian corpus, are regrettably quite fragmentary[120] and, when compared with the Pylian land tenure series, are substantially more limited in number and scope. Nonetheless, they allow the opportunity to compare and contrast the ways in which land tenure is gendered between the two sites to ascertain if the more limited Knossian evidence conforms to the better understood Pylian patterns.

Even with the limitations of the Knossos evidence, the contrast between women's holdings at Pylos and Knossos is striking. No systemic or structural differences between the holding patterns of men vis-à-vis women can be discerned at Knossos. In contrast to the three major conditions constraining women's land tenure at Pylos (land holdings which are limited to short-term leases, to religious officials alone, and by their small size), Knossian men and women seem to hold their orchards in a completely analogous fashion. Compare, for example KN Uf 981 and KN Uf 1031+5738: "Eriklewes (MN) holds an orchard plot"[121] and KN Uf 1031 + KN Uf 5738 "Perijeja (WN) holds an orchard plot"[122] or KN UP 79 where the woman ka-wi-ja has the same DA holding as the man qe-da-do-ro on KN Uf 0121 + KN Uf 6027 + KN Uf 8140 (although her holding is five times the size.) While the corpus is highly fragmentary, our sample size is small, and the risk of over-reading such a small (two dozen tablets) corpus is real; nonetheless in the KN Uf series men and women seem to be incorporated into the Knossian land-holding system in exactly the same way. None of the conditions and restriction placed on women's land holding at Pylos seem to apply here; women's land at Knossos is never described as merely leased nor are any of the women recorded in this series identified with any religious title. This finding stands in direct contrast to Kokkinidiou and Nikolaidou's assertion that women could only acquire status and goods through priesthood.[123] While this pattern appears true for Pylos, it does not fit the evidence from Knossos. Strikingly, no explanations for the establishment of women as land *owners* seem to be necessary at Knossos.

Furthermore, even the brief Knossos land series leaves open economic possibilities for women which are closed to them at Pylos. Left open are the questions of how women obtained the land: at Knossos we cannot unilaterally rule out the possibility of women purchasing or inheriting as we can at Pylos, whether women could bequeath their land holdings to their children, and the limits of Knossian women's land-based economic power. The only discernible difference between men and women at Knossos is their relative frequency. Women certainly make fewer appearances on the orchard tablets than men do; of the 19 tablets where sex and holding can be recovered, 17 list male holders while only two list women.[124] It is difficult to make a strong argument based on relative frequencies when more than half the series' tablets are too fragmentary to read, but perhaps this very difference per se should be regarded as significant. On the other hand, if only complete tablets are assessed, half of that sample would be female orchard holders. Nonetheless, fragmentary evidence and small samples sizes aside, the real difference in gendered land-holding patterns between Knossos and Pylos is one of quality. Even in this brief series, Knossos matches none of the gendered patterns of the Pylos land-tenure system but seems to function in a unique, idiosyncratic way. Above all, while the impression one receives of land-tenure practices at Knossos is of a heavily patriarchal institution, Knossos's land-tenure system appears to have been significantly less circumscribed along gender lines, suggesting an institution which functioned in a far more egalitarian way than did that of Pylos on the mainland.

Conclusions

From this analysis of the land tenure tablets from Pylos and Knossos the following conclusions can be drawn:

The palatially monitored land-tenure system of Pylos was aligned hierarchically not only along status lines,[125] but also according to gender. We can observe a clear and consistent gender asymmetry in the land-tenure system, which strongly suggests the economic subordination of women in the system of land tenure at Pylos. This subordination can be first observed in the types of land-holding categories to which men and women have access. Men have access to all eight land-holding types; women only to one, the smallest and least permanent of the holdings – leased land. Access to these leases is also delineated along gender lines; men from various (civic and priestly) offices have access to land leases, but only women who are explicitly identified as religious officials enter the land-tenure system. The final locus where gender asymmetry can be observed is in the size of men's and women's holdings. Overall, 95 percent of the land recorded in the tenure tablets falls under men's control; only 5 percent is documented as held by women. Furthermore, even in the one common category – leased land – women's plots on average are only two-thirds the size of men's. So while men's access to land appears multivalent, women's control of land is strictly limited, raising the contention that the Pylian land-tenure system is a system designed to reflect a gender ideology where men were the normative land holders and women were, at most, exceptions to be strictly regulated.

In stark contrast to the situation at Pylos, which is highly structured along gender lines, the few texts from Knossos look remarkably egalitarian. While the Knossian corpus of texts relating to land holding is substantially more limited in number and scope than the Pylian texts, the few texts from Mycenaean Knossos seem to show no such restrictions on women's land holding and suggests a more equitable ideology of gender and economic power at Knossos than at Pylos.

Notes

1 Apparently including naval power, as implied by PY An 1, PY An 610, PY An 724, and PY Vn 46 (among others) recording the refurbishing of ships and rowers assigned to serve: Palaima 1991: 273–310.
2 C. Thomas 1976: 101.
3 Killen 1985: 250.
4 L. Palmer 1962: 99.
5 We also see a great deal of interest in land-tenure organization in the Near Eastern Bronze Age economies. Major studies include: deJ. Ellis 1976; Paroussis 1985; Whiting 1991; Killen 1985; Finley 1976. It is important to remember that in the Near Eastern economies the palace-temple complexes owned the majority of the arable land. In contrast, it is not clear in the Aegean palace states how much of the land of each polity was under the direct control of the palatial administrations and how much would have been in "private" or local hands.
6 In the relationship between access to land holdings and women's social status in the historical period, a close correlation is discernible between women's social and economic status and their access to land. Contrast Spartan and Athenian women: land in Athens was well beyond the one medimnus limit of women's purchasing power; in the rare instances where land was part of an Athenian woman's dowry, it functioned more as a trust rather than active use. Spartan women, in addition to their greater autonomy and freedom of movement, according to Aristotle (*Pol.* 1270a20), once owned some 40 percent of the land in Sparta.
7 Nineteen of these tablets are of only peripheral interest to this study since they simply list numbers of certain types of land-holders (such as unidentified ka-ma holders with no references to their names of locations) or mention unspecified types of territory (such as a-ko-ro *agros* "territory) without providing any further, more quantifiable information. See Ventris and Chadwick 1973: 530 for a discussion on a-ko-ro. (These 19 non-utile tablets are PY Ae 995, An 261, An 610, An 616, An 724, An 830 + 907 (pars dextra), Aq 64, Ab 218, Cn 608, Fr 1220, Fr 1226, Fr 1236, Na 406, Na 926, Ua 1413, Un 47, Un 718, Vn 10, and Wa 784.)

8 R. Palmer has recently questioned this reading, noting that the identification of *120 as wheat is not completely secure. R. Palmer 1992: 475–497. For purposes of this study, however, I will be following the conventional identification of *120 as GRANUM/wheat.

9 All of these categories as well as the sex of those attested as controlling them are addressed below.

10 Further studies on the E series land tenure tablets: Bartonek 1957: 115–118; Nosch 1997: 397–403; Bennett 1956: 103–113; Brown 1954: 385–400; Carpenter1983: 1–2; Pugliese Carratelli 1954a: 102–112; Pugliese Carratelli 1954b: 221–222; Deger-Jalkotzy 1988a: 3–52; Deger-Jalkotzy 1988b: 97–122; Del Freo 2005; Dunkel 1981: 18–29; Finley 1957: 135–159; Foster 1981; Furumark 1954: 36–37; Heubeck 1967: 17–21; Hooker 1987a: 313–315; Hooker 1980: 133–150; Kazanskiene 1995: 603–611; Krigas 1987: 23–34; Krigas 1985: 55–59; Lejeune 1976: 81–115; Lejeune 1966: 260–264; Ruijgh 1972: 91–104; Sarkady 1981: 2–3; Sutton 1970; Ventris and Chadwick 1973: 232 ff. ; Webster 1954: 13–14.

11 Hooker refers to the E series of land-holding records "the most impressive single item in the Pylian archive." Hooker 1987: 314.

12 Krigas writes, "we can presume that the Ea, Eb, Ed, and Ep series of tablets in the Pylian archive constitute a certain land-registry, since they refer mainly to lands (cf. *ko-to*-na) [held] (cf. *e*-ke) by individuals from a seemingly land-occupied body, the damos." Krigas 1987: 23.

13 "Though the tablets vary widely in contents, three elements are almost always present: the name of the individual or group owning the land in question, a word or phrase describing the kind of land held or the arrangement by which it is held, and a statement of quantity denoting the size of the holding in question." Sutton 1970: 1.

14 Scholarship is largely in agreement on this reading: see *Docs2*, 236. One minority voice, not widely accepted, reads the GRANUM amounts in land tablets as a tax: Webster 1954: 16. While full consensus has not been achieved, the majority opinion currently leans toward viewing this GRA as the amount of seed wheat needed to sow a particular plot of land, rather than the amount of the land's actual produce. For further discussion, see R. Palmer 1992: 481 and Hooker 1980: 133–134.

15 For these measures, see Ventris and Chadwick 1973: 232.

16 Sutton 1970: iv-v.

17 All tables include notations detailing the sex of the holder as well as the tablet that justifies this identification.

18 In accordance with Scott's call for gender as a category of *historical* analysis: Scott 1996b: 152–180.

19 I have opted not to include the Es series here as they refer to annual and monthly contributions (do-so-mo) of wheat; it is unclear whether the GRA mentioned here functions as a measure of actual plots of land or as a commodity in its own right. In adopting this exclusion I follow Sutton 1970.

20 Palaima 1988b.

21 The normalization of *pa-ro* as πάρο ("from or at the hands of a person") appears undisputed. (πάρο is attested in Alcaeus: Ventris and Chadwick 1973: 568–569; etc.) The interpretation of da-mo has been somewhat more controversial. While all agree on its normalization as δῆμος, its exact meaning is less apparent. At the very least, it appears as a corporate body that can allocate land holdings, and is perhaps best translated as "village." Rutter notes that in the Bronze Age nothing suggests that the term also had political significance, as it came to do in the Archaic and Classical periods with reference to the "common people" as opposed to an hereditary nobility. Rutter 1997: 4.

22 PY Ea 29 is a typical example of a land lease tablet:

e-ro2-qo ra-pte , e-ke , o-na-to , pa-ro , i-ma-di-jo GRA T 1

"e-ro2-qo (MN) the stitcher has a lease from Imadios (MN): 9.6 liters wheat."

E-ro2-qo is a man's name (MN) in the nominative case who is further identified by the occupational title ra-pte (ῥαπτήρ) "stitcher." He "holds" (e-ke ἔχει) a "lease" (o-na-to) from (pa-ro πάρο) Imadios (MN) (i-ma-di-jo man's name in the genitive) of 1T unit of GRA (equals 9.6 liters of wheat). In this tablet the lessee holds land leased from a private individual; in others the "landlord" is the damos itself.

23 PY Ea 817 is a typical example of a ki-ti-me-na tablet:
.a po-me
.b mo-ro-qo-ro-jo , ko-to-na , ki-ti-me-na GRA 2 *T* 1 *V* 3
"The private (ki-ti-me-na) plot of Mologuros (shepherd): 206.4 l. wheat."

24 There is one other E-series subset at Pylos, the Es series which records contributions (do-so-mo) of GRA to Poseidon. These tablets list the names of individual (always male) donors and the amount of wheat they are sending to the god. I have excluded these 16 tablets from consideration as part of the land-tenure system since nothing on these tablets indicates that wheat here is used as a measure of unseen land; instead it appears very likely that the wheat mentioned here is used as a commodity in its own right.

25 He proposes that the other(s) be located rather close to the palace itself, but concedes the difficulties involved in stating this more definitively: Sutton 1970: 1.

26 Killen 1985: 246.

27 Hooker 1980: 139.

28 Ventris and Chadwick 1973: 240.

29 Bennett 1956a: 103–113.

30 Carpenter 1984: 214.

31 Bennett 1983: 41–54.

32 Hooker 1982: 209; Bennett 1956: 109.

33 Scholarly opinion is largely aligned at present against the State of Emergency Theory. The major methodological debate regarding the Pylos tablets is whether a so-called "State of Emergency" existed in the late 13th century Mediterranean and what impact, if any, it had on local Pylian social and economic organization. The evidence for an active emergency currently appears largely inconclusive and the so-called state-of-emergency tablets now seem to indicate less of an emergency than once thought. See Hooker and Palaima for the history of this issue: Hooker 1982: 210–7; Palaima 1995a: 623–633. Shelmerdine in particular reads the tablets as reflecting a period not of sudden emergency but rather of a long and gradual decline: Shelmerdine 1987, 557–568 and 1999: 405. For our purposes, then, we should understand the gender relations attested in the tablets as reflecting a somewhat typical state of affairs for the Pylian state.

34 Sutton 1970: iv-v; L. Palmer 1982: 99; Webster 1954: 14.

35 C. Thomas 1976: 101.

36 Killen 1985: 243; Nosch 1997b: 402–403.

37 I. Tegyey 1987: 365.

38 Nosch 1997b: 403–404.

39 Palaima 1987: 301.

40 Killen 1985: 244.

41 Killen 1985: 244.

42 Nosch 1997b: 397–412.

43 Killen 1985: 244–45.

44 LSJ: 1774, no. II, after Hdt. 2.112, 155; 3.142.

45 If we accept the two masculine names proposed by Lindgren – persuasively, I think – as the holders of the titles wa-na-ka (*wanax*) and ra-wa-ge-ta (*lawagetas*), that is *Enkhelyawon* and *Wedaneus*, respectively: Lindgren 1973, Part II: 134, 150. Furthermore, the other titled group associated with temenos holdings – the te-re-ta – are accompanied solely by the ideogram for "MAN," never "WOMAN."

46 The normalization of wa-na-ka as the Mycenaean form of the Homeric and Classical ἄναξ "lord" is generally accepted as self-evident. Hooker, 1987b: 258; Lindgren 1973, Part II: 150; Palaima 1997 and 1995b. For further discussion on the wa-na-ka, see the introduction to Chapter 3.

47 Scholarly opinion seems to be uniform in accepting the proposed normalization of ra-wa-ke-ta as the contracted form of the later Greek λαγέτας, a compound form combining λαός and ἄγειν,, which should translate literally as "leader of the people:" Szemerenyi 1972: 301–317. Nikoloudis 2008a, 2010 suggests a further function as a mobilizer of human labor in specialized production. Further discussed in Chapter 3.

48 Te-re-ta is generally read as the agent noun τελεστής. Rutter sums up well two of the theories on the meaning of the term te-re-ta: 1.) the *telestai* were religious officials of some kind as they were based at the cult center of Pa-ki-ja-na and the later Greek word tele- has religious connections or 2.) *telestai* were fief-holders, persons who held land from someone (possibly the king) in return for services which they rendered to him. The Greek word tele- also has the meaning of "taxes" or "dues:" Rutter 1997: 3–4. At least two commentators have suggested a *te-re-ta* may have had more than one function: Hooker 1987b: 266; Krigas 1987: 23–34.

49 A further tablet PY Ed 411 lists the aggregate total of all *telestai* holdings, presumably at pa-ki-ja-ne, at a measure of GRA 44 T 2 V [ ] or at least 41,824 l. of wheat; it is unfortunate that we do not have further information as to the precise type of holding this tablet describes, but as the remainder of the Ed series describes o-na-ta holdings, it is likely the telestai have substantial o-na-ta as well as temene.

50 The etymology of ka-ma remains unclear. Some scholars, while identifying it as a kind of agricultural holding, nonetheless refrain from proposing any normalization of this word into Greek. Ventris and Chadwick 1973: 50. Others propose theories none of which are as yet fully accepted. Krigas suggests a special/sacred aspect to ka-ma land, since two persons with apparently religious connections (one titled i-je-ro-wo-ko *ierourgos* and a second whose full title is lacunose but begins with the prefix i-je-ro- which also strongly suggests a religious official) possess this holding. Krigas 1987: 33. Rutter, on the other hand, proposes the polar opposite; emphasizing two of the titles "baker" and "slave of the god," he concludes that ka-ma land was a humbler form of holding. Rutter 1997: 4. Ultimately, we have insufficient evidence as yet to settle on any of these explanations. But while its etymology and sense remain obscure, at very least, we can note that ka-ma is clearly a specialized form of holding distinct from te-me-no and ko-to-na holdings.

51 Rutter 1997: 3.

52 PY Ea 28, PY Eb 152, PY Ep 613 + 1131.3; PY Eb 156 + 157.2; PY Ep 613 + 1131.9; PY Ep 613 + 1131.9; PY Ep 613.9 + 1131.7; PY Eb 839 = PY Ep 613 + 1131.13; PY Eb 495 = PY Ep 613 + 1131.1; PY Eb 169.1 = PY Ep 613 + 1131.11; PY Eb 159.10 = PY Ep 613 + 1131.10; PY Eb 177 + 1010 = PY Ep 613 + 1131.6; PY Eb 842 = PY Ep 613 + 1131.8.

53 Ventris and Chadwick 1973: 262.

54 It is not known what exactly these duties might entail.

55 Recorded in the genitive case.

56 i-je-ro-wo-ko (ἱερουργός) is transparent as a type of priestly office. Morpurgo Davies 1979: 93.

57 Rutter 1997, citing the cook and servant of the god, suggests that this is a holding for those of low social stature, but I consider the mention of the i-je-ro-wo-ko to argue against this.

58 PY An 261 and PY An 616.

59 Ka-ma-e-we are often associated with a different verb used to describe them rather than the more typical e-ke and e-ke-qe; wo-ze "works" more typically modifies them and may imply this type of holding carries with it certain obligations.

60 Ventris and Chadwick equate the term ko-to-na with the Knossian term *ko-to-i-na*, derived from the classical term κτοίνα. They note the use of this term on Rhodes as "a territorial unit equivalent to the Attic deme, glossed by Hesychius in the plural as δῆμος μεμερισμένος or 'subdivided deme'; it is derived from the stem **kti-* 'settle, with buildings and or cultivations' cf. Skt *ksitih* 'settlement', Arm. *sen* 'settled; village'. At Pylos it apparently refers to the smallest unit of cultivation, a 'field' or 'plot.'" Ventris and Chadwick 1973: 232.

61 Krigas 1987: 24.

62 Attempts to identify the etymologies and the meanings of both terms have resulted in a great deal of scholarship with very little consensus reached as of yet. The terms (ke-ke-me-na and ki-ti-me-na) have traditionally been treated as being in opposition to each other. The most common reading has been as "public/communal" (ke-ke-me-na) vs. "private" (ki-ti-me-na). Furumark and L. Palmer in the 1950s and early 1960s connected kekeimenai with κοινός "common": Furumark 1954: 98; L. Palmer 1963: 186.

Ventris and Chadwick next offered as a functional translation for ke-ke-me-na as "belonging to the damos, communal" and ki-ti-me-na as "private, land not administered by the damos", offering as etymologies κτίμεναι, from the same stem as ko-to-na, from **kti-* "settle" κεῖμαι, κείμενος for ke-ke-me-na: Ventris and Chadwick 1973: 232. Also in circulation are Pugliese Carratelli's readings of ke-ke-me-na as "fallow" and ki-ti-me-na as "cultivated": Pugliese Carratelli 1954a: 102–122 and 1954b: 221–2 and Heubeck's ke-ke-me-na as "divided land from existing plots": Heubeck 1967: 17–21; Krigas offers an additional reading of ki-ti-me-na based solely on etymology as "lands held by the *ktitai* (settlers)": Krigas 1985: 57.

Other scholars have attempted to resolve these terms by offering readings which combine etymological derivations and the use of the terms in the tablets. Carpenter proposes "a summary of the framework" where a solution might be found: the "ke-ke-me-na describes a type of land which is usually held by the community, but sometimes by individuals. It is possibly connected with κεῖμαι, but is more likely to be the perfect passive participle of * κίχημι, 'to find, happen upon' or 'bring into cultivation.' Ki-ti-me-na is always associated with private individuals, but on the analogy of ke-ke-me-na it is unlikely to mean 'private'. Its identification as the present passive participle of * κτειμι is practically certain and its meaning is probably close to 'built' or 'inhabited' or 'established.' 'Cultivated' though not impossible is less likely." He combines these with his interpretation that ki-ti-me-na "could refer to the best land, closest to the village, described as 'enclosed' (i.e., 'built') or 'inhabited' (close to the settlement), and held by a few individuals. Ke-ke-me-na could be outlying and perhaps poorer or marginal land, brought into cultivation as needed. Such land might well be described a 'lying' or 'found', 'happened upon.'" Carpenter 1983: 87. This reading is useful in its acknowledgement of the contrasting use of these terms on a functional level; less satisfying is the distance left between the proposed etymologies and the observed usage of both terms in the E series.

Hooker's more limited approach may ultimately be more useful. He prioritizes the functional reading over the less-settled etymology-based ones and offers three observations. First, that the two types of land are mutually exclusive. Second, that ke-ke-me-na ko-to-na refers to a kind of common land, most often "leased" from the da-mo (which he renders as "political community"). He also cuts cleanly through the morass of etymologies proposed to explain the form of the word ke-ke-me-na: " it is plainly a perfect passive participle, but of what verb is impossible to say." (He allows that etymologies from both κοινός "common" or κεάζω "cut" are each possible but not conclusive.) Third, he loosely defines ki-ti-me-na ko-to-na as referring to private land, which is often said by the tablets to be "leased" from named individuals. He is also reluctant to offer a definitive etymology for ki-ti-me-na; "[it] is the present passive participle of an unknown verb; it may be formed from an athematic verb κτίημι or κτεῖμι, which was later replaced by the thematic form κτίζω ('found, establish, inhabit')." Hooker 1980: 138–139. This more functional definition may be the more practical one at present, acknowledging difference between the two terms and tying each most closely to those who command each type, the da-mo with ke-ke-me-na land and named individuals for the ki-ti-me-na.

63 Lane's recent challenge to this reading is addressed in n. 90.

64 Discussed in Ventris and Chadwick 1973: 267. He is here identified by name e-ke-ra2-wo rather than by the title.

65 Already recognized in Ventris and Chadwick 1973: 234.

66 I am distinguishing between holders of ki-ti-me-na plots ("owners") and lessees of ki-ti-me-na plots.

67 Several scholars have proposed that the holders of ki-ti-me-na ko-to-na are the te-re-ta (pl.). See Hooker for caveats. Hooker 1987b: 260–1.

68 These three titles are all genitive singular forms.

69 PY Ea 59.3, PY Ea 305, PY Ea 480, PY Ea 757, PY Ea 801, PY Ea 802, PY Ea 809, PY Ea 539.7.

70 Ventris and Chadwick 1973 trace the etymology of *wo-wo* as follows: ὅρος, Ion. οὖρος, and suggest a possible dissimilation from ὅρος. *Docs2*: 593.

71 Ventris and Chadwick 1973: 593.

72 Discussed in Chapter 3.

73 PY An 424, PY An 615, PY An 656.

74 PY Cn 40, PY Cn 437, PY Cn 453 + 836, PY Cn 599, PY Cn 600.

75 PY La 635.

76 PY Mn 456.

77 PY Na 105, PY Na 525, PY Na 571, PY Na 1053, PY Na 1097.

78 The possible exception is the ke-ra lease given by the priestess to a te-o-jo do-e-ra on PY Eb 416 / PY Ep 704.2, but since the priestess is attested to as a lease-holder herself, it seems more reasonable to read this ke-ra lease as a secondary lease rather than a new holding type.

79 *Diccionario* Vol. 1: 220.

80 It is also possible that the a-pi-me-de of the E-series land tenure tablets might be the same a-pi-me-de in possession of a sizable collection of rams (or in possession of a man in possession of these rams) on the livestock tablet PY Cn 655; it is unclear which term his name in the genitive governs.

81 Ventris and Chadwick 1973: 256.

82 Carlier 1983: 12.

83 Steele 2008.

84 Krigas 1987: 27, 30.

85 *Docs2*: 235.

86 Hooker 1980: 138.

87 Ruijgh 1972: 91.

88 *Docs2*: 235.

89 Dunkel 1981: 22.

90 Lane 2012a: 65.

91 Krigas 1987: 27, 30.

92 Palaima 1997: 412.

93 Hooker 1982: 216–217.

94 See note 33.

95 See Chapter 2, Table 2.6.

96 For all three ki-ti-me-na holders, the combined o-na-ta leased from them do not equal the size of the land provided in each subsection's heading: 98/180 for ru-*83-o, 180/188 for a3-ti-jo-qo, and 96/312 for pi-ke-re-wo. Presumably the ki-ti-me-na holder retains the remainder of the land for his private use.

97 This tablet also receives discussion in Ventris and Chadwick 1973: 244 .

98 In addition to PY En 0074 and its component tablet PY Eo 247, the priest *Westreus* (we-te-re-u) appears on five additional land tenure tablets. He is attested to in individual possession of another four o-na-ta – two of ki-ti-me-na (PY Eb 444/PY En 659, PY Eb 477, and PY Eb 472) and two of ke-ke-me-na (PY Ep 539) origins – measuring a combined total of 656.8 l. wheat. Additionally, the summary holdings tablet PY Ed 317 includes him with three other o-na-te-re – the i-je-re-ja ("priestess"), ka-ra-wi-po-ro ("keybearer(s)"), and e-qe-ta ("follower") – whose combined seed measures clock in at 2073.6 l. wheat.

99 Billigmeier and Turner 1981:7.

100 Billigmeier and Turner 1981:7.

101 Webster 1960: 17

102 Billigmeier and Turner 1981: 9.

103 For etymologies and discussion of i-je-re-ja, ka-ra-wi-po-ro, ki-ri-te-wi-ja, and te-o-jo do-e-ro/ra see Chapter 4.

104 "Builder" and "Armorer" have both been proposed as interpretations for e-te-do-mo. *Diccionario,* I, 254–55.

105 Excluding, of course, the most elite officials and their *temene* holdings.

106 Recent scholarship on this topic has begun to question strongly the reality of seclusion on the level implied by texts such as Lysias 1, etc., arguing that the realities of daily life, ranging from Aristophanes' characterization of women as ferocious bargain hunters (*Lysistrata*), requirements of family life, and the dozens of religious festivals on the Athenian calendar would have had women "out and about" on a fairly regular basis and that the rhetoric surrounding seclusion was just that: rhetoric: Sourvinou-Inwood 1995: 111–120.

107 Perhaps the most cogent example of concessions made for religious practice was the Thesmophoria where matrons not only left the oikos during the day but also for three consecutive nights.

108 Discussed in greater depth in Chapter 3.

109 Morpurgo Davies 1979: 93.

110 This number includes two individual temene holders, plus the three telestai whose holdings average 960 each, ten ka-ma-e-we, three holders of unidentified ko-to-na, 17 owners of ki-ti-me-na land, 12 ke-ke-me-na holders, six male names embedded in compound place names, one e-to-ni-jo holder, and 62 o-na-te-re.

111 The Es series continues to be excluded from this study as the GRANUM recorded in this series refers to grain contributions rather than as a measure of land size.

112 To arrive at these values for *o-na-to* averages – 28 women lessees hold a total of 716.8 l for an average of 25.6 l each while 62 men hold a total of 2358.4 for an average of 38 l. each. (These averages do not include the holdings of priests or priestesses as their holdings frequently appear in aggregate and it is not possible to discern how much land falls under their individual control.)

113 The holdings of priests or priestesses continue to be excluded.

114 Hooker 1987a: 314.

115 Only Gortyn is the exception, and here only an unmarried *patroiokos* (roughly equivalent to the Athenian *epikleros*) could sell or mortgage property (and only to pay off estate debts); otherwise it is unattested elsewhere in Greece that an unmarried woman could sell or mortgage property. Schaps 1979: 45–49.

116 Schaps 1979: 46–47; Connelly 2007: 197–222.

117 Ventris and Chadwick 1973: 267–70; cf. Godart 1968: 56–63.

118 KN F 5079 + 8259, KN Xd 7913, KN Xe 0664, KN X 0039, KN X 5111, KN X 7732, KN X 7753.

119 This series has a total of 41 tablets but 22 of these are too fragmentary to allow the recovery of the name of the holder and the type of the holding.

120 Of the 19 tablets where the sex of the holder can be ascertained, only two (KN UF 836 and Uf 1031 + 5738) appear to be complete.

121 KN Uf 981

.a ko-ṭọ-i-na [

.b e-ri-ke-re-we / e-ke -pu-te-ri-ja [

122 KN Uf 1031 + KN Uf 5738

.a ḳọ-to-i-na

.b pe-ri-je-ja / e-ke , pu-te-ri-ja *DA* 1 ti-ri-to

123 Kokkinidou and Nikolaidou 1993: 163.

124 KN Uf 1031+5738 and KN Uf 79.

125 C. Thomas 1976: 101; Ventris and Chadwick 1973: 232.

7 Women and religion at Knossos and Pylos

Introduction

This chapter explores the intersection of gender and religion in Mycenaean Palatial society to ascertain what role religious affiliation might play on the gender structures of Pylos and Knossos. To date, religion in the tablets has received a fair amount of scholarly attention,[1] and female functionaries have tended to draw a large amount of interest as well,[2] but no study has yet addressed the structures of palatial cult in terms of their impact on gender relations at either state. This chapter focuses on this question, asking how religion impacts gender relations both within and across the two states.

Linear B evidence for cult practice is rich. From the tablets we can recover the names of dozens of Mycenaean – and perhaps also Minoan – heroes and divinities, the names of cult festivals and even the months in which they occur, the forms of cult offerings the states would regularly send to the gods – olive oil, gold vessels, and personnel seem preferred – and even the locations of many of the shrine complexes. We can recover which gods often travel together – Zeus in particular appears with his wife Hera and has a tendency to share his cult sites with his sons, including the familiar Dionysos[3] and the otherwise unknown Drimios. Most importantly for this study, the tablets record people who serve in cult. We can recover approximately 200 individuals assigned to cult-related duties – among them priests and priestesses, keybearers, and sacred slaves and slaves of cult officials – and from examination of the activities they perform, we can recover a framework for how religion and gender intersect in the Mycenaean world.

Religion and the status of women at Pylos

Approximately 900 women are attested in the 1100 Linear B tablets from Pylos – with the vast majority documented in one of two settings: menial labor or cult service. (Only eight women appear outside these two categories.) The two groups largely exist in very distinct social and economic contexts; women belonging to the former group are largely visible via their labor and the systems used to control, feed, and direct them. These women – more than 750 are recorded – typically appear as members of aggregate workgroups, unnamed and undifferentiated, all performing the same tasks in each workgroup alongside their underage children. Strong evidence points to their being slaves, performing unending menial tasks for the benefit of the palace and its representatives, receiving no more in turn than subsistence rations of wheat and figs.[4]

When these women appear in the texts, their lack of economic autonomy is readily apparent, and they are most frequently presented in terms of their production activities, their rations, and their low social status.[5] But another way to approach them, if we shift our lens to focus on religious practice, is to see them as laywomen, inhabiting a different sphere than women assigned to cult activities. As such they compose the largest subset of non-functionary women, but not the only: the seven women considered as wives of high-ranking male officials on PY Vn 34+1191+1006 and PY Ub 1318[6] also appear with no visible cult connections.[7] These two groups of women in many ways would seem opposites – the wives positioned at Pylos's most aristocratic rank, the workgroup women at its lowest. Yet both groups of women share an unexpected attribute: neither group is attested with any real economic authority or autonomy at Pylos. Combined these two groups comprise 85 percent of the women visible in the Pylian records; the only properties we see in their command are subsistence rations – for the workgroup women – and a single pair of leather sandals being prepared for one of the aristocratic wives.

Female cult officials at Pylos

In marked contrast is the visibility and economic power accorded to the 120 Pylian women who are identified as cult officials; these cult officials differ in nearly all regards from their lay counterparts. Religious officialdom not only lends to Pylian women a visibility not accorded to their secular peers but also provides for functionary women an exceptional status where many of the usual restrictions on women's access to resources and economic power are lifted. Functionary women are attested on approximately 100 tablets and hold the following titles: priestess (i-je-re-ja),[8] keybearer (ka-ra-wi-po-ro or *klawiphoros*)[9], servant of the god (te-o-jo do-e-ra)[10] or servant of either the priestess or keybearer, and ki-ri-te-wi-ja (possibly, "barley-women");[11] this last term seems from context to have at least a partly religious function. With the exception of the plural ki-ri-te-wi-ja, all of the other functionary women are consistently differentiated as individuals by name and by title. These are the only women in all of the Pylos texts to be both named and titled.

Functionary women most differ from laywomen in terms of their property holdings.[12] First and foremost, these are the only women who exercise control over land at Pylos; all five types of female cult officials are attested with land holdings. It is difficult to overestimate the importance of controlling land in an agrarian economy, and all categories of cult-affiliated women hold land-leases at Pylos.[13] We have no evidence that establishes these women as land-owners of the land; all are recorded as lease-holders – although it may be that in her official capacity a priestess also had the further ability to redistribute sanctuary resources and/or land.[14] This certainly seems to be the case in terms of the *geras*-lease (apparently some form of honorific grant) the priestess at pa-ki-ja-ne doled out to the female slave of the god u-wa-mi-a.[15]

While "slaves of the god" and "slaves of the priestess or keybearer" – ceremonial titles both – are attested only with land-leases (o-na-ta), higher-ranking female religious functionaries maintained control over other sanctuary goods; the keybearer (ka-ra-wi-po-ro) is listed among donors of bronze in PY Jn 829 and we are told the bronze she contributes is shrine bronze.[16] In addition to controlling property on behalf of their divinities, female religious officials also seem to have had use of property in their own right, for surely this is how we must interpret the dispute between the priestess *Eritha* at pa-ki-ja-ne and the local *damos* over the conditions under which she holds a particular plot of land;[17] this is the sole legal dispute recorded in the entire Linear B corpus.[18] In this dispute, the priestess claims it is e-to-ni-jo ("freehold") land belonging to her divinity (which should presumably render it tax-free), while the damos argues it is actually her own holding, one which carries with it certain obligations. We do not know the outcome of this dispute, but what seems clear is that she must have had legal access to both forms of holdings – private and official – otherwise there could be no dispute. These two officials also exercise control over personnel:[19] the ceremonial, mid-ranking figures known as do-e-ra/ro i-je-re-ja or do-e-ra/a ka-pa-ti-ja (female and male "slaves of the priestess or keybearer") who appear in the land tenure tablets of the E series, and the nameless slaves attributed to them in the personnel series, for example the female slaves of the priestess granted to her on PY Ae 303 "on account of the sacred/shrine gold." Priestesses also receive allocations of the unknown commodity *189 on PY Qa 1289 and PY Qa 1330, and the keybearer and priestess each receive textile allotments in the offering tablet PY Un 6 – these textiles may have been intended either for use in cult, for example as a garment for a cult image, or for the personal use of these women.

Two other named women appear closely connected to cult contexts: mi-jo-qa and a-pi-e-ra.[20] Both women appear on PY An 1281 and PY Fn 50. PY Fn 50[21] records barley distributions to prominent officials at Pylos, affiliated with metals and cult. Both women appear (lines 12 and 13) as the owners of slaves receiving a barley distribution. The position of both women in this text associates them with (other) cult officials. Notably, both appear in ways analogous to the men on this tablet. On their second tablet, PY An 1281,[22] they again appear alongside male officials and, similarly, are assigned slave personnel. Like PY Fn 50, this tablet also has a close linkage to cult service, as documented in the tablet's opening phrase, which places these owners "at the seat of i-qe-ja Potnia,"[23] at the shrine of a local goddess. It is possible that the personnel assigned to a-pi-e-ra and mi-jo-qa on this tablet are the same slaves receiving barley on PY Fn 50. As the cult contexts these women occupy are clear, and as priestesses and keybearers are the only other women at Pylos who have command of do-e-ro/a,[24] it seems likely that these two named women were also priestesses at Pylos.[25]

The women referred to as slaves of gods appear in three tablet series. It is clear from the land tenure tablets where these "slaves" – both male and female – receive land allotments from the damos that at least some of the "divine slaves" differ from "ordinary slaves". In addition to the named divine slaves (te-o-jo do-e-ra) and the slaves of the keybearer and priestess of the land tablets, 14 slave women are also assigned to the priestess "on account of sacred/shrine gold" on PY Ae 303. (That they are actual slaves rather than "slaves of the god" may be surmised from their lack of individual names and the omission of the "slave of the god" formula.) Two additional types of cult slaves may be recoverable from PY An 607 – female slaves of the (likely) goddess do-qe-ja and one slave of the goddess di-wi-ja:

PY An 607
.1a -ja
.1b me-ta-pa , ke-ri-mi-ja , do-qe-ja , ki-ri-te-wi-'ja'
.2 do-qe-ja , do-e-ro , pa-te , ma-te-de , ku-te-re-u-pị
.3 MUL 6 do-qe-ja , do-e-ra , e-qe-ta-i , e-e-to ,
.4 te-re-te-we MUL 13
.5 do-qe-ja , do-e-ro , pa-te , ma-te-de , di-wi-ja , do-e-ra ,
.6 MUL 3 do-qe-ja , do-e-ra , ma-te , pa-te-de , ka-ke-u ,
.7 MUL 1 do-qe-ja , do-e-ra , ma-te , pa-te-de , ka-ke-u
.8 MUL 3
.9–14 *vacat*
Following Nosch's translation:[26]
1. "At *Me-ta-pa*, the *ke-ri-mi-ja's* (likely a male collector), *do-qe-ja* barley workers:
2. The father is *do-qe-ja* slave, but the mother is at **ku-te-re-u:*
3. 6 *do-qe-ja* slave women; [Total] *do-qe-ja* slave women have been sent to the *e-qe-ta*
4. for the purpose of *te-re-te-we* (?): 13 *do-qe-ja* slave women.
5. The father is *do-qe-ja* slave, but the mother is slave of *di-wi-ja*:
6. 3 *do-qe-ja* slave women; the mother is a *do-qe-ja* slave, but the father is a smith:
7. 1 *do-qe-ja* slave woman; the mother is a *do-qe-ja* slave, but the father is a smith:
8. 3 *do-qe-ja* slave women"

Nosch notes that on this record of parents and their daughters, it seems that do-qe-ja slave status is inherited by daughters. She further notes that should do-qe-ja be a goddess, we should understand these slaves to be more akin to the te-o-jo do-e-ra of the land series rather than that of ordinary slaves.[27] This seems a reasonable reading as all the parents identified seem to hold at least a social status of the middle rank.

I think we should also place among the ranks of cult slaves the mysterious women of the notorious PY Tn 316.[28]

PY Tn 316

Recto

.1 po-ro-wi-to-jo ,

.2 i-je-to-qe , pa-ki-ja-si , do-ra-qe , pe-re , po-re-na-qe

.3 pu-ro , a-ke , po-ti-ni-ja AUR *215-VAS 1 MUL 1

.4 ma-na-sa , AUR *213-VAS 1 MUL 1 po-si-da-e-ja AUR *213-VAS 1 MUL 1

.5 ti-ri-se-ro-e , AUR *216-VAS 1 do-po-ta AUR *215-VAS 1

.6–.9: (*vacat*)

.10: pu-ro (*vacat*)

reliqua pars sine regulis

Verso

.1 i-je-to-qe , po-si-da-i-jo , a-ke-qe , wa-tu

.2 do-ra-qe , pe-re , po-re-na-qe , a-ke

.3a -ja

.3b pu-ro AUR *215-VAS 1 MUL 2 qo-wi-ja , ṇạ-[ ] , ko-ma-we-te-

.4 i-je-to-qe , pe-ṛẹ-*82-jo , i-pe-me-de-ja-qe di-u-ja-jo-qe

.5 do-ṛạ-qe , pe-re-po-re-na-qe , a , pe-re-*82 AUR *213-VAS 1 MUL 1

.6 i-pe-me-ḍẹ-ja AUR *213-VAS 1 di-u-ja AUR *213-VAS 1 MUL 1

.7 pu-ro e-ma-a2 , a-re-ja AUR *216-VAS 1 VIR 1

.8 i-je-to-qe , di-u-jo , do-ra-qe , pe-re , po-re-na-qe a-ḳẹ

.9 di-we AUR *213-VAS 1 VIR 1 e-ra AUR *213-VAS 1 MUL 1

.10 di-ri-mi-jo di-wo , i-je-we AUR *213-VAS 1 [ ] *(vacat)*

.11 pu-ro *(vacat)*

.12 *angustum*

.13–.15: *(vacat)*

.16 pu-ro *(vacat)*

reliqua pars sine regulis

No tablet's interpretation has been as hotly contested as PY Tn 316, and many of its terms remain in dispute. This tablet records lists of gifts (do-ra-qe) brought (pe-re) to the shrines of various divinities. On the recto, the first two lines establish our heading; we have a list of "gifts brought and carried" (do-ra-qe pe-re po-re-na-qe) to the shrine at pa-ki-ja-na (i-je-to-qe pa-ki-ja-si) during the month of po-ro-wi-to – Palmer suggests a normalization of "*Plowistos* / the month of sailing."[29] The remainder of the recto lists the divinities at Pylos who will receive these gifts and establish the types of offerings provided: "To Potnia: 1 gold vase (type 215), 1 woman; to ma-na-sa: 1 gold vase (type 213), 1 woman; to Posideia: 1 gold vase (type 213), 1 woman; to ti-ri-se-ro-e: 1 gold vase (type 216); and to do-po-ta: 1 gold vase (type 215).

Offerings continue on the verso, but three new site locations are introduced: the shrine of Poseidon governing lines 1–3 (gifts carried and brought) to Pylos: 1 gold vase (type 215), 2 women; the shrine of pe-re-*82-jo, Iphemedeia, and Diwia (lines 4–7), gifts carried and brought to: pe-re-*82: 1 gold vase (type 213), 1 woman, to Iphemedeia: 1 gold vase (type 213), and Diwia: 1 gold vase (type 213), 1 woman; the shrine of Zeus (lines 8–11), gifts carried and brought to Zeus:

1 gold vase (type 213), 1 man, to Hera: 1 gold vase (type 213), 1 woman, and to Drimios the son of Zeus: 1 gold vase (type 213).

An early controversy broke out over the term po-re-na in the headings, with attempts to read the term as a Bronze Age variant of *pornai* "prostitutes." This reading also envisioned a nefarious fate for these women, seeing them as gifts to the gods, and hence human sacrifices. A less lurid reading, however, would associate po-re-na as an o-grade version of the verb φέρω, and so link it to "bringing" – to my mind a far superior reading, and one that does not introduce an otherwise unattested women's profession to the table. And as for the human sacrifice reading, nothing on either side of the tablet indicates either that these women (and the one man given to Zeus) or the gold vessels are to face ritual destruction. The opening line listing the name of the month allows for a more pedestrian reading, that these are the regular monthly offerings from the palace to the major shrine areas, and a vase and a servant seem to be the standard offering fare. We already know from PY Ae 303 that a priestess receives 13 slaves from the palace e-ne-ka i-je-ro-jo ku-ru-so-jo "for the sake of the sacred – or shrine – gold." This may well be the answer to the mystery; here on TN 316 we have all three elements – women, shrine, gold – once more. These personnel transferred to the gods then are likely to be merely sacred slaves, like the ones previously discussed on PY An 607 belonging to Diwia and do-qe-ja.

So from the tablets documenting the affairs of female cult personnel at Pylos, some important patterns emerge. Priestesses and other cult functionaries are the only women at Pylos, to have access to land holdings, to have the right to challenge their polity in disputes, to represent themselves, to be named, to have access to bronze, textiles, and useful foodstuffs, and to exercise control over low- and mid-ranked personnel. In all these ways, female cult officials differ greatly from the women of the workgroups discussed in Chapter 3. One further difference also emerges: cult officials show no indications of being palace dependents. The palace does not supply them with rations and shows no interest in their children; the tablets do not even note whether these women have children. Their capacity seems, in many ways, to be part of the extra-palatial economy at Pylos; they enter it only obliquely, through land and commodity series.

Thus while at Pylos, laywomen's economic leverage is strictly limited, and women are unattested as high-ranking civic officials, religious affiliation seems to lend to women an exceptional status – the only one where many of the otherwise commonplace constraints on women's access to resources and economic power are lifted.

Religion and the status of women at Knossos

When we pose this same question regarding the impact of religion upon intra-gender hierarchies at Knossos, however, we observe a rather different relationship between gender and religious affiliation than we do at Pylos. While at Pylos, religious affiliation lent women an otherwise exceptional degree of visibility and economic power, at Knossos, religious status does not serve to create a similarly elite class of women. (Women's holdings in Knossian religion appear below.) While we continue to see groups of women in low-status working collectives,[30] we also see a number of women as named property owners. In no instances are any of these female property holders identified with a religious title. On the other hand, it is important to note that the increased visibility and economic viability of Knossian women did not put them on an equal footing with Knossian men. Just in terms of property holdings, men hold about three times as many commodities as women do, and men's holdings include high status items such as armor and chariots. Knossian men are attested at a much higher frequency and the majority of attention in the tablets is paid to them. Overall, we continue to witness a male-dominated society in Mycenaean Knossos – but one that accords greater autonomy and economic clout to women than does Pylos.

Men and women in Cult: The gender politics of Mycenaean religion

While religion had the ability to create and reinforce hierarchies among functionary and laywomen – at least at Pylos – did it have the converse ability to erase gender hierarchies between functionary men and women? That is, what impact did functionary status have on the intra-state gender hierarchy? Are male and female cult officials analogous in their responsibilities and holdings? Does gender trump religion or religion trump gender in the organization and reinforcement of social status among cult officials of different sexes? As always, I begin with the evidence from Pylos.

Men and women in Pylian cult practice

In this section, I present a brief survey of the ways in which men and women function in Pylian religion. Men appear in religious settings on approximately 70 tablets at Pylos. These men hail from a wide range of social positions, from highly elite figures such as the *wanax* and *lawagetas*, to cult officials such as priests and servants of the god or priestess, to lower placed workers who receive food allocations at feasts or who comprise the staff of various divinities or shrines.

Elite men with religious duties: Wanax and Lawagetas[31]

As a function of their stations as the two highest-ranking figures in the Pylian state, both the *wanax* and *lawagetas* are attested either directly or obliquely in the arena of Pylian religious practice.[32] Both men furnish cult festivals with provisions. The *wanax* on PY Un 2 provides the sanctuary at pa-ki-ja-ne with a large assortment of animals – among them an ox – and staples including huge quantities of wine and barley;[33] the *wanax* and *lawagetas* also sponsor a feast on behalf of Poseidon on PY Un 718. On this tablet, they are joined in their sponsorship by the *damos* which commits two units each of wheat and wine (240 l. of each), two rams, cheeses, and unguents. The *lawagetas*'s contribution is similar to that of the *damos* in scale;

he also provides two rams and somewhat smaller amounts of wine and flour. On the other hand, the *wanax's* contribution dwarfs that of the other two entities; he provides 480 l. of wheat, 360 l. of wine, an ox, a variety of cheeses, honey, and a sheepskin.

In terms of more oblique involvement in the area of cult, both men hold *temene* – they are the only figures apart from the gods to have such land holdings – and various (lay) staffers of the *wanax* are attested among the cult officials who hold land in the E series as well.[34]

It is perhaps best not to envision the *wanax* and *lawagetas* as cult servants but rather as the leading sponsors of Pylian religion.

PERSONNEL WITH CULT TITLES

Men's formal cult titles are less varied than that of their female counterparts. While six titles for women involved in Pylian religion are known,[35] only four are attested for Pylian men (i-je-re-u, te-o-jo do-e-ro, do-e-ro i-je-re-ja, and do-e-ro ka-pa-ti-ja[36]). No masculine equivalents for either the keybearer or ki-ri-te-wi-ja are known.

PRIESTS AND PRIESTESSES

Priests appear on 12 tablets at Pylos in contexts including personnel series texts (PY Aq 218), land tenure tablets,[37] Qa allotment texts (PY Qa 1290, PY Qa 1296), and the festival allotment tablet PY Fn 837 + 864. Priestesses appear either directly (representing themselves) or indirectly (i.e. as slaves' owners) on 11 tablets; these include a personnel series text (PY Ae 303), land tenure tablets,[38] Qa texts (PY Qa 1289, PY Qa 1300,) and PY Un 6. Interestingly, the textual contexts occupied by priests and priestesses are virtually identical. Both appear on a single personnel series text, two Qa tablets, and seven or eight land tenure tablets; each has only a single unanswered tablet – the priest's appearance on the Fn festival tablet and the priestesses on the Un.

The treatment of both priests and priestesses in the Pylian tablets is remarkably similar. Both sets are frequently named; two names are attested for priestesses (e-ri-ta and ka-wa-ra on PY Ep 704 and PY Qa 1289)[39] while three priests are named throughout the corpus, with one of these (we-te-re-u who is identified by the titles i-je-re-u and o-pi-ti-ni-ja-ta[40]) mentioned on seven tablets.[41] (He is likely the main priest at the cult site of pa-ki-ja-ne). All other priests are named only once. These remaining priests are named sa-ke-re-u on PY Ea 756 and a-o-ri-me-ne on PY Qa 1296. An additional priest located at se-ri-no-wo-te (PY Qa 1290) is not named.

While more priests are known than priestesses, their proportionate holdings – both in variety and scope – are also very similar. Both are attributed personnel identified only by ideogram in the personnel series texts. Ri-so-wa and ne-wo-ki-to are both recorded as the possessors of an unnamed man (VIR) each on PY Aq 218, while a priestess at Pylos is attributed three women (MUL) "on account of the sacred/shrine gold" on PY Ae 303. The Qa series makes two mentions each of priestesses and priests, all of whom receive the same *189 allotment. Land tenure seems to show many similarities between the holdings of priests and priestesses as well; all hold leases of land, and while the holdings of priests tend to be slightly bigger than those of priestesses, these o-na-ta (lease) holding arrangements seem to be largely gender blind once functionary status is attained. There are, however, two significant differences between priests and priestesses with respect to land tenure. While only the priestess at pa-ki-ja-ne is attested granting a *geras*-lease,[42] one of the priests (sa-ke-re-u on Py Ea 756) is attested in possession of his own ki-ti-me-na ko-to-na – a type of land holding never seen in women's hands.

Overall, however, it would appear that for priests and priestesses, functionary status seems to trump gender. With the exception of the ki-ti-me-na and *geras* holdings, the only real difference seems to be that slightly more priests are active in the tablets. On a one-to-one scale, however, these two officials appear far more similar than different.[43]

SACRED SLAVES[44]

The 45 tablets which record male and female sacred slaves record them in virtually identical contexts – as lessees of o-na-ta land in the Pylian E series.[45] As these holdings are discussed in detail in Chapter 6, I will not repeat my full argument here. Overall, these holdings seem to be held by men and women in identical ways from the same lessors. The only significant difference in their treatment is that on the whole, the sizes of women's lots tend to be on average two-thirds the size of their male counterparts.

LAYMEN AND WOMEN IN CULT CONTEXTS

As discussed in Chapter 4, a number of tablets in the Fn, Fr, and Un series record allocations of food and property to people who do not carry any of the "official" cult titles per se, but who seem to be working within cult contexts. These figures include workgroup women stationed at sanctuary sites or men such as cult heralds. On the few tablets which mention both men and women such as Fn 187 and An 1281 men appear far more often than women, but the women who do appear have holdings identical to their male counterparts. [46]

Gender and religion at Pylos

From this survey, it seems apparent that, at Pylos, religiously affiliated women occupied a social and economic standing highly similar to that of their closest male counterparts – whether these counterparts were men who held the masculine variant of a specific cult title or who appeared on the same tablet within cult contexts.

Where differences emerge along gender lines is in the representation and numbers of women across the entire system of Pylian religion. While female functionaries appear quite analogous to their male counterparts on a one-to-one level, more men than women are incorporated into the official and *de facto* religious systems of Pylos, particularly further down the social scale. Therefore while cult at Pylos appears fairly gender blind on each rung of religious officialdom, the overall system of religion at Pylos continues to be a male-dominated institution. This is further emphasized when the *wanax* and *lawagetas* are included in discussions of Pylian cult. As no female counterpart for either is attested, we should remember that while religious status seems to erase many of the gender boundaries between officials of similar standing, nonetheless women as a sex never achieve the same elite relationship to cult as do the highest-ranking male officials. In short, Pylian women serve in cult, but the *wanax* and the *lawagetas* sponsor it.

Gender and religion at Knossos

Turning to Knossos, we might ask if similar patterns are discernable whereby religion creates a corresponding system of parity among similarly ranked religious officials and the laypeople who enter cultic contexts. Unfortunately, texts pertaining to human involvement in cult at Knossos are few and far between – and to further complicate matters, cult-related tablets from Knossos preferred to record offerings under the names of deities rather than their human attendants.

Priests and priestesses

Only four extant tablets from Knossos mention priests or priestesses. These tablets derive from three different series and have few, if any, points of commonality. A priest is mentioned on a single tablet of the Knossos personnel series.

KN Am 821 + FR.[47]
.1]ra-jo , / e-qe-ta-e , e-ne-ke , ẹ-mi-to VIR 2 // ki-ta-ne-to , / su-ri-mo , e-ne-ka ‘o-pa’ VIR ̣1
.2]si-ja-du-we ,.ṭạ-ṛạ , / i-je[-re-]u, po-me , e-ne-ke , ‘o-pa’ X VIR 1 // ko-pe-re-u., / e-qe-ta , e-ki-‘si-jo’ VIR 1
.3] *vacat*

On this tablet, men (VIR) are being allocated to various officials, among them the elite e-qe-ta-e (“followers,” likely companions to the *wanax*) and a single priest, the i-je-re-u on line 2. The occasion for this tablet, however, is not entirely clear. The repeated e-ne-ke/a “for the sake of” is resolved with e-mi-to (“tribute”?) and o-pa (“obligatory payment”?).[48] The selection of the male officials does much help resolve this tablet so much as further muddle it – what would bring the e-qe-ta-e and a priest together for a transaction? And why are both the words i-je-re-u “priest” and po-me ποίμην/“shepherd” together in the nominative case? Is this priest also a shepherd? Finally, what occasions these allocations? The combination of a political and a cult official is an odd choice; it is not clear that these allocations are tied specifically to their official political and cultish capacities, so much as to their standings as important members of the state. At any rate, there is not much on this tablet to fix it as belonging to the direct performance of cult duties.

The second tablet which mentions a priest also may place him outside of his religious office. Assuming the restoration is correct,[49] a second priest appears on the livestock tablet KN C 7048 in possession of sheep. As this title and the sheep ideogram are the only legible items on this tablet, it is tempting to associate this shepherd/priest with the one on KN Am 821. What is definite, however, is that this tablet once more references a priest, far from his official cult capacity.

All mentions of priestesses derive from tablets in the Knossos Fp series; this series which primarily records allocations of olive oil to specific shrines and deities is the most overtly religious of the entire Knossos corpus. Three priestesses are mentioned on the two tablets Kn Fp 1 + 31 and Kn Fp 13. The first records monthly allocations of grain to a list of divinities in the regions of Knossos and its port Amnisos:[50]

Kn Fp 1 + 31
1 de-u-ki-jo-jo ‘me-no’
.2 di-ka-ta-jo / di-we OLE S 1
.3 da-da-re-jo-de OLE S 2
.4 pa-de OLE S 1
.5 pa-si-te-o-i OLE 1
.6 qe-ra-si-ja OLE S 1[
.7 a-mi-ni-so , pa-si-te-o-i S 1[
.8 e-ri-nu , OLE V 3
.9 *47-da-de OLE V 1
.10 a-ne-mo , / i-je-re-ja V 4
.11 *vacat*
.12: to-so OLE 3 S 2 V 2
1. “In the month of Deukios:
2. To Diktaion Zeus: 9.6 l. oil
3. To the Daidaleion: 19.2 l. oil
4. To Pa-de: 9.6 l. oil
5. To all the gods: 28.8 l. oil
6. To qe-ra-si-ja: 9.6 l. oil
7. Amnisos, to all the gods: 19.2 l. oil
8. To Erinys: 4.8 l. oil
9. To *47-da-: 1.6 l. oil
10. To the priestess of the winds: 6.4 l. oil
11. (blank)
12. (total) 108.8 l. oil”

This tablet includes one priestess – the priestess of the winds – among a list of divinities (and one shrine – the Daidaleion). This priestess of the winds is located at Amnisos, and receives the third smallest portion of oil on this tablet. It seems clear that she is receiving this allocation in her official capacity; she is the only human on this list, and her amount is sufficient only for the tending of a small shrine complex. It is interesting to note that she functions as the embodiment of her divinity here.

The second text which mentions priestesses is very similar.[51]

Kn Fp 13
.1 ra-pa-to 'me-no' , *47-ku-to-de OLE V 1 pi-pi-tu-na V 1
.2 au-ri-mo-de OLE V 4 pa-si-te-o-i S 1 qe-ra-si-ja S 1
.3 a-ne-mo-i-je-re-ja OLE 1 u-ta-no , 'a-ne-mo-i-je-re-ja' S 1 V̩ 3
"In the month of Lapatos: to *47-ko-to: 1.6 l. oil, to Pi-pi-tu-na: 1.6 liters
To Aurimo: 6.4 l. oil; to all the gods: 9.6 liters; to qe-ra-si-ja 9.6 liters
To the priestess of the winds: 28.8 l. oil; At Utanos (PN), to the priestess of the winds: 12.8 liters"

Again, we see priestesses as the only humans referenced on Fp Olive Oil tablets. It is interesting to see that this cult is present in more than one location, and that in both, it is the human priestess who seems to embody the cult. However, as she is doing little other than receiving cult goods on these two tablets, it is difficult to ascertain how the relationship between priests and priestesses is structured at Knossos. It does appear that these priestesses are envisioned as more ensconced in their official capacity on these two tablets than was the priest who was somewhat more obliquely situated.

The other mentions of cult personnel at Knossos are not much more helpful.

Additional cult personnel at Knossos.

Three additional types of cult personnel are attested to at Knossos: one te-o-jo do-e-ro, two mentions of ki-ri-te-wi-ja, and a single do-e-ra of a divinity. The lone te-o-jo do-e-ro ("slave of the god") appears on the personnel tablet KN Ai 966 + 7855 + 7856:

KN Ai 966 + 7855 + 7856
.a te-o , do-e-ro [
.b a-ri-ke-u , / ka-pạ-so ja-[
"Halikeus (obscure) , slave of the god"

This tablet is so brief that perhaps the only real information it provides to us regarding religious structure is that the institution of divine slaves is not specific to Pylos. The second apparent sacred slave at Knossos appears on KN Gg 713+0994.

KN Gg 713 + 994
ma-ri-ne-we , / do-e-ra 'ME+RI' *209-VAS+A [

Here, a female slave of the divinity ma-ri-ne-we[52] is listed as the person to whom the cult offerings are delivered; she receives a quantity of honey in a vessel of type

*209. Again, it is interesting to note that this slave, like the priestess of the winds, is once more treated as the embodiment of her god. (It would be helpful to know if any men affiliated with cult perform this role as well, but our evidence is too limited to venture a guess.)

The final two mentions of cult personnel at Knossos are the ki-ri-te-wi-ja on KN Fp 363 and KN E 777.

KN Fp 363
.1 qe-te-a , te-re-no OLE [
.2 da-*83-ja-de / i-je-ro S 2 ki-ri-te-wi-ja , [
.3 di-wo-pu-ka-ta S 2 [
.4] *vacat* [

This tablet, of the Fp olive oil series, lists olive oil offerings "to be paid" (qe-te-a); the ki-ri-te-wi-ja appear on the second line following the amount due to a shrine (i-je-ro). Again, we see offerings granted directly to female cult officials.

KN E 777[53]
recto
.1 ko-no-si-ja / ki-ri-te-wi-ja-i LUNA 1 GRA 100[
.2 a-mi-ni-si-ja LUNA 1 GRA 100 [
.3 pa-i-ti-ja LUNA 1 GRA 100[

verso
.1 a-ze-ti-ri-ja GRA ̣1̣0[
1: "Women of Knossos (for the *ki-ri-te-wi-ja* women): *ration* for one month 9,600 l. of wheat
2: Women of Amnisos: *ration* for one month 9,600 l. of wheat
3: Women of Phaistos: *ration* for one month 9,600 l. of wheat"
"Decorators: *ration* for one month 960 l. wheat"

On this tablet, the ki-ri-te-wi-ja appear to have a very different function; instead of receiving relatively small offerings of oil – as did all female cult officials previously mentioned at Knossos – here the ki-ri-te-wi-ja of Knossos, Amnisos, and Phaistos are receiving monthly rations of wheat; these wheat rations are sufficient to feed 500 workgroup women for a month. This is the first hint that we have had at Knossos of sacerdotal women performing more civic duties. One would be interested to know whether other cult officials had similar functions.

Overall, the evidence for religious personnel at Knossos is substantially more limited than at Pylos; the Knossian texts tend to name divinities directly rather than their priests/priestesses. The few instances of priests and priestesses, however, record them in very different contexts.[54] The male personnel are all recorded in non-religious contexts; the divinities they represent are not even mentioned. By all indications, priests are invested into the Knossian social structure in a variety of secular roles; they appear as prominent individuals who control both resources and personnel. Knossian priestesses (mentioned a total of three times on two tablets), on the other hand, are only recorded as acting on behalf of their divinities. These priestesses have no non-occupational contact with their palatial administration; nowhere are priestesses attested as entering the Knossos economy on their own behalf, only on behalf of their patron divinity. In short, religion at Knossos was much like – or certainly not different from – other Knossian social institutions.

Perhaps what is most significant about the relationship between gender and religious standing at Knossos is how little impact religion seems to have had in creating and reinforcing status hierarchies.

Conclusions

So, by examining the tablets with an eye to both gender and religious affiliation as categories of organization, it seems that the impact of religion on the gender framework of the two states is not the same. Each state has its own specific gender system which religion affects differently. At Pylos, religious status for a woman served as the locus where otherwise normative gender roles break down. Religious officialdom lent women an otherwise exceptional degree of visibility and economic power. Furthermore, religion is the sole arena of society where men's and women's roles and status appear egalitarian at Pylos. When women acquired religious standing at Pylos, they closely paralleled their male counterparts, particularly the priests and male servants of the gods. In fact, at Pylos the priestesses and priests function as nearly congruent analogs; they exercise quite similar control of land and personnel, and in one instance, even appear on the same tablet where the size of their combined land holdings is listed. Overall, at Pylos, religion functioned as the great equalizer of gender relations; it is the dual axes of religion and gender that determine for a Pylian woman her degree of public visibility, her access to commodities and land, and the amount of autonomy she enjoys within this palatial polity.

In contrast at Knossos, whose gender-based hierarchies are less pronounced than those of Pylos, religion creates no such differences but rather reinforces the regular Knossian gender structure; at Knossos, the impact of religion upon gender is all but negligible. Knossian society in all arenas continues to be strictly gendered; religion is not a game-changer for women at Knossos. Or to put it another way, at Knossos there is no indication that religious status changes social norms for women. Religion seems to function as simply another patriarchal institution reinforcing the overall social structure.

Notes

1 Major works on religion in Linear B scholarship include: Baumbach 1979 :143–160; Bendall 2007; Chadwick 1985: 191–202; Gerard-Rousseau 1968; Goodison 1989; Hägg 1985: 203–225; Hiller 2011; Palaima 2008: 343–361; Hooker 1983: 137–142; Killen 1985; Laffineur and Hagg 2001; Lupack 2011, 2010a, 2008a; L. Palmer 1983.

2 Billigmeier and Turner 1981: 1–10; Carlier 1983; Chadwick 1988: 44–95.

3 Dionysos (di-wo-nu-so) appears on KH 5 Gg alongside Zeus where both receive offerings of gold. Dionysos is not explicitly named as a son of Zeus here, but they are the sole recipients on this tablet.

4 For argumentation, see Chapter 3, pp. 111–13.

5 Billigmeier and Turner 1981; Carlier 1983; Chadwick 1988; Nosch 2003.

6 Hiller 1989.

7 These women are discussed in Chapter 4: Women and property holdings at Pylos.

8 ἱέρεια "priestess." Carlier 1983: 12; *Diccionario*: Vol. 1, 273–74; *Docs2*: 547; Lindgren 1973: Part II, 561; Morpurgo Davies 1979: 93.

9 Ka-ra-wi-po-ro from κλᾳδοφόρος (Attic κλειδοῦχος "priestess"), literally "keybearer." Billigmeier and Turner 1981: 7; Carlier 1983: 12; *Diccionario*: Vol. I, 324–25; Ventris and Chadwick 1956: 396; Ventris and Chadwick 1973: 551; Hooker 1987a: 313–315; Morpurgo Davies 1979: 93.

10 For etymologies, definitions, and further commentary, see Lindgren 1973: Part II, 35.

11 Nosch 2003: 20.

12 Full texts and translations for cult officials and their holding can be found in Chapters 4 (for commodity holdings) and 6 (for land).

13 Cult officials' land holdings are extensively discussed in Chapter 6.

14 Nosch concurs. Nosch 2003: 14.

15 PY Ep 704.2:

u-wa-mi-ja , te-o-jo , do-e-ra , o-na-to , e-ke-qe , i-je-re-ja , ḳẹ-ra , to-so , pe-mo GRA T 1 V 3

"Huamia, slave of the god, holds a geras-lease from the priestess so much grain: 14.4."

This text is cited in its entirety in Chapter 4. This tablet repeats information also found on PY Eb 416.

16 Supra, pp. 140–41.

17 PY Ep 704.5–6

.5 e-ri-ta , i-je-re-ja , e-ke , e-u-ke-to-qe , e-to-ni-jo , e-ke-e , te-o , da-mo-de-mi , pa-si , ko-to-na-o

.6 ke-ke-me-na-o , o-na-to , e-ke-e , to-so , pe-mo GRA 3 *T* 9

"Eritha the priestess holds and she claims that (her) god holds an e-to-ni-jo, but the damos says that she has a plot of ke-ke-me-na ko-to-na (a communal plot): so much seed: 374.4 l. wheat."

This tablet recapitulates information also found on PY Eb 297.

18 Explored further on pp. 136,137 and 216–17.

19 Carlier 1987: 11–12.

20 Full texts for both are provided in Chapter 4, pp. 159–60 fns. 79 and 83.

21 PY Fn 50: 12–13.

.12 mi-jo[-qa] do-e-ro-i HORD V 3

.13 a-pi-ẹ-ṛạ do-e-ro-i HORD V 3

22 PY AN 1281: 1–2; 7–8

.1 po-]ti-ni-ja , i-qe-ja

.2]-mo , o-pi-e-de-i

.7 mi-jo-qa[ ]e-we-za-no VIR 1

.8 a-pị-e-ṛạ to-ze-u VIR 1

23 Ventris and Chadwick 1973 proposes that o-pi-e-de-i be read as two words *opi hedei* "at her seat" (i.e., shrine or temple) ἕδος *Il.* v, 360+]. Ventris and Chadwick 1973: 565.

24 Nosch notes that the keybearer and priestess only hold slaves in cult contexts. Nosch 2003: 14.

25 Nosch 2003: 14 also reads PY An 1281 to place them in contexts of cult.

26 Nosch 2003: 20.

27 Nosch 2003: 20.
28 Select PY Tn 316 bibliography: For overview and history of interpretation see Palaima 2011; 1999. For paleography and physicality of tablet: E. Bennett 1987; Palaima 2011. For the sacrifical victims theory: Baumbach 1983; Chadwick 1976; Hooker 1977. For the votive women theory: Uchitel 1988, 1984.
29 L. Palmer 1963: 254.
30 Although I suggest that the specific work arrangements of low-ranking female workgroup members are operating under two very different arrangements – slavery at Pylos and corvée labor at Knossos. See the conclusions to Chapters 3 and 5 for argumentation.
31 For additional commentary and bibliography on these two figures, see Chapter 3.
32 For the wanax in cultic contexts, see Hooker 1983: 257–267 and Palaima 1995b.
33 The full provisioning of pa-ki-ja-ne by the wanax includes 1968 l. of barley, 18 l. of cyperus, 144 l. of flour, 384 l. of olives, 24 . of ..., 12 l. of honey, 120 l. of figs, one ox, 26 rams, 6 ewes, two he-goats, two she-goats, one fat hog, six sows, 732 l. of wine, and two cloths.
34 These include the wanax's fuller (ka-na-pe-u) on PY En 74, PY Eo 160, and PY Eo 276, his potter on PY Eo 371+1160, and on PY En 609 his e-te-do-mo ("builder" and "armorer" have each been proposed; *Diccionario* p. Vol. 1: 254–55). On the *wanax* and his staff, see also: Palaima 1995b.
35 Priestess, keybearer, ki-ri-te-wi-ja, te-o-jo do-e-ra, do-e-ra ka-pa-ti-ja, and do-e-ra i-je-re-ja.
36 Ka-pa-ti-ja is the name of the best attested (if not only) keybearer at Pylos.
37 Py Ea 756, PY Eb 472, PY Ed 317, PY En 74, PY En 659, PY Eo 247, PY Eo 444, PY Ep 539.
38 PY Eb 297, PY Eb 339+ 409, PY Eb 1176, PY Ed 317, PY En 609, PY Ep 539, PY Ep 704.
39 If we accept Killen's reading of mi-jo-qa and a-pi-e-ra as priestesses, two more named priestesses should join ka-wa-ra and e-ri-ta. Killen 2001: 438.
40 A priestly title, Ventris and Chadwick 1973: 566.
41 PY Eb 472, PY Ed 317, PY En 74, PY En 659, PY Eo 247, PY Eo 444, and PY Ep 539.
42 Supra, pp 138 and 223.
43 This is also the conclusion of Billigmeier and Turner 1981: 10.
44 In this section, I am treating as interchangeable te-o-jo do-e-ro/ra, do-e-ro/ra i-je-re-ja, and do-e-ro/ra ka-pa-ti-ja.
45 Slaves of divinities also appear on An 607. Carlier argues that the status of these functionaries may be hereditary. Carlier 1983: 13. Cf. Billigmeier and Turner 1981: 9; Hiller 1988: 57.
46 Killen 2001: 435–438.
47 Translation from Ventris and Chadwick 1973: 168: "two followers on account of *tribute*; Ki-ta-ne-to at Su-ri-mo on account of *dues* ; .... priest at E-ra (ta-ra), shepherd on account of dues; Kopreus, follower, of Exos."
48 Ventris and Chadwick 1973: 168.
49 Only an i precedes a glide begun with a j in Linear B.
50 Discussed in Ventris and Chadwick 1973: 305–207. Hooker 1980: 152–53.
51 Ventris and Chadwick 1973: 307–308.
52 L.R. Palmer 1981: 8.
53 Translation of the recto is from Ventris and Chadwick 1973: 214.
54 *Pace* Carlier who suggests that both priests and priestesses rarely appear in their official contexts; this is true for priests at Knossos, but not, I contend, for priestesses. Carlier 1983: 11.

8 Conclusions

Women in Aegean prehistory

This book has examined the evidence pertaining to women recorded in the Linear B tablets from Knossos on Crete and Pylos on the Greek mainland and has recovered evidence for nearly 2000 women, documented in over 800 Linear B tablets. In terms of the central research question here, whether the gender organizations of these two states were homogeneous in their integration of women into their economic institutions, there is sufficient evidence to warrant the conclusion that the two states of Mycenaean Pylos and Knossos exhibited significant differences in their gender structures, and that, in these earliest of Greek records, gender organization was a locally specific rather than universalized phenomenon in the Bronze Age Aegean.

Women at Pylos

Pylos offers the best opportunity to investigate the structures and parameters of gender organization in the Mycenaean period. Due to its reasonably good state of preservation, and the tendency of its scribes to sort and compile their data, the Pylos archive provides an opportunity to recover many of the ways Pylian women were integrated into their state economy particularly in the four aspects of the economy where women were most textually visible: in the institutions of production, property, land tenure, and religion.

The picture that emerges from a study of the ways in which these four institutions are gendered is a complex but consistent one. At Pylos, the documents depict an economy and an administration where women consistently occupied a less central position than did their male counterparts and a social structure that was incontrovertibly patriarchal. Of the three overarching status categories which encompassed Pylos's population – the elite, ranking administrators with large property holdings, middle-status officials and artisans, and low-ranking servile laborers, Pylian women appeared only in the two lowest rungs. Nonetheless, the contribution of women to the Pylian economy remained significant with some 900 women attested. All documented women entered the textual record either by means of production or the control of property, and these two categories served as the dividing line between lower and middle-ranked women at Pylos.

As an institution, production activities were consistently assigned to Pylos's lowest-ranking women, specifically the female palace dependents of the personnel series that constituted the majority of women at the site – more than 750 of the nearly 900 documented women. These women functioned as members of 51 single-sex workgroup units, assigned to 27 different tasks. These task assignments were uniformly menial, primarily dedicated to repetitive and labor-intensive work such as textile production (in all stages from wool-carding and spinning, through weaving, sewing, and cloth decoration) and to the maintenance, nourishing, and tending of the palace and its personnel. The low social standing of these women is evident in their textual treatment: these women were never named or differentiated in any way as individuals; they appear only as members of workgroups, recorded by the title of their workgroup, the drawn ideogram for woman and a tally of the number of adult women and underage children belonging to each unit. All these women appear to have little to no social or economic autonomy, and have no property holdings other than the basic subsistence rations of wheat and figs provided to them by the palace.

In terms of the organization of women's labor at Pylos, a complex system of workgroup assignment seems to have been in operation, both in terms of task assignment and in the placement of workgroups throughout the state. What we see is largely a two-tiered system, with each province's outlying villages staffed with a small number or workers, generally in one or two workgroup units. These outer village workgroups appear exclusively devoted to textile production, while the capital centers of Pylos and Leuktron each hosted multiple workgroups with a broader range of assignments.

Each regional capital center hosted a variety of textile workers – both sites housed single-task textile workers (who may have functioned as a type of Bronze Age piecework assembly line) and specialists in particular cloth types. Textile workers were by far and away the most represented type of workgroup women at Pylos's capital sites and were presumably so positioned to meet the textile requirements of each center. The remaining labor categories also clustered at the main sites. Both Leuktron and Pylos had workgroups of flour-grinders, a seemingly perpetual task; as our evidence currently stands, though, it appears that only the Pylian center housed the three types of workers who would seem to have functioned as the center's janitorial and maintenance workers (sweepers, water-attendants, and personal attendants – all tasks which also should be constantly required, perpetual, and never-ending). It would appear that only the main palace site required such a fully standing domestic staff.

In addition to these task-named workgroups were several workgroups identified not by title but by the ethnic origins of the workgroup women. All but two of these ethnics derived from locations far from Pylian control, mainly from the Eastern Aegean and Asia Minor. The geographic distribution of these workgroups seems significant. The ethnically-identified workgroups were clustered disproportionately at the main capital site of Pylos. Moreover neither of the two workgroups that had their origins within Pylian state limits was left at their eponymous villages, but was instead each transferred to secondary locations. If one of the goals of the

Pylian administration had been to monitor and secure these workers, this system of clustering and transfer would make logical sense. While a variety of scholarly positions have been staked out with regard to the status of these women, I find the identification of these dependent workers as palace slaves to be the most persuasive and compelling. Previous scholarly studies have cited several aspects of supporting evidence for this reading: 1.) The presence of palace-provided subsistence rations for both the workgroup women and their children. 2.) The absence of any adult male countrymen accompanying these women – lessening the odds that these women were present as independent contractors. 3.) The palace's interest in, and ability to, reassign the adult sons of these workers. 4.) The menial nature of the tasks involved seems more consistent with a slave rather than free model. To these arguments, I would add: 1.) The decision to cluster women with foreign ethnic titles at the centers rather than the peripheral villages seems strategic and may reveal an interest on the part of the palace to exercise greater control over non-indigenous women. 2.) The never-ending nature of some of the workgroup tasks implies perpetual work – particularly on the part of the women assigned to food production, palace maintenance, and personal attendance. Since these workers are presented with the identical textual formulas as the textile and other workgroup women – they are rostered and rationed in identical ways, and all of their children are monitored by the palace as well – I argue that we must regard the status of all the workgroup women as indivisible. And, if we can identify the status of some of the women, we can extrapolate that status to encompass all of them – and perhaps, finally settle the now 55-year-old debate over their status. I contend that the endless, never-completable nature of the domestic tasks argues for a full-time, everyday workforce and a servile status for these women – and so, as the unity of status of all the Pylian workgroup women is clear, it seems apparent that we should read the work of *all* workgroup women as perpetual and continuous. Therefore, for low-status dependent workers assigned to perpetual tasks, maintained with only subsistence rations, unaccompanied by adult men, and whose sons are reassigned en masse to tasks of the palace's choosing, I see no other reasonable explanation than enslavement.

Other than these women assigned to the collective workgroups, there is no evidence for extra-palatial craftswomen, that is, non-dependent women who conducted their own economic affairs in their own right. The lack of independent craftswomen in the archives stands in direct contrast to Pylian men, who were designated with over a hundred occupational titles. While some Pylian men appeared to have been direct dependents of the palace, the vast majority of them seem to have conducted their labor outside of direct palatial control. While men's titles may serve to designate them within their occupational contexts, such as smiths who receive allotments of bronze, or without, for example, titles used to differentiate two men with the same name – no free, economically independent women were visible to us in production activities. The only female laborers attested to are those who appear without any property or economic autonomy of their own, laboring in the collective workgroups.

The situation changes dramatically for the Pylian women identified as religious officials. Unlike the women of the workgroups, women listed as religious functionaries enjoyed a high level of visibility and economic autonomy at Pylos; one of them, in fact, was involved in the oldest legal dispute known from Europe where she represented herself and her own economic interests against her local government. In many ways, religion functioned as an economic wildcard in terms of Pylian gender roles; this was the sole venue in the Pylos tablets where women demonstrated any economic power in their own right.[1] Priestesses of several types held slaves, both male and female, and acted as supervisors to other free personnel. They also exercised control over property, including food-stuffs, textiles, commodities as important as bronze, as well as property which they administered on behalf of their divinities – including shrines and their contents – and property allocated to them in their own names. Most importantly, this property included leased land (technically, short-term land holdings). Priestesses and other female cult officials were the only women at Pylos with attested access to land holdings, but even within this institution women did not achieve full parity with men. No Pylian women are attested as land-owners; even priestesses were limited to leased, rather than owned, land – but sacerdotal status lent certain women access to land denied to other women. Typically referred to both by their names and titles, these women seem to have been envisioned by the palace primarily within their official capacities; these are the only women who are not recorded in terms of either their marital arrangements or fecundity.

In contrast to priestly women and their economic autonomy were the wives of high-ranking officials. What is interesting is that these women appear to be of high prestige, but their high rank did not seem to be paralleled by a similarly high level of economic power. No real property seems to have accrued to these women – the most we see is an allocation of leather sandals – and the contrast between these wives of elite family and the female religious officials is striking.

So at Pylos, as much later in Classical Athens, it would seem that the institution of religion itself lent certain women an exceptional economic status in that religious practice functioned as the sole locus where ideologies of economic restriction and subordination were superseded by the requirements of cult. Thus, we see two primary economic identities for women at Pylos: low-status workgroup women defined by their status as property-less producers or property-holding religious functionaries for whom the institutions of property, land tenure, and religion intersected.[2]

Women at Knossos

Recovering women's investiture into the economic structures of Mycenaean Knossos is a more difficult prospect that at Pylos. The poor state of preservation of the Knossos tablets is a major obstacle as are the difficulties posed by the apparent lack of unity of the corpus. Consequently, it is not feasible to attempt to fully model the Knossos evidence; more useful is to use the Knossos evidence to assess whether it conformed to or diverged from the more recoverable gender practices of Pylos.

While at first glance, many of the gender practices of Mycenaean Pylos appear to have been mirrored at Mycenaean-era Knossos (e.g., no women appearing among the administrative elite, men controlling far more property than women, a large proportion of Knossian women being recorded in low-status workgroup units, etc.), closer examination of the Knossian evidence reveals that the specifics of its system of gender organization did not in fact conform to those of Pylos but instead differed in several significant ways.

The first differences emerge in their employ of aggregate workgroups. Five major differences can be seen between the two sites: 1.) All the women of the Knossos workgroups appear to have been assigned to textile production; unlike at Pylos, no workers assigned to food- processing or janitorial work are attested. 2.) Only ethnics local to Crete are used to describe the workgroup women; there is no evidence of foreign women composing any of the textile workgroups at Knossos. 3.) None of the ethnically-labeled women were transferred to another location to perform their tasks. 4.) In addition to the rostering records, the Knossos tablets record production targets set for these workgroups (and occasionally the delivery of these products). 5.) Workgroups on occasion produced materials different from those their occupational titles would imply. 6.) Some of the workgroup women are expressly called slaves; in these instances their owners' names appear as their workgroup title.

How might these differences imply a different type of workgroup structure in place at Knossos? To start, it seems significant that none of the necessarily perpetual and year-round tasks were attributed to these workgroups – none of these workgroups were attested to as performing such endless tasks as food-processing or domestic service. Knossos also had production goals for items to be manufactured by these women, targets which were met and their products tallied in completion of these goals. This may well imply that the work of these women was only commanded for certain portions of the year; certainly there is nothing in the extant information pertaining to these workgroups which guarantees their work to have been continuous. The requirement that women produced commodities other than their own workgroup specialties would seem to reinforce this position; why else would they retain the workgroup name unless that they returned to their specialty after fulfilling the targeted goal? Furthermore, since only some of these women were specifically identified as slaves, it seems reasonable to regard the others as not. From all these differences, I think it likely that these workgroups were not a full-time slave labor force, but rather workers commandeered for corvée labor. As such these workers seem to have remained in their home villages, producing textiles for the administration for only part of the year. Again, nothing in these records seems to necessitate understanding them as a permanent labor force; I suggest we keep open the possibility that these were corvée workers instead. If so, these workers would have been of significantly higher social standing than the slave laborers of the Pylos groups – a possibility which should remain open.

Yet, the most significant distinction between the two sites was not with respect to production. The real difference was in terms of property holdings. At Pylos, the only women who exercised control over significant holdings were priestesses and other religious functionaries, but even these women had limits on their holdings – notably, in terms of their access to the most important commodity in an agrarian economy: arable land. Even Pylian priestesses did not own their land; land was granted to them only in the form of short-term leases, a circumstance that would have effectively precluded even sacerdotal women from amassing any major, long-term property holdings. In contrast, ordinary (that it, non-priestly) Knossian women were attested to as owning their own land, and were recorded in ways completely analogous with male land holders. Moreover land was not the only property held by women in Mycenaean-era Knossos. Various women were also attested as having massive amounts of food-stuffs, slaves, raw and finished textile products, and luxury goods such as gold and bronze vessels. These women were also held personally accountable for missing property – further underscoring the notion that the property in question was considered that of these women rather than of their husbands, fathers, or other male relations. Importantly, none of these property holders were attested to in any context that might suggest they held a religious affiliation, nor were they listed as wives of ranking men. In fact, at Knossos, unlike Pylos, there was no discernable social or political institution in place that dramatically elevated certain women to an exceptional status; it would seem that at least some women in the Knossos economy were considered to have had an independent economic identity, and that this was the expected norm. It would seem that Knossos did not require the presence of any social institution to justify the lifting of restrictions on women's economic activities, because the economic activities of women at Knossos were not significantly restricted along lines of gender in the first place.

So, overall, analysis strongly suggests that the gender organization of Mycenaean Knossos did not conform to that of Mycenaean Pylos either in terms of specific practices or in terms of their underlying rationales. While both incorporated large numbers of low- and middle-ranking women into their economies, the structures that created the broad gulf between female laborers and property holders at Pylos seem to have been absent as organizing factors at Knossos. Whereas at Pylos only religious affiliation served to lend a woman an autonomous economic identity, religion seemed to play no such role at Knossos where women with no apparent religious affiliations act as property owners. Unfortunately, the texts are too spare to allow us to recover the mechanisms that drove property ownership at Knossos, but we should at least reject the idea that functionary status had the same meaning for Knossian women that it did for Pylian. and that at Knossos, at least some property holdings were controlled by more "ordinary" women.

Ramifications of this study

This study impacts upon two fields of inquiry in Classical scholarship: the history of women in Greek antiquity and the ongoing Bronze Age discussions regarding the process of "Mycenaeanization" on Crete and the specific workings of the palatial workforce.

Women in antiquity

First and foremost, this monograph is intended to expand the historical frameworks associated with the study of women in Greek antiquity. Collections, textbooks, and classes devoted to the study of women in antiquity to date have had the tendency to begin their inquiries with the Homeric epics with little if any attention paid to the era that preceded them.[3]

Consequently, two of the goals of this study have been to push back the chronological framework for the history of women in Greece to the 14th and 13th centuries BCE. and to render more accessible the lived social and economic realities of women's lives in these oldest of Greek documents. Interestingly, many practices at Knossos seem more in line with Near Eastern models for women in society, especially with regard to labor, but Pylos seems to share more in common with later historical-era Greece – particularly Athens – where it comes to women. Pylos's women, like those of Athens eight centuries later, appear to have had no real property beyond personal effects, and the only women with property and public responsibilities belong to the ranks of priestesses.

In addition to bringing to light specific historical information, such as the competing systems of land tenure for Pylian and Knossian women or the differential impact of religious officialdom on women's social and economic positions, I consider the most important finding of this study with respect to scholarship on ancient women is to note that even in the earliest Greek records we see no unity of gender roles and practices nor any common gender structure shared between the different Greek-administered polities. Instead gender practices are already locally unique and specific to each state, leading to the larger question as to whether there ever was a *koine* of gender practice in the Greek world. From the Linear B evidence, we must conclude that if ever there had been such a *koine*, it was already gone by the Late Bronze Age, replaced by more site-specific structures and driven more by local choices, needs, and histories. In this light, the broad differences in gender practices witnessed at Classical Athens and Sparta may not be all that surprising; it may be rather that the entire idea of a monolithic experience of gender in Ancient Greece is an illusory concept. With this in mind then, a new variable should be added to our interpretative frameworks: in addition to addressing ancient Greek women in terms of era, class, age, servile or free status, we must also adjust for wide variances between localities.

Mycenaean Crete

This study also makes two central contributions to Aegean Bronze Age archaeology:

1 It fleshes out more of the workings of the Bronze Age economy – particularly in identifying the logic behind the stationing of the workgroups in Pylos and its provinces and the differing land-tenure systems of Pylos and Knossos.

2 It contributes to the ongoing debate over the degree of Hellenization in Mycenaean Crete, particularly Mycenaean Knossos, in that it seeks to challenge existing trends in scholarship that would universalize the workings of Mycenaean states.

This trend toward universalizing Mycenaean states is particularly problematic in that it does not allow in particular for Knossos's unique history or the possibility that the process of cultural assimilation (Hellenization) may not be complete at this site. Indeed, how Mycenaean was Mycenaean Crete? While this question alone warrants a book-long study of its own, nonetheless a gender-centric approach to Linear B evidence may be particularly useful as a gauge by which to assess issues of cultural survival and assimilation, offering another means of entry into this question. While previous studies of the institutional framework of the Linear B texts have often emphasized similarities in the political and administrative structures of Pylos and Knossos, examining a gender-centered approach instead shakes out significant differences between the two states – at least insofar as the treatment and social organization of women was concerned. While much of the institutional masculine landscape appears to reflect a high degree of assimilation and acceptance of mainland political institutions and administrators (*wanax, lawagetas, eqetai*, etc.) in Mycenaean Knossos, investigation into the feminine spheres reveals that the process of assimilation was by no means complete. Quite simply, mainland institutions do not appear to be governing women's role in the economy on Crete.

I suggest that the process of making Knossos Mycenaean was far more complicated than previously assumed, and far less complete, in that elements in as central an organizational factor as gender persisted even a century after the introduction of a Greek administration to Knossos. This study suggests that differences in gender practices between the two states provide strong evidence for ongoing *cultural* differences between Mycenaean Knossos and the mainland, and that employing gender – now demonstrated as a useful category of *archaeological* analysis – can be fruitful not just for the study of women per se, but also for broader questions of acculturation and resistance.

Finally, this study may also provide insight into the other great mystery relating to gender studies in Aegean prehistory: the actual roles and status of *Minoan* women. In the absence of a successful decipherment of the Minoan Linear A tablets, debate has largely focused – and stalled out – on images from frescoes, engraved sealstones, and rings. Iconography is always a difficult source for lived realities, but perhaps here we may have a back way into this discussion. If we do indeed see significant differences between Pylos and Knossos, and if Pylos might be regarded as a type site for Mycenaean gender practices – as it was, after all, a palace in which a Mycenaean Greek administration governed a Mycenaean Greek populace, and presumably the choices it made in its administration were designed to fit its own cultural and administrative needs – the differences between the two sites may have wider significance. If these differences in gender organization at Knossos imply a level of cultural assimilation that was at best partial, where might those different practices have come from? I suggest that these differences may likely be holdovers from an earlier period – for would Mycenaean Greeks introduce gender practices not their own – and that the most likely source of those holdovers would be Neopalatial Minoan Crete, where women have long been suspected of enjoying a more egalitarian status than other women of the Eastern Mediterranean. And if our differences are indeed Minoan holdovers, we may now be able to suggest that Minoan women labored in corvée workgroups, maintained property in their own names, and, most importantly, owned land.

Notes

1 It is interesting to note that in those rare instances where women bearing workgroup titles appear in cultic contexts, small amounts of property are also allocated to them. This would seem to reinforce my contention that it is the association with cult practice that permits Pylian women to enter into the institution of property holding.
2 There remains one exception to prove the rule: the elusive *Kessandra* with her large grain holdings appears to be the sole (apparently non-functionary) woman in control of a significant amount of goods.
3 Foley 1981 remains the major exception to this trend.

Appendices

Note on appendices

The following abbreviations are in use throughout Appendices A and B:

WN	=	Woman's name
MN	=	Man's name
PN	=	Place name
WomOcc	=	Women's occupation
ManOcc	=	Men's occupation
FemEthnic	=	Feminine ethnic adjective

Appendix A: All mentions of women in the Pylos Tablets

Title nominative	#	*Name*	*Sex*	*Sex identified*
---	1	*34-ke-ja	F	Feminine name ending -eia
[ ]	1	*35-ke-ja	F, sing	Feminine name ending -eia
---	1	a-*65-ja	F	By analogy with rest of entries on tablet
---	1	a-pi-e-ra *Amphiera*	F	Feminine name ending
---	1	a-pi-e-ra *Amphiera*	F	Feminine name ending
---	1	a-pi-te-ja	F	Feminine name ending
---	1	a-ro-ja	F? M?	Feminine name ending?
---	1	a3-pu-ke-ne-ja	F	Feminine name ending -eia
---	1	e-ti-je-ja	F	Feminine name ending -eia
---	1	e-ti-ri-ja	F?	Feminine name ending?
---	1	ka-pa-si-ja *Karpathia*	F	Feminine name ending -ia
---	1	ka-ra-i (MN or WN) (MN more likely)	M or F, sing	Unclear, form could be fem. but all others on tablet male
---	1	ka-ra-i (MN or WN) (MN more likely)	M or F, sing	Unclear, form could be fem. but all others on tablet male
---	1	ka-ra-i (MN or WN) (MN more likely)	M or F, sing	Unclear, form could be fem. but all others on tablet male
---	1	ke-i-ja	F?	Feminine name ending -eia
		ke-sa-da-ra *Kessandra* Κεσσάνδρα	F	Feminine name ending -a (masc form takes o(s))

Function	*Tablet*	*Tablet identifying sex*	*Designation type*
Receives HORD (barley) [and NI (figs)?]	PY Fn 187.19	Same	WN
Holds an o-na-to ke-ke-me-na ko-to-na from damos	PY Eb 871	Same	WN
Among list of nominative WNs accompanied by MNs in genitive	PY Vn 34+1191+ 1006	By analogy with rest of PN Vn series and same	WN
Listed with MN - she's in genitive as owner	PY An 1281.08	Same	WN
Has male slaves who hold HORD	PY Fn 50.13	Same	WN
Holds HORD and NI (figs)	PY Fn 187.01	Same	WN
Holds HORD [and NI (figs)?]	PY Fn 187.20		WN
Holds HORD and OLIV	PY Fn 79.01	Same	WN
Uncertain	PY Vn 851.10	Same	WN
Uncertain	PY Vn 851.09	Same	WN
Uncertain	PY Vn 851.12	Same	WN
Makes yearly contribution of GRA	PY Es 644.08	Same	WN or MN
Has GRA (for contribution)	PY Es 650.08	Same	WN or MN
Has GRA (for contribution)	PY Es 726.01	Same	WN or MN
Holds (commodity) *189	PY Qa 1303	Same	WN
Personnel series, allocated a MN?	PY An 435 + 1477 + 1060 + 1061 + 1465 + 1033 + 1516	same	WN

Title nominative	#	*Name*	*Sex*	*Sex identified*
---	1	ke-sa-da-ra *Kessandra* Κεσσάνδρα	F	Feminine name ending -a (masc form takes o(s))
---	1	ke-sa-da-ra *Kessandra* Κεσσάνδρα	F	Feminine name ending -a (masc form takes o(s))
---	1	ke-sa-da-ra *Kessandra* Κεσσάνδρα	F	Feminine name ending -a (masc form takes o(s))
---	1	ke-sa-da-ra *Kessandra* Κεσσάνδρα	F	Feminine name ending -a (masc form takes o(s))
---	1	ku-ri-na-ze-ja	F	Feminine name ending -eia
---	1	ma-ra-me-na[*Malamena*	F	Feminine name ending -eia and by analogy with rest of tab.
---	1	mi-jo-qa	F	Feminine name ending (genitive)
---	1	mi-jo-qa	F	Feminine name ending (genitive)
---	1	mi-jo-qa	F	Feminine name ending (genitive)
---	1	pi-ri-ta *Philista* Φιλίστα	F	Feminine ending
---	1	pi-ro-pa-ta-ra *Philopatra*	F	Feminine name ending -a (masc form takes o(s))
---	1	re-u-ka-ta-ra-ja *Leuktraia*?	F	Feminine name ending -aia?
---	1	]-ru-ke-ja	F	Feminine name ending -eia
---	1	te-do-ne-ja	F	Feminine name ending -eia
---	1	wi-ri-ke-ja	F	Feminine name ending -eia, dat?
---	1	wo-di-je-ja *Wordieia*	F	Feminine name Ending
---	1	wo-di-je-ja *Wordieia*	F	Feminine name ending -eia

Function	*Tablet*	*Tablet identifying sex*	*Designation type*
Holds 480 l. GRA, 480 l. NI (Figs)	PY Fg 368	Same	WN
Holds 480 l. GRA	PY Fg 828	Same	WN
Unknown	PY Mb 1380	Same	WN
Holds (commodity) *16	PY Mn 1368	Same	WN
Holds HORD and NI (figs)?	PY Fn 187.07	Same	WN
Among list of nom. WNs accompanied by MNs in genitive	PY Vn 1191+34+ 1006	Same	WN
Listed with MN - she's in genitive - as owner	PY An 1281.11	Same	WN
Has male slaves who hold HORD	PY Fn 50.12	Same	WN
Has a do-e-ro who holds HORD	PY Fn 867	Same	WN
In list of nominative WNs accompanied by MNs in genitive	PY Vn 1191+34+ 1006	Same	WN
In list of nominative WNs accompanied by MNs in genitive	PY Vn 1191.05	Same	WN
Uncertain	PY Vn 851.12	Same	WN
Uncertain	PY Vn 851.05	Same	WN
Uncertain	PY Vn 851.10	Same	WN
Uncertain	PY Vn 851.08	Same	WN
Has leather for sandals (pe-di-ra)	PY Ub 1318	Same (name also with MUL on KN Ap 639.03)	WN
In list of nominative WNs accompanied by MNs in genitive	PY Vn 1191+34+ 1006	KN Ap 639.03 and Same	WN

Title nominative	#	*Name*	*Sex*	*Sex identified*
a-*64-ja (@ Pylos) *Aswiai* ("women of Asia/Lydia"); ethnic adj.	35		F	MUL ideogram
a-*64-ja (@ Pylos) *Aswiai* ("women of Asia/Lydia"); ethnic adj.	35		F	MUL ideogram
a-*64-ja (@ Pylos) *Aswiai* ("women of Asia/Lydia"); ethnic adj.	x		F	Known from MUL ideogram on PY Aa 701, Ab 515
a-*64-ja ri-ne-ja (@ Leuktron) *Aswiai lineiai* ("Aswian women linen-workers")	x		F	Known from MUL ideogram on PY Aa 701, Ab 515
a-da-ra-te-ja	1		F	MUL ideogram
a-da-ra-te-ja	1		F	MUL ideogram
a-ke-ti-ra2 (@ Lousos) *asketriai* ("decorators") [ἀκέστρια]	32		F	MUL ideogram
a-ke-ti-ra2 (@ Pylos) *asketriai* ("decorators") [ἀκέστρια]	38		F	MUL ideogram
a-ke-ti-ra2 (@ Pylos) *asketriai* ("decorators") [ἀκέστρια]	0		F	MUL ideogram
a-ke-ti-ra2 (@ Pylos) *asketriai* ("decorators") [ἀκέστρια]	0		F	MUL ideogram
a-ke-ti-ra2 (@ Pylos) *asketriai* ("decorators") [ἀκέστρια]	0		F	Known from MUL ideogram on PY Aa 815, Ab 564
a-ke-ti-ra2 (@ Pylos) *asketriai* ("decorators") [ἀκέστρια]	0		F	Known from MUL ideogram on PY Aa 815, Ab 564
a-ke-ti-ra2 *asketriai* ("decorators") [ἀκέστρια]	12		F	MUL ideogram
a-ke-ti-ra2 *asketriai* ("decorators") [ἀκέστρια]	0		F	Known from MUL ideogram on PY Aa 815, Ab 564
a-pi-qo-ro *amphiqoloi* ("attendant-women") [ἀμφιπολοι Od. i. 331]	32		F	MUL ideogram
a-pi-qo-ro *amphiqoloi* ("attendant-women") [ἀμφιπολοι Od. i. 331]	0		F	Known from MUL ideogram on PY Aa 804

Function	*Tablet*	*Tablet identifying sex*	*Designation type*
Women's workgroup with accompanying children	PY Aa 701	Same	FemEthnic
Receives workgroup rations	PY Ab 515	Same	FemEthnic
Mothers of tallied men and boys	PY Ad 315	PY Aa 701, Ab 515	FemEthnic
Mothers of tallied men and boys	PY Ad 326	PY Aa 701, Ab 515	FemEthnic WomOcc
Women belonging to the Collector Adrastes	PY Ab 388	Same	WomOcc derived from MN
Women belonging to the collector Adrastes	PY Aa 785	Same	WN? FemAdj?
Women's workgroup with accompanying children	PY Aa 717	Same	WomOcc
Women's workgroup with accompanying children	PY Aa 815	Same	WomOcc
Receives workgroup rations	PY Ab 564	Same	WomOcc
Receives workgroup rations	PY Ab 1099	Same	WomOcc
Mothers of tallied men and boys	PY Ad 290	PY Aa 815, PY Ab 564	WomOcc
Mothers of tallied men and boys	PY Ad 666	PY Aa 0815, PY Ab 564	WomOcc
Women's workgroup with accompanying children	PY Aa 85	Same	WomOcc
Holds/Receives KA 1 unit (in list of offerings)	PY Un 219.04	PY Aa 815, PY Ab 564, etc.	WomOcc
Women's workgroup with accompanying children	PY Aa 804	Same	WomOcc
Mothers of tallied men and boys	PY Ad 690	PY Aa 804	WomOcc

Title nominative	#	*Name*	*Sex*	*Sex identified*
a-pi-qo-ro *amphiqoloi* ("attendant-women") [ἀμφιπολοι Od. i. 331]	0		F	Known from MUL ideogram on PY Aa 804
a-pu-ko-wo-ko *ampukworgoi* ("women headband makers")	8		F	MUL ideogram
a-pu-ko-wo-ko pa-ka-te-ja *ampukworgoi* ("women headband makers"); pa-ke-te-ja: obscure	0		F	Known from MUL ideogram on PY Ab 210
a-ra-ka-te-ja (@ Pylos) *alakateia*, ("spinning women") [ἠλακάτη "distaff" Od. iv. 135+]	0		F	Known from MUL ideogram on PY Aa 89, Aa 240
a-ra-ka-te-ja *alakateia*, ("spinning women") [ἠλακάτη "distaff" Od. iv. 135+]	37		F	MUL ideogram
a-ra-ka-te-ja *alakateia*, ("spinning women") [ἠλακάτη "distaff" Od. iv. 135+]	21		F	MUL ideogram
do-e-ra i-je-r-e-ja *doelai hijereias* ("female slaves of the priestess") [δούλη ἱέρειας]	14		F	Feminine Religious Title
do-e-ra i-je-re-ja pa-ki-ja-na ("slave of the priestess at pa-ki-ja-na") [δούλη ἱέρειας]	1	e-ra-ta-ra	F, sing	Feminine Religious Title
do-e-ra i-je-re-ja pa-ki-ja-na ("slave of the priestess at pa-ki-ja-na") [δούλη ἱέρειας]	1	e-ra-ta-ra	F, sing	Feminine Religious Title
e-ke-ro-qo-no (@ Pylos) *enkheroquoinon* ("wage-earners") [ἐγχειρόποινος]	0		F	MUL ideogram
e-ke-ro-qo-no (@ Pylos) *enkheroquoinon* ("wage-earners") [ἐγχειρόποινος]	0		F	MUL ideogram
e-ke-ro-qo-no (@ Pylos) *enkheroquoinon* ("wage-earners") [ἐγχειρόποινος]	0		F	Feminine genitive plural ending
e-ke-ro-qo-no (@ Pylos) *enkheroquoinon* ("wage-earners") [ἐγχειρόποινος]	0		[F]	[MUL ideogram]
e-ke-ro-qo-no o-pi-ro-qo *enkheroquoinon opiloquoi* "supernumerary wage-earners"	7		F	MUL ideogram
e-pi-jo-ta-na (PN) MUL ("women at PN: e-pi-jo-ta-na")	8		F	MUL ideogram
e-wi-ri-pi-ja Ewipiai ("women from Εὔριπος"); ethnic adj.	16		F	MUL ideogram
i-je-re-ja *hiereia* ("priestess") [ἱέρεια Il. vi 600+]	1	ka-wa-ra	F	Feminine Religious Title
i-je-re-ja *hiereia* ("priestess") [ἱέρεια Il. vi 600+]	14		F	Feminine Religious Title
i-je-re-ja *hiereia* ("priestess") [ἱέρεια Il. vi 600+]	1		F, sing	Feminine Religious Title

Function	*Tablet*	*Tablet identifying sex*	*Designation type*
Holds/Receives olive oil	PY Fr 1205	PY Aa 0804	WomOcc
Receives workgroup rations	PY Ab 210	Same	WomOcc
Mothers of tallied men and boys	PY Ad 671	PY Ab 210	WomOcc
Mothers of tallied men and boys	PY Ad 677	PY Aa 89, Aa 240	WomOcc
Women's workgroup with accompanying children	PY Aa 89	Same	WomOcc
Women's workgroup with accompanying children	PY Aa 240	Same	WomOcc
Holder of 14 female slaves "on account of the sacred gold"	PY Ae 303	Same	WomTitle
Holds an o-na-to ki-ti-me-na ko-to-na	PY En 609.16	Same	FemTitle WN
Holds an o-na-to ki-ti-me-na ko-to-na	PY. Eo 224.06	Same	FemTitle WN
Receives workgroup rations	PY Ab 563	Same	WomOcc
Receives workgroup rations	PY Ab 1100	Same	WomOcc
Mothers of tallied men and boys	PY Ad 691	Same	WomOcc
Women's workgroup with accompanying children	PY Aa 854	Same	WomOcc
Women's workgroup with accompanying children	PY Aa 777	Same	WomOcc
Women's workgroup with accompanying children	PY Aa 0095	Same	PN as WomOcc
Women's workgroup with accompanying children	PY Aa 0060	Same	FemEthnic
Holds (commodity) *189	PY Qa 1289	Same	WomOcc WN
Holds slaves "on account of the sacred gold"	PY Ae 0303	Same	WomTitle
Grants an o-na-to as a ke-ra (gift) to te-o-jo do-e-ra u-wa-mi-ja	PY Eb 0416	Same	FemTitle

Title nominative	#	*Name*	*Sex*	*Sex identified*
i-je-re-ja *hiereia* ("priestess") [ἱέρεια Il. vi 600+]	1		F, sing	Feminine Religious Title
i-je-re-ja *hiereia* ("priestess") [ἱέρεια Il. vi 600+]	1?		F	Feminine Religious Title
i-je-re-ja *hiereia* ("priestess") [ἱέρεια Il. vi 600+]	1?		F	Feminine Religious Title
i-je-re-ja hiereias ("priestess") [ἱέρεια Il. vi 600+]	1	e-ri-ta *Eritha*	F, sing	Feminine Religious Title
i-je-re-ja *hiereias* ("priestess") [ἱέρεια Il. vi 600+]	1	e-ri-ta *Eritha*	F, sing	Feminine Religious Title
i-je-re-ja *hiereias* ("priestess") [ἱέρεια Il. vi 600+]	1	(e-ri-ta?) (*Eritha*?)	F, sing?	Feminine Religious Title
i-je-re-ja ko-to-no-o-o-de *hiereia ktoino(h) okhos* ("priestess ktoina-holder") [ἱέρεια Il. vi 600+]	1	[e-ri-ta] [*Eritha*] named on composite tablet PY Ep 704.05	F, sing	Feminine Religious Title
i-je-re-ja pa-ki-ja-na *hiereia* ("priestess @ pa-ki-ja-na") [ἱέρεια Il. vi 600+]	1		F	Feminine Religious Title
i-je-re-ja pa-ki-ja-na *hiereia* ("priestess @ pa-ki-ja-na") [ἱέρεια Il. vi 600+]			F, sing	Feminine Religious Title
i-je-re-ja pa-ki-ja-na hiereia ("priestess @ pa-ki-ja-na") [ἱέρεια Il. vi 600+]	1		F, sing	Feminine Religious Title
i-je-re-ja pa-ki-ja-na *hiereia* ("priestess @ pa-ki-ja-na") [ἱέρεια Il. vi 600+]	1	(e-ri-ta) (Eritha)	F, sing	Feminine Religious Title
i-je-re-ja pa-ki-ja-na *hiereia* ("priestess @ pa-ki-ja-na") [ἱέρεια Il. vi 600+]	1	(e-ri-ta) (Eritha)	F, sing	Feminine Religious Title
i-je-re-ja pa-ki-ja-na *hiereia* ("priestess @ pa-ki-ja-na") [ἱέρεια Il. vi 600+]	1	[e-ri-ta] [Eritha] named on composite tablet PY Ep 704.03	F, sing	Feminine Religious Title
ka-pa-ra2 description of women cloth-worker(s), ethnic or descriptive term - exact sense uncertain	24		F	MUL ideogram
ka-pa-ra2-de description of women cloth-worker(s), ethnic or descriptive term - exact sense uncertain	24		F	MUL ideogram
ka-ra-wi-po-ro *klawiphoros* ("keybearer") [Dor. Κλακοφόρος, cf. Att. κλειδοῦχος]	0		F	Accompanying feminine name: PY Ae 110, Eb 338, etc.

Function	*Tablet*	*Tablet identifying sex*	*Designation type*
Grants an o-na-to as a ke-ra (gift) to te-o-jo do-e-ra u-wa-mi-ja	PY Ep 0704.02	Same	FemTitle
Holds/Receives *189	PY Qa 1300	Same	FemTitle
Holds/Receives TE-cloth	PY Un 6 v1	Same	FemTitle
Claims to hold an e-to-ni-jo, disputed by damos	PY Ep 704.05	Same	FemTitle WN
Holds an o-na-to ke-ke-me-na ko-to-na	PY Ep 704.03	Same	FemTitle WN
Holds o-na-ta with 4 officials	PY Ed 317	Same	FemTitle
Claims to hold an e-to-ni-jo, disputed by damos	PY Eb 297	Same and PY Ep 704.05	FemTitle
Holds a male slave who has an o-na-to ke-ke-me-na ko-to-na from da-mo	PY Eb 1176	Same	FemTitle
Has a slave woman who holds an o-na-to ki-ti-me-na ko-to-na	PY En 609.16	Same	FemTitle
Holds a female slave who holds an o-na-to ki-ti-me-na ko-to-na	PY Eo 224.06	Same	FemTitle
Holds an o-na-to ki-ti-me-na ko-to-na	PY En 609.18	Same	FemTitle
Holds an o-na-to ki-ti-me-na ko-to-na	PY Eo 224.08	Same	FemTitle
Holds an o-na-to ke-ke-me-na ko-to-na from damos	PY Eb 339 + 409	Same	FemTitle
Appears in list of women and boys	PY An 292.02	PY Aa 788	WomOcc
Women's workgroup with accompanying children	PY Aa 788	Same	WomOcc
Too fragmentary to recover	PY Vn 48.07	PY Ae 110, PY Eb 338, PY Ep 904.07	FemTitle

Title nominative	*#*	*Name*	*Sex*	*Sex identified*
ka-ra-wi-po-ro *klawiphoros* ("keybearer") [Dor. Κλακοφόρος, cf. Att. κλειδοῦχος]	0		F	Accompanying feminine name: PY Ae 110, Eb 338, etc.
ka-ra-wi-po-ro *klawiphoros* ("keybearer") [Dor. κλακοφόρος, cf. Att. κλειδοῦχος]	1	ka-pa-ti-ja *Karpathia*	F	Accompanying feminine name: PY Ae 110, Eb 0338, etc.
ka-ra-wi-po-ro *klawiphoros* ("keybearer") [Dor. κλακοφόρος, cf. Att. κλειδοῦχος]	1	ka-pa-ti-ja *Karpathia*	F, sing	Feminine name ending
ka-ra-wi-po-ro *klawiphoros* ("keybearer") [Dor. κλακοφόρος, cf. Att. κλειδοῦχος]	1	ka-pa-ti-ja *Karpathia*	F, sing	Feminine name ending
ka-ra-wi-po-ro *klawiphoros* ("keybearer") [Dor. κλακοφόρος, cf. Att. κλειδοῦχος]	1	ka-pa-ti-ja? *Karphathia*?	F	Known from WN ending: PY Ae 110, Eb 338, etc.
ka-ra-wi-po-ro *klawiphoros* ("keybearer") [Dor. κλακοφόρος, cf. Att. κλειδοῦχος]	1	(ka-pa-ti-ja)? if sing; *Karpathia*	F, sing or pl	Known from WN ending: PY Ae 110, Eb 338, etc.
[ka-ra-wi-po-ro *klawiphoros* ("keybearer") [Dor. κλακοφόρος, cf. Att. κλειδοῦχος]	1	ka-pa-ti-ja *Karpathia*	F, sing	Feminine name ending
[ka-ra-wi-po-ro *klawiphoros* ("keybearer") [Dor. κλακοφόρος, cf. Att. κλειδοῦχος]		ka-pa-ti-ja *Karpathia*	F	Feminine name ending
ka-ru-ti-je-ja @ PN: Pylos Women belonging to the collector Karustios	0		F	Feminine Title ending - eia
ki-ma-ra description of women, possibly ethnic	3		F	MUL ideogram
ki-ma-ra @ Leuktron description of women, possibly ethnic	0		F	Known from MUL ideogram on PY Aa 63
ki-ni-di-ja @ Pylos *Knidiai* ("women from Κνίδος)"; ethnic adj.Κνίδος	20		F	MUL ideogram
ki-ni-di-ja @ Pylos *Knidiai* ("women from Κνίδος"); ethnic adj.	0		F	Known from MUL ideogram PY Aa 792, Ab 189, etc.
ki-ni-di-ja @ Pylos *Knidiai* ("women from Κνίδος"); ethnic adj.	21		F	MUL ideogram
ki-ni-di-ja @ Pylos *Knidiai* ("women from Κνίδος"); ethnic adj.	21		F	MUL ideogram
ki-ri-te-wi-ja a class of women with a religious function	0		F	Known from MUL ideogram on PY An 607

Function	*Tablet*	*Tablet identifying sex*	*Designation type*
Provides (with other officials - all male) temple bronze for smiths	PY Jn 829	PY Ae 110, PY Eb 338, PY Ep 904.07	WomTitle
Holds/Receives TE-cloth	PY Un 6 v2	PY Ae 110, PY Eb 338, PY Ep 904.07	FemTitle
Holds two ke-ke-me-na ko-to-no	PY EB 338	Same	FemTitle WN
Holds ke-ke-me-no land	PY Ep 704.07	Same	FemTitle WN
Holder of a slave at Pylos	PY Ae 0110	PY Ae 110, PY Eb 338, PY Ep 904.07	WomTitle
Holds o-na-ta with 4 other officials	PY Ed 317	PY Ae 110, PY Eb 338, PY Ep 904.07	FemTitle
Has a do-e-ro who holds an o-na-to ke-ke-me-na ko-to-na	PY Ep 539.09	Same	FemTitle WN
Gives HORD 2	PY Un 443 + 998	Same	WN
Mothers of tallied men and boys	PY Ad 671	Same	WomOcc
Women's workgroup with accompanying children	PY Aa 63	Same	WomOcc
Mothers of tallied men and boys	PY Ad 668	PY Aa 63	WomOcc
Receives workgroup rations	PY Ab 189	Same	FemEthnic
Mothers of tallied men and boys	PY Ad 683	PY Aa 792, PY Ab 189, PY An 292.04	FemEthnic
Women's workgroup with accompanying children	PY Aa 792	Same	FemEthnic
List of women and boys	PY An 292.04	Same	FemEthnic
Holds an o-na-to ke-ke-me-na ko-to-na from da-mo (182.4 l. wheat)	PY Eb 0321 + 0327 + 1153	PY An 0607	FemTitle

Title nominative	#	*Name*	*Sex*	*Sex identified*
ki-ri-te-wi-ja a class of women with a religious function	0		F	Known from MUL ideogram on PY An 607
ki-ri-te-wi-ja do-qe-ja @ me-ta-pa; a class of women with a religious function, do-qe-ja obscure	0		F	MUL ideogram
(ki-ri-te-wi-ja) MUL a class of women with a religious function	6		F	MUL ideogram
(ki-ri-te-wi-ja) MUL a class of women with a religious function	13		F	MUL ideogram
(ki-ri-te-wi-ja) MUL a class of women with a religious function	3		F	MUL ideogram
(ki-ri-te-wi-ja) MUL a class of women with a religious function	1		F	MUL ideogram
(ki-ri-te-wi-ja) MUL a class of women with a religious function	1		F	MUL ideogram
ki-si-wi-ja "Chian (?) women" ethnic adj, (possibly derived from PN: Χῖος]	6		F	MUL ideogram
ki-si-wi-ja o-nu-ke-ja @ PN: Pylos: "Chian women o-nu-ka makers @ Pylos"	7		F	MUL ideogram
ki-si-wi-ja o-nu-ke-ja @ PN: Pylos: "Chian women o-nu-ka makers @ Pylos"	0		F	Known from MUL ideogram on PY Aa 770
ko-ro-ki-ja ethnic adj, describing women	8		F	MUL ideogram
ko-ro-ki-ja ethnic adj, describing women	8		F	MUL ideogram
ko-ro-ki-ja @ Pylos ethnic adj, describing women	9		F	MUL ideogram
ko-ro-ki-ja @ Pylos ethnic adj, describing women	0		F	Known from MUL ideogram on PY Aa 354
ko-wa (part of a-*64-ja workgroup) *korwa* ("girls") [κούρη Il.]	35		F	Feminine Family Title
ko-wa (part of a-*64-ja workgroup) *korwa* ("girls") [κούρη Il.]	11		F	Feminine Family Title
ko-wa (part of a-ke-ti-ra2 workgroup) *korwa* ("girls") [κούρη Il.]	16		F	Feminine Family Title
ko-wa (part of a-ke-ti-ra2 workgroup) *korwa* ("girls") [κούρη Il.]	18		F	Feminine Family Title
ko-wa (part of a-ke-ti-ra2 workgroup) *korwa* ("girls") [κούρη Il.]	33		F	Feminine Family Title
ko-wa (part of a-pi-qo-ro workgroup) *korwa* ("girls") [κούρη Il.]	26		F	Feminine Family Title

Function	*Tablet*	*Tablet identifying sex*	*Designation type*
Too fragmentary to recover	PY Un 1426 + 1428	PY An 607	FemTitle
Listed among women at me-ta-pa	PY An 607.01	Same	FemTitle
Tally of ki-ri-te-wi-ja women and their parentage	PY An 607.2-3	Same	FemTitle
Tally of ki-ri-te-wi-ja women and their parentage	PY An 607.4	Same	FemTitle
Tally of ki-ri-te-wi-ja women and their parentage	PY An 607.5-6	Same	FemTitle
Tally of ki-ri-te-wi-ja women and their parentage	PY An 607.6-7	Same	FemTitle
Tally of ki-ri-te-wi-ja women and their parentage	PY An 607.7-8	Same	FemTitle
Women's workgroup with accompanying children	PY Aa 770	Same	FemEthnic
Receives workgroup rations	PY Ab 194	Same	FemEthnic WomOcc
Mothers of tallied men and boys	PY Ad 675	Same	FemEthnic WomOcc
Women's workgroup with accompanying children	PY Aa 354	Same	FemEthnic
List of women and boys	PY An 292.3	Same	FemEthnic
Receives workgroup rations	PY Ab 372	Same	FemEthnic
Mothers of tallied men and boys	PY Ad 680	PY Aa 354	FemEthnic
Receives workgroup rations	PY Ab 515	Same	FamTitle
Children accompanying women's workgroup	PY Aa 701	Same	FamTitle
Children accompanying women's workgroup	PY Aa 85	Same	FamTitle
Children accompanying women's workgroup	PY Aa 717	Same	FamTitle
Children accompanying women's workgroup	PY Aa 815	Same	FamTitle
Children accompanying women's workgroup	PY Aa 804	Same	FamTitle

Title nominative	#	*Name*	*Sex*	*Sex identified*
ko-wa (part of a-pu-ko-wo-ko workgroup) *korwa* ("girls") [κούρη Il.]	8		F	Feminine Family Title
ko-wa (part of a-ra-ka-te-ja workgroup) *korwa* ("girls") [κούρη Il.]	26		F	Feminine Family Title
ko-wa (part of a-ra-ka-te-ja workgroup) *korwa* ("girls") [κούρη Il.]	25		F	Feminine Family Title
ko-wa (part of e-ke-ro-qo-no o-pi-ro-qo e-wi-ri-pi-ja workgroup) *korwa* ("girls") [κούρη Il.]	11		F	Feminine Family Title
ko-wa (part of e-ke-ro-qo-no o-pi-ro-qo workgroup) *korwa* ("girls") [κούρη Il.]	3		F	Feminine Family Title
ko-wa (part of ka-pa-ra workgroup) *korwa* ("girls") [κούρη Il.]	8		F	Feminine Family Title
ko-wa (part of ki-ma-ra workgroup) *korwa* ("girls") [κούρη Il.]	5		F	Feminine Family Title
ko-wa (part of ki-ni-di-ja workgroup) *korwa* ("girls") [κούρη Il.]	12		F	Feminine Family Title
ko-wa (part of ki-ni-di-ja workgroup) *korwa* ("girls") [κούρη Il.]	20		F	Feminine Family Title
ko-wa (part of ki-si-wi-ja workgroup) *korwa* ("girls") [κούρη Il.]	4		F	Feminine Family Title
ko-wa (part of ki-si-wi-ja o-nu-ke-ja workgroup) *korwa* ("girls") [κούρη Il.]	7		F	Feminine Family Title
ko-wa (part of ko-ro-ki-ja workgroup) *korwa* ("girls") [κούρη Il.]	4		F	Feminine Family Title
ko-wa (part of ko-ro-ki-ja workgroup) *korwa* ("girls") [κούρη Il.]	9		F	Feminine Family Title
ko-wa (part of ku-te-ra3 workgroup) *korwa* ("girls")[κούρη Il.]	0		F	Feminine Family Title
ko-wa (part of lacunose workgroup) *korwa* ("girls") [κούρη Il.]	2		F	Feminine Family Title
ko-wa (part of lacunose workgroup) *korwa* ("girls") [κούρη Il.]	0		F	Feminine Family Title
ko-wa (part of lacunose workgroup) *korwa* ("girls") [κούρη Il.]	0		F	Feminine Family Title
ko-wa (part of lacunose workgroup) *korwa* ("girls") [κούρη Il.]	0		F	Feminine Family Title
ko-wa (part of me-re-ti-ra2 workgroup) *korwa* ("girls") [κούρη Il.]	10		F	Feminine Family Title
ko-wa (part of me-re-ti-ra2 workgroup) *korwa* ("girls") [κούρη Il.]	8		F	Feminine Family Title
ko-wa (part of me-re-ti-ra2 workgroup) *korwa* ("girls") [κούρη Il.]	6		F	Feminine Family Title

Function	*Tablet*	*Tablet identifying sex*	*Designation type*
Receives workgroup rations	PY Ab 210	Same	FamTitle
Children accompanying women's workgroup	PY Aa 89	Same	FamTitle
Children accompanying women's workgroup	PY Aa 240	Same	FamTitle
Children accompanying women's workgroup	PY Aa 60	Same	FamTitle
Children accompanying women's workgroup	PY Aa 777	Same	FamTitle
Children accompanying women's workgroup	PY Aa 788	Same	FamTitle
Children accompanying women's workgroup	PY Aa 63	Same	FamTitle
Children accompanying women's workgroup	PY Aa 792	Same	FamTitle
Receives workgroup rations	PY Ab 189	Same	FamTitle
Children accompanying women's workgroup	PY Aa 770	Same	FamTitle
Receives workgroup rations	PY Ab 194	Same	FamTitle
Children accompanying women's workgroup	PY Aa 354	Same	FamTitle
Receives workgroup rations	PY Ab 372	Same	FamTitle
Children accompanying women's workgroup	PY Aa 506	Same	FamTitle
Children accompanying women's workgroup	PY Aa 759	Same	FamTitle
Receives workgroup rations	PY Ab 946	Same	FamTitle
Receives workgroup rations	PY Ab 1102	Same	FamTitle
Receives workgroup rations	PY Ab 1112	Same	FamTitle
Children accompanying women's workgroup	PY Aa 62	Same	FamTitle
Children accompanying women's workgroup	PY Aa 764	Same	FamTitle
Receives workgroup rations	PY Ab 789	Same	FamTitle

Title nominative	*#*	*Name*	*Sex*	*Sex identified*
ko-wa (part of mi-ra-ti-ja workgroup) *korwa* ("girls") [κούρη Il.]	35		F	Feminine Family Title
ko-wa (part of mi-ra-ti-ja workgroup) *korwa* ("girls") [κούρη Il.]	54		F	Feminine Family Title
ko-wa (part of mi-ra-ti-ja workgroup) *korwa* ("girls") [κούρη Il.]	16		F	Feminine Family Title
ko-wa (part of ne-we-wi-ja workgroup) *korwa* ("girls") [κούρη Il.]	10		F	Feminine Family Title
ko-wa (part of no-ri-wo-ko workgroup) *korwa* ("girls") [κούρη Il.]	10		F	Feminine Family Title
ko-wa (part of o-pi-ro-qo workgroup) *korwa* ("girls") [κούρη Il.]	8		F	Feminine Family Title
ko-wa (part of o-ti-ra2 workgroup) *korwa* ("girls") [κούρη Il.]	12		F	Feminine Family Title
ko-wa (part of o-ti-ra2 workgroup) *korwa* ("girls") [κούρη Il.]	21		F	Feminine Family Title
ko-wa (part of pa-ke-te-ja ri-ne-ja workgroup) *korwa* ("girls") [κούρη Il.]	2		F	Feminine Family Title
ko-wa (part of pa-ke-te-ja workgroup) *korwa* ("girls")[κούρη Il.]	5		F	Feminine Family Title
ko-wa (part of pa-wo-ke workgroup) *korwa* ("girls") [κούρη Il.]	2		F	Feminine Family Title
ko-wa (part of pa-wo-ke workgroup) *korwa* ("girls") [κούρη Il.]	4		F	Feminine Family Title
ko-wa (part of pe-ki-ti-ra2 workgroup) *korwa* ("girls") [κούρη Il.]	7		F	Feminine Family Title
ko-wa (part of ra-mi-ni-ja workgroup) *korwa* ("girls") [κούρη Il.]	7		F	Feminine Family Title
ko-wa (part of ra-pi-ti-ra2 workgroup) *korwa* ("girls") [κούρη Il.]	38		F	Feminine Family Title
ko-wa (part of ra-qi-ti-ra2 workgroup) *korwa* ("girls")[κούρη Il.]	6		F	Feminine Family Title
ko-wa (part of ra-wi-ja-ja workgroup) *korwa* ("girls") [κούρη Il.]	7		F	Feminine Family Title
ko-wa (part of ra-wi-ja-ja workgroup) *korwa* ("girls") [κούρη Il.]	28		F	Feminine Family Title
ko-wa (part of re-wo-to-ro-ko-wo workgroup) *korwa* ("girls") [κούρη Il.]	13		F	Feminine Family Title
ko-wa (part of re-wo-to-ro-ko-wo workgroup) *korwa* ("girls") [κούρη Il.]	37		F	Feminine Family Title
ko-wa (part of ri-ne-ja workgroup) *korwa* ("girls") [κούρη Il.]	4		F	Feminine Family Title

Function	*Tablet*	*Tablet identifying sex*	*Designation type*
Children accompanying women's workgroup	PY Aa 798	Same	FamTitle
Receives workgroup rations	PY Ab 382	Same	FamTitle
Receives workgroup rations	PY Ab 573	Same	FamTitle
Children accompanying women's workgroup	PY Aa 695	Same	FamTitle
Children accompanying women's workgroup	PY Aa 98	Same	FamTitle
Receives workgroup rations	PY Ab 899	Same	FamTitle
Children accompanying women's workgroup	PY Aa 313	Same	FamTitle
Receives workgroup rations	PY Ab 417 + 1050	Same	FamTitle
Receives workgroup rations	PY Ab 746	Same	FamTitle
Children accompanying women's workgroup	PY Aa 662	Same	FamTitle
Children accompanying women's workgroup	PY Aa 795	Same	FamTitle
Receives workgroup rations	PY Ab 558	Same	FamTitle
Receives workgroup rations	PY Ab 578	Same	FamTitle
Receives workgroup rations	PY Ab 186	Same	FamTitle
Receives workgroup rations	PY Ab 555	Same	FamTitle
Receives workgroup rations	PY Ab 356 + 1049	Same	FamTitle
Children accompanying women's workgroup	PY Aa 807	Same	FamTitle
Receives workgroup rations	PY Ab 586	Same	FamTitle
Children accompanying women's workgroup	PY Aa 783	Same	FamTitle
Receives workgroup rations	PY Ab 553	Same	FamTitle
Children accompanying women's workgroup	PY Aa 76	Same	FamTitle

Title nominative	*#*	*Name*	*Sex*	*Sex identified*
ko-wa (part of ri-ne-ja workgroup) *korwa* ("girls") [κοὐρη Il.]	9		F	Feminine Family Title
ko-wa (part of ri-ne-ja workgroup) *korwa* ("girls") [κοὐρη Il.]	5		F	Feminine Family Title
ko-wa (part of ri-ne-ja workgroup) *korwa* ("girls") [κοὐρη Il.]	8		F	Feminine Family Title
ko-wa (part of ti-nwa-si-ja workgroup) *korwa* ("girls") [κοὐρη Il.]	4		F	Feminine Family Title
ko-wa (part of ti-nwa-si-ja workgroup) *korwa* ("girls") [κοὐρη Il.]	9		F	Feminine Family Title
ko-wa (part of to-sa-me-ja workgroup) *korwa* ("girls") [κοὐρη Il.]	2		F	Feminine Family Title
ko-wa (part of to-sa-me-ja workgroup) *korwa* ("girls") [κοὐρη Il.]	8		F	Feminine Family Title
ko-wa (part of we-we-si-je-ja workgroup) *korwa* ("girls") [κοὐρη Il.]	6		F	Feminine Family Title
ko-wa (part of we-we-si-je-ja workgroup) *korwa* ("girls") [κοὐρη Il.]	16		F	Feminine Family Title
ko-wa (part of workgroup at PN: da-mi-ni-ja) *korwa* ("girls") [κοὐρη Il.]	13		F	Feminine Family Title
ko-wa (part of workgroup at PN: e-pi-jo-ta-na) *korwa* ("girls") [κοὐρη Il.]	8		F	Feminine Family Title
ko-wa (part of workgroup at PN: me-ta-pa) *korwa* ("girls") [κοὐρη Il.]	3		F	Feminine Family Title
ko-wa (part of workgroup at PN: ne-wo-pe-o) *korwa* ("girls") [κοὐρη Il.]	3		F	Feminine Family Title
ko-wa (part of workgroup at PN: ne-wo-pe-o) *korwa* ("girls") [κοὐρη Il.]	7		F	Feminine Family Title
ko-wa (part of workgroup at PN: ze-pu2-ra3) *korwa* ("girls") [κοὐρη Il.]	15		F	Feminine Family Title
ku-te-ra3 @ Pylos *Kytherai* ("women of Κύθερα"); ethnic adj.	0		F	MUL ideogram
ku-te-ra3 @ Pylos *Kytherai* ("women of Κύθερα"); ethnic adj.	0		F	Known from MUL ideogram on PY Aa 506
ku-te-ra3 @ Pylos *Kytherai* ("women of Κύθερα"); ethnic adj.	28		F	MUL ideogram
ku-te-ra3 ka-pa-ra2 @ Pylos *Kytherai* ("Kytheran textile- workers")	0		F	Known from MUL ideogram on PY Aa 788
ma-te mater ("mother") [μήτηρ]	1		F	Feminine Family Title
ma-te mater ("mother") [μήτηρ]	1		F	Feminine Family Title

Function	*Tablet*	*Tablet identifying sex*	*Designation type*
Children accompanying women's workgroup	PY Aa 93	Same	FamTitle
Children accompanying women's workgroup	PY Aa 94	Same	FamTitle
Receives workgroup rations	PY Ab 379	Same	FamTitle
Children accompanying women's workgroup	PY Aa 699	Same	FamTitle
Receives workgroup rations	PY Ab 190	Same	FamTitle
Children accompanying women's workgroup	PY Aa 775 + 956	Same	FamTitle
Receives workgroup rations	PY Ab 277	Same	FamTitle
Children accompanying women's workgroup	PY Aa 762	Same	FamTitle
Receives workgroup rations	PY Ab 217	Same	FamTitle
Children accompanying women's workgroup	PY Aa 96	Same	FamTitle
Children accompanying women's workgroup	PY Aa 95	Same	FamTitle
Children accompanying women's workgroup	PY Aa 752	Same	FamTitle
Children accompanying women's workgroup	PY Aa 786	Same	FamTitle
Receives workgroup rations	PY Ab 554	Same	FamTitle
Children accompanying women's workgroup	PY Aa 61	Same	FamTitle
Receives workgroup rations	PY Ab 562	Same	FemEthnic
Receives workgroup rations	PY Ad 390	PY Aa 506	FemEthnic
Women's workgroup with accompanying children	PY Aa 506	Same	FemEthnic
Mothers of tallied men and boys	PY Ad 679	PY Aa 788	WomOcc FemEthnic
Mother of 6 ki-ri-te-wi-ja women	PY An 607.02	Same	FamTitle
Mother of 3 ki-ri-te-wi-ja women (she's also a slave of Diwia)	PY An 607.5	Same	FamTitle

Title nominative	#	*Name*	*Sex*	*Sex identified*
ma-te mater ("mother") [μήτηρ]	1		F	Feminine Family Title
ma-te mater ("mother") [μήτηρ]	1		F	Feminine Family Title
me-ki-to-ki-ri-ta	1		F	MUL ideogram
me-ki-to-ki-ri-ta?	1	]	F	MUL ideogram
me-re-ti-ra2 @ Pylos *meletriai* ("women corn-grinders")	6		F	MUL ideogram
me-re-ti-ra2 *meletriai* ("women corn-grinders")	7		F	MUL ideogram
me-re-ti-ra2 *meletriai* ("women corn-grinders")	6		F	MUL ideogram
me-re-ti-ri-ja @ Leuktron *meletriai* ("women corn-grinders")	0		F	Known from MUL ideogram PY Ab 789, etc.
me-ta-pa (PN) MUL "women at PN: me-ta-pa"	7		F	MUL ideogram
me-ta-pa (PN) MUL "women at PN: me-ta-pa"	3		F	MUL ideogram
me-ta-pa (PN) MUL "women at PN: me-ta-pa"	5		F	MUL ideogram
mi-ra-ti-ja @ Lousos *Milatiai* ("women of PN: Miletus"); ethnic adj.	54		F	MUL ideogram
mi-ra-ti-ja @ Lousos *Milatiai* ("women of PN: Miletus"); ethnic adj.	54		F	MUL ideogram
mi-ra-ti-ja @ Pylos *Milatiai* ("women of PN: Miletus"); ethnic adj.	16		F	MUL ideogram
mi-ra-ti-ja @ Pylos *Milatiai* ("women of PN: Miletus"); ethnic adj.	0		F	Known from MUL ideogram on PY Ab 573, etc.
mi-ra-ti-ja a-ra-te-ja @ Pylos *Milatiai alakateiai* ("Milatian spinning women")	0		F	Known from MUL ideogram on PY Ab 573, etc.
MUL (lacunose occupational title)	0		F	MUL ideogram
MUL (undesignated) @ PN: pe-ra3-ko-ra-i-ja (Further Province) *Peraigolaia*	0		F	MUL ideogram
MUL (unmodified) unspecified woman given to Potnia	1		F	MUL ideogram

Function	*Tablet*	*Tablet identifying sex*	*Designation type*
Mother of 1 ki-ri-te-wi-ja woman (she's also a slave)	PY An 607.5-6	Same	FamTitle
Mother of 3 ki-ri-te-wi-ja women (she's also a slave)	PY An 607.6-7	Same	FamTitle
Woman belonging to the collector *Megistokritas*	PY Aa 955	Same	WN
Woman belonging to the collector *Megistokritas*	PY Ab 575	Same	WN? WomOcc?
Receives workgroup rations	PY Ab 789	Same	WomOcc
Women's workgroup with accompanying children	PY Aa 62	Same	WomOcc
Women's workgroup with accompanying children	PY Aa 764	Same	WomOcc
Mothers of tallied men and boys	PY Ad 308	PY Ab 789, etc.	WomOcc
Women's workgroup with accompanying children	PY Aa 752	Same	PN used as WomOcc
Women's workgroup with accompanying children	PY Aa 779	Same	PN used as WomOcc
Receives workgroup rations	PY Ab 355	Same	PN used as WomOcc
Women's workgroup with accompanying children	PY Aa 798	Same	FemEthnic
Receives workgroup rations	PY Ab 382	Same	FemEthnic
Receives workgroup rations	PY Ab 573	Same	FemEthnic
Mothers of tallied men and boys	PY Ad 689	PY Ab 573, etc.	FemEthnic
Mothers of tallied men and boys	PY Ad 380	PY Ab 573, etc.	FemEthnic WomOcc
Sealing - too fragmentary to identify	PY Wa 1008	Same	MUL alone
Basket Label - monthly rations for Further Province women	PY Wa 114	Same	[WomOcc]
Given to Potnia @ Pylos along with Gold vessel	PY Tn 316 r3	Same	MUL alone

Title nominative	#	*Name*	*Sex*	*Sex identified*
MUL (unmodified) unspecified woman given to ma-na-sa	1		F	MUL ideogram
MUL (unmodified) unspecified woman given to po-si-da-e-ja	1		F	MUL ideogram
MUL (unmodified) unspecified woman given to shrine of di-u-ja	1		F	MUL ideogram
MUL (unmodified) unspecified woman given to shrine of Hera	1		F	MUL ideogram
MUL (unmodified) unspecified woman given to shrine of pe-re-*82	1		F	MUL ideogram
MUL (unmodified) unspecified woman given to shrine@ Pylos	2		F	MUL ideogram
[MUL] (lacunose occupational title)	0		[F]	[MUL restored from rest of PY Aa series]
[MUL] (lacunose occupational title)	0		[F]	[MUL restored from rest of PY Aa series]
[MUL] (lacunose occupational title)	0		[F]	[MUL restored from rest of PY Aa series]
[MUL] (lacunose occupational title)	0		[F]	[MUL restored from rest of PY Aa series]
[MUL] (lacunose occupational title)	3		F	MUL ideogram
[MUL] (lacunose occupational title)	0		F	[MUL ideogram]
[MUL] (lacunose occupational title)	0		F	[MUL ideogram]
[MUL] (lacunose occupational title)	0		F	[MUL ideogram]
[MUL] (lacunose occupational title)	0		F	[MUL ideogram]
[MUL] (lacunose occupational title)	0		F	[MUL ideogram]
[MUL] (lacunose occupational title)	0		F	[MUL ideogram]

Function	*Tablet*	*Tablet identifying sex*	*Designation type*
Given to ma-na-sa along with Gold vessel	PY Tn 316 r4	Same	MUL alone
Given to po-si-da-e-ja along with Gold vessel	PY Tn 316 r4	Same	MUL alone
Given to shrine of di-u-ja along with Gold vessel	PY Tn 316 v6	Same	MUL alone
Given to shrine of Hera along with Gold vessel	PY Tn 316 v9	Same	MUL alone
Given to shrine of pe-re-*82 along with Gold vessel	PY Tn 316 v5	Same	MUL alone
Given to shrine at Pylos along with Gold vessel	PY Tn 0316 v3	Same	MUL alone
Women's workgroup with accompanying children	PY Aa 759	(Same - by analogy with rest of PY Aa series)	[WomOcc]
Women's workgroup with accompanying children	PY Aa 860	(Same - by analogy with rest of PY Aa series)	[WomOcc]
Women's workgroup with accompanying children	PY Aa 863	(Same - by analogy with rest of PY Aa series)	[WomOcc]
Women's workgroup with accompanying children	PY Aa 987	(Same - by analogy with rest of PY Aa series)	[WomOcc]
Women's workgroup with accompanying children	PY Aa 1178	Same	[WomOcc]
Receives workgroup rations	PY Ab 468	(Same - by analogy with rest of PY Aa series)	[WomOcc]
Receives workgroup rations	PY Ab 559	(Same - by analogy with rest of PY Aa series)	[WomOcc]
Receives workgroup rations	PY Ab 580	(Same - by analogy with rest of PY Aa series)	[WomOcc]
Receives workgroup rations	PY Ab 581	(Same - by analogy with rest of PY Ab series)	[WomOcc]
Receives workgroup rations	PY Ab 582	(Same - by analogy with rest of PY Ab series)	[WomOcc]
Receives workgroup rations	PY Ab 584	(Same - by analogy with rest of PY Ab series)	[WomOcc]

Title nominative	#	*Name*	*Sex*	*Sex identified*
[MUL] (lacunose occupational title)	0		F	[MUL ideogram]
[MUL] (lacunose occupational title)	0		F	[MUL ideogram]
[MUL] (lacunose occupational title)	41		F	[MUL ideogram]
[MUL] (lacunose occupational title)	0		F	[MUL ideogram]
[MUL] (lacunose occupational title)	0		F	[MUL ideogram]
[MUL] (lacunose occupational title)	0		F	[MUL ideogram]
[MUL] (lacunose occupational title)	0		F	[MUL ideogram]
[MUL] (lacunose occupational title)	71		F	[MUL ideogram]
[MUL] (lacunose occupational title)	0		F	[MUL ideogram]
[MUL] (lacunose occupational title)	0		[F]	[By analogy with rest of PY Ad series]
[MUL] (lacunose occupational title)	0		[F]	[By analogy with rest of PY Ad series]
[MUL] (lacunose occupational title)	0		[F]	[By analogy with rest of PY Ad series]
[MUL] (lacunose occupational title)	0		[F]	[By analogy with rest of PY Ad series]
[MUL] (lacunose occupational title)	7		F	MUL ideogram
ne-we-wi-ja adj, describing women textile-workers	21		F	MUL ideogram

Function	*Tablet*	*Tablet identifying sex*	*Designation type*
Receives workgroup rations	PY Ab 585	(Same - by analogy with rest of PY Ab series)	[WomOcc]
Receives workgroup rations	PY Ab 946	(Same - by analogy with rest of PY Ab series)	[WomOcc]
Receives workgroup rations	PY Ab 978	(Same - by analogy with rest of PY Ab series)	[WomOcc]
Receives workgroup rations	PY Ab 1102	(Same - by analogy with rest of PY Ab series)	[WomOcc]
Receives workgroup rations	PY Ab 1109	(Same - by analogy with rest of PY Ab series)	[WomOcc]
Receives workgroup rations	PY Ab 1112	(Same - by analogy with rest of PY Ab series)	[WomOcc]
Receives workgroup rations	PY Ab 1113	(Same - by analogy with rest of PY Ab series)	[WomOcc]
Receives workgroup rations	PY Ab 1114	(Same - by analogy with rest of PY Ab series)	[WomOcc]
Receives workgroup rations	PY Ab 1115	(Same - by analogy with rest of PY Ab series)	[WomOcc]
Mothers of tallied men and boys	PY Ad 674	(Same - by analogy with rest of PY Ad series)	[WomOcc]
Mothers of tallied men and boys	PY Ad 681	(Same - by analogy with rest of PY Ad series)	[WomOcc]
Mothers of tallied men and boys	PY Ad 700	(Same - by analogy with rest of PY Ad series)	[WomOcc]
Mothers of tallied men and boys	PY Ad 1450	(Same - by analogy with rest of PY Ad series)	[WomOcc]
Too fragmentary to recover	PY Ae 634	Same	MUL
Women's workgroup with accompanying children	PY Aa 695	Same	WomOcc

Title nominative	#	*Name*	*Sex*	*Sex identified*
ne-we-wi-ja adj, describing women textile-workers	0		F	Known from MUL ideogram on PY Aa 695, Ab 560
ne-we-wi-ja @ Pylos adj, describing women textile-workers	0		F	MUL ideogram
ne-wo-pe-o (PN) MUL ("women at PN: ne-wo-pe-o")	8		F	MUL ideogram
ne-wo-pe-o (PN) MUL ("women at PN: ne-wo-pe-o")	7		F	MUL ideogram
ne-wo-pe-o (PN) MUL ("women at PN: ne-wo-pe-o")	0		F	Known from MUL ideogram on PY Aa 786, Ab 554
no-ri-wo-ko (*-worgoi*) ("women nori-workers")	8		F	MUL ideogram
no-ri-wo-ko @ Leuktron ("women nori-workers @ Leuktron")	0		F	Known from MUL ideogram on PY Aa 98
o-pi-ro-qo @ Pylos *opiloquoi* ("unassigned or supernumerary women") [cf. ἐπίλοιπος Pind.+]	8		F	MUL ideogram
o-pi-ro-qo @ Pylos *opiloquoi* ("unassigned or supernumerary women") [cf. ἐπίλοιπος Pind.+]	0		F	Known from MUL ideogram on PY Ab 899
o-ti-ra2 @ Pylos ("Women *-triai* workers") (name of a trade)	21		F	MUL ideogram
o-ti-ri-ja ("Women *-triai* workers") (name of a trade)	0		F	Known from MUL ideogram on PY Aa 313
o-ti-ri-ja @ Pylos ("Women *-triai* workers") (name of a trade)	21		F	MUL ideogram
pa-wo-ke @ Pylos *pan-worges* ("maids with a variety of tasks", "maids of all work")	4		F	MUL ideogram
pa-wo-ke @ Pylos *pan-worges* ("maids with a variety of tasks", "maids of all work")	0		F	Known from MUL ideogram on PY Aa 795
pa-wo-ke *pan-worges* ("maids with a variety of tasks", "maids of all work")	0		F	Known from MUL ideogram on PY Ab 558
pa-wo-ke *pan-worges* ("maids with a variety of tasks", "maids of all work")	4		F	MUL ideogram

Function	*Tablet*	*Tablet identifying sex*	*Designation type*
Mothers of tallied men and boys	PY Ad 357	PY Aa 695, PY Ab 560	WomOcc
Receives workgroup rations	PY Ab 560	Same	WomOcc
Women's workgroup with accompanying children	PY Aa 786	Same	PN used as WomOcc
Receives workgroup rations	PY Ab 554	Same	PN used as WomOcc
Mothers of tallied men and boys	PY Ad 688	PY Aa 786, Ab 554	PN used as WomOcc
Women's workgroup with accompanying children	PY Aa 98	Same	WomOcc
Mothers of tallied men and boys	PY Ad 669	Same	WomOcc
Receives workgroup rations	PY Ab 899	Same	WomOcc
Mothers of tallied men and boys	PY Ad 691	Same	WomOcc
Receives workgroup rations	PY Ab 417 + 1050	Same	WomOcc @ PN
Mothers of tallied men and boys	PY Ad 663	PY Aa 0313	WomOcc
Women's workgroup with accompanying children	PY Aa 313	Same	WomOcc
Receives workgroup rations	PY Ab 558	Same	WomOcc
Mothers of tallied men and boys	PY Ad 691	PY Aa 795	WomOcc
Holds WOOL	PY La 632	PY Ab 558	WomOcc
Women's workgroup with accompanying children	PY Aa 795	Same	WomOcc

Title nominative	#	*Name*	*Sex*	*Sex identified*
pe-ki-ti-ra2 @ Pylos *pektriai* ("wool-carders")	0		F	Known from MUL ideogram on PY Ab 578
pe-ki-ti-ra2 @ Pylos *pektriai* ("wool-carders")	7		F	MUL ideogram
pe-ki-ti-ra2 *pektriai* ("wool-carders")	0		F	Known from MUL ideogram on PY Ab 578
pi-we-re (PN) MUL ("women @ PN: pi-we-re")	7		F	MUL ideogram
ra-mi-ni-ja @ Pylos *Lamniai* ("women of PN: Λῆμνος"); ethnic adj.	7		F	MUL ideogram
ra-pi-ti-ra @ Pylos *raptriai* ("sewing women") [ῥάπτρια]	38		F	MUL ideogram
ra-qi-ti-ra2 @ Pylos *laqutriai*? women's trade, different from ra-pi-ti-ra2; (sense obscure)	6		F	MUL ideogram
ra-qi-ti-ra2 @ Pylos *laqutriai*? women's trade, different from ra-pi-ti-ra2; (sense obscure)	0		F	Known from MUL ideogram on PY Ab 356
ra-wi-ja-ja @ Pylos ke-re-za *lawiaiai*; sense obscure, possibly "captives"	26		F	MUL ideogram
ra-wi-ja-ja @ Pylos ke-re-za *lawiaiai*; sense obscure, possibly "captives"	28		F	MUL ideogram
ra-wi-ja-ja @ Pylos ke-re-za *lawiaiai*; sense obscure, possibly "captives"	0		F	Known from MUL ideogram on PY Ad 807
re-wo-to-ro-ko-wo @ Pylos: *lewotrokhowoi* ("women bath-attendants") [λοετροχόος]	37		F	MUL ideogram
re-wo-to-ro-ko-wo @ Pylos: *lewotrokhowoi* ("women bath-attendants") [λοετροχόος]	0		F	Known from MUL ideogram on PY Aa 783
re-wo-to-ro-ko-wo *lewotrokhowoi* ("women bath-attendants") [λοετροχόος]	38		F	MUL ideogram
ri-ne-ja @ po-to-ro-wa-pi *lineiai* ("linen-workers")	x		F	Known from MUL ideogram on PY Aa 76
ri-ne-ja @ da-mi-ni-ja *lineiai* ("linen-workers")	0		F	MUL ideogram
ri-ne-ja @ da-mi-ni-ja *lineiai* ("linen-workers")	0		F	Known from MUL ideogram on PY Aa 96

Function	*Tablet*	*Tablet identifying sex*	*Designation type*
Women's workgroup with accompanying children	PY Aa 891	PY Ab 578	WomOcc
Receives workgroup rations	PY Ab 578	Same	WomOcc
Mothers of tallied men and boys	PY Ad 694	PY Ab 578	WomOcc
Women's workgroup with accompanying children	PY Aa 1182	Same	PN as WomOcc
Receives workgroup rations	PY Ab 186	Same	FemEthnic
Receives workgroup rations	PY Ab 555	Same	WomOcc
Receives workgroup rations	PY Ab 356 + 1049	Same	WomOcc @ PN
Mothers of tallied men and boys	PY Ad 667	PY Ab 356	WomOcc
Women's workgroup with accompanying children	PY Aa 807	Same	WomOcc
Receives workgroup rations	PY Ab 586	Same	WomOcc @ PN
Mothers of tallied men and boys	PY Ad 686	PY Ad 807	WomOcc?
Receives workgroup rations	PY Ab 553	Same	WomOcc
Mothers of tallied men and boys	PY Ad 676	PY Aa 783	WomOcc
Women's workgroup with accompanying children	PY Aa 783	Same	WomOcc
po-to-ro-wa-pi	PY Ad 678	PY Aa 76	WomOcc
Women's workgroup with accompanying children	PY Aa 96	Same	WomOcc
Mothers of tallied men and boys	PY Ad 697	PY Aa 96	WomOcc

Title nominative	#	*Name*	*Sex*	*Sex identified*
ri-ne-ja @ e-pi-ja-ta-ni-ja *lineiai* ("linen-workers")	0		F	(By analogy with rest of PY Ad series)
ri-ne-ja @ e-pi-ko-e *lineiai* ("linen-workers")	14		F	MUL ideogram
ri-ne-ja @ e-pi-ko-e *lineiai* ("linen-workers")	x		F	Known from MUL ideogram on PY Aa 94
ri-ne-ja @ e-u-de-we-ro *lineiai* ("linen-workers")	0		F	Known from MUL ideogram on PY Aa 772, Ab 379
ri-ne-ja *lineiai* ("linen-workers")	2		F	MUL ideogram
ri-ne-ja pa-ke-te-ja *lineiai* ("linen measurers?"); pa-ke-te-ja obscure	2		F	MUL ideogram
(ri-ne-ja?) pa-ke-te-ja *lineiai* ("linen measurers?"); pa-ke-te-ja obscure	9		F	MUL ideogram
(ri-ne-ja) @ po-to-ro-wa-pi *lineiai* ("linen-workers")	4		F	MUL ideogram
(ri-ne-ja) @ e-u-de-we-ro *lineiai* ("linen-workers")	6		F	MUL ideogram
(ri-ne-ja)@ e-u-de-we-ro *lineiai* ("linen-workers")	8		F	MUL ideogram
ri-ne-ja@ ke-e *lineiai* ("linen-workers")	6		F	MUL ideogram
ri-ne-ja@ ke-e *lineiai* ("linen-workers")	0		F	Known from MUL ideogram on PY Aa 0093
si-to-ko-wo *sitokhowoi* ("grain measurer(s)")	0		F?	By analogy with rest of tablet - all have MUL ideograms
[te-o-jo do-]e-ra *theoio doela* ("female slave/servant of the god") [θεοîο δούλη]	1	[ ]	F	Feminine Religious Title
te-o-jo do-e-ra (Tab: te-o-[ ])*theoio doela* ("female slave/servant of the god") [θεοîο δούλη]	1	i-do-me-ne-ja	F, sing	Feminine Religious Title
te-o-jo do-e-ra *theoio doela* ("female slave/ servant of the god") [θεοîο δούλη]	1	qe-ri-ta	F, sing	Feminine Religious Title
te-o-jo do-e-ra *theoio doela* ("female slave/ servant of the god") [θεοîο δούλη]	0	[ ]	F	Feminine Religious Title
te-o-jo do-e-ra *theoio doela* ("female slave/ servant of the god") [θεοîο δούλη]	1	[ ]	F	Feminine Religious Title
te-o-jo do-e-ra *theoio doela* ("female slave/ servant of the god") [θεοîο δούλη]	1	[ ]	F	Feminine Religious Title

Function	*Tablet*	*Tablet identifying sex*	*Designation type*
Mothers of tallied men and boys	PY Ad 687	(Same - by analogy with rest of PY Ad series)	WomOcc
Women's workgroup with accompanying children	PY Aa 94	Same	WomOcc
Mothers of tallied men and boys	PY Ad 672	PY Aa 94	WomOcc
Mothers of tallied men and boys	PY Ad 670	PY Aa 772, Ab 379	WomOcc
Receives workgroup rations	PY Ab 746	Same	WomOcc
Receives workgroup rations	PY Ab 745	Same	WomOcc
Women's workgroup with accompanying children	PY Aa 662	Same	WomOcc
Women's workgroup with accompanying children	PY Aa 76	Same	PN used as WomOcc
Women's workgroup with accompanying children	PY Aa 772	Same	WomOcc
Receives workgroup rations	PY Ab 379	Same	WomOcc
Women's workgroup with accompanying children	PY Aa 93	Same	WomOcc
Mothers of tallied men and boys	PY Ad 0295	PY Aa 0093	WomOcc
List of women and boys	PY An 0292.01	Same - by analogy with rest of tablet	WomOcc
Holds an o-na-to ke-ke-me-na ko-to-na from da-mo	PY Eb 502	Same	FemTitle
Holds an o-na-to ke-ke-me-na ko-to-na	PY Eb 498	PY Ep 212	FemTitle WN
Holds an o-na-to ke-ke-me-na ko-to-na	PY Eb 900	PY Ep 613 + PY Ep 1131.17	FemTitle WN
Too fragmentary to recover	PY Ed 411	Same	FemTitle
Holds an o-na-to	PY Eb 859	Same	FemTitle
Holds an o-na-to	PY Eb 916	Same	FemTitle

Title nominative	#	*Name*	*Sex*	*Sex identified*
te-o-jo do-e-ra *theoio doela* ("female slave/ servant of the god") [θεοῖο δούλη]	1	a3-wa-ja *Aiwaia* Αἰαίη	F, sing	Feminine Religious Title
te-o-jo do-e-ra *theoio doela* ("female slave/ servant of the god") [θεοῖο δούλη]	1	a3-wa-ja Aiwaia Αἰαίη	F, sing	Feminine Religious Title
te-o-jo do-e-ra *theoio doela* ("female slave/ servant of the god") [θεοῖο δούλη]	1	e-pa-sa-na-ti (or Tab: i-pa-sa-na-ti)	F, sing	Feminine Religious Title
te-o-jo do-e-ra *theoio doela* ("female slave/ servant of the god") [θεοῖο δούλη]	1	e-pa-sa-na-ti (or Tab: i-pa-sa-na-ti)	F, sing	Feminine Religious Title
te-o-jo do-e-ra *theoio doela* ("female slave/ servant of the god") [θεοῖο δούλη]	1	e-pa-sa-na-ti (also spelled i-pa-sa-na-ti)	F, sing	Feminine Religious Title
te-o-jo do-e-ra *theoio doela* ("female slave/ servant of the god") [θεοῖο δούλη]	1	e-pa-sa-na-ti (also spelled i-pa-sa-na-ti)	F, sing	Feminine Religious Title
te-o-jo do-e-ra *theoio doela* ("female slave/ servant of the god") [θεοῖο δούλη]	1	e-ri-qi-ja	F, sing	Feminine Religious Title
te-o-jo do-e-ra *theoio doela* ("female slave/ servant of the god") [θεοῖο δούλη]	1	e-ri-qi-ja	F, sing	Feminine Religious Title
te-o-jo do-e-ra *theoio doela* ("female slave/ servant of the god") [θεοῖο δούλη]	1	i-do-me-ne-ja	F, sing	Feminine Religious Title
te-o-jo do-e-ra *theoio doela* ("female slave/ servant of the god") [θεοῖο δούλη]	1	i-ni-ja	F, sing	Feminine Religious Title
te-o-jo do-e-ra *theoio doela* ("female slave/ servant of the god") [θεοῖο δούλη]	1	i-ni-ja	F, sing	Feminine Religious Title
te-o-jo do-e-ra *theoio doela* ("female slave/ servant of the god") [θεοῖο δούλη]	1	ko-pi-na	F, sing	Feminine Religious Title
te-o-jo do-e-ra *theoio doela* ("female slave/ servant of the god") [θεοῖο δούλη]	1	ko-ri-si-ja *Korinsia*	F, sing	Feminine Religious Title
te-o-jo do-e-ra *theoio doela* ("female slave/ servant of the god") [θεοῖο δούλη]	1	ko-ri-si-ja *Korinsia*	F, sing	Feminine Religious Title
te-o-jo do-e-ra *theoio doela* ("female slave/ servant of the god") [θεοῖο δούλη]	1	ko-ri-si-ja *Korinsia*	F, sing	Feminine Religious Title
te-o-jo do-e-ra *theoio doela* ("female slave/ servant of the god") [θεοῖο δούλη]	1	ko-ri-si-ja *Korinsia*	F, sing	Feminine Religious Title
te-o-jo do-e-ra *theoio doela* ("female slave/ servant of the god") [θεοῖο δούλη]	1	ko-ri-si-ja *Korinsia*	F, sing	Feminine Religious Title
te-o-jo do-e-ra *theoio doela* ("female slave/ servant of the god") [θεοῖο δούλη]	1	ko-ri-si-ja *Korinsia*	F, sing	Feminine Religious Title
te-o-jo do-e-ra *theoio doela* ("female slave/ servant of the god") [θεοῖο δούλη]	1	ma-*79	F, sing	Feminine Religious Title

Function	*Tablet*	*Tablet identifying sex*	*Designation type*
Holds an o-na-to ki-ti-me-na ko-to-na	PY Eo 160.02	Same	FemTitle WN
Holds an o-na-to ki-ti-me-na ko-to-na	PY En 74.22	Same	FemTitle WN
Holds an o-na-to ke-ke-me-na ko-to-na from damos	PY Eb 1350	PY Ep 212.5: fem title te-o-jo do-e-ra	FemTitle WN
Holds an o-na-to ki-ti-me-na ko-to-na	PY Eo 247.04	Same: fem title te-o-jo do-e-ra; sing verb	FemTitle WN
Holds an o-na-to ki-ti-me-na ko-to-na	PY En 74.13	Same	FemTitle WN
Holds an o-na-to ke-ke-me-na ko-to-na	PY Ep 212.05	Same	FemTitle WN
Holds an o-na-to ke-ke-me-na ko-to-na	PY Ep 539.02	Same	FemTitle WN
Holds an o-na-to ke-ke-me-na ko-to-na	PY Eb 1440	Same	FemTitle WN
Holds an o-na-to ke-ke-me-na ko-to-na	PY Ep 212.09	Same	FemTitle WN
Holds an o-na-to ki-ti-me-na ko-to-na	PY En 609.6	Same	FemTitle WN
Holds an o-na-to ki-ti-me-na ko-to-na	PY Eo 211.03	Same	FemTitle WN
Holds o-na-to ke-ke-me-na ko-to-na	PY Ep 613.15 + 1131	Same	FemTitle WN
Holds an o-na-to ki-ti-me-na ko-to-na	PY Eb 347	Same	FemTitle WN
Holds an o-na-to ki-ti-me-na ko-to-na	PY En 74.18	Same	FemTitle WN
Holds an o-na-to ki-ti-me-na ko-to-na	PY En 74.24	Same	FemTitle WN
Holds an o-na-to ki-ti-me-na ko-to-na	PY Eo 160.4	Same	FemTitle WN
Holds o-na-to ki-ti-me-na ko-to-na	PY Eo 247.3	Same	FemTitle WN
Holds an o-na-to ki-ti-me-na ko-to-na	PY EP 212.4	Same	FemTitle WN
Holds an o-na-to ki-ti-me-na ko-to-na	PY En 74.08	Same	FemTitle WN

Title nominative	#	*Name*	*Sex*	*Sex identified*
te-o-jo do-e-ra *theoio doela* ("female slave/ servant of the god") [θεοῖο δούλη]	1	ma-ra3-wa *Marraiwa?* Μαρραῖα	F	Feminine Religious Title
te-o-jo do-e-ra *theoio doela* ("female slave/ servant of the god") [θεοῖο δούλη]	1	ma-ra3-wa *Marraiwa?* Μαρραῖα	F	Feminine Religious Title
te-o-jo do-e-ra *theoio doela* ("female slave/ servant of the god") [θεοῖο δούλη]	1	ma-re-ku-na*	F? M?	Feminine Religious Title here; but Masculine do-e-ro in PY En 74
te-o-jo do-e-ra *theoio doela* ("female slave/ servant of the god") [θεοῖο δούλη]	1	mi-ra *Smila*?	F, sing	Feminine Religious Title
te-o-jo do-e-ra *theoio doela* ("female slave/ servant of the god") [θεοῖο δούλη]	1	mi-ra *Smila*?	F, sing	Feminine Religious Title
te-o-jo do-e-ra *theoio doela* ("female slave/ servant of the god") [θεοῖο δούλη]	1	mi-ra *Smila*?	F, sing	Feminine Religious Title
te-o-jo do-e-ra *theoio doela* ("female slave/ servant of the god") [θεοῖο δούλη]	1	mi-ra *Smila*?	F, sing	Feminine Religious Title
te-o-jo do-e-ra *theoio doela* ("female slave/ servant of the god") [θεοῖο δούλη]	1	mu-ti (probably error for mu-ti-ri) *Myrtilis*	F, sing	Feminine Religious Title
te-o-jo do-e-ra *theoio doela* ("female slave/ servant of the god") [θεοῖο δούλη]	1	mu-ti-ri *Myrtilis*	F, sing	Feminine Religious Title
te-o-jo do-e-ra *theoio doela* ("female slave/ servant of the god") [θεοῖο δούλη]	1	pi-ro-na *Philona*?	F, sing	Feminine Religious Title
te-o-jo do-e-ra *theoio doela* ("female slave/ servant of the god") [θεοῖο δούλη]	1	po-so-re-ja *Psoleia*?	F, sing	Feminine Religious Title
te-o-jo do-e-ra *theoio doela* ("female slave/ servant of the god") [θεοῖο δούλη]	1	po-so-re-ja *Psoleia*?	F, sing	Feminine Religious Title
te-o-jo do-e-ra *theoio doela* ("female slave/ servant of the god") [θεοῖο δούλη]	1	po-so-re-ja *Psoleia*?	F, sing	Feminine Religious Title
te-o-jo do-e-ra *theoio doela* ("female slave/ servant of the god") [θεοῖο δούλη]	1	po-so-re-ja *Psoleia?*	F, sing	Feminine Religious Title
te-o-jo do-e-ra *theoio doela* ("female slave/ servant of the god") [θεοῖο δούλη]	1	po-so-re-ja *Psoleia*?	F, sing	Feminine Religious Title
te-o-jo do-e-ra *theoio doela* ("female slave/ servant of the god") [θεοῖο δούλη]	1	po-so-re-ja *Psoleia*?	F, sing	Feminine Religious Title
te-o-jo do-e-ra *theoio doela* ("female slave/ servant of the god") [θεοῖο δούλη]	1	qe-ri-ta	F, sing	Feminine Religious Title
te-o-jo do-e-ra *theoio doela* ("female slave/ servant of the god") [θεοῖο δούλη]	1	re-ka *Leskha*?	F, sing	Feminine Religious Title

Function	*Tablet*	*Tablet identifying sex*	*Designation type*
Holds an o-na-to ke-ke-me-na ko-to-na from damos	PY Eb 0866	Same	FemTitle WN
Holds an o-na-to ke-ke-me-na ko-to-na from da-mo	PY Ep 705.01	Same	FemTitle WN
Holds an o-na-to ki-ti-me-na ko-to-na	PY Eo 276.05	PROBLEM: here do-e-ra but in PY En 74.6 te-o-jo do-e-ro	FemTitle? WN? MascTitle? MN?
Holds an o-na-to ke-ke-me-na ko-to-na	PY Eb 905	Same	FemTitle WN
Holds an o-na-to ki-ti-me-na ko-to-na	PY En 74.4	Same	FemTitle WN
Holds an o-na-to ki-ti-me-na ko-to-na	PY Eo 276.3	Same	FemTitle WN
Holds an o-na-to ke-ke-me-na ko-to-na	PY Ep 613.16 + 1131	Same	FemTitle WN
Holds an o-na-to ke-ke-me-na ko-to-na from damos	PY Eb 858	Same	FemTitle WN
Holds an o-na-to ke-ke-me-na ko-to-na	PY Ep 212.6	Same	FemTitle WN
Holds an o-na-to ke-ke-me-na ko-to-na	PY Ep 539.1	Same	FemTitle WN
Holds an o-na-to ke-ke-me-na ko-to-na from MN pa-ra-ko Phalaikos	PY Eb 169	Same	FemTitle WN
Holds an o-na-to ki-ti-me-na ko-to-na	PY En 609.17	Same	FemTitle WN
Holds an o-na-to ki-ti-me-na ko-to-na	PY Eo 224.07	Same	FemTitle WN
Holds an o-na-to ke-ke-me-na ko-to-na	PY Ep 539.04	Same	FemTitle WN
Holds an o-na-to ke-ke-me-na ko-to-na	PY Ep 539.05	Same	FemTitle WN
Holds an o-na-to ke-ke-me-na ko-to-na	PY Ep 613.12 + 1131	Same	FemTitle WN
Holds an o-na-to ke-ke-me-na ko-to-na	PY Ep 613.17 + 1131	Same	FemTitle WN
[Holds o-na-to]	PY Eb 886	PY Ep 212	FemTitle WN

Title nominative	#	*Name*	*Sex*	*Sex identified*
te-o-jo do-e-ra *theoio doela* ("female slave/ servant of the god") [θεοῖο δούλη]	1	re-ka *Leskha*?	F, sing	Feminine Religious Title
te-o-jo do-e-ra *theoio doela* ("female slave/ servant of the god") [θεοῖο δούλη]	1	re-ka *Leskha*?	F, sing	Feminine Religious Title
te-o-jo do-e-ra *theoio doela* ("female slave/ servant of the god") [θεοῖο δούλη]	1	si-ma *Sima*?	F, sing	Feminine Religious Title
te-o-jo do-e-ra *theoio doela* ("female slave/ servant of the god") [θεοῖο δούλη]	1	si-ma Sima?	F, sing	Feminine Religious Title
te-o-jo do-e-ra *theoio doela* ("female slave/ servant of the god") [θεοῖο δούλη]	1	ta-ra-mi-ka *Thalamika, -iska*? Θαλάμικα	F	Feminine Religious Title
te-o-jo do-e-ra *theoio doela* ("female slave/ servant of the god") [θεοῖο δούλη]	1	ta-ra-mi-ka *Thalamika, -iska*? Θαλάμικα	F	Feminine Religious Title
te-o-jo do-e-ra *theoio doela* ("female slave/ servant of the god") [θεοῖο δούλη]	1	te-qa-ja *Theqaia* Θηβαῖα	F, sing	Feminine Religious Title
te-o-jo do-e-ra *theoio doela* ("female slave/ servant of the god") [θεοῖο δούλη]	1	to-ro-ja *Troia*?	F	Feminine Religious Title
te-o-jo do-e-ra *theoio doela* ("female slave/ servant of the god") [θεοῖο δούλη]	1	tu-ri-ja-ti *Thuriatis*	F, sing	Feminine Religious Title
te-o-jo do-e-ra *theoio doela* ("female slave/ servant of the god") [θεοῖο δούλη]	1	tu-ri-ja-ti *Thuriatis*	F, sing	Feminine Religious Title
te-o-jo do-e-ra *theoio doela* ("female slave/ servant of the god") [θεοῖο δούλη]	1	u-wa-mi-ja *Huamia*	F, sing	Feminine Religious Title
te-o-jo do-e-ra *theoio doela* ("female slave/ servant of the god") [θεοῖο δούλη]	1	u-wa-mi-ja *Huamia*	F, sing	Feminine Religious Title
te-o-jo do-e-ra *theoio doela* ("female slave/ servant of the god") [θεοῖο δούλη] (Tab: te-o do-e-ra - error)	1	ma-*79	F, sing	Feminine Religious Title
te-o-jo do-e-ro *theoio doelos* ("male slave/ servant of the god") [θεοῖο δούλῆ]	1	ma-re-ku-na* (but WN in component)	M? F?	Masculine Title te-o-jo do-e-ro (but Fem. in PY Eo 0276.5)
te-pe-ja @ PN: ko-ri-to "women te-pa-makers (type of textile worker)"	0		F	Feminine genitive plural ending
[ ]-ti MUL too fragmentary for identification	20		F	MUL ideogram
ti-nwa-si-ja ("Tinwasian women"); ethnic adj.	9		F	MUL ideogram

Function	*Tablet*	*Tablet identifying sex*	*Designation type*
[Holds o-na-to]	PY Eb 1344	PY Ep 212	FemTitle WN
Holds an o-na-to ke-ke-me-na ko-to-na	PY Ep 212.1	Same	FemTitle WN
Holds an o-na-to ki-ti-me-na ko-to-na	PY Eo 211.05	Same	FemTitle WN
Holds an o-na-to ki-ti-me-na ko-to-na	PY En 609.8	Same	FemTitle WN
Holds an o-na-to ke-ke-me-na ko-to-na from damos	PY Eb 464	Same	FemTitle WN
Holds an o-na-to ke-ke-me-na ko-to-na from damos	PY Ep 705.1	Same	FemTitle WN
Holds an o-na-to ke-ke-me-na ko-to-na	PY Ep 539.6	Same	FemTitle WN
Holds an o-na-to ke-ke-me-na ko-to-na from da-mo	PY Ep 705.1	Same	FemTitle WN
Holds an o-na-to ki-ti-me-na ko-to-na	PY En 659.5	Same	FemTitle WN
Holds an o-na-to ki-ti-me-na ko-to-na	PY Eo 444.4	Same	FemTitle WN
Holds an o-na-to as a ke-ra (gift) from the priestess	PY Eb 416	Same	FemTitle WN
Holds an o-na-to as a ke-ra (gift) from the priestess	PY Ep 704.2	Same	FemTitle WN
Holds an o-na-to ki-ti-me-na ko-to-na	PY Eo 276.7	Same	FemTitle WN
Holds an o-na-to ki-ti-me-na ko-to-na	PY En 74.6	PROBLEM; here te-o-jo do-e-ro but in PY Eo 276.5 te-o-jo do-e-ra	FemTitle? WN? MascTitle? MN?
Mothers of tallied men and boys	PY Ad 921	Same	WomOcc
Too fragmentary to recover	PY Ae 629	Same	MUL
Women's workgroup with accompanying children	PY Aa 699	Same	FemEthnic

Title nominative	#	*Name*	*Sex*	*Sex identified*
ti-nwa-si-ja @ Pylos ("Tinwasian women"); ethnic adj.	9		F	MUL ideogram
ti-nwa-ti-ja i-ta-ja @ Pylos Tinwasiai *histeiai* ("Tinwasian weavers") [from ἱστός]	0		F	Known from MUL ideogram on PY Aa 699, Ab 190
to-sa-me-ja @ (PN) o-wi-to-no ("to-sa-me-ja women at o-wi-to-no"); likely trade title (-*thnioi*)	8		F	MUL ideogram
to-sa-me-ja @ (PN) o-wi-to-no ("to-sa-me-ja women at o-wi-to-no"); likely trade title (-*thnioi*)	0		F	Known from MUL ideogram on PY Aa 775, Ab 277
(to-sa-me-ja) @ o-wi-to-no ("to-sa-me-ja women at o-wi-to-no"); likely trade title (-*thnioi*)	2		F	MUL ideogram
we-we-si-je-ja @ (Pylos) ke-re-za W's women (workgroup belonging to collector)	22		F	MUL ideogram
we-we-si-je-ja @ (Pylos) ke-re-za W's women (workgroup belonging to collector)	16		F	MUL ideogram
we-we-si-je-ja @ (Pylos) ke-re-za W's women (workgroup belonging to collector)	0		F	Known from MUL ideogram PY Aa 762
ze-pu2-ra3 @ PN: Pylos ("Zephyrian women"); ethnic adj. [from PN: Ζεφυρία]	26		F	MUL ideogram
ze-pu2-ra3 ri-ne-ja @ PN: Pylos Lauranthias ("Zephyrian linen-workers"); ethnic adj.	0		F	Known from MUL ideogram on PY Aa 61

Function	*Tablet*	*Tablet identifying sex*	*Designation type*
Receives workgroup rations	PY Ab 190	Same	FemEthnic
Mothers of tallied men and boys	PY Ad 684	Same	FemEthnic WomOcc
Receives workgroup rations	PY Ab 277	Same	WomOcc?
Mothers of tallied men and boys	PY Ad 685	PY Aa 775 + 956, PY Ab 277	WomOcc?
Women's workgroup with accompanying children	PY Aa 775 + 956	Same	PN used as WomOcc
Women's workgroup with accompanying children	PY Aa 762	Same	WomOcc
Receives workgroup rations	PY Ab 217	Same	WomOcc
Mothers of tallied men and boys	PY Ad 318 + 420	PY Aa 762	WomOcc derived from MN
Women's workgroup with accompanying children	PY Aa 61	Same	FemEthnic
Mothers of tallied men and boys	PY Ad 664	Same	FemEthnic WomOcc

Appendix B: All mentions of women in the Knossos Tablets

Title	*#*	*Name*	*Sex*	*Sex identified*
---	1	[ ]	F	MUL ideogram
---	3	[ ]	F?	MUL ideogram
---	0	[ ]	F	MUL ideogram
---	1	[ ]-i-ta-no	F	MUL ideogram
---	1	[ ]-ja-mi-nu	F	MUL ideogram
---	1	[ ]-ja-mu-ta	F	MUL ideogram
---	1	[ ]-ja-si-ja	F	MUL ideogram
---	1	[ ]-ka-na	F	MUL ideogram
---	1	[ ]-ma	F	MUL ideogram
---	1	[ ]-me-no	F	MUL ideogram
---	1	[ ]-na	F	MUL ideogram
---	13	[ ]-ni-ta	F	Part of list of women's names followed by MUL ideogram
---	1	[ ]-ra	F	MUL ideogram
---	13	[ ]-si	F	MUL ideogram
---	1	]ta2-no[	F	MUL ideogram
---	1	*18-to-no	F	MUL ideogram
---	1	*56-po-so	F	By analogy with rest of tablet
---	1	a-de-ra2	F	MUL ideogram

Function	*Tablet*	*Tablet identifying sex*	*Designation type*
Included in roster of women's names	KN Ap 5547 + 8162.02	Same	MUL
Included in roster of women with textiles	KN Ap 5748 + 5901 + 5923 + 8558.02	Same	MUL
Included in roster of WNs accompanied by MUL ideograms	KN Ap 5864.01	Same	MUL [WN]
Included in roster of women's names	KN Ap 769.1	Same	WN
Included in roster of women's names	KN Ap 5547 + 8162.1	Same	WN
Included in roster of women's names	KN Ap 5864.5	Same	WN
Included in roster of women (with some children)	KN Ap 639.14	Same	WN
Included in roster of women's names	KN Ap 5864.3	Same	WN
Included in roster of WNs accompanied by MUL ideograms	KN Ap 5864.4	Same	WN
Included in roster of women (with some children)	KN Ap 639.1	Same	WN
Included in roster of WNs accompanied by MUL ideograms	KN Ap 5864.3	Same	WN
Included in roster of women with textiles	KN Ap 5748 + 5901 + 5923 + 8558.3	Same	WN
Included in roster of WNs accompanied by MUL ideograms	KN Ap 5864.2	Same	WN
Included in roster of women with textiles	KN Ap 5748 + 5901 + 5923 + 8558.1	Same	MUL
Included in roster of WNs accompanied by MUL ideograms	KN Ap 5864.6	Same	WN
Included in roster of women (with some children)	KN Ap 639.4	Same	WN
Holder of TELA-1+TE cloth	KN Ln 1568	Same	WN
Included in roster of women (with some children)	KN Ap 639.11	Same	WN

Title	*#*	*Name*	*Sex*	*Sex identified*
---	1	a-ma-no	F	Part of list of women's names followed by MUL ideogram
---	1	a-nu-wa-to	F	MUL ideogram
---	1	a-qi-ti-ta	F	MUL ideogram
---	1	a-to-me-ja	F	MUL ideogram
---	1	a-wa-ti-ka-ra	F	MUL ideogram
---	1	a3-du-wo-na	F	MUL ideogram
---	1	da-te-ne-ja	F	MUL ideogram
---	1	du-sa-ni	F	MUL ideogram
---	1	du-tu-wa	F	MUL ideogram
---	1	e-ti-wi-ja	F	MUL ideogram
---	1	e-ti-wa-ja	F	MUL accompanies name on KN Ap 639
---	1	i-du	F	MUL ideogram
---	1	i-ta-ja	F	MUL ideogram
---	1	i-ta-ja	F	Known from MUL ideogram on KN Ap 769.2
---	1	i-ta-mo @ do-ti-ja	F	MUL ideogram
---	1	ka-*56-so-ta	F	MUL ideogram
---	1	ka-na-to-po	F	MUL ideogram
---	1	ke-pu	F	MUL ideogram
---	1	ke-ra-me-ja *Kerameia* Κεραμεῖα	F	MUL ideogram

Function	*Tablet*	*Tablet identifying sex*	*Designation type*
Included in roster of women with textiles	KN Ap 5748 + 5901 + 5923 + 8558	Same (but also used as a MN in KN As 1520) - prob. two people	WN
Included in roster of women (with some children)	KN Ap 639.14	Same	WN
Included in roster of women (with some children)	KN Ap 639.12	Same	WN
Included in roster of women (with some children)	KN Ap 639.2	Same	WN
Member of a family - but likely to be a scribal exercise rather than admin. record	KN Am 827 + 7032 + 7618	Same	WN
Included in roster of women's names	KN Ap 769.1	Same	WN
Included in roster of women (with some children)	KN Ap 639.2	Same	WN
Included in roster of women (with some children)	KN Ap 639.3	Same	WN
Included in roster of women (with some children)	KN Ap 639.13	Same	WN
Included in roster of women (with some children)	KN Ap 639.8	Same	WN
Holds wool at Phaistos	KN Od 681	KN Ap 639	WN
Included in roster of women (with some children)	KN Ap 639.7	Same	WN
Included in roster of women's names	KN Ap 769.2	Same	WN
Too fragmentary - may be textile tablet	KN Xe 537	KN Ap 769.2	WN
Among list of missing women	KN Ap 618 + 623 + 633 + 5533 + 5922.1	Same	WN
Included in roster of women's names	KN Ap 769.1	Same	WN
Included in roster of women (with some children)	KN Ap 639.9	Same	WN
Included in roster of women (with some children)	KN Ap 639.13	Same	WN
Included in roster of women (with some children)	KN Ap 639.7	Same	WN

Title	*#*	*Name*	*Sex*	*Sex identified*
---	1	ki-nu-qa @ *56-ko-we	F	MUL ideogram
---	1	ki-si-wi-je-ja	F	Feminine name ending –eia
---	13	ki-zo	F	MUL ideogram (1 of 3)
---	1	ko-pi	F	MUL ideogram
---	1	ku-tu-qa-no	F	MUL ideogram
---	1	ku-tu-qa-no	?	WN on KN Ap 639, but unlikely to be same person
---	1	ma-ku[ ]	F	MUL ideogram
---	1	na-e-ra-ja	F	Feminine name ending –eia
---	13	o-ri-mo	F	Part of list of women's names followed by MUL ideogram
---	13	o-sa-po-to	F	Part of list of women's names followed by MUL ideogram
---	1	pa-i-ti-ja *Phaistia* Φαιστία	F	MUL ideogram
---	1	pa-ja-ni	F	MUL ideogram
---	1	pe-ri-je-ja *Perieia*	F	Feminine name ending –eia
---	1	pi-ja-mu-nu		Part of list of women's names followed by MUL ideogram
---	1	pi-ra-ka-ra *Philagra* Φίλαγρα	F	MUL ideogram

Function	*Tablet*	*Tablet identifying sex*	*Designation type*
Among list of missing women	KN Ap 618 + 623 + 633 + 5533 + 5922.1	Same	WN
Context obscure	KN Xd 98 +196	Same	WN
Included in roster of women with textiles	KN Ap 5748 + 5901 + 5923 + 8558.1	Same	WN
Included in roster of women (with some children)	KN Ap 639.1	Same	WN
Included in roster of women (with some children)	KN Ap 639.9	WN here [but MN on KN Da 1161]	WN
Holds sheep at Phaistos	KN Da 1161 + 7187	WN in KN AP 639 - here uncertain	MN?
Included in roster of women (with some children)	KN Ap 639.3	Same	WN
Holder of PE TELA-1+TE cloth	KN Ln 1568	Same	WN
Included in roster of women with textiles	KN Ap 5748 + 5901 + 5923 + 8558.2	Same	WN
Included in roster of women with textiles	KN Ap 5748 + 5901 + 5923 + 8558.03	Same	WN
Included in roster of women (with some children)	KN Ap 639.4	Same	WN
Included in roster of women (with some children)	KN Ap 639.2	Same	WN
Holds orchard plot	KN Uf 1031 + 5738	Same	WN
Included in roster of women with textiles	KN Ap 5748 + 5901 + 5923 + 8558.2	Same	WN
Included in roster of women (with some children)	KN Ap 639.4	Same	WN

Title	#	*Name*	*Sex*	*Sex identified*
---	1	po-ni-ke-ja *Phonikeia*	F	Feminine name ending –eia
---	1	po-po	F	By analogy with rest of tablet KN Ln 1568 (all WNs)
---	1	po-po	F	By analogy with rest of tablet KN Ln 1568 (all WNs)
---	1	po-po	F	By analogy with rest of tablet KN Ln 1568 (all WNs)
---	1	po-po	F	By analogy with rest of tablet
---	1	po-po	F?	By analogy with rest of tablet KN Ln 1568 (all WNs)
---	1	po-po	F?	By analogy with rest of tablet KN Ln 1568 (all WNs)
---	1	pu-wa *Purwa* Πύρρα	F	MUL ideogram
---	1	pu-zo	F?	Part of list of women's names followed by MUL ideogram
---	1	qe-pa-ta-no	F	By analogy with rest of tablet
---	1	qi-na	F	Chadwick
---	1	ru-ki-ti-ja *Luktia*	F	By analogy with rest of tablet
---	1	ru-ki-ti-ja *Luktia*	F	By analogy with rest of tablet KN Ln 1568
---	1	ru-nu	F	By analogy with rest of tablet
---	1	ru-sa-ma	F	By analogy with rest of tablet

Function	*Tablet*	*Tablet identifying sex*	*Designation type*
Supervisor in charge of wool	KN Ln 1568	Same	WN
Expected to transfer 4 units TELA-2	KN L 513	KN Ln 1568	WN
Supervisor in charge of linen (other supervisor on tablet MN)	KN L 567	KN Ln 1568	WN
Supervisor in charge of linen	KN L 648	KN Ln 1568	WN
Holder of PE TELA-1+TE cloth	KN Ln 1568	Same	WN
Supervisor in charge of 4 units wool	KN Od 689	KN Ln 1568	WN
Supervisor (commodity lacunose)	KN Xe 524	KN Ln 1568	WN
Included in roster of women (with some children)	KN Ap 639.11	Same	WN
Included in roster of women with textiles	KN Ap 5748 + 5901 + 5923 + 8558.02	Same	WN
Holder of PE TELA-1+TE cloth	KN Ln 1568	Same	WN
Supervisor responsible for 4 units TELA-2 (o-pi-qi-na)	KN Ld 584	Same	
Holder of PE TELA-1+TE cloth	KN Ln 1568	Same	WN
Too fragmentary to recover	KN Xd 314	KN Ln 1568	WN
Holder of TELA-1 cloth	KN Ln 1568	Same	WN
Holder of PE TELA-1+TE cloth	KN Ln 1568	Same	WN

Title	#	*Name*	*Sex*	*Sex identified*
---	1	ru-ta2-no	F	MUL ideogram
---	1	sa-*65	F	MUL ideogram
---	1	sa-ma-ti-ja	F	MUL ideogram
---	1	sa-mi	F	MUL ideogram
---	1	sa-ti-qi-to	F	MUL ideogram
---	1	si-ne-e-ja	F	MUL ideogram
---	1	si-nu-ke	F	MUL ideogram
---	1	ta-su	F	By analogy with rest of tablet
---	1	te-qa-ja *Theqaia* Θηβαῖα	F	MUL ideogram
---	1	ti-no	Ḟ	Part of list of women's names followed by MUL ideogram
---	1	tu-*49-mi	F	MUL ideogram
---	1	tu-ka-na	F	MUL ideogram
---	1	tu-ka-na	F	MUL ideogram
---	1	tu-ka-to	F	MUL ideogram
---	1	tu-zo	F	MUL ideogram
---	1	tu-zo	M?	WN on KN Ap 639, but likely to be MN here
---	1	u-jo-na	F	MUL ideogram
---	1	u-pa-ra	F	MUL ideogram
---	1	wa-ra-ti	F	MUL ideogram

Function	*Tablet*	*Tablet identifying sex*	*Designation type*
Included in roster of women (with some children)	KN Ap 639.12	Same	WN
Included in roster of women (with some children)	KN Ap 639.10	Same	WN
Included in roster of women (with some children)	KN Ap 639.8	Same	WN
Included in roster of women (with some children)	KN Ap 639.10	Same	WN
Included in roster of women (with some children)	KN Ap 639.9	Same	WN
Included in roster of women (with some children)	KN Ap 639.12	Same	WN
Included in roster of women (with some children)	KN Ap 639.11	Same	WN
Holder of MI TELA-1+TE cloth	KN Ln 1568	Same	WN
Included in roster of women's names	KN Ap 5864.04	Same	WN
Included in roster of women with textiles	KN Ap 5748 + 5901 + 5923 + 8558.02	Same	WN
Included in roster of women (with some children)	KN Ap 639.7	Same	WN
Included in roster of women (with some children)	KN Ap 639.10	Same	WN
Included in roster of women (with some children)	KN Ap 639.11	Same	WN
Included in roster of women (with some children)	KN Ap 639.8	Same	WN
Included in roster of women (with some children)	KN Ap 639.1	Here WN; on KN C 7698 probably MN	WN
Holds 1 pair of cattle	KN C 7698 + 7892 + 8223 + frr.	F on KN Ap 0639, but would be only female cattle-owner	MN?
Included in roster of women (with some children)	KN Ap 639.10	Same	WN
Included in roster of women (with some children)	KN Ap 639.12	Same	WN
Included in roster of women (with some children)	KN Ap 0639.13	Same	WN

Title	#	*Name*	*Sex*	*Sex identified*
---	1	wa-wa-ka	F?	By analogy with rest of tablet
---	1	wi-da-ma-ta2	F	MUL ideogram
---	1	wi-da-ma-ta2	F	Known from MUL ideogram on KN Ap 639.9
---	1	wi-da-ma-ta2	F	Known from MUL ideogram on KN Ap 639.9
---	1	wi-ja-na-tu	F	MUL ideogram
---	1	wi-so	F	MUL ideogram
---	1	wo-di-je-ja *Wordieia*	F	MUL ideogram
[ ]-ra MUL too fragmentary for identification	0		F	MUL ideogram
[ ]ke-ja too fragmentary for identification	14		F	MUL ideogram
[ ]re-ja MUL too fragmentary for identification	3		F	MUL ideogram
[ ]ja too fragmentary for identification	23		F	MUL ideogram
[ ]ja too fragmentary for identification	0		F	MUL ideogram
[ ]ja MUL too fragmentary for identification	5		F	MUL ideogram
[ ]ja MUL too fragmentary for identification	18		[F]	[MUL ideogram]
[ ]ja MUL too fragmentary for identification	1		F	MUL ideogram
[ ]jo-jo -Too fragmentary for identification, but women in question belong to MN in genitive	50		F	MUL ideogram
]te-ja-ne MUL obscure	0		F	MUL ideogram
a-ke-ti-ri-ja @ ra-su-to *asketriai* (“decorators”)	2		F	MUL ideogram
a-ke-ti-ri-ja *asketriai* (“decorators”)	1		F	MUL ideogram

Function	*Tablet*	*Tablet identifying sex*	*Designation type*
Holder of TELA-1+TE cloth	KN Ln 1568	same	WN
Included in roster of women (with some children)	KN Ap 639.9	Same	WN
Holder of MI TELA-1+TE cloth	KN Ln 1568	KN Ap 639.09	WN
Holder of MI TELA-1+TE cloth	KN Ln 1568	KN Ap 639.09	WN
Included in roster of women's names	KN Ap 769.2	Same	WN
Included in roster of women (with some children)	KN Ap 639.4	Same	WN
Included in roster of women (with some children)	KN Ap 639.3	Same	WN
Women's workgroup with accompanying children	KN Ai 825	Same	WomOcc
Women's workgroup with accompanying children	KN Ak 620 + 6028 (+ fr.)	Same	WomOcc
Receives workgroup rations	KN Ai 752 + 0753	Same	WomOcc
Women's workgroup with accompanying children	KN Ak 7830 + fr.	(Same - by analogy with rest of series)	[WomOcc]
Women's workgroup with accompanying children	KN Ak 8444	Same	[WomOcc]
Women's workgroup with accompanying children	KN Ai 338	Same	MUL
Women's workgroup with accompanying children	KN Ak 7006	(Same - by analogy with rest of series)	[WomOcc]
Women's workgroup with accompanying children	KN Ak 7030 + 9664 + frr.	(Same - by analogy with rest of KN Ak series)	[WomOcc]
Women's workgroup with accompanying children	KN Ak 7827 + frr.	Same	[WomOcc]
Too fragmentary to recover	KN Ai 7962 + 7969	Same	MUL
Women's workgroup with accompanying children	KN Ai 739	Same	WomOcc
Women's workgroup with accompanying children	KN Ak 7001	Same	WomOcc

Title	#	*Name*	*Sex*	*Sex identified*
a-mi-ni-si-ja [MUL] *Amnisiai* ("women from Amnisos"); ethnic adj. from PN: Amnisos	0		F	[MUL ideogram] By analogy with rest of tablet
a-no-qo-ta MUL ("women belonging to MN: a-no-qo-ta")	30		F	MUL ideogram
a-no-zo-jo @ da-*22-ro ("women belonging to MN: a-no-zo-jo")	9		F	MUL ideogram
a-ra-ka-te-ja *alakateiai* "spinning women" [ἠλακάτη "distaff" Od. iv. 135+]	0		F	Known from MUL ideogram on PY Aa 89, Aa 240
a-ra-ka-te-ja *alakateiai* "spinning women" [ἠλακάτη "distaff" Od. iv. 135+]	0		F	Known from MUL ideogram on PY Aa 89, Aa 240;
a-ze-ti-ri-[ja] *asketriai* ("decorators")	0		F	Known from MUL ideogram on KN Ap 694.3
a-ze-ti-ri-ja *asketriai* ("decorators")	0		F	Known from MUL ideogram on KN Ap 694.3
a-ze-ti-ri-ja *asketriai* ("decorators")	0		F	Known from MUL ideogram on KN Ap 694.3
a-ze-ti-ri-ja *asketriai* ("decorators")	0		F	Known from MUL ideogram on KN Ap 694.3
a-ze-ti-ri-ja *asketriai* ("decorators")	0		F	Known from MUL ideogram on KN Ap 694.3
a-ze-ti-ri-ja @ da-*22-to *asketriai* ("decorators")	x		F	Known from MUL ideogram on KN Ap 694.3
au MUL (part of workgroup with lacunose occupational title); au obscure	1		F	MUL ideogram
da-te-we-ja ethnic or occupational term describing women - exact sense uncertain	9		F	MUL ideogram
da-te-we-ja ethnic or occupational term describing women - exact sense uncertain	?		F?	Known from MUL ideogram on KN Ak 612
da-te-we-ja ethnic or occupational term describing women - exact sense uncertain	0		F	Known from MUL ideogram on KN Ak 612

Function	*Tablet*	*Tablet identifying sex*	*Designation type*
Women's workgroup with accompanying children	KN Ai 825	(Same - by analogy with rest of tablet)	WomOcc
Women's workgroup with accompanying children	KN Ak 615	Same	WomOcc
Women's workgroup with accompanying children	KN Ak 627 + 7025 + fr.	Same	WomOcc
Women's workgroup with accompanying children	KN Ak 5009 + 6037 + 8588	PY Aa 89, Aa 240	WomOcc
Appears on cloth production target record	KN Lc 531 + 542	PY Aa 89, Aa 240 and Same	WomOcc
Associated with Wool allotments	KN Ln 1568. lat a	KN Ap 694.3	WomOcc
Receives wheat 960 l. (monthly ration?)	KN E 777	KN Ap 694.3	WomOcc
Associated with o-nu-ke wool	KN M 683	KN Ap 694.3	WomOcc
Lacunose - but tablet lists a MN making a "contribution"	KN Xe 657	KN Ap 694.3	WomOcc
Too fragmentary to recover	KN X 7737	KN Ap 694.3	WomOcc
Unclear; tablet also lists a MN	KN Xe 544	KN Ap 694.3	WomOcc
Part of women's workgroup with accompanying children	KN Ak 617	Same	[WomOcc]
Women's workgroup with accompanying children	KN Ak 612	Same	WomOcc
Either women responsible for linen cloth pieces or the cloth itself	KN L 594	KN Ak 612 and Same	WomOcc?
Holds ko-u-ra cloth pieces, Type 1: 3 units	KN Lc 540 + 8075	KN Ak 612 and Same	WomOcc

Title	*#*	*Name*	*Sex*	*Sex identified*
da-te-we-ja ethnic or occupational term describing women - exact sense uncertain	0		F	Known from MUL ideogram on KN Ak 612
da-wi-ja, ne-ki-ri-de ("da-wian women ne-ki-ri-de workers"); ethnic adj. from da-wo	2		F	MUL ideogram
de ko-wa (part of lacunose workgroup); de - abbrev. of de-di-ku-ja dedeikahuia "instructed"	1		F	Feminine Family Title
de MUL (part of lacunose workgroup); de - abbrev. of de-di-ku-ja dedeikahuia "instructed"	1		F	MUL ideogram
de MUL (part of lacunose workgroup); de - abbrev. of de-di-ku-ja dedeikahuia "instructed"	2		F	MUL ideogram
de MUL (part of lacunose workgroup; de - abbrev. of de-di-ku-ja dedeikahuia "instructed"	1		F	MUL ideogram
de-di-ku-ja MUL (part of to-te-ja workgroup) ("women trained as to-te-ja workers")	1		F	MUL ideogram
di ko-wa (part of [ ]ke-ja workgroup) ("girl undergoing instruction as a [ ]ke-ja worker")	1		F	Feminine Family Title
di ko-wa (part of qa-mi-ja workgroup) ("girl undergoing instruction in the qa-mi-ja workgroup")	3		F	Feminine Family Title
di kowa ("girl undergoing instruction in lacunose occupation"); di (for di-da-ka-re) *didaskalei*	1		F	Feminine Family Title
di [MUL] (part of workgroup at se-to-i-ja) ("women undergoing instruction at se-to-i-ja")	5		F	[MUL ideogram]
di [MUL] (part of workgroup with lacunose title) ("women in training for x workgroup")	0		F	[MUL ideogram]
di za MUL part of workgroup with lacunose title ("women of age this year in x training")	2		F	MUL ideogram
di-da-ka-re ko-wa me-zo-e (part of pa-i-ti-ja workgroup) ("older girls in training with Phaistian women")	X		F	Feminine Family Title
di-da-ka-re [ko-wa] me-zo-e (part of we-ra-ti-ja workgroup) ("older girls in training with we-ra-ti-ja")	11		[F]	Feminine Family Title

Function	*Tablet*	*Tablet identifying sex*	*Designation type*
Too fragmentary to recover	KN Xe 5891	KN Ak 612 and Same	WomOcc
Women's workgroup with accompanying children + two sons come to adulthood	KN Ak 780 + 7004 + 7045 + 7767	Same	WomOcc, Ethnic
Part of women's workgroup with accompanying children	KN Ak 610	Same	MUL
Part of women's workgroup with accompanying children	KN Ak 610	Same	MUL
Part of women's workgroup with accompanying children	KN Ak 5907	Same	[WomOcc]
Part of women's workgroup with accompanying children	KN Ak 5948	Same	[WomOcc]
Part of women's workgroup with accompanying children	KN Ak 611	Same	WomOcc
Part of women's workgroup with accompanying children	KN Ak 620 + 6028 (+ fr.)	Same	FamTitle
Part of list of girls and boys from various towns	KN Ap 5876 + 5928 + 5971 + 6068 + fr.	Same	FamTitle
Part of women's workgroup with accompanying children	KN Ai 190	Same	FamTitle
Part of women's workgroup with accompanying children	KN Ak 634 + 5767	Same	WomOcc
Personnel count: part of women's workgroup	KN Ap 5868 + 8220	Same	[WomOcc]
Part of women's workgroup with accompanying children	KN Ak 616	Same	WomTitle
Part of women's workgroup with accompanying children	KN Ak 828	Same	FamTitle
Part of women's workgroup with accompanying children	KN Ak 784 [+] 8019	Same	FamTitle

Title	#	*Name*	*Sex*	*Sex identified*
di-da-ka-re pe MUL (part of lacunose workgroup) ("women of age last year under instruction as x")	5		F	Feminine Family Title
di-da-ka-re pe MUL (part of lacunose workgroup) ("women of age last year under instruction as x")	2		F	MUL ideogram
do-e-ra (of MN: *56-so-jo at PN: a-mi-ni-so) *doela* ("slave-women of *56-so-jo") [δούλη]	?		F	Feminine Status Title
do-e-ra (belonging to MN: a-ke-u) *doela* ("slave-woman, maid-servant, bondwoman") [δούλη]	4		F	Feminine Status Title
do-e-ra (belonging to MN a-ke-u) *doela* ("slave-woman, maid-servant, bondwoman") [δούλη]	[ ]		F	Feminine Status Title
do-e-ra (belonging to MN: a-pi-qo-i-ta) *doela* ("slave-women of a-pi-qo-i-ta) [δούλη]	32		F	MUL ideogram
do-e-ra *doela* ("slave-woman, maid-servant, bondwoman") [δούλη]	1		F	MUL ideogram
do-e-ra *doela* ("slave-woman, maid-servant, bondwoman") [δούλη]	1?		F	Feminine Status Title
do-e-ra *doela* ("slave-woman, maid-servant, bondwoman") [δούλη]	1?	di-qa-ra	F	By analogy – in WN position and Feminine Status Title
do-e-ra we-ke-sa *doela* ("we-ke-sa slave-women"); we-ka-sa obscure [δούλη]	1		F	Feminine Status Title
do-ti-ja TU MUL ("Adult daughters at do-ti-ja"); tu = abbreviation for tu-ka-te ("daughter")	4		F	MUL ideogram, Feminine Family title
(e-ne-re-ja) Tab: e-ne-ra (description of women: "makers of e-ne-ra")	0		F	MUL ideogram
e-ne-re-ja (description of women: "makers of e-ne-ra")	0		[F]	[MUL ideogram]
e-ra-ja ("Women of PN: e-ra"); e-ra-ja ethnic adj.	7	---	F	Feminine ethnic ending
e-ro-pa-ke-ja (description of women cloth-workers, obscure)	0		F	Feminine Title ending –eia
e-ro-pa-ke-ja (description of women cloth-workers, obscure)	0		F	Feminine Title ending –eia
i-je-re-ja (a-ne-mo) *anemon hiereia* ("Priestess of the winds") [ἱέρεια]	1		F	Feminine Religious Title

Function	*Tablet*	*Tablet identifying sex*	*Designation type*
Part of women's workgroup with accompanying children	KN Ak 7005	Same – by analogy with rest of KN Ak series	WomOcc
Part of women's workgroup with accompanying children	KN Ak 783 + 7011 + 7535 + fr.	Same	WomTitle
Slave woman/women belonging to MN: *56-so-jo at Amnisos	KN Ai 1036	Same	StatusTitle
In list of slaves belonging to men (here to MN a-ke-u)	KN Ap 628 + 5935.1	Same	StatusTitle
In list of slaves belonging to men (here to MN a-ke-u)	KN Ap 628 + 5935.2	Same	StatusTitle
Women's workgroup with accompanying children belonging to MN a-pi-qo-i-ta	KN Ai 824	Same	StatusTitle
In list of slaves belonging to men	KN Ap 628 + 5935.3	Same	StatusTitle
Given (?) as a slave to god Marineus? Or to mar-i-ne-we women	KN Gg 713 + 994	Same	Status Title
In list of slaves belonging to men	KN Ap 628 + 5935.3	Same	StatusTitle
Slave woman/en who have been purchased: qi-ri-ja-to "he bought"	KN Ai 1037	Same	FemTitle
Personnel tallies of children workers at various villages	KN Ap 629.2	Same	[WomOcc]
Women's workgroup with accompanying children	KN Ai 762 + fr.	Same	(WomOcc)
Women's workgroup with accompanying children	KN Ak 638	Same	WomOcc
In personnel list of otherwise named women	KN Ap 639.5	Same	FemEthnic
Hold tu-na-no Cloth type 1, 1 unit	KN Lc 534 + 7647 + 7818	Same	WomOcc
Delivery record of finished textiles	KN Ld 595	Same	WomOcc?
Receives olive oil along with divinities; her amount 6.4 l. is much less than the gods	KN Fp 1 + 31	Same	FemTitle

Title	#	*Name*	*Sex*	*Sex identified*
i-je-re-ja (a-ne-mo) (not at u-ta-no) *anemon hiereia* ("Priestess of the winds") [ἱέρεια]	1		F	Feminine Religious Title
i-je-re-ja (a-ne-mo) @ u-ta-no *anemon hiereia* ("Priestess of the winds at u-ta-no") [ἱέρεια]	1		F	Feminine Religious Title
ka-pa-ra2 description of women cloth-worker(s), either ethnic or descriptive term	0		F	Known from MUL ideogram on PY An 292.2
ka-ra-we *grawes* ("old women") [γρηῦς Od. 1. 191+] (part of workgroup)	1	[ ]	F	MUL ideogram
ka-ra-we (part of lacunose workgroup) *grawes* ("old women") [γρηῦς Od. 1. 191+]	6		F	MUL ideogram
ki-ri-te-wi-ja a class of women with a religious function (literally "barley-women")	0		F	Known from MUL ideogram on PY An 607
ki-ri-te-wi-ja-i (a-mi-ni-si-ja) ("ki-ri-te-wi-ja-i of Amnisos") (literally "barley-women")	0		F	Known from MUL ideogram on PY An 607
ki-ri-te-wi-ja-i (ko-no-si-ja) ("ki-ri-te-wi-ja-i of Knossos") (literally "barley-women")	0		F	Known from MUL ideogram on PY An 607
ki-ri-te-wi-ja-i (pa-i-ti-ja) ("ki-ri-te-wi-ja-i of Phaistos") (literally "barley-women")	0		F	Known from MUL ideogram on PY An 607
ko-ro-ka[ ] too fragmentary for identification	0		F	By analogy w/ rest of KN Ak series
ko-ru-we-ja adj. describing women textile workers	?		F	Feminine Title ending –eia
ko-u-re-ja description of textile workers	0		[F]	Known from MUL ideogram on KN Ap 694.1
ko-u-re-ja description of textile workers	1	]ja	F	MUL ideogram
ko-u-re-ja description of textiles or their makers	0		F	Known from MUL ideogram on KN Ap 694.1
ko-u-re-ja @ a-mi-ni-so description of textiles or their makers	0		F	Known from MUL ideogram on KN Ap 694.1
ko-u-re-ja (tab: ko-[u-re-ja]) description of textiles or their makers	0		F	Known from MUL ideogram on KN Ap 694.1, etc.
ko-wa (part of [ ]re-ja workgroup) ("girl in [ ]re-ja workgroup")	1		F	Feminine Family Title

Function	Tablet	Tablet identifying sex	Designation type
Receives olive oil 96 l. (largest amount on tablet)	KN Fp 13	Same	FemTitle
Receives olive oil: 14.4 l.	KN Fp 13	Same	WomTitle
Women's workgroup with accompanying children	KN Ak 5009 + 6037 + 8588	PY An 292.2	WomOcc
Included in roster of workgroup women	KN Ap 694.2	Same	FamTitle
Tally of women's workgroup (or subgroup)	KN Ap 5868 + 8220	Same	WomTitle
Receive olive oil (amount lacunose)	KN Fp 363	PY An 607	WomTitle (collective)
Allocated huge monthly rations of wheat for women in Amnisos region (9600 l.)	KN E 777	PY An 607	WomTitle
Allocated huge monthly rations of wheat for women in Knossos region (9600 l.)	KN E 777	PY An 607	WomTitle
Allocated huge monthly rations of wheat for women in Phaistos region (9600 l.)	KN E 777	PY An 607	WomTitle
Women's workgroup with accompanying children	KN Ak 5553	(Same - by analogy with rest of KN Ak series)	WomOcc?
Associated with PU-Cloth (folded? double thick?)	KN L 472	Same	WomOcc
Women's workgroup with accompanying children	KN Ak 643	KN Ap 694.1	
Included in roster of women with textiles	KN Ap 694.1	Same	WomOcc
Holds 30 units Wool	KN Lc 581	KN Ap 694.1	WomOcc
Holds cloth?	KN Lc 550 + 7381	KN Ap 694.1	WomOcc
Holds cloth?	KN Lc 548	KN Ap 694.1, etc.	WomOcc
Receives rations as part of women's workgroup	KN Ai 752 + 753	Same	FamTitle

Title	#	Name	Sex	Sex identified
ko-u-re-ja (tab: ko-[u-re-ja]) description of textiles or their makers	0		F	Known from MUL ideogram on KN Ap 694.1, etc
ko-wa (part of a-ke-ti-ri-ja workgroup @ PN: ra-su-to) ("girl in the decorator workgroup")	1		F	Feminine Family Title
ko-wa (part of lacunose workgroup) ("girls of lacunose workgroup")	1		F	Feminine Family Title
ko-wa (part of lacunose workgroup) ("girls of lacunose workgroup")	6		F	Feminine Family Title
ko-wa (part of lacunose workgroup) ("girls of lacunose workgroup")	1		F	Feminine Family Title
ko-wa (part of lacunose workgroup) ("girls of lacunose workgroup")	2		F	Feminine Family Title
ko-wa (part of lacunose workgroup) ("girls of lacunose workgroup")	2		F	Feminine Family Title
ko-wa (part of lacunose workgroup) ("girls of lacunose workgroup")	0		F	Feminine Family Title
ko-wa (part of lacunose workgroup) ("girls of lacunose workgroup")	2		F	Feminine Family Title
ko-wa (part of lacunose workgroup) ("girls of lacunose workgroup")	6		F	Feminine Family Title
ko-wa (part of lacunose workgroup) ("girls of lacunose workgroup")	2		F	Feminine Family Title
ko-wa (part of lacunose workgroup) ("girls of lacunose workgroup")	8		F	Feminine Family Title
ko-wa (part of lacunose workgroup) ("girls of lacunose workgroup")	0		F	Feminine Family Title
ko-wa (part of lacunose workgroup) ("girls of lacunose workgroup")	0		F	Feminine Family Title
ko-wa (part of lacunose workgroup) ("girls of lacunose workgroup")	0		F	Feminine Family Title
ko-wa (part of lacunose workgroup) ("girls of lacunose workgroup")	2		F	Feminine Family Title
ko-wa (part of lacunose workgroup) ("girls of lacunose workgroup")	1		F	Feminine Family Title
ko-wa (part of lacunose workgroup) ("girls of lacunose workgroup")	6		F	Feminine Family Title
ko-wa (part of lacunose workgroup) ("girls of lacunose workgroup")	4		F	Feminine Family Title
ko-wa (part of lacunose workgroup) ("girls of lacunose workgroup")	0		F	Feminine Family Title

Function	*Tablet*	*Tablet identifying sex*	*Designation type*
Holds cloth?	KN Lc 548	KN Ap 694.1, etc.	WomOcc
Children accompanying women's workgroup	KN Ai 739	Same	FamTitle
Children accompanying women's workgroup	KN Ai 194	Same	FamTitle
Children accompanying women's workgroup	KN Ai 338	Same	FamTitle
Rations for women's workgroup with accompanying children	KN Ai 751	Same	FamTitle
Children accompanying women's workgroup	KN Ai 754	Same	FamTitle
Rations for women's workgroup with accompanying children	KN Ai 5543	Same	FamTitle
Children accompanying women's workgroup	KN Ai 7017	Same	FamTitle
Children accompanying women's workgroup	KN Ai 7023 + 7605	Same	FamTitle
Rations for women's workgroup with accompanying children	KN Ai 7026 + 8662 + fr.	Same	FamTitle
Children accompanying women's workgroup	KN Ai 7029	Same	FamTitle
Children accompanying women's workgroup	KN Ak 640	Same	FamTitle
Children accompanying women's workgroup	KN Ak 781 + 8339	Same	FamTitle
Children accompanying women's workgroup	KN Ak 5648 +5967 + 8606	Same	FamTitle
Children accompanying women's workgroup	KN Ak 7005	Same	[WomOcc]
Children accompanying women's workgroup	KN Ak 7008	Same	FamTitle
Children accompanying women's workgroup	KN Ak 7015	Same	FamTitle
Children accompanying women's workgroup	KN Ak 7018	Same	FamTitle
Children accompanying women's workgroup	KN Ak 7019	Same	FamTitle
Children accompanying women's workgroup	KN Ak 8218 + 8336	Same	FamTitle

Title	*#*	*Name*	*Sex*	*Sex identified*
ko-wa (part of lacunose workgroup) ("girls of lacunose workgroup")	0		F	Feminine Family Title
ko-wa (part of lacunose workgroup) ("girls of lacunose workgroup")	1		F	Feminine Family Title
ko-wa (part of lacunose workgroup) ("girls of lacunose workgroup")	3		F	Feminine Family Title
ko-wa (part of lacunose workgroup) ("girls of lacunose workgroup")	0		F	Feminine Family Title
ko-wa (part of workgroup belonging to MN we-we-si-jo) ("girls of we-we-si-jo's workgroup")	0		F	Feminine Family Title
ko-wa [ ] (part of e-ne-re-ja workgroup @ PN Amnisos) ("girls of the e-ne-ra makers")	0		F	Feminine Family Title
ko-wa [me-wi-jo-e] (part of workgroup at PN da-wo) ("younger girls of da-wi-ja workgroup")[μείων]	0		F	Feminine Family Title
ko-wa me-[u-jo] (part of lacunose workgroup) ("younger girls"); *meiwyos*	0		F	Feminine Family Title
ko-wa me-u-jo (part of da-te-we-ja workgroup) ("younger girls"); *meiwyos* [μείων]	1		F	Feminine Family Title
ko-wa me-u-jo (part of lacunose workgroup) ("younger girls"); *meiwyos* [μείων]	0		F	Feminine Family Title
ko-wa me-u-jo (part of lacunose workgroup) ("younger girls"); *meiwyos* [μείων]	0		F	Feminine Family Title
ko-wa me-u-jo (part of lacunose workgroup) ("younger girls"); *meiwyos* [μείων]	2		F	Feminine Family Title
ko-wa me-u-jo (part of lacunose workgroup) ("younger girls"); *meiwyos* [μείων]	0		F	Feminine Family Title
ko-wa me-u-jo (part of qa-mi-ja workgroup) ("younger girls"); *meiwyos* [μείων]	9		F	Feminine Family Title
ko-wa me-u-jo (part of workgroup belonging to MN: a-no-qo-ta) ("younger girls") [μείων]	0		F	Feminine Family Title
ko-wa me-u-jo-e (part of lacunose workgroup) ("younger girls"); *meiwyos* [μείων]	0		F	Feminine Family Title
ko-wa me-u-jo-e (part of lacunose workgroup) ("younger girls"); *meiwyos* [μείων]	8		F	Feminine Family Title

Function	*Tablet*	*Tablet identifying sex*	*Designation type*
Children accompanying women's workgroup	KN Ak 9407	Same	FamTitle
With woman's workgroup receive rations	KN Ap 5077 + fr.	Same	FamTitle
Too fragmentary to recover	KN X 7720	Same	FamTitle
Too fragmentary to recover	KN X 8168	Same	FamTitle
Children accompanying women's workgroup	KN Ak 9173 + 9459 [+?] 9001	Same	FamTitle
Children accompanying women's workgroup	KN Ak 638	Same	FamTitle
Children of slave women workers (belonging to a-pi-qo-i-ta)	KN Ak 621	Same	FamTitle
Children accompanying women's workgroup	KN Ak 7022 [+] 7024	Same	FamTitle
Children accompanying women's workgroup	KN Ak 612	Same	FamTitle
Children accompanying women's workgroup	KN Ak 614 + fr.	Same	FamTitle
Children accompanying women's workgroup	KN Ak 617	Same	FamTitle
Children accompanying women's workgroup	KN Ak 5884 [+] 5896	Same	FamTitle
Children accompanying women's workgroup	KN Ak 7020	Same	FamTitle
Children accompanying women's workgroup	KN Ak 613	Same	FamTitle
Children accompanying women's workgroup	KN Ak 615	Same	FamTitle
Children accompanying women's workgroup	KN Ak <1807>	Same	FamTitle
Children accompanying women's workgroup	KN Ak 616	Same	FamTitle

Title	#	*Name*	*Sex*	*Sex identified*
ko-wa me-u-jo-e (part of workgroup at PN se-to-i-ja) "younger girls" [μείων]	10		F	Feminine Family Title
ko-wa me-wi-jo (part of da-wi-ja ne-ki-ri-de workgroup) me-wi-jo = me-u-jo [μείων]	-1		F	Feminine Family Title
ko-wa me-wi-jo (part of lacunose workgroup) ("younger girls of lacunose workgroup")	4		F	Feminine Family Title
ko-wa me-wi-jo (part of lacunose workgroup) ("younger girls of lacunose workgroup")	2		F	Feminine Family Title
ko-wa me-wi-jo-e (part of lacunose workgroup) ("younger girls of lacunose workgroup")	7		[F]	Feminine Family Title
ko-wa me-wi-jo-e (part of lacunose workgroup) ("younger girls of lacunose workgroup")	14		F	Feminine Family Title
ko-wa me-wi-jo-e (part of lacunose workgroup) ("younger girls of lacunose workgroup")	1		F	Feminine Family Title
ko-wa me-wi-jo-e (part of lacunose workgroup) ("younger girls of lacunose workgroup")	5		F	Feminine Family Title
ko-wa me-wi-jo-e (part of slaves of MN a-pi-qo-i-ta) ("younger girls - slaves of a-pi-qo-i-ta")	15		F	Feminine Family Title
ko-wa me-wi-jo-e (part of workgroup belonging to MN a-no-zo @ PN da-*22-to)	10		F	Feminine Family Title
ko-wa me-zo (part of da-te-we-ja workgroup) ("older girls"); *medzos* "older" [μείζων]	1		F	Feminine Family Title
[ko-wa me-zo] (part of lacunose workgroup) ("older girls"); *medzos* "older" [μείζων]	5		F	Feminine Family Title
ko-wa me-zo (part of lacunose workgroup) ("older girls"); *medzos* "older" [μείζων]	1		F	Feminine Family Title
ko-wa me-zo (part of lacunose workgroup) ("older girls"); *medzos* "older" [μείζων]	1		F	Feminine Family Title
ko-wa me-zo (part of lacunose workgroup) ("older girls"); *medzos* "older" [μείζων]	1		F	Feminine Family Title
ko-wa me-zo (part of lacunose workgroup) ("older girls"); *medzos* "older" [μείζων]	0		F	Feminine Family Title

Function	*Tablet*	*Tablet identifying sex*	*Designation type*
Children accompanying women's workgroup	KN Ak 634 + 5767	Same	FamTitle
Children accompanying women's workgroup	KN Ak 780 + 7004 + 7045 + 7767	Same	FamTitle
Children accompanying women's workgroup	KN Ak 619 +5633+5892 +5963+6010 +8258+8687	Same	FamTitle
Children accompanying women's workgroup	KN Ak 5940 + 8667	Same	FamTitle
Children accompanying women's workgroup	KN Ak 626	Same	[WomOcc]
Children accompanying women's workgroup	KN Ak 783 + 7011 + 7535 + fr.	Same	FamTitle
Children accompanying women's workgroup	KN Ak 2126	Same	FamTitle
Children accompanying women's workgroup	KN Ak 5907	Same	FamTitle
Children of slave women workers (belonging to a-pi-qo-i-ta)	KN Ai 824	Same	FamTitle
Children accompanying women's workgroup	KN Ak 627 + 7025 + fr.	Same	FamTitle
Children accompanying women's workgroup	KN Ak 612	Same	FamTitle
Children accompanying women's workgroup	KN Ak 5884 [+] 5896	Same	FamTitle
Children accompanying women's workgroup	KN Ak 636	Same - by analogy with rest of series	FamTitle
Children accompanying women's workgroup	KN Ak 2126	Same	FamTitle
Children accompanying women's workgroup	KN Ak 5741 + 5895	Same	FamTitle
Children accompanying women's workgroup	KN Ak 7009	Same	FamTitle

Title	#	*Name*	*Sex*	*Sex identified*
ko-wa me-zo-e (part of lacunose workgroup) ("older girls"); *medzos* "older" [μείζων]	3		F	Feminine Family Title
ko-wa me-zo-e (part of lacunose workgroup) ("older girls"); *medzos* "older" [μείζων]	5		F	Feminine Family Title
ko-wa me-zo-e (part of lacunose workgroup) ("older girls"); *medzos* "older" [μείζων]	13		F	Feminine Family Title
ko-wa me-zo-e (part of lacunose workgroup) ("older girls"); *medzos* "older" [μείζων]	0		F	Feminine Family Title
ko-wa me-zo-e (part of lacunose workgroup) ("older girls"); *medzos* "older" [μείζων]	0		F	Feminine Family Title
ko-wa me-zo-e (part of lacunose workgroup) ("older girls"); *medzos* "older" [μείζων]	0		F	Feminine Family Title
ko-wa me-zo-e (part of lacunose workgroup) ("older girls"); *medzos* "older" [μείζων]	10		F	Feminine Family Title
ko-wa me-zo-e (part of ri-jo-ni-ja workgroup) ("older girls"); *medzos* "older" [μείζων]	3		F	Feminine Family Title
ko-wa me-zo-e (part of slaves of MN a-pi-qo-i-ta workgroup) ("older girls"); *medzos* "older" [μείζων]	5		F	Feminine Family Title
ko-wa me-zo-e (part of to-te-ja workgroup) ("older girls"); *medzos* "older" [μείζων]	4		F	Feminine Family Title
ko-wa me-zo-e (part of workgroup at PN da-wo) ("older girls"); *medzos* "older" [μείζων]	4		F	Feminine Family Title
ko-wa me-zo-e (part of workgroup belonging to MN a-no-zo @ PN da-*22-to)	7		F	Feminine Family Title
ko-wa me-zo-e (part of workgroup belonging to MN we-we-si-jo)	0		F	Feminine Family Title
ko-wa me-zo-e (part of workgroup belonging to MN: a-no-qo-ta) ("older girls"); *medzos* [μείζων]	6		F	Feminine Family Title
ko-wa me[ ] (part of ka-pa-ra2 workgroup) ("girls of the ka-pa-ra2 workgroup")	0		F	Feminine Family Title

Function	*Tablet*	*Tablet identifying sex*	*Designation type*
Children accompanying women's workgroup	KN Ak 610	Same	MUL
Children accompanying women's workgroup	KN Ak 614 + fr.	Same	FamTitle
Children accompanying women's workgroup	KN Ak 617	Same	FamTitle
Children accompanying women's workgroup	KN Ak 619 +5633+5892 +5963+6010 +8258+8687	Same	FamTitle
Children accompanying women's workgroup	KN Ak 830 + fr VI	Same	FamTitle
Children accompanying women's workgroup	KN Ak 5893 + 8623	Same	FamTitle
Children accompanying women's workgroup	KN Ak 7022 [+] 7024	Same	FamTitle
Children accompanying women's workgroup	KN Ak 624	Same	FamTitle
Children of slave women workers (belonging to a-pi-qo-i-ta)	KN Ai 824	Same	FamTitle
Children accompanying women's workgroup	KN Ak 611	Same	FamTitle
Children accompanying women's workgroup	KN Ak 621	Same	FamTitle
Children accompanying women's workgroup	KN Ak 627 + 7025 + fr.	Same	FamTitle
Children accompanying women's workgroup	KN Ak 622	Same	FamTitle
Children accompanying women's workgroup	KN Ak 615	Same	FamTitle
Children accompanying women's workgroup	KN Ak 5009 + 6037 + 8588	Same	FamTitle

Title	*#*	*Name*	*Sex*	*Sex identified*
ko-wa me[(part of lacunose workgroup)	0		F	Feminine Family Title
ko-wa of 7 e-ra-ja (PN) women ("girl/ daughter of workgroup@ PN: e-ra-ja")	1	---	F	Feminine Family Title
ko-wa of total 45 women (all on tablet) ("total girls on tablet")	5	---	F	Feminine Family Title
ko-wa of WN: du-tu-wa ("girls of WN: du-tu-wa")	2	---	F	Feminine Family Title
ko-wa of WN: ke-pu ("girls of WN: ke-pu")	2	---	F	Feminine Family Title
MUL (lacunose occupational title)	3		F	MUL ideogram
MUL (lacunose occupational title)	1	[ ]	F	MUL ideogram
MUL (lacunose occupational title)	0		F?	[By analogy with rest of KN Ai series]
MUL (lacunose occupational title)	0		F?	[By analogy with rest of KN Ai series]
[MUL] (lacunose occupational title)	0		[F]	[By analogy with rest of KN Ai series]
MUL (lacunose occupational title)	10		F	MUL ideogram
[MUL] (lacunose occupational title)	0		[F]	[By analogy with rest of KN Ai series]
MUL (lacunose occupational title)	12		F	MUL ideogram
MUL (lacunose occupational title)	x		F	[By analogy with rest of KN Ai series]
MUL (lacunose occupational title)	6		F	MUL ideogram
[MUL] (lacunose occupational title)	0		[F]	By analogy with rest of KN Ai series]
[MUL] (lacunose occupational title)	0		[F]	[By analogy with rest of KN Ai series]
[MUL] (lacunose occupational title)	0		[F]	[By analogy with rest of KN Ai series]

Function	*Tablet*	*Tablet identifying sex*	*Designation type*
Children accompanying women's workgroup	KN Ak 7013	Same	FamTitle
In personnel list, accompanies 7 e-ra-ja women	KN Ap 639.5	Same	FamTitle
In personnel list, accompanies total women	KN Ap 639.6	Same	FamTitle
In personnel list, accompanies WN du-tu-wa (mother)	KN Ap 639.13	Same	FamTitle
In personnel list, accompanies WN ke-pu (mother)	KN Ap 639.13	Same	FamTitle
Women's workgroup with accompanying children	KN Ai 194	Same	MUL
Women's workgroup with accompanying children	KN Ai 321	Same	MUL
Receives workgroup rations	KN Ai 750	Same	[WomOcc]
Receives workgroup rations	KN Ai 751	Same	[WomOcc]
Receives workgroup rations	KN Ai 5543	(Same - by analogy with rest of KN Ai series)	[WomOcc]
Too fragmentary to recover	KN Ai 5849	Same	MUL
Women's workgroup with accompanying children	KN Ai 7014	(Same - by analogy with rest of KN Ai series)	[WomOcc]
Women's workgroup with accompanying children	KN Ai 7017	Same	MUL
Women's workgroup with accompanying children	KN Ai 7023 +7605	Same	MUL
Receives workgroup rations	KN Ai 7026 + 8662 +fr.	Same	MUL
Women's workgroup with accompanying children	KN Ai 7027	(Same - by analogy with rest of KN Ai series)	[WomOcc]
Women's workgroup with accompanying children	KN Ai 7029	(Same - by analogy with rest of KN Ai series)	[WomOcc]
Women's workgroup with accompanying children	KN Ai 7883	(Same - by analogy with rest of KN Ai series)	[WomOcc]

Title	#	*Name*	*Sex*	*Sex identified*
MUL (lacunose occupational title)	0		F	MUL ideogram
MUL (lacunose occupational title)	11		F	MUL ideogram
MUL (lacunose occupational title)	10		F	MUL ideogram
MUL (lacunose occupational title)	30		F	[By analogy with rest of KN Ai series]
MUL (lacunose occupational title)	36		F	MUL ideogram
MUL (lacunose occupational title)	73		F	MUL ideogram
MUL (lacunose occupational title)	22		F	MUL ideogram
MUL (lacunose occupational title)	34		F	MUL ideogram
MUL (lacunose occupational title)	x		F	[By analogy with rest of KN Ak series]
MUL (lacunose occupational title)	x		F	[By analogy with rest of KN Ak series]
MUL (lacunose occupational title)	x		F	[By analogy with rest of KN Ak series]
MUL (lacunose occupational title)	17		F	MUL ideogram
MUL (lacunose occupational title)	3		F	MUL ideogram
[MUL] (lacunose occupational title)	0		[F]	[By analogy with rest of KN Ak series]
[MUL] (lacunose occupational title)	0		[F]	[By analogy with rest of KN Ak series]
[MUL] (lacunose occupational title)	0		[F]	[By analogy with rest of KN Ak series]
MUL (lacunose occupational title)	0		F	MUL ideogram

Function	*Tablet*	*Tablet identifying sex*	*Designation type*
Women's workgroup with accompanying children	KN Ai 7890	Same	MUL
Women's workgroup with accompanying children	KN Ai 7952	Same	MUL
Women's workgroup with accompanying children	KN Ak 610	Same	MUL
Women's workgroup with accompanying children	KN Ak 614 + fr.	(Same - by analogy with rest of series)	MUL [WomOcc]
Women's workgroup with accompanying children	KN Ak 616	Same	[WomOcc]
Women's workgroup with accompanying children	KN Ak 617	Same	[WomOcc]
Women's workgroup with accompanying children	KN Ak 619 +5633+5892 +5963+6010 +8258+8687	Same	[WomOcc]
Women's workgroup with accompanying children	KN Ak 621	Same	[WomOcc]
Women's workgroup with accompanying children	KN Ak 626	Same	[WomOcc]
Women's workgroup with accompanying children	KN Ak 631	Same	[WomOcc]
Women's workgroup with accompanying children	KN Ak 636	(Same - by analogy with rest of KN Ak series)	[WomOcc]
Women's workgroup with accompanying children	KN Ak 781 + 8339	Same	[WomOcc]
Women's workgroup with accompanying children	KN Ak 782	Same	WomOcc
Women's workgroup with accompanying children	KN Ak 783 + 7011 + 7535 + fr.	(Same - by analogy with rest of KN Ak series)	[WomOcc]
Women's workgroup with accompanying children	KN Ak 1807	(Same - by analogy with rest of KN Ak series)	[WomOcc]
Women's workgroup with accompanying children	KN Ak 2126	(Same - by analogy with rest of KN Ak series)	[WomOcc]
Women's workgroup with accompanying children	KN Ak 5604	Same	[WomOcc]

Title	*#*	*Name*	*Sex*	*Sex identified*
[MUL] (lacunose occupational title)	0		F	[By analogy with rest of KN Ak series]
[MUL] (lacunose occupational title)	0		F	[By analogy with rest of KN Ak series]
[MUL] (lacunose occupational title)	0		F	[By analogy with rest of KN Ak series]
[MUL] (lacunose occupational title)	0		F	[By analogy with rest of KN Ak series]
[MUL] (lacunose occupational title)	0		F	[By analogy with rest of KN Ak series]
[MUL] (lacunose occupational title)	10		F	[By analogy with rest of KN Ak series]
[MUL] (lacunose occupational title)	0		F	[By analogy with rest of KN Ak series]
[MUL] (lacunose occupational title)	0		F	[By analogy with rest of KN Ak series]
MUL (lacunose occupational title)	0		F	MUL ideogram
[MUL] (lacunose occupational title)	8		F	[By analogy with rest of KN Ak series]
[MUL] (lacunose occupational title)	0		[F]	[By analogy with rest of KN Ak series]
[MUL] (lacunose occupational title)	0		[F]	[By analogy with rest of KN Ak series]
[MUL] (lacunose occupational title)	0		[F]	[By analogy with rest of KN Ak series]
MUL (lacunose occupational title)	2		[F]	MUL ideogram
MUL (lacunose occupational title)	84		[F]	[By analogy with rest of KN Ak series]

Function	*Tablet*	*Tablet identifying sex*	*Designation type*
Women's workgroup with accompanying children	KN Ak 5611	(Same - by analogy with rest of KN Ak series)	[WomOcc]
Women's workgroup with accompanying children	KN Ak 5648 + 5967 + 8606	Same	[WomOcc]
Women's workgroup with accompanying children	KN Ak 5655	(Same - by analogy with rest of KN Ak series)	[WomOcc]
Women's workgroup with accompanying children	KN Ak 5741 + 5895	(Same - by analogy with rest of KN Ak series)	[WomOcc]
Women's workgroup with accompanying children	KN Ak 5879	(Same - by analogy with rest of KN Ak series)	[WomOcc]
Women's workgroup with accompanying children	KN Ak 5884 [+] 5896	(Same - by analogy with rest of KN Ak series)	[WomOcc]
Women's workgroup with accompanying children	KN Ak 5893 + 8623	(Same - by analogy with rest of KN Ak series)	[WomOcc]
Women's workgroup with accompanying children	KN Ak 5907	(Same - by analogy with rest of KN Ak series)	[WomOcc]
Women's workgroup with accompanying children	KN Ak 5926 + 5933 + 8219	Same	[WomOcc]
Women's workgroup with accompanying children	KN Ak 5940 + 8667	(Same - by analogy with rest of KN Ak series)	[WomOcc]
Women's workgroup with accompanying children	KN Ak 5948	(Same - by analogy with rest of KN Ak series)	[WomOcc]
Women's workgroup with accompanying children	KN Ak 6048	(Same - by analogy with rest of KN Ak series)	[WomOcc]
Women's workgroup with accompanying children	KN Ak 7002	(Same - by analogy with rest of KN Ak series)	[WomOcc]
Women's workgroup with accompanying children	KN Ak 7003	Same	[WomOcc]
Women's workgroup with accompanying children	KN Ak 7005	Same	[WomOcc]

Title	*#*	*Name*	*Sex*	*Sex identified*
[MUL] (lacunose occupational title)	0		[F]	[By analogy with rest of KN Ak series]
[MUL] (lacunose occupational title)	0		[F]	[By analogy with rest of KN Ak series]
[MUL] (lacunose occupational title)	0		[F]	[By analogy with rest of KN Ak series]
[MUL] (lacunose occupational title)	0		[F]	[By analogy with rest of KN Ak series]
[MUL] (lacunose occupational title)	0		[F]	[By analogy with rest of KN Ak series]
[MUL] (lacunose occupational title)	0		[F]	[By analogy with rest of KN Ak series]
[MUL] (lacunose occupational title)	0		[F]	[By analogy with rest of KN Ak series]
[MUL] (lacunose occupational title)	0		[F]	[By analogy with rest of KN Ak series]
[MUL] (lacunose occupational title)	0		[F]	[By analogy with rest of KN Ak series]
[MUL] (lacunose occupational title)	0		[F]	[By analogy with rest of KN Ak series]
MUL (lacunose occupational title)	0		F	MUL ideogram
MUL (lacunose occupational title)	0		[F]	MUL ideogram
[MUL] (lacunose occupational title)	0		[F]	[By analogy with rest of KN Ak series]
[MUL] (lacunose occupational title)	0		[F]	[By analogy with rest of KN Ak series]
[MUL] (lacunose occupational title)	0		[F]	[By analogy with rest of KN Ak series]

Function	*Tablet*	*Tablet identifying sex*	*Designation type*
Women's workgroup with accompanying children	KN Ak 7007	(Same - by analogy with rest of KN Ak series)	[WomOcc]
Women's workgroup with accompanying children	KN Ak 7008	(Same - by analogy with rest of KN Ak series)	[WomOcc]
Women's workgroup with accompanying children	KN Ak 7009	(Same - by analogy with rest of KN Ak series)	[WomOcc]
Women's workgroup with accompanying children	KN Ak 7012	(Same - by analogy with rest of KN Ak series)	[WomOcc]
Women's workgroup with accompanying children	KN Ak 7013	(Same - by analogy with rest of KN Ak series)	[WomOcc]
Women's workgroup with accompanying children	KN Ak 7015	(Same - by analogy with rest of KN Ak series)	[WomOcc]
Women's workgroup with accompanying children	KN Ak 7016	(Same - by analogy with rest of KN Ak series)	[WomOcc]
Women's workgroup with accompanying children	KN Ak 7018	(Same - by analogy with rest of KN Ak series)	[WomOcc]
Women's workgroup with accompanying children	KN Ak 7019	(Same - by analogy with rest of KN Ak series)	[WomOcc]
Women's workgroup with accompanying children	KN Ak 7020	(Same - by analogy with rest of KN Ak series)	[WomOcc]
Women's workgroup with accompanying children	KN Ak 7021	Same	[WomOcc]
Women's workgroup with accompanying children	KN Ak 7022 [+] 7024	Same	[WomOcc]
Women's workgroup with accompanying children	KN Ak 7028	(Same - by analogy with rest of KN Ak series)	[WomOcc]
Women's workgroup with accompanying children	KN Ak 8218 + 8336	(Same - by analogy with rest of KN Ak series)	[WomOcc]
Women's workgroup with accompanying children	KN Ak 8337	(Same - by analogy with rest of KN Ak series)	[WomOcc]

Title	*#*	*Name*	*Sex*	*Sex identified*
[MUL] (lacunose occupational title)	0		[F]	[By analogy with rest of KN Ak series]
[MUL] (lacunose occupational title)	0		[F]	[By analogy with rest of KN Ak series]
[MUL] (lacunose occupational title)	0		[F]	[By analogy with rest of KN Ak series]
[MUL] (lacunose occupational title)	0		[F]	[By analogy with rest of KN Ak series]
[MUL] (lacunose occupational title)	0		[F]	[By analogy with rest of KN Ak series]
[MUL] (lacunose occupational title)	0		[F]	[By analogy with rest of KN Ak series]
[MUL] (lacunose occupational title)	0		[F]	[By analogy with rest of KN Ak series]
[MUL] (lacunose occupational title)	0		[F]	[By analogy with rest of KN Ak series]
[MUL] (lacunose occupational title)	0		[F]	[By analogy with rest of KN Ak series]
MUL (lacunose occupational title)	40		[F]	MUL ideogram
[MUL] (lacunose occupational title)	0		[F]	[By analogy with rest of KN Ak series]
MUL (lacunose occupational title)	0		F	MUL ideogram
MUL (lacunose occupational title)	1		F	MUL ideogram
[MUL] (lacunose occupational title)	0		F	[By analogy with rest of KN Ap series]
MUL (lacunose occupational title)	26		F	MUL ideogram
MUL (unmodified) Too fragmentary to recover	200		F	MUL ideogram

Function	*Tablet*	*Tablet identifying sex*	*Designation type*
Women's workgroup with accompanying children	KN Ak 8338	(Same - by analogy with rest of KN Ak series)	[WomOcc]
Women's workgroup with accompanying children	KN Ak 8341	(Same - by analogy with rest of KN Ak series)	[WomOcc]
Women's workgroup with accompanying children	KN Ak 8726	(Same - by analogy with rest of KN Ak series)	[WomOcc]
Women's workgroup with accompanying children	KN Ak 8795 [+] 8334	(Same - by analogy with rest of KN Ak series)	[WomOcc]
Women's workgroup with accompanying children	KN Ak 9001 + 9035 [+] 9173	(Same - by analogy with/ rest of KN Ak series)	[WomOcc]
Women's workgroup with accompanying children	KN Ak 9002	(Same - by analogy with rest of KN Ak series)	[WomOcc]
Women's workgroup with accompanying children	KN Ak 9407	(Same - by analogy with rest of KN Ak series)	[WomOcc]
Women's workgroup with accompanying children	KN Ak 9409	(Same - by analogy with rest of KN Ak series)	[WomOcc]
Women's workgroup with accompanying children	KN Ak 9410	(Same - by analogy with rest of KN Ak series)	[WomOcc]
Women's workgroup with accompanying children	KN Ak 9417	Same	[WomOcc]
Women's workgroup with accompanying children	KN Ak 9485 [+] 9522	(Same - by analogy with rest of KN Ak series)	[WomOcc]
Women's workgroup with accompanying children	KN Ak 9499	Same	[WomOcc]
Women's workgroup with accompanying children	KN Ak 9500	Same	[WomOcc]
Women's workgroup with accompanying children	KN Ap 5077 + fr.	(Same - by analogy with rest of KN Ap series)	[WomOcc]
Workgroup tally	KN Ap 5868 + 8220	Same	[WomOcc]
Too fragmentary to recover	KN Ai 1805	Same	MUL

Title	*#*	*Name*	*Sex*	*Sex identified*
MUL (unmodified) Too fragmentary to recover	?		F	MUL ideogram
ne di ko-wa (part of ri-jo-ni-ja workgroup) ("young girls under instruction as ri-jo-ni-ja")	3		F	Feminine Family Title
ne di [MUL] (part of lacunose workgroup) ("young women under instruction in x")	1		F	[MUL ideogram]
ne di [MUL] (part of lacunose workgroup) ("young women under instruction in x")	1		F	[MUL ideogram]
ne di [MUL] (part of lacunose workgroup) ("young women under instruction in x")	0		[F]	[MUL ideogram]
ne di [MUL] (part of workgroup@ do-ti-ja) ("young women under instruction at do-ti-ja")	6		F	[MUL ideogram]
ne di [MUL] (part of workgroup@ tu-ni-ja) ("young women under instruction at tu-ni-ja")	3		F	[MUL ideogram]
ne-ki-ri-de ("women ne-ki-ri-de workers"); ne-ki-ri-de describes workers, sense unclear	0		F	Known from MUL ideogram on KN Ak 0780
ne-ki-[ri-de] ("women ne-ki-ri-de workers"); ne-ki-ri-de describes workers, sense unclear	0		F?	Known from MUL ideogram on KN Ak 0780
ne-we-wi-ja adj, describing women textile-workers	0		F	Known from MUL ideogram on PY Aa 0695, Ab 0560
o-du-ru-wi-ja ("women of o-du-ru-we / Zakro")	1		F	MUL ideogram
pa di [MUL] (part of lacunose workgroup) ("old women under instruction as x workers")	4		F	[MUL ideogram]
pa di [MUL] (part of lacunose workgroup) ("old women under instruction as x workers")	3		F	MUL ideogram
pa di [MUL] (part of lacunose workgroup) ("old women under instruction as x workers")	2		[F]	[MUL ideogram] By analogy with rest of series
pa di [MUL] (part of lacunose workgroup) ("old women under instruction as x workers")	2		[F]	[By analogy with rest of KN Ak series]

Function	*Tablet*	*Tablet identifying sex*	*Designation type*
On sealing - too brief to identify	KN Wn 8752	Same	MUL as title
Part of women's workgroup with accompanying children	KN Ak 624	Same	FamTitle
Part of women's workgroup with accompanying children	KN Ak 5926 + 5933 + 8219	(Same - by analogy with rest of KN Ak series)	[WomOcc]
Part of women's workgroup with accompanying children	KN Ak 5940 + 8667	(Same - by analogy with rest of KN Ak series)	[WomOcc]
Part of women's workgroup with accompanying children	KN Ak 8341	(Same - by analogy with rest of KN Ak series)	[WomOcc]
Tally of young women associated with village workgroups	KN Ap 629.2	(Same - by analogy with rest of KN Ap series)	[WomOcc]
Tally of young women associated with village workgroups	KN Ap 629.1	(Same - by analogy with rest of KN Ap series)	[WomOcc]
Associated with wool	KN Ln 1568. lat a	KN Ak 780 + 7004 + 7045 + 7767	WomOcc
Associated with wool	KN Ws 8152	KN Ak 780 + 7004 + 7045 + 7767	WomOcc?
Holds ko-u-ra cloth pieces	KN Lc 560 + 7587 + 7815	PY Aa 695, PY Ab 560	WomOcc
Women's workgroup with accompanying children	KN Ai 982	Same	Ethnic
Part of women's workgroup with accompanying children	KN Ak 614 + fr.	(Same - by analogy with rest of KN Ak series)	[WomOcc]
Part of women's workgroup with accompanying children	KN Ak 619 +5633+5892 +5963+6010 +8258+8687	Same	[WomOcc]
Part of women's workgroup with accompanying children	KN Ak 626	(Same - by analogy with rest of KN Ak series)	[WomOcc]
Part of women's workgroup with accompanying children	KN Ak 626	(Same - by analogy with rest of KN Ak series)	[WomOcc]

Title	*#*	*Name*	*Sex*	*Sex identified*
pa di [MUL] (part of lacunose workgroup) ("old women under instruction as x workers")	1		F	[MUL ideogram]
pa di [MUL] (part of lacunose workgroup) ("old women under instruction as x workers")	0		F	[MUL ideogram]
pa-i-ti-ja ("Phaistian women"); ethnic adj. from PN: Phaistos	0		F	[MUL ideogram]
pe di [MUL] (part of MN a-no-zo-jo's workgroup) ("women (of age last year) under instruction in MN: a-no-zo-jo workgroup")	2		[F]	[MUL ideogram]
pe di MUL (workgroup lacunose) ("women (of age last year) under instruction as x workers")	2		F	MUL ideogram
pe di MUL (workgroup lacunose) ("women (of age last year) under instruction as x workers")	0		F	[MUL ideogram] By analogy with rest of series
pe di MUL (workgroup lacunose) ("women (of age last year) under instruction as x workers")	6		F	MUL ideogram
qa-mi-ja ("Women of qa-mo"); ethnic adj. based on PN qa-mo	0		F	MUL ideogram
ri-jo-ni-ja ("women of ri-u-no"); ethnic adj.	0		F	By analogy with rest of KN Ak series
ri-jo-ni-ja ("women of ri-u-no"); ethnic adj.	0		F	By analogy with rest of KN Ak series
ri-jo-no TU MUL ("Adult daughters at PN: ri-jo-no")	3		F	MUL ideogram, Feminine Family title
se-to-i-ja (PN) MUL ("women at PN: se-to-i-ja")	74		F	[MUL ideogram]
te-pe-ja @ Knossos (tab: ko-no-so te[-pe-ja]) ("women te-pa-cloth makers @ Knossos")	pl?		F	Known from fem. gen. plural ending on PY Ad 921
te-pe-ja ("women te-pa-cloth makers")	pl?		F?	Known from fem. gen. plural ending on PY Ad 921

Function	*Tablet*	*Tablet identifying sex*	*Designation type*
Part of women's workgroup with accompanying children	KN Ak 5907	(Same - by analogy with rest of KN Ak series)	[WomOcc]
Part of women's workgroup with accompanying children	KN Ak 5948	(Same - by analogy with rest of KN Ak series)	[WomOcc]
Women's workgroup with accompanying children	KN Ak 828	(Same - by analogy with rest of KN Ak series)	Ethnic = WomOcc
Part of women's workgroup with accompanying children	KN Ak 627	(Same - by analogy with rest of KN Ak series)	[WomOcc]
Part of women's workgroup with accompanying children	KN Ak 616	Same	WomTitle
Part of women's workgroup with accompanying children	KN Ak 621	(Same - by analogy with rest of KN Ak series)	[WomOcc]
Part of women's workgroup with accompanying children	KN Ak 631	Same	WomOcc
Women's workgroup with accompanying children	KN Ak 613	Same	FemEthnic
Women's workgroup with accompanying children	KN Ak 624	(Same- by analogy with rest of KN Ak series)	FemEthnic
Women's workgroup with accompanying children	KN Ak 624	(Same - by analogy with rest of KN Ak series)	WomOcc
Tally of young women associated with village workgroups	KN Ap 629.1	Same	[WomOcc]
Women's workgroup with accompanying children	KN Ak 634 + 5767	Same	PN used as WomOcc
Holds cloth?	KN Lc 549	PY Ad 921	WomOcc
Delivery record for MI TE-cloth, 3 units	KN Le 641 + frr.	PY Ad 921	WomOcc

Title	*#*	*Name*	*Sex*	*Sex identified*
ti-wa-ti-ja ("Tinwasian women"); ethnic adj.	3	a-*79 ?	F	MUL ideogram
to-te-ja obscure, a women's trade	10		F	MUL ideogram
to-te-ja (Tab: to-te-[ ) obscure, a women's trade	x		F	Known from MUL ideogram on KN Ak 611
TU of WN *18-to-no ("daughter of WN *18-to-no"); TU = abbrev. for *thugater* [Θυγάτηρ]	1		F	MUL ideogram, Feminine Family title
TU of WN [ ]si ("daughter of WN [ ] si") TU = abbrev. for *thugater* [Θυγάτηρ]	1 of 3		F	MUL ideogram, Feminine Family title
tu-ni-ja TU MUL ("Adult daughters @ PN: tu-ni-ja"); TU = abbrev. for *thugater* [Θυγάτηρ]	4		F	MUL ideogram, Feminine Family title
we-ra-te-ja ethnic or occupational term describing women, exact sense obscure	2	---	F	MUL ideogram
we-ra-te-ja [we-ra-ti-ja] ethnic or occupational term describing women, exact sense obscure	2?		[F]	Known from MUL ideogram on KN Ap 618+623+ 633+5533
we-we-si-jo [MUL] ("women belonging to MN we-we-si-jo")	0		[F]	[MUL ideogram]
we-we-si-jo [MUL] ("women belonging to MN we-we-si-jo")	0		[F]	[MUL ideogram]
za di MUL (part of lacunose workgroup) "women (of age this year) under instruction as x")	1		F	MUL ideogram

Function	*Tablet*	*Tablet identifying sex*	*Designation type*
In list of missing women	KN Ap 618 + 623 + 633 + 5533 + 5922.2	Same	FemEthnic, WN?
Women's workgroup with accompanying children	KN Ak 611	Same	WomOcc
Too fragmentary to recover	KN X 7846	KN Ak 611	WomOcc
In personnel list, daughter of WN *18-to-no	KN Ap 639.4	Same	FamTitle
Included in list of women and textiles	KN Ap 5748 + 5901 + 5923 + 8558.1	Same	FamTitle
Tally of young women associated with village workgroups	KN Ap 629.1	Same	[WomOcc]
In list of missing women	KN Ap 618 +623 + 633 +5533 + 5922.2	Same	WomOcc?
Women's workgroup with accompanying children	KN Ak 784 [+] 8019	KN Ap 618 + 623 + 633 + 5533 + 5922.2	WomOcc?
Women's workgroup with accompanying children	KN Ak 622	Same	WomOcc
Women's workgroup with accompanying children	KN Ak 9173 + 9459 [+?] 9001	(Same - by analogy with rest of KN Ak series)	[WomOcc]
Part of women's workgroup with accompanying children	KN Ak 9001 + 9035 [+] 9173	Same	WomOcc

Bibliography

Acheson, P. E. 1999. "The Role of Force in the Development of Early Mycenaean Polities." In R. Laffineur (ed.), 98–104.

Adrados, F. R. 1968. "Wa-na-ka y ra-wa-ke-ta." *Incunabula Graeca* 25:1–3, 559–573.

Alexandri, A. 1994. *Gender Symbolism in LBA Aegean Glyptic Art.* Unpublished Doctoral Dissertation, Department of Archaeology, University of Cambridge.

Arthur, M. 1981. "The Divided World of the Iliad 6." In H. Foley (ed.), 19–44.

Aura, J. F. 1985. *Diccionario micénico.* Vol. 1. Madrid: Consejo Superior de Investigaciones Cientificas.

—— 1993. *Diccionario micénico.* Vol. 2. Madrid: Consejo Superior de Investigaciones Cientificas.

Bachhuber, C. and R. G. Roberts (eds.). 2009. *Forces of Transformation: The End of the Bronze Age in the Mediterranean.* Themes from the Ancient Near East, BANEA Publication Series, 1. Oxford: Oxbow Books.

Bamberger, J. 1974. "The Myth of Matriarchy: Why Men Rule in Primitive Society." In M. Rosaldo and L. Lamphere (eds.), 263–280.

Barber, E. J. W. 1991. *Prehistoric Textiles: The Development of Cloth in the Neolithic and Bronze Ages with Special Reference to the Aegean*. Princeton, NJ: Princeton University Press.

—— 1994. *Women's Work. The First 20,000 Years. Women, Cloth, and Society in Early Times.* London: W. W. Norton & Co.

—— 1997. "Minoan Women and the Challenges of Weaving for Home, Trade, and Shrine." In R. Laffineur and P. P. Betancourt (eds.), 515–519.

Bartonek, A. 1957. "A Contribution to the Problem of Land Tenure in Ancient Pylos." *Sbornik P. F. F. Brnenske Univ.* 6, 115–118.

—— (ed.). 1968. *Studia Mycenaea: Proceedings of the Mycenaean Symposium Brno April 1966*. Brno: Universita J. E. Purkyne.

—— 1983. "The Linear B Series and their Quantitative Evaluation." In A. Heubeck and G. Neumann (eds.), 19–22.

—— 1987. "On the Prehistory of Ancient Greek." *SMEA* 26, 7–21.

Baumbach, L. 1979. "The Mycenaean Contribution to the Study of Greek Religion in the Bronze Age." *SMEA* 20, 143–160.

—— 1983. "An Examination of Personal Names in the Knossos Tablets as Evidence for the Social Structure of Crete in the Late Minoan II Period." In O. Kryzszkowska and L. Nixon (eds.), 3–10.

—— 1992. "The People of Knossos: Further Thoughts on Some of the Personal Names." In J-P. Olivier (ed.), *Mykenaika. BCH Suppl.* 25, 57–63.

Bendall, L.M. 2007. *Economics of Religion in the Mycenaean World: Resources Dedicated to Religion in the Mycenaean Palace Economy*. Oxford: Oxford University Press.

Bennet, John. 1985. "The Structure of Linear B Administration at Knossos." *AJA* 89, 231–248.

—— 1988a. "Approaches to the Problem of Combining Linear B Textual Data and Archaeological Data in the Late Bronze Age Aegean." In E. R. French and K. A. Wardle (eds.), 509–518.

—— 1988b. "'Outside in the Distance': Problems in Understanding the Economic Geography of Mycenaean Palatial Territories." In J-P. Olivier and T. G. Palaima (eds.), 19–41.

—— 1990. "Knossos in Context: Comparative Perspectives on the Linear B Administration of LM II-III Crete." *AJA* 94, 193–211.

—— 1990. "Knossos in Context: Comparative Perspectives on the Linear B Administration of LM II-III Crete." *AJA* 94, 193–211.

—— 1992. "'Collectors' or 'Owners'? An Examination of Their Possibile Functions with the Palatial Economy of LM III Crete." In J-P. Olivier (ed.), 65–101.

—— J. 2001. "Agency and Bureaucracy: Thoughts on the Nature and Extent of Administration in Bronze Age Pylos." In S. Voutsaki and J. Killen (eds.) *Economy and Politics in the Mycenaean Palatial States*. Cambridge: Cambridge Philosophical Society, 25–37.

—— 2007. "The Aegean Bronze Age." In W. Scheidel, I. Morris, and R. Saller (eds.), 175–210.

—— 2008. "Now You See It; Now You Don't! The Disappearance of the Linear A Script on Crete." In J. Bennet and S. Houston (eds.), *The Disappearance of Writing Systems. Perspectives on Literacy and Communication,* 1–29.

—— 2011. "The Geography of the Mycenaean Kingdoms." In Y. Duhoux and A. Morpurgo Davies (eds.), 137–168.

Bennett, E. L. 1955. "The Olive Oil Tablets of Pylos: Texts of Inscriptions Found." *Minos* Supplement 2. Salamanca.

—— 1956a. "The Landholders of Pylos." *AJA* 60, 103–113.

—— 1956b. "Correspondances entres les textes des tablettes pylienne Aa, Ab, et Ad." In M. Lejeune (ed.), *Etudes Mycéniennes, Actes du Colloque de Gif-sur-Yvette*. Paris: Centre national de la recherché scientifique, 121–136.

—— 1976. "The Pylos Tablets Transcribed Part II: Hands, Concordances, Indices. [=PTT]" *Incunabula Graeca* 59. Roma: Edizioni dell'Ateneo.

—— 1983. "Pylian Landholding Jots and Tittles." In A. Heubeck and G. Neumann (eds.), 41–54.

—— 1984. "The Importance of Pylos in the History of Mycenaean Studies." In C. W. Shelmerdine and T. G. Palaima (eds.), 1–10.

—— 1987. "To Take the Measure of Mycenaean Measures." In J. T. Killen, J. L. Melena, and J-P. Olivier (eds.), 89–95.

Bennett, E. L. Jr. and J-P. Olivier. 1973. The Pylos Tablets Transcribed Part I: Texts and Notes. *Incunabula Graeca* 51. Roma: Edizioni dell'Ateneo.

Bennett, Judith. M. 2006. *History Matters. Patriarchy and the Challenge of Feminism.* Philadelphia, PA: University of Pennsylvania Press.

Betancourt, P. P., V. Karageorghis, R. Laffineur, and W-D. Niemeier, (eds.), 1999 *Meletemata. Aegaeum* 20. Liège and Austin, TX: Annales d'archéologie égéenne de l'Université de Liège et UT-PASP.

Billigmeier, J-C. and J. A. Turner. 1981. "The Socio-Economic Roles of Women in Mycenaean Greece: A Brief Survey from Evidence of the Linear B Tablets." In H. P. Foley (ed.), 1–18.

Bloedow, Edmund F. "Itinerant Craftsmen and Trade in the Aegean Bronze Age." In *TEXNH*, eds. Robert Laffineur and Philip P. Betancourt, *Aegaeum* 16, 438–447. Liège and Austin: Université de Liège and University of Texas at Austin, 1997.

Bolognesi, G., E. Evangelisti, A. Grilli *et al.* (eds.). 1969. *Studi linguistici in onore di Vittore Pisani*, Vol. II. Brescia.

Bradford, A.S. 1986. "Gynaikokratoumenoi: Did Spartan Women Rule Spartan Men?" *Ancient World* 14, 13–18.

Branigan, K. 1998. *Cemetery and Society in the Aegean Bronze Age*. Sheffield: Sheffield Academic Press.

Brown, W. E. 1954. "Land Tenure in Mycenaean Pylos." *Historia* 5, 385–400.

Budin, S. 2011. *Images of Woman and Child from the Bronze Age: Reconsidering Fertility, Maternity, and Gender in the Ancient World.* Cambridge: Cambridge University Press.

Burke, R. B. 1997. "The Organization of Textile Production on Bronze Age Crete." In R. Laffineur and P. P. Betancourt (eds.), 413–422.

—— 1998. *From Minos to Midas, The Organization of Textile Production in the Aegean and in Anatolia*. Doctoral Dissertation, Los Angeles, CA: University of California.

—— 1999. "Purple and Aegean Textile Trade in the Early Second Millennium B. C." In P. P. Betancourt, V. Karageorghis, R. Laffineur, and W-D. Niemeier (eds.), 75–82.

—— 2011. "Textiles." In E. Cline, 430–442.

Cameron, A. and A. Kuhrt. 1983. *Images of Women in Antiquity*. Detroit, MI: Wayne State University Press.

Cantarella, E. 1987. *Pandora's Daughters. The Role and Status of Women in Greek and Roman Antiquity*. Baltimore, MD: Johns Hopkins University Press.

Carlier, P. 1983. "La Femme dans la Société Mycénienne." In E. Lévy (ed.), *La Femme dans les Sociétés Antiques, Actes des Colloques de Strasbourg*. Strasbourg: University of Strasbourg, 9–32.

—— 1987. "A Propos de te-re-ta." In P. Ilievski and L. Crepajac (eds.), 65–73.

—— 1995. "Qa-si-re-u et qa-si-re-wi-ja." In R. Laffineur and W-D. Neimeier (eds.), 355–364.

Carpenter, M. 1983. "*Ki-ti-me-na* and *ke-ke-ma-na* at Pylos." *Minos* 18, 81–88.

—— 1984. "Some Reasons for the Double Version of the Pylos Land-Register." *BICS* 31, 214.

Cartledge, P. 1981. "Spartan Wives: Liberation or License." *CQ* 31, 84–109.

Cavanagh, W. and C. Mee. 1998. *A Private Place: Death in Prehistoric Greece*. Jonsered: Paul Åström Förlag.

Chadwick, J. 1954. "Mycenaean: A Newly Discovered Greek Dialect." *TPHS*, 14, 1–17.

—— 1964. "Review of L. R. Palmer, *Interpretation of Mycenaean Greek Texts*." *Gnomon* 36, 323.

—— 1967. *The Decipherment of Linear B*. Cambridge: Cambridge University Press.

—— 1968. "The Organization of the Mycenaean Archives." In A. Bartonek (ed.), 13–21.

—— 1976. *The Mycenaean World*. Cambridge: Cambridge University Press.

—— 1979. "The Use of Mycenaean Documents as Historical Evidence." In E. Risch and H. Mühlestein (eds.), 31–35.

—— 1985. "What Do We Know About Mycenaean Religion?" In A. Morpurgo Davies and Y. Duhoux (eds.), 191–202.

—— 1988. "The Women of Pylos." In J-P. Olivier and T. G. Palaima (eds.), 43–95.

Chadwick, J. and L. Baumbach. 1973. "The Mycenaean Greece Vocabulary." *Glotta* 41, 200.

Chaniotis, A. 1999. *From Minoan Farmers to Roman Traders: Sidelights on the Economy of Ancient Crete*. Stuttgart: Franz Steiner Verlag.

Chantraine, P. 1968. *Dictionnaire Étymologique de la Langue Grecque: Histoire des Mots*. Vols. 1–4.

Christ, C. P. 1998. *Rebirth of the Goddess*. New York: Routledge.

Cline, E. 1994. *Sailing the Wine-Dark Sea: International Trade and the Late Bronze Age Aegean*. Oxford: Oxford University Press.

—— 2011. *The Oxford Handbook of the Bronze Age Aegean*. Oxford: Oxford University Press.

Cline, E. H. and D. Harris-Cline. 1998. *The Aegean and the Orient in the Second Millennium. Proceedings of the 50th Anniversary Symposium Cincinnati, 18–20 April 1997*. Liège and Austin, TX: Université de Liége and University of Texas at Austin.

Cohen, A. and J. Rutter. 2007. *Constructions of Childhood in Ancient Greece and Italy*. Princeton, NJ: American School of Classical Studies.

Cohen, D. 1989. "Seclusion, Separation, and the Status of Women in Classical Athens." *Greece and Rome* 36, 3–15.

Coldstream, N. 1995. "The Rich Athenian Lady of the Areiopagos and Her Contemporaries." *Hesperia* 64, 391–403.

Cole, S. G. 1981. "Could Greek Women Read and Write?" In H. Foley (ed.), 219–245.

Conkey, M. and J. Spector. 1984. "Archaeology and the Study of Gender." In M. Schiffer (ed.), 1–38.

Connelly, J. B. 2007. *Portrait of a Priestess: Women and Ritual in Ancient Greece*. Princeton, NJ: Princeton University Press.

Costin, C. L. 1991. "Craft Specialization: Issues in Defining, Documenting, and Explaining the Organization of Production." *Archaeological Method and Theory* 3, 1–56.

—— 1996. "Exploring the Relationship between Gender and Craft in Complex Societies: Methodological and Theoretical Issues of Gender Attribution." In R. P. Wright (ed.), 111–140.

D'Agata, A. L. 1999. "Hidden Wars: Minoans and Mycenaeans at Haghia Triada in the LM III Period: The Evidence from Pottery." In R. Laffineur (ed.), 47–55.

D'Agata, A.L. and J. A. Moody. (eds.). 2005. *Ariadne's Threads: Connections between Crete and the Greek Mainland in Late Minoan III (LM IIIA2 to LM IIIC)*. Tripodes 3. Athens: Scuola Archaeologica Italiana di Athene.

Damiani Indelicato, S. 1988. "Were Cretan Girls Playing at Bull-Leaping?" *Cretan Studies* 1, 39–47.

Davis, E. N. 1986. "Youth and Age in the Thera Frescoes." *AJA* 90, 399–406.

—— 1995. "Art and Politics in the Aegean: The Missing Ruler." In P. Rehak (ed.), 1995b, 11–20.

Davis, J. L. and J. Bennet. 1999. "Making Mycenaeans: Warfare, Territorial Expansion, and Representations of the Other in the Pylian Kingdom." In R. Laffineur (ed.), 105–120.

de Fidio, P. 1977. I Dosmoi Pilii a Poseidon: Una Terra Sacra di Eta Micenea. *Incunabula Graeca* 65. Roma: Edizioni dell'Ateneo & Bizzarri.

—— 2001. "Centralization and Its Limits in the Mycenaean Palatial System," In S. Voutsaki and J. Killen (eds.) *Economy and Politics in the Mycenaean Palatial States*. Cambridge: Cambridge Philosophical Society, 15–24.

—— 2008. "Mycenaean History." In Duhoux and Morpurgo Davies, Vol. 1., 81–114.

DeForest, M. 1993. *Woman's Power, Man's Game: Essays on Classical Antiquity in Honor of Joy J. King.* Wauconda, IL: Bolchazy-Carducci.

de Ste. Croix, G. E. M. 1970. "Some Observations on the Property Rights of Athenian Women." *CR* 20, 273–278.

Deger-Jalkotzy, S. 1972. "The Women of PY an 607." *Minos* 13, 137–160.

—— 1988a. "Landbesitz und Sozialstruktur im Mykenischen Staat von Pylos." In Heltzer, M. and E. Lipinski (eds.), 3–52.

—— 1988b. "Noch Einmal zur Ea-Serie von Pylos." *Minos* Suppl. 10, 97–122.

—— 2008. "Mycenaean History." In Y. Duhoux and A. Morpurgo Davies (eds.), 81–114.

Deger-Jalkotzy, S. and I. S. Lemos. (eds.). 2006. *Ancient Greece from the Mycenaean Palaces to the Age of Homer.* Edinburgh Leventis Studies 3. Edinburgh: Edinburgh University Press.

deJ. Ellis, Maria. 1976. *Agriculture and the State in Ancient Mesopotamia: An Introduction to the Problems of Land Tenure.* Occasional Publications of the Babylonian Fund, 1. Philadelphia: The University Museum.

Del Freo, Maurizio. 2005. *I censimenti di terreni nei testi in Lineare B.* Pisa and Roma: Instituti Editoriale e Poligrafici Internazionale.

Dexter, M. R. and E. C. Polomé. (eds.) 1997. *Varia on the Indo-European Past: Papers in Memory of Marija Gimbutas.* Washington DC: Institute for the Study of Man.

Dickinson, O. 1994. *The Aegean Bronze Age.* Cambridge: Cambridge University Press.

—— 1999. "Robert Drew's Theories about the Nature of Warfare in the Late Bronze Age." In R. Laffineur (ed.), 21–25.

Donald, M. and L. Hurcombe. (eds.). 2000. *Representations of Gender from Prehistory to the Present.* London and New York: Macmillan and St. Martin's.

Dorsi, P. 1976–77. "Per Una Storia Della Toponomastica Cretese Antica." *Incontri linguistici* 3, 41–62.

Driessen, J. 1985. "La 'Grande Tablette' (As 1516) de Cnossos." *Minos* 19, 169–193.

—— 1989. *The Room of the Chariot Tablets at Knossos. Interdisciplinary Approach to the Study of a Linear B Deposit.* Doctoral Dissertation, Department of Classics, Katholieke Universiteit Leuven. Belgium.

—— 1990. *An Early Destruction in the Mycenaean Palace at Knossos: A New Interpretation of the Excavation Field-Notes of the South-East Area of the West Wing.* Leuven. Acta Archaeologica Lovaniensia Monographiae 2.

—— 1992. "'Collector's Items'. Observations sur l'Élite Mycénienne de Cnossos." In J-P. Olivier (ed.), 197–214.

—— 1997. "Le Palais de Cnossos au M R II-III: Combien de Destructions?" In J. Driessen and A. Farnoux (eds.), 113–134.

—— 1998–99. "*Kretes* and *Iawones:* Some Observations on the Identity of Late Bronze Age Knossians." In J. Bennet and J. Driessen (eds.), 83–105.

—— 2000. *The Scribes of the Room of the Chariot Tablets at Knossos: Interdisciplinary Approach to the Study of a Linear B Deposit.* Salamanca: Ediciones Universidad de Salamanca.

—— 2008. "Chronology of the Linear B Texts." *A Companion to Linear B: Mycenaean Greek Texts and Their World.* Duhoux, Yves and Anna Morpurgo Davies, eds. Louvain-la-Neuve, Peeters. 69–77.

—— 2011. "Chronology of the Linear B Texts." In Y. Duhoux and A. Morpurgo Davies. (eds.), 69–81.

Driessen, J. and A. Farnoux. (eds.). 1997. "La Crète Mycénienne: Actes de la Table Ronde Internationale Organisée par l'École Française d'Athènes (26–28 Mars 1991)." *BCH*

Supplément 30. Athens and Paris: École française d'Athènes and De Boccard Édition-Diffusion.

Driessen, J. and C. Langohr. 2007. "Rallying 'round a 'Minoan' Past: The Legitimation of Power at Knossos during the Late Bronze Age." In W. Parkinson and M. Galaty (eds.), 178–89.

Driessen, J. and C. F. McDonald. 1984. "Some Military Aspects of the Aegean in the Late 15th and Early 14th Centuries BC." *BSA* 79, 49–74.

—— 1997. *The Troubled Island. Minoan Crete Before and After the Santorini Eruption. Aegaeum* 17. Liége: University of Liége.

Driessen, J. and I. Schoep. 1999. "The Stylus and the Sword: The Role of Scribes and Warriors in the Conquest of Crete." In R. Laffineur (ed.), 389–401.

Duhoux, Y. 2011. "Interpreting the Linear B Records: Some Guidelines." In Y. Duhoux and A. Morpurgo Davies (eds.), 1–32.

Duhoux, Y. and A. Morpurgo Davies. (eds.). 2011. *A Companion to Linear B: Mycenaean and Greek Texts and Their World.* Vol. 2. Louvain-la-Neuve/Walpole, MA: Peeters.

Duhoux, Y., T. G. Palaima, and J. Bennet. 1989. *Problems in Decipherment.* Louvain-La-Neuve, Belgium: Peeters.

Dunkel, G. 1981. "Mycenaean ke-ke-me-na, ki-ti-me-na." *Minos* 17, 18–29.

Dyczek, P. 1992. "The Status of Women in Aegean Culture: Some Considerations." In A. Lipska, E. Niezgoda, and M. Zabecka (eds.), *Studia Aegaea et Balcanica in Honorem Lodovicae.* Warsaw: Wydawnictwa Uniwersytetu Warszawskiego.

Earle, T. 2002. *Bronze Age Economics. The Beginnings of Political Economies.* Boulder-Oxford: Westfield Press.

Ehrenberg, M. 1989. *Women in Prehistory.* London: British Museum Publications.

Evans, A. 1921–35. *The Palace of Minos.* Vols, 1–4. London: Macmillan.

Everly, D., H. Hughes-Brock, and N. Momigliano. (eds.). 1994. *KNOSSOS: A Labyrinth of History. Papers presented in Honour of Sinclair Hood.* Oxford: British School at Athens.

Facaros, D. and Pauls, M. 2003. *Crete* (Country and Regional Guides). London: Cadogan Guides.

Fantham, E., H. P. Foley, N. B. Kampen, S. B. Pomeroy and H. A. Shapiro. 1994. "Spartan Women: Women in a Warrior Society." In E. Fantham, N. B. Kampen, S. B. Pomeroy and H. A. Shapiro (eds.), *Women in the Classical World: Image and Text.* Oxford and New York: Oxford University Press, 56–67.

Finley, M I. 1954. *The World of Odysseus.* New York: Viking Press.

—— 1957a. "Homer and Mycenae: Property and Tenure." *Historia* 6, 135–159.

—— 1957b. "The Mycenaean Tablets and Economic History." *Economic History Review* 10. 128–141.

—— 1976. *The Ancient Economy.* London: Chatto and Windus.

Firth, R. J. 1993. "A Statistical Analysis of the Greekness of Men's Names on the Knossos Linear B Tablets." *Minos* 27–28, 83–100.

Foley, H. P. 1981. *Reflections of Women in Antiquity.* New York: Gordon and Breach Science Publishers.

Foster, E. D. 1980. "An Administrative Department at Knossos Concerned with Perfumery and Offerings." *Minos* 16, 19–51.

—— 1981. "The Flax Impost at Pylos and Mycenaean Landholding," *Minos* 17, 67–121.

Foster, K. P. and R. Laffineur. (eds.). 2002. "Metron: Measuring the Bronze Age." Proceedings of the 9th International Aegean Conference/9e Rencontre égéenne internationale, Yale University, 18–21 april 2002. *Aegaeum* 24. Liége: Forlag uden navn.

Foxhall, L. 1989. "Household, Gender and Property in Classical Athens." *CQ* 39, 22–44.

—— 1995. "Women's Ritual and Men's Work in Ancient Athens." In R. Hawley and B. Levick (eds.), 97–110.

Foxhall, L. and J. Salmon. 1999. *When Men Were Men. Masculinity, Power and Identity in Classical Antiquity.* London and New York: Routledge.

French, E. R. and K. A. Wardle. (eds.). 1988. *Problems in Greek Prehistory, Papers Presented at the Centenary Conference of the British School of Archaeology at Athens, Manchester, April 1986.* Bristol: Bristol Classics Press.

Furumark, A. 1954. "Agaische Texte in Griechiescher Sprache." *Eranos* 52, 36–37.

Galaty, M. L. and W. A. Parkinson. (eds.). 1999. *Rethinking Mycenaean Palaces. New Interpretations of an Old Idea.* Los Angeles, CA: The Cotsen Institute of Archaeology.

—— (eds.). 2007. *Rethinking Mycenaean Palaces: New Interpretations of an Old Idea*, rev. ed. Los Angeles, CA: UCLA Press.

Gale, N. H. 1991. "Bronze Age Trade in the Mediterranean." *SIMA* 90. Göteborg: Paul Åströms Förlag.

Galison, P. and D. J. Stump. (eds.). 1996. *The Disunity of Science: Boundaries, Contexts, and Power.* Palo Alto, CA: Stanford University Press.

Garcia Ramón, J.L. 1992. "Mycénien *ke-sa-do-ro/Kessandros, ke-ti-ro/Kestilos, ke-to/Kestor/:* grec alphabétique *Ainesimbrota, Ainesilaos, Ainetor* et le nom de Cassandra." In J-P. Olivier (ed.), *Mykenaika. BCH Suppl.* 25, 239–255.

—— 2011. "Mycenaean Onomastics." In Y. Duhoux and A. Morpurgo Davies (eds.), 253–298.

Gates, C. 1992. "Art for Children in Mycenaean Greece." In R. Laffineur and J. L. Crowley (eds.), 161–171.

—— 1999. "Why are There No Scenes of Warfare in Minoan Art?" In R. Laffineur (ed.), 277–284.

Georgoudi, Stella. 1992. "Creating a Myth of Matriarchy." In P. Schmitt-Pantel (ed.), 449–456.

Gérard-Rousseau, M. 1968. Les Mentions Religieuses dans les Tablettes Mycéniennes. *Incunabula Graeca* 19. Roma: Edizioni Dell'Ateneo.

Gero, J. and M. Conkey. (eds.). 1991. *Engendering Archaeology: Women and Prehistory.* Oxford: Basil Blackwell.

Gilchrist, R. 1991. "Women's Archaeology? Political Feminism, Gender Theory and Historical Revision." *Antiquity* 65, 495–501.

Gillis, C. 1997a. *Trade and Production in Premonetary Greece: Production of the Craftsman.* Proceedings of the 4th and 5th International Workshops, Athens 1994 and 1995. SIMA-PB 143. Jonsered: Paul Åströms Förlag.

—— 1997b. "The Smith in the Late Bronze Age: State Employee, Independent Artisan, or Both?" In R. Laffineur and P. P. Betancourt (eds.), 505–519.

—— 2000. *Trade and Production in Premonetary Greece: Acquisition and Distribution of Raw Materials and Finished Products.* Proceedings of the 6th International Workshop, Athens 1996. SIMA-PB 154. Jonsered: Paul Åströms Förlag.

Gillis, C., C. Risberg, and B. Sjöberg. (eds.). 1995. *Trade and Production in Premonetary Greece: Aspects of Trade.* Proceedings of the Third International Workshop, Athens 1993. SIMA-PB 134. Jonsered: Paul Åströms Förlag.

Gimbutas, M. 1974. *The Gods and Goddesses of Old Europe.* Berkeley, CA: University of California Press.

—— 1997. *The Kurgan Culture and the Indo-Europeanization of Europe: Selected Articles from 1952–1993.* Journal of Indo-European Studies Monograph no. 18. Washington DC: Institute for the Study of Man.

—— 1999. *The Living Goddesses.* Berkeley, CA: University of California Press.

Gould, J. 1980. "Law, Custom and Myth: Aspects of the Social Position of Women in Classical Athens." *JHS* 100, 38–59.

Goodison, L. 1989. *Death, Women and the Sun. Symbolism of Regeneration in Early Aegean Religion. BICS* Supplement 53. London: Institute of Classical Studies.

Grumach, E. 1958. *Minoica. Festschriftzum 80. Geburtstag von Johannes Sundwall.* Berlin: Akademie Verlag.

Hägg, R. 1985. "Mycenaean Religion: The Helladic and the Minoan Components." In A. Morpurgo Davies and Y. Duhoux (eds.), 203–225.

Hägg, R. and N. Marinatos. 1981a. *Proceedings of the First International Symposium at the Swedish Institute in Athens, 12–13 May 1980. SkrAth, 4°,* XXVII. Stockholm: Svenska Institutet i Athen.

—— 1981b. "Sanctuaries and Cults in the Aegean Bronze Age." In R. Hägg and N. Marinatos (eds.), 41–48.

—— 1987. *The Function of the Minoan Palaces.* Stockholm: Paul Åströms Förlag.

Hajnal, I. 1997. "Sprachschichten des Mykenischen Griechischen." *Minos* Suppl. 14, 12–19.

Hall, J. M. 1997. *Ethnic Identity in Greek Antiquity.* Cambridge: Cambridge University Press.

Halstead, P. 1992. "Agriculture in the Bronze Age. Towards a Model of Palatial Economy." In B. Wells (ed.), 105–117.

Hawley, R. and B. Levick. 1995. *Women in Antiquity: New Assessments.* New York: Routledge.

Heltzer, M. and E. Lipinski. 1988. *Society and Economy in the Eastern Mediterranean (c.1500–1000 BC).* Proceedings of the International Symposium held at the University of Haifa from the 28th of April to the 2nd of May 1985. Leuven: Uitgeverij Peeters.

Heubeck, A. 1967. "Myk. Ke-ke-me-no." *AZ* 17, 17–21.

—— 1969. "Gedanken zu Griechisch λαός", In G. Bolognesi, E. Evangelisti, A. Grilli *et al.* (ed.), 535–544.

—— 1976. "Epikritisches zu den Griechischen Ortsnamen mit dem *-went-*/*-wont-* Suffix Besonders zu den Namen Phleius." *SMEA* 17, 127–136.

—— 1985. "Zu den Mykenischen Stoffadjectiven." *Münchener Studienzur Sprachwissenschaft* 46, 123–138.

Heubeck, A. and G. Neumann. 1983. *Res Mycenaea. Akten de VII Internationalen Mykenologischen Colloquium in Nürnberg vom 6–10.* Göttingen: Vandenhoeck and Ruprect. 19–22.

Hiller, S. 1979. "Ka-ko na-wi-jo, Notes on Interdependence of Temple and Bronze in the Aegean Bronze Age." In E. Risch and H. Mühlestein (eds.), 189–195.

—— 1988. "Dependent Personnel in Mycenaean Texts." In M. Heltzer and E. Lipinski (eds.), 53–68.

—— 1989. "Familienbeziehungen in mykenischen Texten." In T. G. Palaima, C. W. Shelmerdine, and P. H. Ilievski (eds.), 40–65.

—— 2011. "Mycenaean Religion and Cult." In Y. Duhoux and A. Morpurgo Davies (eds.), 169–212.

Hiller, S. and O. Panagl. 1997. *Die Frühgriechischen Texte aus Mykenischer Zeit.* Darmstadt: Wissenschaftliche Buchgesellschaft.

Hitchcock, L. A. 1997. "Engendering Domination: A Structural and Contextual Analysis of Minoan Neopalatial Bronze Figurines." In E. Scott and J. Moore (eds.), 113–130.
—— 2000. "Engendering Ambiguity in Minoan Crete: It's a Drag to be a King." In M. Donald and L. Hurcombe (eds.), 69–86.
Hocker, F. and T. G. Palaima. 1993. "Late Bronze Age Aegean Ships and the Pylos Tablets Vn 46 and Vn 879." *Minos* 25–26, 297–317.
Hood, S. 1978. *The Arts in Prehistoric Greece.* Penguin Books. Harmondsworth.
—— 1985. "The Primitive Aspects of Minoan Artistic Convention." In J-C. Poursat and P. Darque (eds.), 21–26.
Hooker, J.T. 1977. *Mycenaean Greece.* London: Routledge.
—— 1980. *Linear B: An Introduction.* Bristol: Bristol Classical Press.
—— 1982. "The End of Pylos and the Linear B evidence." *SMEA* 23, 210–217.
—— 1983. "Minoan Religion in the Late Palace Period." In O. Kryzszkowska and L. Nixon (eds.), 137–142.
—— 1987a. "Minoan and Mycenaean Administration: A Comparison of the Knossos and Pylos Archives." In Hägg, R. and N. Marinatos (eds.), 313–316.
—— 1987b. "Titles and Functions in the Pylian State." *Minos* 21, 257–267.
Hutton, W. F. 1990. "The Meaning of qe-te-o in Linear B." *Minos: Revista de Filología Egea,* 25: 105–132.
Ilievski, P. H. 1979a. "Mycenaean *ka-ra-no-ko.*" *SMEA* 20, 161–169.
—— 1979b. "Vocabulary Words from the Mycenaean Personal Names." In E. Risch and H. Mühlestein (eds.), 134–146.
—— 1983. "Some Structural Peculiarities of Mycenaean-Greek Personal Names." In A. Heubeck and G. Neumann (eds.), 202–215.
—— 1992. "Observations on the Personal Names from the Knossos D Tablets." In J-P. Olivier (ed.), 321–348.
Ilievski, P. and L. Crepajac. (eds.). 1987. *Tractata Mycenaea. Proceedings of the Eighth International Colloquium on Mycenaean Studies, Held in Ohrid (15–20 September 1985).* Skopje: Macedonian Acedemy of Sciences and Arts.
Immerwahr, S. 1983. "The People in the Frescoes." In O. Kryzszkowska and L. Nixon (eds.), 143–153.
—— 1990. *Aegean Painting in the Bronze Age.* London and State College: Pennsylvania State University Press.
Johnson, A. G. 2005. *The Gender Knot: Unraveling Our Patriarchal Legacy*, rev. ed. Philadelphia, PA: Temple University Press.
Jones, B. R. 1998. *Minoan Women's Clothes: An Investigation of their Construction from the Depictions in Aegean Art.* Institute of Fine Arts, New York: New York University.
Jones, S. 1997. *The Archaeology of Ethnicity: Constructing Identities in the Past and Present.* London and New York: Routledge.
Just, R. 1989. *Women in Athenian Law and Life.* New York and London: Routledge.
Katz, M. A. 1995. "Ideology and 'the Status of Women' in Ancient Greece." In R. Hawley and B. Levick (eds.), 21–43.
—— 2000. "Sappho and Her Sisters: Women in Ancient Greece (review essay)." *Signs.* 25, 505–531.
Kazanskiene, V. P. 1995. "Land Tenure and Social Position in Mycenaean Greece." In R. Laffineur and W-D. Niemeier (eds.), 603–611.
Killen, J. T. 1964. "The Wool Industry of Crete in the Late Bronze Age." *BS* 59, 1–17.
—— 1966a. "The Knossos Lc (Cloth) Tablets." *BICS* 13, 105–109.
—— 1966b. "The Abbreviation TU on Knossos Women Tablets." *ZA* 16, 207–212.

—— 1968.'The Knossos o-pi Tablets', in C. Gallavotti (ed.), *Atti e Memorie del 1° Congresso Internazionale di Micenologia* (Roma 27 settembre-3 ottobre 1967), (Incunabula Graeca 25:2), Rome 636–643.

—— 1974. "A Problem in the Knossos Lc (1) (Cloth) Tablets." *Hermathena* 113, 82–90.

—— 1979. "The Knossos Ld (1) Tablets." In E. Risch and H. Mühlestein (eds.), 151–181.

—— 1981. "Some Puzzles in a Mycenaean Personnel Record." *Ziva Antika* 31, 37–45.

—— 1983a. "Mycenaean Possessive Adjectives in *e-jo*." *TAPA* 113 (1983): 66–99.

—— 1983b. "TA and DA." *Concilium Eirene XVI, Mycenaeological Colloquium. Proceedings of the 16th International Eirene Conference*, Vol. III, Section IV, eds. Pavel Oliva and Alena Frolikova, 121–126. Prague: Praha Kabinet pro studia recká, rimská a latinská, 1983.

—— 1984. "The Textile Industries at Pylos and Knossos." In C. W. Shelmerdine and T. G. Palaima (eds.), 49–63.

—— 1985. "The Linear B Tablets and the Mycenaean Economy." In A. Morpurgo Davies and Y. Duhoux (eds.), 241–305.

—— 1988. "Epigraphy and Interpretation in Knossos WOMAN and CLOTH records." In J-P. Olivier and T. G. Palaima (eds.), 167–183.

—— 1995. "Some Further Thoughts on 'Collectors'." In R. Laffineur (ed.), 213–26.

—— 1997. "The Find-Places of the Tablets from the Western Magazines at Knossos." *Minos* 31–32, 123–132.

—— 2001. "Religion at Pylos: The Evidence of the Fn Tablets." In R. Laffineur and R. Hägg (eds.), 435–443.

—— 2008. "Mycenaean Economy." In Y. Duhoux and A. Morpurgo Davies (eds.), 159–200.

Killen, J. T., J. L. Melena and J-P. Olivier. (eds.). (1987) "Studies in Mycenaean and Classical Greek Presented to John Chadwick" *Minos* 20–22. Salamanca: Universidad de Salamanca, 89–95.

Killen, J. T. and J-P. Olivier. 1966. "388 Reccords de Fragments dans les Tablettes de Cnossos." In L. R. Palmer and J. Chadwick (eds.), 47–92.

—— 1989. *The Knossos Tablets*, 5th ed. *Minos* suppl. 11. Salamanca: Ediciones Universidad de Salamanca.

Koehl, R. 1986. "The Chieftain Cup as a Minoan Rite of Passage." *JHS* 106, 99–110.

Kokkinidou, D. and M. Nikolaidou. 1993. Η αρχαιολογία και η κοινωνική ταυτό ητα του φύλου Προσεγγίσει στην αιγαιακή *(Archaeology and Gender: Approaches to Aegean Prehistory)*. Thessaloniki: Banias.

Kopaka, K. 1997. "'Women's Arts – Men's Crafts'? Towards a Framework for Approaching Gender Skills in the Prehistoric Aegean." In R. Laffineur and P. P. Betancourt (eds.), 521–531.

Kopcke, G. 1995. "The Argolid in 1400 – What Happened?" In R. Laffineur and W-D. Neimeier (eds.), 89–93.

Kraemer, R. S. 1988. *Maenads, Martyrs, Matrons, Monastics: A Sourcebook on Women's Religions in the Greco-Roman World*. Philadelphia, PA: Fortress.

Krigas, E. 1985. "Mycenaean ke-ke-me-na, ki-ti-me-na." *Minos* 19, 55–59.

—— 1987. "The Land Registry. A Survey of the Ea-Eb-Ed-Ep Tablets of the Pylian Archive." *SMEA* 26, 23–34.

Kristensen, K. R. 1994. "Men, Women and Property in Gortyn: The Karteros of the Law Code," *C&M* 45, 5–26.

Kryzszkowska, O. and L. Nixon. 1983. *Minoan Society: Proceedings of the Cambridge Colloquium 1981*. Bristol: Bristol Classical Press.

Kunstler, B. 1987. "Family Dynamics and Female Power in Ancient Sparta." *Helios* 13, 31–48.

Kyriakidis, E. 2010. "'Collectors' as Stakeholders in Mycenaean Governance: Property and the Relations between the Ruling Class and the State." *Proceedings of the Cambridge Philological Society.* 56. 140–177.

Laffineur, R. 1995. "Craftsmen and Craftsmanship in Mycenaean Greece: For a Multimedia Approach." In R. Laffineur and W-D. Niemeier (eds.), 189–200.

—— (ed.). 1999. *Polemos: Le Contexte Guerrier en Égée á l'Âge du Bronze. Actes de la 7e Rencontre Égéenne Internationale Université de Liège, 14–17 avril 1998, Aegaeum* 19. Liège and Austin: Histoire de l'art et archéologie de la Grèce antique and Program in Aegean Scripts and Prehistory, University of Texas at Austin.

Laffineur, R. and Basch, L. (eds.). 1991. *Thalassa. L'Égée Préhistorique et la Mer. Actes de la Troisième Rencontre Égéenne Internationale de l'Université de Liège, Station de recherches sous-marines et océanographiques (StaReSo), Calvi, Corse, 23–25 avril 1990, Aegaeum* 7. Annales d'archéologie égéenne de l'Université de Liège. Liège: Histoire de l'art et archéologie de la Grèce antique, Université de Liège.

Laffineur, R. and P. P. Betancourt. 1997. *Τεχνη: Craftsmen, Craftswomen and Craftsmanship in the Aegean Bronze Age. Proceedings of the 6th International Aegean Conference / 6e Rencontre Égéenne Internationale Philadelphia, Temple University, 18–21 April 1996, Aegaeum* 16. Liège and Austin, TX: Université de Liège and University of Texas at Austin.

Laffineur, R. and Hägg, R. (eds.). 2001. *Potnia: Deities and Religion in the Aegean Bronze Age: Proceedings of the 8th International Aegean Conference/8e Rencontre Égéenne Internationale, Göteborg, Göteborg University, 12–15 April 2000.* Liège and Austin, TX: Université de Liège and University of Texas Press.

Laffineur, R. and W-D. Neimeier. 1995. *Politeia: Society and State in the Aegean Bronze Age. Proceedings of the 5th International Aegean Conference / 5e Rencontre égéenne internationale, University of Heidelberg. Archäologisches Institut, 10–13 April 1994, Aegaeum* 12. Liège and Austin, TX: Histoire de l'art et archéologie de la Grèce antique and University of Texas at Austin, Program in Aegean Scripts and Prehistory.

Landau, O. 1958. *Mykenisch-Grichische Personennamen.* Göteborg: Acta Universitatis Gothoburgensis.

Landenius Enegren, H. 1995. "A Prospographical Study of Scribal Hand 103, Methods, Aims and Problems." In R. Laffineur and W-D. Niemeier (eds.), 115–130.

—— 2008. *The People of Knossos. Prosopographical Studies in the Knossos LinearB Archives.* Uppsala: Acta Universitatis Upsaliensis.

Lane, M. F. 2009. "From da-mo to dh=mov: Survival of a Mycenaean Land Allocation Tradition in the Classical Era?" In Bachhuber, C. and R. G. Roberts (eds.), 111–8.

—— 2012a. "Landholding at Pa-ki-ja-ne" *Pasiphae* VI. 59–116.

—— 2012b. "Linear B wo-wo/wo-wi-ja" *Pasiphae* VI. 117–184.

Lang, M. 1988. "Pylian Place-Names." In J-P. Olivier and T. G. Palaima (eds.), 185–212.

Leduc, C. 1992. "Marriage in Ancient Greece." In P. Schmitt-Pantel (ed.), 235–296.

Lee, M. 1995. *Semiotic Approaches to the Iconography of Gender in Minoan Neopalatial Bronze Votive Figurines.* M.A. Thesis, Department of Classical Archaeology, Bryn Mawr College.

Lefkowitz, M. L. 1983. "Wives and Husbands." *Greece and Rome* 30, 31–47.

Lefkowitz, M. L. and M. B. Fant. (eds.). 1982. *Women's Life in Greece and Rome. A Source Book in Translation,* 1st ed. Baltimore, MD: Johns Hopkins.

Lefkowitz, M. L. and M. B. Fant. (eds.). 1992. *Women's Life in Greece and Rome. A Source Book in Translation,* 2nd ed. Johns Hopkins. Baltimore, MD.

Lejeune, M. 1958. *Mémoires de philologie Mycénienne I (1955–57)*. Rome: Edizione dell'Ateneo.

—— 1966. "Le Récapitulatif du Cadastre Ep de Pylos." In L. R. Palmer and J. Chadwick (eds.), 260–264.

—— 1976. "Analyse du dossier Pylien *Ea*." *Minos* 15, 81–115.

—— 1979. "Sur la Fiscalité Pylienne Ma." In E. Risch and H. Mühlestein (eds.), 147–150.

Lerner, G. 1986. *The Creation of Patriarchy.* Oxford: Oxford University Press.

Leukart, A. 1979. "Autour de *ka-ko na-wi-jo:* Quelques Critères." In E. Risch and H. Mühlestein (eds.), 183–187.

Lindgren, M. 1973. *The People of Pylos. Prosopographical and Methodological Studies in the Pylos Archives.* Uppsala: Acta Univeritatis Upsaliensis.

—— 1979. "The Interpretation of Personal Designations in Linear B: Methodological Problems." In E. Risch and H. Mühlestein (eds.), 81–86.

Lipska, A., E. Niezgoda, and M. Zabecka (eds.). 1992. *Studia Aegaea et Balcanica in honorem Lodovicae.* Warsaw: Wydawnictwa Uniwersytetu Warszawskiego.

Lupack, S. 1999. "Palaces, Sanctuaries, and Workshops: The Role of the Religious Sector in Mycenaean Economies." In M. L. Galaty and W. A. Parkinson (eds.), 25–34.

—— 2006. "Deities and Religious Personnel as Collectors." In Perna, M. (ed.). 89–108.

—— 2007a. "Archaeology and Linear B: Finding a Balance." In C. Gillis (ed.). 2007. *The Proceedings of the 7th Annual Conference on Trade and Production in Premonetary Greece.* Gothenberg, pp. 1–16.

—— 2007b. "Palaces, Sanctuaries and Workshops: The Role of the Religious Sector in Mycenaean Economics." In W. Parkinson and M. Galaty. (eds.), 54–65.

—— 2008a. The Role of the Religious Sector in the Economy of Late Bronze Age Mycenaean Greece, BAR International Series 1858, Oxford: Archaeopress.

—— 2008b. "The Northeast Building of Pylos and An 1281," In A. Sacconi, L. Godart and M. Del Freo (eds.), 467–484.

—— 2010. "Minoan Religion," In E. H. Cline (ed.), 251–262.

—— 2011. "A View from Outside the Palace: The Sanctuary and the *Damos* in Mycenaean Economy and Society," *AJA* 115, 207–217.

Lyberopoulou, G. 1978. *Le Costume Égéen.* Doctoral Dissertation, Université de Paris.

Manning, S. W. 1995. *The Absolute Chronology of the Aegean Bronze Age: Archaeology, Radiocarbon, and History,* Monographs in Mediterranean Archaeology. Sheffield: Sheffield Academic Press.

Marinatos, N. 1984. *Art and Religion in Thera. Reconstructing a Bronze Age Society.* Athens: D. and I. Mathioulakis.

—— 1987a. "Offering of Saffron to The Minoan Goddess of Nature: The Role of the Monkey and the Importance of Saffron." In *Proceedings of the Uppsala Symposium 1985. Uppsala Studies in Ancient Mediterranean and Near Eastern Civilizations* 15. Uppsala: University of Uppsala. 123–132.

—— 1987b. "Public Festivals in the West Courts of the Palaces." In R. Hägg and N. Marinatos (eds.), 135–143.

—— 1993. *Minoan Religion. Ritual, Image, and Symbol.* Columbia, SC: University of South Carolina Press.

—— 1995. "Formalism and Gender Roles: A Comparison of Minoan and Egyptian Art." In R. Laffineur and W-D. Niemeier (eds.), 577–585.

Marler, J. 1997. *From the Realm of the Ancestors: An Anthology in Honor of Marija Gimbutas*. Manchester: Knowledge, Ideas, and Trends, Inc.

McDonald, W. A. and G. Rapp. 1972. *The Minnesota Messenia Expedition*. Minneapolis, MN: University of Minnesota Press.

Mee, C. 1998. "Gender Bias in Mycenaean Mortuary Practices." In K. Branigan (ed.), 165–171.

Melena, J. L. 1975. *Studies on Some Mycenaean Inscriptions from Knossos Dealing with Textiles. Minos* Suppl. 5. Salamanca: Ediciones Universdad de Salamanca.

Meskell, L. 1995. "Goddesses, Gimbutas and 'New Age' Archaeology." *Antiquity* 69, 74–85.

Montecchi, B. 2012. "Wool-spinning, Bronze-working and the Peculiarities of Mycenaean ta-ra-si-ja." *Pasiphae* VI. 185–194.

Morgan, K. A. 2004. *Popular Tyranny: Sovereignty and its Discontents in Ancient Greece*. Austin: University of Texas Press.

Morgen, S. (ed.). 1989. *Gender and Anthropology: Critical Reviews for Research and Teaching*. Washington DC: American Anthropological Association.

Morpurgo Davies, A. 1979. "Terminology of Power and Terminology of Work in Greek and Linear B." In E. Risch and H. Mühlestein (eds.), 87–109.

Morpurgo Davies, A. and Y. Duhoux. (eds.). 1985. *Linear B: A 1984 Survey. Proceedings of the Mycenaean Colloquium of the VIIIth Congress of the International Federation of the Societies of Classical Studies (Dublin, 27 August–1st September 1984), BCILL* 26. Louvain-la-Neuve: Cabay.

Morris, H. J. 1986. *An Economic Model of the Late Mycenaean Kingdom of Pylos*. Ph.D. Dissertation, University of Minnesota.

Morris, S. 2004. "Imaginary Kings: Alternatives to Monarchy in Early Greece." In K. A. Morgan (ed.), 1–24.

Nakassis, D. 2008. "Named Individuals and the Mycenaean State at Pylos." In A. Sacconi, M. Del Freo, L. Godart, and M. Negri (eds.). *Colloquium Romanum: atti del XII colloquio internazionale di micenologia, Roma, 20–25 febbraio 2006*. Vol. 2. Pisa/Roma: Fabrizio Serra, 549–61.

—— 2010. "Reevaluating Staple and Wealth Finance at Mycenaean Pylos." In Pullen, D. J. (ed.), 127–48.

—— 2013. *Individuals and Society in Mycenaean Pylos*. Leiden and Boston, MA: Brill.

Nakassis, D., J. Gulizio, and S. A. James (eds.). 2012. *KE-RA-ME-JA: Studies presented to Cynthia Shelmerdine*. Philadelphia, PA: INSTAP Press.

Neils, J. and J. H. Oakley. 2003. *Coming of Age in Ancient Greece: Images of Children from the Classical Past*. New Haven, CT: Yale University Press.

Neumann, G. 1994. "Wertvorstetllungen und Ideologie in der Personennamen der mykenischen Griechen." *AnzWien* 131, 127–166.

Niemeier, W-D. 1983. "The Character of the Knossian Palace Society in the Second Half of the Fifteenth Century B.C.: Mycenaean or Minoan?" In O. Kryzszkowska and L. Nixon (eds.), 217–236.

Nikoloudis, S. 2008a. "The Role of the ra-wa-ke-ta. Insights from PY Un 718." In A. Sacconi, M. del Freo, L. Godart and M. Negri (eds.). 2008. *Colloquium Romanum, Atti del XII Colloquio Internazionale di Micenologia, Roma, 20–25 febbraio 2006*. Rome: Fabrizio Serra – Editore, 587–594.

—— 2008b. "Multiculturalism in the Mycenaean World." In B. J. Collins and M. R. Bachvarova (eds.). *Anatolian Interfaces: Hittites, Greeks and their Neighbours.*

Proceedings of an International Conference on Cross-Cultural Interaction, September 17–19, 2004, Emory University, Atlanta, GA. Oxford: Oxbow Books, 45–56.

—— 2012. "Thoughts on a possible link between the PY Ea series and a Mycenaean Tanning Operation." In P. Carlier et al. (eds.). Études *Mycéniennes 2010. Actes du XIIIe colloque international sur les textes égéens, Sèvres, Paris, Nanterre, 20–23 septembre 2010.* Rome: Fabrizio Serra editore, 285–302.

Nixon, L. 1983. "Changing Views of Minoan Society?" In O. Kryzszkowska and L. Nixon (eds.), 237–238.

Nordquist, G. 1995. "Who made the pots? Production in the Middle Helladic Society." In R. Laffineur and W-D. Niemeier (eds.), 201–207.

—— 1997. "Male Craft and Female Industry, Two Types of Production in the Aegean Bronze Age." In R. Laffineur and P. P. Betancourt (eds.), 533–538.

Nosch, M-L. B. 1997a. "Craftsmen in the Linear B Archives." In C. Gillis, C. Risberg and B. Sjöberg (eds.), 43–55.

—— 1997b. "Pylian Craftsmen: Payment in Kind/Rations or Land?" In R. Laffineur and P. P. Betancourt (eds.), 397–403.

—— 1998. "L'Administration des Textiles en Créte Centrale, Hors des Séries Lc/Le/Ln." *Bulletin de Correspondance Hellenique* 122, 404–406.

—— 2000. "Acquisition and Distribution: ta-ra-si-ja in the Mycenaean Textile Industry." In C. Gillis, C. Risberg and B. Sjöberg (eds.), 43–61.

—— 2003. "The Women at Work in the Linear B Tablets." In *Gender, Culture and Religion in Antiquity.* Proceedings of the second Nordic symposium on women's lives in Antiquity, Helsinki, 20–22 October 2000, SIMA Pocket Book 166. Paul Åström. Jonsered, 12–26.

—— 2008. "The Mycenaean Palace-Organised Textile Industry." In M. Perna and F. Pomponio (eds.), *The Management of Agricultural Land and the Production of Textiles in Mycenaean and Near Eastern Economics.* Napoli: Studi egei e vicinorientali 4. 135–154.

—— 2011. "The Administration of Textiles at Knossos: Observations on the Lc(1) Textile Targets (ta-ra-si-ja)." *American Journal of Archaeology* 115, 495–505.

—— 2012. "Voicing the Loom: Women, Weaving, and Plotting." In D. Nakassis, J. Gulizio and S. A. James (eds.).

Nosch, M-L. B. and E. Andersson. 2003. "With a Little Help from my Friends: Investigating Mycenaean Textiles with the Help from Scandinavian Experimental Archaeology." In K. P. Foster and R. Laffineur (eds.), 197–205.

Nosch, M-L. B. and R. Firth. 2002. "Scribe 103 and the Mycenaean Textile Industry at Knossos: The Lc(1) and Od(1) Sets." *Minos* 37–38, 121–142.

Nosch, M-L. B. and C. Gillis. 2007. *Ancient Textiles. Production, Craft and Society.* Oxbow Press, Oxford. Ancient Textiles Series, no. 1. Oxbow Books. London.

Nosch, M-L. B. and R. Laffineur. 2012. *KOSMOS. Jewellery, Adornment and Textiles in the Aegean Bronze Age.* 13th International Aegean Conference held at Copenhagen, April 2010/13em e Rencontre Égéenne, Copenhague, avril 2010. *Aegaeum* 33. Liège and Austin, TX: Histoire de l'art et archéologie de la Grèce antique and University of Texas at Austin, Program in Aegean Scripts and Prehistory.

Oliva, P. and A. Frolikova (eds.). 1983. *Concilium Eirene XVI, Mycenaological Colloquium. Proceedings of the 16th International Eirene Conference*, Vol. III, Section IV. Prague: Praha Kabinet pro studia recká, rimská a latinská.

Olivier, J-P. 1959. "Etude d'un nom de métier mycénien." *AC* 28, 179.

—— 1960. *A Propos d'une "Liste" de Desservants de Sanctuaire dans les Documents en Linéaire B de Pylos*. Bruxelles: Presses Universitaires.

—— 1967. "Les Scribes de Cnossos: Essai de Classment des Archives d'un Palais Mycénien." *Incunabula Graeca* 17. Roma: Edizioni dell'Ateneo.

—— 1984. "Administrations at Knossos and Pylos: What Differences?" In C.W. Shelmerdine and T. G. Palaima (eds.), 11–18.

—— 1987. "Des Extraits de Contrats de Vente d'esclaves dans les Tablettes de Knossos." *Minos* 20–22, 479–498.

—— 1992. *Mykenaïka. Actes du IXe Colloque international sur les textes mycéniens et égéens, Centre de l'Antiquité Grecque et Romaine de la Fondation Hellénique des Recherches Scientifiques et École française d'Athènes. BCH Suppl. 25.* Paris: Diffusion de Boccard.

—— 1993. "KN 115 = KH 115. Un Même Scribe à Knossos et à La Canée au MR IIIB: du Soupçon à la Certitude." *BCH* 117, 19–33.

—— 1994. "The Inscribed Documents at Bronze Age Knossos." In D. Everly, H. Hughes-Brock, and N. Momigliano (eds.), 165–168.

—— 2001. "Les 'Collecteurs': Leur Distribution Spatiale et Temporelle." In S. Voutsaki and J.T. Killen (eds.), 139–59.

Olivier, J-P. and T. G. Palaima. (eds.). 1988. *Texts, Tablets and Scribes. Studies in Mycenaean Epigraphy and Economy Offered to Emmett L. Bennett, Jr. Minos.* Salamanca: Ediciones Universidad de Salamanca.

Olsen, B. A. 1998. "Women, Children, and the Family in the Late Aegean Bronze Age: Differences in Minoan and Mycenaean Constructions of Gender?" *World Archaeology* 29.3, 380–392.

Ortner, S. 1974. "Is Female to Male as Nature is to Culture?" In M. Rosaldo and L. Lamphere (eds.), 67–88.

Palaima, T. G. 1984. "Scribal Organization and Palatial Activity." In C. W. Shelmerdine and T. G. Palaima (eds.), 31–41.

—— 1987. "Preliminary Comparative Textual Evidence for Palatial Control of Economic Activity in Minoan and Mycenaean Crete." In R. Hägg and N. Marinatos (eds.), 301–306.

—— 1988a. "The Development of the Mycenaean Writing System." In Olivier, J-P. and Palaima, T. G. (eds.), 269–341.

—— 1988b. *The Scribes of Pylos*. Roma: Edizioni dell'Ateneo.

—— 1991. "Maritime Matters in the Linear B Tablets." In R. Laffineur and L. Basch (eds.), 273–310.

—— 1992–1993. "Ten Reasons Why KH 115 ≠ KN 115." *Minos* 27–28, 261–281.

—— 1995a. "The Last Days of the Pylos Polity." In R. Laffineur and W-D. Niemeier (eds.), 623–633.

—— 1995b. "The Nature of the Mycenaean *Wanax*: Non-Indo-European Origins and Priestly Functions." In P. Rehak (ed.), 119–139.

—— 1997. "Potter and Fuller: The Royal Craftsmen." In R. Laffineur and P. P. Betancourt (eds.), 406–412.

—— 1999. "Mycenaean Militarism from a Textual Perspective: Onomastics in Context: *lawos, damos, klewos*." In R. Laffineur (ed.), 367–379.

—— 2003. "'Archives' and 'Scribes' and Information Hierarchy in Mycenaean Greek Linear B Records." In M. Brosius (ed.). 2003. *Ancient Archives and Archival Traditions.* Oxford: Oxford University Press, 153–194.

—— 2009. "Continuity from the Mycenaean Period in an Historical Boeotian Cult of Poseidon (and Erinys)," In S. Pomeroy (ed.), 527–536.

—— 2011. "Scribes, Scribal Hands and Paleography." In Y. Duhoux and A. Morpurgo Davies (eds.), 33–136.

—— 2011b. "Linear B." In E. Cline (ed.), 356–372.

Palaima, T. G., C. W. Shelmerdine, and P. H. Ilievski (eds.).1989. *Studia Mycenaea.* Zica Antika Monographies No. 7. Skopje.

Palaima T. G. and E. Sikkenga. 1999. "Linear A > Linear B." In P. P. Betancourt, V. Karageorghis, R. Laffineur, and W-D. Niemeier (eds.), 599–608.

Palaima, T. G. and J. C. Wright. 1985. "Ins and Outs of the Archive Rooms at Pylos: Form and Function in a Mycenaean Palace." *AJA* 89, 251–262.

Palmer, L. R. 1961. "The Find Places of the Knossos Tablets." *Antiquity* 35, 135–141.

—— 1962. *Mycenaeans and Minoans. Aegean Prehistory in the Light of the Linear B Tablets.* New York: Alfred A. Knopf.

—— 1963. *The Interpretation of Mycenaean Greek Tablets.* Oxford: Oxford University Press.

—— 1981. *Some New Minoan-Mycenaean Gods.* Innsbrucker Beiträge zur Sprachwissenschaft 2. Innsbruck: Institut für Sprachwissenschaft der Universität Innsbruck.

—— 1983. "Mycenaean Religion, Methodological Choices." In A. Heubeck and G. Neumann (eds.), 338–366.

Palmer, L. R. and J. Chadwick. 1966. *Proceedings of the Cambridge Colloquium on Mycenaean Studies 1965.* Cambridge: Cambridge University Press.

Palmer, Ruth. 1989. "Subsistence Rations at Pylos and Knossos." *Minos* 24, 89–124.

—— 1992. "Wheat and Barley in Mycenaean Society." In J-P. Olivier (ed.), 475–497.

—— 1994. *Wine in the Mycenaean Palace Economy. Aegaeum* 10. Histoire de l'art et archéologie de la Grèce antique. Liège and Austin, TX: Université de Liège and Program in Aegean Scripts and Prehistory, University of Texas at Austin.

—— 1998–1999. "Models in Linear B Landholding: An Analysis of Methodology."*Minos.* 33–34, 223–50.

—— 2008. "How to Begin? An Introduction to Linear B Conventions and Resources." In Y. Duhoux and A. Morpurgo Davies. (eds.), 25–68.

Paroussis, M. 1985. *Les Listes de Champs de Pylos et Hattusa et le Régime Foncier Mycénien et Hittite.* Paris: Société D'Edition "Les Belles Lettres."

Patterson, C. 1987. "Hai Attikai: The Other Athenians." In M. Skinner (ed.), 49–67.

—— 1991. "Marriage and the Married Woman in Athenian Law." In S. Pomeroy (ed.), 48–72.

—— 1998. *The Family in Greek History.* Cambridge, MA: Harvard University Press.

Peradotto, J. and J. P. Sullivan. (eds.). 1984. *Women in the Ancient World: The Arethusa Papers.* Albany, NY: State University of New York Press.

Perna, M. (ed.). 2006. *Fiscality in Mycenaean and Near Eastern Archives* Naples: Studi Egei e Vicinorientali.

Perna, M. and F. Pomponio. 2008. *The Management of Agricultural Land and the Production of Textiles in Mycenaean and Near Eastern Economics.* Napoli: Studi egei e vicinorientali 4.

Perpillou, J-L. 1976. "Données numériques des documents Fn de Pylos." *SMEA* 17, 65–78.

Peterson, S. E. 1981. *Wall Painting in the Aegean Bronze Age: The Procession Frescoes.* Doctoral Dissertation, University of Minnesota.

Pomeroy, S. 1975. *Goddesses, Whores, Wives, and Slaves.* New York: Schocken Press.

—— 1991. *Women's History and Ancient History*. Chapel Hill: University of North Carolina Press.

—— 1995. "Women's Identity and the Family in the Classical Polis." In R. Hawley and B. Levick (eds.), 111–121.

—— (ed.). 2009. *Festschrift for Spyros Iakovidis*. Chapel Hill: University of North Carolina Press.

Pope, M. 1975. *The Story of Decipherment*. London: Thames and Hudson.

—— 1989. "Ventris's Decipherment – First Causes." In Y. Duhoux, T. G. Palaima, and J. Bennet (eds.), 25–37.

—— 2008. "The Decipherment of Linear B." In Y. Duhoux and A. Morpurgo Davies. (eds.), 1–24.

Popham, M. R., E. Catling, and H. W. Catling. 1974. "Sellopoulo Tombs 3 and 4, Two Late Minoan Graves near Knossos." *BSA* 69, 37–41.

Poursat, J-C. and P. Darque. 1985. *L'iconographie minoenne*. *BCH Suppl.* XI. Paris: École Français d'Athènes.

Preston, L. 2008. "Mycenaean States: Late Minoan II to IIIB Crete." In C. W. Shelmerdine (ed.), 310–326.

Pugliese Carratelli, C. G. 1954a. "La Decifrazione Dei Testi Micenei." *La Parola del Passato* 35, 102–112.

—— 1954b. "Nuovi studi sui testi micenei." *La Parola del Passato* 35, 221–222.

Pullen, D. J. (ed.). 2010. *Political Economies of the Aegean Bronze Age: Papers from the Langford Conference, Florida State University, Tallahassee, 22–24 February 2007*. Oxford: Oxbow Books.

Redfield, J. 1977–1978. "The Women of Sparta." *Classical Journal* 73, 146–161.

Reeder, E. D. 1995. *Pandora: Women in Classical Greece*. Baltimore, MD: Trustees of the Walters Gallery.

Rehak, P. 1995a. *The Role of the Ruler in the Prehistoric Aegean*. *Aegaeum* 11, Annales d'Archéologie Égéenne de l'Université de Liège, Histoire de l'art et archéologie de la Grèce antique. Liège and Austin, TX: Université de Liège and Program in Aegean Scripts and Prehistory, University of Texas at Austin.

—— 1995b. "Enthroned Figures in Aegean Art and the Function of the Mycenaean Megaron." In P. Rehak (ed.), 95–118.

—— 1996. "Aegean Breechcloths, Kilts, and the Keftiu Paintings." *AJA* 100, 35–51.

—— 2007. "Children's Work: Girls as Acolytes in Aegean Ritual and Cult." In A. Cohen and J. Rutter (eds.), 205–228.

Rehak, P. and J. G. Younger. 1998. "Review of Aegean Prehistory VII: Neopalatial, Final Palatial, and Postpalatial Crete." *AJA* 102, 91–173.

Richter, D. C. 1971. "The Position of Women in Classical Athens." *CJ* 67, 1–8.

Risch, E. and H. Mühlestein. 1979. *Colloquium Mycenaeaum. The Sixth International Congress on the Aegean and Mycenaean Texts at Chaumonnt sur Neuchâtel, September 1–7*. Université de Neuchâtel.

Rosaldo, M. and L. Lamphere. 1974. *Women, Culture, and Society*. Palo Alto, CA: Stanford University Press.

Rougemont, F. 2001. "Some Thoughts on the Identification of the 'Collectors' in the Linear B Tablets." In Voutsaki, S. and J. Killen (eds.), 129–38 and 239–254.

—— 2004. "The Administration of Mycenaean Sheep Rearing (Flocks, Shepherds, 'Collectors')". In Santillo Frizell, B. (ed.), 20–30.

—— 2008. "The 'Collectors' as an 'International Elite' in the Mycenaean World." In C. Gillis and B. Sjöberg. (Abstract, p. 175).

—— 2009. *Contrôle économique et administration à l'époque des palais mycéniens (fin du IIe millénaire av. J.-C.)* (BÉFAR 332). Athens.

Ruijgh, C. J. 1967. *Études sur la Grammaire et le Vocabulaire du Grec Mycénien.* Amsterdam: Hakkert.

—— 1972. "Quelques Hypothèses en Marge des Tablettes En-Ep/Eo-Eb de Pylos." *SMEA* 15, 91–104.

Ruipérez, M. S. 1972. (ed.). *Acta Mycenaea II: Proceedings of the 5. International Colloquium on Mycenaean Studies, held in Salamanca, 30 March–3 April, 1970,* Volume 2.

Rutter, J. 1997. "The Prehistoric Archaeology of the Aegean." http://projects.dartmouth.edu/history/bronze_age June 26, 1997.

—— 2003. "Children in Aegean Prehistory." In J. Neils and J. H. Oakley (eds.), 31–58.

Sacconi, A., L. Godart and M. Del Freo. (eds.). 2008. *The Proceedings of the 12th International Mycenological Colloquium, vol. II.* Rome: Biblioteca di Pasiphae Series.

Santillo Frizell, B. (ed.). 2004. *Pecus: Man and Animal in Antiquity. Proceedings of the Conference at the Swedish Institute in Rome, September 9–12, 2002.* Rome: The Swedish Institute in Rome. Projects and Seminars 1. (http://www.svenska-institutet-rom.org/pecus/)

Sarkady, J. 1981. "Landownership Relations in Pylos." *ActaOrHung* 35, 2–3.

Schaps, D. 1979. *Economic Rights of Women in Ancient Greece.* Edinburgh: Edinburgh University Press.

Scheidel, W., I. Morris and R. Saller. (eds.). 2007. *The Cambridge Economic History of the Greco-Roman World.* Cambridge: Cambridge University Press.

Schiffer, M. (ed.). 1984. *Advances in Archaeological Method and Theory.* New York: Academic Press.

Schmitt-Pantel, P. 1992. *From Ancient Goddesses to Christian Saints*, Vol. 1. Cambridge, MA: Harvard University Press.

Scott, E. and J. Moore. 1997. *Invisible People and Processes: Writing Gender and Childhood into European Archaeology.* London: Leicester University Press.

Scott, J. W. 1996a. *Feminism and History.* Oxford: Oxford University Press.

—— 1996b. "Gender: A Useful Category of Historical Analysis." In J. W. Scott (ed.), 152–180.

Sealey, R. 1990. *Women and Law in Classical Greece.* Chapel Hill, NC: University of North Carolina Press.

Shelmerdine, C. W. 1984. "The Perfumed Oil Industry at Pylos." In C. W. Shelmerdine and T. G. Palaima (eds.), 81–95.

—— 1985. *The Perfume Industry in Mycenaean Pylos.* SIMA-PB 34. Paul Åströms Förlag. Göteborg.

—— 1987. "Architectural Change and Economic Decline at Pylos." *Minos* 20–22, 557–568.

—— 1988. "Scribal Organization and Administrative Procedures." In J-P. Olivier and T. G. Palaima (eds.), 343–384.

—— 1989. "Mycenaean Taxation." In T. G. Palaima, C. W. Shelmerdine, and P. H. Ilievski (eds.), *Studia Mycenaea.* 1988. Ziva Antika Monographies No. 7. Skopje, 125–148.

—— 1997. "Workshops and Record Keeping in the Mycenaean World." In R. Laffineur and P. P. Betancourt (eds.), 387–397.

—— 1998. "Where Do We Go from Here? And How Can the Linear B Tablets Help Us Get There?" In E. H. Cline and D. Harris-Cline (eds.), 291–299.

—— 1999. "Pylian Polemics: The Latest Evidence on Military Matters." In R. Laffineur (ed.), 403–410.

—— 2006. "Mycenaean Palatial Administration." In S. Deger-Jalkotzy and I.S. Lemos. 73–86.

—— (ed.). 2008a. *The Cambridge Companion to the Aegean Bronze Age.* Cambridge University Press. Cambridge, 152.

—— 2008b. "Mycenaean Society." In Y. Duhoux and A. Morpurgo Davies (eds.), 115–158.

Shelmerdine, C. W. and J. Bennet. 2008. "Mycenaean States: Economy and Administration." In C.W. Shelmerdine (ed.), 289–309.

Shelmerdine, C. W. and T. G. Palaima. 1984. *Pylos Comes Alive: Industry and Administration in a Mycenaean Palace.* New York: Archaeological Institute of America.

Sherratt, A. and S. Sherratt. 1998. "Small Worlds: Interaction and Identity in the Ancient Mediterranean." In E. H. Cline and D. Harris-Cline (eds.), 329–342.

—— 1991. "From Luxuries to Commodities: the Nature of Mediterranean Bronze Age Trading Systems." In N. H. Gale (ed.), 351–386.

Sjöberg, B. L. 1995. "The Mycenaean Economy: Theoretical Frameworks." In C. Gillis, C. Risberg, and B. Sjöberg (eds.), 19–32.

Sjöberg, G. 1960. *The Preindustrial City: Past and Present.* New York: The Free Press.

Skinner, M. 1987. *Rescuing Creusa. New Methodological Approaches to Women in Antiquity.* Austin, TX: Texas Tech University Press.

Slater, P. E. 1974. "The Greek Family in History and Myth." *Arethusa* 7.1, 9–44.

Smithson, E. 1968. "The Tomb of a Rich Athenian Lady, ca. 850." *Hesperia* 37, 77–116.

Sourvinou-Inwood, C. 1995. "Male and Female, Public and Private, Ancient and Modern." In E. D. Reeder (ed.), 111–120.

Spector, J. 1993. *What This Awl Means: Feminist Archaeology at a Wahpeton Dakota Village.* Minneapolis: Minnesota Historical Society Press.

Spector, J. D. and M. K. Whalen. 1989. "Incorporating Gender into Archaeology Courses." In S. Morgen (ed.), 69–70.

Steele, P. M. 2008. "A Comparative Look at Mycenaean and Near Eastern Bureaucracies: 'Bilateral' Documentation in the Linear B Archives?" *Kadmos* 47, 31–49.

Stella, L. A. 1965. *La Civiltà Micenea nei Documenti Contemporanei.* Roma: Edizione dell'Ateneo.

Sutton, D. F. 1970. *An Analytical Prosopography and Statistical Guide to the Land Tenure Tablets at Pylos.* Ph.D. Dissertation, University of Wisconsin.

Talalay, L. 1993. *Deities, Dolls, and Devices: Neolithic Figurines from the Franchthi Cave in Greece.* Bloomington, IN: University of Indiana Press.

—— 1994. "A Feminist Boomerang: The Great Goddess of Greek Prehistory." *Gender and History* 6.2, 165–183.

Tartaron, T. F. 2008. "Aegean Prehistory as World Archaeology: Recent Trends in the Archaeology of Bronze Age Greece." *Journal of Archaeological Research* 16.2, 83–161.

Tegyey, I. 1984. "The Northeast Workshop at Pylos." In C. W. Shelmerdine and T. G. Palaima (eds.), 65–80.

—— 1987. "Scribes and Archives at Knossos and Pylos: A Comparison." In P. H. Ilievski and L. Crepajac (eds.), 357–366.

Thomas, C. G. 1973. "Matriarchy in Early Greece: the Bronze and Dark Ages." *Arethusa* 6:2, 173–195.

—— 1976. "The Nature of Mycenaean Kingship." *SMEA* 7, 93–116.

—— 1995. "The Components of Political Identity in Mycenaean Greece." In R. Laffineur and W-D. Niemeier (eds.), 349–354.

Thomas, N. R. 1999. "The War Animal: Three Days in the Life of the Mycenaean Lion." In R. Laffineur (ed.), 297–312.

Tritsch, F. J. 1958. "The Women of Pylos." In E. Grumach (ed.), 406–445.

Tringham, R. 1994. "Engendered Places in Prehistory." *Gender, Place and Culture,* 1: 2, 169–203.

Tsountas, C. and J. I. Manatt. 1966. *The Mycenaean Age: A Study of the Monuments and Culture of Prehomeric Greece.* Chicago, IL:Argonaut Press.

Uchitel, A. 1984. "Women at Work. Pylos and Knossos, Lagash and Ur." *Historia* 33, 257–282.

—— 1988. "The Archives of Mycenaean Greece and the Ancient Near East." In M. Heltzer and E. Lipinski (eds.), 19–30.

van Alfen, P. G. 2008. "The Linear B Inscribed Vases." In Y. Duhoux and A. Morpurgo Davies (eds.), 235–242.

van Leuven, J. 1979. "Mycenaean Goddess Called Potnia." *Kadmos* 18, 112–129.

Ventris, M. 1951–1952. *Work Notes on Minoan Language Research* 1–20 (28th Jan. 1951–1st June 1952). (Privately distributed).

Ventris, M. and J. Chadwick. 1953. "Evidence for Greek Dialect in the Mycenaean Archives." *JHS* 73, 84–103.

—— 1956. *Documents in Mycenaean Greek. Three hundred Selected Tablets from Knossos, Pylos and Mycenae with Commentary and Vocabulary.* Cambridge: Cambridge University Press, 1956.

—— 1973. *Documents in Mycenaean Greek*, 2nd ed. Cambridge: Cambridge University Press.

Voutsaki, S. 1995. "Social and Political Processes in the Mycenaean Argolid: The Evidence from the Mortuary Practices." In R. Laffineur and W-D. Niemeier (eds.), 55–63.

Voutsaki, S. and J. T. Killen. (eds.). 2001. *Economy and Politics in the Mycenaean Palace States.* Cambridge Philological Society Suppl. 27. Cambridge: Cambridge Philological Society.

Walberg, G. 1995. "Minoan Economy: An Alternative Model." In R. Laffineur and W-D. Niemeier (eds.), 157–161.

Walters, K. R. 1993. "Women and Power in Classical Athens." In M. DeForest (ed.), 194–214.

Warren, P. M. 1969. *Minoan Stone Vases.* Cambridge Classical Studies. Cambridge: Cambridge University Press.

Warren, P. and V. Hankey. 1989. *Aegean Bronze Age Chronology.* Bristol: Bristol Classical Press.

Webster, T. B. L. 1954. "Pylos *Aa,* Ab tablets – Pylos *E* tablets – Additional Homeric notes." *BLICS* 1, 13–14.

—— 1960. *Mycenae to Homer.* New York: Barnes and Noble.

Weingarten, H. 1999. "War Scenes and Ruler Iconography in a Golden Age." In R. Laffineur (ed.), 347–357.

Wells, B. 1992. *Agriculture in Ancient Greece: Proceedings of the Seventh International Symposium at the Swedish Institute at Athens, 16–17 May 1990. SkrAth* 4° XLII. Stockholm: Paul Åströms Förlag.

Whiting, R. M. Jr. 1991. *Earliest Land Tenure Systems in the Near East: Ancient Kudurrus.* Oriental Institute Publication 104, I-II. Chicago, IL: University of Chicago Press.

Whitley, J. 1996. "Gender and Hierarchy in Early Athens. The Strange Case of the Disappearance of the Rich Female Grave." *Metis* 11, 209–231.

Withee, D. 1992. "Physical Growth and Aging Characteristics Depicted in the Theran Frescoes." *AJA* 96, 336.

Wright, J. 1995. "From Chief to King in Mycenaean Greece." In P. Rehak (ed.), 63–81.

Wright, R. P. 1991. "Women's Labor and Pottery Production in Prehistory." In J. M Gero and M. W. Conkey (eds.), 233–275.

—— 1996a. *Gender and Archaeology*. Philadelphia, PA: University of Pennsylvania Press.

—— 1996b. "Technology, Gender and Class Worlds of Differences in Ur III Mesopotamia." In R. P. Wright (ed.), 79–110.

Wylie, A. 1996. "The Constitution of Archaeological Evidence: Gender Politics and Science." In P. Galison and D. J. Stump (eds.), 311–343.

Yamagata, N. 1995. "The Gods in Homer and in Linear B." *BICS* 40, 246–247.

Younger, J. G. 1976. "Bronze Age Representations of Aegean Bull-Leaping." *AJA* 80:2, 125–137.

—— 1995. "Bronze Age Representations of Aegean Bull-Games, III." In R. Laffineur and W-D. Niemeier (eds.), 507–545.

Younger, J. J. and P. Rehak. 2008. "The Material Culture of Neopalatial Crete." In C. W. Shelmerdine (ed.), 152.

Zweig, B. 1993. "The Only Women Who Give Birth to Men: A Gynocentric Cross- Cultural View of Women in Ancient Sparta." In M. DeForest (ed.), 32–53.

Subject index

Tablet index

For Product Safety Concerns and Information please contact our EU representative GPSR@taylorandfrancis.com Taylor & Francis Verlag GmbH, Kaufingerstraße 24, 80331 München, Germany

Printed and bound by CPI Group (UK) Ltd, Croydon, CR0 4YY
24/01/2025
01825549-0005